Social Problems

DISSENSUS AND DEVIATION

IN AN INDUSTRIAL SOCIETY

RUSSELL R. DYNES
ALFRED C. CLARKE
SIMON DINITZ
THE OHIO STATE UNIVERSITY

IWAO ISHINO
MICHIGAN STATE UNIVERSITY

New York   Oxford University Press   1964

PREFACE

Some books are written for teachers while others are intended primarily for students. We have compromised by writing a book for the student and a preface for the teacher. At the outset, we should like those teachers who use this book to understand what has been included and excluded, and why.

Our analytic framework is limited to American society, and therefore some broader social problems of traditional concern have been excluded. The implications of a growth in population are treated insofar as they affect American society, but there is no inclusive discussion of the "population explosion" itself. The same is true of a different threat of explosion, the possibility of nuclear war, which is unquestionably the most critical international issue of our times, yet we felt that justice could scarcely be done to it within the scope of these chapters on American society. And, though we describe the general consequences of industrialization, the teacher should not expect direct analyses of specific economic and political institutions; the interested student will examine these areas in detail when taking courses in economics and political science, and therefore this book will concentrate primarily on institutions of traditional sociological concern. Finally, we have included no extensive discussions of questions of values, or of particular "solutions" for specific social problems, because we feel that the individual teacher can best select and present such information as the need arises.

This book, then, provides one approach which the teacher is invited to use in application to contemporary social problems. But today, any special orientation necessarily represents an adjustment to the larger traditions of a discipline, and we must therefore begin by placing our *normative* approach in the context of others. *Social pathology* [1] was one of the earliest approaches to social problems at a time when sociologists tended to be reformers as well as theorists, defending the psychologically halt and socially lame and attempting to rectify the conditions which produced their pathology. Such sociologists have effectively illuminated crucial issues, for today many of their books are dated—either the group in question has organized its own pressure group like

1. John M. Gillin, *Social Pathology*, 3rd ed., New York. Appleton-Century-Crofts, 1946.

the AFL-CIO or the NAACP, or the social problem itself has diminished because of corrective measures like legislation. More recently, this emphasis has largely been replaced by a more abstract concern with a *conflict of values* [2] which allows the sociologist to explicate controversial issues without identifying himself with any single position. Each of these approaches tends to be extreme, however, the first encouraging too much personal involvement and the second discouraging it by permitting the analyst to isolate and compare ideologies in a social vacuum.

A third approach utilizes a concept of *social disorganization* [3] in which behavior is viewed as being problematical to the entent that it lacks, or conflicts with, the consensus of society. This has often been criticized because it implies that consensus is a "normal" condition which precedes "abnormal" disorganization, and thus encourages return to the original state of organization, an unrealistic "solution" because most disorganization is the result of lasting social and technological change. The fourth sociological approach, *social deviation*, [4] is similar to the third because it too deals with behavior deviating from some norm which, presumably, has the consensus of society as a whole. However, both these approaches may be criticized for implying and not stating their normative referent; in disorganization and deviation the norm from which behavior departs is seldom specified so that a theoretical impression of universality is imparted to something which may, in actuality, be relative. The fifth approach to social problems is *cultural lag*, [5] the notion that a state of equilibrium exists in society until technological change disrupts it.

By applying any of these five methods of analysis, sociologists implicitly choose one of two heuristic models of society. The *conflict model* is implicit in the approaches of pathology and value conflict because they both represent society as a mass of groups with conflicting interests which must be held together by force and constraint in their constant rivalry for power. The *integration model* is implicit in the remaining approaches of disorganization, deviation, and cultural lag because they all represent society as a state of order or equilibrium which is constantly being interrupted and then integrated once again. For this book we have chosen the integration model because it

1. provides a common framework suitable for both institutional and individual problems.

2. is more clearly sociological than ideological.

3. requires the newer perspective of sociology which tends to emphasize

2. John F. Cuber, Robert A. Harper, William F. Kenkel, *Problems of American Society: Values in Conflict*, 3rd ed., New York: Holt, 1956.
3. Mabel Elliott and Francis E. Merrill, *Social Disorganization*, 4th ed., New York: Harper, 1961.
4. Marshall B. Clinard, *Sociology of Deviant Behavior*, New York: Rinehart, 1957.
5. Abbott Herman, *An Approach to Social Problems*, Boston: Ginn, 1949.

an integrated or equilibrated system and places social problems within a general scientific tradition, since both the physical and biological sciences employ integrative models frequently.

4. provides the student with a structural point of departure so that he is not plunged in the midst of conflicting institutions and pressure groups or suspended in an ideological vacuum of abstract "values."

By presenting the student with a heuristic model of an integrated society organized in accordance with certain behavioral norms, we hope to combine the best features of previous integrative approaches and minimize their shortcomings. Chapter 1 introduces normative terminology based on the approaches of social disorganization (normative dissensus) and social deviation (behavioral deviation), but also emphasizes normative consensus, the nature of the existing norm, its location in society and its limits. Chapter 1 also presents the concept of technological change as the basic "cause" of dissensus and deviation. But Chapter 2 places this "cause" in its proper historical perspective because, even though we have all inherited the changing norms of a swiftly developing industrial society, every social problem need not be traced to a specific technological advance—in certain cases, other more immediate social factors may be more pertinent.

The remaining chapters of this book will emphasize instances of deviation, when behavior does not follow general conduct norms, and examples of dissensus, when there is a lack of agreement over appropriate norms within a given institution. But an analysis of behavioral deviation requires some knowledge of individuals who do not deviate, and thus focuses attention on the nature of the normative referent itself and on those mechanisms of social control responsible for maintaining it. Moreover, the study of normative dissensus requires an analysis of the nature, as well as the content, of the normative structure of a society, including its historical development—the processes whereby consensus has been achieved. And this, in turn, leads to an analysis of group structures and social relationships, particularly those which tend to reduce and inhibit deviation and dissensus. Throughout this book, the principles established in the first two chapters will repeatedly be used to encourage both teacher and student to consider how societies are organized. Thus, we believe that the normative approach to social problems formulated in terms of the integration model provides a theoretical framework within the best traditions of sociology.

A final comment should be made on the bibliographical references. We have included citations of some of the many paperback books because their price and ready availability provide some hope that students' interest in the literature of social problems will not terminate with the final examination.

We should also record our indebtedness to those who have contributed to this venture. We wish to thank the students in our classes at various universities who have exposed some of the weaknesses inherent in our earlier formulations. We hope we have learned enough from them. We wish to thank our colleagues who have graciously permitted us to try their patience as we were testing our ideas. We are now able to answer their persistent question, "Where's the book?" A special note of commendation must go to Mrs. Laura Cleaver whose typing skill is exceeded only by her skill in deciphering handwriting. We are also grateful for the tolerance of our four wives and thirteen children who too often may have regarded our book as a convenient rationalization for avoiding the obligations, but never the pleasures, of family life. And finally, we appreciate equally the forbearance and the encouragement of those at Oxford University Press, particularly Paul Whitfield.

December 1963   R. R. D.   A. C. C.   S. D.   I. I.

CONTENTS

I INTRODUCTION

II NORMATIVE DISSENSUS

III BEHAVIORAL DEVIATION

EPILOGUE, 583

I INTRODUCTION

CHAPTER 1 THE PROBLEM OF PROBLEMS

It has become part of the mission of sociologists to catch the goings-on of people and institutions at the time; or at least to catch those parts of them which tend to be overlooked by students of politics and economics, and by those who report on and criticize what are considered the serious works of art and of the mind. The lives of the families across the tracks; the reactions of housewives to the morning soap opera . . . the slow moving changes in the level of schooling of those Americans who are called Negro. These things don't make the news, but they make the big story comprehensible when it breaks into the headlines. One might say that part of the calling of sociologists is to push back the frontier of the news so as to get at the news back of, or below the news, not in the sense of getting at the lowdown, but in that of giving the reported events another dimension, that of the perspective of culture and of social processes.[1]

As Everett Hughes says above, it is part of the mission of sociologists to "catch the goings-on of people and institutions." Making "the big story comprehensible" is not the purpose of this book, but this type of understanding may be a by-product of sociology. The events called current are often surface manifestations of social problems requiring deeper analysis, and to understand such problems we need to begin at the beginning.

FOUNDATIONS OF SOCIAL LIFE

Every society must face certain recurrent situations, since certain needs must be met if social life is to continue. Human beings of any society must successfully deal with personal problems, such as sexual activity and reproduction, as well as social problems caused by natural enemies and enemies from other societies. Then, if the members survive long enough, some means of producing and distributing goods and services must be evolved. Some members must do one job, while other members do other jobs; since each person may require the goods and services performed by others, some system of exchange must come into being. To facilitate this exchange, some rudimentary form of government must evolve to determine rights and obligations, and various

1. Everett C. Hughes, "The Improper Study of Man," in Lynn White, Jr. (ed.), *Frontiers of Knowledge in the Study of Man*, New York: Harper, 1956.

3

mechanisms must emerge to control individuals who do not fulfill their obligations. To assure the continuation of a society, each generation must transmit to the next some sense of what it has accomplished and learned. Every society develops ways of meeting the crises associated with the life cycle — birth, illness, death — as well as of providing some collective interpretation of its history and destiny.

As might be expected, different groups of people meet these basic issues in significantly different ways. The members of one society to fulfill their nutritional needs, may hunt, while those in another may gather food. Those in one society may arrange their family patterns monogamously, while their neighbors may practice polygamy. One society may develop a division of labor around family relations, while another may arrange it in terms of village organization. The patterns of behavior that develop around these basic problems are remarkably variable, and are useful for observing differences in societies which, geographically speaking, are actually neighbors.

The patterns of behavior that develop around a society's basic needs constitute a much larger pattern called culture. Culture can be considered as an adaptive tool with which a society meets the basic problems of human existence. The advantage of such a tool for survival is that the members of the society can pass on their experience in meeting these problems to succeeding generations. This means that the succeeding generations can be taught *how* to act when they encounter given situations in the future.

THE NORMATIVE ORDER

Part of this accumulated wisdom — the culture of a society — consists of norms, notions about what individuals *should do* when they find themselves in certain situations. Of course, such notions can be learned in theory by the members of a society prior to any actual experience; one can be taught how a family *should* be organized, or learn how work relationships *should* be structured, before the need for such organization arises.

Members of a society "carry" with them norms as to what their behavior should be in particular situations and whether or not certain behavior is appropriate. It is not sufficient in the analysis of society only to observe how individuals behave. Some attempt must be made to observe how the members of a society *feel* they *should* behave. We will call this "should" aspect of behavior the *normative order*, the norms themselves being *statements of prescription and proscription — statements of how people should and should not act.*

1. *Norms have a group referent.* When any group of persons is in communication over a period of time, a normative structure is developed.

Through communication, agreement on the direction of behavior is achieved and, with the statement of these directions, norms emerge. Thus, a work group, a union, a corporation, or a family, by virtue of the association and communication of its members, develops and transmits a normative structure. While it is possible to analyze many types of groups and their respective normative structures, the focus of this book will be on American society.

2. *Norms are learned.* Since norms have this group referent, they are learned through group experience. Within the family, parents seldom realize they are transmitting norms; but they do, every time they remind their children that they should do this and not that. Every group develops means of indoctrinating "recruits" within its own normative structure: armies have basic training, corporations have training programs, universities have orientation conferences, churches have catechism classes, and fraternities have hazings and initiations. All groups, either formally or informally, develop some mechanism for the inculcation of norms in new members.

3. *Behavior conforming to the norms is maintained through rewards and punishments.* When people act, others evaluate their behavior by means of relevant norms. Behavior consistent with the norm is rewarded with approval, which can range from a mother's smile and a cookie to the power and prestige of promotion in a large corporation. Behavior which departs from those norms may be met with punishment ranging from ridicule to death.

4. *Norms become internalized.* Norms are followed not so much because of the threat of punishment or the promise of reward, but because they become an integral part of an individual's personality. Most behavior within a society is not motivated by the promise of rewards or the threat of punishment, but is an outgrowth of what the members of that society "want" to do, simply because they are accustomed to a life which includes the "shoulds" and "oughts" of behavior. Some behavior may, of course, be determined by a person's conscious estimate of what would happen if he violated a norm — his possible shame or the loss of approval he might experience. But most norms are so subtly embedded in one's personality that they remain unconscious until new norms must be learned or old ones violated.

5. *Norms differ in their importance.* Obviously, a great variety of rewards and punishments is meted out for conformity to, or deviation from, a norm. Murder evokes a strong emotional reaction from the public and is punishable by death or by life imprisonment, while the penalty for yawning in public is little more than personal embarrassment.

6. *Norms can be inferred from behavior which is rewarded and punished.* The rewards and punishments meant to determine behavior give some indication of the relative seriousness with which a group views its norms. Severe

punishments and great rewards indicate the presence of major norms; while mild punishments and slight rewards point to minor, or less important, ones. However, detecting and analyzing a norm by observing what behavior is rewarded and what behavior is punished is often a complex task. Under certain circumstances, actions usually disapproved are approved. Certain types of behavior may, for example, be tolerated because the violator is young or old. Other types of behavior may be tolerated if a person is unfamiliar with the norms, as is the rookie or the newlywed. Certain types of behavior may be rewarded in one group but not in others. We can allow for all these special cases, however, if our *observations focus on the sanctions of others, and not on the person behaving.* Reactions of others to behavior in particular situations provide the best clue to the existence and nature of the norm.

7. *Norms can be inferred from the testimony of the members of a society.* Verbal testimony provides an excellent source of information about the normative order of a society. Individuals, in many instances, can provide explicit statements of the norms of a particular group. In other instances, through a description of the behavior regarded as acceptable and unacceptable, a perceptive observer can formulate the implicit norm.

Testimony from written sources provides further information about the normative order of a society. The Ten Commandments, the Magna Carta, the Declaration of Independence, the Constitution of the United States, and thousands of other lesser documents indicate man's attempts to give a more precise and explicit statement of the norms that provide guides for behavior in a society.

8. *Norms are based on values.* A value is a standard of worthwhileness operating within a society. Values function as over-all designs for behavior. For example, one might state that honesty is a value in American society. This value of honesty is translated into a specific norm, in Biblical terms, in "Thou shalt not steal," or in other terms in the specific language of the law. The value of honesty may also be translated into other norms—such as, "one should be faithful to one's wife, . . . one should not cheat on exams, . . . one should report votes accurately," or "one should honestly describe the specific steps in a scientific experiment."

The values of a society may be inferred from observation of the way certain themes are reflected through many norms. A recurrent theme is competition; for example, in schoolwork children are encouraged to compete for grades, and in dating they are advised to compete for the attention of the opposite sex. Moreover, the food they eat and the television programs they watch also undergo a constant process of competitive selection, on the basis of selling or "drawing" power. By observing the recurrence of a given theme in the normative order, we have inferred one of the values important in a society — in this case, competition as it affects America.[2]

NORMATIVE CONSENSUS AND BEHAVIORAL CONFORMITY

A society in which no social problems exist is, of course, hypothetical, because (1) the members would have to agree on the norms to be followed and (2) never deviate from them in their behavior. The first condition, the agreement of members of a society upon the norms to guide behavior in a particular segment of society, is called *normative consensus*; and the second condition, the agreement of each individual to follow the norms agreed upon within his society, is called *behavioral conformity*.

A society characterized by normative consensus and behavioral conformity operates smoothly because relationships between people are authoritatively defined, attitudes toward important activities and issues are similar, and each individual's behavior corresponds to the expectations of the society as a whole.

NORMATIVE DISSENSUS AND BEHAVIORAL DEVIATION

Suppose a particular norm specifies that all persons must drive on the right-hand side of the highway. If everyone in the society accepts this norm and follows it, thousands of automobiles can move freely from place to place. When predicting such conformity, we must allow for certain variables: (1) some individuals may be uncertain which side of the road to drive on; and (2) others my simply drive on the left-hand side. The first variable, in which there is disagreement or uncertainty about the appropriate norm, is called *normative dissensus*; and the second variable, in which a certain type of behavior conflicts with an accepted norm, is called *behavioral deviation*. These conditions transform the ideal of a trouble-free society into the reality of a society with *social problems*. Deviation and dissensus, then, constitute social problems (see Table 1).

Behavioral Deviation. Even when a norm is clearly and consistently defined and there is normative consensus within a society, certain individuals do not follow this guide for behavior. Norms regulating the preservation of human life are so strict that deviations are often punishable by death, yet about 9000 homicides occur in the United States every year, and these deviations constitute a social problem.

Mental illness could also be considered a behavioral deviation. A norm of

2. The student may have already learned that competition is one of the social processes, along with co-operation, accommodation, assimilation, and conflict. But this does not negate the fact that *some societies* may view competition, or any other of these processes, as a value.

everyday life specifies: "Every person should develop an image of himself and of social reality which is acceptable to others." Yet, individuals whose concept of themselves is far removed from the way others define them range from the borderline neurotic who defines himself as inadequate, to the psychotic who defines himself as Napoleon or Moses. The behavior of such individuals is considered problematic because it departs from the norm suggesting socially appropriate levels of mental health.

TABLE 1-1

Concepts and definitions

Concept	Definition
Norms	Statements of prescriptions and proscriptions concerning how members of a society should act
Institutions	Systems of social norms arising around basic social functions
Normative Consensus	Agreement among the members of a society on norms
Normative Dissensus	Disagreement among the members of a society on norms
Behavior	Actions of individuals and groups
Behavioral Conformity	Condition where the behavior of individuals conforms to norms
Behavioral Deviation	Condition where the behavior of individuals does not conform to norms

Deviant behavior is popularly explained by the characteristics of the deviant person himself — the criminal, the psychotic, the alcoholic, or the drug addict. The deviant, however, must be understood in terms of the specific norm that defines his deviation. Since deviation involves behavior contradictory to a stated norm, it is most easily identifiable when the norm is written and specific, as in a legal, ethical, or moral code. In the complexities of contemporary societies, however, many norms are not specifically stated, and what appears to be deviation from one norm is sometimes only behavior consistent with another norm not recognized by the observer.

While the concept of deviation ordinarily includes any departure in behavior from any norm in a society, our analysis will be restricted to such major deviations as crime and mental illness, whose seriousness can easily be determined because of the public's emotional attitude or the specification of punishment. Such behavior is so seriously regarded by societies that it is usually a clear-cut case of deviation from a norm stated in terms of "shall not." The individual is proscribed from acting in a particular way, whether he is engaging in family behavior, economic behavior, or recreational behavior. Such norms are based on what society considers crucial values and thus tend to resist change.

Normative Dissensus. While deviation consists of actual behavior which departs from norms specifying certain types of conduct within a society, normative dissensus reflects differing ideas about the types of behavior permissible within that society. In studying deviation we analyze the actual behavior of individuals, and in studying normative dissensus, we must examine conflicting ideas of what behavior *should be* within a society.

As indicated previously, every society faces certain recurrent situations that require normative definitions: the preservation of life through sexual activity and the birth of children, the distribution of goods and services, the maintenance of social order through the control of behavioral deviation, and the transmission to future generations of those social norms which have evolved and have been maintained. Around such basic needs, societies develop certain systems of social norms termed *institutions*. Social norms concerning the production and distribution of goods constitute the economic institution; other norms prescribe and proscribe socially acceptable ways of organization and behavior for the institutions of politics, religion, education, family life, and even leisure. Within various institutions, there may not be complete consensus as to the appropriate norms, and this may make deviation impossible to determine. If some in a society think marriage should be a permanent relationship, they may view divorce as clearly deviant behavior. But, at the same time, others within a society, who see marriage as an attempt to attain maximum happiness, may regard divorce as an appropriate way of avoiding unhappiness or of seeking future happiness. Within the institution centering in marriage and the family, we may have dissensus because the same behavior, divorce, is viewed as a deviant act by some and an acceptable act by others. The question is which of these alternatives *should* prevail within the society. Such questions constitute what we call normative dissensus.

Normative dissensus is, at times, a matter of disagreement between groups within a society. For example, specific groups within the economic institutional area, such as labor and management, may possess conflicting norms and may attempt to gain support for them through "propaganda," public relations, discussion, and any of the various methods of persuasion utilized in a democratic society. Normative dissensus may also be seen in the competing claims of voluntary associations organized around particular interests, which also seek through the various methods of persuasion to gain consensus for the particular norms they advocate. Of course, normative dissensus can also exist within a group. For example, within a family there may be conflicting opinions about the direction of a wife's behavior; the husband may feel that "a woman's place is in the home," while the wife may view her role quite differently. Disagreement within the family may also arise over priority — what part should elderly relatives play in making decisions, and to what extent should children be expected to support, or defer to, their elders?

Normative dissensus is not always reflected in group disagreement, however, because different norms within a society are not necessarily totally embodied by any specific group. When studying social problems, we should remember that since normative dissensus reflects conflicting ideas we will therefore concentrate on the *content* of the divergent norms, not on their location or acceptance by particular groups. Normative dissensus reflects contradictory beliefs about certain institutions and creates chaotic behavior, undefined and unsanctioned. Contradictory standards in a specific group often reflect the dissensus within the society as a whole.

Within any society, normative consensus may alternate with normative dissensus. New social arrangements stemming from technological change may require new norms and reduce the importance of older ones. The dissensus that results creates a social problem until a new consensus has been achieved. Viewed in this way, normative dissensus requires some historical perspective since a shift in norms is not achieved within a short period of time and, in retrospect, this shift can be regarded as cultural change. Conflict among specific groups may constitute only one small part in a larger pattern of change. Consequently, throughout the discussion of normative dissensus in the following chapters, we shall emphasize the sweeping changes in norms affecting an entire society.

THE "CAUSE" OF SOCIAL PROBLEMS — SOCIAL CHANGE

Societies are never static. While social change may make many norms obsolete, the previous effectiveness of other norms persuades some members of a society to retain them as guides for behavior, while others, recognizing the impact of change, begin to explore new normative possibilities. By examining the impact of social change on the small community of Caliente, we can illustrate the sort of normative shifts which have affected whole societies in the past and continue to affect every industrialized society in the present.

Caliente was a town built at a break of a railroad across an eighty mile canyon. Caliente owed its existence to the railroad, whose development was a product of a long adaptation to the technological requirements of the steam engine. The number and position of depots for the railroad were determined by the frequency with which engines had to be serviced and crews changed, and Caliente flourished because of the certainty that it was necessary for railroad maintenance. A water system was laid to supply the needs of the town for centuries. The townspeople used their life savings to build houses, and businesses built stores with past profits in anticipation of even greater profits in the future. The town built churches, schools, and a hospital, and developed a combined park and playfield for future generations.

The tempo of town life was set by the daily arrival and departure of trains. In every area of community life, norms developed defining behavior, appropriate for the "good" citizen, businessman, or engineer. Caliente developed into a normal small town, stressing in its normative order all the virtues society regarded as "solid" and "sound."

When the railroad was built, depots were necessary at 100-mile intervals. But immediately after World War II, improvements in technology made it possible for trains to increase the distance between stops. Fortunately, Caliente was located between terminals about 600 miles apart and, as other service centers were closed, Caliente became even more important because fewer stops meant increased services for long-range travel.

But other technological developments during World War II made it possible for railroads to convert to diesel engines in a relatively short time, and Caliente's new prosperity was misleading; diesels required few stops for water and fuel so Caliente itself soon became a victim of "progress." The valuation of railroad property was three-fifths that of the town and the railroad could discount this as a capital loss, which it might then recover through the increased efficiency of the new engine. But the townspeople could not regard *their* loss as a deficit useful for decreasing their taxes. Boilermakers, for example, found their skills no longer needed and had to become unskilled laborers, while apprentices found themselves training for jobs which no longer existed. Since work now had to be sought outside the community, the merchants lost their customers, the churches lost their congregations, and the town lost its taxpayers.

What modifications occurred in Caliente's social norms can only be partly inferred. Those who had raised families and built their lives around the values of the community internalized the norms and transmitted them to their children because such norms had proved to be reliable guides in developing an acceptable standard of living. But dieselization ended much of the "good life" and normative dissensus followed. Those who had followed the older norms most diligently began to question their adequacy when they found their work disintegrating and saw that only the deviants from the old norms — the childless and the selfish — could escape because they had no interest or investment in the community. While those who stayed continued to profess their belief in "the American way" of progress, they felt that the railroad's sudden decision to withdraw solely on the basis of profit showed a cynical disregard for the loyalty of its employees developed through years of good service and good citizenship. The people of Caliente looked to the leadership of "pressure groups" for new norms to guide behavior, and soon saw the value of political action in softening the consequences of technological change. Union members became enthusiastic supporters of new work rules, such as requiring three men in a diesel cab, even though outsiders who had not experienced normative dissensus regarded such practices as needless inefficiency. The old norms no longer made sense to the people of Caliente and they now faced the struggle of developing a new consensus in almost every institutional area of the community.[3]

What happened in Caliente overnight has happened in every society more gradually. Social change makes obsolete old norms which many people con-

3. Based on W. F. Cottrell, "Death by Dieselization: A Case Study in the Reaction to Technological Change," *American Sociological Review*, vol. 16, no. 3 (June 1951), pp. 358–65.

tinue to follow because of their value in guiding previous behavior. But since social change makes behavior in accordance with old norms impossible, new norms are sought. The problems that emerged in Caliente were a result of changes which most people would evaluate as "progress." While the people of Caliente continued to approve of progress, they had not anticipated that it would affect them so directly; and their reaction illustrates the important point that social problems are not created by "evil" forces but by the forces which have created the modern world.

TYPES OF SOCIETIES

Sociologists and anthropologists have developed many different ways to describe societies. All societies have some features in common. This makes it possible to conceive of an ideal type — that is, no one society would possess all of the characteristics included in the type, but each one would have a portion of the traits suggested. While it is possible to construct types to illustrate many different traits, we shall restrict ourselves to the folk society and the industrial society, which can be used to demonstrate the impact of social changes and its consequences for behavioral deviation and normative dissensus. In this book, we will concentrate upon the industrial society, whose traits can best be developed by contrast with an opposite type, the folk society.

The folk society is so small and limited that its members know each other well because they remain in close contact all of their lives. Communication is by word of mouth, and few individuals stray beyond the geographical limits of their own society so that they seldom realize that those in other societies have different norms. Their own normative order is in the custody of elders and is transmitted from generation to generation with little change. The primary unit of social organization is the kin group, the center of all activity within the society, which makes all decisions and preserves and transmits all norms. Thus, the folk society as a whole is composed of economically self-sufficient groups that face life's problems in conventional ways with traditional and automatic behavior which is expected and is seldom questioned or criticized. Because of their isolation and continuous interaction, the members of a folk society are all very much alike, both genetically and socially. Norms are clear and consistent and deviation is minimal. The society as a whole is characterized by a strong sense of identification and belonging together as members of the same group.[4]

The industrial society, as exemplified by many of the countries of the West, including the United States, directly contrasts with the folk society. The kin

4. Robert Redfield, "The Folk Society," *American Journal of Sociology* (January 1947), pp. 293–308.

group as the sole source of norms is, to a great extent, replaced by other distinct and specialized economic, political, religious, and educational organizations. An industrial society is a large society, characterized by differentiation and specialization, so that many new institutional areas are created which have no precedent in the past and thus require new norms. The society is so complex that, within the institutions themselves, groups such as labor and management evolve and utilize social, economic, or political pressure to maintain or extend their own norms. In such a society normative dissensus is constant and inevitable.

The complexity of an industrial society is reflected in its dominant pattern of settlement — city life. In urban areas, large numbers of individuals become dependent upon one another regardless of their own wishes. And, even though people are interdependent, they do not know each other; during his lifetime a city dweller may never even see those who would have been relatives or neighbors in a folk society. Extensive interaction with specific individuals is minimal. Impressions of social norms come impersonally from the radio, the newspaper, or television.

Because of the different levels of experience necessary for a complex division of labor, an industrial society is characterized by a heterogeneous population. To fulfill the specialized tasks which a division of labor requires, individuals must often move from place to place, leaving those with whom they have shared common experiences. Thus, the mobile heterogeneous population of an industrial society is often confronted with new norms which arise from unique experiences, or different norms which conflict with traditional patterns and create dissensus, since the presence of new norms compels a re-evaluation of older ones. Since an industrial society must co-operate with other industrial societies, having their own social norms, a situation emerges which invites comparisons of norms between societies as well as within them.

An industrial society, then, is far more complex than a folk society because of shifts in population, an extensive division of labor, economic interdependence with other societies having other norms, and technological change which create innovations in experience and behavior for which traditional norms are inadequate. The social control of the kin group is replaced by complex sets of institutional norms which often conflict, so that dissensus and deviation are plentiful and social problems arise.

In emphasizing social complexity and change, we must not ignore the continuity and consistency of values within industrial societies; the most complex society can change without flying apart. The next chapters portray the types of change in an industrial society and indicate the directions those changes have taken in American society.

THE PLAN OF ANALYSIS

The analysis in subsequent chapters centers on American society as one example of an industrial society. The choice of concentrating on American society is dictated by convenience and consistency. Broadening the analysis to include other societies would require shifting cultural contexts. Restricting the analysis may reinforce provincialism since it treats the society as a self-contained, independent social system. However, this limitation allows a more intensive focus and may be of value in understanding other societies.

Throughout the analysis, industrialization is viewed as a force creating social problems. The following chapter depicts the silent revolutions which have produced industrial societies. In subsequent chapters, each institutional area is analyzed in terms of the consequences of industrialization. A society can be viewed as a system of interconnected parts. Because of these interconnections, change in one part of society produces strain and frequently change in other parts. Each institution serves a different function but, because of interconnections among institutions, a change in one ultimately has the effect of a pebble thrown into still water. Industrialization is the pebble in this analysis of social problems.

Since industrialization is viewed as a "causal" factor, the economic institution is not treated separately. Nor is there a separate discussion of political institutions. While normative changes have occurred in these two institutional areas, we have chosen to concentrate on those areas which traditionally have been of sociological concern.

In each chapter dealing with normative dissensus, a similar pattern is followed. The *normative problem* is stated, centering on the adaptation demanded of each institution by the development of an industrial society. A normative conception is suggested, based on pre-industrial social conditions. These *historical normative conceptions* derive from several sources; some had their roots in the European cultural heritage diffused to the society through its immigrant populations; other elements emerged during the colonial experience and from the early farming frontier conditions. In general, these historical conceptions developed prior to the beginning of the twentieth century.

These normative conceptions achieved a high degree of consensus because of the stability of pre-industrial America. The precise degree of consensus must remain unknown without the existence of data such as public opinion and attitude studies; these techniques were a by-product of later stages of industrialization. However, even without such data, it is possible, through the use of historical materials, to reconstruct these normative conceptions and to infer their widespread consensus in American society. By this reconstruction, the historical norms serve as a starting point for analyzing each institution.

This consensus in each of the institutional areas was undermined by the gradual changes brought about by industrialization. The social conditions on which these historical conceptions were based were transformed, creating the opportunity, and even the necessity, for change. Newer *contemporary normative conceptions* emerged, taking these changes into account, and, thus produced the problematic condition of normative dissensus. The contemporary conceptions are, in most instances, treated as a contrast to the former ones. In some institutions, there has been a reaction not only to the historical conception but to the contemporary one also, which is called the *emergent normative conception*. In most institutions, however, only two dissident conceptions are treated.

The plan of analysis, then, consists of discussion of the evolution from a historical to a contemporary normative conception produced by the modifications in the social structure created by increasing industrialization. Figure 1-1 summarizes the plan of analysis.

Fig. 1-1. The Analysis of Normative Dissensus.

Type of Normative Conception

Type of Social Structure

Time Dimension

----------1860---1880 --1900---1940---1960--------

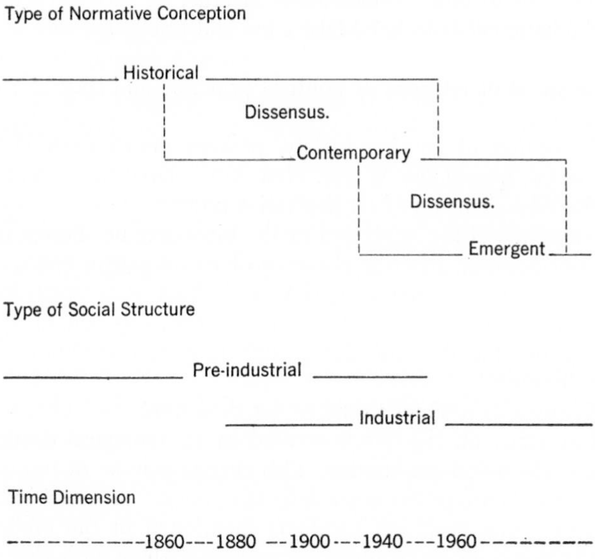

The next chapter further explores the forces creating the industrial society which necessitated normative change. Starting with the normative changes in the American community, subsequent chapters discuss the family, education, religion, mass communication, science, leisure, and medical care. Two chapters deal with norms in racial and ethnic relations. The analysis then turns to behavioral deviation, emphasizing mental illness and crime.

SUMMARY

Every society responds to certain needs. The way these needs are met vary from society to society and constitute cultural differences. In every society, norms specify the way members of a society should behave within various institutions. Norms are learned through the transmission of culture and are shared, creating predictability of behavior when there is consensus on and conformity to them.

Some behavior may not conform to important norms within a society, and may be considered deviant. There may be disagreement as to what norms are appropriate to guide behavior within a particular institution. This disagreement is called here normative dissensus. Conditions of deviation and dissensus constitute social problems.

Social change creates opportunities for deviation and dissensus. Folk societies are characterized by little social change, but in rapidly changing industrial societies the conditions producing deviation and dissensus are maximized.

QUESTIONS AND SUGGESTIONS FOR FURTHER STUDY

1. Every society has to meet certain needs in order to survive. What would you consider the basic needs to be? Make a list and briefly indicate why each is essential.
2. Take a statement of religious or political principle and state the norms which can be inferred.
3. Read a description of another society, perhaps drawn from Howard Becker (ed.), *Societies Around the World*, New York: Dryden, 1956, and from this account, describe elements of its normative order.
4. Read a community study, suggested in the bibliographic sources in Chapter 3, and from this account, describe elements of its normative order.
5. Observe a group over a period of time and, from your observations, write a list of norms which apply. Based on these norms, can you show instances of deviation of the members of the group? Can you determine examples of normative dissensus?
6. Why is dissensus sometimes mistaken for deviation?
7. Write a case study on the effects created by technological change in a community with which you are familiar. This change may be of the type described in the case of Caliente or one created by the "boom" of a new industrial plant.
8. Take another social problems text, one mentioned in the bibliography, and compare the theory of social problems presented there with that presented in this chapter.

SUGGESTED READINGS

(Note: In this and subsequent bibliographies, a number of paperback books are included. They are designated by   P.   While many of these are not "standard" sociological works, this does not mean that they are not worthwhile. Their accessibility often compensates for the gaps of many libraries.)

Bernard, Jessie, *Social Problems at Mid Century: Role, Status and Stress in a Context of Abundance*, New York: Dryden, 1957. This text views social problems in terms of shifts in roles and changes in status within a society.

Clinard, Marshall B., *Sociology of Deviant Behavior*, 2nd ed., New York: Rinehart, 1963. This book concentrates on various forms of deviant behavior. It is especially strong in its discussion of crime.

Cuber, John F., *Sociology: A Synopsis of Principles*, 4th ed., New York: Appleton-Century-Crofts, 1959. A popular introductory text. It includes a discussion of social norms in Chapter 14.

Horton, Paul B., and Gerald R. Leslie, *The Sociology of Social Problems*, 2nd ed., New York: Appleton-Century-Crofts, 1960. This widely used text employs three different approaches to social problems: (1) the social disorganization approach, (2) the personal deviation approach and (3) the conflict in values approach.

Mead, Margaret, *Cultural Patterns and Technical Change*, New York: New American Library. (A Mentor Book)   P   This work was originally prepared as a UNESCO publication. The author, a well-known anthropologist, describes some of the consequences of technological changes in folk societies.

Redfield, Robert, *The Primitive World and Its Transformations*, Ithaca: Cornell University Press, 1957.   P   A discussion of the impact of change and its transformation of folk societies.

Social Problems, Official Journal of the Society for the Study of Social Problems. This journal contains the best continuing treatment of various aspects of social problems now available.

Sumner, William Graham, *Folkways*, New York: Dover, 1962.   P   This classic, written by one of America's pioneer social scientists, was published in 1906. Sumner introduced the concepts of *folkways* and *mores* to indicate different types of norms.

CHAPTER **2** THE DEVELOPMENT OF
AN INDUSTRIAL SOCIETY

The world revolution of our time is "made in U.S.A." It is not Communism, Fascism, the new nationalism of the non-Western peoples, or any of the other "isms" that appear in the headlines. They are reactions to the basic disturbance, secondary rather than primary. The true revolutionary principle is the idea of mass-production. Nothing ever before recorded in the history of man equals, in speed, universality and impact, the transformation this principle has wrought in the foundations of society in the forty short years since Henry Ford turned out the first "Model T."

Though "made in Detroit," the impact of the new principle is not confined to the United States or to the old industrial territory of the West. Indeed, the impact is greatest on the raw-material-producing, pre-industrial civilizations which have no resistance to the new forces, no background or habit-pattern of industrial life to cushion the shock. In China the mass-production principle, swept into the hinterland from the coastal cities by the forced migration of industries during the Japanese invasion, is destroying the world's oldest and hitherto its stablest institution: the Chinese family. In India, industrialization has begun to corrode the Hindu caste system: ritual restrictions on proximity and intercourse between castes simply cannot be maintained under factory conditions. Russia uses the new mass-production principle to try again where Byzantium failed: to mate Europa and the Bull, the technological fruits of Western thought with oriental despotism, to produce a new world order which claims to be the legitimate heir to both East and West. In our own country the Old South, hitherto least touched by industry and still living in the ruins of its ante-bellum rural order, is speedily being "tractored off." Indeed, conversion of the Southern farm into a rural assembly line seems on the verge of "solving" the Southern race problem in a manner never dreamed of by either Southern Liberal or Southern Reactionary: by pushing the Negro off the land into the industrial cities.[1]

SILENT REVOLUTIONS

Most of us have probably never thought of "the Negro problem" in the way described above, as the particular result of a world-wide shift to industrialism. Our society is full of such problems, however, and this chapter will

1. Peter F. Drucker, *The New Society: The Anatomy of the Industrial Order*, New York: Harper, 1949, p. 1. Reprinted by permission of Harper & Row, Publishers.

trace their source to a series of "silent revolutions," gradual changes in the normative standards of behavior that resulted from America's emergence as an industrial nation.

The impact of these revolutions can best be traced from the historical and economic conditions which preceded them. Before industrialization the Western world was feudalistic, being composed of small communities formed about the land holdings of a particular lord which were called a "manor." The manorial court governed economic relationships and settled disputes over the way in which land and labor were to be distributed and used. The court was also responsible for the morality of the entire community, and even controlled the serf's right to marry and to leave the manor. Feudalistic life was, therefore, only slightly more complex than life in the "folk society" described in Chapter 1. Behavioral norms which gained consensus within the manorial community were transmitted from generation to generation by "kin groups," and people were isolated in their self-sufficient communities so that life was reasonably simple and secure. Even the serfs, who had no political rights, could not be forced off their land without just cause; and, though both serfs and free landholders earned little more than enough to live by, they could depend on the manor for defense and protection against the unjust actions of other manors.

The feudalistic hierarchy of a single lord and his landholders was replaced by the development of small towns and cities long before the machine age. But, when industrialism emerged toward the end of the eighteenth century, there were still large landholders, and "kin groups" still controlled normative standards of behavior throughout society. Only with the advent of the factory system was the importance of the kin group de-emphasized, because the industrial worker could live apart from his community and family; because he now earned wages and often he no longer felt directly responsible even to close relatives. Young workers, especially, began to receive wages which made them economically equal, and even superior, to their parents. They were attracted to cities, where the jobs were, and lost all identification with their old home environment, suddenly finding themselves self-sufficient and isolated.

Life in the industrial cities demanded new responses to new social norms. Men could no longer own the tools with which they worked. Their tools were in the factories. Therefore, work and "life" became increasingly separate, and the economic necessities of work made it the basis of life's responsibilities; the breadwinner was removed from home, and family life began to center on his workday because the rewards he received in terms of wages determined his family's standard of living and his children's chance for happiness and future success. The moral worth of an individual came to be evaluated in terms of wages, and the differences among people occupying different occupational levels began to be reflected in the community where one lived and the sort of activities engaged in after the workday had ended: the "kin group" was rapidly supplanted by the community itself as the source and ultimate judge of norms because behavior was now being evaluated in terms of economic and social "status."

Toward the end of the eighteenth century, and continuing through the nineteenth, our economic norms were undergoing radical change, and people needed moral and political justification for their new way of life. Economically, it seemed that every man possessed enough sense to serve his own best interests and, in doing so, to benefit society as well; and politically it followed that all men deserved equal rights and that the people themselves should be the best judge of their society, its laws and government. The technological change from hand to machine labor which we know as the Industrial Revolution was, in reality, a series of silent revolutions which altered family and community norms and created innumerable social problems. In this section, we shall examine these silent revolutions first descriptively, in terms of "mobility" within our society, and then interpretively, to determine the psychological impact on workers. Next, we shall consider the revolution in technology itself which resulted in science as a method and symbol of progress and which also required a system of mass communication, with resulting problems and new responsibilities. Finally, we shall examine the effects of these silent revolutions on the organizational structure of our whole society.

THE MOBILITY REVOLUTION

Geographical Mobility. An industrial society depends upon a large working force, and, in the United States, this need has been partly satisfied by immigration. Apart from the remnants of Indian tribes, all Americans are either immigrants or the descendants of immigrants. At the time of the Revolutionary War, there were only 4 million people to begin our nation; but, during the next hundred years, over 35 million people left Europe and came to the United States because of the unrest and displacement caused by industrialization. The large land holdings in most European countries had been broken up as they passed from generation to generation, and with agriculture becoming mechanized, fewer workers were needed. Widespread depression provided further incentive for emigration: word about industrial employment in America spread throughout Europe, was echoed by friends and relatives already there, and fell on receptive ears of many who had little to lose and much to gain. They came by the millions, found jobs or created them, and stayed. Although this mass movement from Europe was interrupted by World War I, and virtually halted by restrictive legislation in 1921 and

1924, our country retained a heritage of 8 million people from Central Europe (Germany, Poland, etc.), six million from Eastern Europe (U.S.S.R., Latvia, etc.), 5 million from Italy, 4.5 million from Ireland, 4 million from England, 3 million from the Balkan countries, and 2 million from Scandinavia.[2]

The need for labor throughout America also created a high rate of internal migration. People took literally Horace Greeley's advice to "go West" where land could be acquired cheaply and developed, at first for agriculture and later for industry. From 1935 to 1940, the net migration West included about one million people, and from 1940 to 1957 it was over twice that number. From 1950 to 1960, the average increase in population for the United States was 18.5 per cent, but California increased 48.5 per cent, and Nevada and Arizona equaled Alaska, at 70 per cent. These figures are somewhat influenced by variable birth rates, of course, but the trend toward Western migration undoubtedly accounts for most of the increase.

Industry's needs created another geographical shift; from rural to urban areas. In fact, America has always had difficulty keeping people "down on the farm." At the first census in 1790, only 5 per cent of the population lived in urban areas. By 1960 this figure had increased to 70 per cent, largely because industry could satisfy the financial needs of so many farmers who never really earned net profit, except in years of postwar adjustment. From 1920 to 1961, this country's population increased by over 75 million to a total of 182 million, and yet the number of people living on farms dropped to half of the 1920 farm population. In 1961 there was approximately the same number of farmers as there had been during the Civil War, when only 32 million people lived in the United States.

But geographical mobility has greater total significance than these patterns of westward and rural migration. From 1950 to 1960, over 30 million people moved *each year*; and, though two-thirds of this movement was local, from block to block or across town, 5 million people went to another county and another 5 million moved to different states. Thus, almost one American in five moves every year, usually in search of industrial opportunity; and, if this total pattern of mobility were distributed equally throughout the United States, our entire population would be reshuffled every five years. We can no longer consider migration "abnormal," merely because it increases during such crises as wars and depressions. In fact, those who stayed at home in 1950 were slightly below the average educational level of nine years, while those who moved farthest away were well over two years above it. Professions requiring a great deal of education are characterized by a high rate of mo-

2. Oscar Handlin, *The Uprooted: The Epic Story of the Great Migrations That Made American People*, Boston: Little, Brown, 1951, p. 3.

bility, partly because the bulk of industrial opportunity is still concentrated in a few sections of our country. In 1961, for example, three states — New York, New Jersey, and Pennsylvania — accounted for more than a quarter of all jobs in heavy industry and manufacturing. And, since the states with greater industrial opportunities generally have lower birth rates, the supply of workers with specialized skills in a given area seldom corresponds with the demands of industry. People often assume that "migrants" are shiftless and irresponsible. But today, the man who leaves home is often the key to the industrial way of life,[3] for he is usually a worker or manager who has *accepted* the responsibility of being "interchangeable," of being able to function efficiently wherever he may be moved by the changing pressures of competition and of industrial decline or expansion.

Many changes in technology also are responsible for geographical mobility. Eventually atomic energy may decentralize industry by supplying a new means of power for areas not having the water or fuel which is now needed to generate electricity. Moreover, factories producing atomic materials for defense have already begun a trend toward large-scale employment in outlying, and even isolated, areas of the country. Automation is another technological advance which may radically influence geographical mobility. The completely automatic factory is controlled by electronic brains which require the supervision of only a few operators and technicians, so new buildings can often be constructed away from older densely populated centers. And, even though the American economy as a whole generally supplies new resources for employment despite increased technical efficiency, workers in newly automated plants obviously face job readjustment, which usually means relocation as well.

America's high rate of geographical mobility is still viewed by some people as a mere passing phase. But, for the reasons previously noted, it is difficult to conceive of a fixed and stable population in this country, at least in the near future. On the contrary, geographical mobility is an integral factor in the development and maintenance of the entire industrial system.

Social Mobility. As we have seen, one aspect of the mobility revolution has been geographical mobility. But, once he obtains employment, the individual may experience another type of mobility. For this process, by which workers move from one position to another within a hierarchy of prestige, we shall use the general term *social mobility.* Most American industries feel they constitute little societies within our society; employees are part of an industrial "family," and are expected to act according to behavioral norms agreed upon by management and unions. There is a complex division of labor within the

3. William H. Whyte, *The Organization Man,* New York: Simon and Schuster, 1956, p. 297.

industrial community just as there is in society, and some jobs have more prestige than others. Generally, positions of leadership and responsibility command the most prestige, and other jobs are evaluated by the amount of special training and intelligence required to perform them. Though this hierarchy of prestige tends to remain constant, the people and jobs affected by it are socially mobile because of rapid changes within competitive industries. Jobs increase or decrease according to financial pressures within an industry, and technological change creates new jobs or demands new skills and places extra responsibility on workers in old ones. And, just as there are changes in the demand for specialized skill and experience, there are shifts in the supply of manpower. No elite group can control the distribution of intelligence and talent, and individuals with high ability in lower positions will eventually displace, or even replace, those above them.

Because of this consensus about the importance of ability, a number of norms traditionally used to determine one's status in society are not valid when applied to occupational placement. Rapid technological change within an industry prevents the "inheritance" of jobs, so that being able to do what one's father did is not enough. And, since who you are becomes less important than what you can do, job placement is not a matter of social status; a person's family background, age, sex, race, and religion are important only if they affect his work. But often the norms of industry and society conflict over this aspect of social mobility, producing considerable dissensus. For example, most immigrants entered the American economy at its lowest level of employment because of language difficulties and a lack of specialized industrial training. In comparison with his European experience, of course, the immigrant probably regarded his position as one of unlimited opportunity, particularly because his children had "no place to go but up" in a new and rapidly expanding economy. But American society did not receive the immigrant with the same amount of enthusiasm as American industry, and this lack of social acceptance created problems of adjustment. Many immigrants tended to form self-contained ethnic communities which preserved the old norms and provided some continuity with their past. And, while the first generation could satisfactorily combine the new economic rewards of the industrial society with an older way of life imported from Europe, the second generation found itself caught between two systems of norms. By requiring attendance at public schools, the society began to indoctrinate the sons of immigrants into the mysteries of American speech and behavior, while their parents insisted that they speak "the language of home" and retain the old customs. Today, other so-called "minority groups" such as Negroes, Jews, Mexicans, Puerto Ricans, and Southern rural whites have assumed the role of immigrant in matters of normative conflict between the status ascribed to one by society, and the potential status one may achieve in industry.

Despite particular cases of prejudice and social injustice, there are solid economic reasons for optimism concerning social mobility in an expanding industrial society. Since industrial expansion is usually based on technological development, more people are constantly being called upon to perform clerical, technical, and professional services within growing corporations. Thus, there is an increase in professional, managerial, and "white-collar" positions and a decrease in manual tasks which demand less skill, and thus receive less reward. But, even without this increase in occupations of higher status, the birth rate insures favorable conditions for social mobility. Since workers in higher positions of responsibility tend to have smaller families than those working at lower levels of skill and prestige, an industrial society needs upward social mobility merely to fill the *same number* of high level positions.

Given a healthy economy, there should be little *real* difference in social mobility among the industrial societies of the Western world. But the fact remains that America has always *seemed* to be more socially mobile than other countries.[4] If the value of the dollar had remained constant from 1900 to 1950, America's standard of living would have doubled itself,[5] and individuals tend to regard the widespread availability and abundance of consumer goods as an index of this progress and of their own success. For example, even though a worker has not improved his occupational position in five years, he will probably feel that his ability to buy a home on a forty-year mortgage or a car on thirty-six "easy" monthly installments constitutes genuine social mobility — and such purchases would probably convince his neighbors as well. It has also been estimated that between 20 and 30 per cent of the American urban work force has, at some time, been self-employed.[6] And, while small business has a high mortality rate in the United States, such ventures prove that many people still take a chance on remaining at least semi-independent within the normative hierarchy of our industrial society.

This constant attempt to achieve seems to typify "the American way of life." In the past, America's immigrants saw endless opportunity, in spite of objective difficulties; today, this country's minority groups again carry the heavy burden of poverty and social and racial prejudice, but believe fervently in social mobility as a means of personal betterment. In any industrial society, of course, the attainment of goals through competition results in higher social and financial status for the individual. But in America, special emphasis is constantly being placed on the inevitable achievement of such

4. Seymour M. Lipset and Reinhard Bendix, *Social Mobility in Industrial Society*, Berkeley: University of California Press, 1961, pp. 13–77.
5. William Ogburn, "Technology and the Standard of Living in the United States," *American Journal of Sociology*, LX, 4 (1955), pp. 380–86.
6. Lipset and Bendix, op. cit. p. 102.

status: people compete for jobs, for mates, for wealth, recognition, and power so that one must "earn the grade" in school, and then "earn the right" to every position sought in later life.

The norms centering on achievement can reflect a society's weakness as well as its strength. As we learned in Chapter 1, the importance of a norm can usually be determined by society's punishments for deviation as well as by its rewards for conformity; and many of America's problems are caused by those who punish themselves, or are punished by others, for not "living up" to these aspirations. People whose status remains inferior may utterly reject the goals of their society, relying solely on a theory of ultimate equality embodied by a religious or political ideal. Others may find their way blocked by racial or religious barriers, and then violate still more serious norms in protest, becoming criminals to gain some measure of substitute satisfaction. Parents may deny themselves both the spiritual and financial rewards of life, investing all their hopes in their children who quickly sense that they must succeed to please their parents. In general, emphasis on achievement strains conventional morality in many otherwise ordinary areas of American life; material ends often are sought by tainted means, and the football player is too often tempted to foul a star opponent in order to win, just as the student often is tempted to cheat for the sake of a better grade. Small wonder that a society which places such emphasis on mobility is characterized by an extremely high rate of mental illness and by much prejudice, a feeling that others (particularly minority groups) have too much power and constitute an unfair threat to one's own status.[7]

Thus, the mobility revolution has been an inevitable component in the making of our industrial society and has introduced new problems of psychological tension, behavioral deviation, and normative dissensus. The geographically mobile person tends to be somewhat isolated, having no permanent roots in society; and the socially mobile person lives between two worlds, feeling alienated from the social level he desires to leave and unaccepted by the higher level he aspires to reach. For Americans, one of the costs of mobility is chronic insecurity because the individual is taught to be dissatisfied with his current status and position in life.

THE BEHAVIORAL REVOLUTION

Previously we have seen how mobility creates conflict among the members of an industrial society; now we shall see how work itself can create dissensus and deviation. The term "mass production" evokes an image of a long con-

7. A. B. Hollingshead, R. Ellis, and E. Kirby, "Social Mobility and Mental Illness," *American Sociological Review*, XIX (October 1954), pp. 577–84. Also, see Joseph Greenbaum and L. I. Pearlin, "Vertical Mobility and Prejudice" in *Class, Status, and Power*, Reinhard Bendix and Seymour M. Lipset (eds.), Glencoe, Ill.: Free Press, 1953, p. 492.

veyer belt attended by rows of people, each putting a slightly different part into something which will eventually emerge as a finished product. But the factory assembly line of mass production is only one aspect of *bureaucratization*, an industrial society's system for organizing all levels of social life.[8] Before industrialization, people performed their work largely at home, set their own pace, and started and stopped whenever they wished, within the limits of necessity. But, when the worker moved to factory or office, he became one part of a larger economic organization, and his task was only part of a broad operation requiring the combined efforts of other parts. The clerk in a department store depends on others who take a desired item from stock and pass it to a shipping clerk who wraps it and gives it to the truck driver who will deliver it. And this, in turn, necessitates paper work since other people must prepare a bill, inventory the item purchased, and re-order another so the entire process can begin again. Moreover, bureaucratization is not confined to sales organizations. Today, for example, a single story in a magazine or newspaper is the product of a group of specialists — columnists, rewrite men, copy and photo editors, pressmen and linotype operators — who must be co-ordinated by a "managing" editor. The principle of mass production, a complex division of labor among individuals whose tasks are co-ordinated under managers, has permeated our entire society. Through bureaucracies we "produce" education, governmental activities, recreation, and even religion; and we shall next see how this organizational system has necessitated a behavioral revolution, changing the individual's feelings about himself and his responsibilities toward society.

The work world is specialized.

> . . . men differ in personality, intellect, and potential
> . . . no man can do two things at the same time
> . . . no man can be in two places at the same time
> . . . no man knows everything [9]

These few simple assertions are the main reasons for the development of specialization within an industrial society. Men are different, and their individual strengths must be cultivated and utilized so they can function with maximum efficiency as parts within bureaucracies. Specialization, then, is a principle which makes possible bureaucratization. There are probably fewer

8. The term "bureaucracy" throughout the book is used in its sociological meaning — that of a type of organization which systematically co-ordinates the work of many individuals. It is not used in its popular meaning of inefficiency and red tape in government. For a summary discussion of this concept, see Peter Blau, *Bureaucracy in Modern Society*, New York: Random House, 1956.

9. Luther Gulick, "Notes on the Theory of Organization," in *Papers on the Science of Administration*, New York: Institute of Public Administration, Columbia University, 1937, p. 3.

totally unskilled and untrained workers in our society now than ever before, and technological developments lessen the number of workers relying solely on manual skills, while increasing the demand for the intellectual and social skills of co-ordinators and organizers. Thus, today management is becoming increasingly concerned about effective communication along the growing "chain of command"; and, in this age of increasing specialization, our society is often affected by a broader lack of communication between the individual worker and the company he works for. In its initial stages, industrialization destroyed traditional skills because individual workers were not sufficiently specialized; for example, a cobbler with the whole range of special skills needed to make a pair of shoes suddenly found himself faced with the task of running a machine which performed only one of the many operations he knew so well. Such adjustment was difficult because the new specialized task often was mechanical and repetitious, requiring little thought or attention, and the worker no longer had personal responsibility for the finished product. Even today, industrial workers who have never known the satisfactions of individual craftmanship often feel dissatisfied because they cannot visualize their own role in terms of a complete product or service without feeling dwarfed, restricted, and incomplete; ultimately, it is the factory or the company which produces and, whether it be conscious or unconscious, an individual's dissatisfaction with the narrowness of specialization can often result in dissensus and deviation — idleness, or a search for more meaningful work.

The work world centers around a regular routine. It has been suggested that the clock, not the steam engine, is the machine that made industrialization possible.[10] On entering or leaving the factory, many workers must punch a time clock, and all of us compete with the clock as well as with each other; even the university professor is expected to "produce" a certain amount of information per hour in the classroom. Workers, managers, teachers, and students must all be on time or be penalized, and even doctors "schedule" operations. Time has become an invaluable commodity in industrial society; Benjamin Franklin insisted that "time is money," and we tacitly agree every time we worry about "spending" or "saving" it. We get up not with the chickens, but with the alarm clock, eat not when we feel hungry but during lunch hour, and go to bed, sleepy or not, whenever it is "bedtime."

The norm of being "on time" is so much a part of our lives that we really notice it only in contrast with norms of other societies. When Southern migrant workers or Mexican laborers do not bring to the centers of industry the normative standards of regularity and punctuality, we find their attitude puzzling and frustrating. An even broader contrast is provided by newly in-

10. Lewis Mumford, *Technics and Civilization*, New York: Harcourt, Brace, 1934, p. 14.

dustrialized nations like China, where centuries of tradition do not support norms of regularity and the society must enforce them by governmental discipline.

The work world is impersonal and contractual. The intense interest in time results from the regularity and precise co-ordination expected at all levels of life. Society's demands include tax forms, insurance forms, and endless applications and examinations which cover everything from drivers' licenses to charge accounts, just as industry's activities are guided by normative work rules specified in contracts, training manuals, and numerous "memos from the boss." Since the principle behind such routines is efficiency, the individual may at times be depressed by the vast amount of impersonal planning which attends every stage of his career.

The individual worker's relationships with his fellow workers and his superiors reinforce this impersonality. In folk society the individual could share the risks involved in earning a living with his kin group or with the whole community. But the worker in an industrial society is valued chiefly for his labor. The employer who hired him can also fire him, and accidents or illness cause temporary, but just as crucial, unemployment since there is little family or community support to depend on. Labor unions have been organized to offer the support during an emergency which, in folk societies, is still supplied by the kin group or community. But today, most unions are bureaucratized, and provide "sick pay" according to the same impersonal economic norms that management uses for wages. This sharp division between the individual's personal fortunes and his work activities is accentuated by his position in the hierarchy of industrial prestige. All workers are expected to leave their personal problems, activities, and attitudes at the door when they report for work. The very terms "lunch hour" and "coffee break" imply a new and more personal situation in contrast with the formal work relationships which prevail throughout the day. "The boss" is expected to be fair, impartial, and objective, avoiding all personal considerations in evaluating and supervising those under his authority; and the worker, in return, is expected not to "butter him up," to use one of the hundreds of phrases which disparage the seeking of favors or approval beyond the call of duty.

Another aspect of impersonality in industry is represented by the contract, an implicit or written agreement between the worker and his company which limits each to those formal responsibilities and activities which constitute a specific job. If an individual worker were to ask for additional wages solely because he needed the money more than his employer, neither his union nor his company would pay much attention because the demand is plainly outside the work contract. But, if a kinsmen of the employer asked for money on the same grounds of need, the employer could not refuse him solely because he had no right to ask. He might still refuse the request, of course, but he would at least have to grant his kinsman the *right* to ask because of family ties. Since industrial norms are removed from home and kin group, they are uncomplicated by diffuse personal considerations; favoritism for "the Boss's son" is a classic example of flagrant violation because every employee's rights and obligations are specific and definite; neither the employer nor the worker can ask for more than is agreed upon in the contract.

If all social relationships were as formal and impersonal as those in industry, family life would be impossible because individuals would have no emotional ties or loyalties extending beyond a contractual agreement. Thus, many educators, authors, and clergymen have been dismayed by the behavioral revolution. For specialization and routinization destroys spontaneity when it influences leisure, art, sex, education, and even religion; and many thoughtful people wonder whether man is becoming "depersonalized" and "dehumanized" because of increased mechanization and bureaucratization.

THE COMMUNICATIONS REVOLUTION

Americans cannot spend a day without being near a radio or watching a television program, and hardly ever sit down without picking up a book, newspaper, magazine, or comic book. They find it difficult to go from one place to another without receiving advice from a billboard or loudspeaker, and seldom go a week without seeing a movie at a theater, a school, or even a church. In 1962 over 1700 daily, and 10,000 weekly, newspapers were published in the United States, along with almost 8000 magazines and periodicals. Every year book publishers issue about 15,000 new books or editions which can be purchased directly or borrowed from one of the 10,000 public libraries. To put it another way, those whose primary concern is conserving our forests would be shocked to know that every American consumes annually 300 pounds of reading matter. Moreover, at least one out of every four Americans goes to a movie every *week*, and over 97 per cent of our homes have radio, while television is quickly catching up, with 55 million sets in 90 per cent of the homes.

Most Americans take these facts for granted and seldom think of their influence as being the result of a silent revolution in the ways of disseminating information and ideas throughout an industrial society. But not too long ago, most people could not read and received their information largely by word of mouth. The few who could read received information from newspapers which were expensive and scarce, being hand printed on handmade paper. It was only after technological advances in printing that printers began to look for news instead of waiting for it to come to them. Their circulation increased, being promoted by growing literacy, and advertisers were attracted to the expanding enterprise, offering financial assistance so that more pages and readers, and advertisers, could be added. The new industries of publishing and advertising emerged and developed a common interest in communicating with new groups who were becoming increasingly important in the industrial society. Women were influential, so newspapers, advertisements, and features were addressed to them. New magazines catered to the special interests of farmers, workers, and many other groups who were becoming conscious of their part in an expanding economy. The thousands of immigrants coming to work in the factories found that their loyalty to America was often judged by their literacy, so they, too, became readers. Since people regard papers and magazines as far more than a mere factual source of news, it is easy to understand the successful debut of the comic strip in 1893.

Prints and photographs underwent a development similar to newspapers, for they began as advertising vehicles until technological advances and increased circulation made them a potential medium for entertainment as well. In the early 1900's, a way was found to project an image on a screen so that thousands could view the same picture and an industry dedicated to entertainment for the masses came to be symbolized by the word "Hollywood."

The emergence of our industrial society created the need for a quick and efficient message service. The telephone and the telegraph aided the rapid geographical expansion of business, and when radio was developed it was considered another message service of great value. However, radio had one fatal weakness — a lack of privacy. In the 1920's radio transmitters were operated primarily for the purpose of testing transmitting equipment and, when eavesdroppers began to make comments on the quality of the test signals, they soon found themselves being addressed as "ladies and gentlemen of the radio audience." Such listeners quickly grew tired of hearing test signals and soon "programs" were being presented. By 1930, two large broadcasting networks linked stations together, and advertisers saw another promising medium of mass communication.

Throughout the development of radio, the idea of transmitting pictures to accompany sound was also being considered. After World War II, factories geared to wartime production of electronic equipment became available for peacetime use. Television quickly became the medium to which sponsors turned because its novelty created sales almost overnight. Television antennas went up on almost every house, living rooms were rearranged, and soon television chairs and snack tables became essential equipment for quick-frozen "TV dinners."

In the development of these communications media, a common trend prevails. Each began as the result of a simple desire to inform people, then expanded into a large-scale commercial enterprise, and became a medium of entertainment as well. Thus, today, American newspapers, radio, and television all face the task of maintaining a balance among education, commercialism, and entertainment.

Historically, in the United States, the analogy of the "free market" in industry has also been applied to ideas. In the mass communication of ideas, individuals could express many conflicting opinions, and from this free interchange "truth" could emerge and the democratic process be confirmed. But once the town meeting was replaced by world-wide news coverage and the ice cream social by the local movie theater, one flaw in this theory became apparent. People who received views through the mass media could not answer back; they could only respond to the presentations as they occurred, and too often became the passive recipients of others' opinions. Moreover, within the last few years, another change has occurred in the communications revolution. Just as the competitive economic market has gradually been diminishing due to a concentration of production in a few large corporations, the communications market of ideas is narrowing because public opinion is concentrated in fewer sources of supply. Fewer people are able to give opinions through the mass media because the advertisements of many small "independent" shopkeepers are being replaced by advertising contracts with large corporations, and the opinions of local politicians are being supplanted by those of national party leaders who have the means to purchase time and space in the mass media. This gradual reduction presents the possibility that groups controlling the various channels of communication can offer their special and unique view of the world as the only "real" one, and have their opinions passively accepted. In fact, most of our ideas *are* derived from the mass media; today, people often refuse to believe in an event at all until they read about it or "actually see it" on television. In totalitarian societies leaders often maintain power by distorting facts, or by diverting public attention from important issues. When, in an industrial society, the mass media begin to take sides, the opposition has no comparable ideological weapons with which to reply. As it becomes easier for the "message from our sponsor" to become the program itself, the media of mass communication assume greater responsibility for developing normative consensus.

THE SCIENTIFIC REVOLUTION
Chapter 1 has illustrated how advances in technology can affect industry and society, so in this section we shall attempt only to describe the role applied science has played in our society's silent revolutions, and the way in which science itself has revolutionized norms. In the form of medical and sanitation measures, applied science has checked the spread of many diseases, promoting

a rapid growth of population. Improvements in sanitation, particularly, have enabled people to live more closely together in healthful circumstances, and, have thus facilitated rapid urban growth. Medical research also has increased our life span with the result that we have a new segment of the population with unique interests and problems, the aged.

Science also facilitates mobility throughout an industrial society. Technological innovations are often responsible for geographical mobility and advances in transportation have supplied the means; just as the railroads once promoted the westward movement, today cars, trains, and buses have created the "commuter movement" from cities to suburbs. So-called "labor-saving devices" have also promoted changes in the role of women, giving them more free time for social activities and enabling some housewives to enter industry.

In the United States, science has noticeably affected normative standards. When discussing the behavioral revolution, we noticed how industrialization tends to mechanize human behavior, but the influence of machines extends to our social life as well. The automobile has revolutionized patterns of courtship and partly released adolescents from adult supervision. Machines stand between a person and his daily life. The vacuum cleaner, the washer and dryer are between the housewife and her daily chores, and at the market she no longer faces the grocer and the butcher, but rows of cans and neatly packaged meat. Heating plants and air-conditioning systems separate the inside world from the outside, and our entertainment and conversation come increasingly from radio, television, movies, or magazines — all the result of industrial technology.

How, then, do we appear to other societies less influenced by technology? A Spanish encyclopedia contains the following entry:

> AMERICANISM: a way of life characteristic of the citizens of the United States who are commerce-minded, have a commercial soul, and are biased in favor of practical success and intense technicization and automation of all the processes of life, frequently neglecting higher values.[11]

Medieval man's primary loyalty was to God because that which was above and beyond one's earthly existence was believed to be better, more significant, and more *real*. But, as a more pragmatic outlook toward reality yielded impressive technological advances, some people began to suppose that man could manage without God. A process of secularization began, as science lent support to certain ideas (summarized historically by such labels as the Enlightenment and the Renaissance) which helped to displace religious conceptions about the nature of man and society. However, some European societies were unable or unwilling to exploit this change from an emphasis on

11. *Encyclopedia Universal Herder*, Barcelona, 1954.

eternal life to an emphasis on the improvement of man's present lot. Thus, the so-called "New World" *was* new because the American Puritans considered hard work and progress to be definite virtues, and our industrial society continued to stress these principles as an economic necessity. Older European societies tend to judge the United States in terms of their own traditional norms, lamenting our emphasis on material progress at the expense of the "higher" emotional and spiritual values represented by the arts, philosophy, and religion.

For us, however, such attitudes seem incorrect because technology and material progress are integral parts of an industrial society; today we seem to be on the verge of creating life itself in a test tube and of traveling through space to visit whole worlds not our own. Man seems to be the center of the universe and the measure of all things. The British philosopher and mathematician, Bertrand Russell, has eloquently summarized this position as follows:

In the prescientific world, power was God's. There was not much that men could do even in the most favorable circumstances, and the circumstances were liable to become unfavorable if men incurred the divine displeasure. This showed itself in earthquakes, pestilences, famines, and defeats in war. Since such events were frequent, it was obviously very easy to incur divine displeasure. Judging by the analogy of earthly monarchs, men decided that the thing most displeasing to the Deity is a lack of humility. If you wished to slip through life without disaster, you must be meek: you must be aware of your defenselessness and constantly ready to confess it. But the God before whom you humbled yourself was conceived in the likeness of man, so that the universe seemed human and warm and cozy — like home, if you are the youngest of a large family — painful at times, but never alien and incomprehensible.

In the scientific world, all this is different. It is not by prayer and humility that you cause things to go as you wish, but by acquiring a knowledge of scientific laws. The power you acquire in this way is much greater and much more reliable than that formerly supposed to be acquired by prayer, because you never could tell whether your prayer would be favorably heard in heaven. The power of prayer, moreover, had recognized limits; it would have been impious to ask too much. But the power of science has, so some people think, no known limits. We were told that faith could remove mountains, but no one believed it; we are now told that the atomic bomb can remove mountains and everyone believes it.

It is true that if we ever did stop to think about the cosmos we might find it uncomfortable. The sun may grow cold or blow up; the earth may lose its atmosphere and become uninhabitable. Life is a brief, small, and transitory phenomenon in an obscure corner, not at all the sort of thing that one would make a fuss about if one were not personally concerned. But it is monkish and futile — so scientific man will say — to dwell on such cold and unpractical thoughts. Let us get on with the job of fertilizing the desert, melting the arctic ice, and killing each other with perpetually improving technique. Some of our activities will do good, some harm, but all alike will show our power. And so, in this godless universe, we shall become gods or devils.[12]

Science, then, has created the most important silent revolution of all. As technological advances began to secularize man's view of the world, his social, religious, and political norms had to be redefined. God no longer seemed the source and delegator of political power and, to some degree, the history of the Western world is the gradual, sometimes halting, movement by "the people" toward some form of constitutional government. Once the power of its Puritan theocracy had been broken, the United States was also very careful to keep religion and politics separate.

But the question remains whether, by affecting our social, religious, and political norms, the scientific revolution has permanently altered other values. That a significant alteration has occurred is suggested in this modification of a traditional form.

The Twenty-third Psalm

(Materialist's Version)

Science is my shepherd;
I shall not want;
He maketh me to lie down on foam-rubber mattresses;
He leadeth me beside six lane highways.
He rejuvenateth my thyroid glands;
He leadeth me in the paths of psychoanalysis for peace of mind's sake.
Yea, though I walk through the valley of the shadow of the iron curtain,
I will fear no communist; for thou art with me; thy radar screen and thy hydrogen bomb, they comfort me.
Thou preparest a banquet before me in the presence of the world's billion hungry people.
Thou anointest my head with home permanents.
My beer-glass foameth over.
Surely prosperity and pleasure shall follow me all the days of my life; and I will dwell in Shangri-la forever.[13]

Some have already proclaimed science a new form of religion, both as a means of salvation and as a hope for "eternal" progress on earth, and we might well ponder their secular image of a "Good Life" full of material comforts and possessions.

THE ORGANIZATIONAL REVOLUTION

Our present era has been called the "second age of the Brontosaurus" because of the great rise in the number, size, and power of organizations in American

12. Bertrand Russell, *The Impact of Science on Society*, New York: Columbia University Press, 1951, pp. 17–18. Reprinted by permission of Columbia University Press.
13. "In a Spiritual Vacuum," *The Christian Century*, 73 (March 7, 1956), p. 300. Copyright 1956 by the Christian Century Foundation. Reprinted by permission.

society.[14] A hundred years ago, since there were few corporations and large businesses, labor unions were almost nonexistent, and there were few organizations for employers or professional men. No farm organizations of any importance existed, there was no American Legion or Veterans of Foreign Wars and, with the exception of the Masons, no fraternal organizations. Except for the government, the only organizations were churches, political parties, and a few local philanthropic societies. Government itself touched only a few areas of social life. There were no Departments of Labor, Agriculture, Commerce, Defense, or Health, Education, and Welfare, no agencies regulating aviation or communications, no FBI, and none of the countless other agencies, authorities, commissions, and boards we know today.

Today, the few organizations which existed a hundred years ago have taken their place among thousands of new ones. Every conceivable type of economic activity is represented by its own trade or occupational association. The corporation is dominant, nearly 18 million people belong to labor unions, and over half the farmers belong to one of three large farm organizations. Governmental agencies and departments have proliferated, and voluntary associations are created daily to aid distressed animals or investigate comic books. Veterans' organizations and fraternal orders have multiplied; clubs and charitable organizations have been created, and everywhere organizations are becoming larger, better organized, and more efficient. In this section, we shall attempt to discern the larger outlines of this organizational revolution in the emergence of big business, big government, big unions, and our smaller but important voluntary associations.

The Corporation. In the early days of the industrial revolution, industries were frequently organized by an individual who had money to invest and the ability to supervise the factories himself. Thus, his friends called him a "captain of industry," and his enemies, a "robber baron." Soon, however, the expanding economy carried most industries beyond the control of any single individual; and, though the lone entrepreneur has not completely disappeared, most economic activity today is carried out by the corporation. From a sociological standpoint, the corporation represents a unique principle in social organization because it has assumed certain legal rights which ordinarily belong only to individuals. While corporations are actually owned by many people, they can engage in contracts as individuals; and, in return for granting this privilege, the actual owners of a corporation — its stockholders — are held responsible only to the extent of their stock, and not for the total success or failure of the corporation. With such an arrangement, businesses no longer had to depend on the limited capital of one individual, and their existence was never threatened by the death of an owner. Though employees

14. Kenneth Boulding, "The Jungle of Hugeness," *Saturday Review* (March 1958), p. 8.

changed jobs and owners sold their stock to others, businesses continued and grew, as large amounts of capital began to accumulate within the corporate structure. Today, approximately 50 per cent of American manufacturing is held by about 150 corporations, most of which have individual assets of over $250 million. About two-thirds of the productive assets of the United States, excluding agriculture, are owned by an aggregate of not more than 500 corporations. Many single corporations in America today produce more than the combined industries of other countries; General Motors produces more cars than the British, German, and French automobile industries, and the United States Steel Corporation produces more than the entire British steel industry! In fact, with their budgets and payrolls, some of our corporations affect more people than most American states and many foreign countries; the budget of the American Telephone and Telegraph Company, for example, would place it about thirteenth in the annual expenditures of the various states.

Thus, through physical size and financial strength the corporation has had a revolutionary effect on America's norms of ownership and responsibility. While the stockholder has a theoretical right to share in the control of the organization, he does not own a factory or even a machine; and, particularly in the largest corporations, there are so many "owners" that no single coalition of stockholders can exercise effective control. To bridge this gap between theoretical ownership and actual management, a relatively new and powerful group of industrial managers has emerged. Today management is industry's true source of control and power; and since, at best, these men are only one of several owners, they seldom act in the self-seeking manner attributed to the owner-manager during the early stages of industrial development. Management has become a profession in which technical and scientific skills are of secondary importance because the manager himself is primarily valued for his ability to co-ordinate the skills and activities of others.

The Federal Government. Most corporations insist that they live dangerously, while other economic groups like workers and farmers are only interested in security. In reality, however, corporations have reduced many of the risks which made smaller business operations so insecure in the past. To protect their products against sudden shifts in consumer demand, most large corporations conduct large-scale advertising campaigns to create new tastes or reinforce old ones. Through the sponsorship of industrial research, corporations also control technological change; and their sheer size enables them to spread marketing risks over a diverse line of products and to diminish the dangers of faulty leadership by centering authority in the organization itself, and not in individual managers. Thus, the corporation has managed to minimize practically all of the risks arising from a competitive economic system, while workers and farmers have had to depend on government support or intervention to reduce their insecurity.[15] In a real sense, it is proper to consider government a major economic organization because its own increased activities have, in part, checked the growth of other organizations. Federal antitrust legislation has reduced the size of some corporations and prevented mergers by others; and, through its regulation of competition, banking, public utilities, unions, and the stock market itself, government has assumed a major role in the distribution of the country's wealth.

The federal government attempts to stimulate, or at least stabilize, the economy as well as to control and limit big business. Through tariffs it has sought to limit foreign competition with our own industries, and has encouraged farmers to produce more by extending agricultural credit, offering direct subsidies, and purchasing surplus crops. Social security programs have been developed to ease the economic pressures formerly softened by the kin group and the community, and government insurance today protects one out of every ten workers from the rigors of unemployment due to physical disability or old age. In 1961 there were 15 million beneficiaries under this program alone, and 8 million more people received at least one unemployment insurance payment averaging $33.85 a week. Moreover, such figures can be expected to increase because of the lengthening life span. Particularly because of increases in national defense contracts, the government itself has also become a major source of employment. From 1910 to 1961 the government's share in national employment has risen from 5 to over 16 per cent, and in 1961 almost 9 million persons employed in the United States had government jobs. One-fifth of the gross national output passes through the hands of local, state, and federal employees; and over 40 per cent of the country's families receive checks from the Treasury at the end of each month because they contain at least one federal employee or security beneficiary.

Today the government takes part in such a multitude of activities that it would take the rest of this book to enumerate them. A selected list of government agencies responsible for the most prominent of these activities is, in itself, enough to dull the mind and tire the eyes: the antitrust, wage and hours, and labor standards divisions of the Department of Labor, the Internal Revenue Service, the Federal Communications Commission, the Interstate Commerce Commission, the Federal Reserve System, the Securities and Exchange Commission, the Atomic Energy Commission, the Civil Aeronautics Board, and the National Aeronautical and Space Administration. Today, our government is obviously a major economic force. Many of the more current conflicts over the role of government in an industrial society will be reflected in the following chapters, but here we shall merely

15. John K. Galbraith, *The Affluent Society*, Boston: Houghton Mifflin, 1958, pp. 100–106.

observe that, while both unions and corporations frequently resist any government intervention in their respective areas of influence, they both continue to seek governmental aid.

The Unions. The Industrial Revolution put the individual worker on his own to sell his labor to the highest bidder. He could bargain with his employer, and, under the assumptions of the free market, both would work out a contractual relationship defining their economic obligations. But, with the rise of the large corporation, these theories concerning equal bargaining between employer and employee became less realistic. One of the effects of the behavioral revolution was the worker's increasing dissatisfaction with his narrow and impersonal contractual obligations, and unions emerged to provide more equality in bargaining for wages and for such security benefits as unemployment compensation and hospitalization. Unions arrived somewhat late on the American industrial scene but, aided by governmental policies designed to encourage collective bargaining, they have increased sixfold in the past 25 years. Only in recent years has union membership failed to increase. Unions claim nearly 18 million workers, or about 34 per cent of the nonprofessional and nonsupervisory employees of American industry and, as we might suspect, have been most successful in organizing the production workers in large plants. About half of the 21 million "blue collar" workers (craftsmen, operatives, repairmen, and laborers) are union members.

Labor unions have been responsible for the introduction of many new industrial norms like collective bargaining and rules and procedures for hiring and firing which are intended to eliminate the personal likes and dislikes of individual managers. Today, at every level of government, labor organizations and their leaders represent an interest group to be considered, and their support is often actively sought. While no political party concerned solely with union interests has yet emerged, unions, like management and other economic interests, seek to influence legislation through political pressure.

The growth of union membership has made them almost as important economically as industry and government. Membership dues, mostly deducted from payrolls with the same efficiency as withholding taxes, provide unions with around $600 million a year, and existing union treasuries contain more than a billion dollars. Through pension and welfare funds obtained by collective bargaining, millions of dollars — much of it invested in stock — often remain under the control of union officials. In fact, the extent of union ownership of stock in various corporations has recently raised speculation that union representatives might someday enter a bargaining session about wages only to find themselves representing both labor *and* management! [16]

Unionization cannot be viewed solely in economic terms, however. For

16. A. H. Raskin, "New Issue: Labor as Big Business," *The New York Times Magazine* (February 22, 1959), p. 9.

many workers the union represents a sense of belonging and of participation which compensates for the isolated and impersonal economic relationships in our industrial society. In some sense, labor unions constitute a new "community" serving many of the same functions as the manor under feudalism. Through union membership the worker can obtain a hearing for his complaints, some control over working conditions, and have some protection against arbitrary supervisors.

Voluntary Associations. People who have common interests may meet and call society's attention to certain conditions they consider problematical. Such voluntary associations are not strictly economic; they are usually formed to focus on social issues and they permit individuals to express special interests. For example, a man may join a sports club which must put pressure on the local government to obtain satisfactory recreational facilities, or he may belong to an organization expressly dedicated to the health or education of his community. Such local voluntary organizations concerned with special or limited interests tend to have a short life. But others, organized to defend or improve the status of an occupation or profession, may have a more lasting existence. In fact farmers' and trade associations, and even labor unions, were once voluntary associations, though today it is more fitting to recognize them as permanent economic organizations because of their size and scope.

Voluntary organizations organized for the purpose of social reform resemble those concerned with economic advancement. They can be limited to "improving" divorce laws or passing zoning laws in a particular city or community; or, like the National Association for the Advancement of Colored People or the National Conference of Christians and Jews, they can represent relatively permanent ethnic, racial, and class interests.

There are well over 100,000 voluntary associations in the United States [17] and, for a number of reasons, most of them seem to thrive best in industrial societies. Few organizations of any sort exist in homogeneous areas of a society, and those that do tend to cover a wide variety of interests and activities. But, in urban centers of industrial societies, segments of the population with divergent interests and activities evolve which must be organized within narrower limits. The development of voluntary associations also is inhibited in societies dominated by particular institutions like the state, church, or family. But, in industrial societies, the individual can seldom express all of his own needs and interests within the family, the church, or the community, and therefore he seeks out organizations of others with similar special interests. Too, voluntary associations emerge when normative dissensus exists and, since they are composed of potential blocs of voters, exert a powerful influence for various kinds of social and economic change.

Due to the organizational revolution, an increasing number of Americans

17. Arnold Rose, *Sociology*, New York: Knopf, 1956, p. 309.

will spend their lives working within large economic organizations which, in turn, will respond by developing larger groups of co-ordinators to "direct traffic" and reinforce organizational norms. Managers are becoming increasingly important as a source of corporate power, and labor leaders are especially prominent today. Federal administrators are assuming greater responsibility because the government is an independent source of economic power. Even voluntary associations become influential and self-perpetuating when they are organized around issues of lasting importance. In a now famous book, the title of which — *The Organization Man* — has virtually become a part of our language, William H. Whyte suggests how our executives represent a broader tendency toward the bureaucratization of society as a whole.

If the term [organization man] is vague, it is because I can think of no other way to describe the people I am talking about. They are not the workers, nor are they the white-collar people in the usual, clerk sense of the word. These people only work for The Organization. The ones I am talking about *belong* to it as well. They are the ones of our middle class who have left home, spiritually as well as physically, to take the vows of organization life, and it is they who are the mind and soul of our great self-perpetuating institutions. Only a few are top managers or ever will be. In a system that makes such hazy terminology as "junior executive" psychologically necessary, they are of the staff as much as the line, and most are destined to live poised in a middle area that still awaits a satisfactory euphemism. But they are the dominant members of our society nonetheless. They have not joined together into a recognizable elite — our country does not stand still long enough for that — but it is from their ranks that are coming most of the first and second echelons of our leadership, and it is their values which will set the American temper.

The corporation man is the most conspicuous example, but he is only one, for the collectivization so visible in the corporation has affected almost every field of work. Blood brother to the business trainee off to join Du Pont is the seminary student who will end up in the church hierarchy, the doctor headed for the corporate clinic, the physics Ph.D. in a government laboratory, the intellectual on the foundation-sponsored team project, the engineering graduate in the huge drafting room at Lockheed, the young apprentice in a Wall Street law factory. They are all, as they so often put it, in the same boat. Listen to them talk to each other over the front lawns of their suburbia and you cannot help but be struck by how well they grasp the common denominators which bind them. Whatever the differences in their organization ties, it is the common problems of collective work that dominate their attentions, and when the Du Pont man talks to the research chemist or the chemist to the army man, it is these problems that are uppermost. The word *collective* most of them can't bring themselves to use — except to describe foreign countries or organizations they don't work for — but they are keenly aware of how much more deeply beholden they are to organization than were their elders. They are wry about it, to be sure; they talk of the "treadmill," the "rat race," of the inability to control one's direction. But they have no great sense of plight; between themselves and organization they believe they see an ultimate harmony and, more than most elders recognize, they are building an ideology that will vouchsafe this trust.[18]

Whether or not Mr. Whyte is exaggerating the plight of a "company man," the age of the organization unquestionably is here, and the work world for almost all of its employees — semi-skilled, clerical, managerial, and professional — is characterized by the specialization, routinization, and impersonality formerly associated with factory workers.

EVALUATIONS OF AN INDUSTRIAL SOCIETY

The development of industrial societies is one of the most important facts of the contemporary world, and thus has not gone unevaluated. Some have viewed the Industrial Revolution as progress, while others have seen in it the seeds of human destruction. We shall now consider these contradictory evaluations, and then list some general characteristics of industrialism as it exists today.

Industrial Societies as Progress. Some people see the material by-products of industrial societies as constituting an important advance in the history of mankind. Many of the traditional concerns of pre-industrial societies like poverty, illness, and sufficient housing can now be "solved" by these tremendous productive forces. Such an evaluation is particularly characteristic of those who have begun to receive some of the material benefits of industrialization.

The idea that the new or the changed constitutes progress is a familiar one to contemporary Americans because every year thousands of new products come on the market whose very newness is constantly advertised as a material improvement. Popular ideologies provide the assurance that "every day in every way, things are getting better and better," even though mankind has not always regarded change in this way. The Greeks felt that they were moving away from, not toward, their Golden Age, and medieval man felt that social progress was irrelevant because only Divine Judgment was of great importance. It was only when industrial society emerged that men began to seriously consider that the changes they were experiencing might be viewed as "progress."

The idea of progress received support from other emerging beliefs about the physical world. The evolutionary ideas of Darwin and others provided an orderly way to interpret social change. Just as man could be seen as having evolved from lower animal forms, society could be considered as evolving from "lower" folk societies to the "higher" forms of industrial societies. Such ideas were comforting, of course, because the scholars formulating them were in societies standing at the "peak" of the evolutionary scale.

18. From *The Organization Man*. Copyright © 1956 by William H. Whyte, Jr. By permission of Simon and Schuster, Inc. pp. 3–4.

Industrial Societies as Chaos. As industrial societies developed, they were subjected to criticism as well as praise. Often they were viewed as a mass of inconsistencies which confused the individual at every turn. As each institution developed and became autonomous, conflicting norms seemed to emerge — the family often demanded one thing and the economic system another. Each institution also develops within it groups seeking special interests, and there are always a number of voluntary associations clamoring for additional attention.

Few people denied the material benefits which industrial societies made possible, but many criticized their methods of production. Increasing complexity seemed to be alienating man from some of the basic processes of social life. In a folk society an individual lived within the security of his kin group, but his whole existence was circumscribed by limited choices. The emergence of industrial societies enabled the individual to gain a degree of freedom never before obtained, but at the cost of traditional sources of security — his friends and his kin group. Consequently, man's increased choices only create confusion, and his existence lacks meaningful direction. Theologians and psychologists represent modern man as being "in search of a soul," while novelists like Dostoevsky and philosophers like Kierkegaard feel he is isolated and tormented by a hostile world. Karl Marx was more specific, suggesting that the worker was becoming increasingly alienated from the means of production. All of these theorists placed the blame on the emergence of an industrial society.

Many have used this image of modern man as an explanation of all types of contemporary behavior. The younger generation is "beat" or "silent," afraid to speak up except to chronicle their irresponsibility and their anxiety; and, when our youth can no longer avoid adult responsibilities, they can move into the womb of a large organization where decision-making can be avoided, or at least shared. Even the movement away from heavily populated industrial centers can be seen as an attempt to seek security. In the suburbs, one can buy a house like everyone else's and live in a community where children are dressed alike, conversation is uniform, and voting behavior is similar, and where participation in identical leisure activities is mandatory. Again, anxiety is reduced because the group has already made most major decisions. Indeed, if one is inclined, most of our present-day behavior can be interpreted as some form of escape from the anxiety created by industrial society. The appeal of Disneyland is not restricted to children because in Frontierland one can recapture the simplicity of the past; or, if one rejects the past, he can always go to Tomorrowland, or to Adventureland, where life is exotic. In all of these "lands," life is colorful and harmless, clever and not challenging, safe and sterile, pretty and artificial — in short, unlike "Todayland." And, if the various appeals of Disneyland are not enough, there are other escapes.

Movies, martinis, soap operas, tranquilizers, political conservatism, Zen Buddhism, alcoholism, and neurosis have all been viewed as attempts to escape the anxiety created by an impersonal industrial freedom which is often isolation.

SOLUTIONS OFFERED FOR THE CHAOS OF INDUSTRIAL SOCIETIES

Some theorists have suggested that the growth of totalitarian governments within the twentieth century can be interpreted as an attempt to "solve" the problems modern society poses. Industrialization has created the demand for a new kind of existence where isolation and anxiety would be minimized and maximum consensus could exist. Authoritarian government offers individuals a sense of security; it has risen not only in situations where a small group of leaders seized power by force and subterfuge; many Germans and Italians relinquished their freedom willingly, not under force. Authoritarianism offered a "folk society" with which the individual could identify, and which gave him direction and consistency. Of course, the sources of direction and identification were as vague and nonexistent as Hitler's ideal of an Aryan culture. But through mass meetings and controlled hysteria, the individual could at least *feel* himself to be a part of something large and purposeful. He could identify with strong leadership and, in this way, escape from his own insignificance. Russian Communism can be seen in a similar context. A consistent ideology provides people with a sense of relatedness and mission; the Communist Party selects the immediate goals and, through the activities of the various collectives, the security of a folk society is recaptured. Such are the "gains" which people can achieve by an "escape from freedom." [19]

Opportunities to escape also exist in nontotalitarian societies. Many political movements stress the shortcomings of industrial societies and, while not explicitly suggesting an authoritarian solution, implicitly suggest that an elite group should control society and offer the people security by protecting them from the ravages of industrialization. Other political movements simply consider modern freedom too great a price to pay, and plead for a return to the past and those old "tried and true" norms which men could live by.

SOCIAL PROBLEMS AND STABILITY

While neither the diagnosis that industrial societies are inherently disorganized nor the various cures ranging from reactionary measures to authoritarianism are accepted here, such criticisms focus attention on the lack of cohesiveness within industrial society. The lack of consensus on norms among a heterogeneous population does create a number of choices for the individual and, with traditional norms constantly being challenged by newer ones, confusion

19. Erich Fromm, *Escape from Freedom*, New York: Rinehart, 1941.

and anxiety can result. The looseness of social relationships also make deviation easier and more appealing and, in this sense, social problems are an integral part of the "chaos" of industrial societies.

The task of this book is to analyze social problems within the context of industrial societies and not to give a summary judgment about the relative
state of progress or "chaos" within such a society. However, certain general
conclusions can already be drawn:

1. Industrial societies have already survived, at least for a moderate length
of time.

2. World history seems to be moving toward the development of more industrial societies. The much discussed notion of "underdeveloped" countries
implies that their present economic performance could be improved by
means which are known and understood in existing industrial societies. These
means are transmitted through technical assistance, and are being accepted
by societies at all stages of underdevelopment. While the impact of industrialization has already been great, further technological progress is still actively
sought all over the world.

3. It is unlikely that existing industrial societies will move back toward a
type of society with "folk-like" characteristics unless this occurs in the context
of some authoritarian type of social system with pseudo folk-like emphasis.

4. We reject the alternative of a society which "solves" the social problems
of industrialization by means of an authoritarian social system because such
a solution violates our values of human freedom and responsibility.

Industrial societies do present, in one sense, a picture of disorganization and
chaos. But the mere fact that they have survived and continue to grow indicates that they have developed techniques for achieving some type of
stability.

SUMMARY
The Industrial Revolution involved a shift from small communities in which
kin groups regulated norms to large cities where individuals were forced to
acknowledge impersonal organizations as the source and judge of norms. The
forces which created this change in the normative order of an industrial
society constitute a number of silent revolutions — silent because they
achieved their impact gradually and revolutionary because they created
drastic changes. The mobility revolution was geographical because industrial
expansion drew immigrants across the sea and migrants across state lines
toward large industrial centers or toward the West where new industries were
to be built. The mobility revolution was social because factories needed new
and special skills. The behavioral revolution denotes a change in the individ-

ual's attitude toward his work; because of bureaucratization (an industrial society's way of co-ordinating the work of many individuals), many workers tended to feel they were insignificant parts of a vast industrial machine. The communications revolution began because of the continual need for efficient contact throughout a mass society. The scientific revolution refers to the increasing technological advances which have enabled us to populate cities, mechanize industry, and give great numbers of workers a higher standard of living and considerable leisure through the use of "labor-saving" devices. The organizational revolution refers to the fact that activities increasingly take place within large-scale organizations.

Observers offer contrasting evaluations of industrial societies, suggesting that industrialization is either the apex of progress, or a chaos of insecurity and anxiety. Since the principal purpose of the following chapters is a deeper understanding of social problems, the subject matter of the book will be dissensus and deviation. The reader should remember that, by studying such problems, we are *not* lending support to the virulent critics of industrial societies. One of the important by-products of the study of social problems should be an increased understanding of the way in which societies are organized.

QUESTIONS AND SUGGESTIONS FOR FURTHER STUDY

1. How accurate is the concept of the "silent revolutions"? Do you feel that these changes have been unnoticed by those individuals who have experienced them?
2. Is mass production incompatible with craftsmanship? In industrial societies are there any indications that workers seek out opportunities for craftsmanship off the job?
3. Consider different types of employment you may have had. Did the requirements for these jobs fit the characteristics of the work world described in this chapter? If you have had several types of jobs, how are the differences in the requirements explained by the nature of the job?
4. Why do you think that migration is often viewed as "abnormal"? Are there any historical reasons which may have created this impression?
5. Why does an industrial society require mobility?
6. Social mobility in American society is generally viewed as "good." Can you see any negative consequences of mobility?
7. Make a list of the voluntary associations that exist in your community. You may have to consult newspapers for notices of meetings as one guide. If you live in a large city, you may have to restrict your listing to a neighborhood. Determine the function of each of the associations.
8. To measure the impact of the organizational revolution, ask the seniors you know what type of job they expect to obtain when they enter the labor market.
9. Taking the period of one day, keep a record of the time and nature of your exposure to the various media of mass communication.

10. Go through an issue of a current magazine and make a count of advertisements that make specific reference to science in their copy.
11. Taking some written criticism of an aspect of contemporary life, like a letter to the editor, assess to what extent the criticism is directed toward characteristics that result from the development of an industrial society.
12. What we have termed "silent revolutions" are often summed up by the term "Industrial Revolution" because changes in the factory system preceded or created the others. With this in mind, explain how all of the silent revolutions are interrelated.

SUGGESTED READINGS

Bell, Daniel, *Work and Its Discontents*, Boston: Beacon Press, 1956. A brief essay on the nature and problems of work in industrial society.

Blau, Peter M., *Bureaucracy in Modern Life*, New York: Random House, 1956. p   An interesting short summary of various aspects of bureaucracy. It contains a chapter on "Bureaucracy and Democracy."

Boulding, Kenneth, *The Organizational Revolution*, New York: Harper, 1953. A discussion of the implications of the organizational revolution.

Friedmann, Georges, *The Anatomy of Work: Labor, Leisure and the Implications of Automation*, New York: Free Press of Glencoe, 1962. An analysis of the nature of work and the effects of automation. It draws on data from several industrial societies.

Handlin, Oscar, *The Newcomers*, Garden City: Doubleday, 1962. This book discusses the problems of the new migrants, Negroes and Puerto Ricans, in the New York metropolitan area.

———, *Immigration as a Factor in American History*, Englewood Cliffs, N.J.: Prentice-Hall, 1959. This historical work focuses on the years between 1840 and 1920. It discusses the old world background of immigrants and their subsequent adjustment to American life. It contains a number of personal documents.

Lipset, S.M., and Reinhard Bendix, *Social Mobility in an Industrial Society*, Berkeley: University of California Press, 1961.   p   A survey of existing research on social mobility plus original research. Concludes the rates of mobility are relatively similar in all industrial societies.

Mills, C. Wright, *White Collar*, New York: Oxford University Press, 1956. p   Always a stimulating writer, Mills describes the emerging importance of managers, professionals, and white collar workers in American society.

Walker, Charles R. (ed.), *Modern Technology and Civilization: An Introduction to Human Problems in the Machine Age*, New York: McGraw-Hill, 1961.   p This is a collection of readings exploring the relationship between man and machine. It has sections dealing with technology in non-Western countries and on technology and human values.

Weber, Max, *From Max Weber: Essays in Sociology*, translated by H. H. Gerth and C. Wright Mills, New York: Oxford University Press, 1958.   p   This book contains the classic essay on bureaucracy. It also includes an introduction by the translators to Weber's various contributions to understanding the modern world.

Whyte, William H., Jr., *The Organization Man,* New York: Simon and Schuster, 1956.   P   This provocative book describes the impact on society of the organizational revolution and the increased bureaucratization of life. It touches on a number of aspects ranging from the education of the organization man to the organization man at home in suburbia.

II NORMATIVE DISSENSUS

Students of the American community in the fifties have had their attention drawn to the suburbs much as the attention of their counterparts in the twenties was drawn to the slums. On the face of it, the reasons would appear to be quite different: the slum is the center of urban disorganization while the suburb would appear to be that of urban aspiration. Closer attention to the details of suburban life suggests, however, that it is actually the setting for the dominant "disorders" of our time.[1]

In one sense, the story of what has happened to the community is a restatement of what has happened to the total society — the decline of the small community, the decline of personal relationships, the loss of local autonomy, the collapse of mutual help, the accentuation of mobility, the urbanization of the community, plus the industrialization and bureaucratization of community life.

Communities in American society have always been organized around the tools of work. In the early settlement patterns in the United States, the lines of the political unit, the county, were frequently drawn so that the small community designated as the county seat would be no further than one day's horseback ride from the most distant point in the county. Most communities grew up around the activities of transportation. Some towns grew on the riverbanks or along the oceans. Others grew along the post roads or along the growing railroads. Even today, many communities still derive their existence from being close to some highway link, while every community is being built and rebuilt to serve the automobile. In every large city, huge areas are being torn down to make way for new expressways to accommodate hundreds of thousands of automobiles. Since these automobiles eventually must stop, parking space must be made available, so houses must be demolished to make parking lots.

While the fact that economic functions fashion the community may be obvious, it is not so obvious that, as economic functions change, the community also changes. The development of an industrial society has included

1. Maurice R. Stein, *The Eclipse of Community, An Interpretation of American Studies,* Princeton: Princeton University Press, 1960, p. 199.

what can be called an urban revolution. This has meant broadening the community to include more people. More people usually mean different kinds of people, with different ideas about what a community should be. Too, if the economic functions change, the old ideas of what a community should be are undermined and become difficult to achieve. With changing conditions, new normative conceptions emerge, conflicting with the older ones. This chapter, then, is concerned with normative dissensus about the nature of the community — what the community should be.

The normative problem: what should the community be in an industrial society?

From its inception, American society was a rural society based on an agricultural economy. In this context the independent farm and the small town seemed very natural. The initial pattern of scattered settlements was carried westward with the expanding frontier. Along the frontier, the Homestead Act gave 160 acres to a homesteader and required him to live on the land to retain title. Each farm was separated from others by considerable distance. Clusters of farms, however, were soon tied together when the school and the church provided a focal point for the farm community.

In many sections of the United States the small town emerged. The farmer, in spite of his considerable independence, needed the small shopkeeper, the grain and feed dealer, the blacksmith, and, with growing mechanization, the farm implement dealer. Other small towns emerged at the bends of the rivers or at other intersections of trade routes. This settlement pattern scratched indelibly into American society certain images of what a community should be. Since the agrarian economic base lasted a long time, the resulting conceptions of community life persisted as normative even as America became urbanized.

> *Historical Normative Conception: The Small Town* — The community should be characterized by personalized relationships. Community problems should be solved by mutual help and with minimal governmental assistance. Community growth should be "natural" and unimpeded.

The conception suggested that the rural small-town community constituted the model for the good life. Embedded in this was the notion that the community was, and should be characterized by, friendly, personal relationships. In an environment of friendly relationships, it was possible for individuals to be independent and self-sufficient. The need for organized community life was minimal. Most community problems could be solved by mutual help so governmental "interference" was held to a minimum. If government had to exist, it must be a local government responsive to the needs of one's friends and neighbors. Government, too, must operate on a face-to-face basis. The growth of such a community would come from the independence and success of its individual members. Where houses were built and shops established was a consequence of impersonal economic forces. The development of the community was a consequence of accumulated "success" of individuals best able to fulfill the requirements of independence and its result — economic affluence. The core of this historical normative conception of the community, then, consisted of (1) an emphasis on personal relationships; (2) an emphasis on solving community problems by mutual help and a minimum of assistance from a local government responsive to the needs of the local community; and (3) an emphasis on the growth of the community being dictated by impersonal economic forces.

This normative conception of the "good" community that emerged in the rural small town has governed America's reaction to urbanization. It has impeded the understanding of communities as they changed in the growing cities. Just as the rural small-town complex was a by-product of certain social factors, a new type of community emerged better suited to the demands of an industrial society. These newer communities, the cities, were a denial of all held dear in rural small-town America.

THE END OF THE RURAL DREAM AND THE BEGINNING
OF THE URBAN NIGHTMARE

In 1790, about 5 per cent of the population was classified as urban. Between 1790 and 1840, the urban population doubled. In the next 50 years, it tripled. In 1920, the census indicated that over 50 per cent of the growing population was urban (Fig. 3-1). At every period except 1810–20, the growth of the urban population has exceeded the growth of the total population in the United States (see Table 3-1).

This growth created a threat to the historical conception of the community. Smallness and homogeneity gave way to largeness and heterogeneity. Many came to the cities who would have been "out of place" in the small town. Much of the urban growth came via immigration. From 1820 to 1955, some 40.4 million immigrants were admitted to the United States. In some years, more than a million came annually. Since the United States never developed a policy of settling immigrants, most immigrants landed on the Atlantic seaboard and settled into coastal cities. These immigrants found their economic future in the growing industries in urban areas. Earlier settlers with a stake in the small towns were content to see these immigrants exposed to the evils

Fig. 3-1. Urban-Rural Population, 1890-1960.

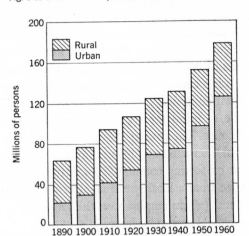

of the city, particularly since their "foreign" background would violate the homogeneity of the small community. Since many immigrants had come originally from peasant backgrounds in Europe, they were faced with the problem of adapting to the city, as well as to the new way of living called America. Their difficulty in making that dual adaptation reinforced the normative conception of the rural small town as "normal."

These foreign immigrants were joined in the city by migrants from rural areas coming to work in growing industries. Since large rural families often could not divide their land among their many children, the "surplus" children sought their fortunes in the city. To those who had internalized the rural small town model for living, it was inconceivable that people would voluntarily go to the city. When this farm-to-city movement continued, it was often assumed the city must have some unnatural hold on those "unfortunate" people. Just as an insect flew crashing to its death against a lighted window, the bright lights of the city were seen as a lure leading rural migrants to their ultimate destruction.

Cities, perhaps not ready for formal attention to the pressing problems of urban life, developed a rather spontaneous compromise between personal relationships and governmental structure. This was the political machine. As the immigrant arrived in the city, friendless and alone, his first contact with American institutions was often with the ward heeler. This ward heeler made it his business to lend a helping hand to the newcomer. He was the contact for relief, for jobs, and for entry into the promised land of American citizenship. He became the intermediary to the landlord and to all the complexities of urban life. When a deserving family asked for aid, there were no forms to

TABLE 3-1

Percentage increase in population growth, United States, 1790–1960

Period	Percent increase		
	Total population	Urban population	Rural population
1950–1960 *	18.4	29.3	−0.8
1940–1950	14.5	20.6	6.5
1930–1940	7.2	7.9	6.4
1920–1930	16.1	27.3	4.4
1910–1920	14.9	29.0	3.2
1900–1910	21.0	39.3	9.0
1890–1900	20.7	36.4	12.2
1880–1890	25.5	56.5	13.4
1870–1880	30.1	42.7	25.7
1860–1870	22.6	59.3	13.6
1850–1860	35.6	75.4	28.4
1840–1850	35.9	92.1	29.1
1830–1840	32.7	63.7	29.7
1820–1830	33.5	62.6	31.2
1810–1820	33.1	31.9	33.2
1800–1810	36.4	63.0	34.7
1790–1800	35.1	59.9	33.8

Source: U.S. Census of Population, U.S. Summary, Number of Inhabitants, P1-A, 1952, *Statistical Abstract of the United States*, 1961, Washington, D.C.: U.S. Government Printing Office, 1961.

* *Note:* In the 1950 Census, a change in definition of urban resulted in the net transfer of 7,540,222 persons or 5.0 per cent from rural to urban classification. This change came primarily from the densely populated urban fringe. For exact definition, consult *Statistical Abstracts.*

complete, no eligibility requirements, nor any delays to expect and accept. The political machine was built on the principle of personalized relationships amidst the impersonality of the city. The contact between the ward boss and his followers was based on mutual help — "you do favors for me and I will vote for you so that you can continue to do favors for me." This was almost a restatement of the obligations between neighbors in the small town. The political machine emerged in almost every large city in America at one time or another. The Tammany Hall machine in New York has a long history, starting with Boss Tweed and continuing to the present. Other machines have been bossed by Crump in Memphis, Hague in Jersey City, Pendergast in Kansas City, and Curley in Boston. In each of these, the end result was personal service based on political considerations.

The activities of the political machine plus the problems of increasingly concentrated populations finally give rise to different normative conceptions. Many of these new ideas were the result of a consciousness created by a group of writers known as the muckrackers. The muckrackers — writers like Upton

Sinclair, Ida Tarbell, and Lincoln Steffens — exposed to the apathetic public some of the evils they found in the factories and slums. By forcing people on the right side of the tracks to face the "muck" — the consequences of urbanization and industrialization, they often stimulated the development of municipal planning and the initiation of programs of economic security which recognized the demise of mutual help.

These changes, however, have been frustrated at almost every step by continued rural domination of governmental bodies. Cities are creatures of individual states and can only engage in activities permitted under charters granted by state legislators. If the legislatures are sensitive to the needs of cities, then helpful legislation can be passed. If state legislatures are not sensitive to the needs of cities, legislation may be rejected because it is new or because it centers on problems unfamiliar to nonurbanites. Cole has suggested:

As cities developed in the United States, and they did develop rapidly, they became the unwilling victims of legislative restriction and legislative acts. This lack of home rule and lack of adequate representation has existed until the present. Today, 64 percent of the people, that is, the urban population, elect 25 percent of the state legislators. To put it another way, 36 percent of the population, the rural, elects 75 percent of the members to state legislatures. . . On the other hand, city people and corporations pay 90 percent of the taxes. Fulton County, Georgia, which contains the city of Atlanta, and which has a population of almost 400,000, had three representatives in the lower House in the Georgia Legislature in 1947. Echols County, Georgia, with a population of 3,000 had one. In California, the people of Los Angeles, considerably more than four million in number, elect one senator. The smallest senatorial district in California, composed of less than 15,000 population, elects one.[2]

Changes in representation, however, may occur. A group of city dwellers in Tennessee brought suit to force the first redistricting in 60 years. In 1962, the Supreme Court ruled that the federal courts have the right to review the distribution of seats in state legislatures (*Baker* v. *Carr* 369 U.S., 186).

The same problem exists on the national level. While almost 70 per cent of the national population is urban, it is represented by only 42 per cent of the seats in the U.S. House of Representatives. The House is supposed to represent existing population distribution (see Figs. 3-2 and 3-3). It is not surprising that, in 1962, a new Department of Urban Affairs, to be of cabinet status, was rejected by Congress.

In the city, a new normative conception emerged. It recognized the breakdown of the mutual help which had occurred in the town and the fact that the pattern of spontaneous growth based solely on economic considerations could no longer be applied in the same fashion. This newer definition was

2. William Cole, *Urban Society*, Boston: Houghton Mifflin, 1958, pp. 298–300.

Fig. 3-2. Contrasts Between 1960 Urban-Rural Composition and Representation in the U.S. House of Representatives, 1962.

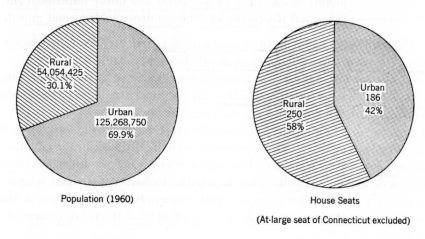

Population (1960)

House Seats

(At-large seat of Connecticut excluded)

Fig. 3-3. Urban-Rural Population by States, 1962.

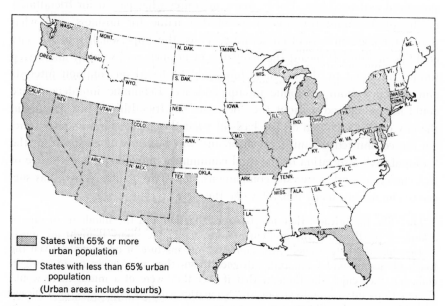

slow in developing because it contradicted many of the older assumptions based on the rural small town.

Contemporary Normative Conception: Urbanism — The community should value impersonality and utilize impersonal governmental techniques in solving urban problems and growth.

The word community has two meanings which have been used interchangeably. The term refers to a group of people living in a particular area and dependent upon one another. The term also refers to a type of relationship with others, a sharing of ideas and values. In the rural community, these two dimensions of the community coincided. The individuals who were interdependent were also those who shared the same values, so the "spatial" and the "social" dimensions of the community were intertwined. In the city, they became increasingly separated. The web of interdependence was much larger and made it more difficult, if not impossible, to have personalized relationships in the same fashion as in the rural community. This separation in the city had many implications for the conception of what the urban community should be.

1. *Personal Relationships.* Social relationships in urban areas seemed superficial and transitory. But to many urbanites what passed for friendliness in the rural community was often another name for nosiness, and what passed for concern was often scrutiny. Thus, the impersonality of the city could be of value. It meant the avoidance of nosiness and scrutiny and a step toward increased freedom. Friendship could be based on common interests and detached from economic interdependence. Economic interdependence could be maintained without the "necessity" of friendship. Thus, friends in the city could be chosen on the basis of *what* they were, not *who* they were. To the committed urbanite, impersonality was a means of escape from the "compulsory" association of the rural community, providing a wider range of free choice of work, interests, companions, and style of life. Whyte has suggested the reasons many urbanites *like* the city.

They like the privacy; they like the specialization and the hundreds of one of a kind shops; they like the excitement — to some, the sirens at night are music — they like the heterogeneity, the contrasts, the mixture of odd people. Even the touch of Sodom and Gomorrah intrigues them; they may never go to a nightclub, but they enjoy the thought that if ever they were of a mind, there would be something interesting to go out to. "No matter what goes on," says one Chicago man, "it goes on *here*." [3]

The impersonality of cities is exaggerated. Much stems from the separation of work from the residential neighborhood. The literature depicting the assimilation of immigrant groups suggests that the "impersonal" city might best be characterized as a collection of neighborhoods — warm, friendly, and per-

3. The Editors of *Fortune, The Exploding Metropolis,* Garden City: Doubleday, 1958, p. 19.

sonal — but neighborhoods tied to the fortunes of the industrial world. Thus, the stress on impersonality ignores many personal relations based on choice rather than convenience. A recent study indicates that, even in the most urbanized areas, informal, face-to-face relationships centering on family and friendship continue.[4]

2. *Community Problems.* Growth meant two different things for the problem-solving process in the community. First, the traditional mutual help pattern collapsed in the city and, in its place, a formalized, largely governmental program of security emerged. Second, the city became the hub of problems unknown in the rural community.

The initial reaction in cities was to depend on mutual help. Collective action demanded a person take into account the plight of his neighbors — neighbors he had not seen and did not know. The mutual help pattern in its informal sense collapsed.

Although problems of economic security are present in all types of communities, in the city they took on added significance. Industrialization created new dimensions of economic security — hours and wages, industrial accidents, problems of the employment of older workers, and problems of periodic unemployment. While these were issues primarily in the city, they emerged from the changes which industrialization had created. Cities found themselves confronted with many migrants who sought work and then economic assistance.

These new problems created by forces larger than the community could only be solved by the "larger" society — the state and federal governments. This appeal to "higher" levels of governmental authority conflicted with traditional notions of local and minimal governmental responsibility. The conception emerged in the city that the risks from industrial employment would have to be reduced by formal methods and with governmental responsibility. The specific problems centered on (a) legislation covering the employment of women and children, (b) wage and hour regulation, (c) workman's compensation, (d) unemployment compensation, and (e) assistance to the older person no longer employable in the industrial system.

(a) *Female and child labor legislation.* Industrialization created employment at all levels of skill. Particularly in cities, where family members were not busy in agricultural pursuits, there were opportunities for industrial employment for both women and children. Early in industrialization, urban businessmen offering employment to children were considered public benefactors, teaching children good work habits early. While child labor was practiced in rural areas, people were slow to recognize that working on the

4. Scott Greer and Ella Kube, "Urbanism and Social Structure: A Los Angeles Study," in Marvin Sussman (ed.), *Community Structure and Analysis*, New York: Crowell, 1959, pp. 93–112.

family farm was not the same as working in a textile mill. Gradually, the realization came that arduous work might be damaging to the child's health and that children should be in school rather than being burdened with industrial employment.

The employment of women was also singled out for legislative attention. Such attention was based on the belief that women were physically weaker than men and that their health must be protected against unsuitable work conditions. Laws were passed fixing minimum wages for women and children, fixing maximum hours, specifying certain working conditions, and prohibiting certain types of hazardous employment.

(b) *Wage and hour legislation.* Protective legislation concerning women and children was also extended to men. The argument for shorter hours assumed that excessive working hours led to escapist leisure to reduce overfatigue and that it took attention away from family life. The argument for a minimum wage was that the adequacy of wages determined the standard of living. If jobs provided low wages, workers might reduce their food intake and their health expenditures which would make for greater costs to the society. For these reasons, various state laws governing wages and hours were passed. In 1938, the Federal Fair Labor Standards Act was passed covering all employment involved in interstate commerce and providing a minimum wage for a basic work week of forty hours. In effect, this act covered employment in large industries in large cities.

(c) *Workman's compensation.* Accidents are inevitable in modern industry. There are difficulties attending recovery from injury and from the loss of income during the period of recovery. Early handling of industrial accidents required the employee to show that the employer had been negligent. The employee generally received little or no compensation. Later legislation abolished the legal notion of negligence and provided cash benefits for medical care for any injury arising in the course of employment.

(d) *Unemployment compensation.* Unemployment was chronic in urban industrial society. During the early development of industrial society, unemployment was viewed as an inherent risk in such a society. Coupled with the value of individualism, it was assumed that anyone who wanted a job could find one if he looked hard enough. The care of the unemployed was handled by private welfare agencies or by relatives. In 1929, however, the volume of unemployment in the United States reached almost 3 million. Instead of being a temporary peak, by spring of 1933 the number of unemployed had risen to a peak of 15 million. Private agencies, which usually carried the load, were swamped. The few public agencies in existence were also swamped. At this point the federal government began to provide grants to states to be used for temporary relief. In addition, the federal government began to undertake work programs for the unemployed — the Works Progress Administration, the Civilian Conservation Corps, and the National Youth Administration. Finally the federal government, in the Social Security Act of 1935, made provisions which stimulated individual states to pass laws providing unemployment benefits. This act provided that the cost of administrating such a program would be borne by the federal government but set minimum requirements to be followed by the various states. In general, such laws provided that if an individual became unemployed he would be paid compensation of about half of his previous average salary. This would be paid until another job was obtained or for a period related to the amount of credit built up by previous employment. Unemployment compensation was financed by a tax on employers. Such compensation was not intended as a substitute for a job and could be terminated if a suitable job was offered and rejected. While Wisconsin was the only state with an unemployment compensation law prior to this time, by the end of 1937 all states had passed laws providing unemployment compensation. Thus, one of the most persistent problems of an industrial society was lessened. While unemployment was not abolished, the economic penalties of unemployment were reduced.

(e) *Old age assistance and benefits*. Industrialization and urbanization placed increasing emphasis on youth. It was difficult for all workers to maintain their skill, their employment, and their security, but the burden of unemployment fell most severely on "older" workers — individuals whose skills and training could not keep pace with advancing industry. Just as the depression helped prepare the way for unemployment compensation, it advanced the passage of laws providing pensions and benefits for the dependent aged. The Social Security Act of 1935 provided aid to states for assistance to dependent aged. As in unemployment compensation, the various states were to set up and administer programs within limits set by the federal government. Since 1939, the federal government has matched the sums supplied by the local and states agencies.

The Social Security Act also initiated a social insurance system to prevent economic dependency in the future. In Old Age Insurance, provision was made to assure the worker of an annuity upon retirement. Later, in 1939, Survivors' Insurance was added, providing payment for wives and dependent children. Contributions to this insurance were made by both employer and employee. While the initial programs covered most employees in urban commerce and industry, other types of employment have since been covered.

This legislation was viewed by many urbanites as a rational solution to changing community forms. The security of the urban industrial worker still made little sense, however, to farmers and small shopkeepers. Concern with the conditions of work was seen as an invasion of the values of independence. Concern for older persons could not be fathomed easily by those who remained on family farms. The idea that assistance other than the Christmas basket or donated labor at a barn raising was necessary, was seen as an indication that independence would be undermined, especially when assistance was provided by government. As governmental concern passed from the local community to the state, and finally to the remotest of all governmental units, the federal government, all that was dear to the rural community seemed to be disintegrating. This assistance was offered impersonally. Helping became an occupation — social work — and even became professionalized, requiring training and standards of performance. The emergence of these newer conceptions was resisted in the city itself, but they found increasing favor as the older rural community showed its inability to cope with city problems.

Governmental action extended beyond problems of economic security. In the city, the government became an active force in planning the community. The older assumption of spontaneous community growth became increasingly untenable in the city. The conception of how city services would be provided and how cities would grow underwent change.

3. *The Growth of the Community.* Increased density of population had many meanings for the city. It produced many innovations unnecessary in the small town. It led to the development of (a) municipal services, (b) city planning, (c) zoning, (d) public housing, and more recently (e) urban redevelopment and renewal.

(a) *Muncipal services.* The density of population in cities necessitated services unnecessary in the rural community. The congestion of cities made individuals liable for the consequences of the acts even of Mrs. O'Leary's cow. Gradually, cities evolved organized protection for fires in the form of fire departments. Fire codes were enacted specifying in detail how buildings might be erected and equipped. These codes had to be enforced by inspectors. They protected the individual from his own and his neighbors' fires and protected the tenant from the carelessness of his landlord and vice versa.

Although cities only emerged when a certain level of sanitation was achieved, historically, one of the curses of urban living has been epidemics. In time, cities developed programs of municipal health which included inspection powers, quarantining powers, inoculations, and other preventive measures.

Traffic control has been another problem which first emerged in the great cities. While horse racing on highways had been prohibited long before the advent of the automobile, only within the past 30 years have cities developed specialized groups and techniques to formulate and enforce the rules governing the use of the streets.

Other concerns emerged more recently. Cities lately have made attempts to limit noise from the congestion of hundreds of thousands of people and automobiles. Also, cities have become increasingly aware of the pollution of both air and water. The smog in Los Angeles and the polluted water which has closed beaches in New York and Cleveland have stimulated both concern and action.

Urban congestion, however, had other more favorable consequences. The concentration of population allowed the co-operative solution of what traditionally had been individual problems in rural communities. The pump handle could be replaced by the faucet, the back yard dump by the weekly garbage collection, the path by the sidewalk, and the two ruts in front of the house by pavement. The kerosene lamp could be replaced by the light bulb, and the dinner bell by the telephone. While these may not all be counted as gains, certainly they cannot be counted as losses. All gradually became the concern of municipal government, either in providing the service or by regulating the efforts of others to provide it.

With the growth of such municipal concerns, people in cities could not long be passive. Some individuals began to suggest that cities could exercise some control over how they grew, how they looked, and how the parts of the urban puzzle were put together. These notions about controlling and directing urban growth have come to be known as city planning.

(b) *City planning.* In one sense, city planning was not new in America. Washington and Jefferson were perhaps the first American city planners, since many of their thoughts were incorporated in the final design of the capital city. Many cities copied William Penn's plan for Philadelphia. It was a simple plan with a city hall in a plaza located at the intersection of wide streets going north and south and east and west; the rest of the city was planned on a gridiron of streets. Most urban growth in America, however, was unplanned.

During the first decade of the twentieth century, a number of citizen groups began to devote themselves to developing plans for city growth. In fact, a city plan for San Francisco was published immediately before the earthquake, but was ignored in the scramble to rebuild. Many of the citizen groups found their plans ignored by elected officials. It became apparent that, despite citizen enthusiasm, no city plan would be carried out without official governmental sanction. Then the attempt was made to create official planning commissions within urban governments to bring about a combination of planning and official action.

Today, the idea of a planning commission is well established. All major cities of the United States have planning programs implemented by continued staff operations. Planning has spread also to many smaller communities. Planning in smaller cities in recent years has been stimulated by federal aid providing funds on a matching basis to establish planning operations. Since the problems of planning seldom coincide with the actual political boundaries of communities, recent attention has been given to planning for regions or for total metropolitan areas requiring the co-operation of several political units.

City planning is essentially a process of substituting foresight for hindsight. Through planning, a community attempts to anticipate future developments and to plan for them. Planning includes concern for streets, housing, recreation, industrial location, and types of construction. It is not simply the preparation of a "master" plan for creating a "city beautiful," but is best seen as a continual process which guides development to maximize the best cities can offer and to minimize the worst that cities can achieve. The fact that city planning cannot be static is underscored by continued urban growth. New people in a city set off a series of implications for the community. Let us assume that a factory comes to a community and creates a hundred new jobs. These hundred new jobs will bring 450 people to that community. This would include about 100 children — 67 in elementary school and 33 in high school. This would call for 2.2 new rooms in the grade school and 1.65 new rooms in the high school, which would cost about $120,000. Four new teachers would have to be hired. The 100 families will add about $30,000 to the school budget.

Besides the teachers, the city will need four-fifths of a new employee in the police department and two-thirds of a new fireman, upping the police budget by $4510 and the fire department by $2820. Many new jobs need to be done also, from collecting taxes to collecting garbage. This would add four new city employees at the total cost of from $12,000 to $15,000. Too, the water department will have to pump 10,000 gallons more each day. Traffic will be increased by 140 cars. The city will have to add 500 more volumes to its library, part of a visiting nurse, and a fraction of a new cell down at the city jail.[5]

Since the implications of city growth are so extensive and the lag in solving city problems so great, city planning utilizes a number of tools. Among these tools are zoning, the encouragement of standards in private housing, the construction of public housing, and urban redevelopment and renewal. Each requires further explanation.

(c) *Zoning.* While the use of land in the rural community was left to individual choice, the owner was still limited by the informal pressures of his neighbors. In the city, this control became ineffective and land use became chaotic. European countries, with their longer urban experience, enacted zoning laws early. Then large metropolitan areas in the United States gradually began to control land use through zoning laws. The City of New York, for example, enacted its first comprehensive ordinance in 1916. The idea of zoning is to control the destiny of every parcel of land within a city. The

5. "So Your Town Doesn't Need Planning?" *Changing Times* (September 23, 1955).

municipal government seeks to limit, by districts, the character of buildings to be erected and seeks to prescribe the areas of land which may be built on. Many early zoning laws were declared invalid when the courts held that they deprived property owners of their rights and privileges, but in the well-known case of the *Village of Euclid* v. *Ambler Realty Company* (1926), zoning ordinances were provided a legal foundation. Since that time, zoning ordinances have been passed in most cities and in many smaller communities. By legal action certain sections of the community can be set aside for industrial development, others for single residences, others for multiple residence dwellings, and others for small business use. In this way, some order could emerge. Unfortunately, most urban areas were already chaotic when zoning ordinances were put into effect. In almost every area, some existing buildings are "nonconforming." For example, a factory may already exist in an area now zoned for single residences; such a factory cannot be torn down to make the area more homogeneous but neither can they be torn down and replaced by another factory or some other nonconforming building. Zoning depends upon the premise that time will correct past mistakes, but mistakes have a long lifespan.

The effectiveness of zoning also depends upon the consistency with which zoning ordinances are enforced. As the community changes, provision must be made to allow some change in the original intent of the law. Changes made at the request of particular property owners are known as "spot zoning" — when, for example, an apartment house is allowed in an area set aside for single dwelling units. Spot zoning, if permitted extensively, can destroy the effectiveness of the original zoning ordinance. Ironically, zoning is most effective in impersonal situations, as in large cities, where decisions are based upon principle and not upon the status of the individual requesting the change. In many small towns and suburbs, where personalized relationships take precedence over legal requirements, the result is often constant spot zoning and the perpetuation of a crazy-quilt pattern of land use.

(d) *Public housing.* Gradually cities found it necessary to become concerned with the quality of housing. New York City in 1879 passed a law prohibiting windowless rooms and later added provision providing for light, air, fire protection, and sanitation in new construction. During World War I, a few states and the federal government built a limited amount of buildings to house war workers. Some public housing was built in New York state in the 1920's, but not until the depression of the 1930's did housing, both public and private, become a matter of concerted governmental action.

The Federal Housing Administration was established in 1934 to encourage improvement in housing standards and conditions. Although the FHA did not make loans or build houses, it insured mortgages and property improve-

ment loans made by private lending institutions. Its intent has been to encourage lending so that construction of housing would be stimulated. From
1934 to 1957, the FHA insured the mortgages of 4.4 million homes. Of these,
2.5 million have been new homes. In addition, the FHA has insured almost
700,000 housing units in apartment projects and insured about 20 million
loans for property improvements. Normally, FHA-insured mortgages are
used in financing between 20 to 30 per cent of all housing built each year.

In addition to this aid to private lending institutions, the federal government also moved into public housing during the 1930's. Public housing was
facilitated by federal loans to local housing authorities for the construction
of publicly owned houses. Also, the federal government paid local housing
authorities an annual subsidy to meet the difference between low rent
charged for the units and the cost actually needed to cover carrying charges
and operating expenses. This housing aid, which has been carried on through
a number of agencies, is now the responsibility of the Public Housing Administration. Until 1957, there were in the United States almost 535,000
dwelling units in low-rent public housing projects.

Public housing, unlike many innovations of the 1930's, has not become
an integral part of the urban environment nor has it, like some other innovations, disappeared as an acknowledged failure. Public housing has been
and is opposed by some private builders and lenders as "governmental interference" in a free housing market. These same critics, however, often do
not object to governmental aid to private building in the form of FHA assistance. The lack of acceptance of public housing may be in terms of design.
Many projects comprise high density, multi-storied apartments, appealing
neither to the tenants nor to those who drive by. While, in fact, these projects
are probably no more monotonous than many suburban developments, they
do have a quality marking them as "institutions" devoted to "caring" for low
income groups. This appearance of segregation by income is accentuated by
rigid income limits used as a qualification for tenancy. When a tenant increases his income over the limit, he is requested to move. Minority group
members who have difficulty in finding other types of private housing may
refuse to accept higher income to stay in the project. With recent Negro
migration to cities, an increasing proportion of the units is occupied by
Negroes. The lack of a free private housing market for the Negro makes
public housing increasingly segregated. Because of these and other reasons,
public housing in the United States has not become as integral a part of the
city as it has in Europe.

Housing in urban areas has, in recent years, continued to improve. It is
interesting to note, in light of the general assumption that housing is primarily
an urban problem, that most of the dilapidated dwellings in the United

States in 1956 were outside the metropolitan areas. In addition, if home ownership is considered a value, there has been an increase in home ownership with increasing urbanization (see Table 3-2).

TABLE 3-2

Occupied dwelling units in the United States, 1890–1960

Year	Total	Per cent owner occupied
1890	12,600,000	47
1900	15,900,000	46
1910	20,200,000	45
1920	24,300,000	45
1930	29,900,000	47
1940	34,800,000	43
1950	42,800,000	55
1960	53,000,000	62

Source: Bureau of Census and *Britannica Book of the Year*, 1962, Chicago: Encyclopaedia Britannica, Inc., 1962, p. 137.

(e) *Urban redevelopment and renewal.* During the 1930's, new housing, both public and private, was seen as the solution to depressed housing conditions and the resulting pall they cast over a whole city. Slum areas were to be cleared and new neighborhoods were to be created. Many plans for rehabilitation were disrupted or inhibited by World War II.

Since World War II, city problems have been summarized under the label of urban redevelopment. This term came into usage after the passage of housing acts in 1949 and 1954. These acts included what was considered best from the depression legislation. They also indicated that redevelopment should not only clear slum areas but renew deteriorating areas. Every part of a city is in the process of deterioration. This rate of deterioration can be slowed down by differing techniques. There may be areas where the housing is old, but of satisfactory design. Since many of these areas are basically sound, these features can be conserved by a minimum amount of clearance or by the enforcement of minimum housing standards. More blighted older areas may require more drastic measures to forestall their becoming slums. This may be achieved by enforcing legal standards of repair, maintenance, and occupancy. This might require making credit available for property improvements. It might also require neighborhood organization to try to rally the area owners to revitalize neighborhood self-respect with regard to property standards. These phases of redevelopment are often given the name of urban renewal.

Other areas of the city are beyond conservation and rehabilitation. They must be cleared and rebuilt. One persistent barrier to slum clearance has been the high cost of slum property. Landlords make profits from rentals and are not willing to sell for low prices. Neither are they willing to clear their land, because its poor location deflates its value. By assuming the job of acquiring and clearing slum property, a city can assemble a large enough tract so that any rebuilding will not be engulfed by slum buildings left standing. The city buys slum property, clears it, and then sells it to a private developer at a reduced price. The federal government covers two-thirds of this loss and the city puts up the other third. The private developer builds commercial and industrial buildings or middle-income apartment houses.

For the first time the Housing Act of 1949 showed a concern for the families displaced by clearance and rebuilding operations. It required, as a condition of federal aid, that the families be relocated in areas of somewhat equal facilities and at rents within their financial means. While existing private or public housing is used in relocation, additional credit was extended for those families to purchase new or rehabilitated low-cost private housing. In addition, low-cost public housing has been encouraged for those families unable to afford private housing. Businesses are also given relocation payments to cover moving expenses.

It seems clear, as America enters into the latter part of the twentieth century, that the problems of cities will be continuing ones of adaptation. Many of the earlier problems — fire, public health, tenement regulation — have been "solved" in the sense that continuous attention is devoted to these problems on the part of some branch of municipal government. Deterioration of cities will obviously not be solved by the simple act of slum clearance, since slums are constantly being created. The problem, then, becomes not just building a growing city, but rebuilding a deteriorating one. This is no small task. "Designing a dream city is easy; rebuilding a living one takes imagination." [6]

Thus, a new normative conception emerged with the growth of urban areas. With the breakdown of the traditional mutual help pattern, many devices to assure economic security emerged. These techniques almost always involved governmental initiation and action, violating the traditional limited role of government in the rural community. The tradition of "spontaneous" growth or, more correctly, the determination of community growth through the operation of the market was replaced by city planning where economic values took their place alongside humanitarian and aesthetic considerations.

Throughout the growth of cities, the traditional conception persisted. Tomars, in a perceptive article entitled "Rural Survivals in American Urban Life," has indicated a number of ways in which certain practices and beliefs,

6. The Editors of *Fortune*, op. cit. p. 168.

in cities, reflect rural rather than urban norms.[7] He suggests that the preference for "a home of your own" in the city reflects the values of rural self-sufficiency. This might explain, in part, rejection of apartment-like public housing projects. In a home of your own, one central feature of urban architecture is the fireplace, which has little function in the days of central heating, except rural nostalgia. This survival becomes more ludicrous when the fireplace is filled with imitation logs and red lights that flicker. Many rural aphorisms still are used even though they have lost their meaning. "Early to bed and early to rise" made sense in a rural environment but it persists to make those on "artificial" schedules feel guilty for "lolling" in bed in the morning or staying up late at night. Rural origins and/or identification are still important in urban and national politics. Franklin Roosevelt, with all his urbanity, gave his occupation as farmer and Eisenhower had his Gettysburg farm. Many urbanites who cannot point to rural origins buy farms to plant their roots and to spread their tax loss. Every spring, another rural survival is seen when thousands of urbanites spend $150 on garden equipment to grow ten cents' worth of radishes.

TABLE 3-3

Preference for type of community by size of community

	Where they would like to live				
Where they live now	Large city	Small city	Close to city	Far from city	Out in country
Over 100,000	36.2	10.4	36.5	2.8	11.1
25,000 to 100,000	6.8	43.3	26.9	4.4	16.4
2500 to 25,000	6.9	27.8	46.5	3.2	12.4
Under 2500 and rural non-farm	6.1	16.4	49.0	6.9	20.5
Rural farm	0.6	6.5	18.1	1.1	71.7
national average	14.7	17.6	35.8	3.5	26.0

Source: "The Fortune Survey," *Fortune* (April 1946), p. 277, nation-wide sample.

The persistence of the traditional rural conception and the discomfort with the developing conception of the city is shown, in another way, in the expression of where people preferred to live. Table 3-3 shows that, of those in large cities over 100,000, only a little over one-third were content with living in a large city. The rest expressed a desire to get away from the city. Those who lived in smaller communities desired the bright lights of the city even less.

The traditional normative conception persisted during the emergence of the conception of urbanism and created dissensus. Impersonality, that is,

7. Adolph S. Tomars, "Rural Survivals in American Urban Life," *Rural Sociology* (December 1943), pp. 378–86.

impersonalized solutions to community problems and planned urban growth, has never been completely accepted, even in the city. As such, this continued disagreement concerning the nature of the community constitutes a social problem. In addition, urban growth has created problems of implementing the traditional conception in any community. Two types of contemporary communities, the small town and suburbia, attempt to retain elements of this traditional conception in a society dominated by cities. The normative conceptions of these types of communities and their success in implementing these conceptions will be discussed below.

> *Contemporary Normative Conception: The Contemporary Small Town* — The small town should resist the inroads of urban-industrial society and reaffirm the historical conception of the community.

Even with the growth of cities, the small town has persisted. In these small towns, much of the historical conception persists, coupled with a rejection of urbanism. There is the continued emphasis upon the importance of personalized relationships. But, in the contemporary small town, the economic base upon which a network of friendship was historically based has disintegrated. The small town increasingly finds itself without the autonomy it once had in American society. The economic life of most contemporary small towns is oriented toward urban products and urban producers. Political life is no longer autonomous but adapts local affairs to the demands of state and federal government. Nevertheless, the small town continues to cherish autonomy and self-sufficiency.

1. *Personal Relationships.* The small town still values personal relationships. Many small town inhabitants think of themselves and of their neighbors as being "just plain folks." [8] This implies that the small town has no false or artificial values. Thus, neither money, status, family background, nor education is assumed to have any effect upon one's contact with another. A premium is placed on those who are average, friendly, and open. The intellectual, the bookish, and the introverted are defined as being difficult to understand, since they are not "just plain folks." Both as a description of what the small town is and what it should be, it is implied that people are equalitarian, honest, helpful, and clean living. This model of social relationships is held up to the whole urban industrial society. It is assumed in the twentieth-century small town that:

(a) The basic traditions of American society — grass roots democracy, in-

---

8. This discussion follows closely Arthur Vidich and Joseph Bensman, *Small Town in Mass Society*, Garden City: Doubleday, 1960.

dividualism, etc. — are most frequently found in the small town. If the "American heritage" is to be preserved, it can be preserved best in the small town safe from urban influences.

(b) The small town also is the best defense against various "isms" — Communism, Socialism, Secularism, Totalitarianism, Atheism, and perhaps, one might add, Industrialism.

(c) Most of the progress made by American society has come from rural talent that migrated to the city. The few virtues in urban life are attributable to rural migrants able to withstand the deterioration of the city.

(d) If more people lived in small towns, the problems of the contemporary world would not exist.

The truth of these reaffirmations is not important in this context. The fact that they are a part of the belief system of the small town makes them significant. This reaffirmation contrasts with the small towners' image of the city. Their image of the larger urban industrial society includes the following:

(a) Cities breed corruption and, with their impersonality, are unable to solve the problems they create. Thus, cities are unwholesome environments for children and family life.

(b) The large political centers, particularly Washington, are populated by bureaucrats and "fast-buck" operators, who live like parasites off the "hardworking" people. Urban politicians do not reflect the wishes of America.

(c) Industrial workers are paid too much for doing too little work. Union leaders foment trouble and are anti-democratic forces in American life.

(d) Cities, in general, are hot-beds of un-American sentiment and their universities and churches are centers of atheism and secularism.

(e) Most of the problems of small town and country life have their origins in the effects urban life has had upon rural ways.[9]

2. *Community Problems.* In the contemporary small town, mutual help is still valued. In times of crisis, neighbors still show concern for those in distress. Most of this mutual help centers on birth, death, and illness, but is no longer left to the spontaneity of friendship. Practically all organizations, from the church to the American Legion and the Grange, have committees organized to facilitate mutual help. Whether admitted or not, mutual help has been formalized and perhaps impersonalized.

Other than personal and family crises, most of the problems traditionally handled in the small community by mutual help have been passed on to other governmental units — the county welfare office, the state bureau of unemployment compensation, the federal system of Social Security. This means that the solutions to the more important community problems are now originating outside the small town. Most of the improvements being made in small towns

9. Ibid. p. 32.

require qualifying for federal or state aid. If a federal agency rules that a
community can no longer continue to dump sewage into the nearest stream,
political activity will center on this ruling for many years. Local political action takes on the character of seeking favors, subsidies, and special treatment
from outside agencies. Local political power rests on local political leaders
having access to sources of decision-making in larger governmental units.
Informal political power goes to those who can understand the technical and
legal language which characterizes the requests from larger governmental
units. Thus, the lawyer and the engineer become informal political leaders
although they may not hold office. The lawyer can understand the legal
demands and the engineer can understand the technical demands. Local
political leaders often simply reaffirm the advice of these experts skilled in
the techniques of the urban industrial world. The informal political power
of the technical expert is, of course, a denial of grass roots democracy and
another indication of the dependency of the small town on the larger society.

This dependency on the larger society is shown in many ways. Tax rates
are set by outside agencies. The construction and maintenance of roads is
under state and county supervision. The location of highways is set by state
departments while local communities exercise slight veto power. Even the
last bastion of small-town politics, the school, has fallen under outside and,
in larger part, urban influences. School standards are set by state agencies.
Certification of teachers and salary schedules are defined for the local community. The range of flexibility for the local community is guided by the
superintendent and the principal, who — by virtue of their urban training
and their extra-community contacts — define standards of educational performance to the school board and to the town. Thus, in the contemporary
small town, while local autonomy is reaffirmed, the conditions to support
these conceptions have disappeared.

3. *Community Growth.* By definition of the small town, problems of
growth are not significant for most of these communities. Most small towns
experience relative stability in population size or have declining populations.
A favorite topic of conversation in many small towns centers on the "things
they used to have" — the band concert in the park, the hotel, the railroad
station, and where people used to live before they went to the city. Some small
towns, however, face the problems of community growth in an acute way.
Decisions made in some city a thousand miles away to locate a plant in a
small town often mean that this small town will be doubled or tripled in
population. In spite of the fact that such a plant location brings the "taint
of urbanism and industrialization" to the town, it is generally accepted by the
residents as a good thing and the solution to many community problems. It
will provide a larger tax base, a means of keeping young people from going

to the cities, and new opportunities for employment. The reaction to these problems of growth is to continue the tradition of spontaneous development. By following the tradition, it is assumed that a new and larger community will be infused with the existing "goodness" of the small community. During this rapid growth, the need for urban techniques such as zoning and planning become apparent, but, by then, growth is completed and the small town finds itself a large town, poorly planned and with an accumulation of new problems which will take another generation to solve. As one illustration of the process, consider what happened to two small towns in Ohio:

Many still talk about August 12, 1952, as the day the A-bomb hit Pike County. What they mean is . . . that on that date the United States government, through its Atomic Energy Commission, announced it would build its gaseous diffusion plant there. This plant, costing approximately $1,219,000,000, just about doubled the total value of all public and tax exempt property in Ohio. Largest of all atomic plants, the Pike County project swallowed up an entire village, 34 farms, seven partial farms, two cemeteries and a church. The buildings for the plant were larger than the combined buildings of the Pentagon in Washington, D.C., and the Willow Run Building in Michigan.

Pike County, which bore most of the impact of this plant, had two small towns which had, for the past 50 years, been relatively static in their size and composition. In 1950, Piketon had 768 residents while Waverly had 1679. Percentagewise, Piketon was to become the fastest growing town in America when it grew to 3000 within a few short months. Its village corporation limits were extended and city water, sewer, police and fire protection had to be provided. Not counting the permanent housing to be developed nor the several thousands of trailers which were to cluster around it, the size was to be tripled just by the building of a five-hundred family Public Housing Unit. Waverly, too, grew to 6500 people.

While in the schools of the county the population doubled, Piketon schools increased 346 per cent. This was accomplished by putting students two at a desk. When this possibility was exhausted, other space was sought out. In one school district, a jail was pressed into service. Waverly continued to use an elementary building which had been built in 1867 and which had been condemned for a number of years.

While much of the increase was from 100,000 construction workers who were in the area only a short period of time, local officials flushed by such a "boom" tended to forget that they would soon be gone. The net result of the plant on the total permanent population was not as dramatic since the plant was automated and would only require 4000 workers, many of them to be employed from the area. Many of these permanent residents, engineers, executives, technicians, when they came to settle down rejected the small towns, such as Waverly and Piketon, close to the plant and settled in small cities, much further away. A number of factors affected this settlement pattern. Many of the new permanent residents with urban experience expected certain community services and were also repelled by the "floundering" of local officials in handling admittedly difficult problems of rapid growth. A hospital was needed, but the traditional rivalry between Waverly and Piketon delayed its completion until the fight over its location could run its course. In addition to the lack of medical resources, these towns lacked many services which urbanites take for granted. Local political leaders viewed the newcomers as outsiders and, hence, could not and would not communicate with them in the solution of community problems. Many local merchants used a two-price system — higher for newcomers and lower for their "neighbors." The housing that was built was not attractive to those permanent residents who had developed urban expectations.

One newcomer, who was to be a permanent resident, said, "I brought my family out of a highly congested metropolitan area into this rural life and learned how the other 'half of the world' lives. We have seen floods, drought, and have learned the importance of the school bus driver. We never appreciated the schools, the medical ability of the nearby professional men, and shopping centers, telephone and transportation. To be truthful, I'm doubtful if many realize how far behind the county is. It isn't the horde of newcomers; there was a problem here but it's easier to move away than try to better conditions. Now conditions are better but they are still inferior to most counties to the north." One of the local residents summed up the consequences of the plant as follows: "Financially, we have benefitted from the plant in a small way. Physically, it has been a headache — schools, streets, housing, sewage, utilities, higher taxes, etc. What was once a quiet little town has been turned into a madhouse, good for the druggist and the nerve medicine company." [10]

Admittedly, few small towns experience such dramatic growth, but the process goes on continually in an industrial society. Population mobility will increase and more and more small towns will experience rapid growth. By rejecting urban techniques and by accepting unplanned, spontaneous growth, these small towns find themselves with problems which could have been attenuated by accepting the experience of the city.

> *Contemporary Normative Conception: Suburbia* — The community should retain personalized relationships and solve community problems by grass roots government while accepting advantages and techniques of the urban industrial world.

As American cities grew, they presented an image of depressed humanity. Factories spewed forth smoke and dirt which settled down on row after row of company houses. To avoid the dirt and to see something green again became an understandable goal. The automobile added to this dirt and congestion, but it also offered the opportunity to escape the ugliness and to seek the space, the green, and the cleanliness of a new community form. As Table

10. Adapted from Russell R. Dynes, *The Consequences of Population Mobility for School and Community Change*, School-Community Development Study, Columbus: Ohio State University, 1956.

3-3 indicates, living in cities does not mean *liking* cities. Still, for all groups, there is a peculiar fascination about the city. The city is the dominant focus of an industrial society. The city is where the jobs are. How to combine motives of escape from the city with one's economic dependence on the city provided a persistent dilemma which the automobile helped solve. The automobile made it possible for Americans to solve the conflict of their dependence on the city and their rejection of it. The solution was suburbia.

For increasing numbers of people, moving to suburbia has meant the opportunity to combine the best of both worlds — the simplicity of the rural small town and the fascination of the city. That this alternative has strong appeal is obvious when the growth around the large cities of the United States is observed. Table 3-4 indicates the rate of this population increase.

TABLE 3-4

Population of the United States by area of residence: percentage increase

Area	Percentage increase	
	1940–50	1950–60
United States	14.5	18.4
Standard Metropolitan Areas	22.0	26.4
Central Cities	13.9	10.6
Outlying Parts	35.6	49.0

Source: Bureau of Census, 1950 Census of Population (Advance Reports), "Population of the Standard Metropolitan Areas: April 1, 1950," Series PC-9, No. 6 (November 24, 1952), p. 1. *Statistical Abstract of the United States,* 1961, Washington, D.C.: U.S. Government Printing Office, 1961, Table 10.

"Standard metropolitan area" is a census term developed to take into account the dependence on a city of a large segment of a population even though this population might reside outside the political boundaries of the city. The term is used to indicate an area that contains one or more cities of 50,000 or more population and includes contiguous areas economically integrated with the central city. Most population growth in the United States has taken place within these standard metropolitan areas but most of the growth of the metropolitan areas has been in the outlying areas and not in the central cities. Over a fifty-year period, growth rates in the metropolitan areas have moved outward. Hawley indicates that in the 1900–1910 decade the most rapidly growing areas were the central cities. In the next decade, the highest rates of growth were in the 0–5 mile zones around the central city. From 1920 to 1930, growth rates shifted to the 5–10 mile zones, where they remained for the next two decades. Today, there is rapid population growth in the even more distant zones, especially in the zones over 35 miles from the central city.[11] This growth has created a new type of community: suburbia.

1. *Personal Relationships.* The advantages of suburbia are often seen in their personalized relationships. With the city as the source of income and the automobile as the means of travel, where to live can rest on other considerations. Suburban families are different from those who stay in the central cities. Duncan and Reiss have noted that, "The suburban population is relatively homogeneous, ethnically; that is, a high proportion is native white. It enjoys relatively high socio-economic status, as indicated by occupational composition, average educational attainment, and income. The suburban population shows evidences of a stronger familistic bent than the urban population, in its comparatively high proportions of married, its levels of fertility, and its lower rate of female labor-force participation." [12] In a study of suburban Chicago, Bell found that those who had moved to the suburbs looked for a place which was "better for the children" and where they could "enjoy life more." Since most of these residents had recently moved from apartments, many were concerned with the "more space" inside and outside which suburbia would provide. In addition, almost three-fourths of the respondents indicated a "quest for community" — the idea that with their move they would get more friendly neighbors and would have access to greater community participation. As a consequence, they felt they would have a greater sense of belonging to the community.[13]

Studies of suburbs indicate a pattern of rather intense neighboring.[14] Since the men are in the city or driving back and forth, neighboring centers on the wife and children. Riesman has characterized the suburb as somewhat like a fraternity house at a small college.[15] Just as one's fraternity brothers are similar in age, ethnic background, and income, neighbors in suburbia do not have to overcome the barrier of differences. While critics of suburbia have called it a "homogenized" community unlike the real (urban) world, seemingly most suburbanites feel that this is its strength. One's neighbor is not a stranger as he might be in the city but he is someone like you — with the same kind of education, the same kind of car and house, the same kinds of interests, the same number of children, and the same political and social

11. Amos H. Hawley, *The Changing Shape of Metropolitan America*, Glencoe, Ill.: Free Press, 1955, pp. 15–17.
12. Otis Dudley Duncan and Albert J. Reiss, Jr., *Social Characteristics of Urban and Rural Communities, 1950*, New York: Wiley, 1956, p. 6.
13. Wendell Bell, "Social Choice, Life Styles and Suburban Residence," in William M. Dobriner (editor), *The Suburban Community*, New York: Putnam, 1958, pp. 225–47.
14. See, for example, Sylvia Fleis Fava, "Contrasts in Neighboring: New York City and a Suburban Community," ibid. pp. 122–31.
15. David Riesman, "The Suburban Sadness," ibid. p. 386.

ideals. Again, this is the traditional appeal of the rural community in more modern terms.

2. *Community Problems.* Part of the ideology of suburbia is that community problems can best be solved at the grass roots and that small political units are more democratic. In contrast to the anonymous operation of municipal government, suburbanites assume that many problems can be solved on the basis of mutual help and that the rest should be dealt with by personalized governmental service.

Since much of the life of suburbia revolves around children, many community problems focus on them. While their neighbors in the central city grapple with urban renewal, suburban communities find their greatest community concern in schools. The larger number of children and the recent emphasis upon education in American society combine to produce a major preoccupation with education. Schools, however, are "beyond" politics and therefore school affairs are carried on in a "nonpartisan" manner. While insisting on grass roots and "nonpartisan" support, suburbanites place primary responsibility for schools on a school superintendent and accept and implement his policies. Suburbanites in their escape from the urban industrial world, thus implicitly accept one of its prime tenets, professionalization of function. Concern for schools, usually, does not raise the issue of the ends of education — what education should be directed toward. School superintendents, supported by the suburban PTA, generally avoid this issue and concentrate on physical problems. In most suburban communities, the direction of the educational concern is cast in terms of more buildings, more teachers, and more money. In suburbia, as in the rest of American society, it is difficult to be against "progress." This grass roots support of larger and "better" schools is encouraged not only by the informal pressures of the PTA but by the school board, one's friends and neighbors or at least friends of friends, or neighbors of neighbors.

"Grass roots" government extends beyond the school. The mayor, the councilmen, the chief of police, the fire chief, the building inspector, — perhaps everyone except the garbage collector — are considered approachable. In this way, all the elected officials and all of the appointed employees are open to public view and supervision. It is assumed that small governmental units with their few "exposed" individuals provide the best government possible.

Critics of suburbia, however, point out that this model for the solution of community problems has several drawbacks. The earlier small town was both a social and a spatial unit. While contemporary suburbia represents a social community — at least for women and children — the extended absence of the breadwinner in the central city betrays the notion that the economic unit coincides with the political or social boundaries. Suburbs have no independent economic status. They contain only a fraction of the labor force, facilities, and equipment that provide the raw materials for an industrial society. As a production unit, the suburb contributes nothing and the separation of work and residence indicates its utter dependence on the central city. Too, suburbanites are dependent on the city for cultural advantages. With this inherent dependence, suburban governments, with all their personalized services, avoid most of the major problems which confront the central city.

Other critics of personalized suburban government have suggested that, while it can be effective, it can also be offensive. Wood has suggested that:

Grass roots government may or may not be good government then; it is difficult to say. It depends on whether the town is good or not. The smaller the town, the more justice is a matter of public opinion in the community itself, rarely formalized, rarely examined, rarely permanently established, depending on the sentiment of the moment. It is little wonder that the local justice of the peace is the laughingstock of the legal profession. Even if he knows his duties, how can he possibly impartially administer justice in an atmosphere of overwhelming intimacy? . . .

[In personalized government] the notion of contractual relations is replaced by the reality of personal relations, who belongs and who does not. The individual depends on the sanction of the group and remains uncertain of his rights and prerogatives. In the end, he has no fixed standard to indicate how he stands in the face and eyes of his neighbors.[16]

Preoccupied with schools and indifferent to the problems of the central city, suburbanites generally accept state and national solutions to the problems of economic security. These are not, however, crucial issues for most suburbanites. They are in an age category which can disregard social security and they are in an occupational and income category in which unemployment makes little sense. Nor are suburbanites faced with oppressive working conditions in their air-conditioned offices in the city.

3. *Community Growth.* By and large, suburban communities have accepted controlled community growth and have used many of the controls developed to regulate the growth of cities. These controls were initiated to shape land use and to prevent blight, but many suburbs have used them to exclude "undesirable elements." While legal restrictive covenants have been declared unconstitutional, by setting severe zoning restrictions and stringent building requirements, exclusion of particular racial and/or income groups can be accomplished.

Planning has spread to suburbia. Nearly 80 per cent of all incorporated

16. Robert C. Wood, *Suburbia, Its People and Their Politics*, Boston: Houghton Mifflin, 1958, p. 280.

places with populations over 5000 now have planning boards. But most of these planning boards operate informally and without technical professional personnel. Less than half of the smaller communities have technical staffs or consultants. Of these, only about one-third have full-time professional planning directors.

Many suburban developers do utilize the insights accumulated in urban areas and often maintain reasonable standards. Some suburbs, however, develop standards only when the developer is gone, leaving behind a pent-up demand for municipal services — streets, sewers, water, garbage collection, and schools. Since most suburbs are without industries, municipal services must be based on a residential tax. With increasing population, costs often sky-rocket and the suburbanite finds himself with higher and higher tax rates. Since municipal services can be provided more economically on a larger geographical base, the proliferation of suburbs substitutes local responsibility and increased costs for administrative and economic efficiency. Suburbanites also create increased costs for the central city. Most suburbanites work in the central city, and most use the city for trade and recreation, but this use is not "paid" for by taxation. The suburbanite, thus, gets a "free ride" down the freeway and into the city. Some central cities have instituted income taxes based on the principle that if one "uses" the city, one must help support its services. Thus the suburbanite is caught in a double responsibility — increased costs in his residential area and added costs for his use of the city.

It is clear, however, that planning for community growth cannot be done effectively if suburbia is considered separately from the larger metropolitan area. The effectiveness of planning is restricted by the multiplicity of political units. In 1960, in the 17 towns that comprise Denver's four-county suburban area, for example, there were 27 school districts, 35 water districts, 59 sanitation districts. The suburbia of Portland, Oregon, embraced three counties, 178 special districts, 60 school districts, 12 city governments. None of these, however, approached Los Angeles, which contains 72 separate governments in addition to assorted districts, authorities, and unincorporated communities.[17] In recognition of this interdependence, planning increasingly is done on a regional basis or by joint city-county effort. Cities have tried to solve the problem of multiplication of political units in many ways. One response has been annexation. This alternative is usually rejected by suburban areas on the basis that it undermines grass roots democracy. In order to meet this objection, recent attempts have established special districts assuming functions which are metropolitan in character, while the suburbs retain their autonomy in other areas. In a few places, such as Dade County,

17. *Time* (June 20, 1960), p. 17.

Florida, which includes Miami and its suburban areas, attempts have been made to establish the inclusive governmental unit at the county level. While suburbs are sometimes willing to surrender some functions to special districts, a new larger governmental unit for the growing metropolitan areas violates the notion of grass roots government. The most recent attempt to make sense of the conflicting political authorities has been the metropolitan federation. In 1950, Toronto established the first federated government. It gave the federated government authority to carry out programs obviously metropolitan in character — transportation, water, sewage, land use, planning — and it gave the suburbs representation in the federated system. Federated government has not spread dramatically since that time. Perhaps one reason for its lack of success is that the important problems of the suburbs are obviously metropolitan in character and in order to solve them suburbia has to lose its local autonomy. The total metropolitan area must be considered as a functional unit. Suburbia's claim to autonomy in the face of metropolitan interdependence remains one of the most important unsolved issues of contemporary America.

THE CONSEQUENCES OF SUBURBANIZATION FOR THE CENTRAL CITY
One result of suburbanization has been to change the nature and character of the central city.[18] The result has been to turn central cities into lower class, primarily Negro slums. The largest metropolitan areas in the United States have attracted large numbers of Negro migrants from the South. Between 1940 and 1950 the 14 largest metropolitan areas, those with a population over one million, increased their total population 19 per cent. Within these areas, however, the total Negro percentage gain (65.1 per cent) was more than four times greater than that of the white increase (15.6 per cent). While this increase is spread through the whole metropolitan area, the greatest impact has been in the central cities where the whites increased 3.7 per cent and Negroes increased 67.8 per cent.

Between 1950 and 1960, this trend continued. Of the ten largest *central* cities, eight lost population. The Negro population of these cities grew spectacularly and in eight of the cities constituted one-fifth of the population. In Washington, Negroes constitute a majority (see Table 3-5).

This growth of the Negro population in the central city follows a regular pattern. Negroes live in segregated residential areas. Given an increase in Negro population, housing must be found in predominantly white areas. Once Negroes begin to move into a white area, the area gradually changes from predominantly white to predominantly Negro. This pattern of Negro expan-

18. This discussion follows closely Morton Grodzins, *The Metropolitan Areas as a Racial Problem*, Pittsburgh: University of Pittsburgh Press, 1958.

sion starts from the core of the city and moves out. The Negro population generally moves into an area already characterized by high residential mobility. Many white residents of these areas interpret this movement as their being "pushed" out of an area but, in most instances, the new resident simply fills up vacancies. Some white residents will not accept Negroes as neighbors and move out. Many, however, stay until the proportion of non-whites reaches the "intolerance" level. This level of neighborhood tolerance is often given the name of the "tip point" and some real estate operators, who profit from the higher income that comes from Negro overcrowding, exploit this tip point by selling a house to a "block busting" family that "tips" that block toward all Negro occupancy. The result of this "tipping" is to perpetuate segregation and to extend the "black belt" farther away from the central core of the city.

TABLE 3-5

Per cent change in the total and Negro population
in the ten largest cities, 1950–60

City	Per cent Negro in total population		Per cent change	
	1950	1960	Negro population	Total population
New York	9.5	14.0	45.5	−1.4
Chicago	13.6	22.9	65.1	−1.9
Los Angeles	8.7	13.5	95.6	25.8
Philadelphia	18.2	26.4	40.7	−3.3
Detroit	16.2	28.9	60.5	−9.7
Baltimore	23.7	34.8	44.6	−1.1
Houston	20.9	22.9	72.4	57.4
Cleveland	16.2	28.6	69.6	−4.2
Washington	35.0	53.9	46.6	−4.8
St. Louis	17.9	28.6	39.4	−12.5

Source: *Britannica Book of the Year*, 1962, p. 136, Table IV.

Suburban living is effectively "closed" to Negro families. While cost is one factor, Negroes are excluded by a variety of devices. The hostility of surburban residents prevents many Negroes from attempting a move. Developers planning to build Negro housing often find themselves harassed by zoning, subdivision, and building codes. These codes are enforced differently, however, for "desirable developers." Even if houses are built, banks often refuse to give mortgages to Negro buyers. These devices and others keep Negroes in the central cities.

The consequences of this growing segregation are many. By its very nature, it separates people within the city on the basis of skin color. More than this, it spreads the slums throughout the central city since there is no free housing market. With the increase in non-white population and "escape" to the suburbs closed, existing housing and even new areas secured by "tipping" are overcrowded. Overcrowding leads to a more rapid deterioration of areas. Overcrowding pushes teenagers into the street and into the influence of the street gang. Some of the migrants are unaccustomed to urban life in general, and to slum conditions in particular. Family patterns begin to disintegrate. Drinking increases. Aggression emerges. This disorganization has been common to many groups who came to the city as migrants — the Irish, the Italians, the Poles. In this instance, however, disorganization is associated with skin color. Unlike the other immigrants who lost their "undesirable" attributes, Negroes cannot lose their skin color and escape the slums to a better life somewhere else.

This population shift has other consequences for the city. Retail sales expand in suburban areas and contract in the central city. New downtown businesses are more likely to be hamburger joints or discount houses, spreading the slums to the central business districts. Motels in suburban areas undercut the hotels, and new highways make it easier for offices to move out and be followed by banks and other services. This decline of the downtown area decreases the tax valuation and adds the additional problem of seeking new sources of revenue.

The segregation of a large, primarily Negro, lower-class population in the central city also has political consequences. Negroes in these areas are not politically disfranchised as they are in some areas of the South. They may become the majority group politically. While political lines traditionally have not been drawn on a racial basis, the equivalence of political boundaries and racial groups may focus political action on the activities of the Negro community. While there is no evidence that Negroes are more self-interested politically than other groups, the undeniable visual impact of the Negro would lend credence to any charge of political domination. While existing city councils may be dominated by one particular interest — perhaps business — this is never as obvious to voters as a city council dominated by Negroes would be. Such domination might aggravate existing conflict in state legislatures, so that Negro-white conflict would be added to the conflict between rural and urban areas. This racial dimension may further impede the legislative solution to the relationship between city and suburb.

Grodzins has suggested a number of steps toward the solution of this racial concentration.[19] One step would be to remove the restrictions on where Negroes might live. While this can be conceived as a simple act of justice, it would go far in eliminating the social costs of present concentrations. If Negroes had free residential movement, there would be less overcrowding in

19. Ibid.

existing Negro areas and there would be smaller and fewer all-Negro neighborhoods. If Negroes were free to move in the same fashion whites do, they would go to areas where the social characteristics of others are similar in income, education, etc. While income factors confine many Negroes to less desirable residential areas, there are Negroes living in existing segregated areas simply because they have no place to go. With the gradual economic improvement of Negroes, free access to housing markets would result in the scattering of Negro families throughout the entire central city and suburban areas. If a free housing market were achieved, it would slow the panic flights of whites since they could be sure that no matter where they moved a similar situation would develop. The knowledge that a similar situation would occur wherever they might move would focus the attention of new and old residents alike on maintaining the standards of the neighborhoods, eliminating the concentration of attention of old residents on preventing Negro occupancy. Laws banning discrimination in housing could effect such widespread dispersion of non-white populations, but probably would be effective only if they covered large jurisdictions.

The case for a free housing market, implemented by nondiscrimination laws, rests on the assumption that non-whites in relatively small numbers would move into existing white areas. The tipping mechanism mentioned earlier perhaps indicates that interracial communities exist only if some limit on non-white migration occurs. In some cases, the limits are placed by economic factors — only a few Negroes can afford to live in certain expensive interracial communities. In other instances, migration has been limited by quotas placed on Negro occupancy and indirectly on white occupancy. In Philadelphia, the developers of the suburbs of Concord Park and Greenbelt Knoll have announced their intention of maintaining a white-Negro ratio of 55-45. Seemingly on the basis of past experience, where controlled migration has been achieved, interracial communities have been achieved. While controlling Negro migration would be a limitation on freedom, it perhaps substitutes a smaller discrimination for a larger one.

Since one of the reasons for the drift of the central city toward a non-white slum has been suburban movement, one way to reduce this drift would be to encourage the movement of white populations back into the central city. Many individuals go to the suburbs to achieve things the city does not provide — modern housing, space, and good schools. It is the young married couples who are typically candidates for suburbia. Certain advantages of the central city, at some later date, may pull many of these couples back, when they have exhausted the advantages and become aware of the disadvantages of suburbia. For older suburbanites, when the children are grown and gone, the house seems empty and the task of keeping the place up becomes no longer a family task but a nuisance. The crabgrass is never really conquered and the hedge always needs trimming. As Whyte suggests: "The grass, particularly, seems to become a Thing, and it is sometimes mentioned with such animosity as to suggest that the suburban lawn may be the salvation of the city." [20] The older suburban wife, no longer absorbed in PTA, finds her neighbors less engrossing when she no longer shares the problems of parent-hood with them. Her work load is lightened and she looks again to the advantages of living in the city. Too, she can, by moving into the city, see more of her husband, perhaps two hours more a day. The husband's mood is improved by not having to fight traffic or the frustrations of commuting delays. For these individuals, city living can provide a new lease on life.

In addition, other types of families may find city living attractive. Many parents, finding the efficiency or, more aptly, the smallness of the suburban ranch house no answer for their increasing herd of children, look toward the big old houses in the city as an answer to their immediate problems. What they sacrifice in modern design, they may gain in extra bedrooms, a cellar, and the vanishing American institution, the dining room. Still other parents may react against the homogenization of the suburbs. While suburbs are generally viewed as a good place to rear children, suburbia is an artificial world — a world where every adult is young, and where everyone owns a station wagon and a backyard barbecue. It is not a world where old people live, where minority groups live, or where people differ in their worldly possessions. Some parents suggest that if their children are to learn to live in the "real" world as adults, they must become familiar with this world as children.

To capitalize on the desires of these individuals, already drawn to advantages of the city, would facilitate the return of non-white populations to the central cities. Some migrants to suburbia have suggested that their movement was not motivated because they had Negroes for neighbors but because of housing and educational deterioration. Perhaps if urban redevelopment programs can attract families back into the city so that heterogeneity can be achieved without overcrowding, the advantages of the city can be achieved without the disadvantages, and the metropolitan population can be concentrated without being segregated.

THE FUTURE OF COMMUNITY

No observer of community life would predict a reversal of the growth of urban areas. While this growth may not occur in the central city, metro-

20. The Editors of *Fortune*, op. cit. p. 11.

politan growth in general seems assured. As metropolitan areas increase, continued suburbanization will aggravate the already serious problems of traffic, overlapping political units, and the lack of co-ordination in metro-politan planning. Metropolitan areas will increasingly dominate rural areas and the small towns. Perhaps the future of the community lies in the changes and modifications which will be made in these metropolitan areas and their core, the central cities. One English observer apparently sees some hope for the community.

Much of the apathy about the metropolitan explosion is often attributed to the supposed American aversion to planning anything not dedicated to a specific purpose; no one has apparently decided what the purpose of the city is. Now, however, the idea seems to be taking hold, both in print and in concrete, that it should be a cultural centre attracting the intellectual and artistic flower of the nation to a Utopian existence. Some cities have made impressive starts on urban renewal along these lines and on the construction of inspiring city centres. Given enough enthusiasm, the American city could presumably become as efficient and decorative as the automobile.[21]

SUMMARY

Communities have always been organized around the tools of work. Early American communities reflected an agricultural economy. The normative pattern for community relations centered on personalized relationships and emphasized mutual help and "natural" growth. This conception has lasted throughout much of American history.

Urban growth made this conception difficult to implement. Instead of personalized relationships, the city emphasized impersonality. Natural community growth created problems which could not be solved by mutual help. Through increasing experience with urbanism a new normative conception emerged which saw value in impersonality. In response to population concentration, impersonal governmental techniques met the new problems and guided urban growth.

In the face of continued urban growth, elements of the older normative conception persist within the contemporary small town and in suburbia. In each, these older norms exist in spite of their almost complete dependence upon the urban industrial world. Continual suburbanization has a tendency to turn the central city into a low-class Negro slum. This will complicate resolution to the conflict of the valued autonomy of suburbia and its dependence upon the central city. What has happened to the community reflects many of the changes created by industrialization in the total society.

21. *The Economist* (January 4, 1958), p. 36.

QUESTIONS AND SUGGESTIONS FOR FURTHER STUDY

1. What was the nature of community structure which facilitated the development of the historical normative conception?
2. In what type of existing community could one find the closest approximation of the historical normative conception?
3. Read Lincoln Steffens, *The Shame of the Cities*. What modifications have taken place in American cities that have alleviated some of the "shame" about which he wrote?
4. Analyze the relation between population size and representation within the legislature of your state. Are urban areas under-represented?
5. Interview a number of voters on their attitudes toward a proposed welfare levy or a zoning law. Do they see them as proper functions of the local government? How do their attitudes toward these issues relate to their conception of the nature of the community?
6. Interview residents of a small town to explore their dependence on urban areas for goods and services. Also explore the images they have of the city — its values, its disadvantages, etc.
7. In the quotation at the beginning of the chapter, why does the author suggest that suburbia represents the setting for the dominant disorders of our time?
8. Read the sections on suburbia in William Whyte's *The Organization Man*. How do these observations fit the suburbs with which you are familiar?
9. Do you think the residents of small towns tend to repress the fact that they are dependent on the urban industrial world?
10. Select a large metropolitan area and, from census data, trace the changes in its structure over a period of years. Observe not only changes in size but also changes in the composition of the population.

SUGGESTED READINGS

Dobriner, William (ed.), *The Suburban Community*, New York: Putnam, 1958. A collection of articles on the growth, the social organization and the style of life in American suburbs.

Dobriner, William, *Class in Surburbia*, Englewood Cliffs, N.J., Prentice-Hall, 1963.   P   A book which emphasizes the diversity of types of suburbs which exist today in American society.

Editors of *Fortune*, *The Exploding Metropolis*, Garden City: Doubleday, 1958. P   A collection of essays on various aspects of metropolitan life written by "people who like cities." It is critical of many of the directions of urban redevelopment.

Hatt, Paul K., and Albert J. Reiss, Jr., *Cities and Society: The Revised Reader in Urban Sociology*, Glencoe, Ill.: Free Press, 1957. A collection of readings on the nature of the urban community and urban life. A widely used text.

Hoover, Edgar M., and Raymond Vernon, *Anatomy of a Metropolis*, Garden City, Doubleday, 1962. P This is a discussion of the changing distribution of people and jobs within the New York metropolitan area. While it focuses on a particular area, it indicates many of the processes occurring in cities and suburbs over the country.

Lynd, Robert S., and Helen M. Lynd, *Middletown*, New York: Harcourt, Brace, 1929. One of the classic community studies. It should be followed by *Middletown in Transition*, the Lynds' restudy of the same community ten years later.

Vidich, Arthur, and Joseph Bensman, *Small Town in Mass Society*, Garden City, Doubleday, 1960. P An attempt to show how small communities adapt to their increasing dependency on the urban industrial world.

Weimer, David (ed.), *City and Country in America*, New York: Appleton-Century-Crofts, 1962. P A collection of readings dealing with urban and rural life. It includes a number of "classic" statements.

Weber, Max, *The City* (trans. and ed. by Don Martindale and Gertrud Neuwirth), New York: Collier Books, 1961. P This book traces the origins of urban life and discusses the role of cities in the development of modern life.

West, James, *Plainville, U.S.A.*, New York: Columbia University Press, 1961. P One of the classic community studies. It includes a description of class structure in this rural community.

Wood, Robert C., *Suburbia: Its People and Their Politics*, Boston: Houghton Mifflin, 1958. P An analysis by a political scientist of the implications of suburban development for politics. It points out the difficulties of "grass roots" democracy in these areas.

CHAPTER 4 THE CHANGING FAMILY:
PROBLEM OR SOLUTION

> Although readjustment is a slow process for any institution caught in
> the conflict of shifting social patterns, it is especially difficult for the
> family, which has no national organization — no central board of di-
> rectors — to issue directives to individual families. Hence, families ex-
> periment, fail, try again; and eventually conduct is stabilized, norms are
> established, and new values accepted.[1]

Without overstating the case, we can safely say that the demands of modern
industry and the "traditional" family system are incompatible. The historical
sequence is clear. Whenever a society becomes highly industrialized, it
inevitably breaks up the economically self-sufficient extended family. This
has occurred in every country that has experienced rapid industrialization, but
what has happened to the American family since shortly after the Civil War
affords a particularly vivid example.

The normative problem: how should the family adapt to an industrial world?

Recent years have served to quicken social change, and along with it concern
about changing family patterns. One can hardly pick up a newspaper or a
magazine without finding some aspect of contemporary family life subjected
to vigorous scrutiny or criticism. Some people decry the fact that the family
has lost its close-knit character and its self-sufficiency. Some criticize mothers
for preferring to work outside the home, and condemn fathers for relinquish-
ing their traditional authority. Others complain about the "brashness of
youth" and seem willing to assume that delinquency is a product of the
contemporary family. Since the Kinsey Report became a best seller, the
charges of some groups give the impression that the book was the cause of
the results it reported. There are writers who suggest that modern marriages
are not taken seriously, and who would tighten divorce laws. Others argue
that this would be attacking a symptom rather than a cause. Neighborhood
stability is prized by many, and families are criticized for moving from job
to job and from community to community. They are said to be rootless, but

1. Ruth S. Cavan, *The American Family*, New York: Crowell, 1953, p. 29.

88

only symptomatic of the rootlessness of modern family life. The list of criticisms and concerns could be extended since almost everyone is for or against specific changes in marriage and family behavior. But few try to understand why the changes have occurred.

Why is it that people worry about these changes? And why is it that some people do not worry about them — and even welcome change? Why is it that some believe the family is falling apart while others, using the same data, conclude that the family is becoming even more meaningful than it was a generation ago? Concern about any social issue does not exist in a vacuum. Any evaluation, whether positive or negative, has to have a basis — an image of what is good — what is normal. Our discussion in this chapter centers on the fact that the contemporary family is often judged on the basis of an image derived from the rural, pre-industrial family. Since the modern, urban family has departed from this image in many ways, it is often assumed that family life today is incomplete. Stated conceptually, contemporary family norms conflict with historical normative prescriptions. Problem aspects of the family, therefore, involve a comparison between two conceptions of what the family should be. We start with the historical answer.

> *Historical Normative Conception: Familism* — The family should be characterized by economic self-sufficiency. Since family objectives are more important than individual interests, decisions should be made by the head of the family, the husband and father.

The basic features of the family today represent the end-products of a long historical process. To understand what has happened to the urban-industrial family it is necessary to look first at its historical roots. For what we see today is the family attempting to adapt to a rapidly changing world. Many of its present features developed in an agricultural economy and represented a practical adjustment to a way of life that no longer exists. A historical perspective will sharpen our awareness of the impact of the "silent revolutions" upon the family.

ECONOMIC SELF-SUFFICIENCY

One of the outstanding characteristics of the early American family was its ability to thrive as a self-contained economic unit. It did so because the time-period demanded it. Before the development of a complex technology and urban way of life, American society was made up for the most part of large, independent, widely separated farming families. The home was the center of production as well as consumption, and family life was organized around agricultural work. In fact, the home was not only the central social unit, it was a kind of miniature factory as well. Everyone had a specific job to do and there was a clear-cut division of labor. Skills were developed early in life through instruction by elders. Furthermore, every family member was needed, from the smallest child to the oldest grandparent. In short, the early rural household was as much a business enterprise as it was a family. The following description vividly illustrates this kind of family.

At the close of the Civil War, my father bought a small farm in Southern Illinois. I was 9 years old at the time. We had two horses, two cows, and three brood sows. The sows were turned loose in the woods. We also had a small flock of sheep. From the wool of these sheep, and cotton from a small patch, my mother spun, wove, and made up the clothing for the entire family.

We planted 10 to 12 acres of corn. There was no market for corn, we raised only enough for our own use. We also sowed four or five acres of wheat. This was cut with a cradle and threshed out with a flail. There was but one wheat fan in the neighborhood. We borrowed this and fanned the chaff from the wheat. We took the wheat to the mill and had it ground into flour for our own use, the miller taking a toll of the wheat to pay for the grinding. We sold no farm produce for the simple reason there was no market.

We had the yard full of chickens, geese, and turkeys. My mother occasionally traded some of these, together with butter and eggs, to peddlers for groceries and other small needs.

During the summer months we children — there were four of us — dug ginseng, while in winter the older members of the family trapped small fur-bearing animals. Ginseng and pelts were the two things we could sell for cash. From the sale of these we purchased the family shoes and paid taxes.

Winter always found us with at least 2,500 pounds of smoked meat, plenty of potatoes, turnips, cabbage, and apples "holed up" to last us until we had spring vegetables.

When we wanted to go anywhere, our only conveyance was a farm wagon or a home-made sleigh. Our only recreation or amusement was going to a log-rolling, house-raising, or "coon hunting." We did cut an occasional "bee tree." We had no money, and in our method of living needed very little. . . .

. . . We were warmly clothed, comfortably housed, and usually had a year's food supply. When we wanted fresh meat, we killed the wild game in the woods about us. Above all, we were not in debt. When crops were bad, we put up no "wailing wall." We asked nobody for help. We helped ourselves.[2]

In an agricultural economy economic factors influenced people to marry. A wife and children were necessary if a man aspired to become a successful farmer. A bachelor was severely handicapped in economic competition with a man who had sons. For the single woman, marriage was the only socially

2. From a letter to the St. Louis Post-Dispatch in the 1930's, reprinted in Seba Eldridge and Associates, Fundamentals of Sociology: A Situational Analysis, New York: Crowell, 1950, pp. 506–7. Reprinted by permission of Thomas Y. Crowell Company and the St. Louis Post-Dispatch.

acceptable alternative, unless she preferred to play the role of maiden aunt and to help her sisters raise their children. In the choice of a mate, emphasis was placed on practical rather than personal considerations. The man wanted a wife who was a good cook and housekeeper and the woman sought a man who was a "good provider." Since marriage and a large family were economic assets, most couples married early — which, in itself, contributed to larger family size. In fact, the size of the family often determined the size of the farm. If a large family represented an effective way for a farmer to acquire a labor source, the size of his enterprise could be increased by adding children who, in turn, would produce children of their own. If the farmer could persuade his sons (and their wives) to help work the family farm, then he could expand his operations even further — all with a minimum of capital. The emphasis upon a larger family was also buttressed by religious as well as economic thinking, for the Old Testament decreed, "Be fruitful and multiply and replenish the earth." This commandment was formulated in a pre-industrial era and it had a utilitarian as well as a sacred meaning for an agricultural people.

FAMILISM

The fact that occupational roles merged with family life in rural America meant that family members were fused together in a closely knit working team. The individual achieved status in proportion to his or her contribution to the family's welfare and not according to achievements in the outside world. The well-being of all superseded the well-being of an individual. Sociologists have used the term *familism* to describe this type of in-group feeling, or belief, that the pursuit of common family objectives should have priority over individual interests.[3]

In agricultural society familism was also strengthened by the isolation of most families on scattered farms. Furthermore, roads were poor and transportation slow. Even in the villages there were few buildings other than those occupied by families. Under such circumstances, the home became the central social unit. It was "factory and marketplace, schoolhouse, playground, chapel, hospital, and courtroom, all combined in one."[4] Family members depended upon each other for association, conversation, and recreation because few other facilities were available. Farming as an occupation also limited

3. Burgess and Locke describe familism in terms of five characteristics: (1) a feeling of belonging to the family group; (2) integration of activities of family members for attainment of family objectives; (3) the utilization of family resources to help needy members; (4) rallying to the support of a member, if he is in trouble; and (5) the maintenance of continuity between the parental family and new family units. Ernest W. Burgess and Harvey J. Locke, *The Family, From Institution to Companionship,* 2nd ed., New York: American Book, 1953, pp. 71-2.

4. Meyer F. Nimkoff, *Marriage and the Family,* Boston: Houghton Mifflin, 1947, p. 81.

greatly the farmer's opportunity for travel, particularly if he had livestock to care for. Sometimes the yearning for the company of others became very great, which may help to explain the extreme hospitality often accorded travelers by isolated groups.

PATRIARCHAL-AUTHORITARIAN RULE

To manage a farm someone has to give orders, to be responsible, to direct and co-ordinate activities. In short, a farm needs a boss, a foreman — and the husband-father was this. In this sense we can say that "agricultural life breeds patriarchy." [5] The husband was the acknowledged head of the family and his wife and children were his subordinates. He was the final authority and disciplinarian, and his decisions were not to be questioned. [6] To the early American family, the phrase, "father knows best," was no cliché — it was a way of life.

A recent autobiographical account of an elderly woman teacher reflects the historical normative conception of women.

My father's word was law in our house. I never resented this, but rather felt that whatever he said was all right. I believed that men were wiser than women or children, that they really knew what was best. I wanted him to make decisions on everything. When my husband asked me to marry him, I went to my father to have him make my decision. After I was married I expected my husband to make all my decisions. Now that he has gone, I am having an awful time trying to make decisions for myself. [7]

The father's status was closely tied to his knowledge of farming and to his role as provider. This information, partly acquired from earlier generations and partly through years of experience, was passed on to his sons. Boys had higher status than girls, for they were the carriers of the family name and would be future heads of families. The greater muscular strength of the male was important in an agrarian economy and contributed to his status.

Patriarchal rule has a long history in Western societies. The Roman husband-father was extremely powerful, with powers of life and death over his children and wife. Roman law was the prototype for English law, which in turn became the basic model for American family legal codes. Thus in

---

5. James H. S. Bossard and Eleanor S. Boll, *The Sociology of Child Development*, New York: Harper, 3rd ed., 1960, p. 308.
6. Commenting on the functional importance of patriarchal rule in the pioneer family, Blood and Wolfe add, "In general, the more stark the conditions for survival, the more crucial the family decisions which must be made, so the more unchallenged the authority-figure is likely to be. Disobedience to the husband-father in the wilderness was like mutiny on a ship at sea, when all hands might be lost under inexperienced leadership." Robert O. Blood, Jr., and Donald M. Wolfe, *Husbands and Wives: The Dynamics of Married Living*, Glencoe,: Free Press, 1960, p. 16. Reprinted by permission of The Free Press.
7. Paul H. Landis, *Introductory Sociology*, New York: Ronald Press, 1958, p. 570.

terms of its historical traditions the rural family could have been little other than male-dominated.

The subordinate position of women was in keeping with widely believed notions about the "natural superiority of the male." Little was known about the psychology of individual differences, and I.Q. test scores did not exist. The view that women were inherently inferior was simply accepted as correct and was not seriously challenged. This viewpoint was also supported by traditional religious beliefs. Kirkpatrick points out that, "The prevailing account of creation was unfavorable to women, since Eve, the prototype of the feminine sex, was portrayed as a mere side issue created from the rib of Adam. Furthermore, Eve played the role of the temptress in the Old Testament story, urging Adam to eat of the apple which, to the early Christians, probably symbolized sex temptation." [8] Women were honored as housewives and mothers, but they were not to meddle in men's affairs.[9] It was believed that women should not aspire to understand the intricacies of economics or be concerned with legal and political rights. For these reasons, it was argued, women needed little formal education. Although early patriarchal-authoritarian conceptions of family life were soon challenged in a rapidly changing society such as the United States, the impact of patriarchal thinking is still clearly a part of much family organization today.

The discussion thus far has emphasized the close relationship between typical features of the early American family and the type of society in which it existed. The large, close-knit, self-sufficient patriarchal family was well adapted to a predominantly rural, pre-industrial way of life. These characteristics, however, not only describe the way the family *was*, but they have become the basis for describing the way the family *ought to be*. Thus the historical conception of the "good family" today is based in large measure on an image of the early American farm family. But the emergence of an industrialized way of life meant that many of the traditional features of the family became increasingly difficult to attain, or no longer served a useful purpose. As the family adapted to the demands of an industrial society, new conceptions of what a family should be emerged and began to conflict with

8. Clifford Kirkpatrick, *The Family as Process and Institution*, New York: Ronald, 1963, p. 105.
9. On this point, Williams has made a pertinent observation: "Many discussions of the position of women in our social order have failed to make certain essential distinctions. Probably the most frequent and important source of confusion is failure to distinguish among the *evaluation of women*, the *legal rights of women*, and the *roles actually expected of women*. It is possible to have a society in which women are highly valued, yet do not share many of the formal rights exercised by men or play masculine roles. In early America, for example, women did not lack a place of high honor and esteem, although they were confined to distinctly feminine roles and were without many legal rights that have been since acquired." Robin M. Williams, Jr., *American Society*, New York: Knopf, 1960, pp. 61–2.

earlier conceptions, thus creating normative dissensus and a social problem. In short, the traditional family came into existence for practical reasons, and declined for other practical reasons. It is understandable, therefore, that each way of life should have its strong adherents. We turn now to a discussion of these changes and the way in which the family adapted to its new social setting.

THE IMPACT OF INDUSTRIALIZATION ON THE FAMILY

An expanding industrialism, along with continual social change, imposed a new set of demands and brought about fundamental changes which affected the family. The growth of factories and large-scale business organizations meant that occupational roles, especially for the male, were removed from the family scene. Homemade products could not compete effectively with those produced by assembly line techniques. Mass-produced products, in turn, decreased the need for an extended family with parents, brothers, sisters, and others living in the same household. The family no longer needed to serve as a business partnership and family members ceased to be partners in production.

When work shifted from the home to the factory the family began to shed many of its other functions—educational, religious, recreational, and protective. Although the family has added new functions (a point we will return to later), the growth of industrialized America meant that activities were slowly but steadily taken away from the family and turned over to other organizations. Or to state what has happened more precisely, other organizations arose which performed many of the traditional family functions more effectively in an urban-industrialized setting. A man's home may still be his castle, but it is a less self-contained castle than it was.

An industrialized economy requires a highly specialized division of labor outside the home. To keep pace with the growing need for a wide variety of skills, additional years of formal training became essential. This led to the appearance of specialized schools and they largely replaced the educational function of the family. Parents could no longer train their children for vocational roles or serve as meaningful models for guiding their behavior. Traditional family ties were further weakened by the fact that parental viewpoints now had to compete with other interests and values acquired by children from schools and newly emerging mass media.

With the decline of farming and the growth of cities the usefulness of children diminished sharply. Widespread use of machinery eliminated much of the need for children in industry, and the introduction of child-labor laws, along with compulsory school attendance, served further to remove children from the labor scene. Not only did the economic value of children decline sharply, but the cost of rearing them increased tremendously. During the deflationary years of the 1930's "it was estimated that raising a child through the age of eighteen, *before* he went to college, cost the average family between $9180 and $10,485." [10] At present, rearing a child to maturity, again before college expenses, costs well over $20,000.[11] The development of more effective methods of contraception helped parents plan their families and made possible early marriage without the burden of children. All these changes contributed to smaller families. Census data show that the average-size family decreased from 5.8 persons in 1790 to 3.6 persons in 1958.

The type of housing in American cities also had an impact on family size. As urban population continued to expand and land became more expensive, an increasing proportion of families began to live in multiple family dwellings. One can correlate the declining birth rate with the type of family dwelling available. Most urban homes have only two or three bedrooms, and the demands of apartment living often run counter to the needs of children. Landlords seldom welcome large families. Many couples living in apartments would have to move elsewhere with the arrival of their first child. Many renting couples who have children would be required to move if they had an additional child. These features of urban living help explain why few relatives today are encouraged to become permanent household members, and why aging parents, especially those who are dependent upon others for care, are left stranded by the contemporary, small, independent family.

Modern technology is based on a large, mobile labor force. Vocational success frequently involves moving to another job as new opportunities appear, and this usually means moving one's family to another community. Large corporations often transfer their personnel to another district when they promote them. Thus the demands of job mobility alone have had a powerful influence on the traditional American family structure. If one is expected to move every few years he cannot bring along a retinue of sisters, brothers, uncles, and cousins.

At the same time that technological advancements were revolutionizing work outside the home, the products of mass production were radically changing the nature of work within the home itself. In keeping with the emphasis on technological efficiency, a variety of labor-saving devices appeared and became regarded as "standard equipment" in many homes. Today, automatic refrigerators, dishwashers, disposal units, electric mixers, frozen foods, and eye-level ovens in split-level homes are a familiar part of the family scene. These innovations, along with central heating, hot- and cold-running water, and the specialized services of cleaners, laundries, and bakeries, have all made

10. Arnold W. Green, *Sociology: An Analysis of Life in Modern Society*, 3rd ed., New York: McGraw-Hill, 1960, p. 394.
11. *Newsweek* (May 16, 1955), p. 68.

housework less time-consuming and physically exhausting. In short, house-work, along with other jobs, has become mechanized. As one observer put it: "I, who remember my grandmother spending two hours washing the dishes after a family meal, now hear my own daughters arguing about whose turn it is to put them into the dishwasher." [12] And some wag has even claimed that a husband's traditional pre-dinner remark, "What's cooking?" is chang-ing to "What's thawing?"

Even though labor-saving machines have facilitated women's work, it does not follow that the modern wife-mother necessarily devotes less time to household responsibilities. Though cleaning is easier, standards of cleanli-ness are higher. A study by Nimkoff shows that women with more labor-saving devices spend more time, not less, on housework.[13] He reasons that, "with efficient machines at her disposal for cleaning, cooking and washing, the modern housewife can perform her domestic duties in less time and with less energy and is, therefore, in a position to perform them more often. The availability of the labor-saving devices invites their use as does the ease of operation . . . The effect of the household appliance is, then, to make it possible for the housewife to do a more thorough job of housekeeping *as well as* to provide her with more leisure for out-of-the-home pursuits." [14]

Although the family has lost most of its productive function, it retains its consumption function. And in an affluent society whose economy is easily threatened by underconsumption, this function assumes increasing im-portance. It should be remembered that the family, not the individual, is the unit of consumption. The largest proportion of consumer goods is pur-chased by families for family consumption. This is reflected in the emphasis advertisers place on family values in their promotion of automobiles, boats, appliances, camping equipment, and other consumer items. A more recent trend, however, is the increasing proportion of consumer goods purchased by women. This indicates the emergence of a new role for wives, since it was not much more than a generation ago when the decisions to buy all major items were made by the husband. Increasingly manufacturers are recognizing this new role of women and are designing both the product and the sales approach with her in mind. Consumption patterns have become so com-plicated, with the additions of new brands and new products, that wise selec-tion has become an important family function. Bossard and Boll note:

For example, when the first women's college was instituted in the United States, there were no closets, but only three hooks on the walls of the students' rooms. One was for the Sunday dress; one for the nightdress, and one for the school

12. Bossard and Boll, op. cit. p. 310.
13. Meyer F. Nimkoff, "What Do Modern Inventions Do to Family Life?" *Annals of the American Academy of Political and Social Science* (November 1950), p. 56.
14. Ibid.

dress. Most of these were painstakingly made at home. Now, in late August and early September, women's clothing stores are bombarded by entering college girls and their mothers, spending hours in careful selection of this year's college wardrobe. In much the same way, the earlier family menu was the result of choice of what had been grown on the farm and whatever meat, fish, and poultry were available. Now, it would seem that in order to make the best nutritional choice for one's family, one should have at least a course in Elementary Physics, Chemistry, and Home Economics.[15]

The nineteenth and twentieth centuries also witnessed sweeping changes in the role of women and in courtship and dating patterns. Although the changing status of women will be discussed later, it is important that several observations be made here. Though the pre-industrial conception of women cast them in a generally inferior role, another part of this earlier image attributed to women a moral and spiritual quality superior to that of men. It was believed that women possessed an inherent sense of dignity and purity, and the male's role was to protect them in all situations. In effect, women were placed on a pedestal, and at social gatherings chaperones were considered indispensable. Ladies were also expected to act like "ladies." They were supposed to be "reserved," gracious, and dignified—never "forward."

The pre-industrial conception of women is vividly portrayed in the clothing that "ladies" wore. Noting the extreme modesty of that era, Leuba reports that:

she covered herself from top to toe with numerous layers of clothing and an abundance of fluff and ruffles. Her body was not only concealed, it was made almost impregnable; it was a fortress with outworks of crinoline and an inner citadel protected by tightly laced corset through which ran strips of bone or steel. The perfect young lady was one who moved and dressed in a manner that would not reveal the existence of her body.[16]

This attire was designed to minimize sexual appeal and was in keeping with the strict chastity codes for women in the nineteenth century. Virginity was highly valued and premarital coitus was considered to be one of the most serious offenses a woman could commit. Ideally, at least, she was not supposed to be interested in sexual matters. Most courtship behavior was highly formalized, and the terms "necking" and "petting" had not yet been coined. Doubtlessly, there were those who did not conform to these normative expectations, "as the once-popular terms 'flirt' and 'siren' indicate. But . . . insofar as public opinion was concerned, such females were unlikely to be considered 'ladies.' " [17]

15. James H. S. Bossard and Eleanor Boll, *The Sociology of Child Development*, New York: Harper, 3rd ed., 1960, p. 312. Reprinted by permission of Harper & Row, Publishers.
16. Clarence Leuba, *The Sexual Nature of Man*, New York: Doubleday, 1954, p. 5.
17. William M. Kephart, *The Family, Society, and the Individual*, Boston: Houghton Mifflin, 1961, p. 245.

Industrialization drastically changed these conceptions of womanhood, courtship practices, and sexual behavior. Women achieved greater equality with men on all fronts. Courtship and dating behavior was liberalized, and sex became a subject which even "nice" people discussed openly.[18] Somewhere between World War I and II, the pedestal began to crumble. The ladylike role was supplanted by that of the "good sport" and again, changes in women's fashions mirrored the new normative conception of women. Kephart's description shows how complete this transformation was.

It became mandatory for the modern miss to wear modern clothes. Little by little the various layers of petticoats were pared. Bustles disappeared and corsets were put away. As the armor was removed, feminine clothing took on a more functional look. Frills and ruffles were replaced by the simplicity of design. Dresses no longer contained yards of bulky material. Necklines became lower, sleeves and hemlines were shortened. As women discarded the more indirect methods of attraction — flattery, feminine mannerisms, an air of dependence — a frontal approach soon came to prevail. Sweaters and short skirts were utilized, as were high heels and sheer stockings. Hats were chic. Make-up became a self-styled art, with lipstick, powder, rouge, eye shadow and mascara, perfume, facial creams, and nail polish the outward symbols of the new femininity. Hair-styling and hair-coloring became national fetishes, and the local female headquarters often came to be centered in the Beauty Shop.[19]

An urban setting provided numerous opportunities for young people to meet without the constant surveillance of parents, and it is not necessary to dwell upon the ways in which the automobile and modern highways (as well as not so modern roads) influence dating behavior.

These changes undermined the historical normative conception of the American family. Each challenged some aspect of earlier conceptions of women and family life. Cumulatively, they set the stage for the contemporary view of what the family should be in an industrial world.

> *Contemporary Normative Conception: Individualism* — The family should be characterized by satisfying interpersonal relationships. Since individual differences should be respected, major decisions should be based on democratic-equalitarian principles.

A recurring theme of this chapter has been that marriage and family life takes place today in a fundamentally different social setting. The norms of

18. Commenting on the pervasive nature of man's sexual drive, Homans observes, "In modern America there is no danger of our underrating it. Indeed we exaggerate its power, perhaps because so many of us have forgotten what it is to be hungry." George C. Homans, *The Human Group*, New York: Harcourt, Brace, 1950, p. 232.
19. Kephart, op. cit. p. 245.

the earlier family system do not fit neatly into a highly mobile, impersonal, urban society. They were developed and buttressed by a pre-industrial way of life that no longer exists. The family no longer represents the necessary unit for survival in a frontier economy. Although urban living is not without its problems and insecurities, much of the stern harshness of early America has disappeared. With the increase of leisure and luxury, new family norms have appeared to meet new situations.

SATISFACTORY INTERPERSONAL RELATIONS

The high degree of movement in both occupation and place of residence among members of an industrial society has brought on new conditions of living which challenge the establishing of meaningful interpersonal relations. When some persons move in search of a better job or a better climate they are often separated from their families by several states and hundreds of miles. Residential and vocational changes produce further changes in interests, goals, and "style of living." It is not surprising, therefore, to find that brothers, sisters, and other relatives often have little in common during their adult years. Furthermore, when these people move, the chances are that they will move into a large city and that they will know few, if any, people in the new location. This breaking of family and neighborhood ties, usually in the early adult years of life, means that a set of emotionally comfortable relationships has to be left behind and a new set cultivated. In a very real sense the modern adult must face his crises alone. He can no longer count on the stabilizing support of an integrated kinship system and the feeling of belonging to a primary group neighborhood. Earlier generations had to cope with other problems, but not with this one.

Life in a large city can be delightful, but it can also be lonely. This is especially true for the unmarried. Although the bachelor's life is often portrayed in fiction as gay and carefree, in reality this is far from the case. Living alone—or with roommates—is seldom preferred to marriage as a life pattern. Marriage, it should be noted, is the only relationship that survives mobility, and insulates persons against the loneliness of modern urban living. Many observers feel that "this is one of the main reasons why more Americans are marrying today than ever before." [20] In short, a man's best friend has become his wife. It is this way of life — involving a sense of isolation and loss of affectional bonds — that has produced the need for companionship, happiness, and the attainment of meaningful interpersonal relationships in family life.

Just how important the need for a compatible partner has become is shown by a study of 909 Detroit wives. Forty-eight per cent choose "companionship

20. Blood and Wolfe, op. cit. p. 150.

in doing things together with the husband" as the single most valuable aspect of marriage.[21] The researchers also found that, "This far outstrips the other four aspects — love, understanding, standard of living, and the chance to have children. The latter (having children) is a poor second with only 27 per cent first choices. In addition to being overwhelmingly popular as the first-choice item, companionship [22] is chosen second by 21 per cent more, and third by 16 per cent, leaving only 14 per cent who do not choose it as one of the three most valuable parts of marriage." [23]

There has occurred, then, a normative shift in the purpose and function of marriage, and in the standards by which family life is judged successful. Today these standards are defined by the ability of family members (especially husband and wife) to meet each others' psychological, emotional, and companionship needs. But these needs are subtle and evasive. When the criterion of marital success is happiness, the rewards are great for those who achieve it, but it is more difficult to achieve than the objectives sought by the traditional family. Couples today make much greater demands upon each other, and seek in a marriage partner all of the friendship and security that stable primary groups once provided.

Even mate selection has changed. The wide contrast between contemporary and traditional normative expectations is evident in the following reply of a traditionally oriented wife, when asked about the qualities of a good spouse. She remarked, "I am sick of all this talk of choosing and choosing . . . If a man is healthy and does not drink, and has a good little handful of stock, and a good temper, and is a good Christian, what great difference can it make to a woman which man she takes? There is not so much difference between one man and another." [24] Such an attitude greatly simplifies mate selection because criteria of this sort can be readily determined and do not depend largely upon personal preferences. But in a highly mobile society, a sense of mutual acceptance and response have become crucial. The increased importance of personality factors in the family as it has moved from a pre-industrial to an industrial era is unmistakable.

21. Ibid.
22. The term, companionship, as used here does not necessarily mean what sometimes comes to mind. "The primary emphasis is on companionship in leisure-time activities, not on merging every aspect of married life. In this respect, a wife can be enthusiastic about companionship even though she stays home while her husband goes to work, does most of the housework without his help, and in general plays a quite different role in life. In other words men and women don't have to be identical in order to have a good time together." Robert O. Blood, Jr., and Donald M. Wolfe, *Husbands and Wives, The Dynamics of Married Living*, Glencoe: Free Press, 1960, p. 173. Reprinted by permission of The Free Press.
23. Ibid. p. 150.
24. James G. Leyburn, *Frontier Folkways*, New Haven: Yale University Press, 1935, p. 129, quoting Olive Schreiner, *Thoughts on South Africa*, New York, 1897, p. 193.

The idea that people can be married and happy at the same time is a new and radical notion. Throughout most of history, romantic love and affection have been associated with courtship rather than marriage. Literature has not portrayed the great "love affairs" as occurring among husbands and wives. It should be remembered, for example, that Romeo and Juliet, and Antony and Cleopatra were not married. In a pre-industrial era, few couples approached marriage with the idea of achieving great personal happiness. Compared to today's couples, those of earlier generations expected very little in the way of personal satisfaction. This does not mean that companionship, affection, and happiness were absent from the traditional family. These qualities were there in greater or lesser degree, but the focus was different. They were not regarded as primary objectives. They were not, because they could not be — the time period did not permit it. The emphasis was on economic survival, not individual happiness. As relations outside the home have become increasingly impersonal in an industrialized world, the need for emotionally comfortable experiences has increased, and the modern family represents the last remaining major social setting where this need can effectively be met.

GREATER INDIVIDUALISM

The family in pre-industrial society was oriented around familistic values. Emphasis was placed on family unity and solidarity rather than on individual interests and preferences. As industrialization proceeded, it was accompanied by a new and greater emphasis upon individual rights and privileges. Much of American culture reinforces individualistic norms, and they fitted in well with prevailing conceptions of democracy, laissez-faire economics, and various theories of progress. The tendency today is to regard oneself primarily as an individual, and only secondarily as a family member. Simply stated, familism has been replaced by individualism.

This normative shift has been described in several ways. One expression of the idea uses the phrase "personalization of the family." As the economic significance of the family diminishes, the importance of the individual person increases.[25] Another way of stating this is to say that economic functions have given way to personality functions. The historical prescription emphasized the spouses' work role. In effect, the husband as producer in a rural economy married essentially a housekeeper — and implicit in the normative view was the idea that any capable housekeeper could do the job adequately.

25. William F. Ogburn and Meyer F. Nimkoff, *Technology and the Changing Family*, Boston: Houghton Mifflin, 1955, p. 54.

But as economic functions declined, a husband or wife was selected more on the basis of personality characteristics. Still another way of looking at it is to view the modern urban family as an "association of individuals" — an association in which individual aspirations and potentials are recognized and encouraged. Impetus for this type of individualism has been provided by the many opportunities existing in urban areas, and by the ability of wives and children to support themselves independently. The amount of time that family members spend away from each other also increases their independence and their ability to make decisions independently of other family members.

The importance of individualism in the modern family is evident when historical and contemporary views of child training are compared. The historical conception viewed the child essentially as a worker — a contributor to the economic production of the family. Household chores were increased as the child grew older, and concepts of duty and responsibility — especially responsibility for his parents and their welfare — were deeply instilled early in life. "The training of the child was so shaped as to give the parent maximum benefit and security." [26] The contemporary conception sees the child as a very different kind of person. Parents emphasize individual accomplishments of their children, attend child-study courses, search for hidden talents, and generally pour their best efforts into their childrens' personality development. Even more basic is the different conception of the child which has emerged in recent years. Contemporary thinking does not view the child as a minature adult, but as a growing, developing, and ever-changing individual, whose treatment must differ not merely in degree but in kind from that received by the adult.[27] His normal childish impulses are not discouraged, and he is introduced to adult tasks and responsibilities in keeping with each stage of growth. Respect for individual differences has taken priority over the need for maintaining a particular type of parent-child relationship. The contemporary parent, in contrast to the traditional parent, expects little or no return in the way of work or income — or even security for himself in his old age. Much of his satisfaction comes from seeing his child move into a successful marriage and achieve the vocational goals that have become meaningful to him. With these normative differences, parents who have internalized earlier prescriptions now find it difficult to understand the behavior of their children.

The importance of individualism can also be seen in the emphasis placed on personal selection of a mate. Marriage based on a mutually satisfying love relationship necessarily exerts strong pressure upon each person to choose his own spouse. Since there is no other individual who can readily share his

26. Paul H. Landis, *Introductory Sociology*, New York: Ronald, 1958, p. 569.
27. Ogburn and Nimkoff, op. cit. p. 195.

feelings, he must select someone with whom he can establish an intimate continuing relationship. Romantic love, therefore, becomes functional in a family system stressing the importance of individual happiness and the ability of husband and wife to meet each other's affectional needs.

Not only is mate selection based on the highly individualistic attractions of romantic love, but the continuation of the marriage itself is now largely a matter of personal choice. This is in keeping with individualistic norms, which emphasize the freedom to terminate a relationship which has become intolerable. In other words, those who marry on the grounds of individual choice may go to the divorce courts on the same grounds. Persons who have internalized the idea of individual initiative in business and individual salvation in religion apply this reasoning to marriage. It is perhaps inevitable, therefore, that a high rate of divorce will be found in a family system where the mutual meeting of personality needs is valued more highly than family tradition and unity. Yet this tendency toward disorganization may be offset by the depth of affection often existing among family members today. Some observers feel that the strong emotional ties that are developed between husband and wife and their children "are the strongest safeguards of family unity in the contemporary United States." [28]

DEMOCRATIC-EQUALITARIAN PHILOSOPHY

Greater emphasis upon companionship and individual rights has contributed to the emergence of more equalitarian relationships within the family. If emotional needs are important in a mobile, competitive society, then it would appear that the idea of individual rights would have a better chance of thriving in a democratic-equalitarian setting than in the traditional patriarchal family with its emphasis upon masculine authority. In addition, as a study by Elizabeth Bott revealed, those who establish few close ties with persons outside the family are more likely to draw close together within the family and to develop an equalitarian relationship than are those involved in a more complete social life outside.[29]

Other changes within the family and in the larger society help explain the growing trend toward more equalitarian family norms. Probably the greatest impact has come from the accent on women's rights and probably the most important single factor has been the status that women have achieved through greater economic independence. Clearly, the increase in the number and kinds of jobs now open to women accounts for much of the increase in their status. Since occupation and income are the major indices of male prestige, it is easy to see how gains on this front have enhanced the

28. Blaine E. Mercer, *The Study of Society*, New York: Harcourt, Brace, 1958, p. 250.
29. Elizabeth Bott, *Family and Social Network*, London: Tavistock, 1957.

status of women. The Women's Bureau of the United States Department of Labor publicizes the gains made by women in jobs traditionally held by men, and their data point up some of the occupational changes that are an important part of the contemporary family picture. For example, the number of women bank officials increased from 4605 in 1944 to 6013 in 1950, and the number of women employees on Wall Street as customers' brokers nearly doubled from 1946 to 1951 [30] — and these trends have simply continued in recent years.

Data from the Women's Bureau also show that the proportion of women in the labor force has increased gradually during the past decades — equaling 18 per cent in 1900 and about 25 per cent in 1940. It reached a high of 36 per cent during World War II and then dropped sharply to 28 per cent with the return of war veterans to civilian jobs — before starting to climb again. Today, one out of every three workers is a woman, and in 1949, for the first time, the number of married women at work exceeded the number of single women. Women are also occupying a variety of important political offices. "The number of women serving in appointive state positions of responsibility runs into the thousands, while the number in county and municipal offices is too large even to estimate." [31] Although husbands are still the major breadwinners in most families, it is also true that the increasing economic contribution of wives has been accompanied by an increase in their status and authority.

Despite earlier objections, the new job patterns for women have become accepted and even preferred by most men. Ogburn and Nimkoff report the results of a *Fortune* poll in which

men were asked which of three girls equally good-looking a man would prefer to marry: a girl who had never held a job, a girl who had held a job and been moderately successful at it, or a girl who had held a job and had been extremely successful. The balloting ran: 33.8 per cent for the moderately successful, 21.5 per cent for the extremely successful, and only 16.2 per cent for the girl who never held a job. Most men, then, want their woman to work, which increases the authority of women: but they do not so often want their women to be more successful than they are.[32]

The increasing productivity of the American economy has created a demand for educated women as well as men, and "today more girls than boys graduate from high school, since the latter often drop out to go to work. Even at the college level there are now nearly half as many women as men enrolled." [33] This increase in level of education for women may mean that the modern wife is a better conversationalist than the submissive rural-farm

30. Ogburn and Nimkoff, op. cit. p. 182.
31. Kephart, op. cit. p. 235.
32. Ogburn and Nimkoff, op. cit. p. 184.
33. Blood and Wolfe, op. cit. p. 18.

wife, and hence a better companion to her husband. More education for her has tended to minimize earlier attitudes of inferiority and superiority between the sexes, and this has helped bring about the necessary equality which companionship requires. It is also likely, however, that increase in the wife's educational level increases the probability that quarrels and arguments will occur in today's marriages. Since quarreling assumes equality, very little occurred in the traditional family system. With greater freedom and informality in modern marriages, spouses feel freer to discuss controversial topics and "level" with one another.

In the area of parent-child relationships, a democratic-equalitarian philosophy has largely replaced the earlier authoritarian pattern. This change is especially noticeable in the relationship between father and child. In an earlier era it was usually on the basis of man to dependent child — and as the child grew, the relationship developed into man to man.[34] Contemporary norms, however, urge the father to be a "pal" to his children — especially to his sons. In effect, the parent is expected to come closer to developing a child-to-child relationship. This does not mean that the contemporary family norm allows the child to do anything he pleases. But the present-day parent is expected to be something more than a disciplinarian. It is currently believed that the child needs more than discipline. He needs other influences such as limits placed on his behavior, a set of consistent expectations, and stimulating experiences.

The influence of democratic-equalitarian norms is evident in the way decisions are made in the contemporary family. Today there is much more sharing of power between husband and wife. This does not mean that all decisions are made jointly — which is usually not feasible and probably not desirable. What has happened is that a new balance of power has emerged. The way in which it operates in the contemporary family has been observed by Blood and Wolfe in their study of Detroit families. They discern a shift from what they term the ideological theory of power to the pragmatic theory. The former notion, in keeping with historical norms, held that both the power to make decisions, and the authority to do so, should reside in the husband. The pragmatic theory holds that the balance of power "is determined by the comparative resourcefulness of the two partners and by the life circumstances in which they live." [35] The contemporary husband runs into trouble when he tries to exercise power just because he is "the man of the house." "Rather, he must prove his right to power, or win power by virtue of his own skills and accomplishments in competition with his wife." [36] In an effective summary statement Blood and Wolfe write:

34. Bossard and Boll, op. cit. p. 339.
35. Blood and Wolfe, op. cit. p. 29.
36. Ibid.

This reflects a new unpredictability in family life. Under former historical circumstances, the husband's economic and social role almost automatically gave him pre-eminence. Under modern conditions, the roles of men and women have changed so much that husbands and wives are potential equals — with the balance of power tipped sometimes one way, sometimes the other. It is no longer possible to assume that just because a man is a man, he is the boss. Once upon a time, the function of culture was to rationalize the predominance of the male sex. Today the function of culture is to develop a philosophy of equal rights under which the saying goes, "May the best man win!" — and the best man is sometimes a woman. The role of culture has shifted from sanctioning a competent sex over an incompetent sex to sanctioning the competent marriage partner over the incompetent one, regardless of sex.[37]

This does not mean that all features of the traditional family system have disappeared. Many aspects of it still remain. For example, marriage vows remain essentially the same — but ministers today seldom mention obedience to brides, and the word "obey" has disappeared from most marriage pledges. What we see, then, in the contemporary family is a mixture of old and new normative expectations. This means that men and women today can never be quite so sure as grandma and grandpa were that their decisions are the "correct" ones.[38] We turn now for a closer look at some of the consequences of this normative dissensus.

THE AMBIGUOUS STATUS OF THE AMERICAN WOMAN

With few exceptions, the phrase "changing American family" can almost be restated as the "changing status of women." [39] Recent significant changes in the family have been more closely associated with changes occurring in women's status than with those taking place in men's status. Despite much opposition to "women's rights" from the press, pulpit, and males generally, a remarkable increase in women's status occurred in a relatively short period of time. While few persons would deny women the economic, legal, political, and educational equalities they have won since the 1800's, these gains have not been without their cost. Industrialization placed a larger proportion of the entire population in the labor force, and it has provided women, especially married women, with unprecedented job opportunities. Not very long ago women had only one role in the home. Now they are capable of occupying a number of roles in and out of the home. There are socially acceptable alternatives to the traditional role of housewife. As a result, women today can not be quite so sure they have selected the "right" role once they have

---

37. Ibid. pp. 29–30.
38. There is evidence, however, that men have experienced greater difficulty in making the transition between family systems than have women. Most research in this area clearly shows that women are more ready and willing for the new roles than are men to accept women in them.
39. Green, op. cit. p. 387.

made a choice. As one observer has put it, "the female sex is here to stay, but where is 'here'?" [40]

Historical normative expectations were clear-cut. A woman's place was in the home. Her job was secure. Furthermore, the activities she performed, such as cooking, canning, and caring for children, were those approved by the whole society. The modern woman, however, faces a very different set of expectations. On the one hand, there is the strong pull of the past. Marriage, family, and homemaking are still regarded by most women as preferable to full-time careers. Research shows that few single women prepare seriously for professional positions. One typical study showed that an entering class of freshmen in a women's college expressed little feeling for any job as a career; 90 per cent of them hoped to marry within five to ten years after graduation. [41] On the other hand, the traditional activities of women have lost considerable prestige in a society which stresses the importance of specialized training, a pay check, and professional status. It is not surprising, therefore, that the modern woman who answers the question, "Now what do you do?" replies defensively by saying, "I am just a housewife." Despite the exhortations of the traditionalists the term "housewife" has come to signify relatively low status.

This defensiveness may be especially common in "intellectual" groups such as university faculties, where wives sometimes feel compelled to go to school, join social causes, or remain politically aware and active, *but it is by no means restricted to them.* The urban suburban middle-class housewife who enjoys her home and family and does not *want* to be a committee chairman for the Parent-Teacher Association, or canvass for the Heart Fund, or belong to the League of Women Voters, is all too often characterized by her peers as refusing to accept the civic responsibilities of female status. [42]

The mass media in an industrial society may be training women to be wives, but hardly housewives. The image of women portrayed in much of the mass media reinforces the low position assigned to their traditional household role. Women are usually shown in a recreational setting, enjoying a cigarette between dances at a ski lodge, or happily motoring with their family along a lake-shore highway. McGee notes that,

The heroines of magazine serials and magazine and television advertisements are uniformly single or young-marrieds of the upper income brackets, and barring only advertisement for cleansing agents guaranteed to "lighten the drudgery of housework," there is seldom a hint of dirty diapers and unending processions of soiled dishes and linen, sinks and toilet bowls to be scrubbed, and the eventual

40. Reece McGee, *Social Disorganization in America*, San Francisco: Chandler, 1962, p. 149.
41. See Irene M. Wightwick, *Vocational Interest Patterns*, New York: Columbia University Press, 1945.
42. Ibid.

agony of deciding — for ten thousand nights — what to cook for dinner and then cooking it. Yet these, and a multiplicity of similar tasks *are* the housewives' jobs, and are the jobs that most women perform for most of their lives.[43]

The devaluation of the traditional activities of married women is relatively new in American society, and it is in the role of "wife" or "wife and mother" that most women today are confused. It is important to keep in mind, therefore, that the conflicting roles of women are more clearly related to being *married* than to being employed. Most women marry (approximately 88 per cent), and it is precisely at this point that modern women encounter problems not experienced in rural America. Today married women — and especially mothers — do not face a consistent set of normative prescriptions to guide their behavior.[44] Basically, they face three alternative roles — each one largely incompatible with the others. Kirkpatrick has described them and has pointed out the privileges and obligations each involves.[45] Since these roles represent ideal types, few women may be classified in terms of one role to the total exclusion of the other two — but these formulations are useful for analysis.

The wife and mother role reflects the historical normative expectations for the woman. Her world is bounded by her home, her husband, and her children. Its privileges include: security, the right to support, respect as a wife and mother, a certain amount of domestic authority, and the right to alimony in the case of divorce. Corresponding obligations include: bearing and rearing children, making a home, rendering domestic services, acceptance of a dependent social and economic status, loyal subordination to the economic interests of the husband, and acceptance of a limited range of activities.

The other roles have emerged along with the development of an industrialized society, and together with the wife-mother role embody basic features of contemporary normative expectations.

The companion role thrives best where there is leisure time, and occurs more often in urban and suburban settings. The privileges include: sharing pleasures with the husband, a more romantic emotional response, admiration,

43. Ibid. p. 148.
44. In some segments of the population housewifery seems to have already disappeared as a recognized part of the woman's role. The newspaper account quoted below describes a contest designed to select women "outstanding" in various areas of activity. It is significant that traditional roles such as homemaking, child-rearing, and cooking are not even considered.

   "Six Austin women will be named as 'outstanding' January 1 by the women's staff of the *American-Statesman*. They will really be named by the City of Austin, however, because Austinites will select them. Below is a ballot.

   Nominate the woman you think should be named 'outstanding' in each of these fields — clubwoman, hostess, gardener, volunteer service worker, arts, career." Austin, Texas, *American*, December 8, 1960. Cited in Reece McGee, op. cit. p. 149.
45. Kirkpatrick, op. cit. pp. 168-9.

adequate funds for dress and recreation, and certain amounts of chivalrous attention. On the other hand, it implies: the preservation of beauty under penalty of marital insecurity, rendering of ego and sexual satisfactions to the husband, the cultivation of social contacts advantageous to his career, and the maintenance of intellectual alertness.

The partner role depicts essentially the career oriented woman. This alternative is a more recent innovation, and occurs more frequently in families where both husband and wife are college educated. This role includes the privileges of: economic independence, acceptance as an equal, exemption from one-sided domestic service to the husband, equal voice in determining location of residence, equal control of family finances, and equality in regard to social and moral freedom. The obligation side of the balance sheet includes: financial contribution to a common family fund in proportion to earning ability, responsibility to achieve success in a career, acceptance of equal responsibility for the support of children, willingness to forgo appeals to chivalry, and renunciation of alimony except in the case of dependent children.

The fact that these roles overlap, and that some sort of choice has to be made among them, is a source of conflict in modern families. Certainly there is no easy, simple solution to these problems. Yet it is clear that the trend is toward higher levels of formal education for more and more women, which essentially prepares them for professional careers. In terms of Kirkpatrick's classifications, they are educated to become better partner-wives, but at the same time they are urged by society to be companion-wives, and the weight of tradition tells them to be mother-wives. With these inconsistencies and ambiguities in the normative system, it is not surprising that women today are confused.[46] A common problem is the frustration experienced by the woman who performs one role through duty and habit but who yearns for a different role. Thus the talented woman, with abilities equal to her husband's, sometimes becomes envious of the woman who has successfully become a partner-wife. Or, there may be conflict between spouses. For example, a wife who expects to find her life answers in a mother role and prefers to spend her time at home with five children may find that her husband expects her to be a companion-wife, available to accompany him on fishing trips and to ball games.

Another form of conflict involves what Kirkpatrick calls "ethical inconsistency," which refers to an unfair distribution of privileges and obligations. "Since a privilege to the husband involves an obligation to the wife, and

46. Some observers contend, "it is impossible to state what is the proper role and function of a specific woman or mother in the United States. The possibilities are so varied that there is no longer a set pattern and the question of what it should be is highly argumentative." Bossard and Boll, op. cit. p. 309.

vice versa, any tendency on the part of a spouse to claim the privileges of more than one role brings about marital dissatisfaction." Research shows that women tend to emphasize role *privileges*, while men would prefer them to stress marital role *obligations*. In other words, women frequently feel entitled to the security of a mother-wife, the leisure of a companion-wife, and the financial independence of a partner-wife. Men, on the other hand, often prefer their mates to have the submissiveness of a mother-wife, the vivaciousness of a companion-wife, and the income-producing quality of a partner-wife.

Not only does each of these roles have its critics and admirers, but some combinations seem more workable than others. The companion-wife, for example, may spend winters in Miami and summers in Canada, but this role is only possible for the wealthy, and it overlooks the existence of children. It is similar to what Parsons calls the "glamor girl," and represents an unstable basis for marriage, since it places much emphasis on short-lived physical beauty and sexual attractiveness. The traditional wife-mother role, oriented to home and children, is the one played by most women throughout history, but it is becoming more difficult to maintain in the face of contemporary expectations which stress equality, a relatively small family, and the desirability of preparing for a stable vocation. The contemporary normative conception pushes women toward acceptance of the partner role—or toward combining this role with another one. In fact, some observers believe that the most general form of conflict in modern marriage stems from disagreement between husband and wife over what aspects of the wife-mother role and the partner role she shall combine.[47] The successful performance of the partner role alone, let alone in combination, has its own unique difficulties. The full-partner role seems best suited to childless couples, or if there are children it can be fulfilled more easily after the children are well along in school and are essentially self-directing. Certainly the partner-wife with pre-school children *is* largely dependent upon her husband, much as the wife in the traditional family is. A further difficulty, which is seldom discussed, "is that equality in decision-making often does not work. It is very well for the husband and wife to *agree* how to spend their money or where to take their vacation — but what if they do not agree? A vote is always a tie. In the case of true equality of decision and action, the impasse is unresolvable save by unilateral capitulation or the interruption of the marriage relationship." [48]

Dissensus has special implications for the college-educated woman. The fact that she has the ability, training — and often the desire — to pursue other alternatives in addition to homemaking makes her decision particularly

47. Green, op. cit. p. 413.
48. McGee, op. cit. p. 152.

difficult.[49] She approaches graduation early — sometimes earlier than men, whose college years may be interrupted by military service. She arrives early, therefore, at a crucial "crossroad," involving basic life decisions. Furthermore, for her it is especially difficult to separate the alternative pathways and pursue them one at a time.

Destiny comes in a prepared package for college women as compared with college men. For the college women, love, marriage, and motherhood tend to be wrapped up together with homemaking in a package which often must be accepted or rejected as a whole. The package can be unwrapped and sorted out according to taste, but that is not the general expectation, and the sorting-out process is not easy.

There is no time for the college woman to experiment with designs for living. The period of sex attractiveness and reproductivity is briefer for women than for men; hence thorough experimentation with a career may rule out marriage and motherhood. Experimentation with children, who grow slowly, does not leave time to try out a career as well. Homemaking is not something to be picked up and laid down like a hat on a bargain counter. For women as compared with men, it is always "later than you think." [50]

THE AGED: CAUGHT BETWEEN TWO FAMILY SYSTEMS

In addition to the dissensus centering on husbands, wives, and children, a new source of concern has developed in the modern family: the aged parent. The remarks of Wilensky and Lebeaux place the basic issues in perspective.

Of all the social problems created by the impact of industrialism on the family, none is more certain to increase in importance than the problem of the aged. First, there are more older people than ever before. Second, the emancipation of the married couple, of women, and the accent on youth, leave the old folks stranded. Here again the conflict between generations may be intensified, because the changes are not complete — the old ways and the new co-exist, and the generations therefore have conflicting expectations.[51]

In a pre-industrial society, old age was not a social problem. The needs of aging parents could easily be accommodated in the extended, large family system. They could find useful activities in the home or on the farm, and their experiences and suggestions were highly valued. In short, they could continue to be productive and to feel that they occupied an important place in the family.

49. In a nation-wide sample of women, Weiss and Samelson found that the percentage of women "who refer to housework as a role which makes them feel useful and important" decreases with increasing education. Robert S. Weiss and Nancy Morse Samelson, "Social Roles of American Women: Their Contribution to a Sense of Usefulness and Importance," *Marriage and Family Living*, 20 (Nov. 1958), p. 359.
50. Clifford Kirkpatrick, *The Family as Process and Institution*, New York: Ronald, 1963, p. 444. Copyright 1963 The Ronald Press Company.
51. Harold W. Wilensky and Charles N. Lebeaux, *Industrial Society and Social Welfare*, New York: Russell Sage Foundation, 1958, p. 77.

But the development of an industrial world changed all this. The mobile, nuclear family, with its emphasis upon career success and independent households, finds it difficult to "fit" grandparents into this way of life. In fact, the aged, today, are usually not considered an intrinsic part of the family.[52] Available evidence suggests that relatively few children today feel a sense of obligation for their parents. A study of 100 Midwestern families showed that "in only 11 per cent of the cases were children caring for their parents." [53] This is in striking contrast to the norms of the traditional, extended kinship system where parents could expect their children to provide for them in their later years. Furthermore, literally millions of older persons living today are not many years removed from the land — despite the rapid growth of cities. Approximately one out of every three urban residents today grew up on a farm. It is, therefore, not surprising that aged parents and adult children, who are products of conflicting family systems, clash over questions about "rights" and "responsibilities." The disappointments of the old, and "the guilty consciences of the young . . . are painful evidence of the clash." [54]

At the same time that the independent, nuclear family finds itself unable to meet the needs of the aged, the proportion of older people in the population is increasing rapidly.[55] Since 1900, the population in the United States has approximately doubled, but the number of persons 45 to 64 has tripled, while the number 65 years and older has quadrupled. And as the data in Figure 4-1 show, the projected estimate for 1980 for those over 65 is 24 million. These circumstances also largely explain why so much of current welfare spending goes to the aged, which, in effect, is "the by-product of an increased emphasis on the nuclear family, the rapidity of social change, and the aging population." [56]

Industrialization has made it possible for more people to reach old age and at the same time it has made it more difficult for the aged to become a meaningful part of modern life.

DIVORCE: SYMPTOM OR CAUSE

A relatively high divorce rate may be expected in a society which values "romantic love" as a basis for mate selection, and regards individual happiness as the best measure of successful marriage. In effect, divorce is a function

52. Belle B. Beard, "Are the Aged Ex-family?" *Social Forces*, 27 (1949), pp. 274–9.
53. Paul Landis, *Social Problems in Nation and World*, New York: Lippincott, 1959, p. 655.
54. Wilensky and Lebeaux, op. cit. p. 78.
55. The nuclear family system is not, of course, the only source of difficulty for elderly people in our society. Those who are in the 60–70 age range include some of the wealthiest persons in the United States but this age span also includes the poorest, and the poor far outnumber the rich. The health, housing, and recreational needs of the aged are also serious problems.
56. Wilensky and Lebeaux, op. cit. p. 79.

Fig. 4-1. Number of People Sixty-five Years of Age and Over in the United States, 1870 to 1960 and Predicted Numbers to 1980.

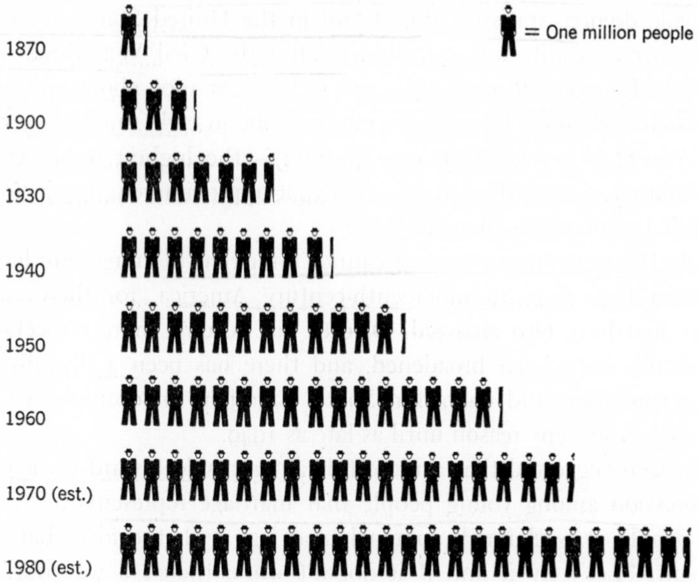

Sources: Data for years 1870-1950 from, U.S. Bureau of the Census, *Historical Statistics of the United States, Colonial Times to 1957*, Washington, D.C., 1960, Series A 71-85, p. 10. Data for year 1960 from U.S. Bureau of the Census, *U.S. Census Population 1960, General Social and Economic Characteristics*, Table 65, p. 199. Projected data for 1970 and 1980 from *Current Population Reports*, "Illustrative Projections of the Population of the United States, by Age and Sex 1960-1980," by M. Zitter and J. Siegel, series P-25, no. 187 (November 1958), p. 17.

of the kind of courtship-marriage system we have in contemporary American society. Sometimes the high divorce rate is interpreted as an indication of the inadequacy of love as a basis for marriage, but it is probably more accurate to say that "the figure reflects not so much the failure of love as the determination of people not to live without it." [57]

According to Kephart, the divorce trend during the nineteenth and twentieth centuries can be summarized in eight words:

> Nineteenth century — more grounds
> Twentieth century — more divorces

Kephart does not imply a cause-and-effect relationship. During the nineteenth century, divorce legislation began to appear in the Southern and Middle states, and New England increased the number of grounds for obtaining a divorce. "By the Civil War, divorce jurisdiction had generally been taken out of the hands of the state legislature and placed under the control of the courts." [58]

57. Morton M. Hunt, *The Natural History of Love*, New York: Knopf, 1959, p. 342.
58. Kephart, op. cit. p. 255.

Unfortunately there are no data on divorce rates prior to the Civil War but during the unsettled period immediately following the war, divorce began to increase, and in 1867 for the first time the Census Bureau collected nation-wide divorce statistics. The trend in the United States, for the most part, has been steadily upward. Shortly after the Civil War there was only one divorce for every 36 marriages, and in the year 1900 about one in twelve were ended by divorce. In 1922 the rate was one in eight, and in 1945, at the end of World War II, it was one in three — the highest it has ever been in this country. Currently it is assumed that approximately one in four marriages will terminate in divorce.[59]

Despite this general increase we cannot infer that marriages are less happy today than they were in nineteenth-century America, for there are other variables that have also changed. Divorce has become more respectable, the legal grounds have been broadened, and there has been a liberalization of their interpretation and character. South Carolina, for example, would not grant a divorce for any reason until as late as 1949.

It has been suggested that a more tolerant attitude toward divorce creates the impression among young people that marriage represents a "trial run." Young people, it is claimed, approach marriage with the idea that it is impermanent. "Let's try it and if it doesn't work, there's a way out." There is no evidence that this is the reasoning young people use. None of the studies of divorce support the notion that marriage (or divorce) is approached casually. Most competent observers believe that young people expect their marriages to last and give no thought to divorce unless serious problems arise in their marriage.

Most divorces occur during the first two or three years of marriage, which means that divorces generally separate couples rather than families. As the graph in Figure 4-2 shows, all divorces do not involve children. Nevertheless, thousands of children are involved in divorces every year, and this constitutes the main problem created by divorce. The nuclear family, as compared with an extended family, has great difficulty in providing a stable social setting for children when the parents have been divorced. Davis sums up the multiple problems involved:

. . . the child's future must be decided in each case by the discretion of the court, with few principles other than the vague "welfare of the child" to guide it. The

59. Comparative data show that the United States has the highest divorce rate among Western nations, but "various countries in the past have had higher rates than the United States; e.g., Israel (1935–1944), Egypt (1935–1948), Japan (1887–1919), Algeria (1887–1940)." Thus the increase in divorce rates during the past two or three generations has not been limited to the United States. It has been generally similar for all Western countries permitting divorce, especially for those who have experienced rapid industrialization. Robert K. Merton and Robert A. Nisbet (eds.), *Contemporary Social Problems*, New York: Harcourt, Brace and World, 1961, p. 405.

Fig. 4-2. Divorce Rate for Couples With and Without Children Under 18, According to Duration of Marriage

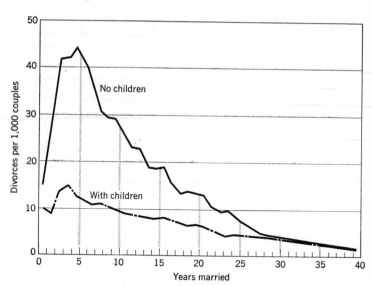

Source: Metropolitan Life Insurance Company, "Divorce and Size of Family," *Statistical Bulletin*, Vol. 31, No. 2 (February, 1950), p. 3.

parents often use the child as an instrument of mutual conflict. They also compete for his custody, though not for his support . . . In our culture, therefore, the child of divorce is a social problem in the sense that societal machinery for dealing with him does not operate automatically or satisfactorily. Though he is really better off than the child whose parent has died, he is more of a problem because his condition is felt to be somebody's fault, with all that this implies.[60]

An overwhelming majority of divorced persons remarry — and do so rather quickly — which suggests that they are not disenchanted with marriage per se, but simply with the one they had. At every age level, even through the seventies, marriage rates for the divorced are higher than for the rest of the population. In fact, about 94 per cent of divorced women over thirty eventually remarry. And in connection with the "child's welfare," the remarriage rate of divorced mothers is not significantly lower than that of female divorcees generally. Commenting on this fact, Goode notes that despite the high rate of divorce in the contemporary family, "the existing kinship institutions indirectly move both child and mother back into relatively well-defined statuses, thus fixing responsibility for maintenance, status placement, and socialization of the child."

A further point should be added to any discussion of the impact of divorce

60. Kingsley Davis, H. S. Bredemeier, and Marion J. Levy, Jr. (eds.), *Modern American Society*, New York: Rinehart, 1949, pp. 673, 686.

on the modern family. Contrary to the impression given by divorce statistics, marriages today last longer than at any other time in history. While it is obvious that the divorce rate is higher than it used to be, it is not so obvious that the far lower death rate of today more than offsets it. *The average married couple, therefore, actually lives together longer than did their great-grandparents.* In 1890, for example, 33 marriages in each thousand in the United States were broken each year. Of these marriages, 30 were terminated by death. Today, only 27 marriages per thousand are broken each year, and the proportion broken by death has been reduced to 17.5 per thousand. Divorce does not break 3 per thousand, as then, but 9.3. As a result, 6 more marriages per thousand survive today than survived in 1890.[61] Thus, measured by this standard of stability, it can be argued that longer life and modern technology have brought about more rather than less permanence in family relationships.

Thus far our basic concern has focused upon differing normative conceptions of what the family should be, and the type of impact that widespread industrialization has made upon traditional family norms. But what does the future hold? What is more likely to happen? What are the implications of continuing industrialism for the family? We turn now to a consideration of these questions.

THE FUTURE OF THE FAMILY

The changes discussed in this chapter illustrate that the family is an adaptive institution. That is, it does not create change so much as it adapts to changing social conditions. We have described a number of the adjustments the family has made to an urban-industrial world. In the light of recent trends, however, it would appear that the contemporary family will have to adapt to another feature of successful industrialization — that of increased leisure time. Although this innovation will be treated in greater detail in a later chapter, several observations are relevant to our discussion here.

In recent years the emphasis upon technological efficiency has increased production rates so fast that the hours of labor have been radically shortened and leisure time has become available to large segments of the population for the first time in history. Furthermore, as work becomes more specialized, it becomes increasingly difficult to utilize work experiences as a common bond uniting family members. If the husband's job involves complex procedures there is a tendency not to bother with long explanations of what he is doing. Consequently, his wife and children may know almost nothing about his job — and may even prefer it that way. But along with this trend

---

61. Paul H. Landis, *Making the Most of Marriage*, 2nd. ed., New York: Appleton-Century-Crofts, 1960, p. 26. An additional point worth noting in regard to marital stability is the fact that most marriages last longer than most business partnerships.

goes the fact that working hours seem destined to shrink even further. As a result husbands will be able to spend more time at home, and probably with even fewer job interests to share with other family members. Such bonds as common interests and family solidarity must come increasingly from sources other than work. Furthermore, in a society with more automation, shorter hours, and better transportation to home, the urban worker will have more energy at the end of the day to engage in nonwork activities. In this setting, recreation becomes more than a mere diversion. It becomes an increasingly important family function around which common values and goals can be developed.[62]

Another characteristic of an industrial society, namely, the concentration of economic activity in large bureaucratic organizations, holds important implications for future family relationships. Miller and Swanson base their study of *The Changing American Parent* on this trend, and provide a speculative model of an emerging type of family which they have termed the *colleague* family. This formulation takes into account the fact that the United States has moved from an entrepreneurial society of small shopowners to a society dominated by large-scale bureaucratic organizations. In adjusting to this new setting, and in keeping with the conception of the family as an adaptive institution, family relationships are likely to be compatible with the essential features of a bureaucracy. For example, Miller and Swanson claim that industrial specialization — a necessary part of any bureaucratic corporation — has created new conditions for family relationships. The underlying assumptions upon which job specialization is based have been taken over by the family. Women and men are increasingly equal, but they are also separate and different. They are beginning to realize "that differences in talent, interest, and function, as long as they are complementary, do not threaten equality. Instead, they may enrich and promote the common life." [63] It is for this reason that the term "colleague" family is used, because it suggests co-workers "with equal, interdependent, but distinct and mutually recognized competencies." As specialists [64] working in a bureaucracy "may

63. For a more complete discussion of the impact of increased leisure on the family, see Max Kaplan, *Leisure in America: A Social Inquiry*, New York: Wiley, 1960, chap. 5.
63. Daniel R. Miller and Guy E. Swanson, *The Changing American Parent*, New York: Wiley, 1958, p. 200.
64. Despite the fact that increasing specialization worries some people, the point should be added that a specialized occupation has beneath it a fairly broad general background. For example, the graduate chemist whose work demands a high order of specialized knowledge has attended school for a considerable period. Whether he ever gets enough literature, history, philosophy, etc., is now and will remain a burning issue within academic circles. But he does get more of these than if he left school at 15 to go to work as a farmer, small merchant, or general salesman. And the way in which the chemist has been exposed at an early age to a broad variety of interests is likely to promote a type of urbanity that may come otherwise only in occasional instances. And any movement in the direction of a more cosmopolitan outlook should promote a better understanding of interpersonal relationships.

find in each other skills they lack, but skills they equally need, and as they may defer to one another's judgment on the grounds of differing competence without feeling that they have personally lost in prestige, so husband and wife may now relate in this way."

In Miller and Swanson's view, the contemporary, or companionship type, family began as a demand that women should be able to do all the things open to men. "It was still a man's world and women tried to enter it by becoming masculine." But the conditions that brought equality and companionship also changed the male role. The older norms that required the male to be aggressive, independent, and dominating decreased with the growth of greater job security, "and of routinized channels of occupational advance through the more passive means of education and faithful service. In large areas of life it became acceptable and even required that men, like women, have the same skills and preoccupations traditionally associated with the other sex." [65]

As husbands (and wives) are increasingly employed in large organizations, Miller and Swanson hypothesize that the organizational requirements for personal stability and their provision for greater economic security will serve to lower the rate of divorce and separation. They believe further that children will not be as subordinated in the household as they were in the past, nor will they be the equal decision makers that they are in some contemporary families. They will be "more in the nature of junior partners who are wanted and needed and whose opinions are sought and given careful consideration, but who must have proper seniority before being admitted to full participation in deciding the family's course." Furthermore, the fact that proportionally more children will spend their future working lives in a large organizational setting means that they must understand the intricate human relations of the bureaucracy. Modern parents who have accumulated a lifetime of experience working for large organizations have acquired valuable skills in assessing bureaucratic behavior and in making critical judgments of social situations which their children will need. "We may expect, then, the reappearance of the parent as the counselor and aid of the children after they have become adults and parents in their own right." [66] In this respect it is likely that an industrialized society may enhance some of the traditional functions of the family. The family may again become the school for the job, but it will be the school for the job's human relations, not its technical skills.

SUMMARY

The contemporary family is particularly vulnerable to criticism and evaluation since it is both directly involved in the lives of most people and recently

65. Miller and Swanson, op. cit. p. 200.
66. Ibid. p. 204.

changed in almost every phase of its life by industrialization. Much of contemporary family life is evaluated on the basis of an image derived from the rural, pre-industrial family. The modern urban family has departed from this image in many ways. Thus, normative dissensus arises from conflicting conceptions of what the family should be.

The basic features of the traditional American family were consistent with the demands of an agricultural way of life. Economic self-sufficiency, familism, and patriarchal-authoritarian rule were emphasized. The home was the center of production, family goals were more important than individual interests, and patriarchy was a way of life. But the impact of industrialization meant that the family had to adapt to a fundamentally different type of social setting. The locus of work shifted from the home to the factory and the business office. Industrial opportunities helped to increase the status of women and specialized schools undermined the family's educational function. Since an industrial society is based upon a large, mobile labor force, traditional kinship ties were weakened under the impact of vocational and residential mobility. Family size decreased, housing changed, and in the small, independent nuclear family system the aged were left stranded.

As the society changed the family continued to adapt to increasing industrialization. In keeping with other normative shifts, the family system that emerged emphasized democracy rather than patriarchy, individualism rather than familism, and affection rather than production. But in spite of widespread change, many aspects of family life have been modified rather than drastically changed. In effect, the modern family reflects a curious mixture of both historical and contemporary features.

Some consequences of normative dissensus can be clearly seen in the confused status of American women, the high rate of divorce, and the insecure role of the aged. Although the family has changed, the evidence, on balance, does not suggest that the family has become a less important social institution. In an impersonal, mobile industrial world, the affectional function has become more important, and with increasing leisure and the high value placed on marriage and children, family life may become more meaningful.

QUESTIONS AND SUGGESTIONS FOR FURTHER STUDY

1. In what ways are the demands of an industrial society incompatible with the traditional family system?
2. To what extent are the major features of the early American family still a part of the contemporary family?
3. Analyze your own family in terms of the frame of reference presented in this chapter. What evidence is there of normative dissensus among family members? How does this effect your role in the family?
4. Interview several mothers in your neighborhood who are working outside the

home and try to determine the advantages and disadvantages of the mothers' outside employment.

5. What is the relationship between the impersonality of modern society and the importance of the affectional function of the contemporary family?

6. What is meant by the statement, "For the rural farm family, patriarchy was 'a way of life' "?

7. Is the emphasis upon individualism in the modern family inconsistent with family stability? Defend your point of view.

8. Do you think that a more tolerant attitude toward divorce is causally related to the present divorce rate? Why?

9. Why does the married woman experience greater role confusion today than the unmarried woman?

10. Read several contemporary novels and short stories with the purpose of analyzing the conflicting demands on the modern wife.

11. Make a study of a television program or a motion picture, noting the areas in which family dissensus develops most frequently. How are these problems usually resolved?

12. Describe the events leading to the devaluation of the wife's traditional activities.

13. What are some of the implications of a democratic-equalitarian conception of family life for (a) mate selection, (b) child rearing, and (c) divorce?

14. In your opinion, is the family becoming more important or less important in the life patterns of its members? What are the reasons for your answers?

SUGGESTED READINGS

Goode, William J., *After Divorce*, Glencoe: Free Press, 1956. A comprehensive research study based on an urban sample of divorced women.

Miller, Daniel R., and Guy E. Swanson, *The Changing American Parent*, New York: Wiley, 1958. A provocative study relating child rearing practices to recent shifts in the occupational structure of American society. Data are analyzed in terms of families in which the father is employed in an entrepreneurial or a bureaucratic setting.

Kephart, William M., *The Family, Society, and the Individual*, Boston: Houghton Mifflin, 1961. This book focuses on the clash between individual needs and societal requirements.

Kenkel, William F., *The Family in Perspective*, New York: Appleton-Century-Crofts, 1960. Describes the family in terms of several different frames of reference. Discussion of the early American family and contemporary urban family life is especially relevant.

Kirkpatrick, Clifford, *The Family as Process and Institution*, New York: Ronald, 1963. An excellent analysis of American family patterns and dilemmas. A wealth of research data is presented.

Komarovsky, Mirra, *Women in the Modern World*, Boston: Little, Brown, 1953. This analysis illustrates the normative dissensus discussed in this chapter.

Nye, Ivan F., and Louis W. Hoffman, *The Employed Mother in America*, Chicago: Rand McNally, 1963. A compilation of research articles dealing with many significant questions regarding women's employment outside the home and its effect on the children and on the husband-wife relationship.

Ogburn, William F., and Meyer F. Nimkoff, *Technology and the Changing Family*, Boston: Houghton Mifflin, 1955. Surveys a wide variety of material related to the impact of industrialization on the family.

Waller, Willard, *The Old Love and the New: Divorce and Readjustment*, New York: Liveright, 1930. This book has become a classic in its field. Still one of the most insightful discussions of divorce appearing in the sociology of the family literature.

CHAPTER 5 EDUCATION

> When we look over some of the literature and listen to the criticism of
> the American schools, we sometimes wonder how this great institution
> manages to keep going and fulfill its functions. The teacher is hedged
> about with all kinds of "do's" and "dont's" many of them opposing, so
> that he is bound to land in trouble whatever he does. The administrators
> are subjected to a variety of community pressures that ask variously for
> more religion in school, less athletics, or higher or lower standards. All
> their expected activities are inhibited by interruptions and investigations
> by public-spirited citizens. The public school is exhorted, cajoled, and
> pleaded with to do better and fulfill many divergent, inconsistent, and
> unrealistic goals. Failing to perform, voluminous abuse is heaped upon it,
> and it is held at bay by the fact that the public always holds the purse
> strings.[1]

The writers quoted above are strongly identified with the present system of
education in America. There are others who are considerably more critical
of present educational theories and practices. Whatever the case, both the
defenders and critics of contemporary education agree that today's school
must be modified to prepare America's youth for a complex and dynamic
future which is only vaguely perceived at the present time. In the past when
social change was more leisurely, the future seemed more predictable, and
consequently the kind of education necessary to train the young seemed more
comprehensible. Realizing that tomorrow's scientific achievements, technological progress, and social well-being are determined in large measure by the
educational programs now in process, the American public has become keenly
aware of the key role of education in fostering national and industrial growth.
While this awareness is high, dissensus exists on the particular kind of education that will accomplish the task. It is this normative problem that concerns
us here.

The normative problem: how should members of an industrial society be educated?

Although education has long been viewed in the United States as one of the
society's key institutions, its philosophical conceptions have shifted from time

1. Reprinted from *Educational Issues in a Changing Society*, edited by August Kerber
and Wilfred Smith, by permission of the Wayne State University Press. Copyright ©
1962 by Wayne State University Press, p. 355.

to time. American public schools have lacked the centralized authority of the German system, the orderly administrative practices of the French system, and the coherent guiding principles of many church-controlled schools. American education is rather an expression of the organic growth of American experiences and experiments.

As conditions in the society changed so did educational practices and functions. Education in America began in the colonial period as a direct copy of the European system. Formal schooling was limited to a privileged few and the curriculum was designed to prepare youth for a few professions, such as the ministry, and for leadership positions in the society. Products of this educational system assumed the task of maintaining the cultural traditions of Western civilization.

There was of course the necessity for transmitting the various occupational skills and crafts. But most of this training was conducted outside the school by apprenticeship and on-the-job training.

About the middle of the nineteenth century, the rise of cities and industries stimulated the demand for education, and the schools responded to this demand. When the privilege of voting was extended to all males, public schools were established to teach future adults the rights and responsibilities of citizenship. When millions of immigrants arrived with different languages and customs, the schools were the principal agents for introducing them to a common language and a common appreciation of the American way of life. When the ideology developed that talents were to be rewarded on the basis of ability, not social class, economic privilege, or national origin, tax-supported schools were established to optimize equal educational opportunities. When industrialization created a demand for new professions and skills, hundreds of colleges, universities, and graduate schools were established to provide training. When such social problems as juvenile delinquency, divorce, and mental illness rose sharply, efforts were made by the schools to stem the tide by means of counseling and allied services. When new knowledge was required for adults who were already in business or in various other vocations, the schools developed a wide assortment of "adult education" courses, both on and off campus. Education was seen as necessary for every type of skill and for every stage of the life cycle.

By such ever-expanding educational and vocational services, the American school has reflected the dynamic character of American society.[2] The public now relies heavily upon the school for a wide variety of functions that the traditional school never attempted to cover. The public seems to feel that "education pays off." It is almost a commonplace that social problems such

2. For example, see "Public Opinion on Education," *National Education Association Research Bulletin* (October 1958), p. 74.

as delinquency, anti-Semitism, labor-management strife, and even war can be solved "only by education." [3]

Yet, there are disquieting signs on the horizon. There is, for example, a serious shortage of classrooms, of competent teachers, and of operating funds. Over half a million children still go to school on a reduced program because facilities are lacking. Should we emphasize quality and become more selective in permitting access to education, or should we maintain the customary equality of opportunity in education? If the latter, where should the funds come from? From the federal government? There is also the rapid expansion of knowledge so vast in scope and complexity that even the best university instructors have difficulty in absorbing it. Are present instructional methods so obsolete that new methods must be devised to transmit this exploding knowledge? Too, some feel that today's youth lacks moral fiber and a sense of personal responsibility for maintaining our free institutions. Should the schools be responsible for character training in addition to their other responsibilities? [4]

These are some of the issues in American public education. Solutions and recommendations offered are varied and controversial because they are based on different normative conceptions of education. In the late 1700's and early 1800's such issues did not exist because the conception of a proper education was sharply defined. Among the severest critics of today's schools are those who still hold the view of education that was popular in the early 1800's — a view called classicism.

In the development of a normative conception of education, the answers to four basic questions must be sought. These questions are: (1) What is the aim of education? (2) Who should be educated? (3) What should be taught? and (4) What methods of instruction should be used? Classicism developed one set of answers to these questions.

> *Historical Normative Conception: Classicism* — The principal aim of education is to transmit the cultural heritage of the past. Education should be restricted to an elite capable of pursuing classical studies.

In the early days of the republic the aim of education was explicit: to pass on the cultural heritage of the past. This heritage came from Europe and stressed the ideas, literature, and languages of classic Western civilization. Educated people in the first decades of the new republic were expected to be literate in Greek and Latin and to be familiar with the humanistic traditions

3. Max Lerner, *America as a Civilization*, New York: Simon and Schuster, 1957, p. 733.
4. Raymond P. Harris, *American Education, Fact, Fancies, and Folklore*, New York: Random House, 1961.

of the Renaissance period. Whatever their profession or employment, they shared this common cultural background by which they measured the aims and ideals of their contemporary life.

But only a few people were privileged to have such education. It was a concept of education far removed from the practical affairs of life and oriented to the achievements of the past. Moreover, education was expensive. Schools were privately controlled and established as profit-making institutions. Accordingly, few could afford the leisure or the price to be in school. Pennsylvania, for example, in 1834, had only 20,000 children in school out of a population of 400,000 of elementary school age.[5] Thus, concerning the question of who shall be educated — a controversial modern issue — the traditional answer was to educate a limited number exceedingly well and let the others acquire as much as they could under the circumstances.

Given a definition of education for the wealthy, the curriculum was limited and logically integrated so that each level of courses led systematically to the next higher level. The first years taught the pupil the fundamentals of reading, writing, spelling, and arithmetic. Then came the so-called Latin school, which was a secondary school designed to prepare students for college. Latin, Greek, and the classical literature of Western civilization were studied. To these were added the study of mathematics, philosophy, and history. This curriculum has come down to modern times as "liberal education." With the exception of Latin and Greek, these subjects are taught today in high schools and colleges as part of the "general education" curriculum.

Seen in modern perspective, the early pedagogical techniques seem harsh, authoritarian, and dull. At lower levels, the schoolmaster depended on constant drilling, rote-memory work, and harsh methods of discipline. These techniques were relieved somewhat at the higher levels by emphasis on lectures, written examinations, and essays. Nevertheless the instructor assumed, in accord with the prevailing belief about the separateness of mind and body, that his main duty was to discipline the minds of his charges. It was believed that the mind was composed of separate faculties — such as memory and will — which could be strengthened through judicious exercise. Just as the muscles in the body could remain healthy by regular exercise, it was thought the mind required daily drills and mental exercises. Modern learning theory no longer subscribes to such simplistic notions, but in America's earlier years, these pedagogical methods were fundamental. They were believed to be nearly foolproof because they leaned upon the writings and wisdom of the best minds of Western civilization.[6]

5. Tyrus Hillway, *Education in American Society*, Boston: Houghton Mifflin, 1961, p. 31.
6. For an excellent history of American education, see Lawrence Cremin, *The Transformation of the School*, New York: Knopf, 1961.

What, then, happened to those who could not afford this costly education? Was there no need for schooling children of farmers and working class people? Until about 1850, the majority of these children received very little formal schooling. Parents either assumed responsibility themselves or paid a local instructor to provide the rudiments of reading, writing, and arithmetic. The manifest purpose was to have their children acquire sufficient literacy to read the Bible. As for their vocational training, parents often decided their children's careers and sent them as apprentices to appropriate craftsmen and tradesmen. Technical and vocational schools were scarce.

THE DECLINE OF CLASSICISM

Classicism was brought to America from Europe and flourished through the early decades of the nineteenth century. Gradually, however, territorial expansion and the associated growth of the economy gave rise to a different concept of education. The transition did not take place without struggle, and even today there are many people who still subscribe to the norms of classicism. The struggle to establish a new normative order will be considered below.

The Need for Public Education. As much as public education is an accepted part of American life today, it is not a norm which was established overnight. It took nearly a century to complete. By the middle of the nineteenth century, however, the trend toward this goal seemed set, at least in the northern states. A number of factors accounted for this movement.

One contributing factor was the gradual spread of suffrage. When George Washington was first elected to the presidency, only one free male in every seven was eligible to vote. Gradually all males became eligible — and later women, too — as provisions were made in the constitutions of the frontier states and as the older states on the east coast held constitutional conventions for the same purpose. But as the number of voters expanded, it became necessary to educate more than a small group in the society in order that wise decisions and responsibility in government could be guaranteed.

On another level, the demand for a greater spread of education came from businessmen, factory operators, and even trade unions. The growing industries and commerce required not only manually skilled workers, but also workers who could read, write, and do the computations involved in industrial production.

The pressure for raising the educational levels of the working class came also from intellectuals who became increasingly fearful that the wealth of the rising industrialist segment was crystalizing into a rigid social class system. At the same time the rising living standard, combined with greater humanitarian motives associated with industrialization brought about changes in child labor laws which took children out of the factories and put them into the schools. Meanwhile, in response to growing wealth and industrialization in America, millions of new immigrants arrived from Europe. These newer immigrants came from southern and eastern Europe where the cultural and religious background differed from that of the earlier arrivals. These differences in linguistic, religious, and ethnic characteristics motivated Americans of older stock to seek compulsory public education so that the children of immigrants would learn the language, values, and citizenship responsibilities of the new country. These immigrant children, it was believed, would benefit from the common school experience along with other American youngsters.

These historical facts — the trend toward universal suffrage, the need for general literacy among the working class, the arrival of new immigrants, and, in general, the rising industrial culture — led to the decline of private schools, the consequent growth of public education, and the conception of common schools.

The Rise of Public Schools. The situation at the beginning of the 1800's was as follows: privately sponsored, fee-charging schools based on classical precepts available for the wealthy. For the less wealthy there were no formal schools, but vocational training chiefly by means of the apprenticeship system. However, many local governments, concerned for the welfare of destitute children and orphans, established special schooling from tax funds. Thus public schools were first established for charity cases.

This was unfortunate because the early movements to establish public schools were hindered by this precedent. Nevertheless, educational reformers — such as Horace Mann, Henry Barnard, Calvin Wiley, Caleb Mills, Samuel Lewis, and John D. Pierce — were able by the middle of the 1800's to gain public acceptance for tax-supported schools.[7] Their task was particularly difficult because the principle of state control of the schools was well established, and the states in turn delegated responsibility to local school districts. These local school districts, particularly in the Midwest where a district was often composed of a single "red schoolhouse," exercised considerable autonomy. There was no central educational authority for the nation, so each state and the thousands of districts within each state had to be converted to the revolutionary idea of public tax-supported schools.

Incorporated with this notion of tax-supported schools were several other innovations. One was the principle of compulsory education for all children up to a certain age, generally age sixteen. Since children could satisfy the

7. For a history of the public school system in America, see Lawrence A. Cremin, *The American Common School: An Historic Conception*, New York: Teachers College Bureau of Publications, 1951. Lawrence A. Cremin (ed.), *The Republic and the School: Horace Mann on the Education of Free Men*, New York: Teachers College, Columbia University, 1961.

requirements by attending either private or parochial schools, another innovation was involved. This was the "common school" principle, a principle which many countries have since emulated. The idea was to encourage all children in the community to attend its public schools so that they would share a common educational experience and so that children of all nationalities, religions, and economic levels would mix together in the same classroom. Here is how one speaker put it in 1839:

> I want to see the children of the rich and the poor sit down side by side on equal terms, as members of one family — a great brotherhood — deeming no one distinguished above the rest but the best scholar and the best boy — giving free and natural play to their affections, at a time of life when lasting friendships are often formed, and worldliness and pride have not yet alienated heart from heart.[8]

When this common school philosophy became an accepted fact another basic principle was instituted, that of equal educational opportunity. When the tax-supported public schools provided an education equal to or better than the private schools, a long step toward a democratic education was taken.

By 1850, the common school philosophy was prominent in all the northern states, despite many objections from people identified with classical education. (The South, troubled by the Civil War and its aftermath, delayed full acceptance of public education until later.) By 1860, the idea of common schools had spread from elementary to secondary education, though it continued to be disputed until the famous Kalamazoo Case in Michigan in 1874 decided the right of school districts to use tax funds for secondary education. Several hundred high schools were established in the North where they soon replaced the popular, privately sponsored academies. At the same time, girls were given the same opportunities as boys, who formerly had been the primary beneficiaries of public education. As tax-supported schools for secondary education increased, this movement extended to college and university levels. Many states recognizing the need for more institutions than those available under private sponsorship now began to establish state universities and colleges. The trend was given impetus by the Morrill Act of 1862, which provided federal aid. By the middle of the nineteenth century then, the idea of common schools and equal educational opportunity had gone far to destroy the conception of private control of education.

Despite the growing popularity of the common school idea and the advances in literacy levels it made possible, there was and continues to be con-

8. Quoted in Lawrence A. Cremin, "The Future of the American Common School," in George Z. F. Bereday and Luigi Volpicelli (eds.), *Public Education in America*, New York: Harper, 1958, p. 38.

siderable opposition to this basic idea. In the earlier days of public education, opposition to it came from many quarters and was argued on many grounds. The Catholic clergy and some Protestant denominations, for example, viewed the common school as a "Godless" institution, and they claimed they could not in good conscience send their communicants to such institutions. These groups were strongly identified with the ethnic enclaves associated with immigration — the Irish in the case of Catholics, and German Lutherans in the case of Protestants. In the South, following the Civil War, whites balked at the common school idea and established "separate but equal" schools, mainly for racial reasons. (More will be said about this in Chapter 12.) A more subtle type of resistance came from those who argued on social class and intellectual grounds. Many families did not want their children to "mix" in school with those of different backgrounds. Similarly, parents who thought they had children with superior intellectual abilities were inclined to place them in private schools rather than have their talents dulled by the assumed mediocrity of the common school.[9]

The Growth of Colleges and Universities. Despite such outspoken opposition to the common school idea, the principle of tax-supported education was spreading beyond the secondary levels to the college and graduate school. Mention has already been made of the Morrill Act and the consequent establishment of state colleges. This Act provided federal grants to several states for establishing schools of engineering and agricultural science. Justin S. Morrill, who introduced the land grant bill unsuccessfully in 1857, recalled that Congress had appropriated money for mental hospitals. He asked: "If we can legislate for the insane, may we not legislate for the sane?" [10]

In 1890 the second Morrill Act provided that these grants could not be used by a college that barred Negroes, unless it also established separate facilities for them. The result was that Negro colleges were founded in 16 states. Today, the land-grant colleges enjoy a status they did not have when liberal art colleges were the prestigious institutions. Hechinger notes: "As tangible proof of their arrival, the land-grant colleges proclaim that they award nearly 40 per cent of the Ph.D.'s given by all institutions in all disciplines, more than half of all engineering doctorates, a third of those in mathematics and the social sciences and a fourth of those in English." [11]

9. Even if Negro segregated schools are not considered, common schools are avoided by a substantial proportion today. In October 1961, some 15 per cent of all elementary school pupils, 10 per cent of all high school students, and 35 per cent of all college and university students were enrolled in private or parochial schools. *Encyclopedia Britannica Yearbook*, 1962, p. 138.

10. See Fred M. Hechinger, "Land Grant College Story Traces Nation's Education Growth," *New York Times*, November 12, 1961.

11. Ibid.

Along with this expansion of professional training came another modification. The basic college curriculum which concentrated on the humanities and classical studies was included in a curriculum which embraced the developing sciences. The sciences — chemistry, physics, geology, astronomy and biology — were frequently combined in the college of science and arts. The "arts" represented the cultural heritage of Western civilization, while the "sciences" represented both new knowledge and new cosmology. A little later, the growth of "social science" — economics, sociology, psychology, anthropology, political science — did even more to challenge the existing "truths" and beliefs about man, his nature and his world.

As the area covered by these college courses expanded, many American college graduates went to Europe, especially Germany, seeking advanced work and degrees. As increasing numbers of European-trained students returned to the United States, they actively promoted the idea of graduate schools, a concept that not only extended education beyond the baccalaureate degree, but also emphasized original research for the advancement of science and letters. Up to this point, higher education remained isolated from the inventive and creative outside world. To implement the concept of research, graduate schools were superimposed on undergraduate colleges; faculties with research capabilities were added; libraries for assembling new information were established; and facilities for publishing scholarly works and research findings were made available.[12]

With the establishment of graduate schools, the universities — both state and private — quickly spread through the country and in many cases several new colleges and professional schools were brought under the control of a single administration. Such universities typically included colleges of agriculture, engineering, education, business, and home economics and many professional schools such as those of law, medicine, theology, dentistry, library science, journalism, architecture, and speech. By expanding in such directions, higher education in the United States departed radically from the classical tradition and incorporated the principle of vocationalism into its curriculum. These new directions and these new pragmatic concerns were not confined to the campus. The idea of service to the community and nation, first made explicit in land grant colleges, was carried forward by a system of extension programs.

These expanding activities of the universities, together with the contributions of lower level educational institutions, reflect the pragmatic value of the schools for American society. Public opinion has supported the educational system because it has served the community and nation well.

12. Nevitt Sanford (ed.), *The American College*, New York: Wiley, 1962.

The Effects of Social Science on Education. As the number of public schools increased, as the demand for competent school teachers rose, and as the growing colleges and universities provided training for teachers, the developing social sciences began to force revision of classical theories of instruction and education. Building on the contributions of Darwin, Wallace, Mendel, and other biological scientists, social scientists began to use methods of observation and experimentation on problems of human behavior. The developing fields of intelligence testing, field theory, behaviorism, gestalt psychology, psychoanalysis, and the broader concepts of culture and social structure did much to guide teaching away from rote memory, frequent recitation, and harsh discipline toward a more experimental and research-oriented approach. They also began to question many of the assumptions about human behavior held by the classicist.[13] As their perspective broadened, the educational researchers initiated investigations that ranged from limited problems of improving instruction in spelling to broader problems of curriculum design and child development for entire school systems. In brief, where formerly teaching under classicism was considered an art, it was now being conceived of as a science.[14]

By the second half of the nineteenth century, the American educational system was involved in experimentation and diversification. Private education continued, but the common school idea was also popular. Classicism prevailed as the ideal of education, but vocational and technical training added significant dimensions to the curriculum.

The American educational system began with roots nourished in the tradition of European classicism and continued in this mold until about the mid-nineteenth century. From that time, the practical demands of industrialization called for increased technical and vocational training, particularly for those who could not afford private education. While much of higher education was still privately controlled, the pervasiveness of the common school idea in the rest of the system did much to destroy the earlier tendency toward a class-oriented educational system. It departed significantly from the European system. Having thus rejected the ancestral model, Americans now sought to establish a new normative conception to replace the old. This new conception came to be known as pragmatism.

13. David Riesman, "Some Observations on the 'Older' and the 'Newer' Social Sciences," in Leonard D. White (ed.), *The State of the Social Sciences*, Chicago: University of Chicago Press, 1956, pp. 319–39.
14. Carroll Atkinson and Eugene T. Maleska, *The Story of Education*, New York: Chilton, 1961.

Contemporary Normative Conception: Pragmatism — Everyone should be educated to the maximum of his ability and
interests. Education should have as its purpose the understanding of the changing world and the adjustment of the individual to that world. Teaching methods should be guided
by scientific considerations.[15]

What is the aim of education? Pragmatism, being greatly influenced by
contemporary research and scientific investigation,[16] takes a nondogmatic
view of classical values. As Nagel writes: "Ideals and values are not self-
certifying; they are not established as valid by appeals to dogmatic authority,
to intuitions of moral imperative, or to undisciplined preference. Proposed
moral ideals must be congruous with the needs and capacities of human
beings . . . if those ideals are to serve as satisfactory guides to a rich and
satisfying human life." [17] Nagel admonishes humanists and other educators in
the classical tradition: "It is therefore preposterous to maintain, as many
professed humanists in effect do, that ignorance of the conclusions of science
is a desirable condition for projecting or pursuing a good life. . . . It is not
an exaggeration to claim that the theoretical understanding that the sciences
provide is the foundation for a liberal civilization and a humane culture." [18]

For pragmatists, values do not rest on absolutes and have no *a priori* claim
to truth. Pragmatists maintain that truth is something that is good for
definite and practical reasons. Furthermore, they believe that values, like
other beliefs, are subject to change, and values of another era are not necessarily appropriate for the present day.

Applied to education, pragmatism suggests that educators should not
"teach" absolute truth and values, but rather that they help their pupils
learn how to discover worthy values for themselves. This aim of education
seems consistent with the changing views of man and society resulting from
recent advances in scientific knowledge.

15. Perhaps more than any other person John Dewey gave expression to some of the
central ideas of pragmatist educational philosophy. See, for example: John Dewey,
Reconstruction in Philosophy, New York: Holt, 1920, and *Experience and Education,*
New York: Macmillan, 1939. There are many testimonials to Dewey's contributions;
one is: Joe Burnett and others, "Dewey and Creative Education," *Saturday Review*
(November 21, 1959), pp. 19–25. Oscar Handlin has written a book summarizing
Dewey's contribution: *John Dewey's Challenge to Education,* New York: Harper,
1950.
16. John L. Childs, *American Pragmatism and Education,* New York: Holt, 1956.
17. Ernest Nagel, "The Place of Science in a Liberal Education," *Daedalus* (Winter
1959), p. 58.
18. Ibid p. 58.

Who should be educated? Though in the days of classicism, education might have been thought desirable for every citizen, practical considerations prevented the realization of the ideal. Under frontier conditions, the exploitation of the country's rich natural resources depended on human muscle power and the working class did not have sufficient leisure to pursue education. Only the leisure classes had much access to education.

When pragmatism emerged, however, industrialization was permitting more leisure for all citizens. Economic conditions and living standards had improved so that the ideals of educational opportunity could be put into practice. Thus, pragmatism is in a better position to acclaim and to put into practice the ideal that everyone, regardless of social and economic background, should have as much education as he wants and can absorb.

American education has avoided the establishment of an educated elite or a gentleman class that acts as a special court to pass judgment on the morals, culture, and values of the society. While education is becoming accessible to a large proportion of the citizenry, it is also building an image that views the school as a practical road to success, prestige, and honor. "One needs a good education in order to have a good job," goes the popular saying. This suggests that the degree of equal educational opportunity in America determines the extent to which job opportunities are equalized.

Some scholars are worried that with such an orientation, education is no longer seen as a desirable pursuit in itself, but only as a means to some other goal. To this extent they believe the idealism and true value of education are being undermined. Those who feel this way would like to make education more rigorous, where high academic standards are maintained and the pursuit of excellence is held constant. This in turn suggests concern with the curriculum.

What should be taught? Under the former conception of classicism, the general answer to this question was to teach subjects which would impress upon pupils the traditions and ideals of the past, particularly history, literature, and philosophy. The newer conception takes a broader view and sets no arbitrary limits on subject matter, provided that each course or program has some practical value, either to the individual or the community.

Thus, under pragmatism, schools can assume some responsibility for encouraging physical fitness, for inculcating values of respect for law and authority, and for guidance in mate selection, family obligations, and community responsibility. Under earlier conceptions, such responsibilities were not within the purview of the schools. They were functions of the family, church, and other organizations.

Under pragmatism, not only does the school assume a great many functions, but it seems to be engaged in what is popularly regarded as "social reconstruction." [19] That is, the schools not only teach courses which help pupils understand their present social environment, but they also function in many subtle ways as an agency of social reform. For example, the schools are partly responsible for developing among the present adult population a general appreciation of the possibilities for world government. Similarly, there is a strong bias toward creating in the minds of children a general receptivity to new ideas, inventions, and change. For better or worse, educational institutions are encouraging a progressive outlook.

What methods of instruction should be used? The general teaching methods of classicism were developed by the sophists of ancient Greece, with innovations by Renaissance scholars. The classicist teachers of the early 1800's, considered their profession an art; their techniques emphasized strict discipline and much memorization of facts, particularly at the primary and secondary levels. In the higher grades, essays, formal lectures, and written examinations were the standard techniques. These methods are still used in many schools today. Under pragmatism, the influence of social science has been strongly felt. The general principle is to arrange course materials in such a way that the pupils' interests and motivations are enhanced. Ideally, learning is to be a pleasurable experience, rather than drudgery. Educators with the pragmatic orientation believe that in the past schools have turned out students with "unfulfilled talents" because they have not been properly motivated to learn and study. How then could motivation be increased?

One pattern of the pragmatists is to regroup the traditional course content into a curriculum providing a more "meaningful" framework than the artificial, historically developed divisions of subject matter. Mathematics, for example, could be approached, not by analyzing abstract relationships, but by examining problems of buying stocks, computing taxes, and measuring interest on an installment plan. The teaching of the natural and social sciences is not divided into historically derived compartments, but is treated comprehensively in a way that has a direct relevance to the kind of world people face every day. Thus, under the influence of pragmatism, courses tend to become "practical" and "relevant" to the daily experience of the learner. "Concreteness" is favored over abstraction.

There is another difference between the older and newer conceptions. Under classicism, the method of teaching was focused on training the mind and developing the intellect. This idea stemmed from the classical notion that mind and body were separate entities. In contemporary thought, the mind-body distinction is not stressed; mind and body are considered so inter-

19. George S. Counts, *Dare the School Build a New Social Order?* New York: John Day, 1932.

dependent that the "health" of one affects the other. Consequently, pragmatism has focused on training not the mind alone, but the "whole child." In this view, the child is considered a malleable individual seeking a *modus vivendi* in a complex, changing world as a total, integrated, mind-body organism. The schools are seen as a social agency simultaneously providing both intellectual and physical orientation toward the social environment. Children are encouraged to acquire social skills, moral outlook, and other learned habits that would provide them with optimum total adjustment in adult life. Thus, courses in courtship, leisure-time activities, and even driver education are justified on the basis that the schools should give some guidance to the intellectual, emotional, physical, and other aspects of the total personality.

Thus we see the various aspects of pragmatism influencing the growth of modern education in America. Today nearly 30 per cent of all Americans — more than one out of every four — depend upon education either as a full-time occupation or as a time-consuming avocation. More than 51 million of these are students, another two million are teachers and school administrators, and nearly 200,000 are board members of local school systems.[20] The number of people involved in education is growing faster than the population as a whole. (see Table 5-1).

The budget for the 1959–60 academic year for the public elementary and secondary schools alone came to $15.6 billion.[21] Yet, in spite of such growth, there looms on the horizon considerable dissensus concerning contemporary education. What lies behind this dissatisfaction and what is being done to reduce criticism will be examined next.

THE DECLINE OF PRAGMATISM

Pragmatism, which challenged the older conception of classicism in the 1890's, is itself being attacked by modern critics. Paradoxically, these critics subscribe to some of the basic principles of classicism.

One factor behind the present criticisms is the rising population. The contemporary schools and colleges are over-burdened and the demand for education is greater than at any other time in history. There arises a fundamental question of whether, in the face of educational shortages, present education is realistic. Another factor is the growing concern about the present well-being and the future welfare of the society. The modern industrial world requires a vast range of complex skills and knowledge and demands high performance and sustained productivity at almost all levels of the occupational structure.

20. U.S. Office of Education and the National Education Association. "The Magnitude of the American Educational Establishment," *Saturday Review* (September 15, 1962), p. 55.
21. *Encyclopedia Britannica Yearbook*, 1962, p. 219.

TABLE 5-1

The magnitude of the American educational establishment, 1963–64

The Institutions		The Teachers	
Elementary Schools	94,860	Public School Teachers	
Secondary Schools	30,000	Elementary	901,820
Universities, Colleges & Junior		High School	607,460
Colleges	2,100	Non-Public School Teachers	190,000
		College and University Teachers	
Total Institutions	126,960	For resident degree-credit	
		students	312,900
The Learners		Other teaching faculty	
		(extension courses, non-	
Pupils in Elementary Schools		credit courses, etc.)	50,000
(through grade 8)			
Public Schools	29,400,000	Total Teachers	2,062,180
Non-Public (Private &			
Parochial)	5,400,000		
Other	200,000	Administrators and Supervisors	
		Superintendents of Schools	13,130
Total Elementary	35,000,000	Principals and Supervisors	86,540
		College and University Presidents	2,100
Secondary School Students		Other College Administrative	
		and library staff	48,400
Public High Schools	10,700,000		
Non-Public	1,300,000	Total	150,170
Other	100,000		
		Board Members	
Total Secondary	12,100,000		
		Local School Board Members	147,860
College and University full- and		State Board Members	840
part-time students enrolled		College and University Board	
for credit toward degrees		Members	35,000
Public Institutions	2,631,600		
Private	1,754,400	Total	183,700
Total	4,386,000		
Grand Total			
Students Enrolled	51,486,000		

Source: *Saturday Review* (September 21, 1963). Figures are based on latest available estimates from the U.S. Office of Education and the National Education Association.

Does pragmatism provide the necessary educational guidelines for directing
the training of youth today to assume the complex tasks of tomorrow? Finally,
the sheer bulk of new knowledge is so vast that the schools are finding it
difficult to assimilate this information and pass it on to the younger generation. Are current methods of instruction so obsolete that they can no longer
disseminate the exploding scientific and technical knowledge? These factors
have emerged as important in the context of Cold War competition and have
contributed to contemporary dissensus.

1. *The Shortage of Educational Facilities and Teachers.* Despite continuing prosperity since the end of World War II, most competent observers agree on some very basic shortages in education. Some of these include:

(a) *Shortage of qualified teachers.* Of the 1,467,000 qualified teachers needed in 1958–59, there was a shortage of 132,000 teachers.[22] Since that time this number has been reduced somewhat, partly as the result of salary increases which attracted more talent into the profession. Between 1959 and 1960, the number of teachers increased 4 per cent.[23] Yet the shortage continues to plague the schools.

(b) *Shortage of classrooms.* In the fall of 1960, there was a shortage of 142,000 classrooms, a number decreased by only 1000 since 1957. The number of pupils in excess of normal capacity was 1,868,000, or some 122,000 more than in the fall of 1959. At least 685,000 pupils attended schools half-days only or on a reduced program. As for high schools, they will face by 1970 from 50 to 70 per cent more students than they can now accommodate. Institutions of higher learning similarly expect a doubling or tripling of present enrollments.[24]

(c) *Shortage of funds.* School expenditures have been climbing steadily since 1940. Public expenditures for elementary and secondary schools are as follows: 1940, a little more than $2 billion; 1950, slightly less than $6 billion;[25] and 1960, more than $15.5 billion.[26] These educational costs are borne mainly by local governments. For example in 1957 schools received $6.2 billion from local governments, $4.5 billion from state governments, and $0.4 billion from the federal government. Since local governments obtain revenue primarily from property taxes, their ability to pay for school expenditures is directly related to this source. Unfortunately, school expenses are rising faster than property tax revenue. In 1956, for example, property tax revenues had increased only 170 per cent over 1940 figures, while school expenses had increased 374 per cent during the same period.

These shortages are in part due to the failure to keep up with construction demands during the depression years and World War II. Another factor is population increase. Between 1950 and 1960 the American population has grown from 150.7 million to 179.3 million. This is equivalent to an increase of more than 300 per hour, or 7600 per day. Such increases are being felt in growing school enrollments.

In the fall of 1960 some 46 million people, aged 5 to 34, were enrolled in schools and colleges in the United States. This was an increase of 53 per

22. *The New York Times*, August 31, 1958.
23. *Encyclopedia Britannica Yearbook*, 1962, p. 222.
24. *Encyclopedia Britannica Yearbook*, 1962, p. 219.
25. *The New York Times*, September 28, 1958.
26. *Encyclopedia Britannica Yearbook*, 1962, p. 219.

cent over 1950.[27] The rate of increase between 1950 and 1960 for elementary school was 48 per cent, for high school, 54 per cent, and for higher education, 61 per cent.[28] The increases over a five-year period are equally striking. The following statistics are for public and private school enrollments: [29]

	1955–56	1960–61
Elementary	29,000,000	33,800,000
High School	8,000,000	10,100,000
Higher Education	3,000,000	4,000,000

The above shortages and financial problems seem endemic to the present educational organization. Does this mean free public education should be curtailed and other aspects of pragmatism be revamped?

2. *Increasing Demands for Higher Skills*. Not only is the population increasing and placing greater demands upon existing educational facilities, but there is also an increasing demand for higher skills. This in turn requires more years of training. Automation in factory and office is reducing routine work to a minimum. Specialized skills are required to produce, maintain, and operate the machines which make the labor-saving machines possible. Executives are no less independent of the organizational and automated demands of our day. Expanding operations in business, government, and industry are placing greater reliance on efficient office procedures and complicated electronic computers that "think out" solutions to administrative problems. The rising urban population demands of the individual greater dependence upon a wide range of professional services. Accordingly, the demand for unskilled laborers is declining while the need for professional skills is climbing rapidly. The National Education Association estimates the demand for laborers will decline from more than 12 million in 1900 to about 4.6 million by 1975. During the same period the demand for professional skills will climb from 1.2 million to 12.2 million.[30]

The increased demands for professional skills are already being felt in the colleges and universities. Perhaps this can be summarized by the following comparison.[31] In 1900, only 4 per cent of high school graduates went to college. In the fall of 1962, the incoming freshman class constituted 58.6 per cent of the previous academic year's high school graduates. More men than women of the 1962 graduates entered college — 70.7 per cent as compared with 47.4 per cent — but the difference is shrinking. Furthermore,

27. Ibid. p. 137.
28. Ibid.
29. Ibid. p. 218.
30. Reported in *The New York Times*, August 9, 1959.
31. All the statistics and generalizations in this paragraph are taken from Fred M. Hechinger, "Colleges Face Dramatic Changes in Student Population," *The New York Times*, September 16, 1962, p. E-9.

the estimates indicate a changing pattern of enrollment: (a) a sharp increase in part-time study which indicates an "earning-while-learning" pattern; (b) a growth of graduate students in every discipline; and (c) a substantial increase in the number of those who take courses, not for a degree, but for "catching up with the changing world." Some statistics are:

Total college enrollment, estimated in 1962–63: 4,729,000

For degree credit:	
On campus, undergraduate	67.4%
On campus, graduate	7.9
Off-campus	7.9
For non-degree credit:	16.8
	100.0%

In a critical situation where existing school facilities are already overcrowded, can pragmatism provide the necessary training for professional workers and still maintain high standards of education?

3. *The Rapid Accumulation of Knowledge.* Of major importance in the present school controversy is the quickened pace at which new knowledge is being accumulated. This topic will be discussed at length in Chapter 7, but a few comments are appropriate here. According to some scientists, the time interval in the nineteenth century between one major advance and another was about fifty years. Today the time lag in many fields is only about five years. As a result, there is not enough time to teach the new generation the latest scientific and technical knowledge as thoroughly as was done in the past. Science teachers have difficulty in assimilating this new knowledge. The difficulty is compounded by the fact that the language and the concepts of science are becoming so esoteric and specialized that effective communication to nonspecialists is hindered. "We are, in fact," writes Margaret Mead, "in danger of developing special esoteric groups who can communicate only with each other and who can accept as neophytes and apprentices only those individuals whose intellectual abilities, temperamental bents, and motivations are like their own." [32]

As scientists push back the frontiers of knowledge about outer space, human genetics, atomic energy, and electronic computers — to name only a few — even the highly educated public is finding it difficult to be literate in all areas. In today's world, literacy in one field does not necessarily assure literacy in another.

The pursuit of new knowledge demands special intellectual talents, and the search for talent becomes increasingly vigorous. At the same time,

32. Margaret Mead, "Closing the Gap Between the Scientists and the Others," *Daedalus* (Winter 1959), p. 140.

pressure is mounting to provide special education for those who are suited for these special intellectual pursuits. Can these be accomplished without upsetting the existing patterns of education?

These developments, which point to the increasing demand for educational facilities and talent, suggest that some collapsing of responsibilities and functions of the school will be necessary if the main goals of education are to prepare today's youth for tomorrow's tasks. Yet, as late as 1955, some 1800 delegates to the White House Conference on Education expressed the following viewpoint on the purpose of schools in American society: [33]

It is the consensus of these groups that the schools should continue to develop:

1. The fundamental skills of communication — reading, writing, spelling as well as other elements of effective oral and written expression; the arithmetical and mathematical skills, including problem solving. While schools are doing the best job in their history in teaching these skills, continuous improvement is desirable and necessary.

2. Appreciation of our democratic heritage.

3. Civic rights and responsibilities and knowledge of American institutions.

4. Respect and appreciation for human values and for the beliefs of others.

5. Ability to think and evaluate constructively and creatively.

6. Effective work habits and self-discipline.

7. Social competency as a contributing member of his family and community.

8. Ethical behavior based on a sense of moral and spiritual values.

9. Intellectual curiosity and eagerness for life-long learning.

10. Esthetic appreciation and self-expression in the arts.

11. Physical and mental health.

12. Wise use of time, including constructive leisure pursuits.

13. Understanding of the physical world and man's relation to it as represented through basic knowledge of the sciences.

14. An awareness of our relationships with the world community.

This long list seems to be in accord with pragmatic philosophy. It fails to provide a clear order of priorities in the responsibilities and functions of the schools. Concerned about the demands being placed upon education today, numerous critics are asking that changes be made and priorities established. With the exception of some of the more irresponsible criticisms, most of recent recommendations for modifying contemporary educational

33. Quoted in Paul Woodring, *A Fourth of a Nation*, New York: McGraw-Hill, 1957, pp. 108–9.

goals and practices are in reaching basic agreement as to the changes needed. This emerging conception is labeled here, "essentialism."

> *Emergent Normative Conception: Essentialism* — The principal aim of education is to develop the mental capacities, not the "whole" child. Not every subject or skill is equally important and education should concentrate on the "essentials." Since individual capacities differ, special attention should be given to maximize the learning opportunities of the gifted.

In the last ten or fifteen years a number of articles and books have appeared criticizing existing education and making specific recommendations for improving the schools.[34] Many of their recommendations already have been incorporated into the existing school system. Congress also has passed the National Defense Education Act in 1958 adding further stimulus to this new movement and providing for better selection of talent and improved education in basic subjects such as mathematics, science, and foreign languages. The following are some components of essentialism:

What is the aim of education? Most Americans would agree that the purpose of education is to enable the child (a) to make wise decisions throughout his life; and (b) to become a productive member of society. Essentialism emphasizes the former proposition while pragmatism favors the latter.

Pragmatism, it will be recalled, argues that the mind-body distinction is false and that education is a process which engages the "whole child." Pragmatists argue that a child's health, interests, emotions, and family background are involved in his learning. Failure to pay adequate attention to the total child thus may block effective learning.

Essentialism agrees that the teacher cannot ignore the child's health, character, and personal development as factors in learning. However, it maintains that the teacher cannot assume total responsibility for the child. Rather, this responsibility must lie with the parents. The main function of the school is to help the child learn to make wise decisions. In order to make wise

34. Some of the critics of the contemporary conceptions include: H. G. Rickover, *Education and Freedom*, New York: Dutton, 1959; Arthur E. Bestor, *Educational Wastelands: The Retreat from Learning in Our Public Schools*, Urbana: University of Illinois Press, 1953; Robert M. Hutchins, *The Conflict in Education*, New York: Harper, 1953; A. Lynd, *Quackery in the Public Schools*, New York: Grosset & Dunlap, 1956; Rudolf Flesch, *Why Johnny Can't Read*, New York: Harper, 1955; Frederick Neff, "John Dewey and the Luce Ends of Education," *Phi Delta Kappan*, 40 (December 1958), pp. 130–31. Sidney Hook, however, attempts to answer the critics. See his: "Modern Education and Its Critics," *Seventh Yearbook*, Washington, D.C.: The American Association of Colleges for Teacher Education, 1954, pp. 141–52.

decisions, essentialists state that the child must learn to think clearly and to draw valid conclusions from evidence. As his education advances, he should acquire facts and information from various branches of knowledge. At the same time, he must acquire certain skills. At the lower levels of education, these skills include the ability to read, to use oral and written expression, and to grasp quantitative and qualitative concepts of mathematics. At higher levels, mathematics, science, language training, history, and philosophy impart essential skills.

In a word, the goal of education for essentialists is to develop the mind. They favor the cultivation of the mind, the promotion of disciplined thinking, and the pursuit of intellectual inquiry. Thus, this aspect of essentialism is a revival of classicism, and essentialism could be designated as "neoclassicism."

Who should be educated? Like pragmatism, essentialism favors equality of educational opportunity. Every American child, regardless of sex, color, or religion, has a right to as much free public education as will be of benefit to him and to his community. But essentialism argues that this does not mean that the same *kind* of education and the same *amount* of education should be provided to everyone. Essentialists emphasize that individuals differ in their capacities for learning and in specific talents. The difference between essentialism and pragmatism thus focuses on the issue of identifying learning capacity and talent.

The pragmatists argue that learning capacity is not easily identified, not only because present testing methods are inadequate, but also because of the different maturation rates among growing children and the wide variety of special talents that need to be taken into account. Moreover this opinion holds that identification of talent is not sufficient in itself, but proper educational *guidance* must be given in order to realize a student's full potential. Pragmatists generally follow the principle of promotion based on chronological age, particularly at the elementary levels, unless they have conclusive evidence that the child suffers from some auditory, visual, or other measurable handicap. In such cases, pragmatists favor special schools and provisions for the education of handicapped children.

On the other hand, essentialists seem generally satisfied with currently available techniques for identifying gifted children. For these "fast learners," the essentialists believe special attention is desirable.[35] Such special attention includes provision for additional assignments, advanced courses, and in general, a rigorous college preparatory curriculum. Essentialists also favor some form of "ability grouping," or segregation of the academically talented into

35. Woodring, op. cit. pp. 143–58.

separate classes, but not necessarily into separate schools.[36] Woodring, for example, would separate high school students into A, B, and C classes for academic subjects such as mathematics, foreign languages, and science according to academic achievement. The course content would vary for these groupings. The A classes would be strictly intellectual and college-oriented; the C class would be more applied and practical; while the B class would be somewhere in-between. Allowance is made for the possibility of a given student being in different alphabetical groupings in different subjects, for instance, in A class in mathematics and B class in foreign language.

Conant also favors "ability grouping," and suggests that only the top 15 per cent of the graduates of the "comprehensive high schools" should aspire to college education and accordingly their talents should be recognized early so that they can be guided into college preparatory courses.[37] The remaining 85 per cent, he writes, should be channeled into a terminal education at the high school level.

These ideas concerning who should be educated appear to involve a choice between "mass education" and "selective education." The choice can be summarized in this fashion: The essentialists favor "educating a few people exceedingly well and letting the rest try to live up to the standards the few establish." This conception is replacing the older one which says in effect: "Educate a great number somewhat less than perfectly, and do what can be done under the circumstances for the bright students."

What should be taught? In recent years, as indicated in a previous section, the schools have taken on additional tasks such as driver education and accelerated athletic programs. There has also been a growing tendency for the schools to promote musical programs, basketball games, dramatics, and other activities which contribute to the entertainment of the adult members of the community. In the light of classroom shortages, limited number of qualified teachers, and the great expansion of knowledge, those who subscribe to essentialism charge that these "newer" programs detract from the fundamental educational aims of the school. Even the many technical training and vocational courses, especially in the high schools, are considered by some essentialists to be a subversion of the intellectual aims of education.

36. Some recent studies of gifted students include: John Gardner, *Excellence*, New York: Harper, 1961; Donald L. Thistlethwaite, "The Conservation of Intellectual Talent," *Science*, 128 (October 10, 1958), pp. 822–6; Jonathan R. Warren and Paul A. Heist, "Personality Attributes of Gifted College Students," *Science*, 132 (August 5, 1960), pp. 330–37; David C. McClelland, "Encouraging Excellence," *Harvard Alumni Bulletin* (November 11, 1961), pp. 161–65.

37. James Conant and others, *The Identification and Education of the Academically Talented Students in the American Secondary School*, Washington, D.C.: National Education Association, 1958. See also James Conant, *The American High School Today*, New York: McGraw-Hill, 1959.

If such technical courses must be taught, essentialists argue that standards of achievement and the intellectual content of such courses be raised to approximate the standard academic courses. Essentialists in general urge school administrators to resist pressures to divert school time to activities of "minor academic significance." They contend that the responsibility for such programs belongs to the home, the church, and other community agencies.

Essentialism maintains that some academic subjects are more important than others for the complex world in which we live. Gardner believes that reading should be given top priority in elementary schools, followed by mathematics.[38] He recommends not only an increase in hours devoted to these subjects, but also prompt and generous remedial work when necessary. As for secondary education, Gardner would stress science, foreign language, and social studies followed by reading, writing, and mathematics. Most essentialists favor the pursuit of these subjects to the extent of the students' capabilities.

At college levels, essentialism favors a heavier investment of time in the liberal arts, including science, history, foreign language, literature, and social science. As noted earlier, these courses emphasize the cultural heritage of Western civilization and are designed to provide humanistic orientations for educated people. Essentialists are critical of the tendency in certain state universities to develop a wide range of "elective courses" which offer academic credit for vocational courses such as hotel and restaurant management, food packaging, and dancing. The presence of such "snap courses," essentialists contend, develops a climate that detracts able students from doing their best and discourages striving for excellence. In agreement with their goals of education as being a disciplining of the mind, essentialists stress subjects that "stretch the mind," require rigorous thinking, and provide a historical perspective for "continuity between the past and the unknown future."

What methods should be used? Where pragmatism still holds sway, the teaching methods involve presentation of subject matter so that it has practical significance and direct relevance to the experiences of the learner. Essentialism, consistent with its philosophy of training the intellect, believes a good teacher can lead any normal child to become interested in almost any subject within the range of his understanding and need not be limited to the life experiences the learner brings to school. Some essentialists are rapidly incorporating new material from the psychology of learning and concept formation into their teaching methods.[39] The technology of teaching

38. John Gardner, "Goals for Education," in *Commission on National Goals, Goals for Americans*, Englewood Cliffs, N.J.: Prentice-Hall, 1961.
39. Jerome Bruner, *The Process of Education*, Cambridge: Harvard University Press, 1961. See also J. McV. Hunt, *Intelligence and Experience*, New York: Ronald, 1961.

has also been advancing. So-called teaching machines, or more accurately, programmed learning devices, the use of electronic computers for certain kinds of advanced problem solving, and the greater use of learning resources (such as motion pictures, slides, and other audio-visual materials) reflect ways in which some kinds of knowledge and information can be more easily transmitted.[40] Some essentialists like Woodring and Gardner look upon these technical tools as a great aid to education; others, like Conant, are less optimistic.

While not all essentialists agree on these new technologies, they are in basic agreement over the need for accelerating learning, particularly for gifted students. Their recommendations, some of which are already in practice in some schools, generally focus on the "ability grouping" plan. Some high schools, for example, provide college mathematics and science courses for their "fast learners." Foreign languages, formerly begun in secondary schools, are being taught in many elementary schools. Language laboratory facilities are being built. Some administrative changes are also being instituted by essentialists. Small secondary high schools which cannot provide adequate teaching staff and facilities are being reorganized so that comprehensive high schools covering larger districts can be established. Teachers, because of their important role in the learning process, are receiving particular attention.[41] Their competence is being improved with substantial grants provided by the National Defense Education Act in the fields of science, mathematics and foreign language. Educational television is being used with the idea that the services of highly competent instructors can be more efficiently diffused. Teaching assistants, with lower qualifications than professional teachers, are being hired to relieve instructors of some of the time-consuming clerical and nonacademic duties related to teaching. In this way the principal teacher can devote greater attention and time to the essential job of instruction.

THE FUTURE OF EDUCATION

With so many complex problems facing modern industrial society and so many of these problems impinging on educational institutions, it seems that the contemporary conception of pragmatism will eventually be recast into something that resembles essentialism. Most educational reformers already

40. Eugene Galanter (ed.), *Automatic Teaching: The State of the Art*, New York: Wiley, 1959. For a brief survey, see James Cass, "New Tools for Teaching," *Saturday Review* (February 18, 1961), pp. 60–61.
41. Paul Woodring, *New Directions in Teacher Education*, New York: Fund for the Advancement of Education, 1957.

have been able to institute some of their recommendations, especially in some of the larger metropolitan schools.[42]

There are, however, some persisting problems of education which do not directly enter into the pragmatism-essentialism controversy. One of these is the question of federal aid to education. The Democratic party has pledged in its platform to support a general program of federal grants to education. This position is also advocated by the National Congress of Parents and Teachers as well as various teachers' organizations. In general, the opposition comes from those who fear the growth of big government. Although such bills have been introduced, many Congressmen have thus far been reluctant to pass them because they are involved in another controversy of whether the aid should be extended to parochial schools. At this time, observers feel broad and extensive federal aid to education is not likely to pass Congress. But special federal grants for vocational education, for education related to national defense, and specialized needs of higher education will probably be continued.[43]

Another persisting problem of education concerns religion in the public schools.[44] This controversy appears in relation to federal aid for parochial schools, as just noted, but it has other aspects which will be discussed in the following chapter.

Finally, there is a growing controversy among teachers as to which kind of organization best represents their interests. As noted before, there are nearly two million school teachers and college professors. The two principal organizations — the National Education Association and the American Federation of Teachers — are competing for membership and support. The latter, a small organization, has been growing in large metropolitan areas where considerable teacher discontent is found. The controversy between these organizations, observers say, will become more bitter and spill over into more public issues. The New York teachers' strike of April 1962 illustrates this point. Though only 6 per cent voted for it, and though the strike was illegal, some 20,000 teachers out of 40,000 refused to cross the picket lines.[45] Such labor disputes may be expected to increase. Schools, like every organization in industrial

42. For example, Fred M. Hechinger, "Basic Reforms: Reading and Mathematics Changes Underline Grade School Trend," *The New York Times*, March 4, 1962, p. E-9. See also Martin Mayer, *The Schools*, New York: Harper, 1961; Richard P. Kleeman, "Five Years of Change," *Saturday Review* (March 18, 1961), pp. 50–51.

43. Bentley Glass, "The Academic Scientist," *Science*, 132 (September 2, 1960), pp. 598–603.

44. Donald E. Boles, *The Bible, Religion and the Public Schools*, Ames: Iowa State University Press, 1962; Don J. Hager, "New Problems in Intercultural Education," *Journal of Educational Sociology*, 30 (December 1956), pp. 166–67.

45. Paul Woodring, "The New York Teachers' Strike," *Saturday Review* (May 19, 1962), pp. 51–2; National Education Association, "NEA Reply to AFL-CIO Charge," *School and Society*, 59 (October 1957), p. 146.

societies, are undergoing bureaucratization. Teachers find themselves employees in large administrative units where status is accorded to those farthest removed from the teaching-learning process. This raises a problem of identity for teachers. Are they employees who need the "protection" of a labor union? Or are they "professionals" who find such unionization unnecessary?

The foregoing are some of the persisting controversies of modern education. They arise from time to time because the issues have been stalemated by opposing sides. This is not the case, however, with regard to the struggle between the followers of pragmatism and essentialism.[46]

The challenge to education in this modern industrial society is greater than in the past. Never has the population been so large and never has knowledge exploded so rapidly. If equality of educational opportunity is to be maintained and the quality improved, modern methods of instruction, new organization of schools, greater support of the schools by an informed public, and greater specification of essentials of education would seem mandatory.

SUMMARY

Looked at in its broadest implications, normative prescriptions for education in the past have evolved from classicism to pragmatism. The first focused on the preservation of the cultural heritage and the transmission of this legacy to succeeding generations. The other emphasized the need to reflect the contemporary culture and give the society what it currently seemed to want. With the growing complexity of modern technology and social institutions, and urgent need to maintain a viable nation in a world torn by conflict, the goals of education are being shaped into a new form: to train youth creatively so they can acquire the exploding knowledge with a minimum of friction and develop science and learning for the improvement of national welfare. This is to be accomplished, according to this emergent conception, by a clear definition of essential subjects to be taught, maximum encouragement to those with special academic ability, better preparation for teachers, more efficient use of the teacher's time, and a willingness to forgo programs that do not contribute substantially to intellectual development.

QUESTIONS AND SUGGESTIONS FOR FURTHER STUDY

1. Examine any history of a particular college or university. Have its goals and curriculum been influenced by significant events in American history?
2. Discuss among your friends what they think are the most important educational issues of the day. To what extent do their evaluations coincide with the normative conceptions given in this chapter?

46. Rockefeller Brothers Fund, *The Pursuit of Excellence: Education and the Future of America*, New York: Doubleday, 1958.

3. How would you explain the present concern about educational philosophy and aims?
4. To what extent has the federal government supported or influenced the teaching and research carried on in your college or university?
5. Why do most Americans value education highly and yet seemingly permit the continuation of shortages in classrooms and other educational resources?
6. What are the arguments for and against "mass education" at the college level?
7. Review in your mind three or four instructors you have had. See if you can fit their educational philosophy into one or another of the normative conceptions described in this chapter.
8. Interview an elementary or secondary school teacher to find out what recent changes in educational practices have been instituted in his school.

SUGGESTED READINGS

Barzun, Jacques, *Teacher in America*, New York: Anchor Books, 1954.   P
An insightful examination of teaching and learning in the classroom.

Berelson, Bernard, *Graduate Education in the United States*, New York: Mc-Graw Hill. A brilliant defense of graduate education, the result of a two-year study.

Bestor, Arthur E., *Educational Wastelands: The Retreat from Learning in Our Public Schools*, Urbana: University of Illinois Press, 1953. This book is an indictment of pragmatism by one of its most vocal and persistent critics.

Brameld, Theodore, *Education for the Emerging Age: Newer Ends and Stronger Means*, New York: Harper, 1961. Some interesting and valuable proposals for strengthening our schools.

Bruner, Jerome, *The Process of Education*, Cambridge: Harvard University Press, 1961. Bruner has been the leading exponent of the development of programmed learning based upon developing psychological theories.

Conant, James Bryant, *Slums and Suburbs*, New York: McGraw-Hill, 1961.
P   Conant describes the educational implications for metropolitan areas of the suburbanization movement described in Chapter 3. Increasing emphasis on the "gifted" may have serious consequences in ignoring the "culturally deprived" in the slums.

Conant, James Bryant, *The American High School Today*, New York: McGraw-Hill, 1959. A report that has influenced the present changes in the American high schools.

Dworkin, Martin S. (ed.), *Dewey on Education*, New York: Columbia Teachers College, 1959.   P   A worthwhile selection of John Dewey's contributions to education.

Gardner, John, *Excellence*, New York: Harper, 1961. This book typifies the growing emphasis upon seeking "excellence" in education. A careful and balanced criticism of existing practices.

Hodenfield, G. K., and T. M. Stinnett, *The Education of Teachers: Consensus and Conflict*, New York: Spectrum Books, 1962.   P

Peddiwell, J. Abner, *The Saber-Tooth Curriculum, A Satire on American Education*, New York: McGraw-Hill, 1939.   P   A hilarious examination of a serious topic; yet the message is not funny.

Rickover, H. G., *Education and Freedom*, New York: Dutton, 1959.   P   An outstanding critic of pragmatism explains why he favors essentialism.

Riesman, David, *Constraint and Variety in Education*, New York: Anchor Books, 1958.   P   A sociologist examines the cultural context of our schools and colleges.

Sanford, Nevitt (ed.), *The American College*, New York: Wiley, 1962. A comprehensive sociological and psychological analysis of higher education in the contemporary society. A monumental work.

Scott, Winfield C., Clyde M. Hill, and Hubert W. Burns, *The Great Debate: Our Schools in Crisis*, New York: Prentice-Hall, 1959. An anthology of criticisms of the schools that appeared in popular magazines between 1955 and 1959.

> . . . the immigrant was not expected to change his faith upon arrival in this country not because Americans were indifferent to religion or were committed to theological views which called for non-interference in religious matters, but because almost from the beginning, the structure of American society presupposed diversity and substantial equality of religious associations.

> . . . the Protestant pattern will in all probability continue to define the American religious pattern in general, to which American Catholic and Jew will increasingly conform, each in his own way and from his own direction.[1]

It is common to speak of three religions in American society — Catholicism, Protestantism, and Judaism. This is somewhat oversimplified since it excludes the Greek Orthodox, Mormons, Christian Scientists, and others who disclaim membership in any of the categories. It is also an oversimplification to imply that these three religious groups are unitary in their outlooks. Within each of the three, there is and has been normative dissensus as to what they should be or become. Within American Protestantism, the most dominant group numerically, there are over 250 denominations and sects. This diversity can be misleading, however, since 80 per cent of all American Protestants are included in the membership of thirteen denominations. In fact, in dealing with normative dissensus in Protestantism, the concern will be with differences which cut across Protestantism and not differences along denominational lines.

Protestantism, the dominant religious ideology of colonial America, maintained its dominance by adapting well to the moving western frontier and to an agrarian economy. With growing industrialization, the nation changed and Protestantism faced a very different America. With the development of science, new ideas challenged some traditional religious assumptions vital to the very existence of Protestantism. Its adaptations to the industrial and scientific world were not accomplished without normative confusion.

Catholicism and Judaism faced a different adaptation. Although both re-

1. Will Herberg, *Protestant-Catholic-Jew*, Garden City: Doubleday, 1956, pp. 40 and 240.

ligions were represented in America at the time of the Revolution, they have been considered "foreign" religions since their greatest growth occurred through great waves of immigration during the late nineteenth century and the early twentieth. They did not face the shift from rural to urban patterns since they were urban religions from the beginning. They did face, however, problems of reconciling certain conceptions about their religions with the existence of the already established pattern of separation of church and state and the implicit separation of the religious and the secular. The fact that, in contrast to Protestantism, one thinks of Catholicism and Judaism as being more unitary in outlook does not obviate the fact that within each of these religious traditions normative dissensus exists.

PROTESTANTISM

The normative problem: how should Protestantism adapt to an industrial society?

Protestantism was woven into the fabric of early American life. Although the various Protestant groups often had little in common except their opposition to established European churches, they held certain common attitudes, some of them stemming from the Reformation, others from their experience in America. This core of Protestantism was expressed in the following conception.

> *Historical Normative Conception: Traditional Protestantism* — Protestantism should accept the authority of the Bible and the necessity for individual salvation.[2]

Protestantism in America lost much of the imprint of its European origins early. In part, this happened because conditions in America allowed Protestant groups to achieve goals denied them in Europe. In the New World, a tradition developed in which the various churches were entirely on their own, free from governmental restriction or support. The American Revolution provided a barrier and a reason for cutting European ties. Religious groups were so diverse that no single group could gain power. Even though some churches had hoped for direct governmental support, even they altered this idea, either voluntarily or forcibly. Religion became a matter of conscience and decision. There were no territorial or state churches. Each church was a voluntary organization composed only of those who freely professed their faith. A person could, if he wished, change his faith. This Protestant principle, of course, fits well with emerging political democracy and emerging economic individualism.

---

2. This statement obviously oversimplifies the issue. The construction is stated in this fashion in order to sharpen the contrasts with modifications made in later conceptions.

While the separation of church and state was encouraged or at least accepted as the dominant normative pattern in the United States, this, in many respects, led to a serious weakening of Protestantism. For many, this separation meant that religion had no relevance for political institutions. Secularization was accentuated by the fact that education was becoming increasingly the province of the state and less a function of the churches. Actually, public education was encouraged by early Protestantism since it provided the individual believer with access to the source of spiritual strength, the Bible. Not only was there the feeling that the decisions of the faith have little relevance to political institutions, but also that faith had little relevance to economic decisions. Industrialization further contributed to this sense of irrelevance. The astounding miracles of production and technology led to reasonable hope that the Kingdom of God was close at hand. These miracles were man-made and, therefore, man could be master of his fate without dependence on divine assistance.

In effect, there came a sharp separation not only of church and state, but of the religious and the secular. Religious life was a thing apart from the decisions of the market place or the government or the school.

In the latter part of the nineteenth century, the progress of science — biology, anthropology, psychology, geology, and sociology — raised many questions about the traditional Christian world view, and of the Biblical account of the origin of the earth and of mankind. It is easy to see why Darwinism was the focus of controversy between science and religion. This theory seemed to conflict with the Protestant faith at a particularly vital spot — the Biblical story of creation. This theory detracted from the dignity of man as a special creation of God and, by setting back the date of the origin of mankind thousands of years, it led to doubts as to the crucial role of the Christian tradition in the history of man. In addition, this new view of the origin of man cast doubts on the Christian conception of man as a sinner and of the redeeming grace of God. Instead of considering man as "fallen in sin" in the orthodox sense, man could be viewed as actually having accomplished a great deal during his existence and, with industrialization and new scientific discoveries, man had the hope of even greater accomplishments. The success of the scientific method of acquiring knowledge suggested also that the means to all truth had been finally found and that religious truths would be made obsolescent by the new superior model of science.

This challenge of science to traditional religious conceptions and authority, and the growth of cities with their industrial plants and problems created new conditions for Protestantism to face. Protestantism had adapted well to the growing frontier, keeping up with people's movement by providing a circuit-riding ministry. The new cities, however, provided a contrast to the "naturalness" of rural life and a new set of social relationships difficult to understand in terms of individual morality. The reaction to these conditions in the last quarter of the nineteenth century and the first part of the twentieth century is called liberal Protestantism. This "reaction" was not universally accepted. Some disapproved and called for a return to "fundamentalism." Another segment of Protestantism claimed that liberal Protestantism oversimplified the task and had overlooked certain traditional Christian ideas that still had relevance — this segment of Protestantism is generally called neo-orthodoxy. To understand the reactions of fundamentalism and neo-orthodoxy, it is necessary to understand liberal Protestantism.

> *Contemporary Normative Conception: Liberal Protestantism* — Protestantism should accept science and remake the industrial world into the Kingdom of God.

While science and particularly Darwinism challenged Protestantism, there were already changes occurring within Protestant theology which allowed these scientific ideas to be absorbed and accepted. Biblical criticism was being accepted as a method and source of knowledge. Biblical criticism did not mean to attack or find fault with the Bible, but applied the methods of the literary expert toward an understanding of the meaning of the Bible. In Biblical criticism, one would raise such questions as — who wrote the books of the Bible? When? What were the relationships of the Biblical events to other accounts of ancient history? What were the historical circumstances and context of the various writings? For example, it was found that the Gospel of John was not as accurate an account of the life of Jesus as were the other three synoptics, but written later not so much as fact but as a theological interpretation. The acceptance of Biblical criticism meant the abandonment of the belief that the Bible was an infallible record of divine revelation to men. There was much of the Bible that was inspired, even divine, but there was much that was human and in error. It was a very human book including differing conceptions of God plus valuable historical documents, but it also included "fiction" such as legends and myths which contradicted each other and known historical events.

These newer views, stemming from Biblical criticism, were accepted by the major bodies of Protestantism and this made it possible to accept Darwinism and other scientific theories more easily. Evolution could be viewed as a process by which the creative ability of God was expressed. While the traditional idea of how God created the world had to be modified, this did not displace God as creator. The Bible, properly seen, was not a textbook in science; it was a text in religion. The science expressed in the Bible was the science of 2000 years before. The Genesis story of creation was not God's own description of the origins of man to be uncritically accepted, but it was to be understood as an explanation more in keeping with ancient Hebrew traditions and conceptions of that time period. God could still be viewed as working in and with such natural processes as evolution. God was still the source of all truth and nothing known by science could be in final contradiction to faith in God. Liberal Protestantism thus accepted the scientific method as the method of truth of the physical world and used the scientific method itself in Biblical criticism and in historical studies of religion.

Protestantism was not only making an adjustment to the impact of science, but also undergoing a change in its understanding of the role of the church in an industrial society. This movement, generally known as the Social Gospel, called for the reconstruction of society in terms of the ideal of the Kingdom of God. To understand this movement and its meaning, it is necessary to go back in Christian history. In medieval times the Christian could achieve salvation only by abjuring the world. He could, by removing himself from society, avoid the impurity of the world and escape to the purity of some monastic order, where he could contemplate God and live a simple austere life. Luther emphasized, however, that man could serve God in any situation in which he found himself. He did not have to retire to the monastery. Calvin gave this idea another dimension. The purpose of man in this world was to glorify God and he could do this in every aspect of life. While it was not Calvin's intent, these ideas meant that a person's economic activities in the world could be considered as religious as monastic service and thus were properly a field within which a person could fulfill his religious duties. One's economic success could be interpreted as religious virtue. One could work for God and get paid for it. This meant, of course, that one's religious demands and one's economic interests were one and the same. In this conception of salvation, Protestantism sanctioned almost all existing economic practices and interests.[3] Christian goals became identical with the goals of free enterprise. Protestantism made no criticism of the social order. It accepted the society as a positive good and Christian ethics were increasingly cast in individual moral terms of avoiding the excesses of the flesh, being honest and thrifty, reading the Bible, and keeping the Sabbath.

Other ideological movements noted this identification of Protestantism with the status quo. Marx, for example, suggested that "religion was the opiate of the people." But already within liberal Protestantism there were the beginnings of the Social Gospel. The emergence of the Social Gospel was

3. For a discussion of the relation of religious ideas to economic behavior, see Max Weber, *The Protestant Ethic and the Spirit of Capitalism*, New York: Scribners, 1960.

facilitated by the problems created by increasing industrialization, the rapidly growing cities, unemployment, labor management difficulties, and immigration. To those interested in the Social Gospel, it made little sense to talk about personal morality when individuals were being damaged by the economic system. Protestantism must not only talk about honesty, but it must also talk about justice for those who labor. There could be no divine sanction for an inequitable distribution of wealth nor should the poor accept meekly their lowly station in life. Neither could they accept the view that their interests would be protected by the Christian men who owned property. As the intellectual leader of the Social Gospel, Walter Rauschenbush, stated in 1892:

> My first proposition is that the whole aim of Christ is embraced in the words the "kingdom of God"; that this ideal is for this side of death, and not for the other side; that it is a social ideal and not an individualist idea; and that in the idea is embraced the sanctification of all life, the regeneration of humanity and the reformation of all social institutions.[4]

To Protestants interested in the Social Gospel, it made little sense for the church to save souls one by one when society was corrupting them by the thousands. Instead of recommending that Christians seek salvation outside the world, as the monastics did, or gain salvation in their daily routines, as Calvin did, the Social Gospelers saw their mission as the need to change the existing social order. Society must be remade after the pattern of the Kingdom of God as seen by the Hebrew prophets and as revealed by Jesus in the Sermon on the Mount. The social order could become an earthly kingdom of social justice, brotherhood, and democracy.

The Social Gospel considered society more sinful than man. Society, since it was the source of evil, must be changed. Man was essentially a creature of divine worth and dignity possessing intelligence and potential good will. He sinned, but was not inherently a sinner and he was capable of being perfected. Evil could be removed as society moved toward the Kingdom of God on earth. Man could realistically hope for this kingdom and could make it come closer to reality by turning his attention to "good works" in various areas of life. Religious motivation could be turned into social reform.

This shift in normative conception had a profound effect on American Protestantism. In 1908, the Federal Council of Churches of Christ in America was formed, in part, to provide an interdenominational agency for the expression of these liberalized conceptions of religion. In 1912, the Council published its social creed in which it supported the unionization of labor, shorter hours, and higher wages. Both the Council and individual denominations extended their social concerns to race relations, marriage and family,

4. Republished in *The City Church* (September–October 1956), p. 11.

international affairs, political action, and war. In addition, many traditional Protestant concerns which were once seen as purely individual matters, such as drinking, began to be viewed in terms of a social concern.

While the Social Gospel reached its peak immediately prior to World War I, the successful conclusion of that war, the prosperity of the 'twenties, and the reduction of some of the acute problems stemming from industrialization reduced its appeal. During the 'twenties also, it was caught in the battle with fundamentalism. But the determination of the Social Gospel to save the world and establish the Kingdom of God still showed itself in the attitudes many Protestants, particularly clergymen, took prior to World War II. They insisted that war solved nothing, particularly since it would not aid the establishment of the Kingdom of God. While pacifism had been a part of the Protestant tradition through historic peace churches such as the Quakers, many Social Gospelers viewed pacifism as part of a renunciation of a sinful, warlike world. They felt it possible to "convert" other nations — enemy nations — to the way of Christ by applying good will to all and by seeking negotiations among reasonable men. It was the sinfulness of societies which "created" war, and since men were basically good, reasonable men could sit down and solve their differences with Christian charity.

In these ways, then, Protestantism was remade and "liberalized." It made peace with science, accepting its findings and methods. While science might describe the process of evolution of man, God was not displaced as creator. Liberal Protestantism accepted Biblical criticism and abandoned the idea that the Bible was without error. It viewed science as an ally in the search for truth. Within Protestantism, the Social Gospel spread a new concern for the problems of people in society. It emphasized that Christians had a social responsibility and that Christian ethics could not deal solely with individual morality. The nature of moral life was seen to be dependent upon the social context in which Christians found themselves. Society did not have to be accepted as a given standard but could be changed, not by changing individuals, but by changing the society. In addition, the Social Gospel stressed a continuous concern for minority groups — immigrants, migrant laborers, and racial groups.

These ideas were generally accepted by major Protestant groups in the United States. The scientific revolution was, thus, a valuable ally of Protestantism and gave Protestants a concern for the problems emerging from the industrial revolution. These shifts did not occur without reaction nor without opposition. Fundamentalism claimed that liberal Protestantism had sold out to science. Neo-orthodoxy claimed that liberal Protestantism was too optimistic about the perfectibility of society. It is to these two reactions and criticisms of liberal Protestantism to which we now turn.

Contemporary Normative Conception: Fundamentalism —
Protestantism should reject science where it conflicts with a
literal interpretation of the Bible and should remake the industrial world by individual salvation.

Reaction to the liberalization of Protestantism was strong. Some individuals not only rejected scientific evidence, but rejected all religious scholarship using the scientific method. They felt that "saving souls" was the main
task of Protestantism, not concern with social problems. Both of these themes
are indicated by the attitude of Billy Sunday. Sunday's position in American
Protestantism was assessed by the *New York Times* as being "the greatest
high pressure and mass conversion evangel that America or the world has
known." [5] During his forty-year career, he held almost 300 revivals and, in
his twenty most successful revivals, almost 600,000 persons came forward to
shake his hand.[6]

Sunday dismissed the evolutionary concept of the importance of environment
upon human development with a simple, dogmatic denial: "I don't believe in the
bastard theory that men came from protoplasm by the fortuitous concurrence
of atoms." And he denounced the "higher critics" as "high-brows" who "dreamed
out" their theories about the historicity of Jesus and the existence of two Isaiahs
"over a pipe of tobacco and a mug of beer at Leipzig or Heidelberg. When the
word of God says one thing and scholarship says another, scholarship can go to
hell!" With evolutionists and Modernists thus conveniently ostracized from consideration by decent society, Sunday was free to apply the Mosaic laws to contemporary manners. Where he could not quote chapter and verse, he applied his
own small-town morality. . . .

In Sunday's mind the whole universal brotherhood and Social Gospel notion,
with its doctrine of "social service," was nothing more or less than socialism. The
fact that certain of the more liberal ministers like George Herron and Walter
Rauschenbusch actually praised socialism and spoke of their work as "Christian
Socialism" seemed to Sunday to prove his point though he was just as vehement
against men like Lyman Abbott and Washington Gladden who spoke merely of
"Christianizing the social order" and whose reform ideas were comparatively
mild. Sunday called Gladden "that bald-headed old mutt" and damned the whole
Social Gospel movement as sacrilegious, un-American quackery.

The view of postmillenialists like Gladden and Abbott that the church must
play a role in relieving the distress of the poor by undertaking "social service,"
and creating "institutional churches" with gymnasiums, dormitories, and educational classes was, declared Sunday, putting the cart before the horse: "It is an
entirely good and Christian thing to give a down-and-outer a bath, a bed, and a
job," he said, but "the road into the kingdom of God is not by the bathtub nor
the gymnasiums, nor the university, but by the blood red hand of the cross of
Christ." With an anti-intellectualism which was inherent in all his preaching,

5. *New York Times*, November 7, 1935, p. 1.
6. W. G. McLoughlin, Jr., *Modern Revivalism*, New York: Ronald, 1959, p. 415.

Sunday said: "Thousands of college graduates are going as fast as they can straight to hell. If I had a million dollars I'd give $999,999 to the church and $1 to education." The way to help the poor in the downtown slums was to convert them, not to educate them. "The trouble with the church, the YMCA, and the Young People's Societies is that they have taken up sociology and settlement work but are not winning souls to Christ." [7]

In the struggle between religion and science, some individuals gave up religion and others gave up science. This last reaction, in effect, was the position of those who have come to be known as fundamentalists. To meet the changes in liberal Protestantism and its acceptance of science, the fundamentalist moved back to the authority of the Bible as the revealed word of God. As a result of a number of Bible conferences among individuals dissatisfied with the "liberalization" of Protestantism, a series of volumes called *The Fundamentals* were published.[8]

These books emphasized five essential points considered necessary for Christian witness: (1) the infallibility of the Scriptures, (2) Christ's virgin birth, (3) the substitutionary atonement of Christ, (4) Christ's physical resurrection, and (5) his bodily return to earth. To fundamentalists, Biblical criticism was a denial of the uniqueness of Christianity. To admit that the Bible was the work of man was to admit that there is no universal truth. To deny the virgin birth denied the deity of Christ. His resurrection and return were other manifestations of this divinity. To deny that Christ died for the sins of man would mean that God could not forgive men without compromising Himself. Over two million copies of *The Fundamentals* were distributed in the United States during the 1910's and 1920's.

Within almost every Protestant denomination, the fundamentalists made a bid for control — to turn out the liberals and to re-establish the fundamentals. In particular, the fundamentalists concentrated on seminaries as hotbeds of liberalism and demanded that the liberals be dismissed from their responsible jobs. Many fundamentalists viewed any expression of liberal Protestantism as being "communistic, socialistic, and heretical." The fundamentalists did not succeed in gaining control of the major Protestant denominations in the 1920's. Instead of pushing the liberals out, they were pushed out themselves and the leading theological seminaries and larger Protestant denominations remained centers of liberalism. The fundamentalists, however, formed their own denominations, established their own Bible Schools to teach the "truth," and finally began to form their own co-operative organizations.

7. W. G. McLoughlin, Jr., *Billy Sunday Was His Real Name,* Chicago: University of Chicago Press, 1955, pp. 132, 137. Copyright 1955 by The University of Chicago.
8. *The Fundamentals: A Testimony to the Truth* (12 vols.) Chicago: Testimony Publishing Company, 1910–15.

In 1941, several groups split off from major denominations and organized the *American Council of Christian Churches* (ACCC), dedicating themselves to battling "soul-destroying modernism." Its leader and principal spokesman was and is Carl C. McIntire, pastor of the Bible Presbyterian Church in Collingswood, New Jersey. Expelled from the Presbyterian Church in the U.S.A., McIntire has taken the lead in branding the activities of the National Council of Churches, the center of liberalism, as being communistic and ungodly. This attitude is typified by the following statement of a southern evangelist:

The Federal [National] Council is a Goliath of Power, a wild Absalom of rebellion, a loathsome Judas of treachery, a deceiving Sapphira of falsehood, a cruel Ahab of covetousness, a bold Belshazzar of Irreverence, a merciless Nero of evil, a haughty Nebuchadnezzar of pride and a painted Jezebel of murder. . . . I ask you again, will we tolerate such? I say a thousand times, No, and again I say BY THE GRACE OF GOD, THEY SHALL BE EXTERMINATED! [9]

This group also looks at ecumenical attempts as simply compounding an initial error. Since 1948, they have attempted to hold their meetings at the same time and place that larger, ecumenical groups were meeting. Thus, they organized the International Council of Churches, which met in the same city a week before the first meeting of the World Council of Churches. These attempts seemingly are to create confusion.

McIntire, at a meeting in 1952, preceding a meeting of the National Council in Denver, complained that the Revised Standard Version of the Bible (sponsored by the National Council) was "the work of Satan and his agents." In particular, he objected to the substitution of the word "young woman" for "virgin" in Isaiah 7:14. This verse is often seen by fundamentalists as a prophecy of the virgin birth of Jesus. In addition to the "new" Bible, McIntire, of course, rejects the Social Gospel and insists that one must preach "Salvation, not Society; Redemption, not Reform."

The strength of the ACCC is not known. It has claimed as many as 18 denominations and 2 million members. Several of these denominations seemingly exist only on paper. McIntire's own group, the Bible Presbyterians, number about 8000. Two other groups, the Independent Fundamental Churches of America and the Regular Baptists, each claim over 50,000 members. Some individual churches within the General Association of Regular Baptists have become a part of the ACCC. It seems safe to say that the claim of 2 million members is highly exaggerated.

In McIntire's battle against liberals, he has enlisted the support of many religious malcontents. Many of them interpret it as their Christian duty to include anti-Semitism and anti-Catholicism, and they ally themselves with

9. Statement by J. Harold Smith appearing in the *Christian Beacon*, May 9, 1946.

politically "right" and racist groups, such as the John Birch Society and the Ku Klux Klan. These groups have been called "Apostles of Discord" with their "ministries of hate and disruption." [10] It is from these associations and, because of McIntire's own excesses, that other fundamentalist organizations have emerged.

The *National Association for Evangelicals* (NAE) was formed in 1942 in an attempt to provide co-operative expression to groups who could not accept existing co-operative organizations such as the National Council of Churches or the American Council. Of the more than 250 denominations, only 25 have accepted membership in the National Council. Although these 25 denominations included 30 million members, the NAE hoped to be able to speak for the remaining 25 million Protestants and also to speak for many others within denominations affiliated with the National Council. Because the fanaticism of much earlier fundamentalism had been toned down, the NAE attracted the more "respectable" fundamentalists. Instead of attacking the National Council or withdrawing from established groups, they hoped to reform from within. The NAE, however, does not ignore the National Council since one of their spokesmen declared "it is almost implicit that the National Council carries a soft spot for Communism. For even while they deny it, as they must in these days, their socialistic proclivities make them inescapably akin." [11]

In the attack on liberalism, they have found it useful to drop the emotional label of "fundamentalism" and replace it with the term "evangelical." These "evangelicals" seek to be less dogmatic and less anti-intellectual than other fundamentalists. This is indicated by a statement that:

> It is important to insist that obscurantism in all its forms is wholly out of keeping with true Evangelicalism. The Evangelical is not afraid of facts, for he knows that all facts are God's facts; nor is he afraid of thinking, for he knows that all truth is God's truth, and right reason cannot endanger sound faith . . . It is not his business to argue men into faith, for that cannot be done; but it is his business to demonstrate the intellectual adequacy of the biblical faith and the comparative inadequacy of its rivals, and to show the invalidity of the criticisms that are brought against it. [12]

While they emphasize an intellectual tradition, they do not have a high opinion of American higher education. The editor of one of their magazines said: "Today on the great American campuses, Biblical religion is engaged in a constant struggle for survival." Evangelicals should "adopt a new strategy

---

10. Ralph Lord Roy, *Apostles of Discord*, Boston: Beacon Press, 1953.
11. *Newsweek* (April 28, 1958), p. 58.
12. J. I. Packer, *"Fundamentalism" and the Word of God*, London: Inter-Varsity Fellowship, 1958, p. 34.

in academic affairs . . . to challenge the citadels of modern unbelief." [13]
Evangelicals frequently support their own colleges and seminaries, of which
Fuller and Westminster are the better known. Occasionally, an evangelical
will attend a liberal theological school as a means of gathering material for
continuing his theological arguments against liberalism.

The NAE claims to speak for 30 denominations with a membership of one
million and claims to speak for some 10 million other Protestants. Among
the largest of these denominations are the Assemblies of God, the Church
of God (Cleveland, Tenn.), National Association of Free Will Baptists,
International Church of the Foursquare Gospel, Free Methodist Church of
North America, and the Pentecostal Holiness Church. In speaking of the organization and development of the NAE, McLoughlin suggests:

> The time was ripe for this consolidation among the moderate fundamentalists.
> The "ultra-fundamentalists," represented by McIntire, had been discredited by
> twenty years of bluster and bombast. Modernism was undergoing a sharp reorienta-
> tion under the influence of the neo-orthodox movement. The social gospelers
> (among whom were many of Niebuhr's followers), having achieved many of their
> goals through the New Deal, were facing a ground swell of theological and politi-
> cal conservatism which reached a climax during the furor over McCarthyism and
> the presidential election of 1952. But most important, the steady growth of a
> network of fundamentalist schools, publishing houses, journals, radio stations, Bible
> conferences, missionary alliances, and interchurch evangelistic activities of all
> sorts over the years had at last provided the institutional basis upon which a
> united, militant, and prosperous new fundamentalist crusade could be con-
> structed.[14]

The NAE supported another movement to organize fundamentalists. This
was the Youth for Christ movement. This movement attempted to win young
people from the older denominations and their youth groups. Youth for
Christ organized flashy rallies in large auditoriums and emphasized "lively"
musical programs. In general, it was fundamentalism tailored to adolescent
needs.

Billy Graham, the most widely publicized current revivalist, came from an
"evangelical" family background, was educated in "evangelical" schools (Bob
Jones College and Wheaton College), was a "field representative" for Youth
for Christ, and received his primary support from members of the NAE.
Graham tries to avoid the label "fundamentalist" primarily because of its
negative connotations, but his intellectual position is clearly indicated by a
quoted statement in Look Magazine. He said: "If by fundamentalist you

13. Newsweek (April 20, 1959).
14. W. G. McLoughlin, Jr., Modern Revivalism, New York: Ronald, 1959, p. 476. Copyright 1959 by The Ronald Press Company.

mean 'narrow,' 'bigoted,' 'prejudiced,' 'extremist,' 'emotional,' 'snake handler,' 'without social conscience' — then I am definitely not a fundamentalist. However, if by fundamentalist you mean a person who accepts the authority of the Scriptures, the virgin birth of Christ, the atoning death of Christ, His bodily resurrection, His second coming and personal salvation through grace, then I am a fundamentalist. However, I much prefer being called a 'Christian.' " [15] This is, of course, a reiteration of the five fundamentals stated in 1912. That Graham follows the tradition against which the Social Gospel rose is seen in his insistence that all problems — race, war, or labor trouble — would disappear if individuals were converted to Christ. While he does not attack the National Council of Churches, he does not praise it. He does not attack scientific knowledge nor does he use it. He is concerned with personal salvation. Recently, however, Graham has been criticized by some fundamentalists as being too "liberal." [16]

While the ACCC and the NAE represent different brands of fundamentalism, they are united on the five fundamentals. They want to reduce Protestantism to an orthodoxy in a world changed by science and industrialization. They are, in large part, representative of a general resistance to change and an attempt to preserve religious certainty through this change. Part of their appeal is to the uneducated, unacquainted with science, so that lack of knowledge is made a virtue. Part of their appeal is to rural people in the cities, experiencing a dramatic change of social worlds and needing stability. Seemingly there are enough people in an industrial society to make fundamentalism attractive. Their simple rules of personal and social salvation offer an easy solution to complex problems.

Fundamentalism is not dead within the major Protestant denominations. Disputes over doctrines relating to the "fundamentals" are aired in denominational meetings. "Heresy" trials are infrequent but they do occur. More frequently, charges of "liberalism" are made and the various official religious groups listen and then vote down the charges. When a former editor of *The Christian Century* resigned to accept the presidency of a theological school of the United Presbyterian Church, for example, his appointment was challenged because he had once written an editorial declaring that the virgin birth was not an important doctrine. After some discussion, the Assembly confirmed his appointment.[17]

In 1962, in response to "dangerous" Biblical criticism in some of their seminaries, the Southern Baptist Convention passed two resolutions. One of these reaffirmed the faith of the church in the "*entire* Bible as the authori-

---

15. *Look* (February 7, 1956).
16. For documentation of Graham's social and political views, see McLoughlin, *Modern Revivalism*, op. cit. pp. 505–12.
17. *The New York Times*, May 23, 1959.

tative, authentic, infallible word of God" and the other ordered trustees and officials of seminaries to waste no time in stamping out "theological views which would undermine faith in the historical accuracy and doctrinal integrity of the Bible." The resolutions were not without their critics. One minister commented that this would make the church "the laughing stock of the Christian world." [18] While fundamentalism remains critical of the dominant trends in liberal Protestantism, another movement also critical of liberalism has emerged. It is generally referred to as neo-orthodoxy.

> *Emergent Normative Conception: Neo-Orthodoxy* — Protestantism should accept science, but in remaking the industrial world, the sinful nature of man obstructs utopian social reconstruction.

Like fundamentalism, neo-orthodoxy is a reaction against liberalism. But its reaction is not an attempt, as fundamentalism's was, to keep Protestantism faithful to precepts of the seventeenth and eighteenth century. It attempts to go beyond liberalism. Neo-orthodoxy holds that contemporary Protestantism's task is to understand the tragedy and misery of man and the disorder and conflict in society. The neo-orthodox feel that the rise of fascism and communism, and the occurrence of the Second World War shattered the liberal's hope of the establishment of the Kingdom of God on earth. As early as 1934, Reinhold Niebuhr suggested that:

The liberal culture of modernity is defective in both religious profundity and political sagacity . . . [It] understands neither the heights to which life may rise nor the depths to which it might sink . . . It is quite unable to give guidance to a confused generation which faces the disintegration of a social system and the task of building a new one.[19]

Biblical criticism has shown that religious knowledge, like all knowledge, is conditioned by the times. Since the roots of liberal Protestantism lay in the optimism of the late nineteenth and early twentieth centuries, the liberals' answers are not the answers needed for the tragedies of mid-twentieth century. Neo-orthodoxy points out that the Social Gospel, patterned after the Sermon on the Mount, was much more applicable to the simple society in which Jesus lived than to the complexities of modern industrial society. While it is relatively easy to love a long-time neighbor, it is more difficult to love a whole nation in another part of the world, particularly when national and economic barriers intrude. Neo-orthodoxy is thus critical of establishing the

18. *Time* (June 15, 1962).
19. Reinhold Niebuhr, *Reflections of the End of an Era*, New York: Scribner, 1934, pp. ix, 14.

Kingdom of God on earth. Part of the difficulty lies in the fact that man is a sinner. Sin, however, is not interpreted as succumbing to the evils of the flesh, as emphasized by fundamentalists, nor is sin located in corrupt social institutions, as seen in the Social Gospel. Sin to neo-orthodoxy is egocentrism, because the individual puts his own will ahead of God's. Sin is the opposite of love. In this conception, sin is universal since no aspect of life, even religion, is free from pride and self-centeredness. Neo-orthodoxy claims liberals overlook the fact that the social institutions they attacked were being maintained by "sinful" individuals. Even if liberals could change institutions, sinful people would create other evils. In this conception of sin, both science and fundamentalism are self-righteous and self-deifying. The same is true of nations. This does not mean that men have no good in them, but the standard against which they are judged is Jesus.

While this conception of sin shook the Social Gospel's ideas of building a Kingdom of God, it does not mean a return to the fundamentalist gospel of individual salvation. Some neo-orthodox theologians have effectively advocated continuation of the emphasis of the Social Gospel, but they suggest that "perfection" cannot be hoped for. No institution can be free from sin, and, therefore, utopian attempts at social reconstruction are naïve. Alleged solutions to societal ills simply transfer power, with its potential for good and evil, to certain groups — capital, labor, government, or religion. This is expressed in a statement issued by the First World Council of Churches meeting in Amsterdam in 1948:

> The Christian churches should reject the ideologies of both communism and laissez-faire capitalism and should seek to draw men away from the false assumptions that these extremes are the only alternatives. Each has made promises which it could not redeem. Communist ideology puts the emphasis upon economic justice, and promises that freedom will come automatically after the completion of the revolution. Capitalism puts the emphasis upon freedom, and promises that justice will follow as a by-product of free enterprise; that, too, is an ideology which has been proved false. It is the responsibility of Christians to seek new, creative solutions which never allow either justice or freedom to destroy the other.[20]

Neo-orthodoxy views the duty of the church as continually to confront society with "the law of love" while working toward more just relations between men. The depth and power of evil in man, however, require a more sober estimate than Christian Liberals gave of the possibilities for a just social order. Christians should not expect the Kingdom of God to be realized on earth.

Neo-orthodoxy suggests that social situations confront man with mixtures of good and evil, in which no position is completely correct or morally abso-

20. *Man's Disorder and God's Design*, New York: Harper, 1949, p. 195.

lute. Confronted with the rise of dictatorship, was the only alternative to turn the other cheek? Liberals often implied that it was. In this and other situations, the neo-orthodox suggested that the only alternative may be to compromise with evil and then find some way to compensate for the evil done. Neo-orthodoxy tried to temper the optimism of the Social Gospel by drawing attention to the reality of man's evil and sin. While this conception is pessimistic in its outlook for reform, it bases its hope on the activity of Christian love in situations that appear otherwise hopeless.

Although very complex, neo-orthodoxy is presented here primarily as a reaction against the optimism of the Social Gospel. Neo-orthodoxy reintroduced certain traditional Protestant conceptions such as sin, but this does not mean the neo-orthodox agree with fundamentalists. Neo-orthodoxy accepted Biblical criticism and the theory of evolution. It saw science as a valid attempt to understand the nature of man and the physical world but inserted the qualification that man's understanding is always limited by his finite nature. Neo-orthodoxy rejected the Social Gospel not because of its intent but because of its method. The method was naïve, lacked understanding of human nature, and, therefore, was doomed to fail. The fundamentalists' solution to social problems through personal conversion was just as naïve since it promised complete salvation and a freedom from future temptation which was illusory.

It is difficult to assess the impact of neo-orthodoxy on American Protestantism. Like the earlier liberals, those who accept neo-orthodoxy are found in major denominations and seminaries. In fact, many of the liberals of yesterday are the neo-orthodox leaders of today. An example is Reinhold Niebuhr, perhaps the most widely known theologian in America. Neo-orthodoxy is strongest in the more prominent seminaries such as Union, Chicago, Harvard, and Yale. These institutions, in turn, produce teachers for denominational schools. This does not mean that there has been a conscious attempt to "infiltrate" the seminaries as the fundamentalists did in the 1920's. It only indicates the natural evolution of ideas and the continual remaking of Protestantism to meet new and changing conditions. Conflict between neo-orthodoxy and liberalism is not group conflict, for there are no neo-orthodox churches as there are fundamentalist churches. The "conflict" has been over ideas about the nature of Protestantism. Whether neo-orthodoxy with its pessimistic outlook will ever characterize the beliefs of the large body of Protestant laymen is a question which cannot now be answered.[21]

21. This treatment oversimplifies the complexity of Protestantism. Ignored here are an existentialist emphasis found in theologians such as Paul Tillich and a more recent modification of liberalism, sometimes called neo-liberalism, which represents an attempt of liberals to take into account some neo-orthodox criticisms.

THE NON-PROTESTANT RELIGIONS

The problems of Judaism and Catholicism rest in large part on the fact that they exist in a society structured around Protestant norms. The priority and predominance of Protestantism created problems of adjustments for both religious groups. It was this Protestant background, rather than the immediate impact of industrialization, that called for adjustment. For Protestantism, religious belief was a matter of free choice and was symbolized by the conversion experience. Religious truth was not tied to the dogma of a particular church nor was it identified with any group of people. American society had come to see itself as being a religiously plural society where religious groups competed for the allegiances of the population with their versions of religious truth. It was to this type of society that the non-Protestant religions had to adapt. Further elaboration of this adaptation is discussed in reference to ethnic minorities in Chapter 12.

JUDAISM

The normative problem: how should Judaism adapt to a religiously plural society?

From both the historical experience recorded in the Old Testament and the subsequent experience of isolation created by persecution, a historical normative conception developed among Jews.

> *Historical Normative Conception: Traditional Judaism* — Judaism represents the religious experience of the Jewish people.

Judaism presents a paradox, for "Jew" refers to both a religion and a people. The interplay between these two conceptions provides the focus of normative dissensus within American Judaism. While many of the Protestant groups who came to America tied religion and nationality together, none of these Protestant groups felt the connection between "nationality" and religion as intensely as the Jews. Over several generations the Protestant groups with unique national heritages dropped the national touch from their religious ceremonies. Abandoning the cultural uniqueness of Judaism, however, became a religious issue since "foreignness" could not be given up without modifying the religion.

The Old Testament is the history of the Jews as a people and a large part of contemporary Judaism celebrates this history. Many traits derived from group living have become religious customs. In fact, Judaism is less a doctrine than it is a system of practices and customs. In this respect, it differs significantly from both Protestantism and Catholicism.

Christianity broke away from Judaism, and in so doing "modernized" and "westernized" many Jewish practices. Certain practices such as the segregation of the sexes during worship seemed "out of date" when they were reintroduced into America by Judaism. Further, Jews did not distinguish between the religious and secular spheres of life as did Protestantism. The traditional legal system of Judaism still regulated many areas of life, such as clothing and diet. Judaism, then, with its historical continuity, presented a dramatic contrast to the Christian religions. The tension between the Jews as a people with a unique cultural tradition and Judaism as a religion has been resolved in three different ways on the American scene.

Contemporary Normative Conception: Reform Judaism —
Judaism is a religion, one among many in America.

While Jews came to America as early as 1654, early immigration was slow, spasmodic, and slight. By 1840, it was estimated that there were only 15,000 Jews in America. Starting about 1836, there was a mass migration of German Jews to the United States, and by 1880, it was estimated that there were 250,000 here. These Jews found it easier to divorce the idea of Jews as a people from Judaism as a religion than did many of the Jews who came later. Most of these immigrants had been minor merchants in Germany. Since they had few ties in America and little money, many began to move West along with other pioneers. Many of them established small stores in the new towns. Since there were few established Jewish communities to absorb them, their settling across the face of America gave them little reason to retain their "old" ways. When these immigrants left Germany, an attack on traditional Judaism had already begun and attempts were being made to adapt it to a more modern form. Biblical criticism had tended to undercut the traditional basis of Jewish authority. The Talmud and many traditional Jewish laws and customs were being dropped.

These trends were further elaborated on the American scene by what is called Reform Judaism. The elements which marked Jews as a "peculiar" people in the new environment were singled out to be changed. The adaptation of Reform Judaism to American society is seen clearly in a declaration of principles adopted by a group of Reform Rabbis in 1885. They declared:

Third — We recognize in the Mosaic legislation a system of training the Jewish people for its mission during its national life in Palestine, and today we accept as binding only its moral laws and maintain only such ceremonials as elevate and sanctify our lives, but reject all such as are not adapted to the views and habits of modern civilization.

Fourth — We hold that all such Mosaic and Rabbinical laws as regulate diet, priestly purity and dress originated in ages and under the influence of ideas altogether foreign to our present mental and spiritual state. They fail to impress the modern Jew with a spirit of priestly holiness; their observance in our day is apt rather to obstruct than to further modern spiritual elevation.

Fifth — We recognize in the modern era of universal culture of heart and intellect the approach of the realization of Israel's great Messianic hope for the establishment of the Kingdom of truth, justice and peace among all men. We consider ourselves no longer a nation but a religious community, and therefore expect neither a return to Palestine, nor a sacrificial worship under the administration of the sons of Aaron, nor the restoration of any of the laws concerning the Jewish state.

Sixth — We recognize in Judaism a progressive religion, ever striving to be in accord with the postulates of reason. We are convinced of the utmost necessity of preserving the historical identity with our great past, Christianity and Islam being daughter religions of Judaism, we appreciate their mission to aid in the spreading of monotheistic and moral truth. We acknowledge that the spirit of broad humanity of our age is our ally in the fulfillment of our mission, and therefore we extend the hand of fellowship to all who co-operate with us in the establishment of the reign of truth and righteousness among men.[22]

Reform Judaism moved toward Protestantism. By dropping many traditional practices and ideas which they felt to be "un-American" in nature, Jews found themselves more acceptable in the non-Jewish world. Accordingly, Reform Judaism rejected the historic goal of the establishment of a separate Jewish nation — Zion — where Jews could worship and live in peace. Reform Judaism had found its Zion in America. By becoming Americanized, Jews could retain their religion in a country allowing individuals to worship as they please. At least, it would allow a group to worship as it pleased if its religious forms were not too different. Reform Judaism, in many respects, had become one of the many denominations in America.

Contemporary Normative Conception: Orthodox Judaism — Judaism is more than a religion, it is a unique cultural tradition.

While German Jews who created Reform Judaism felt that their peculiar customs were all that was standing in the way of their acceptance into American society, the Eastern European Jews, who provided the basis of Orthodoxy, did not assimilate as rapidly. Their motive for coming to the United States was more frequently escape from persecution rather than the hope of economic fortune. They came from towns in Russia and other Eastern European countries which had been primarily Jewish. Within these towns, they had developed their own distinctive customs unaffected by the larger society around them. They came to America after the expansion of the West was slowing down. Since cities were growing, they tended to stay in the cities and

22. *Yearbook of the Central Conference of America Rabbis* XLV (1935), pp. 198–200.

not to spread out as the German Jews had done earlier. With their earlier enforced isolation in Eastern Europe, religion was embedded in the total fabric of their social life and could not be dropped easily in response to a request to "Americanize." They could also resist more easily because they tended to settle in ethnic enclaves.

The enforced isolation in Eastern Europe had cut off avenues of social mobility for these Jews and kept them primarily in positions as employees. Consequently, many of them became interested in political and economic movements as a means of improving their rather tenuous social position. They were often more interested in unionism and political movements as suitable outlets for their aspirations than they were in religion.

Reform Judaism, however, did not appeal either to religious Jews or to the politically and economically oriented Jews who came to America. To the religious-minded, Reform Jews were too much like Gentiles. To the politically and economically oriented, the financial success of Reform Jews made for increased social distance. To Reform Jews, these new immigrants represented everything Reform Judaism had tried to avoid, and their presence might destroy everything that Reform had accomplished.

These Eastern Europeans became numerically the largest Jewish group in America and the core of Orthodox Judaism.

Between 1880 and 1920, American Jewry was completely transformed. In 1880, they numbered about 250,000, approximately one-half of one per cent of the total population . . . In 1920, about 3,500,000 of the 106,000,000 inhabitants of the United States were Jews — nearly 3½ per cent of the population. Moreover, in 1880 the relatively small number of Jews blended with the American environment. They were members of the respectable middle class, not too concentrated in any particular locality, and at home in the language and mores of the country. However, during the last two decades, and especially after the turn of the century, as the flood of east-European immigration continued, the mass of American Jewry became conspicuous as an immigrant element. In several large cities, they lived huddled together in "ghettos," spoke their own tongue and perpetuated customs and ideas which appeared alien to many of their co-religionists . . .[23]

Orthodox Judaism rejected the path taken by Reform and attempted to retain the image of Jews as a separate people. Residentially isolated in cities, they continued to speak Yiddish, developed separate community institutions, imported traditional religious scholars from Europe, and maintained traditional ideas about establishing a Jewish state. The memory of their past was not dispelled by the novelty of their new home. Judaism was not just another religion among the many in America but it was the organizing focus for the Orthodox Jews. Judaism was different from other American religions. This

23. Oscar I. Janowsky, *The JWB Survey*, New York: Dial Press, 1948, p. 239.

difference did not merely include religious ideas and practices, but it was a religion encompassing their total life activities.

Orthodoxy did not go unchallenged among the second generation, whose memories did not reach back to the problems faced in Eastern Europe. Those ties became less important as new generations came along. World War I and, more importantly, new immigration laws reduced the flow of immigrants from Eastern Europe. In time, there was movement out of the original settlements in the cities. This movement weakened religious sentiments since geographical mobility was often tied to social mobility. Economic opportunities were available in a growing industrial America. Resentment against the attempt of Orthodoxy to make Judaism a distinctive cultural tradition appeared. This resentment, coupled with discontent among other Jews with what they considered the excesses of Reform, gave impetus to another compromise between Judaism as one religion among many and Judaism as a distinctive cultural tradition.

> *Contemporary Normative Conception: Conservative Judaism*
> — The uniqueness of Judaism can be maintained through perpetuating distinctive religious differences.

Just as Reform had appealed to the German Jews earlier, Conservative Judaism offered a compromise more acceptable to second- and third-generation Eastern European Jews. To its adherents, Conservatism combined the best of Reform and Orthodoxy but avoided their excesses.[24]

Conservatism accepted many of the "modern" practices pioneered by Reform while it retained traditional content in its religious services. For example, Conservatism rejected the segregation of the sexes practiced by Orthodoxy and allowed women to participate in services. In addition, certain types of communal fund raising were eliminated or reduced during religious services and, in general, a greater distinction made between secular and sacred areas of life. The religious service, in contrast to that of Orthodoxy, became more conventionalized, dignified, and formal.

On the other hand, Conservatism retained or revitalized many Orthodox ideas. Certain traditional forms of worship were used and, while in most instances English was used, Hebrew was reintroduced for certain rituals. Religious education became an integral part of Conservatism and emphasized learning Hebrew. Many dietary laws rejected by Reform were retained, but often a distinction was made between keeping a kosher home and "eating outside" when these laws were not observed. Conservatism also took an active

---

24. To use a Protestant parallel, Orthodoxy would represent fundamentalism. Reform would represent liberalism, while Conservatism would represent neo-orthodoxy.

interest in Zionism, stressing the common interest of Jews regardless of their present status. All of these factors tended to emphasize Judaism as a people with a unique cultural tradition.

Conservatism, then, represents a compromise between Judaism as a religion and Judaism as a distinct cultural tradition. By re-emphasizing many traits dropped by Reform but by rejecting many of the "foreign" elements of Orthodoxy, Conservatism created a new synthesis. Ethnic differences have been reduced in American society and every new immigrant group has felt pressure to "rid" itself of these elements of distinctiveness. On the other hand, religious differences could remain since, in America, it was every man's prerogative to worship as he pleased. Many immigrants, in the initial insecurities of transplantation, dropped their religious affiliations and many immigrant groups made religious modifications stemming from their fear of rejection. Conservatism, in one sense, tries to perpetuate ethnic differences through religious differences. By centering Jewish life in the synagogue and elaborating traditional themes there, Conservative Jews have attempted to maintain a distinctive cultural-religious tradition but, like Reform, they have yielded in areas where their adjustment to the new society was most difficult. Thus Conservative Judaism is more than a religion but less than a cultural group with a really distinctive tradition.[25] It has a position similar to that which Catholicism has sought in American society, as being more than another religious group in a secular society.

CATHOLICISM

The normative problem: how should Catholicism adapt to a religiously plural society?

The problem for Catholicism was somewhat similar to that of Judaism. While Protestantism has claimed that Christ is the only true road to salvation and Judaism that it was the true way for Jews, Catholicism emphasizes another conception.

> *Historical Normative Conception: Traditional Catholicism —*
> The Catholic Church is the *one* true Church.

The Catholic Church claims to be the only institution with knowledge of religious and moral law. Christ is the bridge between God and man. The Biblical phrase "Thou art Peter and, upon this rock, I will build my church"

25. Ignored here is the Reconstructionist movement founded by Mordecai Kaplan. Kaplan argued that Judaism was not a religion but a religious civilization. While rejecting his reasons, Conservativism has accepted many of his suggested practices.

is interpreted as singling out an individual to establish spiritual power in the world, and this power is carried on through the papacy.

In early America, Catholicism found other authorities already established. Certain Protestant churches, notably Anglican and Congregational, received support from various state governments. In part, the First Amendment, which stated that "Congress shall make no law respecting the establishment of religion," eliminated the advantages of these Protestant groups. What role, then, should Catholicism, as the one true Church, play in a society where other religious groups were numerically superior and generally looked upon with more favor?

Ethnic factors complicated the issue. Colonial Catholicism was English with a clergy that was predominately French, so from the beginning in America Catholicism had a foreign taint. During the early nineteenth century, when Protestantism was making its greatest gains, Catholicism was struggling to exist but, like Judaism, it became revitalized through immigration. The struggle to exist as a minority religion left it little opportunity for concern with doctrinal issues of the one true Church. The type of immigrants who came before the Civil War, however, helped Catholicism partly to overcome its minority position and its "foreign" stamp. Between 1820 and 1865, almost 2 million Irish came to America, almost all of them Catholics. Because of their cultural and linguistic similarity to the American population, the Irish were one of the few immigrant groups who could assimilate easily. But these immigrants were poverty-stricken, ignorant, and of peasant origin as well as Catholic. Their poverty forced them to seek housing in slum areas, while their ignorance and lack of urban skills kept them at low economic levels. Hostility was directed toward the Irish and this hostility was transferred to the Catholicism linked with their low status. Anti-Catholicism developed and Protestants looked upon the Irish as potential converts to be freed from Catholicism. Many Catholics who attended public schools became critical of many aspects of Protestantism which had become part of public education — prayers and hymns, with readings from the King James version of the Bible. Catholic objections to these practices, which were justified in view of a consistent "separation of church and state," [26] intensified Protestant hostility toward these newcomers.

Gradually, Irish Catholics began to move into the American priesthood. Irish Catholicism became more "Americanized" and was better able to cushion the impact of later waves of immigration from countries with less cultural similarity. Catholicism did allow certain Catholic churches to cater to particular immigrant groups, however. These "national" parishes with "native"

26. Today, it is also ironic that Catholics object because public schools are secular since their objections to existing Protestant religious practices helped create the "secularism."

priests were the attempt of the church to meet the varied needs of its members. Thus a particular church might draw all Poles, have a priest trained in Poland, use Polish in the sermon, and celebrate certain saints' days that were particularly venerated by Polish people. In that way, the continuity of religious and cultural experiences was emphasized much as it had been in Orthodox Judaism. But in the process of adaptation to American society, another normative conception of Catholicism had begun to emerge. Instead of a minority religion fighting a battle of acceptance, Catholicism had become an integral part of the American religious scene.

Contemporary Normative Conception: Modern Catholicism
— The Catholic Church is one of the three American religions.

Sociologically, Catholicism has become one of the three religions of American society. The stigma of foreignness gradually has been lifted from Catholicism and it has achieved a position of implied equality on the American scene. In part, this was a result of the assimilation of the various waves of immigration which provided its numerical growth. Historically, to be a Protestant was to be an American and to be a Catholic was to be foreign, but, by a process of assimilation, both Catholicism and Judaism became respectable and achieved a degree of equivalence. The equivalence is manifest in various public and semi-public affairs where a minister, a priest and a rabbi are assembled and given "equal time." Another sign of equivalence is seen in the election of John F. Kennedy to the Presidency of the United States. His campaigns stressed the fact that his being a Catholic did not disqualify him for the highest office in the society. While some voters were not convinced, a sufficient number of them accepted the fact that being a non-Protestant was not automatic disqualification.

Throughout this period of growing equivalence Catholics have worked toward a redefinition of the doctrine of the one true Church. Contemporary Catholic theologians suggest that, historically, this doctrine has been misunderstood. The doctrine, derived from St. Augustine, is that the Church is Catholic and One. The word "One" was intended to stress the unity of the Church but it has often been used in the exclusive sense of "only." The word "Catholic" was intended to stress the universality of the Church, not to identify the true Church by name. Thus the intent of the doctrine was to emphasize the unity of the Church amidst the diversities of different historical periods and of different and complex societies and the universality of a church able to incorporate all into its unity.

Non-Catholics have often felt that this theological doctrine has been used to demand that Catholicism be recognized as the religion of the state. They cite evidence drawn from history and from contemporary societies where Catholicism has been the dominant force. Catholics emphasize, however, that the American situation is unique and that one cannot generalize from the Church's behavior in other periods and in other societies. They add that in America the state historically has had no anti-religious bias and that the Church has enjoyed greater freedom for its activities here than in other supposedly Catholic societies. Because of this experience, the Church has no desire to use the state to enforce its religious decisions. Catholicism thus accepts its place as one of the three religions in the United States. This acceptance does not imply to the Catholic, anymore than it does to other religious groups, that all religions are equally true, Catholics still claim religious truth for their faith, but religious liberty for the Catholic depends on protecting persons who are in error, i.e. those with other religious beliefs. Too, Catholics would not attempt to coerce others into accepting this truth since such intolerance violates the judgments of God. This adaptation of Catholicism to a pluralistic society has not been without strain. Dissensus on the limits of religious authority has occurred not only within religious groups but among religious groups. It is to this discussion which we turn.

INTERFAITH DISSENSUS — THE LIMITS OF RELIGIOUS AUTHORITY
Religious groups exercise authority over their members. Societies, through the state, exercise authority over their citizens. These authorities, historically and currently, have often conflicted, creating a normative problem for society.

The normative problem: what are the limits of religious authority in a religiously plural society?

Every industrial society has developed some normative solution to this problem. The overlap of religious and secular authority necessitates drawing limits. Since there are competing religious authorities in American society, drawing limits becomes complicated since there is dissensus *among* as well as *within* the three major religious groups. Catholicism, however, tends to be at the center of controversy for several reasons. It encompasses a much broader area of behavior subject to religious authority than do other groups. Too, earlier normative solutions in American society were basically Protestant so that many Catholics feel that these solutions were not "American" but only Protestant. Protestants, in turn, feel threatened when older definitions are challenged, since they identify them as American creations, not just Protestant ones. Jews, having thrived in what they define as the religious freedom of American society, often draw the strictest line between religious and secular authority. Many of these issues, however, are not viewed similarly within each religious group. This lack of agreement will be indicated in the following sections.

The issue of the limits of religious authority is quite complex. It obviously involves the relationships between religious and political institutions — the "separation of church and state." It involves the use of tax funds to support religious education. It also involves attempts to legislate morality and regulate family life.

Confusion about the relation between religion and the state is one focus of normative dissensus. In taking his oath of office the President calls on God to help him protect and defend the Constitution — that fundamental law which the Supreme Court has held forbids the Lord's Prayer in public grade schools. Young people are criticized for forsaking the Godliness of their fathers while the public schools are instructed to shun the advocacy of Godliness lest freedom be invaded. Religious content is restricted in public education which started in a theocratic New England. Tax money is not to be used for religious purposes while on the money itself is advertised a trust in God.

The separation of church and state derives from the First Amendment which states that "Congress shall make no law respecting an establishment of religion." No religious group in America recommends that church and the state should be unified, but there are varied interpretations of the desirable limits of separation. Indeed, to many this phrase means that religion has nothing to do with the state (society). However, even in Protestant America there was no complete separation. The norms of Protestant morality (or more accurately Puritan morality) were built into the legal structure — through prohibition laws, blue laws, and gambling laws.

There are, in addition, a number of ties between church and state which indicate either an interest in or toleration of religion. Whether these constitute violations of separation of church and state is problematic. Some of these are:

1. U.S. coins bear the words "In God We Trust."
2. The pledge of allegiance to the flag declares that the United States is "One nation under God."
3. Churches are tax exempt and contributions to churches are deductible from income tax.
4. The President and other governmental officials take their oath of office on the Bible.
5. Congress has a chaplain and has opened with prayer since the founding of the country.
6. Chapels are built at military academies and military installations.
7. Ministers are exempt from military service.

8. Ministers are commissioned as chaplains in the armed forces and employed as chaplains at penal and other governmental institutions.
9. Legal documents are dated "in the year of our Lord" and witnesses are sworn in "so help me God."
10. Religious holidays — Christmas — are legal holidays.
11. Under veterans' benefits for education, GI's could receive support at denominational schools.
12. Under hospital construction acts, denominational hospitals could receive support.
13. Most states have laws restricting some types of behavior on the Sabbath.
14. Most state legislatures have chaplains.
15. Most states recognize God in their constitutions.
16. The Declaration of Independence says the "Creator" is the source of rights and liberties.
17. The Supreme Court of the United States commences its sessions with "God save the United States and this honorable court."

While some of these "violations" of separation of church and state have been the subject of both verbal and legal controversy, generally they have not been felt to be important violations.

The exact meaning of the First Amendment is still unclear. In 1947, the U.S. Supreme Court interpreted it in this way in the Everson bus case:

The "establishment of religion" clause of the First Amendment means at least this: Neither a state nor the Federal Government can set up a church. Neither can pass laws which aid one religion, aid all religions, or prefer one religion over another. Neither can force nor influence a person to go to or to remain away from church against his will or force him to profess a belief or disbelief in any religion. No person can be punished for entertaining or professing religious beliefs or disbeliefs, for church attendance or non-attendance. No tax in any amount, large or small, can be levied to support any religious activities or institutions, whatever they may be called, or whatever form they may adopt to teach or practice religion. Neither a state nor the Federal Government can, openly or secretly, participate in the affairs of any religious organizations or groups and *vice versa*. In the words of Jefferson, the clause against establishment of religion by law was intended to erect "a wall of separation between Church and State." [27]

The First Amendment has been informally interpreted in two different ways — that the state cannot give any *preferential* aid to one group over another, and that the state cannot give *any* aid to religious groups. The Everson case specifically states that it is improper to "aid all religions," not just improper to favor one religion. The difference between these interpretations has real meaning for the relation between religion and education. Regardless of the legal meaning, various religious groups in American society have their own preferred interpretation of the First Amendment.

27. 330 U.S. 1 at page 15 (1947).

Contemporary Normative Conceptions: Catholicism — The separation of church and state means only that preferential aid to religious groups is prohibited. It is appropriate for government bodies to support religious education without favoritism. Moreover, the public schools have a responsibility to teach religion and it is appropriate for the United States to send an ambassador to the Vatican.

Protestantism — The separation of church and state means no aid to parochial schools and no appointment of an ambassador to the Vatican. For many Protestants, however, religious education in public schools does not constitute a violation of separation.

Judaism — The separation of church and state means no tax funds for parochial schools nor religious instruction in public schools. Judaism remains silent on the appointment of an ambassador to the Vatican.

The issue of the separation of church and state is seen in (1) the involvement of public tax-supported schools in teaching religion, (2) the provisions for tax support for parochial schools, and (3) the appointment of an ambassador to the Vatican.

1. *The Involvement of Public Tax-Supported Schools in Religious Instruction and Observance.* There are a number of ways in which religious education has been introduced into the public schools. Some have been ruled unconstitutional, but continue to be practiced. In addition, certain practices have been held to be constitutional in Court rulings where the First Amendment is interpreted more loosely than in the Everson case. Some of the ways religion is currently taught in the public schools are:

(a) *Religion is taught by a public school teacher or by a religious teacher supplied by a church group.* This practice is prevalent in many parts of the country, particularly in rural areas and in the South. It is more common in areas where one religion is dominant and would be ruled unconstitutional if challenged.

(b) *Religion is taught through a released time program.* This is a plan whereby pupils are dismissed perhaps one hour earlier than usual one day a week to attend such religious instruction as they and their parents wish. In a widely publicized case before the U.S. Supreme Court, *McCollum* v. *Board of Education*, an Illinois school board had adopted a program permitting teachers from various denominations to come to the school premises.[28] The teachers were paid not by tax funds but by their respective denominations, but they taught on the public school premises. The children who wanted to go were excused from their other studies; the remaining children continued at their regular studies. The Supreme Court ruled 8 to 1 that this violated the First Amendment on the grounds that state laws required children to go to school and, therefore, it was a compulsory use of the law to provide religious instruction.

Four years later, however, in *Zorach v. Clauson*,[29] the Court upheld a program in which the students were released from the school's physical premises to attend instruction at their respective religious centers. This decision seemingly gave a much looser interpretation of the First Amendment. Justice Douglas, in writing the majority opinion, said:

We guarantee the freedom of worship as one chooses. We make room for as wide a variety of beliefs and creeds as the spiritual needs of men deem necessary. We sponsor an attitude on the part of government that shows no partiality to any one group and that lets each flourish according to the zeal of its adherents and the appeal of its dogma. When the state encourages religious instruction or co-operates with religious authorities by adjusting the schedule of public events to sectarian needs, it follows the best of our tradition.[30]

In this instance the Supreme Court was emphasizing the last part of the First Amendment, "Congress shall make no law regarding an establishment of religion, or *prohibiting the free exercise of religion*." Under the Zorach decision, released time seems to be constitutional *if* the religious instruction takes place off public property, and does not involve tax funds.

(c) *Religion is taught through Bible reading and reciting the Lord's Prayer.* While forbidding denominational instruction, some states and municipalities have permitted and others have required Bible reading and prayers in the daily opening exercises. Most of these observances have a generalized Protestant orientation. Some states have tried to write "neutral" prayers which would offend no religious group. In 1962, the U.S. Supreme Court ruled unconstitutional a neutral prayer composed by the Board of Regents for New York State schools (*Engel v. Vitale* 370 U.S. 421). At that time there was considerable public clamor that the removal of the prayer made the schools "godless," and this continued when, in 1963, the Court, in two separate cases, ruled that the mandatory requirements of Bible reading and the use of the Lord's Prayer in the public schools was unconstitutional. The Court ruled 8 to 1 that these requirements were a violation of the First

28. 333 U.S. 203 (1948).
29. 343 U.S. 306 (1952).
30. 343 U.S. at pp. 313–14.

Amendment. Whether this ruling will prohibit the voluntary use of the Bible or prayer will not be known until it can be tested in the courts, but the Court, in the Maryland and Pennsylvania cases, stated that their decision did not preclude the objective study of religion but only refered to the use of religion in a sectarian manner (*Murray v. Curlett* and *Abington School District v. Schempp*, 372 U.S. 901). It is assumed here that the use of the Lord's Prayer and the reading of the Bible are still widespread in the public schools and, while it cannot be legally required, it is still used informally.

(d) *Religion is taught through the observance of religious holidays.* Jews, in particular, object to public school observance of Christmas and Easter since they feel these programs represent infringements upon non-Christian children. Some communities have joint Christmas-Hanukkah celebrations in the schools. In the light of religious criticism of the commercialization of Christmas and Easter, one might properly raise the question whether these holidays are religious or secular.

Some conflict over religion in the public schools occurs through informal pressures brought to bear upon school officials. Only rarely does some parent feel strongly enough to protest publicly, and the legality of only a few practices has been tested. Sutherland has suggested:

The Supreme Court of the United States during its 167 years, has considered only ten cases involving the religious problems of publicly maintained schools. The brevity of this list (considered in the light of the observances in many hundreds of schools in many states) suggests that the Federal Constitution as actually applied may not have seriously hampered moderate religious manifestations in the public schools of the nation. . . . The Supreme Court has indicated that it will listen only to a complainant with some discernible personal grievance. The Court is not maintained to judge debates on abstract questions, even when these concern the separation of Church and State . . .[31]

The Federal Constitution, as interpreted in the McCollum Case, and the state constitutions in all their variety, impose on public teaching limits more formidable in theory than they may be in practice. The great multitude of comparatively minor religious manifestations which obtain in many grade and high schools probably thrive on local public approval. Most of them escape official interference because of the sheer inertia of the legal machinery, which tends to discourage prosecution, by disgruntled taxpayers and parents, of more than a few cases. No one should welcome judicial delay, expense, and uncertainty. Nevertheless the difficulties met by citizens who start lawsuits on constitutional grounds to enjoin local authorities from conducting some minor religious observances in the public schools may have some good aspects. The practical impossibility of consistent and doctrinaire constitutional literalism in matters of Church and State through-

31. Arthur Sutherland, "Public Authority and Religious Education," *Religious Education* (July–August 1957), p. 260. Presented at a symposium on *The Study of Religion in the Public Schools*, sponsored by The American Council on Education, March 10–12, 1957.

out our federal nation may be one of the curious benefits of the system. It seems to be one of those benign paradoxes which permit an adjustment of localism to national policy, and so make life reasonably tolerable in our widespread and diverse nation.[32]

2. *The Use of Tax Funds To Support Religious Education.* While the right of parents to educate their children in either private or parochial schools is generally assumed in American society, the method of payment for this education is not a settled question. Catholics feel that the right to educate their children in parochial schools is an integral part of religious freedom. They feel that Catholic parents who pay taxes but cannot afford to pay tuition to a parochial school are deprived of religious liberty, and that Catholics who pay tuition for their children are in effect doubly taxed. Catholics feel that parochial schools relieve the taxpayers of a financial burden and that parochial schools should enjoy tax support.

Protestants tend to see the whole issue of the separation of church and state in terms of excluding tax funds from parochial schools. They claim that allowing such support would constitute compulsory taxation for religious purposes. Protestants see the public school system as the cornerstone of democracy — a unifying factor in a society settled by diverse groups. Jews tend to see the problem in similar terms.

Catholics recently have sought welfare and educational services for parochial schools instead of seeking tax support. The Everson case, mentioned earlier, concerned the validity of a New Jersey law which reimbursed parents for the expenses of transporting their children to public and parochial schools. The law was declared valid since the tax money went to the children rather than directly to the schools. In another case the Supreme Court upheld a Louisiana statute providing for the tax purchase of textbooks by children in public and parochial schools. This decision too was based on the ground that the aid went to the children and not to the schools.[33] In other ways, Catholics have sought to furnish children in parochial schools with lunches, medical and dental supplies, as well as with books, supplies, and transportation, from tax funds.

Jews generally accept Catholic claims for welfare services but see the provision of books, supplies, and transportation as a violation of the separation of church and state. Protestants generally do not accept the legitimacy of either welfare or educational services. After the Everson case on the constitutionality of providing bus transportation for parochial schools, an organization called the Protestants and Other Americans United for Separation of Church and State was formed, dedicating itself to maintaining the "sep-

32. Ibid. p. 264.
33. *Cochran* v. *Louisiana,* 281 U.S. 370 (1930).

aration of Church and State under the American form of Government." This organization declared that the Catholic Church was attempting to gain a position of special privilege. While founded primarily by liberal Protestants, many of the rallies sponsored by this organization have been supported by fundamentalists. The movement has been criticized by Catholics as another form of anti-Catholicism and as aiding secularism. Some Protestants have criticized it on the basis that the complete separation of church and state might be a greater danger to Protestantism than aid to Catholic schools.

The court rulings that benefits which go to children rather than to parochial schools, are constitutional have encouraged one Catholic educator to suggest a plan whereby parochial education could be supported in the same way. His plan would give parents of parochial school children certificates of money value to be spent at the school of their choice. This plan, he suggests, would not raise constitutional questions since it is similar to the educational provisions of the G.I. Bill of Rights. It would allow the child freedom of choice in choosing his education. It would assure the liberty of parents to control the religious education of their children. It would, he suggests, pay for the benefits society derives from the education of children in parochial schools.[34]

The conflict over the use of tax funds for religious education has been one of the more important barriers to federal aid to education. Certain federal grants, however, have been given to individuals rather than to schools thus avoiding the issue. While feelings are obviously divided, there may be more support for parochial school aid than can be inferred from the clamorous literature on the subject. In 1949, a Gallup poll showed 41 per cent of the American people favored federal aid to parochial schools, 49 per cent were against it, and 10 per cent had no opinion. Seventy-nine per cent of Catholics were in favor, but so were 31 per cent of Protestants.[35]

3. *The Appointment of an Ambassador to the Vatican.* With the exception of not providing tax funds for parochial schools, there is probably no other issue that unites Protestantism more than opposition to the diplomatic recognition of the Holy See. Even Protestants who would accept nonpreferential aid to religion by the state see in this issue preferential treatment for Catholicism. The issue revolves around whether the Vatican is an ecclesiastical organization or a political organization — a state. If it is an ecclesiastical organization, then Protestants argue that an ambassador from the United States would represent preferential treatment of one religious body. Prot-

---

34. Virgil Blum, S.J. "Freedom of Choice in Schools?" *U.S. News and World Report* (Oct. 25, 1957). It is interesting to note that this article was not presented by the magazine as an argument for parochial schools, but as a possibility for adaptation in southern states wanting to maintain segregated schools.
35. *Public Opinion News Service,* August 17, 1949.

estants disclaim the conception of the Vatican as a political state since it has none of the economic and commercial responsibilities of other states. Because the Vatican is a unique combination of secular political power and ecclesiastical authority, Protestants oppose the presence of an ambassador. Some Protestants insist that, if the Vatican is a political state, American Catholics in the Vatican hierarchy, should renounce their American citizenship.

Catholics find it difficult to understand Protestant feelings on this issue. They point out that the United States maintains diplomatic relationships with other nations which merge church and state and 48 nations maintain diplomatic relations with the Vatican. They point out that the Pope not only possesses moral but political (temporal) authority in Vatican City, and therefore his state qualifies for the establishment of diplomatic relations. Catholics also argue that the refusal to give diplomatic recognition indirectly helps Communism, since the Vatican and the United States are the two principal opponents of international Communism.

While Catholics sometimes draw parallels between recognition of the Vatican and recognition of the state of Israel, Jews have remained silent on this issue. In general, Jews might be expected to oppose the exchange of ambassadors.

> *Contemporary Normative Conceptions: Public Morality* — For most Catholics, Protestants, and Jews, there should be no legal restrictions contrary to religious convictions of morality. For some Catholics and some Protestants, religious conceptions of morality should be strengthened by legal regulation.

It has been said that religious organizations in the United States are less concerned with the morality of politics than with the politics of morality. Religious groups seek to transfer their moral standards into legal regulations and, thus, differing moral standards have led to religious conflict.

Much morality legislation in the United States was based on puritanical Protestant standards. Early Protestants viewed morality in terms of not drinking, not gambling, and keeping the Sabbath. The Eighteenth Amendment was almost exclusively a Protestant creation. States which passed prohibition laws were states with predominately Protestant populations. Catholics and Jews generally do not consider the moderate consumption of liquor immoral. It will be recalled that, outside the South, the Democratic party included many Catholics and Jews. It was dubbed the "Wet" party and, during the F. D. Roosevelt administration, federal prohibition was finally ended. The issue is still relevant in many states maintaining local option.

Anti-gambling laws were also an expression of Protestant morality. Catholicism does not view gambling in moderation as wrong. The use of lotteries, particularly bingo, as a source of funds for the Catholic Church and for parochial schools has led to Catholic demands that they be legalized. Their demands have stimulated Protestant groups to intensify their attacks on the immorality of gambling — and to insist on keeping it illegal.

On two issues, Catholicism and Protestantism somewhat agree. National sex codes reflect Protestant morality, but the Catholic Church has become the most vigorous proponent of strengthening these laws. Catholics have been particularly active in supporting movie censorship and censorship of allegedly pornographic publications. In their attempts to extend controls, Catholics have often been supported by Protestants.

Catholics have also become the foremost defenders of Sunday "blue" laws, originally a Protestant creation. All states except Nevada have some type of Sunday laws. Sunday supposedly is a day for religious observance, not for labor and business. Jews, however, are caught in a dilemma since they do not observe Sunday as their Sabbath. Jews insist that such laws should exempt merchants who, for religious reasons, refrain from doing business on Saturday. In New York, Protestant City Council members joined with Jewish members in insisting on this exemption. At times, the motivation for the extension or enforcement of blue laws is not strictly religious. Many businesses closed on Sunday object to other businesses, particularly "discount" houses remaining open seven days a week.

> *Contemporary Normative Conceptions: Family Relationships* — Many Catholics, considering family life a religious concern within the authority of the church, seek to (a) oppose the liberalization of divorce laws and prevent the use and dissemination of knowledge about artificial birth control, (b) make religious affiliation the most important factor in adoption, and (c) oppose welfare legislation interfering with the concerns of the church. Most Protestants and Jews consider both birth control and divorce matters of individual conscience and religion as only one factor in adoption procedures. In addition they relegate much welfare activity to the responsibility of the "secular" community.

The Catholic Church claims authority over a large portion of family behavior. The claim of the Church extends to issues concerning the legal control of divorce, the dissemination of birth control information, and legislation concerning children, particularly adoption.

While individual states control marriage and divorce laws in the United

States, the attitudes of religious groups are often at variance with state regulations. The Catholic Church does not recognize absolute divorce with the right to remarry. It does recognize "limited" divorce, generally termed separation, under certain circumstances. This practice allows the couple to live apart without the right to remarry. Catholics generally oppose attempts to "liberalize" the divorce laws. This is often done by putting political pressure on state legislators. In turn, legislators are often hesitant to sponsor or vote for certain bills for fear of alienating sizable blocs of voters. Protestant and Jewish groups generally do not oppose the liberalization of divorce laws.

Birth control presents another area of conflict. Catholic doctrine emphasizes sexual relations for the purpose of procreation and therefore maintains that to thwart that purpose is a contradiction of God's will. Birth control by mechanical or medicinal means is absolutely forbidden by the Catholic Church. Women for whom childbearing is a health risk are enjoined to practice abstinence, either total or periodic, from sexual intercourse. Catholic medical personnel are forbidden to prescribe contraceptive devices, even to non-Catholic patients.

Most state laws do not effectively prohibit the dissemination of birth control information. Two states — Connecticut and Massachusetts — do, however, impose a complete ban upon physicians' giving information about birth control methods. Fifteen states have no state birth control legislation, while the remainder generally restrict the dissemination of birth control information to physicians only. While the Connecticut and Massachusetts laws were enacted earlier by legislatures subject to Protestant rather than Catholic influence, attempts to repeal the laws have been blocked.

Catholic objections to birth control information have wider consequences than in supporting or objecting to legislation. In New York City, non-Catholic doctors have been prevented from prescribing contraceptives for non-Catholic patients in municipal hospitals. In one of these hospitals, a physician attempted to fit a patient with a contraceptive device. The patient, Protestant and diabetic, had recently borne her third child, her second by Caesarean section. In the physician's opinion, her life would have been endangered by another pregnancy. His attempt was stopped by his superior. While New York law authorized such a prescription, city hospital administrators had an unwritten ban on providing contraceptive advice within the hospital, seemingly to pacify Catholic opposition. The hospital commissioner's ruling was attacked by a number of Protestant and Jewish organizations. These organizations argued that freedom of religion must work both ways and that hospitals must remain neutral, neither imposing birth control measures on anyone to whom it is religiously repugnant nor withholding it from those who find it religiously acceptable. A number of Catholic organizations, however, supported the commissioner's ruling. The ruling was changed to "give contraceptive advice to those who were 'in genuine need of it.' " [36]

Evidence for rather general agreement on the dissemination of birth control information is supplied by poll data. In 1963, it was reported that 74 per cent of a nation-wide sample favored the availability of such information, but while 80 per cent of the Protestants favored the proposal, only 53 per cent of the Catholics did so. [37]

Since the Catholic Church sees much of family life as being religious life, it views with suspicion attempts on the part of the state to regulate parent-child relationships. Thus, Catholics generally oppose restrictions on child labor as an unwarranted interference of the state. In general, it opposes welfare legislation which goes beyond the granting of funds to families and discourages the development of public welfare institutions supported by tax funds. It also is hostile to legislation to establish governmental supervision of religious welfare institutions.

Protestants and Jews do not view social legislation in this way. The development of public welfare institutions in the United States has, in large part, been the result of social concerns arising from the Social Gospel in Protestantism and strong social concerns within Judiasm. In general, they see public welfare organization as a means to serve all religious groups. They argue that particular religious interests in welfare work should be supported by private funds. In fact, some Protestants have raised the question of whether Protestant welfare organizations should depend upon support from such community-wide fund raising drives as United Appeals since contributions to such funds have almost become a quasi-tax.

Another important area of conflict concerns child adoption. Catholics assume that religion is a matter of status — a person is born into a particular religion and this is immutable. [38] Protestants assume that religion is a matter of election — one chooses his religion on achieving the age of reason. (This distinction is reflected in Catholic and Protestant membership statistics. Catholics count all persons baptized; most Protestant groups count only "full" members, generally only those over 12.) Catholics insist that any child born to a Catholic mother should not be adopted by non-Catholics. Seeing the child's religious faith as crucial, Catholics have urged that adoption laws specifically ban all inter-religious adoptions.

Many states specify that, if possible, children should be placed with adoptive parents of the same religious affiliation. Generally this is interpreted to mean that religion, among other considerations, should be taken into ac-

36. *The New York Times*, August 4, 1958.
37. *Cleveland Press*, June 13, 1963.
38. Orthodox Jews also make this assumption.

count in the placement of adoptive children. If, for example, two sets of adoptive parents were equal in every way except religion, the adoptive agency should give preference to the couple having the same religion as the child's natural parents. But in situations without this equivalence, and particularly when the choice is between placement and institutional care, the adoptive agency need not make the religious affiliation of prospective parents a crucial consideration.

Occasionally these different conceptions become the focus of legal action. In a widely publicized case in Massachusetts, an unwed Catholic mother gave her child for adoption to Jewish parents. Two weeks after signing the papers, claiming she had not known the couple was Jewish, she instituted legal action to turn the child over to a Catholic agency. The Massachusetts courts ordered the child returned. The adoptive parents left the state with the child but the courts ordered extradition. The court battle extended over a six-year period, ending only when the governor of Florida refused to allow the parents to be extradited.[39]

RELIGIOUS DISSENSUS — THE FUTURE

Issues relating to religion are often a no man's land for intellectual discussions. This is due, in part, to the fact that the issues are not intellectual but emotional. The participants in such a discussion have a history conditioning their responses. All religious groups in American society have developed certain minority group reactions of defensiveness and aggression toward those who threaten their position. In part, existing dissensus has to be understood in these terms.

The difficulties of immigration and assimilation in a country already Protestant gave Catholics and Catholicism a "foreign" label. This was accentuated by the development of separate institutions — schools, welfare institutions, and youth organizations — which eased assimilation but isolated Catholics from members of other faiths. Over the years, however, Catholicism has lost most of its foreign identification and has become one of the three "American" religions. In identifying Catholicism as a legitimate American religion, many Catholics were overenthusiastic about this identification and now see Catholicism as a first line of defense against the enemies of America. In particular, Catholicism likes to identify itself as a "bulwark" against international Communism. This often implies that anyone who opposes the views of Catholicism on national or domestic issues is, therefore, a "secularist" and implicitly un-American. Under the term "secularism," Catholicism has condemned humanism, totalitarianism, public schools, Communism, relativism, atheism, and Protestantism.

39. *Time* (June 3, 1957), p. 53.

Protestants, after years of equating America with Protestantism, tend to take the acceptance of Catholicism in American society as a defeat. In particular, they view the Catholic lack of acceptance of the public school system as a threat to American unity. They view Catholicism as still somewhat un-American and interpret any act of charity shown by Catholicism as only diversionary action preceding a strategic move to gain more power.

Minority group feeling has been strong, of course, among Jews. Cutting across the differences between Orthodox, Conservative, and Reform Jews, organizations have emerged to serve the Jewish community in their common task of living in a Christian world. Jews have been concerned not only with preventing anti-Semitism but with preserving the separation of church and state. Jews generally hold a more strict interpretation of the separation of church and state than do Protestants. Since they are numerically the smallest major religious group and, since the peculiar and particular pattern of "secularization" in American society has caused Judaism to flourish, Jews together with Protestants have viewed Catholicism as a threat to the continuation of a congenial pattern.

With this background of "minority" group defensiveness, normative issues are sometimes dismissed as simply being anti-Catholicism, anti-Semitism, or anti-Protestantism. While prejudice does occur, it does not provide an adequate explanation of normative differences between religious groups concerning the role of religion in American society. Not all issues are a product of misunderstanding. They sometimes result from differences in beliefs which cannot be reduced by charging prejudice.

Many normative differences between religious groups may become accentuated in the future. In the past, ethnic communities were numerous, but these communities found it difficult to maintain themselves with increasing industrialization and with the normative conception of Americanization. In the place of these disappearing ethnic communities, religious groups seemingly have emerged as an important point of location for the person. At the turn of the century, a person might consider himself a Pole or an Italian; today he is more likely to see himself as a Catholic. Observing marriage patterns in New Haven from 1870 to 1940, Kennedy found a growing tendency for ethnics to marry outside their own group, indicating the lessening hold of ethnic communities.[40] This increasing pattern of intermarriage, however, did not extend to marriage into different religious affiliations. While the person might marry outside his ethnic community, he stayed within his religious community.

40. Ruby Jo Reeves Kennedy, "Single or Triple Melting Pot?, Intermarriage Trends in New Haven, 1870–1940," *American Journal of Sociology*, 49 (January 1944), pp. 331–9.

The religious community, thus, has become an increasingly meaningful affiliation within an industrialized society. These religious groups represent an inclusive commitment. Religious groups are basically endogamous so that a person's interaction with his family means interaction with members of the same religious group. The norms and values learned within the religiously homogeneous family are also reinforced by a friendship group from the same religious tradition.

In a Detroit sample, Lenski found that, among Jews, all had married within the same religious group. Ninety-six per cent of their close relatives and 77 per cent of their close friends were all or nearly all Jews. The comparable figure for marriage among Catholics was 84 per cent and for Protestants, 86 per cent. For close relatives, 79 per cent for the Catholics and 76 per cent of Protestant drew all or nearly all from within the same religious tradition. For close friends, the figures were 44 per cent for Catholics and 38 per cent for Protestants. While the friendship group was not as homogeneous for Catholics and Protestants as for Jews, the degree of familial homogeneity for all groups was impressive.[41] Lenski documents the fact that each of these religious sub-communities limits communication to those of the same faith and facilitates the development and transmission of distinctive political and economic norms. Its effect was to produce an increasingly parochial view of the world.

This homogeneity within religious groups tends to accentuate normative differences. The controversy centering on the Catholicism of President Kennedy during the election of 1960 and the issues of federal aid to parochial schools may not be the last gasps of bigotry in an increasingly enlightened America, but instead they may indicate the heightening of latent dissensus within a society increasingly compartmentalized by religion. In some industrialized societies, Holland for example, every institutional area of the society has to take into account religious distinctions. Political parties, athletic teams, and even business establishments are identified with one or another religious group. Such a trend toward compartmentalization in America may increase "interest" in religion, but it will be a parochial interest accentuated by an increasing distance from those of other religious traditions.

SUMMARY

Protestantism, because of its priority and early numerical superiority, set the dominant religious pattern in American society. With growing industrialization, traditional Protestantism was challenged in many ways. A new normative conception, that of liberal Protestantism, accepted the knowledge derived from science and turned its attention toward applying the Social Gospel to

41. Gerhard Lenski, *The Religious Factor*, Garden City: Doubleday, 1961, pp. 33–9.

a world being remade by industrialization. Fundamentalism, however, rejected this remaking of Protestantism and stressed what it considered to be the fundamentals of the faith. It also rejected the social concern of liberalism. Neo-orthodoxy, while accepting the insights of science, felt that liberals were too optimistic about the perfectibility of society in the face of the sinfulness of man.

The non-Protestant religions had to come to terms with a religious pattern set by Protestantism. Judaism presented a paradox of being both a religion and a people. Reform Judaism moved in the direction of detaching the religion from the cultural tradition of Judaism — in effect, it "Americanized" the religion. To those immigrants who were to form the base of Orthodoxy, Reform went too far. For the Orthodox, Judaism was embedded in a total cultural tradition and could not be compartmentalized. But, many of the older Orthodox traits seemed outmoded to second- and third-generation Orthodox Jews. For them, Conservatism provided a half-way house, rejecting many of the Orthodox practices but retaining many of the traditions Reform had discarded.

The adaptation of Catholicism has centered on the conception of the one true church. Because of the structure of the Church, a more unitary position on religious authority is maintained. Catholicism's adaptation to the American scene was complicated by the fact that many of its members were recent immigrants and had to make a parallel adjustment to the newness of another cultural tradition. Gradually, Catholicism has come to be viewed as one of the three American religions.

The multiplicity of religious groups has produced different definitions of the limits of religious authority. Specifically, dissensus exists on where to place the "wall" separating church and state, on the extent to which morality should be legislated, and on the extent to which religious factors should guide family policy.

With the decline of ethnic communities, groups reflecting religious differences have become increasingly important in American society. Since these groups foster isolation from other religious traditions, this may result in increasing dissensus.

QUESTIONS AND SUGGESTIONS FOR FURTHER STUDY

1. Read a history of a specific Protestant denomination. From this account, describe the nature of the conflict between liberalism (sometimes called modernism) and fundamentalism.
2. What is meant by the Social Gospel?
3. Observe the patterns of co-operation among Protestant religious organizations

— Council of Churches, ministerial associations, etc. Do these lines of co-operation cut across the liberal-fundamental distinction?

4. Why is the term "neo-orthodoxy" used to describe a recent conception of Protestantism?

5. What were the factors that led eastern European Jews to reject the adaptation made by Reform Jews in the United States?

6. Consult the legal code of your state. From existing legislation and court decisions, describe the pattern of church-state relations found in these documents.

7. Do you think Catholicism has been the major focus of dissensus concerning the separation of church and state? Why?

8. Why have Jews been more consistent in maintaining the separation of church and state?

9. Is there any justification for considering each of the major religious groups in the United States a minority group? Illustrate minority reactions on the part of the various groups.

10. Observe the patterns of co-operation among the various major religious groups within your community. In what areas do they co-operate? In the areas in which they do not co-operate, do these reflect normative differences among the groups?

SUGGESTED READINGS

Clark, Elmer T., *The Small Sects in America*, Nashville: Abingdon Press, 1949 (Apex Books).   P   A classification and description of the small sectarian groups in the United States. The existence of many of these groups can be traced to splits in groups created by normative dissensus.

Dillenberger, John D., and Claude Welch, *Protestant Christianity*, New York: Scribner, 1960.   P   This book contains a useful historical and theological history of Protestantism. It contains a good summary of various theological positions.

Ellis, John Tracy, *American Catholicism*, Chicago: The University of Chicago Press, 1956.   P   A good concise history of Catholicism in the United States.

Gasper, Louis, *The Fundamentalist Movement*, The Hague: Mouton and Co., 1963. A useful account of the fundamentalist movement in the United States since 1930.

Glazer, Nathan, *American Judaism*, Chicago: The University of Chicago Press, 1957.   P   A brief, lucid sociological and historical account of Judaism. Part of the Chicago History of American Civilization Series.

Lenski, Gerhard, *The Religious Factor: A Sociologist's Inquiry*, Garden City: Doubleday, 1961.   P   This study of religious behavior in Detroit includes a wide variety of data. Of particular interest are the images those in one religious group have of others. The book impressively documents the effect of membership in what he terms "socio-religious" groups.

Niebuhr, Richard H., *The Social Sources of Denominationalism*, New York: Meridian Books, Inc., 1957.   P   An excellent account of the various social influences on denominations during their historical development in the United States.

Underwood, Kenneth, *Protestant and Catholic*, Boston: Beacon Press, 1957. P   This is a study of an industrial city and the relationship between religious groups in this community. It focuses on the relationship between Protestants and Catholics.

Weber, Max, *The Protestant Ethic and the Spirit of Capitalism*, New York: Scribner, 1960.   P   This book discusses the relation of religious ideas to the emergence of capitalism and to many of the characteristics of industrial societies. It presents an idea which, while still debated, must be included among the great ideas of the century.

Wickham, E. R., *Church and People in an Industrial City*, London: Lutterworth Press, 1957. A historical and sociological study of Sheffield, England, during nineteenth-century industrial growth and its consequences for religion. Chapter Six, "The Mission of the Church in an Industrial Society," provides some unique ideas about the role of the church.

Yinger, J. Milton, *Religion, Society and the Individual*, New York: Macmillan, 1957. An excellent introduction to the sociology of religion. It contains a collection of articles in addition to text material covering a wide range of topics.

CHAPTER 7   SCIENCE: TECHNOLOGY OR KNOWLEDGE

> The Congress shall have the power . . . ;
>
> To promote the Progress of Science and the useful Arts by securing for limited times to authors and inventors the exclusive right to their respective writings and discoveries.
>
> The Constitution of the United States, Article 1, Section 8

> We must also be alert to the . . . danger that public policy could itself become the captive of the scientific-technological elite.
>
> Dwight D. Eisenhower, Farewell Address, January 17, 1961

> Let (us) seek to invoke the wonders of science instead of its terrors. . . . Let us explore the stars, conquer the desert, eradicate disease, tap the ocean depths and encourage the arts and commerce.
>
> John F. Kennedy, Inaugural Address, January 20, 1961

From the Founding Fathers' concern in the Constitution to "promote the progress of science" to the more recent preoccupation with the "wonders of science," political leaders have been aware of some of the implications of science for public policy. These implications have been important enough so that some have commented on the potential threat of an emerging scientific elite in a democratic society. To consider science within the purview of social problems, however, might seem strange. The concern here is with the normative conception held within an industrial society concerning the nature of science and its relation to the larger society. This conception is a by-product of certain conditions in industrial society. In turn, this conception determines certain paths of implementation within a society. It is to the normative problem that we now turn.

The normative problem: what should be the role of science in an industrial society?

In the latter half of the twentieth century, the concern for science seems to amount almost to a craze. Advertisers insist that our prosperity is the result of science and that in the future, science will make life even better. Business firms assure consumers that their products have been tested by an "independent scientific laboratory" and that they therefore are trustworthy. High school students are admonished by guidance counselors to take more science. News magazines devote separate departments to scientific news. Toymakers rush to make "scientific" toys. Television and magazines try to meet the demand for science fiction on the part of viewers and readers. Politicians warn that the future of the nation and the world is dependent upon developments in science. Political leaders seek scientific advisers while their governments support atomic research so they can join the nuclear "club." The reactor and the rocket may be symbols of our time as great cathedrals were symbols in the past.

Throughout American history there has been a clash between the idea of science as a technique that promotes technological development and the idea of science as the pursuit of knowledge. Neither conception has ever been absent, but the relative emphasis given to one or the other has varied. While the dominant conception of science has traditionally centered in technology, in recent years it has moved toward the emphasis on knowledge. The development, the consequences, and the shift between these normative conceptions is the subject of this chapter. The roots of these conceptions go back as far as the Founding Fathers.

The Founding Fathers came to grips with the relationship between science and society in the Constitution. The framers of the Constitution had the power to make the federal government the patron of science. They knew that European governments had often supported science, and their view of science tended to be broad, including all branches of what was then called "philosophy." Benjamin Franklin, familiar with both English and French intellectual life, thought that all knowledge should be studied and understood. Early in his life he had been instrumental in establishing groups to explore and gain new knowledge. His interests and the organizations founded on these interests combined in 1769 to form the American Philosophical Society, with Franklin as president. Jefferson later served as its third president. This society was national in scope and included all branches of learning. Its four sections dealt with mathematical and physical sciences, geological and biological sciences, social sciences, and the humanities. Elsewhere, such men as John and Samuel Adams and John Hancock were instrumental in the formation of the American Academy of Arts and Sciences, founded in Boston in 1780.

During the Constitutional Convention, suggestions were made to encourage the acquisition of knowledge. Madison asked for the power to create a national university and to "encourage by premiums and provision, the advancement of useful knowledge and discoveries." The importance of science for the new country was not challenged by any of the delegates but most of the proposals to implement it were lost in the struggle over issues that had little connection with science. Most of the delegates concluded that the role of the federal government should be limited, so any support of science finally was looked upon as being beyond the scope of the new government. The final draft of the Constitution did include the word "science" once. It declared that it was in the power of Congress to "promote the Progress of Science and useful Arts. . . ." This would have given Congress a mandate had it stopped at that point, but the phrase "by securing for limited Times to Authors and Inventors the exclusive Right to their respective Writings and Discovery" was added.

While the Constitution gave little explicit attention to science other than for patent provision, there is the irony that the whole Constitution and the whole structure that emerged was based upon a scientific approach to government. In discarding the traditional theory of a hereditary sovereign, the Constitution was based on the idea that the people would rationally build their governmental institutions to suit themselves. The people were the ultimate political power. These people had to be counted and, thus, the census became the ultimate basis of sovereign power in the United States. The Constitution, by ordering the census, made the federal government the most important collector of social science information in the world. Every ten years, the redistribution of political power in the United States is accomplished on the basis of this information.[1]

As the country moved into the nineteenth century, further changes occured. Jackson became the first of a new type of indigenous leader, who lacked Jefferson's, Adams's, and Franklin's appreciation of science as knowledge. The "common" man was beginning to have a voice in public affairs; manufacturers and businessmen were becoming powers. In addition, the growing complexity of knowledge made it increasingly difficult for those who aspired to universal competence in all knowledge. Nor was it possible for men to shift from abstract knowledge to practical invention as both Franklin and Jefferson had done. Science became increasingly a pragmatic venture with the ultimate goal of technological results. In a very real sense, American society developed the normative conception that science was technology. It is to the development of this normative conception that we now turn.

Historical Normative Conception: Technology — Science should be seen as the pursuit of practical knowledge.

While American history is written around political and not technological events, this history is dotted with inventors and their inventions; there is

---

1. It is true, however, that in many state governments, the redistribution of political power lags far behind population shifts. See the discussion on rural-urban representation in the chapter on Community.

something about early industrial development and its political repercussions; there is something about railroad expansion and the expansion of the frontier; there is something about the growth of big business and big labor. Technological consequences, woven into the fabric of American life, are considered identical with science. When the casual student is asked to identify the folk-heroes of science in American history, he is more likely to suggest someone, like Edison or Ford, having little formal education and inclined to be somewhat scornful of the scientific method. Few have heard of Willard Gibbs. It is perhaps no accident that the favorite synonym for technical skill is "know-how," because in America a higher premium has been placed on knowing *how* than on knowing *why*.[2] By and large, Americans have been content to let most of the basic discoveries in science — knowing why — originate in Europe while they have followed the policy of "adapt, improve and apply." This inattention of Americans to science as basic knowledge has long been apparent to foreign scholars. In 1850, Tocqueville observed, "It must be confessed that among the civilized peoples of our age, there are few in which the highest sciences have made so little progress as in the United States."

This emphasis on technology goes back to the very beginnings of the country. Most of the early legislative concern for science was in the form of protecting the inventor so that he would continue to develop technology. The Constitution specified that inventors should be encouraged and protected. In addition, Washington in his first inaugural address in 1789 spoke about the "expediency of giving effective encouragement as well as the introduction of new and useful inventions from abroad as to the exertions of skill and genius in producing them at home." This early concern with inventions was implemented in the first patent law, enacted in 1790. Until 1836, when this law was revised, patents were acted upon perfunctorily. After that time, patents were scrutinized with legal and technical care; only after a search through the previous literature of invention could the applicant's claim be verified. Thus, the Patent Office became a source of cumulative technological information.

Technology was responsive to the pressing needs of the times, and with new technological developments came social and economic changes. America in the first part of the nineteenth century was a country of unfolding natural resources and a relatively small population. America had the space and the resources but not the labor to exploit them. Consequently, much technological growth centered on labor-saving machinery. Besides the cotton-gin, Eli Whitney devised the system of interchangeable parts without which

2. John B. Rae, "The Know-How Tradition: Technology in American History," *Technology and Culture*, Vol. 1, No. 2 (Spring 1960), pp. 139–49.

Henry Ford later would have been helpless. McCormick and his imitators and rivals perfected the reaper. Morse gave up portrait painting and turned his attention to the telegraph — a welcome addition to a country of such vast area. Howe patented his sewing machine and transferred the making of clothes from the home to the factory. Shoemaking machines were devised by McKay just when a huge army was being drafted for the Civil War. Gatling turned up with his machine gun at about the same time.

After the war, new products were numerous. Sholes perfected the typewriter and thereby put women in offices. Westinghouse demonstrated that trains could be stopped by his airbrake and could brag that he had saved more lives than Napoleon destroyed with all his armies. Then came the telephone of Alexander Graham Bell and the hundreds of patent applications from Edison for new models of the telegraph and telephone, the phonograph, and the electric light.

Some of these inventors founded industries and a few became captains of industry. McCormick was the father of the International Harvester Company. Out of Morse's inventions came the Western Union Telegraph Company. The General Electric Company had its origins in Edison's electric light patents. Bell's work was responsible for the American Telephone and Telegraph Company. There is scarcely a company with shares listed on the New York Stock Exchange today that is not in some way indebted to the pioneer inventors of the period 1836–1900.

The patent system allowed the inventor to have a 17-year monopoly on his invention before it became public property. While there were legislative attempts to control other types of monopoly, this patent monopoly was always spared. It was assumed that the inventor of a patentable object was not exercising restraint of trade, but was giving the public something it had never had before. Corporations that developed around the acquisition of patents found that they could effectively control the market for these products. Because technological innovations were valued, this control was not viewed as being monopolistic.

Industrial concerns, to protect their investments, gradually began to support research in product improvement. This research was not science, in the sense of developing basic knowledge, but was directed toward technological development. Thus, the industrial research laboratory became an integral part of the American scene. These industrial research organizations have taken as their mission, to paraphrase Du Pont, "better things for better living through science."

The federal government also was more interested in research that promised immediate practical results than in more abstract scientific endeavors. When James Smithson bequeathed his fortune to the United States so that an institution might be founded for "the increase and diffusion of knowledge amongst men," there was much congressional discussion as to the appropriateness of accepting such a gift. John C. Calhoun and others argued that Congress had no power under the Constitution to accept it. After ten years of debate, Congress finally accepted the trust and founded the Smithsonian Institution. While the first director tried to make the Institution a center for fundamental scientific research, he noted that "though many excel in the application of science to the practical arts of life, few devote themselves to the continued labor and patient thought necessary to the discovery and development of new truths." [3]

Before the Civil War, several attempts were made by the federal government to establish colleges that might become scientific centers. The bills were defeated by states' rights legislators who viewed federal grants of land to individual states as a threat to the powers of the individual states. In 1862, when southern states' rights enthusiasts were absent from Congress, the Morrill Act was passed. The bill provided for the foundation and maintenance of colleges "where the leading object shall be . . . to teach such branches of learning as are related to agriculture and mechanic arts." There was, at first, no provision for research in these areas, only the intent that existing technological knowledge be transmitted to the "liberal and practical education of the industrial classes in the several pursuits and professions of life." Later in 1887, the Hatch Act provided federal funds to support state agricultural experiment stations as a part of this college structure. The emphasis of these experiment stations has been upon practical knowledge. A recent evaluation suggests that:

> Much of this research work is applied rather than basic research. For example, an animal nutrition research worker may utilize the basic scientific findings in chemistry and physiology and apply these to the practical problems of how to secure higher animal gains from less feed. Likewise the agricultural economist attempts to apply the basic economic principles to the cost and return problems of farm business. Seldom do Experiment Station employees see their role as that of developing basic research projects.[4]

At about the same time, the National Academy of Sciences was chartered by Congress with the object that it "shall, whenever called upon by any department of the government, investigate, experiment and report upon any subject of science or of art." Those instrumental in establishing the Academy saw it in terms of its technological advantages. In 1851, the president of the American Association for the Advancement of Science argued that "There

3. Quoted in S. F. Mason, *Main Currents of Scientific Thought*, New York: Henry Schuman, 1953, p. 478.
4. Everett Rogers, *Social Change in Rural Society*, New York: Appleton-Century-Crofts, 1960, p. 308.

are few applications of Science which do not bear on the interests of commerce and navigation, naval or military concerns, the customs, the lighthouses, the public lands, post offices and post-roads, either directly or remotely." [5]

In the half-century following the Civil War, there was a steady growth in governmental activities, particularly in data-gathering services such as the Coast and Geodetic Survey, the Weather Bureau, and the Census Bureau. In addition some scientific work was carried on by the government in order that governmental agencies could perform their duties. The army needed experimentation in communications and in medical services. Both the Department of Agriculture and the National Bureau of Standards required analysis and testing and developed their own research staffs.

Immediately before World War I, the National Advisory Committee on Aeronautics was established. It developed a program of research which formulated plans that in subsequent years guided the construction of commercial and military aircraft. During World War I, a new quasi-governmental organization, the National Research Council, was established by the National Academy of Sciences with the co-operation of national scientific and technical societies, to make scientific resources more fully available to the government.

In the period between the first and second world wars, the government's scientific activities increased. Various Institutes of Health were created as part of the Public Health Service. The various arms of the War Department built a number of research installations. The social sciences began to play an important role in the Departments of Commerce, Labor, and Agriculture.

During World War II, several new organizations carried out the great bulk of all military research and development: the Office of Scientific Research and Development (OSRD) and the Manhattan Engineering District of the War Department's Corps of Engineers. The latter took over the research and development program on nuclear fission begun by a segment of the OSRD.

Throughout this increase in the role of science within the federal government, it should be noted that most of the concern was for application — in the development of better planes and in the traffic control of aircraft; in the production of better crops; in the development of better communication systems for the armed forces; and in the development of medical techniques for military casualties. While basic knowledge often was an outgrowth of the solution of these practical problems, it was considered incidental — solu-

5. Quoted in Don K. Price, *Government and Science: Their Dynamic Relation in American Democracy*, New York: New York University Press, 1954, p. 18.

tions to the immediate problem provided the justification for governmental interest and support.

FACTORS LEADING TO A TECHNOLOGICAL EMPHASIS

These developments, both in industry and government, illustrate the fact that America, although indifferent to the notion of science as basic knowledge, was making tremendous developments in technology. Several explanations have been given for this. One, the notion that America was a primitive country, would have to be rejected, since by 1860 it had 30 million people, large cities, and several learned institutions. Yet none of the large cities became centers of science as London, Paris, and Berlin were at that time. Tocqueville felt that America did not develop basic knowledge because it was always easy to borrow ideas from Europe. Europe represented the source of culture and knowledge for the new developing country. Others have suggested that Americans were too busy "subduing" nature to be occupied with abstract ideas about the nature of the universe.

Another explanation suggested that religion inhibited the development of pure science in America. But the active attacks of religious groups upon science did not occur until the early twentieth century when the doctrine of evolution was seen as a threat to literal interpretation of the Bible. Even this dispute involved only a small section of Protestantism. In fact, there is evidence that Calvinist religious and philosophical ideas actually facilitated the development of modern science.[6]

The lack of an established church and the development of denominationalism prevented any unified attack upon science. Thus, while some denominations might attack certain scientific fields, they were supported by other denominations. Organized religion may have inhibited the development of science as knowledge by channeling the better minds of the nineteenth century into theological studies, but the church cannot be blamed for the lack of development of basic science.

One factor that contributed to the lack of development of science as knowledge was the dependence of educated Americans upon European, particularly German, graduate schools. The late development of graduate education in America has been discussed in Chapter 5. The absence of such a system of graduate education, in which basic research is valued, inhibited the development of science as knowledge and left technological development primarily to the practical inventor.

Possibly the best explanation for the lack of development of science rests

6. See, for example, Robert K. Merton, *Social Theory and Social Structure*, Glencoe,: Free Press, 1957, Part IV: Studies in the Sociology of Science.

in the social structure of nineteenth-century America. In Europe, basic science was primarily the by-product of an aristocracy or leisure class. In America there was no leisure class with the tradition and time to cultivate the more contemplative theoretical scientific ideas. The vestiges of an aristocracy brought to America from Europe disappeared in the equalitarian tendencies of Jacksonian Democracy. The aristocracy that emerged in its place was based on wealth and, in America, wealth came increasingly from the development of new technological devices exploiting the nascent natural resources.

Paradoxically, the Civil War was both a spur to the development of technology and the last hope for the development of an aristocracy that might have developed basic science in America. Lerner has suggested that if the South had triumphed in the Civil War and had spread its "peculiar institution" — slavery — over the nation, a paralysis would have overtaken American technology.[7] It would have created an aristocracy not faced with the necessity of looking for labor-saving devices and having the time and money to develop abstract science. But the dream of Southern leaders for a slave-based plantocracy was shattered by the superior technology of the North, and business leaders became the dominant ruling group instead. The basis of power and prestige became more economic than social. This new aristocracy based on economic power did not develop basic science as had aristocracies in Europe. Shyrock, in assessing the American indifference to basic science during the nineteenth century, has suggested that:

Industrial leaders, on the other hand, were in a position to support basic science if they so desired. Without waiting for mass enlightenment or possible government aid, they could have provided philanthropic endowments or direct subsidies for corporation research. But of all intellectual or cultural interests, theoretical science was the least likely to appeal to them. The most ruthless magnate might enjoy literature of some sort and appreciate the ornamental quality of the fine arts, but why should he encourage the "idle curiosity" of research men? Such curiosity, to him, was neither interesting nor ornamental. There was nothing in his own experience to suggest that out of basic science would come — ultimately — applications and profits. And although this probability already had been demonstrated in the past, the self-made industrialist was not usually familiar with so "impractical" a subject as the history of science.[8]

It is clear that, through the nineteenth century and during the first part of the twentieth, the normative conception of science as technology was accepted and implemented in American society. Throughout this period, there was, of course, some encouragement and development of basic science. Certain

7. Max Lerner, *America as a Civilization*, New York: Simon and Schuster, 1957, p. 216.
8. Robert Shyrock, "American Indifference to Basic Science during the 19th Century," *Archives Internationales d'Historie des Sciences*, No. 5 (October 1948), p. 61.

events in the twentieth century and certain changes in the level of industrial development have, in recent years, created a normative shift toward science as knowledge, which will now be discussed.

ATOMIC BOMBS, SPUTNIKS, AND SCIENCE AS KNOWLEDGE

At the end of World War II there was a critical turning point in the conception of science. The atomic bomb was an impressive technological feat, but gradually it became known that the theoretical groundwork for atomic fission had been laid in Germany and that the achievements of Oak Ridge and Los Alamos were based on theoretical knowledge that started with Einstein's contribution to theoretical physics and had been continued by other European scholars. The atomic bomb was, thus, a triumph of American engineering aided by America's hospitality to refugee scientists fleeing from the tyranny of European dictators. The realization that such wartime weapons development had depended so much upon basic science caused considerable anxiety. It suggested that the political and military fate of a nation might depend upon its progress in knowledge. Vannevar Bush, the wartime director of the Office of Scientific and Research Development, was asked by President Roosevelt to report on scientific progress. He said:

Our national pre-eminence in the fields of applied research and technology should not blind us to the truth that with respect to pure research — the discovery of fundamental new knowledge and basic scientific principles — America has occupied second place . . . In the next generation, technical advance and basic scientific discovery will be inseparable; a nation which borrows its basic knowledge will be hopelessly handicapped in the race for innovation.[9]

On the basis of the recommendation of several scientific committees, Dr. Bush prepared a report entitled *Science: The Endless Frontier*, which laid down certain guides toward the creation of a National Science Foundation. This report suggested a number of elements of a new normative conception:

1. The pursuit of science is a national concern.
2. The scientist must be free to pursue his inquiries in his own way.
3. The dissemination of scientific findings is essential.
4. The internationalism of science should be increased.
5. The control of a Science Foundation should be left to a board of scientists who are accepted as authorities in their fields.
6. The research, sponsored by such a foundation, should be in basic rather than applied sciences.
7. A system of scholarship aid would be necessary to ensure a steady flow of personnel into various scientific fields.

9. Quoted in Mason, op. cit. p. 479.

These recommendations were implemented in many ways in subsequent years.

While American society was moving toward the normative conception of science as knowledge, a second event added impetus to this conception. In October and November 1957, the Soviet Union launched its first space satellites. This came at a time when American failures in the same areas were publicly evident. In the national reassessment that occurred afterwards, one point was repeatedly stressed — that the Soviet Union's success in the space field could be attributed to its rapid development of basic science. Its accomplishments were not isolated technological accomplishments but the result of a long-term emphasis on basic research. While every year 20,000 Soviet workers entered the basic research fields, the U.S. added less than half this number. The bulk of American research talent was being channeled into the development of technological improvements such as air conditioning and the noiseless commode. The Soviet emphasis had not been accidental, for, at the end of World War II, Russia had deliberately started a national policy to develop basic research. Through lavish support basic research was encouraged and rewarded. Dr. M. H. Trytten of the U.S. National Academy of Sciences observed: "Somehow a system of government based on materialism has found a way to bestow its highest rewards on men who deal in abstract ideas." Scientists are, except for top political and industrial leaders, the most favored group in the Soviet Union. Moreover, there is evidence that these scientists operate with considerable freedom. The recruitment of scientists in the Soviet Union is facilitated by an educational system geared to discover and develop potential scientists. This example of a social system mobilized around science and its visible accomplishments circling the earth re-emphasized for American society the necessity of stressing science as knowledge.

The emphasis on external factors creating a shift in the normative conception of science suggests that it is simply a response to wartime and to cold war competition. The shift in American society was, in large part, created by factors similar to those which produced the emphasis on basic research in Germany and in Russia. The similarity of response was due mainly to the high level of technological development common to all industrial societies.

In folk societies, technological skills are relatively static and the knowledge upon which these skills are based is passed on from one generation to another — from father to son, from master craftsman to apprentice. This knowledge and these skills over a period of time are cumulative and gradually become more complex. At a certain level of technological development, not easily specified but certainly a level achieved by most contemporary industrial societies, further technological development depends less and less upon trial and error accumulation and more and more upon abstract knowledge. Technological changes today are more likely to be related to Einstein's theory of relativity than to Goodyear's accidental discovery of the vulcanization process.

The continual elaboration of a complex technology thus depends increasingly on abstract knowledge and on full-time specialists in this field. In this sense, advanced technological development generates its own need for science as knowledge. Continued technological development becomes more than a specific need for a particular industrial segment, it is rather a general need of the entire society for continued economic development.

> *Contemporary Normative Conception: Knowledge* — Science should be seen as the pursuit of basic knowledge.

The idea of science as knowledge is as old as science itself. The distinction carried over into science from Greek philosophy. To the Greeks, the intellect counted far more than the senses. Since the senses were always coupled with material things, thought was considered of greater worth than experience. Coupled with this was the contempt in which the Greek philosopher held the craftsman and the manual laborer. Experimenting was manual work, primarily the work of slaves. Thus thought (basic knowledge) was considered a higher order than application (technology).

This distinction had been recognized by some during the ascendance of the earlier conception of science as technology. The previous quotations by Tocqueville and by the first director of the Smithsonian Institution indicate that they saw a difference between science as knowledge and science as technology. The normative conception of science as knowledge is difficult to convey, particularly in a society still oriented toward practicality. Its meaning is conveyed by Thomson in the following way:

> The scientific worker has elected primarily to know, not do. He does not directly seek, like the practical man, to realize the ideal of exploiting nature, and controlling life — though he makes this more possible; he seeks rather to idealize — to conceptualize — the real, or at least those aspects of reality that are available in his experience. He thinks more of lucidity and formulae than of loaves and fishes. He is more concerned with knowing Nature than with enjoying her. His main intention is to describe the sequences in Nature in the simplest possible formulae, to make a working thought-model of the known world. He would make the world translucent, not that emotion may catch the glimmer of the indefinable light that shines through, but for other reasons — because of his inborn inquisitiveness, because of his dislike for obscurities, because of his craving for a system — an intellectual system in which phenomena are at least provisionally unified.[10]

10. Arthur Thomson, quoted in *Science and Social Change*, Jesse E. Thornton (compiler), Washington, D.C.: The Brookings Institution, 1939, p. 2.

The conception of science as knowledge is not necessarily antithetical to the conception of science as technology. There is no necessary "thinker–slave" dichotomy inherent in the distinction. In fact, it can be argued that technology can best be based on knowledge. In other words, theory is the father of practice. There is nothing as practical as a theory that works. Without theory, certain technological improvements — television, plastics, nylon, transistors, and many others — would not exist. Few scientists today would advocate following the example of Goodyear, who performed hundreds of experiments before he stumbled on a way to vulcanize rubber by sulphur. While technological improvements may come about by "accident" or by concentration on the immediate practical improvements of products, this approach is not as likely to produce "practical" results as a concern for basic knowledge is. It has often been said that basic research is the most practical research since it brings understanding. Understanding is useful, for it provides the means of answering a large number of practical problems. New products and new processes do not emerge fully grown. They are founded on new knowledge.

These practical considerations are not, however, the only justification for basic research. Possibly the most distinctive characteristic of man is his attempt to understand the world he lives in — his past, his future, his universe, himself. Science is part of the long tradition of man's attempt to understand the world he lives in. It is in this sense that Oppenheimer calls scientific activity ennobling.[11] Because of this, it is suggested that the conception of science as basic knowledge deserves the best and most imaginative efforts of scholars and deserves being implemented within our society.

IMPLEMENTING SCIENCE AS KNOWLEDGE

If new knowledge leads to practical use and if the search for knowledge is one of man's most creative endeavors, how, then, can this conception be implemented within a society? A number of suggestions and forms of implementation have emerged in recent years. These suggestions have been centered in four different areas:

1. *Changing the Intellectual Environment.* The development of science as the pursuit of basic knowledge depends on the over-all social and intellectual climate of a society. Since science is a part of intellectual effort, the climate conducive to intellectual effort in general is conducive to the development of science. While the intellectual in American society seemingly is accorded high status, he is also viewed with distrust.[12] As Morris Cohen suggested,

---

11. Dael Wolfle, *Symposium on Basic Research,* Washington: American Association for the Advancement of Science, 1949, p. 3.
12. For a discussion of the status of intellectuals, see Seymour M. Lipset, *Political Man, The Social Bases of Politics,* New York: Doubleday, 1960, pp. 310–33.

"In no other country is the word intellectual so often used as a term of derision and opprobrium." [13] Seeman has shown that intellectuals often use the "language of minorities" in talking about themselves and their activities.[14]

Periodically, in American history, politicians have exploited this latent hostility toward intellectuals as part of a general resentment toward those with power and prestige. One such attack, known as McCarthyism, emerged in the early 1950's.[15] A more recent manifestation has been the rise of the John Birch Society, building on the same sources as the earlier McCarthy movement. Analysis of these movements indicates that they draw their strength from people who feel "lost" among the rapid changes in industrial societies. They attack those in power within the society. Their hostility is often directed toward new power sources, big business or big labor, or toward certain minority groups, such as Catholics, Jews, or Negroes. Their hostility is also directed toward those who deal with ideas. The scientist, since he deals with ideas and since his activities have become increasingly important in American society, often serves as a target. These movements, building on the tensions of international relations, often add to the "normal" hostility toward intellectual endeavor.

A complete analysis of the intellectual environment for science would, of course, have to include the factors which impede intellectual efforts in general within the society. Here discussion will be limited to certain factors which have inhibited the freedom of scientific communication. The development of science depends on the cross-fertilization of ideas. Any factor which impedes this cross-fertilization inhibits the development of knowledge. Certain factors — secrecy, security measures, and limitations on the movement of people — have tended to restrict the cross-fertilization of ideas.

(a) *Secrecy.* While international tensions facilitated science, such tensions have also erected barriers to the development of science as knowledge. Research in atomic energy and secrecy are almost synonyms. When the American atomic energy program was initiated during World War II, the secrecy was a necessity because the United States was the sole possessor of the atom bomb. When control of atomic energy was shifted to civilian control after the war, the secrecy surrounding research had become a habit. The basic legislation controlling atomic energy specified a number of types of information that could be classified as secret. One such classification, defined as secret "any information in any category determined by any government

13. Morris Cohen, *American Thought*, Glencoe: Free Press, 1954, pp. 27–72.
14. Melvin Seeman, "The Intellectual and the Language of Minorities," *American Journal of Sociology*, Vol. 64, No. 1 (July 1958), pp. 25–35.
15. For an analysis of McCarthyism see Daniel Bell (ed.), *The New American Right*, New York: Criterion Books, 1956.

agency authorized to classify information, as being information respecting, relating to, or affecting national defense." [16] Such a definition allowed various government agencies to "classify" basic research as secret even though it might bear only a tangential relation to national defense. Since much basic research, particularly in atomic energy, was supported by various governmental agencies, this meant that almost all knowledge could be seen as "affecting" national defense and, thus, be kept secret. The consequences of secrecy, according to one of Britain's prominent scientists, are as follows:

It is all too easy to see the advantages of secrecy; it stops an adversary from acquiring one's knowledge. The advantage is more apparent than real, however, for development research is something that any nation can do, given sufficient money, scientists and engineers. What secrecy really does is to induce a wholesale disruption of a country's own endeavors whether in development or creativity. [17]

(b) *Security measures.* In the context of post-World War II distrust, loyalty of certain governmental employees was questioned. In response to charges that the government was infiltrated by Communists, President Truman issued a "loyalty" order calling for a police investigation of the political and moral responsibility of all governmental officials. Since most nuclear and other research was directly or indirectly financed by the federal government, this means that many scientists were affected by this order. Under this program, the FBI made loyalty checks on federal employees and transmitted its information to a loyalty board which determined if there were "reasonable grounds" for the belief that an employee was disloyal. This loyalty procedure depended on anonymous accusers, and the accused person could appeal the decision of the loyalty board only after he had been dismissed from government employ. During the operation of the loyalty program, not a single act of espionage or any disloyal act was discovered. [18]

Jungk has suggested, in his personal history of atomic scientists, that these procedures had other consequences.

There were hundreds of such cases in these "bitter years." Statistics alone cannot describe them, for no figures can comprise the whole burden of anxiety, fear and grief borne by those who were involved, because of some unsupported denunciation or by some long forgotten episode in the past. [19]

16. Clinton P. Anderson, "Top Secret — But Should It Be?," *The New York Times Magazine* (May 3, 1959), p. 101.
17. Fred Hoyle, "We Can Take the Lead in Science If —." *The New York Times Magazine* (Jan. 12, 1958), p. 64.
18. According to Seth Richardson, Chairman, Loyalty Review Board, cited in John C. Wahlke, *Loyalty in a Democratic State*, Boston: Heath, 1952, p. 54.
19. Robert Jungk, *Brighter Than a Thousand Suns: A Personal History of the Atomic Scientists*, New York: Harcourt, Brace, 1958, p. 257.

In such an atmosphere of distrust, scientific communication was disrupted. Friendships between scientists broke down under the strain of mistrust. Scientific correspondence sharing information often came to an end. The atmosphere in various laboratories was characterized by suspicion or by the fear that investigators were close at hand. Being "politically safe" became a more important criterion for government employment than being scientifically competent.

The initial anxiety that surrounded the loyalty and security program was aggravated by aspiring politicians who saw themselves as defenders of "democratic" ideals. They found scientific personnel a rich source of "odd" beliefs, international connections, "peculiar" habits, and "weird" interests which they equated with political disloyalty. While many of the excesses of early security programs have been overcome, elements of this fear of disloyalty continue to persist.[20]

(c) *Limits on movement of scientists.* Personal contacts between scientists have been hampered in several different ways. The State Department, which traditionally issues passports, has at times refused to allow certain citizens to leave the country. While primarily directed at Americans suspected of Communist activities, this procedure contradicts the Declaration of Human Rights, which the United States signed as a member of the United Nations, and which states that "Everyone has the right to leave any country, even his own." While the refusal of passports has not been used in many cases nor always been applied to scientists, such barriers can impede the internationalism of science.

A more important barrier has been the refusal to grant visas to "Communists and subversives" to the United States by the McCarran-Walter Immigration Act of 1952. Since such restrictions prohibit visas to individuals who signed petitions or who have lent their "name" to the letterhead of some organization, many European scientists as well as those from Communist countries are not allowed to visit the United States. Since special State Department permission is required for the admission of these scientists to scientific meetings, United States scientists often feel it is too much trouble to do this and prefer to go to another country. A spokesman of the Canadian National Research Council said, "Before the McCarran Act, we rarely had an international congress. Now we have at least a major one a year." [21]

Generally, the scientific community opposes such restrictions as secrecy,

20. The National Defense Education Act of 1958, designed to encourage higher education through loans to students, many of them oriented to scientific fields, required the student to sign a loyalty oath plus an oath "disclaiming support of organizations dedicated to the overthrow of the government."

21. Associated Press release, September 14, 1960.

limitations of travel, and loyalty investigations and suggests that the final test must always be in scientific, not political, terms. The President of the American Association for the Advancement of Science said:

> Given the present grave divisions among nations, classified experiments in military technology seem inevitable, transitory though the secrets prove in practice. Even in dealing with them, however, I would hope that we have learned that we simply cannot enforce loyalty by lining up those we suspect and purging them from us. Loyalty depends on a vast complex of inter-personal relations involving common standards and ideals. For us in the United States this means loyalty to the democratic way of life as exemplified in the history and traditions of the American people. One of these traditions is the tradition of science to find the truth about ourselves and the world about us. Our concept of national security must develop toward maximizing scientific gains rather than minimizing losses.
>
> Now that we are face to face with unassailable evidence that the withholding of publication of our basic research findings does not prevent others from overtaking us, we may be able to look at secrecy in reverse. It is quite possible that by reporting our experiments openly we could work a deterrent effect on irresponsible politicians abroad . . . And there is always hope that, with time, exchange of scientific intelligence may become a bridge for peaceful intercourse between eastern and western civilizations.[22]

2. *Increasing the Supply of Scientific Personnel.* As American society becomes more dependent upon science there is a growing shortage of scientific personnel. Since 1900, the number of persons engaged in scientific, professional, and technical work has been growing twice as fast as the total population. Schoolteachers have increased one and a quarter times as rapidly as the population. The number of professional health workers has increased two and a half times as rapidly; engineers, five times; scientists, ten times. Even with these tremendous increases, there are shortages. During this period, the population increased and economic growth has been in industries where there is high utilization of professional personnel. For example, both the electronics industry and the antibiotics industry scarcely existed prior to World War II.

Since the need for scientists increases faster than the production of scientists, the shortage grows. This shortage has been the subject of much discussion and action. While increased economic rewards might increase the supply of scientists, particularly in a society that values economic rewards, the issue is more complicated than this. Scientific personnel need talent and years of training. Many plans to alleviate the shortage of scientific personnel deal with their recruitment and training.

Attempts to increase the supply of scientific personnel have taken a number of directions. One approach has been to try to reduce the loss of talent,

22. Chauncey D. Leake, "What We Don't Know Hurts Us," *Saturday Review* (January 4, 1958), p. 40.

particularly those who do not go on to higher education. A second approach has been to locate sources of scientific talent. A third approach has been to try to change the rather unfavorable image of the scientist. A fourth approach has been to encourage scientific talent within the educational system. Each of these approaches will be discussed further.

(a) *Reducing the loss of talent.* Many have been concerned with the loss of talent resulting from students who fail to go on to college. Since scientific endeavor requires higher education, those who fail to go to college represent a potential source of scientific personnel. A study of American high school seniors in 1955 determined which students possessed the ability to do college work.[23] Students with the ability to do college work were asked to indicate their plans for college attendance. Among those with the highest academic aptitudes, over 30 per cent did not plan to attend college. While the study did not probe their reasons, some could be inferred. Those students most certain of going to college were those whose parents could provide the most financial and motivational help. For example, 83 per cent of the sons of physicians planned to attend college while only 25 per cent of the sons of semi-skilled workers did so. The students most certain of attending college were those in high schools where the students, the curriculum, and the guidance program were all oriented toward college preparation. Those unable or unwilling to attend college represent a loss of talent not only for science but for the total society.

(b) *Locating sources of scientific talent.* One approach to alleviating the shortage of scientific personnel has been to analyze the origins of existing scientific personnel. Some studies have approached the problem by ascertaining if scientists have different values and attitudes. Generally such studies indicate that interest in science is associated with an interest in theoretical values but a disinterest in political and economic values. In contrast, those with business talents show strong interests in political and economic values.[24] Another approach to locating scientific personnel has been to analyze the types of education and the types of educational institutions attended by the men listed in *American Men of Science*.[25] This study, widely quoted (particularly by institutions which ranked high in the study), found that certain educational institutions — the small private liberal arts college in the Midwest and the West — showed a high productivity of scientists. This study has caused much comment and further research.

Another study challenged the "institutional productivity" hypothesis and

23. Charles C. Coles, Jr., "Current Loss of Talent from High School to College: Summary of a Report," *Higher Education*, XII, No. 3 (November 1955).

24. See, for example, Anne Roe, *The Psychology of Occupations*, New York: Wiley, 1956.

25. Robert H. Knapp and Hubert B. Goodrich, *Origins of American Scientists*, Chicago: University of Chicago Press, 1952.

suggested that differences between the high and low productive institutions are due to the greater concentration of bright students with exceptional scientific motivation at such "highly productive" institutions. This study indicated that the "productive" institutions tend to attract students whose fathers work with their hands and/or with scientific ideas. By contrast, the less productive schools draw students whose fathers' work tends to be in supervisory and ownership positions in business, law, and government.[26] Regardless of whether institutional productivity or a selective student body accounts for the differences, these studies point to differentials in the production of scientific talent. It is known that scientists come disproportionately from certain population categories, e.g. middle-class Protestant males from professional family backgrounds in small towns. Other categories — lower class and upper class women, Catholics, Negroes, those from family backgrounds emphasizing verbal and supervisory skills — are underrepresented in scientific talent. This kind of knowledge could be used in two different ways — first, to reduce the barriers which some groups encounter, e.g. discrimination against women, Catholics, and Negroes, or second, as a basis for understanding what values facilitate scientific endeavor, e.g. whether or not the values taught children in supervisory and/or Catholic families are antithetical to the choice of a scientific vocation.[27]

(c) *Changing the public image of the scientist.* Part of the problem of recruitment of scientific personnel lies in the lack of appeal scientific roles have for prospective recruits. While occupational choice is complex, one important element in recruitment is the image of the occupation held by the public and by those who are in the process of making an occupational choice. Some occupations are valued highly and are chosen early by students. While little boys choose to be cowboys or firemen, they find more parental approval of such choices as doctor or engineer, occupations that have a "good image." Occupations with low prestige often change their titles to change the image. Thus a janitor becomes a custodian or a maintenance engineer, and a beautician becomes a cosmetologist. Too, some occupations, such as that of a sociologist, are relatively unknown, so that early occupational choice is almost impossible. For example, in the study of high school seniors quoted earlier, 25 per cent said they wished to become engineers, while only 6 per cent wished to become physical scientists and only one per cent wished to

26. John L. Holland, "Undergraduate Origins of American Scientists," *Science*, 6 (September 1957), Vol. 126, No. 3271, pp. 433–7.
27. For an interesting discussion of psychological factors in the choice of scientific careers, see Lawrence S. Kubie, "Some Unsolved Problems of the Scientific Career," in Maurice R. Stein, Arthur J. Vidich, and David Manning White (eds.), *Identity and Anxiety*, Glencoe: Free Press, 1960, pp. 241–68.

become social scientists.[28] At least part of these preferences could be explained by the greater public knowledge of the role of engineers.

Since occupational image plays a part in occupational choice, those concerned with the recruitment of scientific personnel have given some attention to the images of the scientists held by high school and college students.[29] The images revealed by these studies indicate a preference among American students for the "practical," "down-to-earth" role played by the engineer — the technologist — while they reveal a mixture of admiration and doubt about the scientist — the man of knowledge. The image the students had of the scientist was of a highly intelligent individual devoted to his studies at the expense of interest in his friends and his family. While some value was placed on the scientist's intellectual abilities, he was also seen as being emotional and radical on political and social issues. While the students saw the scientist as having increasing power in public affairs, they viewed him as being only moderately responsible — someone not to be trusted. These facets of the image perhaps serve as the basis for the questions some people raise about the loyalty of scientists. The scientist was seen as a man with few friends, great determination, and an unusual set of values. He was seen as being basically uninterested in people — and, therefore, out of touch with the "realities" of life. This image was persistent. It was common to both high school and college students. Even those who had already chosen scientific careers accepted this image.

In contrast to the image of the scientist, the student's image of the engineer had few negative aspects. The engineer was seen as being more concerned with people. The engineer was not as self-sacrificing as the scientist and was characteristically wealthier. The engineer was a "more regular" guy. He was clean-cut, played poker, had good taste — revealed in part by his pretty wife. His normalcy was reflected by the fact that he was seen as less intellectual than the scientist. In fact, the authors of the study reported that the image of the engineer was that of the "simonized scientist" — possessing all of the good qualities and none of the bad.

These images, of course, are a reflection of and commentary on the society's value system. It would be interesting to explore the implications of the finding that while self-sacrifice is devalued, the possession of wealth is viewed as being an integral component of a "regular" guy in American society. The point to be emphasized here, however, is that the more favorable image of

28. Coles, op. cit.
29. Margaret Mead and Rhoda Metraux, "Image of the Scientists among High School Students," *Science*, 126 (August 30, 1957), pp. 384–90, and David C. Beardslee and Donald D. O'Dowd, "The College Student's Image of the Scientist," *Science*, 133 (March 31, 1961), pp. 997–1001.

the engineer indicates the persistence of the normative conception of science as technology.

How to overcome this image of the scientist has been the subject of some discussion. There has been an attempt to present the scientist as a "regular guy" — one who has a pretty wife and friends; and one who prefers poker to chess. In other words, the attempt has been made to normalize him — in the previous idiom, to "simonize" him. Some, however, object to such "public relations" attempts to "disguise" scientific inquiry. They suggest that an attempt should be made to place a higher value on intellectual activity and to provide special inducements to students who pursue scientific careers.

(d) *Encouraging scientific talent within the educational system.* A number of suggestions and programs have emerged in recent years to try to encourage scientific talent. One suggestion has been to encourage excellent teaching at all levels of education. This implies that the recruitment of scientific personnel is influenced by teachers who are able to instill a desire in the student to gain and create knowledge. By keeping good teachers from being attracted to more highly paid but perhaps less socially significant jobs and by attempting to upgrade the skills of existing teachers, some scientific talent may be encouraged.

In addition to the stress on improved teaching, there is concern over the early identification and motivation of scientific talent. This requires greater dependence upon guidance and counseling within the schools. Here again one finds shortages — this time a shortage of counselors who have both the skills of testing and awareness of the limitations of existing tests. The federal government has attempted to develop educational programs for the training of counselors and also to sponsor workshops for the continuing education of present counselors.

A number of modifications and extensions of present educational practice have been suggested — the development of summer institutes, the development of honors programs, work acceleration for gifted children, and the establishment of college level courses for able high school students. The encouragement of academically related extracurricular activities, such as science clubs and science fairs, has been recommended to develop latent scientific interests.

In addition to attempts to create interest and motivation on the part of capable students, there is still the problem of providing the financial means for many students to attend college. It has been proposed that a minimum of 100,000 scholarships be provided each year. While this may seem monumental, the cost every four years would be only slightly larger than the cost of one aircraft carrier. The problem of the encouragement of scientific talent, however, cannot be detached from the general encouragement of intellectual endeavor within the school system and within the larger society.

3. *Developing a Science Policy for the Government.* Scientific and technological changes have both economic and political consequences. It is obvious that technological research has increased the capacity of an industrial society to expand its productivity. The repeated story of the somewhat informal letters and visits by Einstein, Szilard, and others to President Roosevelt apprising him of the military potentials of atomic fission which led to the development of the atomic bomb, illustrates the political and military implications of science. The importance of science in government has been recognized since World War II by the establishment of the Atomic Energy Commission, the National Aeronautics and Space Administration, the National Science Foundation, and the Department of Health, Education and Welfare.

To communicate scientific information to the executive branch, a complicated set of administrative machinery has developed. The President has a Science Advisory Committee. There is the Federal Council for Science and Technology responsible for over-all planning and co-ordination in research and development among agencies in the federal government. Both organizations are chaired by a Presidential Assistant for Science and Technology. This assistant to the President attends meetings of the cabinet and is available to the President as a consultant in those areas where science bears on critical questions of policy and action. In addition, several government departments, including the Department of State, maintain Science Advisers.

With the increasing importance of science for government policy, there have been a number of proposals to create a Department of Science and Technology. Such a department would have the same status as any other and would be headed by a secretary, a regular member of the President's cabinet. While many reasons are offered, among them are suggestions that the establishment of such a department would enhance the status of science as a government activity and would encourage greater Congressional support. In addition, proponents of such a change imply that the merger in a single department of a number of agencies would reduce duplication of effort and would bring about better co-ordination. Several different bills establishing a Department of Science have been introduced into Congress.[30] Such a department has been opposed in a report of the President's Science Advisory Board and by a majority of the participants of the American Association for the Advancement of Science Parliament of Science meeting in 1958. If such a department became a reality, one could expect opposition from other gov-

30. S. 676, 86th Congress, First Session; S. 586, 86th Congress, First Session.

ernmental agencies which would lose functions or personnel to the new department. Whether a government department with cabinet status is the answer is not certain, but the effort to provide more effective and better coordinated scientific activities within the government will be of continuing importance in the future.

The problems of the relation of science to government are not simply organizational. To gain support, Congressional or otherwise, requires some understanding by policy makers of the dimensions of the scientific task. With the complexities of knowledge, meanings are often hard to communicate — mathematics cannot be translated phrase for phrase like French. The frustrations of communication have been reflected in a senator's lament, after coming from a hearing on the exploration of space — "This is the only place I know where a senator can't ask questions." [31]

4. *Developing Support for Science.* As indicated earlier, Vannevar Bush, at the end of World War II, called for the establishment of a National Science Foundation. President Truman, in September 1945, called for the creation of such a foundation. In 1947 he ordered an examination of the nation's scientific research effort by a Presidential Scientific Board. Primarily on the basis of both the Bush and the Board reports, legislation was introduced into Congress for the establishment of a foundation. After lengthy debate, the Foundation was enacted into law in 1950 and in 1951 operating funds were voted.

While thirty-eight federal agencies are concerned with scientific activities, as an outcome of the long-lived definition of science as technology, only two of them, the National Science Foundation and the Smithsonian Institution, are not directly concerned with practical problems. The powers of the Foundation were defined by Congress as follows:

> To develop and encourage the pursuit of a national policy for the promotion of basic research and education in the sciences; to initiate and support basic scientific research in the mathematical, physical, medical, biological, engineering, and other sciences . . . ; to award . . . scholarships and graduate fellowships in the mathematical, physical, medical, biological, engineering and other sciences; to foster the interchange of scientific information among scientists in the United States and foreign countries; to evaluate scientific research programs undertaken by agencies of the Federal Government, and to correlate the Foundation's scientific program with those undertaken by individuals and by public and private research groups; to maintain a register of scientific and technical personnel and in other ways provide a central clearinghouse for information covering all scientific personnel in the United States, including its Territories and possessions. [32]

31. David Bergamini, "The Language of Science," *The Reporter* (March 31, 1960), p. 36.
32. Public Law 507, 81st Congress, The National Science Foundation of 1950.

The implementation of the scope of the Foundation has taken a number of directions during its years of operation.

(a) *Support of research facilities.* While government support for research facilities has been extensive in technological areas, little has been expended for tools for basic research. Consequently, nuclear reactors, computer installations, radio and optical telescopes, and other facilities have been provided by the Foundation to universities to encourage and facilitate basic research.

(b) *Support of research.* The general pattern of research support used by the NSF has been the grant system. It operates in the following ways. Proposals from individuals or groups of scientists are submitted, which are reviewed by advisory panels and evaluated on the basis of scientific merit. In 1953, the Foundation was able to support only 8 per cent of the proposals it received, giving an average grant of $11,156 for an average period of 1.9 years. In 1960, it was able to support 26 per cent of the proposals received, at which time the average grant was $30,600 for an average period of 2.3 years.

(c) *Programs for education in the sciences.* From 1950 to 1960, the Foundation expended an estimated $175 million for support of programs directly related to education. More than half this money was spent on institutes to train and retrain teachers in science and mathematics. By 1960, 72,000 teachers had attended such institutes. In addition, support was given through fellowships to graduate students and to advanced scholars for further study. The Foundation has also made available traveling science libraries and demonstrations to high schools. It has provided opportunities for undergraduates to obtain research experience. It has provided for students in small colleges opportunities to come into contact with visiting scientists. It has defined education broadly, not confining it to formal courses in educational institutions, and recently it has given support to raising the level of scientific literacy of the general public. This latter activity is based on the assumption that, in order to participate fully in the democratic process, citizens must have at least a general knowledge and understanding of the nature of science and its implications for national policy.

(d) *International co-operation in science.* Co-operative activities with scientists in other nations have been supported, as illustrated by participation in the International Geophysical Year. The Foundation provided some of the funds for this activity and from this co-operative effort continuing international programs are operating in Antarctic research.

(e) *Other programs.* The Foundation has also been active in formulating improvements in the content of science courses. It has maintained a Register of Scientific and Technical Personnel and information on the number and characteristics of scientific personnel.

The Foundation has also developed programs seeking to disseminate scientific information through translation and publication. The problem of the scope and complexity of scientific literature has become an important one. Scientific literature in languages other than the traditional German and French has become increasingly important. This requires the scientist to become a linguist. Too, the sheer number of professional journals reporting research findings requires almost the full time of a scientist in reading what others have done. This inability to keep up with the scientific literature is both frustrating and costly. The National Science Foundation reported that a group of American research laboratories spent five years and more than $200,000 researching a problem in electrical circuitry, only to discover after the conclusion of the work that the research had long since been done and the results published in Russia. In order to prevent such duplications, the National Science Foundation has begun to support existing abstracting services of scientific societies.

THE CONSEQUENCES OF FEDERAL SUPPORT OF SCIENCE

While the National Science Foundation represents the major entry of the federal government into the support of basic research, it represents only a small part of total federal involvement in research and development. The federal government supports about 50 per cent of the research in the United States. Funds for the other half are supplied by industrial firms, foundations, state and local governments, and by private gifts. Federal funds for research have increased tremendously. In 1940, federal research and development expenditures constituted less than one per cent of the total federal budget while in 1960, it represented almost 7 per cent of the budget, amounting to almost $5.5 billion. These funds go to federal laboratories, industrial laboratories, and to laboratories of nonprofit organizations. In 1959, 37 per cent of all federal funds went to federal laboratories, 45 per cent went to industrial laboratories, 15 per cent to educational institutions, and 3 per cent to other institutions. While increasing support solves some problems, it creates others, for it tends to (1) perpetuate the imbalance between science as knowledge and science as technology; (2) create problems for universities, perhaps diverting them from their basic functions; (3) perpetuate differential emphasis on certain scientific areas at the expense of others.

1. *Perpetuation of the Imbalance Between Science as Knowledge and Science as Technology.* While total expenditures for research have increased rapidly, there are few indications that this increase means an *actual* increase in support for basic science. Between 1953 and 1957, the funds for basic research doubled, but in each of these years these funds represented only about 8 per cent of the total research and development funds in the United States. This means that, regardless of the increase in funds available for basic research,

over 90 per cent of all research funds in the United States still are used for technology. Since about four-fifths of the total national budget is now spent on agencies concerned with national defense, the aim of these agencies — the Department of Defense, the atomic energy and space programs — is to draw the attention of their scientists and research workers to problems having direct military application. While these segments concerned with techno-logical application have increased in their supply of funds, other govern-mental agencies more closely related to basic science, such as the Bureau of Standards, the Weather Bureau, and the Geological Survey, have remained at an appropriation level at which they were in the 1930's. In essence, while the total funds for research and development have increased substantially in recent years, still over 90 per cent of these funds are expended for techno-logical application — thus perpetuating the traditional preoccupation with technology.

2. *The Disruption of Traditional University Tasks.* As indicated previously, about 15 per cent of all federal funds for research and development go to universities. While this percentage has remained relatively constant in re-cent years, the funds have almost doubled, from $260 million in 1954 to almost $500 million in 1959. This means that universities are being offered increased opportunities for financing research. This increased availability of research funds has implications for the mission of the university.

Universities pride themselves on being communities of scholars designed to preserve, transmit, and create knowledge. As such, they represent the "natural" home for implementing the normative conception of science as knowledge. This function of a university is supplemented in American society by the notion of service to the community. In fact, the Morrill Act — establishing the state university system — was cast in terms of a university service agency in agriculture and mechanical arts. Universities, both public and private, have had a tradition of undertaking tasks for governmental agencies. Thus, while the university sees itself as the creator of knowledge, it also defines its mission as one of service.[33]

Universities accepting governmental and industrial funds are often con-fronted with research problems having little immediate relevance to the creation of new knowledge. In 1959, almost 70 per cent of all research funds used in universities were from the federal government, while industry financ-ing and university financing each supplied about 9 per cent. Foundation sup-port and private gifts supplied the rest. This means that the bulk of research activity in universities is focused on technological problems or at least on basic research of interest primarily to the government. Of the federal funds

33. This idea is expressed in Charles V. Kidd, *American Universities and Federal Re-search*, Cambridge: Belknap Press, 1959, Chap. 2, "Functions of Universities."

given to universities for research, about one-third comes from the Department of Defense, another third from the Atomic Energy Commission, and most of the remainder comes from the Department of Health, Education and Welfare, the Department of Agriculture, and the National Science Foundation. The money from the National Science Foundation, most likely to be in support of basic research, represents only 7 per cent of the federal total to universities.[34]

Given the traditional functions of the universities, does the preoccupation with financed research detract from the function of the university as a teaching institution? The teacher-researcher has traditionally been the same person but now these roles are becoming increasingly separated and specialized. There has been a rapid growth of university personnel who have nothing to do with teaching. What are the implications of this rapid growth of research activity when universities face rapidly increasing enrollments? Does federal money raise questions about the authority and autonomy of state and private universities — in other words, the whole issue of federal control? It is interesting, in view of the arguments about federal financing of education, that few questions have been raised about the predominance of federal financing for university research. Finally, and particularly pertinent if science is to be directed to the creation of knowledge, does the availability of funds oriented toward technological application detract and divert the university from its role as the creator of knowledge?

The conflict between the role of the university in the creation of knowledge and its role in needing and receiving financial support for research is nowhere better seen than in a report of the National Science Foundation:

University officials estimate that, during the academic year 1953–1954, academic departments of colleges and universities and agricultural experiment stations received about $85 million for basic research from the Federal government. But Federal officials estimate that they provided barely half of that amount to universities for that same purpose and during that same period.[35]

While part of this discrepancy reveals the difficulty of categorizing research as either "basic" or "applied," certainly part of it reveals the attempt of universities to maintain their image as a place of knowledge without biting the hand that feeds them.

3. *The Perpetuation of Differential Emphasis on Certain Scientific Fields.* As indicated before, men like Franklin and Jefferson saw scientific inquiry as extending to all branches of knowledge. However, the word "science"

34. This concentration does not affect each university equally. In 1962, it was reported that roughly 75 per cent of all government research contracts go to 25 institutions out of over 2000 in the U.S. In addition, fewer than 100 institutions account for 95 per cent of the funds.
35. National Science Foundation, *Basic Research, a National Resource*, Washington, D.C.: Government Printing Office, 1957, p. 25.

generally evokes the image of the chemist with his test tubes, the physicist with his reactor, or the biologist peering through his microscope. Rarely does the word "science" create the image of the social scientist working with demographic data, price indices, or questionnaire data. Thus, the word "science" is most strongly associated with the physical sciences, next with the biological sciences, and less frequently with the social sciences.

In the Congressional debate concerning the establishment of a National Science Foundation, the specific provision which created a Division of Social Sciences was deleted. George Lundberg concluded that the debate "should perhaps not be taken as reflecting any considered hostility or opposition on the part of the Senate, but simply as a reflection of the common feeling that the social and physical sciences have nothing in common and that at best the social sciences are a propagandist, reformist, evangelical sort of cult." [36]

In the Congressional hearings, witnesses confused social science with socialism, suggested that social science was not science, that social science would be used for manipulating human behavior, and added many other misunderstandings to the record. Most witnesses, however, supported the inclusion of the social sciences. While the resultant legislation establishing the Foundation in 1950 did not *exclude* the social sciences it took a "permissive, not mandatory" position toward them. Even though support of social science research was permissible, during the early years of the Foundation's operation there was sole concentration on the physical and biological sciences. Gradually the Foundation began to support social science research in areas of convergence between the physical and social sciences. The inclusion of the social sciences also began to receive support from Congressional sources.

With this support, and with the expansion of social science projects in convergent areas, the NSF staff, in 1958, asked for limited funds for the social sciences as a separate budget item. When these funds were obtained, a consolidated program for the Social Science Research became a part of the NSF.

Table 7-1 indicates that, in terms of actual support, social science is still a stepchild. The physical and biological sciences receive from 13 to 17 times as much money for basic research as do the social sciences.

The disparity between the physical and biological sciences and the social sciences is reflected elsewhere too. In 1953–54, federal money for social science research constituted only about 4 per cent of the total of all federal expenditures for research in universities. One discipline, physics, received over seven times as much as all of the social sciences combined.

While the social sciences are receiving increased support as society shifts its normative conception toward the advancement of knowledge, the continual disparity between support of the social and other sciences may have

36. G. A. Lundberg, "The Senate Ponders the Social Sciences," *The Scientific Monthly*, 64 (May 1947), p. 399.

TABLE 7-1

Expenditures of the National Science Foundation, 1952–60
(to the nearest thousands)

	1952	1954	1956	1958	1960
Total appropriations	3,500	8,000	16,000	49,750	154,773
Biological and medical sciences					
Basic research	736	1,966	4,793	8,540	24,405
Research facilities	—	—	125	987	2,000
Mathematics, physical and engineering sciences					
Basic research	311	2,033	4,700	9,536	33,489
Research facilities	—	—	397	5,404	11,671
Social sciences					
Basic research	—	—	—	554	1,925
Research facilities	—	—	—	—	—

Source: Table I, Alan Waterman, "National Science Foundation: A Ten-Year Resume," *Science*, 6 (May 1960), Vol. 131, No. 3410, p. 1344. Reprinted from *Science* by permission.

important consequences. These were well stated by Lt. Gen. Trudeau, Chief of Research and Development, Department of the Army, in his testimony before a Congressional appropriations committee:

We can never afford to neglect basic research and the Army wants to do more of it whenever we find applicable projects to further this increase in knowledge. Such research is not confined to the physical sciences. Investigations of the social sciences to help us utilize more effectively our manpower and insure man-machine compatibility with complex engines of war being developed is vital. Should we neglect these vital considerations we only aggravate the trend in which the physical sciences are outstripping the social sciences and may, in time, reach a point where the machine may destroy its maker.[37]

SCIENTIFIC DISSENSUS — THE FUTURE

The emergence of science as a national preoccupation has been recent and rapid. Science as knowledge is increasingly seen as a necessity for the continuation of industrialization, but now criticisms are being made about this enhanced status paralleling those made earlier of big business, big labor, and big government. Critics suggest science is too big, too costly, and perhaps too preoccupied with tasks which have little to do with the continuing welfare of the society.

Big science needs broad public support for its continuance and growth. To obtain public support, it has to be popularized. Popularization often makes

37. *Department of Defense Appropriations for 1960.* Hearings before the subcommittee on Appropriations, House of Representatives. 86th Congress, 1st Session, Washington, D.C.: Government Printing Office, 1959, p. 339.

scientific issues a matter of public, rather than professional, controversy. With the growth of science, organizational problems emerge. The scientist, deep in thought solving a problem in knowledge, is being replaced by the scientist-administrator, deep in a conference solving an organizational problem. Administrators, drawn away from the search for knowledge, often find it easier to spend money than thought. Big science is costly, too. Federal expenditures for research and development, mostly for defense, now constitute about 10 per cent of the total national budget. However, if the increase in these expenditures continues at the same rate as it has during the 1950's, it is estimated that in about 65 years the total federal budget would be spent on science and technology.

Even with this rapid increase in expenditures, choices still have to be made as to what areas of knowledge to explore. In the 1960's, the "pet" projects involve high-energy physics and manned space flight. The estimated cost to put a "man on the moon" is $30 billion. Using this sum on other projects could accomplish the following: provide a 10 per cent raise in salary over a ten-year period for every teacher in the United States, from kindergarten through university, in both public and private institutions (about $9.8 billion); give $10 million each to 200 of the better smaller colleges ($2 billion), finance seven-year fellowships (freshman through Ph.D.) at $4000 per person per year for 50,000 scientists and engineers ($1.4 billion); contribute $200 million each toward the creation of ten new medical schools ($2 billion); build and largely endow complete universities, with medical, engineering, and agricultural faculties for all fifty-three of the nations which have been added to the United Nations since its original founding ($13.2 billion); create three more permanent Rockefeller Foundations ($1.5 billion); and still have $100 million left over to popularize science.[38]

The most significant projects are not necessarily those which provide the most interesting publicity or the most enthusiastic public and congressional support. It has been suggested that:

Those cultures that have devoted too much of their talents to monuments that had nothing to do with the real issues of human well-being have usually fallen upon bad days; history tells us that the French Revolution was the bitter fruit of Versailles and that the Roman Colosseum helped not at all in staving off the barbarians.

It is for us to learn well these lessons of history. We must not allow ourselves, by short-sighted seeking after fragile monuments of Big Science, to be diverted from our real purpose, which is the enriching and broadening of human life.[39]

38. Warren Weaver, "What a Moon Ticket Will Buy," *Saturday Review* (August 4, 1962), p. 38.

39. Alvin M. Weinberg, "Big Science — Marvel or Menance?," *The New York Times Magazine* (July 23, 1961), p. 51.

SUMMARY

Science in American society has been viewed as technology and as knowledge. Early development in American society emphasized science as technological progress. The Patent Office provided protection and encouragement for inventions which became the basis for many industrial enterprises. Science was viewed as a continuous source of inventions and gadgets.

The development of the atomic bomb and of earth satellites underscored for American society the importance of science as knowledge. Also continued technological innovation in an industrial society is more and more dependent upon abstract knowledge. To facilitate the conception of science as knowledge many forms of implementation have emerged. These include attempts to change the intellectual environment to encourage the pursuit of knowledge; attempts to increase the supply of scientific personnel; the development of a science policy for government; and the development of support for science. The federal government has been particularly important in increasing support. This increased support has continued to emphasize technological research and the physical and biological sciences. Because of the availability of increasing research funds to universities, the traditional function of the university as the creator of knowledge is threatened. The efforts to implement science as knowledge have become an increasingly important segment of an industrial society, both as a key to further industrialization and as a source of change for other institutional areas.

QUESTIONS AND SUGGESTIONS FOR FURTHER STUDY

1. Read an account of the Lewis and Clark expedition. Show how the different conceptions of science were reflected in the planning. What were Jefferson's reasons for encouraging the expedition and what reasons did he give to Congress to gain its support?
2. Why was the early emphasis in American society on science as technology?
3. Read an account of the origin and development of an early American industrial enterprise. How did technological innovation and patent protection figure in this development?
4. Why was the end of World War II a crucial time for the reassessment of the consequences of different conceptions of science?
5. Examine a history of the United States to see to what extent technological factors are used as an explanation of changes. To what extent does the conception of science as knowledge play in this history?
6. Analyze the "letters to the editor" in a newspaper over a period of time. In it, are there reflections of anti-intellectualism? Are there comments on "dangerous ideas," "impractical theories," "disloyal teachers," etc.?
7. To what extent does the emphasis on scientific careers detract from other equally significant and equally necessary vocations?

8. What advantages are given for initiating a Department of Science and Technology in the federal government?

9. Why do differences exist in the amount of support among the various scientific fields? Are these differences related to historical priorities? To relative differences in status accorded to the fields?

10. Consult a summary of activities of the National Science Foundation. What types of activities have been supported? Does this represent an increase or a change in types of activities from previous years?

SUGGESTED READINGS

Barber, Bernard, *Science and the Social Order*, New York: Collier Books, 1962. p   A textbook discussion of the sociology of science.

———— and Walter Hirsch (eds.), *The Sociology of Science: A Reader*, New York: Free Press of Glencoe, 1962. This reader treats science as a social phenomenon and describes the social process of scientific discovery. It includes readings which extend many of the topics in this chapter.

Dupree, A. Hunter, *Science in the Federal Government*, Cambridge: Belknap Press, 1957. A discussion of the development, up to 1940, of the federal government's involvement in science. This history illustrates the stress placed upon science as technology.

Elbers, Gerald W., and Paul Duncan (eds.), *The Scientific Revolution, Challenge and Promise*, Washington, D.C.: Public Affairs Press, 1959. A collection of articles stimulated by Soviet accomplishments in science. The articles suggest a number of changes, many now implemented, necessary to respond to this challenge.

Kidd, Charles V., *American Universities and Federal Research*, Cambridge: Belknap Press, 1959. This book indicates the extent of increasing support for science and raises a number of questions of this support for the traditional functions of universities.

Kornhauser, William, *Scientists in Industry*, Berkeley: University of California Press, 1962. Analyzes the major areas of strain and accommodation among scientists in the organizational setting of industrial research.

Knapp, Robert H. and Hubert B. Goodrich, *Origins of American Scientists*, Chicago: University of Chicago Press, 1952. Report of a study of the social origins and educational backgrounds of scientists in the United States. This has provided an impetus for other studies.

McCamy, James L., *Science and Public Administration*, University, Ala.: University of Alabama Press, 1960. A consideration of the complex problems of how science relates to public policy. Written with wit and clarity.

Price, Don K., *Government and Science, Their Dynamic Relation in American Democracy*, New York: New York University Press, 1954.   p   A general discussion of the relation of government and science with emphasis on the difficult problems posed by the government's utilization of science.

CHAPTER 8

MEDICAL CARE: INDIVIDUAL OR ORGANIZATIONAL PROBLEM

> . . . we cannot avoid the fact that we are finding ways to prevent and cure disease faster than we can find dollars to pay for them. Since what we want seems to be beyond our present means, we have become a nation of medical window-shoppers — the goods are on display, our motivation to buy has been stimulated, but our pocketbooks won't meet the price tag. Even if we trim away at other items in our budget — a painful bit of surgery that no anesthesia can deaden — we still won't be able to keep up with the rising cost of health as long as the present inefficiencies in our medical plant persists.[1]

There are few social problems whose importance exceeds that of ill health. And there are few whose proposed solutions have evoked more bitter controversy. Medical care has become more than a personal problem; today it is regarded as a public concern. The impressive array of medical discoveries has been accompanied by equally impressive demands for their prompt and wide utilization. This reappraisal of medical services has not been limited to the United States, for questions regarding the over-all improvement of health and medical care have become important in all industrial societies.

The very success of medical achievements has served to intensify the problem. Too, the increased desire for medical service has a short history. Only within the past generation has medicine been able to do much in the way of prevention and cure of disease. Dr. Lawrence Henderson of Harvard has been quoted to the effect that 1912 was the first year in history in which the random patient with a random disease consulting a random physician had better than a 50-50 chance of benefiting from the visit. Before the turn of the century, diagnosis was largely guesswork, anesthesia had just been discovered, surgery was limited to emergencies, and hospitals were for the poor or dying. But with a rapidly expanding medical technology came new techniques, new discoveries, and new specialization. With precise methods of diagnosis and a better understanding of the cause and cure of disease, along with reduced surgical risk and the discovery of wonder drugs, traditional pessimism has been replaced by a new, and sometimes naïve, optimism.

1. Donald B. Straus, "Can We Afford To Be Healthy?" cited in *The Crisis in American Medicine*, Marion K. Sanders (ed.), New York: Harper, 1960, 1961, p. 56.

Today medical care can contribute so greatly to human well-being it is desired by almost everyone. It is regarded as a necessary commodity. Dr. Alan Gregg of the Rockefeller Foundation speaks of this redefinition as the "fourth necessity." He points out that "Three-legged stools used to be common. Now we prefer four-legged chairs. Food, clothing and housing used to be the three necessities of life. Now life rests more solidly on four necessities — food, clothing, housing and health services. Medical science, by its concern for protecting and enhancing life and by its proven dependability in so doing, is making medical care something that everybody wants."

The normative problem: how should medical knowledge be utilized so that it can meet the health needs of the nation more effectively?

Analysis of medical care issues in the United States today discloses a paradox. On the one hand, there is mounting evidence of impressive scientific discoveries. Almost daily, magazines, books, and reports describe new techniques and treatments. On the other hand, there is growing dissatisfaction with medical and hospital care. There is widespread criticism of rising medical costs, and signs of increasing disagreements between patients and doctors. At the very time when technological advances in medicine are mushrooming, the medical profession is also receiving greater criticism.

Dissensus today centers on changes in the doctor-patient relationship. A frequent criticism of physicians is that they do not give enough personal attention. The fact that medicine today is practiced in a much more complex social setting compounds the problem of interpersonal relations. However, a less obvious but equally important reason is the increasing number of people who suffer from psychosomatic or "functional" illness. In these cases the patients' problems are mainly emotional, rather than organic, and such patients are likely to be especially demanding of the physician's time and attention. They often constitute a "reservoir of ill-will." Also, the fact that much medical care now consists of treating chronic disorders means that greater demands are placed on the patient's co-operation. Furthermore, difficulties in the patient-physician relationship occur at a time when the stresses of an industrial society have intensified the need of everyone, with or without neurotic tendencies, for guidance and understanding. Thus the weakening of the sources of support traditional in pre-industrial societies has made many people seek more personal attention from their physicians. It is in this setting, then, that we have the paradox of increasing medical knowledge proceeding simultaneously with — and even creating — a sharp rise in the need and demand for medical care.

Current dissatisfactions rest on underlying assumptions of what medical care should be. Frequently these conceptions are based on a simpler, less complex type of society in which the country doctor was able to establish an informal, continuing relationship with his patients, without the bewilderment (or benefit) of modern methods of diagnosis and hospital procedure. Indeed, the present system of medical practice has its roots in a society vastly different from the one in which both physician and patient find themselves today. This earlier setting provides a necessary background against which contemporary and emerging conceptions can be understood.

HISTORICAL BACKGROUND OF THE PHYSICIAN AND MEDICINE

The image of the "country doctor" about the turn of the century was a very favorable one — probably more favorable than at any time since. He was appreciated, respected, and even revered. The key to this laudable reputation lay in the relationship he was able to establish with his patients. It was a personal relationship. His patients were impressed and satisfied with his attitude toward them *as persons* — in addition to the prescriptions he left for their illnesses. He was receptive to their concerns, their pains, and their anxieties. He was "available" and not in a hurry to leave. He would offer "sensible suggestions" for their emotional difficulties and life problems. He was completely accepted. His fees were "reasonable." And he sometimes forgot to send a bill.

Probably a higher percentage of patients received more personal attention in rural America than they do today. The country doctor could spend more time in those days with each case because there were more physicians in proportion to the population. In 1909 there was one doctor for every 568 persons. In 1961 there was only one for every 709.[2] Even though the horse-and-buggy doctor led a busy life, old fashioned efficient communications insulated him against the almost constant pressure from patients and hospitals that the modern urban physician faces. Without telephones, it was often difficult to locate the country doctor. This permitted him to "sit awhile" and chat with each patient he visited, without danger of the visit being abruptly ended by an emergency phone call.[3]

2. David D. Rutstein, "Do You Really Want a Family Doctor?," *Harper's Magazine*, 221 (October 1960), p. 144.

3. This does not imply, however, that the rural physician was able to move from patient to patient at his own pace. Word still got around and some rather effective methods of communication were devised. Dr. Arthur E. Hertzler tells of one such method in his book, *The Horse and Buggy Doctor*, New York: Harper, 1938, p. 78. "In those days there were no telephones. Neighbors knew by the grapevine message when the doctor had been called to one of their number and if members of their families needed a doctor they hung a sheet on some conspicuous object. If it was at night a lantern was hung up. I knew these signals and answered the call. I remember that one trip I visited seven patients in addition to the one for whom I was originally called."

Probably there was greater continuity of medical care in earlier days. The lack of specialists permitted the family doctor to supervise his patients' health continuously. The same doctor was called for appendicitis or a headache. Furthermore, most people lived their entire lives in the same community, contributing to continuity of medical care and enhancing the doctor-patient relationship. The early practice of medicine occurred almost entirely in the patient's home. The doctor was able to observe his patients in a family setting and to use this in his diagnosis and treatment.

But in spite of this, medical care was poor in pre-industrial America. Tuberculosis was the most common cause of death. Mothers frequently died in childbirth, and infant mortality was higher than most popularized accounts of "the good old days" reveal. While the doctor remained at the patient's bedside, there was little else he could do. Indeed, the genial country doctor knew that compassion and bedside manner were all-important, since he understood little about curing most illnesses. He had limited equipment and only a handful of truly effective drugs — the two most potent ones being digitalis and morphine. He knew how to use his few drugs and to apply sympathy. Beyond that, he could do little.

The uncertainty in medical treatment helps to explain why the physician has been regarded as part healer, part priest, and part family counselor. Illness produces insecurity. The patient finds himself completely dependent upon the physician's skill and knowledge — a situation conducive to reliance on hope, faith, and other subjective factors. Anthropologists have observed that magical beliefs and practices cluster about situations where there is an important uncertainty factor and where there are strong emotional interests in the success of action.[4] Problems associated with medical care provide a classic example. This is why patients deeply desire to have confidence in their doctors, idealize them, and sometimes endow them with superhuman powers. This also helps to explain why the physician-patient relationship is an intimate and complex one, and why changes in this relationship created by new social conditions have produced new problems for physicians and patients alike.

Even though the conditions that sustained the early image of medical care and the physician are no longer present, the image itself remains. It not only remains but serves as a standard against which doctors and medical care today are evaluated. Its influence is still reflected in the kind of doctor selected by the American Medical Association for its coveted "Physician of the Year" award. Invariably, the winner is a general practitioner living in a small community — despite the fact that the doctors on the selection

4. See Bronislaw Malinowski, *Magic, Science and Religion and Other Essays,* Glencoe, Free Press. 1948.

committee are usually urban specialists, and that the "GP" no longer is the typical American physician. The orientation of much contemporary medical practice draws heavily upon this earlier image in other more generic ways, and serves as the basis for the contemporary normative answer to medical care problems.

> *Contemporary Normative Conception: Individual Responsibility* — Illness and medical care problems are essentially matters of individual responsibility and should be resolved through the solo, fee-for-service system of medical practice.

Problems of medical care should be met and solved within the framework of traditional medical practice. The guiding principles of this system are found in a resolution issued by the American Medical Association's House of Delegates in 1934.

All features of medical service in any method of medical practice should be under the control of the medical profession. No other body or individual is legally or educationally equipped to exercise such control.

No third party must be permitted to come between the patient and his physician in any medical relation. All responsibility for the character of medical service must be borne by the profession.

Patients must have absolute freedom to choose a legally qualified doctor of medicine who will serve them from among all those qualified to practice and who are willing to give service.

However the cost of medical service may be distributed, the immediate cost should be borne by the patient if able to pay at the time the service is rendered.

Underlying these principles is the basic conviction of the AMA that medical care is an individual problem, and that payment for medical services should be the responsibility of the individual patient. This position was stated succinctly by Dr. Walter B. Martin when he was president-elect of the AMA. He said, "Medical care is a very complicated problem. It is not just a matter of buildings and equipment and technicians. It is a matter of the individual preserving a sense of responsibility for his own health and participating in providing the cost of it to the extent of his ability to pay. . . ." [5]

The concept of medical care as an individual, personal matter is behind another basic belief of contemporary medicine, namely, the importance of maintaining what is termed "the traditional doctor-patient relationship." This concept is also embodied in the above-mentioned principles, and in-

5. Statement by Dr. Walter B. Martin, January 28, 1954, when he appeared before the House Committee on Interstate and Foreign Commerce as an expert witness on health insurance. Cited in Richard Carter, *The Doctor Business*, New York: Doubleday, 1958, p. 54.

volves essentially three elements: (1) free choice of physician, (2) fee-for-service method of payment, and (3) no third party. In short, the contemporary normative view asserts that the doctrine of individual responsibility can best be realized through the preservation of a voluntary, private relationship between doctor and patient which is free from external influence. It is also widely believed that the maintenance of the traditional relationship is basic to competent medical care, and if it is modified, the quality of medical service will inevitably be lowered.

Thus the contemporary normative conception views medical care as an individual problem. The cost of medical service should be borne by the patient or his family. In keeping with this perspective, the treatment process is viewed as consisting essentially of two individuals — a doctor and a patient. The doctor, a solo practitioner, should be freely chosen and directly paid by the patient, without the intercession of a third party. Any departure from the individualistic, private practice of medicine is viewed as harmful to the quality of medical care.

At this point, some consideration should be given to the technological changes which have created difficulties for the contemporary conception and have led to an emergent conception.

CHANGES AFFECTING THE CONTEMPORARY CONCEPTION

Three sources of change have created difficulties for maintaining the contemporary normative conception. These are (1) changes in the role of the physician, (2) changes in medicine itself, and (3) changes in the larger society.

1. *Changes in the Role of the Physician.* The expansion of medical knowledge inevitably led to specialization. Practicing physicians and medical students alike were forced to add years to their training simply to "keep up" with the growing medical knowledge. Their fields of interest had to become progressively smaller because no man could keep up with the medical literature. Doctors began to resemble laboratory scientists and increasingly concentrated upon minute aspects of the human body, such as cells, tissues, the functions of specific organs, or a particular part of a special illness. As knowledge advanced, specialization became widespread. Whereas in 1900 virtually all American physicians were general practitioners, by 1949 only 38 per cent were so categorized by the American Medical Association. In 1958 the American Medical Directory listed 33 distinct specialities, the standards of which are set by 19 separate examining boards. And if the more common sub-specialities are added to this list, there are today some 50 different types of doctors.[6]

6. Herman M. Somers and Anne R. Somers, *Doctors, Patients, and Health Insurance,* Washington, D.C.: The Brookings Institution, 1961, p. 29.

Other developments, consistent with the major characteristics of an industrial society, have contributed to specialization. One factor concerns the way in which medical students are selected. As research abilities become highly valued, this is reflected in the preferences medical schools give to students who have completed original research in college and who have high classroom grades in the sciences. Too, medical training is characterized by almost constant exposure to research scientists and specialists. The trend toward specialization is also reinforced by the qualifications sought in full-time professors of internal medicine. Dr. David Rutstein, head of the Department of Preventive Medicine at the Harvard Medical School, recently stated, "Demonstrated competence in the basic sciences — particularly in one of the sub-specialities of biochemistry — is almost a prerequisite. Ability to manipulate the gene, the hemoglobin molecule, or an enzyme system is prized far above skill in management of a patient with a complicated disease."[7]

Other circumstances have exerted powerful pressure. Probably one of the most important influences has been patients' enthusiastic acceptance of the specialist and their willingness to pay more for his services than for those of the family doctor. There are also the greater conveniences associated with specialist practice, such as fewer night calls and greater control over daily work schedules. In addition, there is the increased difficulty experienced by many general practitioners in obtaining hospital appointments. "Some of the best hospitals keep them out entirely or restrict them to minor care. And hospital connections are essential in this day of hospital-oriented medicine, if the GP is not to lose all his 'interesting' cases, to become a sort of traffic officer for the specialists and hospitals, to deal with the trivial and manage the hopeless."[8] The emphasis modern physicians place on adequate hospital facilities points to another change which further explains why the image of the elderly, bearded, family physician has given way to the young, clean-shaven surgeon in white surrounded by aseptic assistants and equipment. This is the trend toward hospital-centered medical care. With more elaborate technology and the need for concentrating medical equipment in a central location, the hospital has assumed primary importance as the place for medical treatment. This became necessary when the doctor's equipment began to outgrow his little black bag.

With treatment in a hospital, the doctor-patient relationship also changed.[9]

7. Rutstein, op. cit. p. 147.
8. Somers and Somers, op. cit. p. 31.
9. Some observers feel that an important symptom of deteriorating doctor-patient relationships is reflected in the growth of malpractice suits. AMA Law Department records show that about 18,500 living physicians — one out of seven AMA members — have been the object of a malpractice suit or claim. In California the ratio is one out of four. "Review of Medical Professional Liability Claims and Suits," *Journal of the American Medical Association*, 171 (May 10, 1958), p. 227.

During a "house call" the doctor could evaluate the patient's illness in a significant social setting, and this opportunity frequently aided the diagnosis. However, the more specialized that treatment became, the less the patient was seen as a whole person. And although medical miracles are now frequently performed between strangers, both doctors and patients agree that the absence of continuity and personal attention is not in keeping with the best of medical care. Yet with all the faults of fragmented specialization and the somewhat impersonal doctor-patient relationships, the seriously ill patient today is far better off in the hands of the modern physician than he was with the country doctor.

2. *Changes Within Medicine.* The changing features of medical care are based on (a) the growth of medical knowledge, (b) increased complexity in the organization of medical care, and (c) increased costs. These changes create some of the considerations upon which the emerging conception of medical care rests.

(a) *Growth of medical knowledge and technology.* The sheer increase in medical information and technical equipment since the beginning of this century has been staggering. In the United States alone, there are more than a thousand journals devoted to medicine as a whole or to its numerous branches. The total is even higher if journals in fields related to medicine, such as physiology, are included. A medical editor recently pointed out that if a surgeon were to devote every evening in the month to reading only the principal journals of general surgery in the English language, he could not get through one month's issues before the next crop arrived. The time-consuming aspect of this problem is mirrored in the fact that there are now digests of medical reports recorded on tape for doctors to play while driving about on house calls.

Along with the increase in medical knowledge, there has been a proliferation of new equipment. In grandfather's day the only mechanical equipment available to most physicians included a few simple surgical instruments and such aids as a stethoscope, a clinical thermometer, and a head mirror. The physician's office equipment required little besides ordinary furniture. A doctor starting practice needed relatively little money to equip himself, and he could carry most of his professional equipment in his handbag. But advanced technology has changed all of this. Today the little black bag has been replaced by a battery of mechanical diagnostic tests requiring specialized skills and complicated hospital procedures.

The beneficial results of new medical know-how are often emphasized, but the very achievements which we have witnessed have brought with them some of the most pressing problems confronting medicine today. As we have already indicated, with new knowledge has come new specialization and further fragmentation of the doctor-patient relationship. It has also produced conflict over solo versus group practice, the trend toward involved hospital treatment, disagreements over "corporate medicine," and other conflicts to be discussed later in this chapter.

(b) *Increased complexity in the organization of medical services.* The rapid growth of medical science and technology has brought about widespread change in the organization and administration of medical services. With new knowledge accumulating at an ever increasing rate, medical care has evolved from a simple doctor-patient relationship into a complex business requiring expensive capital equipment and the co-ordination of a vast array of skills. The nineteenth-century picture of the physician maintaining his private office in his home or in an office building, with a nurse and a secretary, is rapidly becoming more nostalgic than real. Not only do one-third of the practicing physicians now work entirely with organizations, but a much larger number — about five-sixths, including the preceding group — work part-time or full-time with organizations, especially hospitals and clinics. In addition to these groups, a large proportion of physicians are now brought into working relationships with public health, public welfare, industrial, and other public and private organizations.

The modern hospital has enabled medical technology to perform more proficiently, but it has also plunged patients and doctors into new and often frustrating relationships. It has also meant that a large army of specialized personnel has appeared along with the new equipment. In an advanced technology, most medical personnel have become attendants to gadgets and machines as much as to patients directly. A perceptive classification of those engaged in specialized medical roles has been made by Simmons:

> If the patient can gain sufficient composure to observe carefully what is going on around him, he will recognize two kinds of specialists. They are (1) the scientific specialists who have learned more and more about less and less in the field of disease and patient problems, the experts who are, of course, indispensable and expensive, and (2) the "factory-trained" specialists who, to do it passably well and cheaply, have been quickly taught a little about a small task. They used to be called attendants and were dispensable and replaceable but are now moving up the prestige ladder, with more dignified titles and labels and increased prerogatives and pay.[10]

The increased complexity of hospital organization has served further to fragmentize health care and has contributed to stresses and conflicts between medical personnel and patients. It has reinforced the feeling on the part of many patients that their personal characteristics are often overlooked or

10. Leo W. Simmons, "Important Sociological Issues and Implications of Scientific Activities in Medicine," *Journal of the American Medical Association,* 173 (May 1960), p. 120.

neglected. These complications are products of our times and constitute unsolved issues in medical care.

One of the most striking changes in the over-all growth of medicine is the degree to which the proportion of physicians has declined, while that of all other medical personnel has expanded. In 1900 there were eleven doctors to every graduate nurse, whereas in 1940 there were two graduate nurses for every physician. In fact, the declining proportion of doctors in the population has come about as a result of the sharp increases in specialized and general assistants.

Changes in medical organization represent a movement away from an entrepreneurial conception of medicine as a profession practiced by individual craftsmen. The present trend is toward an ever increasing division of labor, made necessary by a highly developed technology. But all is not on the liability side of the social ledger. Beyond the machines and attendants, these changes also reflect the growing emphasis on comprehensive care and preventive medicine, which, by their very nature, require the skills of a great variety of paramedical and medical personnel.

(c) *Increased costs.* In medicine, just as in any other field since the nineteenth century, advances have led to increased costs. Measured in terms of the consumer price index, the cost of medical care from 1950 to 1960 has risen much more sharply than the over-all cost of living. Throughout the postwar years a steadily increasing proportion of personal income has been going into medical and hospital care (see Fig. 8-1). For example, private expenditures jumped from $7.7 billion in 1947 to $20 billion in 1961. The sharpest rise has been in payments to hospitals, which have more than tripled during this period. Payments to doctors and dentists have approximately doubled.[11]

This increase, of course, does not mean that Americans are in poorer health than they used to be. The greater complexity of medical services and improved skills and facilities come at high cost. Consider, for example, the fact that modern care often involves a medical "team," consisting of a physician in charge, but with high-salaried specialists in consulting capacities. The resulting care is usually superior, and this feature alone increases costs. However, other members of the team, including nurses, laboratory technicians, dieticians, and other skilled personnel compound costs. Add to this the costs of new medicines and drugs, and the picture becomes very expensive for most patients — even though the product is superior to what it used to be.

The family doctor as recently as two generations ago could do little for a persistent cough except advise prolonged rest. This advice cost perhaps $2, at the most $5. It was inexpensive and usually ineffective. Modern diagnostic and treatment procedures are much more effective, and even if the patient

11. *Fortune* (November 1959), p. 137.

Fig. 8-1. Costs of Medical Care; Percent Change in Cost of Living
Index Since 1950.

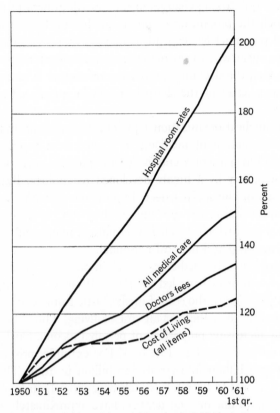

Source: *Time* (July 7, 1961), p. 58. *Time* chart by R.M.Chapin, Jr.,
reproduced by permission; Copyright Time, Inc. 1961.

has lung cancer, he still has a chance to recover. But the diagnosis itself
might cost up to $300 and the cost of the operation, which requires the serv-
ices of two highly skilled doctors with a roomful of technicians and a re-
cuperation period of several weeks in the hospital, could amount to $3000.

Hospital costs have been climbing more rapidly than any other single
item. A Bureau of Labor Statistics study has shown that in the thirty years
from 1926 to 1956 hospital room rates rose 265 per cent. In most hospitals
today a standard private room costs about $25 per day. One of the chief rea-
sons for higher hospital costs is the fact that hospitals offer more services than
ever before — more diagnostic and treatment services, more private and semi-
private accommodations, more out-patient service — and these new and expanded functions are expensive to maintain. Furthermore, hospitals deal in
highly personal services and are unable to profit from labor-saving machinery

which leads to increased industrial efficiency. Automation will never replace the nurse.

There is also the fact that more people are using hospitals than ever before. Today the annual admission rate is 12 per cent of the total population against 8 per cent a generation ago. And finally, room rates are higher because the room itself has changed. Patients used to be satisfied with a bed and four plain walls. But today, a hospital room has to be at least as comfortable as a motel room, including television and other conveniences. Even though medical expenditures have soared in recent years, there are no signs of abatement in this trend. In fact, all available data show that medical and hospital costs are accelerating. Between June 1958 and June 1960 medical prices rose over three times as much as the general price index.[12] By 1970 consumers probably will be spending almost twice as much on medical care as they are now, about $38 billion.

The economics of medical care is a large subject and its many ramifications cannot be pursued here, but an additional word should be added on one other matter that frequently becomes a part of any discussion involving rising health costs.

It is often pointed out to the disgruntled consumer that while he is paying more, he is getting a better buy for his money than ever before; he is receiving a better quality of medical care and more of it. This has not proved sufficient assuagement. Even if he appreciates the fact that he is receiving a far better product, it does not necessarily make it easier to pay for. The intelligent consumer may be well aware that compared to its predecessors the new medical product is as a new Cadillac to an old Model T. But unlike the Cadillac, the purchase of which is optional, modern medical care is essential, irrespective of one's means. This makes the difficulty all the more aggravating. As science and technology continue to serve us with ever-improving medical care, and as consumers become more conscious of its essentiality, the concomitant higher costs become a sorer and sorer point.[13]

These issues are receiving greater attention today and they have generated a steadily increasing public debate. Central to these discussions is "the search for a mechanism for effective pooling of risks and sharing of costs." As we shall see later, the emerging normative answer attempts to come to terms with these issues.

3. *Changes Within Society.* Other changes shaping the problem of medical care have their roots in broader social trends. They involve changes in expectations which have accompanied higher standards of living. These changes also reflect shifts in economic and political viewpoints and a reappraisal of the role of government in medical care. It should be clear, however, that no

12. Somers and Somers, op. cit. p. 403.
13. Ibid. p. 216.

sharp distinction exists between these changes and those just discussed. Society and medicine are interrelated. Changes in either affect, and are affected
by, changes in the other. Of greater importance is the way in which these
trends provide insight into the role played by normative dissensus in medical
care problems.

(a) *Broadened conception of medical care.* Technological developments
have not only led to higher expectations on the part of patients; they have
expanded the concept of medical care to include preventive and rehabilitative
measures. The earlier conception focused on the treatment of acute illnesses,
but as people begin to live longer, more attention is directed to the chronically
ailing and to the degenerative diseases of old age. The fact that more people
reach old age is itself an index of the effectiveness of preventive measures.
But it also means that people now have a better chance of being afflicted with
other disorders later in life. Thus, paradoxically, increasing medical knowledge has increased the need for medical care — particularly among the aged.

The broadened conception of care is reflected in changing definitions of
health. Earlier definitions were negative, defining health as the absence of
disease or disability. There is a trend, however, toward a more positive definition. The World Health Organization provides a representative example:
Health is "a state of complete physical, mental, and social well-being and not
merely an absence of disease or infirmity." The emphasis upon positive aspects of health and what this means in terms of good medical care have been
defined more specifically by Roger Lee and Lewis Jones. They point out that
adequate care (1) limits itself to rational medicine based on the medical sciences; (2) emphasizes prevention; (3) requires intelligent co-operation between the lay public and its practitioners; (4) treats the individual patient as
a whole; (5) maintains a close and continuous personal relation between
physician and patient; (6) makes use of and collaborates with social welfare workers; (7) co-ordinates all types of medical services; and (8) implies
application of all the necessary services of modern scientific medicine to the
needs of all the people.[14]

The more important role played by the modern hospital with its expanded
treatment facilities also buttresses the broadened conception of patient care.

While we must continue to operate and improve our hospitals as repair shops
for the sick and injured, that should no longer be our primary interest and responsibility. We must concern ourselves with the total health needs of the individual in the broadest sense, with much greater emphasis on our out-patient

14. Roger I. Lee and Lewis W. Jones in *Readings in Medical Care*, edited by the Committee on Medical Care Teaching of the Association of Teachers of Preventive Medicine, Chapel Hill: University of North Carolina Press, 1958, cited in Leo W. Simmons, "Important Sociological Issues and Implications of Scientific Activities in
Medicine," *Journal of the American Medical Association*, 173 (May 1960), p. 118.

services extending beyond the hospital into the community. Social changes and the findings resulting from medical research are forcing upon us a changing hospital and a changing system of medical practice by physicians.[15]

Furthermore, the changing normative conception of health has changed patients' attitudes in ways that contribute to new demands upon the doctor's work-load. Urged by health organizations and insurance companies and encouraged by the concept of preventive medicine to see their doctor before serious trouble develops, patients do just that. They see their doctor not only when they are sick, but before they become sick. Today's patients visit doctors twice as often as they did thirty years ago.

(b) *Growth of prepayment plans for medical care.* Rising costs have spurred the growth of voluntary health insurance programs. This fact, plus the cumulative effect of the technological revolution, made it inevitable that some method would have to be found for spreading the risk and sharing costs. Less than a generation ago health insurance was controversial, but today it is fully accepted and Blue Cross has become a household word. The rapid growth of the four basic categories of health insurance is shown in Figure 8-2. The proportion of the population with hospital coverage, which is the most prevalent form of medical protection, rose from 10 per cent in 1940 to 72 per cent in 1957.[16]

Although three out of four families carry some health insurance, these statistics do not tell the whole story. *Insurance benefits cover only 25 per cent of the total medical expenses even of the insured families.*[17] Furthermore, 28 per cent of the population, about 49 million people, have no protection at all. These are usually those who need protection most but are unable to meet minimum payments — the aged, the disabled, the unemployed, and low-income workers. More than 10 million have insurance only against the costs of hospitalization and carry none against the costs of doctors' services. Most plans do not offer "complete" coverage. In most cases, they do not pay for drug and dental bills. Psychiatric care — which is needed by more Americans each year — is not covered to any appreciable extent. Furthermore, most of the programs are limited so that either the first or the last costs of a serious illness are not included. This situation has been compared to a shapely girl trying to conceal herself behind a small towel — "she can move the towel up to cover the top, or lower it to cover the bottom, but it simply won't stretch far enough to give decent coverage." [18] The demand for more comprehensive and balanced medical care plans is growing rapidly.

But protection against illness involves some unique features. Since the

15. Somers and Somers, op. cit. p. 61.
16. Somers and Somers, op. cit. p. 11.
17. Ibid. p. 12.
18. Donald B. Straus, op. cit. p. 40.

Fig. 8-2. Private Health Insurance Enrollment: Percentage of Civilian Population With Hospital, Surgical, "Regular Medical" and "Major Medical" Coverage, 1940-1959[a]

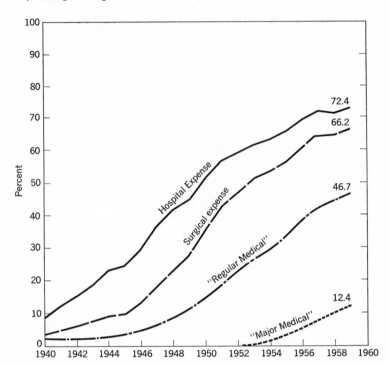

[a] Data based on end of year population and enrollment figures. For definitions see Chap. 13, p. 250.
Source: Health Insurance Council and U.S. Dept. of Health, Education, and Welfare, Social Security Administration.

costs of personal health services cannot be known in advance, these items cannot be budgeted in the same way that a family pays the monthly payment on an automobile or a television set. Moreover, since everyone is a potential hospital case — and the costs are so great — the usual principles of risk do not apply. Some informed observers contend that the term "health insurance" is misleading. Straus feels that it has led us into a semantic trap. He points out that,

You can, for example, insure a $30,000 house against fire for about $30 a year. In a lifetime your premiums will amount to only a fraction of the cost of replacement because, luckily, very few houses burn down. But most bodies will suffer one or more major illnesses and many minor ones in a lifetime. Consequently, it costs from $270 to $300 a year to get insurance protection just for hospital and doctor's bills which account for less than 60 percent of all personal health expenditures. Since illness is almost a sure thing it is not an insurable risk in the same sense as fire, flood, and other accidents and catastrophes.[19]

19. Ibid. p. 41.

There are other unique features about budgeting for medical care. Although it is regarded as a necessity by most people, medical care is not purchased with the same kind of motivation associated with the purchase of other necessities such as food, clothing, and shelter. Medical care is a necessity, but it stands out in the average consumer's budget as the one *undesired* necessity. Furthermore, when medical costs strike with their full weight on the unfortunate minority, the burden can be so staggering that no amount of foresight would make a real difference. Very often a lingering terminal illness, such as cancer, costs from $5000 to $10,000, or even $15,000. In fact, illness is the biggest single threat of financial disaster for most people. Despite the difficulty of budgeting medical expenses, the price of patient care is now so great that it becomes as urgent, if not more so, to insure against sickness as to insure against death. Illness may actually produce greater financial strain on the family than death.

The growth of prepayment plans brings about a change in hospital-patient relations. Under the earlier system of payment, when a dispute arose between patient and hospital authorities, the patient was frequently told to go elsewhere if he did not like the treatment he received. But this "take it or leave it" attitude has an unfair ring about it when the patient has been paying for his service for 10 to 20 years, or longer, and has now come to receive his prepaid medical care. As Simmons has said, "It is entirely out of order to make a proposition to 'take it or leave it' to the medically insured patient. He has a stake in the firm." [20]

(c) *Increased role of government in medical care.* Controversy and debate continue with regard to the proper role of government in health matters. What is often overlooked is the extent to which federal, state, and local government expenditures are currently used in meeting health needs. The federal government provides medical care for members of the armed forces and their dependents under a plan known as Medicare. Government medical responsibilities also extend to eligible veterans, to members of the merchant marine, to Indians, to inmates of federal prisons, and to civilian employees disabled in government service. There are also federal grants-in-aid to states for various medical care programs and support for research, hospital construction, and public health activities. State governments are responsible for the administration of federal grant-in-aid programs, the operation of state hospitals and, through established agencies, participate in such work as the treatment and control of tuberculosis, mental disease, and other illnesses. Local governments work primarily with those in lower income categories and the medically indigent, but also provide public health and preventive services to the general public. On a nation-wide basis, recent data

20. Leo W. Simmons, op. cit. p. 120.

show that twenty-five cents out of every dollar spent for health services is government money, and one in every six Americans looks to the government for all or part of his medical needs.[21] The issue today, therefore, is not whether the government should assume a role in medical care, but how much, if any, enlargement of this role is necessary.

There are large segments of the population who find it increasingly difficult to cope with rising medical costs. The health needs of the aged are a case in point. Recent data show that four-fifths of those over 65 have incomes under $2000, three-fifths under $1000. But they have two to three times more illness than the rest of the population, and half of them are not covered by any form of health insurance. [22] It is significant that during the 1960 Presidential campaign, the leaders and platforms of both political parties were pledged to federal financing of medical care for the aged, and that the Kennedy Administration has continued to stress the need for expanding the social security system to provide additional services for the aged.[23]

Some feel that a federal program for the aged would represent the entering wedge of a steadily growing government involvement in health insurance, while others feel that a program financed out of social security contributions is entirely appropriate. The aged have been surveyed on this issue, and a majority appear to be in favor of government insurance.[24]

Moreover, a considerable body of opinion today recognizes as inevitable the extension of the role of government in the fields of health and medical care, especially in the realm of support for hospitals, medical education, and research. In regard to the government's role, Straus has made an important distinction:

. . . if we are sensible, we will not permit the debate to dwell on "socialized medicine." In the past that slogan has served little purpose except to raise tempers and cloud over the real issues. After all, nobody wants to disturb the precious professional relationship between doctor and patient — and practically nobody wants any more government intervention than is absolutely necessary. (We already have a great deal of piecemeal, unplanned government intervention right now.)

21. Donald B. Straus, op. cit. p. 42.
22. Edward T. Chase, "Politics and Medicine: Is Medical Practice a Profession or a Business?," *Vital Speeches of the Day*, 27 (April 1, 1961), p. 375.
23. Horton and Leslie note that, "Every modern nation except the United States has some form of comprehensive medical care financed by taxation." For documentation and further discussion of this point see, Paul B. Horton and Gerald R. Leslie, *The Sociology of Social Problems*, 2nd ed. New York: Appleton-Century-Crofts, 1960, pp. 537–8.
24. The findings of a Health Information Foundation–National Opinion Research Center survey showed 54 per cent in favor, and other appraisals of public opinion among the aged suggest that this figure is conservative. See for example, "Elderly Voters in St. Petersburg Hit Medical Bill," *New York Times*, September 8. 1960.

So it is time for all of us to recognize that the choice is not between the old-fashioned, strictly private practice of medicine (which has been dwindling for a long while) or a completely government-run setup (which no responsible student of the problem advocates). The real choice will be between: (1) a patchwork containing a wide and confusing variety of unplanned and largely unregulated insurance schemes — none of them wholly adequate — and (2) a program which encourages a variety of medical plans that meet standards of quality and economy, which recognizes that some government aid is inevitable, and which is designed to keep the government's role as economical and unobtrusive as possible.[25]

The changes which have been described in this section served to undercut many basic features of the contemporary normative conception. Earlier images of the physician and medical care were challenged, and normative dissensus was inevitable. The current medical-care scene represents a combination of earlier features which have been adapted to the new setting, as well as certain innovations which are consistent with increased industrialization. It is to this newer, emergent conception that we now turn.

> *Emergent Normative Conception: Organizational Responsibility* — Adequate medical care is of fundamental importance and should be available to everyone. In a society possessing advanced medical knowledge, ill-health represents a social as well as an individual problem. Increased complexity of modern society has limited the effectiveness of traditional methods of medical care. Emphasis should be placed upon ways of developing more effective distribution systems that meet standards of quality and economy.

Changing meaning of "free choice" of physician. As we observed earlier, the freedom to choose one's doctor is regarded by most traditionally oriented physicians as essential to high quality medical practice. Indeed, without this freedom it is claimed that a satisfactory doctor-patient relationship cannot exist. The emerging normative position, in contrast to the contemporary view, maintains that the practice of medicine today is so complex that the traditional method of selecting a physician does not guarantee a close relationship or high quality medical care, and may even be inimical to the patient's own interests. It has been pointed out that the circumstances surrounding the patient's choice of a doctor in a large city today are very different from those in the unspecialized medical practice of several generations ago.[26] In an age of specialization the patient is rarely able to judge the

25. Donald Straus, op. cit. p. 44.
26. Michael M. Davis, *Medical Care for Tomorrow*, New York: Harper, 1955, p. 323.

quality of the services he receives.[27] Many patients consider personal attention more important than antisepsis and precision, and a pleasing bedside
manner may be valued above diagnostic ability. In a study conducted by
the Division of Health Affairs at the University of North Carolina, it was
found that some of the least able doctors had the highest incomes.[28] However, the emerging normative view holds that a sense of freedom is clearly
beneficial for promoting a responsible doctor-patient relationship, and an
informed choice of physician by the patient further safeguards the quality
of care. Although every licensed physician has the legal right to perform any
medical procedure or surgical operation he chooses, it is unprofessional for
him to treat patients outside his area of professional competence. And it is
unwise for the patient to make a self-diagnosis which takes him directly to a
specialist. Thus the growth of complexity of medical services has greatly increased the need for an adequately informed initial choice and for professional guidance of subsequent choices.

The free choice issue has arisen largely in connection with the trend toward various forms of group practice prepayment medical-care plans. The
American Medical Association has, for the most part, maintained that such
plans represent a denial of "free choice" and result in poor medical care.
In 1959, however, this policy was officially changed, and in keeping with the
emergent normative view the concept of "free choice" was enlarged to include "free choice of system or plan." Some medical care plans include a
group of fifteen, twenty-five, or more doctors, and supporters of the emerging
norm point out that those who use "solo" practitioners seldom have such
a range of choice within their geographic and financial limitations. Also,
the appearance of "dual choice" and "multiple choice" systems of medical
coverage permits the insured person to choose individually between two or
more plans or systems of care. Those who support this viewpoint suggest
that these emerging arrangements of medical services have created a method
for combining meaningful freedom with quality and cost controls. Some observers report "it appears on balance that these modern trends constitute an
increase in real freedom and hence enhance the opportunities for responsible
doctor-patient relationships." [29]

The essential features of free choice of physician in an industrial society
can be seen in bold relief when they are compared with the working procedures of a democratic government.

27. It is obvious, of course, that the patient's freedom of choice is further limited by
the field of specialization of physicians in his vicinity and by his financial ability to
pay for their services.
28. Selig Greenburg, "The Decline of the Healing Art," in *The Crisis in American Medicine,* op. cit. p. 24.
29. Somers and Somers, op. cit. p. 487.

Free choice in medical care — like democracy in government — is frequently misunderstood. For a government to be democratic it is not necessary that every administrative officer be chosen by the people. It would scarcely increase the democratic nature of our own government if we were to elect the heads of the executive departments, the joint chiefs-of-staffs, and the justices of the Supreme Court. The essence of democracy is accountability to the electorate and the availability of a practical alternative to the party in power.

The essential factors in free choice of medical care are accountability on the part of the provider of service — whether a solo practitioner or an organized group — to the consumer and the existence of a practical alternative. It does not require individual choice of every individual specialist or technician.[30]

It is in this context that economy, quality, and free choice are compatible. As long as the patient has the alternative of choosing a "solo" practitioner or a physician who is a member of a group medical plan, and has the possibility of changing to a different plan, the right of free choice has not been violated. Thus the emerging normative conception stresses that new forms of medical organization should not be regarded as denials of free choice, but as forms of adaption to changing conditions. Proponents of this view also point out that probably the best medicine in the United States today is practiced in closed-staff hospitals and clinics such as Mayo, Lahey, and Columbia-Presbyterian Hospital, where patients do not have the choice of individual doctors. Patient care is of high quality because the standards of the institution are high.

Changing methods of paying for medical services. One by-product of specialization and increased complexity of medical services has been the development of new methods of remunerating doctors. Although the traditional fee-for-service method still predominates, other methods are spreading rapidly.[31] As the data in Table 8-1 show, the proportion of physicians in private practice has declined from 86 per cent in 1931 to 66 per cent in 1962. During this period, the number of hospital-employed doctors has increased

30. Somers and Somers, op. cit. p. 412.
31. The traditional fee-for-service system has come under increasing criticism in recent years. Donald Straus, vice president of Health Insurance Plan of greater New York (HIP), has described it as based "on the unusual economic doctrine that medical care should be available to each according to his need, and, should be paid for by each according to his ability to pay. The rich are expected to pay high fees and in addition to contribute the bulk of the charity dollar used in medical care. The middle income are expected to pay fees roughly approximating their ability to pay. The poor are expected to pay what they can, when they can. The administrator of this most complex pricing mechanism is the individual solo practitioner, each exercising his own judgment of the many complicated factors that must be considered in any such means test. Not since Robin Hood has any group of men been expected to make a living according to so difficult a set of economic, moral, and ethical standards." *A Framework for Developing a National Policy on the Financing and Organization of Physicians' Services*, 1957, p. 22, cited in Somers, op. cit. p. 53.

greatly. In 1931 only one physician in 16 was so employed; in 1957 the ratio
was one in 5.[32]

TABLE 8-1

Physicians by type of practice, 1931–62

Type of practice	1931	1940	1949	1957	1962
	Number of physicians				
Total	156,406	175,163	201,277	226,625	257,035
Private practice	134,274	142,939	150,417	155,827	170,066
General practice and part-time specialty	112,116	109,272	95,526	81,443	70,471
Full-time specialty	22,158	33,667	54,891	74,384	99,595
Not in private practice	16,151	22,351	41,160	60,137	86,969
Hospital service	9,700	14,209	24,887	36,371	42,710
Teaching, research, public health ..	2,900	3,349	3,737	7,168	12,438
Federal government	3,551	4,793	12,536	16,598	19,581
Retired, not in practice	5,981	9,873	9,700	10,661	12,240
	Per cent of physicians				
Total	100.0	100.0	100.0	100.0	100.0
Private practice	85.9	81.6	74.7	68.8	66.2
General practice and part-time specialty	71.7	62.4	47.4	36.0	27.4
Full-time specialty	14.2	19.2	27.3	32.8	38.8
Not in private practice	10.3	12.8	20.5	26.5	33.8
Hospital service	6.2	8.1	12.4	16.0	16.6
Teaching, research, public health ..	1.8	1.9	1.9	3.2	4.8
Federal government	2.3	2.8	6.2	7.3	7.6
Retired, not in practice	3.8	5.6	4.8	4.7	4.8

Source: U.S. Department of Health, Education and Welfare, Public Health Service, *Health
Manpower Source Book*, Section 14, "Medical Specialists" (1962). Data adapted from
Table 1, p. 3.

During the past few decades there has been a slow but steady shift toward
salaried practice, despite long-standing opposition by much of the medical
profession. The Weiskotten-Altenderfer annual survey of medical school
graduating classes, made after each class has had time to establish itself,
shows that 43 per cent of the 1945 class is employed on salary, full-or-part
time, as compared to 32 per cent of the 1915 class.[33] Furthermore, the increase was almost entirely in the full-time category, and part-time salaried
work showed only a slight decline — which suggests that the increase in
institutional practice reflects a basic reorientation toward medical service
rather than simply a method of supplementing income.

32. Interest in individual practice as well as in general practice appears to decline as schooling advances. *Medical Economics* (September 1957), pp. 306–7.
33. G. H. Weiskotten and M. E. Alterderfer, "Trends in Medical Practice," *Journal of
Medical Education* (July 1956), Pt. 2, p. 78.

It has been argued that the salaried doctor will do less good work than the doctor who is on the fee-for-service basis; that his incentive will be stifled if he receives a salary. Those who adhere to the emerging normative conception argue that this claim is not borne out by experience. They point out that the strong motivating force behind most professionals is the respect of their colleagues, pride in their work, and devotion to duty, as well as an interest in financial gain. Emphasis is also placed on the fact that most creative work in science today is done by men on salaries working in private corporations, large universities, or government settings. Increasing numbers of scientific advances are the result of teams of scientists working together on a problem, rather than the result of a single individual working in isolation.[34] Furthermore, staff doctors at the Mayo Clinic, and at other such groups known for the excellence of their medical care, work for salaries — and there are no financial transactions between patient and physician.

Adherents of emerging norms claim that the greatest rewards under a fee-for-service method of payment "go not necessarily to the person who is practicing the best quality, but rather the greatest quantity of medical care." [35] A further difference is that a fee system tends to emphasize curative medicine, and as a result preventive medicine seldom becomes the driving force behind most physicians' efforts, and public health services are often resisted by the medical profession because of fear of encroachment.

The emerging position, in contrast to the contemporary view, holds that people do not lose their appreciation for medical care when paying for it on other than an individual fee basis. Nor is the doctor-patient relationship less adequate than under the traditional system. With the growth of various group and prepayment insurance plans a new segment of the population is getting a substantial amount of professional medical care for the first time. Consequently these patients have not had time to learn how one "should" behave toward doctors and what it is that they ought to appreciate — and this represents an opportunity for doctors to educate and help these patients who enter into a relationship with them. It is felt that perhaps many new groups of people can be reached and educated through group medical care plans who would otherwise never have come in contact with a doctor. Minority groups, or immigrants, for example, may not know how to find accredited practitioners; without the help of a plan, they may easily fall

34. One observer, a lawyer, writing on some relationships between law and medicine, asks, ". . . why is it that doctors are troubled by this doubt [the effects of a salary on their work] when university professors, lawyers in public service, officials who make government a life work, never even raise the question . . . It is easy enough to answer the argument that a salary will kill the urge to serve; it is hard to understand why the question is ever asked." Wendell Berge, "Social Organization of Medical Care," *Readings in Medical Care*, op. cit. p. 667.
35. Caldwell B. Esselstyne, M.D., "Principles of Physician Remuneration," in National Conference on Labor Health Services, *Proceedings*, 1958, p. 126.

prey to quacks and charlatans. Where patients are systematically given appointments by virtue of their membership in or employment by some organization, many may become accustomed to regular medical care and become self-directing in these matters. In this way, ideas about preventive medical care and health habits can be disseminated in groups otherwise indifferent or ignorant. And perhaps a better doctor-patient relationship can then be established.

Thus proponents of the emerging normative view maintain that high quality care depends upon no one single way of organizing medicine or paying for medical services. In fact, this premise strikes directly at a fundamental difference between the emergent and the contemporary conceptions of who should control the *financial* and *administrative* features of medical care. The contemporary position, which reflects the view of most physicians, says essentially that all aspects of medical practice should be controlled by the medical profession.[36] In contrast, the emergent normative conception, which is supported by some younger physicians says that doctors are experts in medical diagnosis and therapy, but not necessarily in economics or organizational procedures. As long as medical economics remained a relatively simple matter, doctors had no difficulty directing their financial as well as their technical practice. But with the emergence of a highly complex society, the question arises whether a profession largely untrained in economics and social organization should continue to be the sole judge of these phases of medical care. The insistence of most traditionally oriented physicians that only well-trained men should deal with medical questions is beginning to be turned against them when they themselves now deal with economic problems. One physician, an early member of the Mayo Clinic staff, has summarized the argument in this manner:

36. Since the lay public helps to finance in one way or another the construction of most hospitals, there is a growing awareness that this investment is placed at the disposal of the medical profession with exceedingly few controls over quality and quantity of service. The uniqueness of this situation is pointed out by Carter: "Our non-profit hospitals . . . having been built by government, religious groups, and philanthropists at a cost approaching $13 billion . . . represent a huge investment by the non-medical public in its own health. Run purely for service and administered by community leaders responsible for capitalization and maintenance, the hospitals stand as free workshops in which the medical profession toils for its own profit. Efforts by hospital trustees to police the price and quality of the medicine practiced in their institutions are not willingly accepted by the profession. It insists on policing itself, and the results are uneven.

"Michael M. Davis . . . once calculated that, in building and equipping its hospitals, the public has put at the disposal of each practicing physician a capital investment worth about $70,000 . . . Dr. Davis observes: 'If the use of this capital were on a business basis, the annual interest charge for each physician would be at least $3,000. Doctors and laymen alike take this situation for granted. It is a wholesome situation, but sometimes it is worth thinking about.'" Richard Carter, op. cit. p. 35.

The American Medical Association is on wholly sound ground as long as it insists that the physicians in this country are the only experts upon whom the country can depend for expert [medical] opinions. But, by the same token, it would not, I think, be difficult to deny their title as experts in social, economic and financial fields. In these fields they are, at best inexpert and perchance prejudicial witnesses. They cannot there be relied upon as experts and they ought not to aspire to that distinction.[37]

Yet the assumption by the profession that it could continue all phases of its practice, economic as well as medical, is consistent with the laissez-faire society in which medicine in America has its roots. With the shift toward specialization within an industrial society this assumption was bound to be challenged.

The "third party" issue. Increasingly, the basic issues confronting American medicine center on the expansion of third party medical-care financing. Although opinions vary widely concerning its appropriate role, the third party represents an integral feature of present medical practice. As one observer has recently remarked:

It may be pleasant to daydream about rolling history back to the time — if it ever existed — when the only elements in the medical care picture were the physician and the patient. It may be fashionable in some quarters to refer to the third party in medical care as if it were a social disease. However, excluding the State and other institutional purchasers from the medical care field is about as unlikely as limiting the purchase of stocks to individuals, and eliminating such institutional buyers of stocks as the insurance companies, pension funds, trusts, and mutual funds.[38]

A discussion of the changing role of the third party in modern medical care necessarily involves consideration of emerging forms of medical organization. In fact, adherents of the emergent normative view start with the premise that most medical care problems resolve themselves into finding more effective methods of organizing medical services. They point out accumulating evidence that new institutional arrangements, including group practice, hospital practice, and other forms of combined practice, offer the greatest potential for maintaining and improving the quality of medical care.[39] Basically, group practice refers to "the application of medical service by a number of physicians working in systematic association, with joint use

37. A statement by Dr. Hugh Cabot, in "Freedom and Interference in Medicine," by Richard H. Shryock, *The Annals of the American Academy of Political and Social Science*, Philadelphia (November 1938,) p. 19.
38. Statement by Arthur Weissman, cited in Somers and Somers, op. cit. p. 218.
39. The following statement represents another phrasing of the emerging normative viewpoint: "In broadest terms, the issue confronting the medical profession and the nation is how to achieve the advantages of large-scale organization and large-scale financing without sacrificing the essential values of a highly professional and individualized service." Somers and Somers, op. cit. p. 501.

of equipment and technical personnel, and with centralized administrative and financial organization." [40] Although clinics in hospitals can be called group practice, the term usually applies to private-practice groups, organized and administered by doctors. Medical groups range all the way from small rural partnerships to large-scale private enterprises such as the Mayo and Lahey clinics. Payment to the group is usually on the fee-for-service basis, although the doctors are salaried. Group practice without prepayment has for the most part been sanctioned by the AMA, and it is estimated that there are more than 1000 medical groups including about 13,000 physicians rendering private fee-based service in this way.[41]

Commenting on some of the features of group practice, the President's Commission on the Health Needs of the Nation reports:

> The patient benefits through having his entire health service concentrated in one place. This gives greater unity and continuity to his care, encourages consultation whenever it is needed, and minimizes travel. The patient also gets more service per dollar spent through the economy of group practice.
>
> Physicians working together in a group continue the best features of their training period throughout their professional lives — the stimulation to keep up with medical progress through constant appraisal by informed colleagues and ready access to consultations and technical assistance. On the personal side the physician in group practice has greater opportunity to take time off for study and vacation in addition to a more stable income throughout his years of practice.[42]

Another form of emerging medical organization is the *group purchase* of service by large numbers of consumers whose aggregate prepayment of fees is sufficient to provide a medical team combining high standards of service with professionally acceptable salaries. This approach combines group practice with group purchase of service under a prepayment plan. But it is precisely at this point that differences between contemporary and emerging conceptions become great. Prepaid medical service plans provide reasonably comprehensive medical care ranging from home and office calls to hospitalized illnesses, at a fixed, all-inclusive annual price. This service is usually financed by wage deductions or employer contributions, or a combination of the two. Examples of prepaid group practice plans include the Kaiser Foundation Health Plans of California and Washington, the Health Insurance Plan of Greater New York (HIP), the Ross-Loos Clinic (California), and the Group Health Association of Washington, D.C. This form of medical organization is controversial, not because of group practice or even because of

---

40. James H. Means, *Doctors, People, and Government*, Boston: Little, Brown, 1953, p. 71.
41. Richard Carter, op. cit. p. 147.
42. President's Commission on the Health Needs of the Nation, *Building America's Health*, Washington, D.C.: Government Printing Office, 1953. vol. 1, pp. 33–4.

prepayment of fees, but because the combination of these two features results in what nonparticipating physicians call a "closed panel" system of medical practice. This means that the patient has to choose from among doctors who are employed with the service plan.

Another objection set forth by the AMA and adherents to the contemporary normative view, is that most of these plans are controlled by employers, unions, or other lay groups.[43] Even though this control is almost always confined to financial and other nonmedical phases of the plan, and the administration of medical affairs is the responsibility of a medical director, the arrangement has not generally satisfied the medical profession. The controversy over "lay-controlled" (or third party controlled), "closed panel" plans therefore continues. Organized medicine feels that it should have the sole prerogative to decide the way in which medicine should be paid for, as well as the way it should be practiced — and deeply resents the intrusion of a third party as a critical observer.

On the other hand, the emerging normative position maintains that the most promising method for upgrading current medical care lies in better organization — co-ordinating and augmenting the individual physician's skills with institutional arrangements whose efficiency has been adequately demonstrated. This viewpoint assumes that the number of physicians in proportion to the population will probably decline in the foreseeable future, and this places a higher premium on increasing the productivity and effectiveness of a limited supply of doctors. However, it is hardly realistic to increase their productivity by working harder or faster, since they already work longer than most other professional groups. Thus new forms of organization become of utmost importance.[44] Therefore, proponents of the emergent normative view see group practice as the best opportunity for better medical care, and as a possibility for reversing the deteriorating doctor-patient relationship. It is argued that the doctor can treat a patient more effectively when he is not compelled to be thinking about what he should charge for his services, or

---

43. In regard to this type of reasoning, Loomis has remarked, "The objection . . . to 'lay control' is related to the physician's desire not to experience interference or evaluation as he practices. This is of particular interest since the universities at which the physicians train are under lay control." Charles P. Loomis, *Social Systems: Essays on Their Persistence and Change,* Princeton, Van Nostrand, 1960, p. 321.

44. These remarks are particularly relevant to this discussion: "It is unlikely that better organization alone will be able to meet the anticipated physician deficit. The magnitude of the problem appears to require a major push along several parallel lines — more doctors, more paramedical personnel, more mechanical equipment, more rational organization, and more money . . . the obstacles to achievement of these goals are still great. In particular the absence of planning on a scale large enough to meet the needs and backed by the principal centers of professional power and prestige is conspicuously lacking. Nevertheless, the slow, and often painful, process of accommodation to the demands of the new technology is apparently under way." Somers and Somers, op. cit. p. 129.

Fig. 8-3. Physicians Per 100,000 Civilians in Each State, 1957.[a]

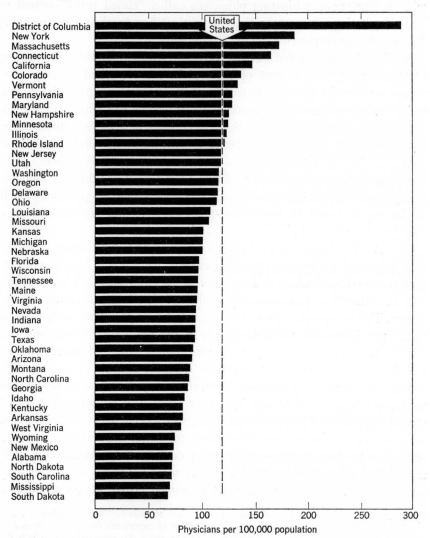

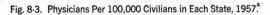

[a] Excludes the retired and those in federal service.
Source: U.S. Public Health Service, *Physicians for a Growing America*, Publ. 709 (1959), pp. 80-81.

what the patient can afford to pay. Organization transfers administrative details to other personnel, thus maximizing the time the doctor can spend with his patients.

However, not all group practice plans have been able to combine a meaningful patient-doctor relationship with efficient medical care, and some of the new approaches are still caught up with a tendency toward assembly-line treatment. "But on the whole," notes a long-time student of health problems, "though group practice is still in the throes of experimentation, its shortcomings seem far easier to correct than those of solo practice which is rapidly becoming an anachronism with the advance of scientific knowledge and the inevitable trend toward more and more specialization." [45]

The following remarks by Somers and Somers effectively point up the basic theme of the emergent normative conception of medical care.

In American culture neither the recognition of science nor the willingness to translate it into technological tools is a major problem. In medicine, as in other fields, we have institutionalized scientific exploration. We apply an unprecedented and increasing portion of our national income to new investigation. Rarely has a society been so ready to experiment with new materials and techniques . . . We are the apostles of rapid obsolescence — even when the superiority of the new has not been established.

Our difficulty lies in another area, not as readily recognized and not as adaptable — the area of social organization and of financing. These factors ultimately determine the extent to which scientific and technological advances can be transformed into diagnosis, prevention, and treatment of disease. But, unfortunately, this is the area where the efficacy of alternative methods is most difficult to demonstrate empirically and where habit, tradition, self-interest, and the relative inflexibility of human institutions are most likely to act as barriers.[46]

DISSENSUS OVER MEDICAL CARE — THE FUTURE

Some observers have pointed out that attitudes toward illness and medical care rest ultimately on "the significance that death holds in a given culture at a particular time. The more that a society as a whole values success in life and fears death the higher its demand for medical care in some form or other." [47] It is likely that few societies, if any, place a higher value than ours on "success," or fear death more. If population continues to outstrip medical facilities and personnel, future demands and expectations will be proportionately higher than they are today.

Indeed, one of the most far-reaching developments, and potentially the most potent, has been the new degree of public concern about medical care issues. There is a growing awareness of the fact that our ingenuity for discovering new medical techniques has not been matched by equally ingenious techniques for meeting the new mass demand for medical care.

What form of medical organization will eventually prove most effective is currently a matter of normative dissensus.[48] Probably considerable variety

45. Selig Greenberg, op. cit. p. 26.
46. Somers and Somers, op. cit. p. 494.
47. Statement by Professor Richard M. Titmus, British social philosopher, cited in Somers and Somers, op. cit. p. 162.
48. In 1950, Willard C. Rappelye, then dean of the Faculty of Medicine of Columbia University, wrote: "It would be short-sighted and, in the long run, futile to ignore the

will be required, and the newer forms will certainly be different. But over and above these issues a larger pattern emerges. In all industrialized countries, medical care is changing from a private relationship involving two individuals, into a network of interdependent, specialized institutions which hold the possibility of providing better service to more people than ever before. This is the overriding fact of twentieth-century medical care.

SUMMARY

Modern medical achievements, broadened conceptions of health, and generally rising social expectations have created a new mass demand for comprehensive, high quality medical care. However, specialization and greater complexity of medical services have led to increased costs. During the past decade the cost of medical services has increased more rapidly than the cost of living, and increasing proportions of family income are being spent for medical and hospital care.

Rising costs have led to the growth of voluntary health insurance programs, but insurance benefits cover only one-quarter of the total medical expenses for most insured families. And among the aged, whose illnesses are more numerous than those of any other group, 50 per cent do not have any form of health insurance. These and other events associated with a more complex, industrialized way of life, have brought about a reappraisal of current medical services and organizational procedures.

Dissensus over medical care is centered in differences between contemporary and emergent viewpoints. The contemporary conception is based in large measure on a pre-industrial image of the physician and medical practice. Ill health is viewed as an individual problem. The patient alone should be financially responsible for his medical needs. He should personally choose his physician and directly pay him on an individual fee basis. The physician should be self-employed and conduct his practice on a fee-for-service basis. A third party, such as a consumer-sponsored medical care plan or government agency, should not be involved in financing or otherwise modifying the traditional doctor-patient relationship. All aspects of medical service should be under the control of the medical profession.

Many features of the contemporary viewpoint have been challenged. The emergent conception argues that illness represents a social as well as an individual problem and maintains that high quality care depends upon no single way of organizing medicine or single way of paying for medical service.

broad implications of medicine, which must be recognized as much a social as a biological science." He stated further that, "anyone who today disregards the relationship of medicine to current social, economic, and political conditions must be literally unwilling to face the facts." Commenting on this observation, Leo W. Simmons remarks, "This statement was made a decade ago; its truth is even more obvious today." Simmons, op. cit. p. 170.

Proponents of the emergent viewpoint question whether the traditional method of selecting a physician necessarily guarantees a close doctor-patient relationship or competent medical care. It contends that salaried physicians do work as good if not better than those working on a fee-for-service basis, and the Mayo and Lahey clinics are cited as examples of medical organizations where standards are high, physicians are salaried, and payment is not made directly to individual doctors. With the trend toward specialization, group practice is viewed as a more effective and efficient form of medical organization.

Supporters of the emergent view state that doctors are experts in diagnosis and therapy but not in financial matters or organizational procedures. They question whether a profession largely untrained in economics and social organization should continue to be the sole judge of these aspects of medical care.

Growing public concern about medical care, and the awareness that more effective methods of distributing available knowledge and techniques are needed, have slowly but steadily produced new forms of medical organization and new ways of financing medical care.

QUESTIONS AND SUGGESTIONS FOR FURTHER STUDY

1. Compare and contrast the "images" of the country doctor, the modern family doctor, and the specialist. What do you feel explains the basic differences?
2. What is meant by the "doctor-patient relationship"? Do you think there have been significant changes in this relationship in recent years? What are the reasons for your answer?
3. Select an example of a health insurance medical plan, e.g. Health Insurance Plan of Greater New York, and compare its features to the traditional system of medical practice.
4. Some observers think that the term "health insurance" has led us into a semantic trap. What is the reasoning behind this statement?
5. What role should government play in medical care programs? Conduct a survey of classroom opinion on this topic. Discuss the reasons for opposing viewpoints. Are most of the viewpoints more consistent with the contemporary or emergent viewpoint?
6. Do you feel that an expansion of the role of government in the fields of health and medical care is inevitable? What are the reasons for your position?
7. Discuss the major differences between group practice and individual practice. What are the advantages and disadvantages of each form of medical organization?
8. To whom does the term "third party" usually refer in the physician-patient relationship? Give several illustrations.
9. Dr. Willard G. Rappelye maintains that medicine "must be recognized as much as a social as a biological science." What are your reactions to this statement?

10. In regard to medical care services, are the "advantages of large-scale organization and large-scale financing" inconsistent with the "essential values of a highly professional and individualized service"? Defend your viewpoint. Cite relevant evidence.

11. Analyze current newspaper accounts discussing the role of the federal government in financing additional medical services for the aged. Determine the specific issues of controversy. How do these issues reflect the dissensus described in this chapter?

SUGGESTED READINGS

Carter, Richard, *The Doctor Business*, New York: Doubleday, 1958. The author raises critical and provocative questions about the contemporary organization of medical practice.

Committee on Medical Care Teaching of the Association of Teachers of Preventive Medicine, *Readings in Medical Care*, Chapel Hill: The University of North Carolina Press, 1958. A useful sourcebook covering a wide variety of health and medical care topics.

Freidson, Eliot, *Patient's View of Medical Practice*, New York: Russell Sage Foundation, 1961. This study describes three types of medical practice in the Bronx and patients' attitudes toward them. The author views medical care as involving a system of relationships which includes not only the patient and the doctor, but the organization of medical practice and the patient's community life as well.

Jaco, E. Gartly (ed.), *Patients, Physicians and Illness*, Glencoe: Free Press, 1958. A collection of readings emphasizing the contributions of the social sciences.

Journal of Health and Human Behavior. A relatively new and very useful source of information. Emphasizes the findings of social science research studies.

Sanders, Marion K. (ed.), *The Crisis in American Medicine*, New York: Harper, 1960, 1961. Contains a collection of timely and forthright articles examining current national medical and health controversies.

Simmons, Leo. Wm., "Important Sociological Issues and Implications of Scientific Activities in Medicine," *Journal of the American Medical Association*, 173 (May 1960). An insightful discussion of social factors affecting medical care.

Somers, Herman M., and Anne R. Somers, *Doctors, Patients and Health Insurance*, Washington, D.C.: The Brookings Institution, 1961. An extremely thorough and competent analysis of the organization, distribution, and financing of medical care services. This book may well become a classic in its field.

Abuses of the freedom on speech ought to be prevented but to whom dare we commit the power of doing it?

Benjamin Franklin

An able, disinterested, public-spirited press, with trained intelligence to know right and courage to do it, can preserve that public virtue without which popular government is a sham and a mockery.

Joseph Pulitzer

Effective communication is essential to society, and technology now makes it possible to communicate with millions. This change has been called the "communications" revolution. Its consequences are apparent every time one picks up a newspaper or magazine, uses the telephone, goes to a movie, or turns on the radio or television.

The normative problem: what should the mass communications present and how should they be controlled in an industrial society?

Most of the mass media are new. After movable type was invented the large-scale production of books and newspapers developed very slowly. By contrast, the motion picture, radio, and television have all developed rapidly in the twentieth century, and they present certain problems different from those presented by print.

Early norms governing the mass media would today be considered authoritarian. In England and many parts of Europe during the sixteenth and seventeenth centuries, truth was not defined as correspondence to reality, but as conformity to rule, the rules being determined by those in power. The public would be informed of what its leaders felt it should know and should support. Monarchies presented the divine right of kings as "truth," the Church presented divine revelation as "truth," but the basic idea was the same — "truth" was limited and the dissemination of "false" ideas was restricted.

As printing became more widespread, those in power developed ways to

255

ensure its conformity to "truth." To maintain control, permits were granted allowing only certain individuals to engage in printing. For example, in England in 1636, the Oxford University Press, was granted the privilege of printing the Authorized King James Version of the Bible. The authorities were particularly careful of those entrusted to print material concerning the affairs of state. These privileged printers were also given the authority to control those entering the printing profession. Books in the areas of religion and politics were examined by various authorities for their compliance with established canons of truth. This type of official permit is retained today by the Catholic Church under the title of *imprimatur*, "let it be printed."

Those in power also had recourse to law. A newspaper publisher who attacked the government could be tried for treason. Under certain regimes publishers could be tried for sedition for almost any public criticism of political authorities. The primary function of the press was to announce decisions after they had been made.

In short, early norms permitted no publishing which, in the opinion of the authorities, would not be good for the state. Criticism, which might disturb citizens, had no right to be published, since by political criticism, the state might be undermined, and by religious criticism, faith might be undermined. "Unfounded ideas" would undermine a society.

In parts of the Western world, however, authoritarian norms regulating mass media were discounted and new normative conceptions developed. One of these may be called the libertarian conception, which, in effect, reversed the authoritarian conception. Rather than publicizing the views of those in power, the press began to present evidence so the public could determine truth for itself and then demand that policies consistent with it be implemented by their leaders. Allied with the press, the public became judges of competing opinions, rather than passive recipients of authoritarian directives. This libertarian conception was written into the Bill of Rights in the United States.

> *Historical Normative Conception: Libertarianism* — The function of the mass media is to provide a market place for ideas. The media must be free of government control.

Libertarianism was a by-product of intellectual currents that helped shape early America.[1] These ideas included the notion that individual happiness and welfare are of supreme importance, that the role of the state was thus to

---

1. The following sections are dependent upon Wilbur Schramm, *Responsibility in Mass Communication*, New York: Harper, 1957; and Fred S. Sibert, T. B. Peterson, and W. Schramm, *Four Theories of the Press*, Urbana: University of Illinois Press, 1956.

serve the individual citizen, who would control the state by democratic processes. American statesmen of the eighteenth century believed that men were rational animals who could understand and control the world without supernatural assistance. By using their reason men could determine truth and use their knowledge to govern themselves.

With this image of man, the Founding Fathers felt it necessary for men to have access to all ideas, to decide for themselves which were true. To silence an opinion was perhaps to silence a truth; even a "wrong" opinion might contain some element of truth. Only in the give and take of open debate could this be determined. Since, historically, government had restricted the free dissemination of ideas, its power over the press must be removed. Thus, when the United States Constitution was written, freedom of the press became a part of the Bill of Rights. All opinions could enter the market. While some would be false, the state could not determine this. "Good" opinions, like good products, would be "bought" more often than "bad," and by and large the majority would make sound decisions.

In theory, anyone was free to start a newspaper and attempt to convince others of the validity of his ideas. Newspapers would encourage the search for truth and, rather than being agents of the state, would protect the individual *from* the state. Criticism of those in political power is no longer considered seditious. The press has established its right to report on decision-making within government and to present political deliberations, not just final decisions.

The new media that developed in the twentieth century — motion pictures, radio, and television — fell heir to this libertarian heritage. Although they provide entertainment as well as news and opinion, these media also seek to avoid governmental "interference" and claim to serve the public in the same fashion that newspapers do.

Broadcasting developed a system of commercial sponsorship by which air time is sold to advertisers. This allowed broadcasters to provide radio and television programming without listeners' license fees or some type of government support. In return for the advertiser's support, the consumer was to listen or see the commercials and to be motivated to buy the product or service. This means of support has been defended as being democratic. The various media have developed marketing research which indicates to advertisers how many people watch their programs and buy their products. Programs with high ratings — those that many people watch — produce more advertising exposure and therefore are considered to be better programs. Since more popular programs attract the support of advertisers, this means that these media are oriented to the majority taste. Broadcasters argue that critics of programming — those who say it is tasteless or even pernicious —

try to impose their own minority tastes upon the majority. Thus the system of support and programming is seen to accord with the libertarian conception since it avoids governmental control and it caters to majority tastes.

The libertarian conception experienced three types of difficulties as the society became more industrialized. First, it has been perplexed by problems of libel, obscenity, and responsibility for national security, which seem to compromise its "absolute freedom." Second, the concentration of ownership in various media has made the expression of opinion more difficult. Third, the development of radio and television has created problems unanticipated by earlier thinking about the nature of newspapers.

1. *Problems of Libel, Obscenity, and National Security.* Traditionally, governments have accepted as one of their duties the protection of the reputation of individuals. To do this, most states developed libel laws to protect the individual from false and derogatory imputations. Libel is often defined as "a statement about an individual which would tend to lower his esteem in the eyes of others and would cause him to be shunned or exposed to hatred and contempt." Persons who feel libeled can bring civil suit and ask for damages. Under the threat of libel suits, the media lose the right of unhampered expression. In practice, however, a judgment of damages against a newspaper is difficult to obtain and with radio and television, because so many individuals are involved in the preparation of scripts, it becomes almost impossible to fix liability for damages. In spite of this, expressions of the mass media do face the threat of action for libel.

Another troublesome area has been the dissemination of obscene and indecent material. In 1873, Congress passed the Comstock Law, which stated that anyone who knowingly sends or receives obscene material through the mail may be punished by five years in jail or a $5000 fine or both. While this law provided for criminal prosecution, the Post Office has interpreted it to mean that the Postmaster can *prevent* mail from being sent, as well as prosecute the person who sent it or asked for it. In effect, the Postmaster is a censor. Generally the Post Office has employed three techniques in eliminating what it considers obscene. First, it impounds suspicious material and then holds a hearing to determine if it is obscene and unmailable. Second, it impounds all first class mail sent to a person who runs a mail order house specializing in obscene literature. Third, it denies second class mailing rights to any periodical that, in its opinion, continually prints obscenity. The constitutionality of such censorship has been relatively untested in federal courts. In 1957, the Supreme Court ruled that the First Amendment does not protect obscenity. Justice Brennan said that obscenity is "utterly without redeeming social importance." At that time, the Court also stated that the judgment as to whether material was obscene depended upon "whether to the average person, applying contemporary standards, the dominant theme of the material taken as a whole appeals to prurient interest." [2] In 1959, the Postmaster General refused mailing privileges to D. H. Lawrence's *Lady Chatterley's Lover.* A federal judge, using the previous Supreme Court definition, decided that the book was not obscene, but he did not rule on the constitutionality of the Postmaster's censorship powers. The censorship powers of the Post Office are based on interpretations, not on actual Congressional approval and not on tested constitutionality.[3]

The ease with which this discretionary power excluding obscenity can be transferred to other material is seen in its application to prevent the mailing of "foreign propaganda material." The Post Office, basing its action on national security, destroyed all Soviet mail during the Korean War but later changed its policy to hold such mail until the addressee signs a statement signifying that he requested the material. This policy resulted not only in the confiscation of *Pravda* but also of a Soviet book entitled *Chess for Beginners.* Such "political" censorship by the Post Office points to another area of difficulty in the libertarian conception — that of issues dealing with national security.

The libertarian conception has rarely made provision for curtailing the liberties of the press in time of war. During World War I, the government set up a system of censorship of messages coming in and going out of the country, but no attempt was made to control the mass media. Magazines and newspapers put into operation a system of voluntary censorship.

After World War I, in 1919, the Supreme Court stated that limitations on freedom of speech and press during wartime would be justifiable only in situations involving "clear and present danger." [4] The government could only impose restrictions where there was urgent danger to the security of the nation in wartime.

After World War II, the legislature passed several bills penalizing discussions that advocated the overthrow of the government "by force and violence." The Supreme Court seemingly accepted these limitations. This legislation has been used more frequently to silence Communist party leaders than to prohibit the publication of Communist party newspapers. These limitations,

---

2. Quoted in Stanley Mesiler, "Hidden Censors," *The Nation* (October 10, 1959), p. 208.
3. The Supreme Court, in a ruling June 23, 1962, said that magazines may be "unpleasant, uncouth, and tawdry, but this does not make them obscene." Three Justices also pointed out that Congress had not given the Postmaster General power to determine what is obscene.
4. *Schenck* v. *United States,* 249 U.S. 47 (1919).

of course, would be acceptable under an authoritarian conception of the press but represent, an uneasy compromise between the libertarian ideal and the problem of meeting the threat of an enemy.

In one sense, the restrictions on the mass media created by considerations of libel, obscenity, and national security have not been considered a threat to libertarian ideas. To argue against these restrictions almost places a person in the position of being *for* libel, obscenity, and subversion. The libertarian conception has not included the "freedom" to be libelous, obscene, and subversive. Considerable criticism, however, has been evoked when realistic works of art have been equated with pornography and when political nonconformity has been equated with political subversion. A more serious problem for libertarianism stems from the limitations on the freedom of expression that have occurred through concentration of ownership.

2. *Problems of Concentration of Ownership of Mass Media.* Until about 1850, newspapers representing a wide variety of shades of political opinion could be bought. A hundred years ago, it was possible to start a newspaper in New York City with $15,000 capital. Today it would take over $5 million of risk capital. *Life*, one of the few large magazines initiated in recent times, lost more than $5 million before it started to make money. Today, starting even a small newspaper would require a capital outlay of up to $250,000, and starting a television station would require $500,000. Thus, freedom to add to the variety of opinions becomes increasingly difficult.

A hundred years ago a publisher could be his own editor, reporter, and typesetter. This is no longer possible, and these jobs have become separate and independent. Newspapers have become concentrated in larger and larger units as a result of industrialization. Greater profits can be made by selling mass-produced newspapers. Also profits can be increased by reducing competition. This has happened in the ownership of newspapers. Table 9-1 shows that, since 1900, there has been a steady decline in the number of daily newspapers, while the population in the United States has doubled and the total circulation of newspapers has increased sixfold. As Table 9-2 indicates, the decrease in the number of daily newspapers has been accomplished at the expense of competition. The number of cities with competing dailies has steadily declined. In 1953–60, there was no competitive ownership of newspapers in 96 per cent of the cities in the United States. Competition is most frequently found in cities with over 300,000 people. Another measure of concentration of ownership is found in the existence of newspaper chains — organizations that own and control two or more newspapers in different cities. In 1945, about 20 per cent of all newspapers belonged to one chain or another. While all papers belonging to a chain do not necessarily have similar editorial policy, they often do. By the very nature of the newspaper chain,

TABLE 9-1

Number of daily Newspapers, total circulation and population
in United States, 1900–1960

Year	Number of dailies	Total circulation	U.S. population
1900	2120	9,330,930	75,994,575
1914	2442	25,426,911	96,000,000 (est.)
1920	2042	27,790,656	105,710,620
1930	1942	39,589,172	122,775,046
1940	1878	41,131,611	131,669,275
1950	1772	53,829,072	150,697,361
1960	1763	58,080,000	179,323,175

Source: Raymond B. Nixon and Jean Ward, "Trends in Newspaper Ownership and Inter-
Media Competition," *Journalism Quarterly*, Vol. 38, No. 1 (Winter 1961), pp. 3–14. Reprinted by permission.

the owners do not live in the cities where most of their papers appear, making
it more difficult for them to know and understand local conditions. These
trends indicate the concentration of ownership in fewer hands, and the
elimination of local competing points of view.

Concentration is also found in the other mass media. Major news is
gathered by two large press associations. Control of radio is concentrated in
three radio networks which own most of the powerful clear-channel stations
and furnish more than three-fourths of the day's radio programs to other
stations. A similar pattern occurs in television — three networks own stations in the larger cities and supply programs to other stations. Most movies

TABLE 9–2

Concentration of newspaper ownership, 1909–1960

Year	Total dailies	Total daily cities	Cities with competing dailies	Percentage of cities with non-competitive ownership
1909–10	2202	1207	689	42.9
1920	2042	1295	552	57.4
1930	1942	1402	288	79.4
1940	1878	1426	181	87.3
1944–45	1744	1396	117	91.6
1953–54	1785	1448	87	94.0
1960	1763	1461	61	95.8

Source: Raymond B. Nixon and Jean Ward, "Trends in Newspaper Ownership and In-
ter-Media Competition," *Journalism Quarterly*, Vol. 38, No. 1 (Winter 1961), pp. 3–14.
Reprinted by permission.

are made by six large studios. And book and magazine publishing is concentrated in a relatively few large publishing houses. Radio and television stations frequently are owned by newspapers.

This concentration sets limits on freedom of expression. In one sense, a person with a minority opinion can still communicate it to his neighbors and to those who might come to hear him speak on a street corner or in a rented hall. He can find a printer who, for a modest fee, will publish his leaflet. But access to the platforms of national opinion through newspapers, radio, and television is another matter. The mass communications agencies must exercise some selection in deciding who is to use their facilities. Those who control the media now have great power to limit and exclude opinion.

Concentration has other consequences. The libertarian conception assumed that the "opinions" of a paper would ultimately have to stand the test of attracting readers with similar views, but with the elimination of local competition, the remaining newspaper will experience an increase in readers who differ in political opinion. What responsibility does a newspaper have to these diverse consumers? Does it have an obligation to present a variety of opinions or should it maintain the single editorial policy of its owners? Newspaper readers no longer are an important source of financial support. Since newspapers depend primarily upon advertising and not circulation for support the threat of "not buying" a newspaper is worthless.[5] By tradition, newspapers will not allow their editorial policies to be affected by the opinions of their advertisers. However, while the editorial page of a newspaper is not sponsored by toothpaste, one still has difficulty in finding the page among the advertisements.

3. *Problems Concerning the Growth of New Media.* When the motion picture, radio, and television were developed, an entertainment function became as important as the opinion forming function of these media. With new function and with new forms of reaching a mass audience, new problems emerged concerning the freedom and the function of mass communication.

Movies have generally been excluded from the libertarian conception. For centuries, the theater was controlled by the state. In the sixteenth and seventeenth centuries, governments regulated theatrical entertainment for political and religious reasons as well as to protect morality. Since motion pictures are a direct continuation of the theater, it was felt that the same limitations should apply. The movie industry acquiesced in state censorship, which was approved by the United States Supreme Court as early as 1915. In fact, proposed federal censorship of motion pictures was averted only when the industry organized its own regulatory body, which was then referred to as the Hays Office.

5. Advertising rates, however, are set on the basis of circulation.

The first effective move to break the censor's hold came in 1952, when a picture, *The Miracle*, was banned in New York State on the basis that it was "sacrilegious." The Supreme Court not only rejected "sacrilege" as a basis for censorship but went on to declare that motion pictures were as entitled to the freedoms granted under the First, Fifth, and Fourteenth Amendments of the Constitution as was the press. Since that time, most legal censorship of movies has been eliminated, but informal measures still remain in the form of pressure groups which threaten exhibitors with boycott. Only gradually have motion pictures been given the same freedom of expression as newspapers.

Radio and television presented even more difficulties to the libertarian conception. These media transmit messages and, in this way, are similar to newspapers and motion pictures, but this transmission of messages is accomplished by utilizing electromagnetic waves, which are limited in supply. If everyone tried to establish a radio or television station it would create chaos. Someone had to distribute the channels, and since the channels belonged to the "people," the logical choice was for government to act as allocator. Some standard also had to be set for allocation. The standard of other public utilities was borrowed — that operation must be consistent with the "public interest, convenience, or necessity."

Stations are considered only the custodians of the channels, not the owners. The channels are a natural resource, to be utilized only in the "public interest." The Federal Communications Commission (FCC) was given the responsibility of putting this standard into practice. The Commission sought to find some basis on which to judge "public interest." They came to interpret this, in part, by a station's program content. A person granted a radio or television channel must make an effort to give to all segments of the population the best program content. This represents a departure from the traditional libertarian conception, because the FCC, an agency of the government, is allowed to judge the content of a medium. Many broadcasters, however, insisted that the role of the government was solely to assign frequencies and not to judge program content. It should be noted that this "mixed" solution to the problem of broadcasting in the United States is probably more consistent with the libertarian conception than solutions in many other countries. France has a government monopoly on broadcasting. Great Britain established a public corporation that is indirectly responsible to the government in power. Canada operates its networks as a public corporation and owns some stations, while other stations are operated by private groups. In countries other than the United States, the media are supported, in large part, by licensing and fees on radio and television receivers.

In spite of these difficulties, the growth of this libertarian normative conception paralleled the development of democratic government. More recently, however, there has emerged a new conception of the functions of the mass media. In modern industrial societies, norms regulating the mass media cannot follow the model which emerged in colonial times based on freedom of the press. The problem still remains: how can we make a restricted market an *actual* free market? The various media of mass communication have certain responsibilities in an industrial society which are not achieved by operating them as private property. This newer norm here is called the concept of Social Responsibility.

> *Contemporary Normative Conception: Social Responsibility*
> — Freedom of the press carried with it not only the right to avoid government control but also certain obligations to the society. The emphasis should be on the freedom to carry out these obligations.

The idea of social responsibility is not a denial of the libertarian conception but an extension of it. Because of certain problems in the libertarian conception, modifications have to be made concerning how the mass media are to operate to make them fit the demands of industrial society.

CRITICISMS OF THE MEDIA
Siebert has summarized the various criticisms of the press — "press" here refers to all of the media — as follows:

1. The press has wielded its enormous power for its own ends. The owners have propagated their own opinions, especially in matters of politics and economics, at the expense of opposing views.

2. The press has been subservient to big business and at times has let advertisers control editorial policies and editorial content.

3. The press has resisted social change.

4. The press has often paid more attention to the superficial and sensational than to the significant in its coverage of current happenings, and its entertainment has often been lacking in substance.

5. The press has endangered public morals.

6. The press has invaded the privacy of individuals without cause.

7. The press is controlled by one socio-economic class, loosely speaking, the "business class," and access to the industry is difficult for the newcomer; therefore, the free and open market of ideas is endangered.[6]

John Crosby, in the early days of television, criticized the "seven deadly

6. Siebert, Peterson, and Schramm, op. cit. pp. 78–9.

sins of the air" which he felt television might inherit from radio.[7] Prophetic in retrospect, these "sins" were as follows:

1. Radio has sold its soul to the advertisers. Crosby illustrated this point by a story of an advertiser sponsoring a dance orchestra who used to make the president of NBC dance to test whether the tempo was right. In a real sense, he who pays the piper calls the tune.

2. Radio has never exploited its enormous potentialities. By standard programming and pat "successful" formulas of soap operas and whodunits, radio has presented, in Crosby's words, "amnesia in the afternoon and death in the evening."

3. Radio has consistently pandered to the lowest tastes and has almost ignored the highest.

4. Radio is morally irresponsible. The defense of programming by the fact that many people listen is not proof of adequacy. Counting heads does not lead to creativity since any program will have a large audience if there are no alternatives. The rating system becomes an elaborate cover up for a lack of standards.

5. Radio is avaricious. Its prime goal has become to make money for advertisers and the owners of the stations. While this goal may be consistent with other business enterprises, the frequencies that broadcasters use are not their property. Thus, radio, as a semipublic institution, has a responsibility to the public to produce programs in their best interest. As radio has operated, however, broadcasters often conceive of the "loan" of the frequency as their "inherent" right to make money.

6. Radio has created an insulting picture of the American people. It has simplified reality so that what is presented on the air has little relationship to reality. When Wolcott Gibbs resigned as motion picture reviewer for the *New Yorker*, he claimed that the world portrayed by motion pictures is "an astounding parody of life devoted to a society in which anything is physically and materially possible, including perfect happiness, to a race of people who operate intellectually on the level of the *New York Daily News*, morally on that of Dayton, Tennessee, and politically and economically in a total vacuum." [8] By catering to the lowest common denominator, radio deals with the trivial rather than the important. It pictures a society in which right always triumphs and wrong is always punished. It promises that romance is a solution to personal tragedies. It presents the "good" life as acquisitive, and personal happiness as equivalent to having possessions. It presents mar-

7. John Crosby, "Seven Deadly Sins of the Air," *Life*, 29 (November 6, 1950), pp. 147–8.
8. Wolcott Gibbs, quoted in Ruth Inglis, *Freedom of the Movies*, Chicago: University of Chicago Press, 1947, p. 8.

riage as adultery or bickering but seldom as love and affection. It presents "solutions" to problems which have little relationship to causes. It creates the illusion of humor either by canned laughter or by audiences "warmed up" and "cued." In these and other ways radio distorts reality.[9]

Television has continued this image of the American people. It presents a world in which minority groups are seldom seen. It is a world in which most people live in big cities and work in high status occupations. It is a world in which there is little religious life and little sickness but where almost everyone dies a violent death and homicide is even more popular than rape.

7. Radio is cowardly. In attempting to appeal to as many groups as possible, it is overly sensitive to criticism. It is afraid to offend Negroes, Jews, Protestants, Catholics, doctors, lawyers, policemen, senators, the PTA, the National Association of Manufacturers, the AFL-CIO, and almost every organized interest in American society. This fear is fed by the continual complaints of these groups to broadcasters. However, if all complaints were heeded, it would be impossible for any program to portray a villain, since villains must be located in some social group. While the risks of stereotyping minority groups are real, politeness can be carried too far. As Crosby said, "Sheer inoffensiveness is so small a virtue as to be no virtue at all."

These criticisms have created the desire for other normative arrangements. While many of the norms from the libertarian conception were acceptable, the seriousness of the criticisms has created the necessity to explore other normative possibilities.

THE EMERGENCE OF SOCIAL RESPONSIBILITY

The social responsibility conception accepts the libertarian ideas that the various media should provide information and discussion, that they should enlighten the public so that they can make the decisions demanded of citizens, and that they should protect the rights of individuals; but it points out that the media have often been deficient in performing these functions. It accepts the idea that mass media should bring the producers and the consumers of goods together through advertising, but insists that this should not be more important than informing and enlightening the public. It concedes that one function of the various media is entertainment but urges that it be "good" entertainment. It recognizes that the various media should be financially self-sufficient, but it argues that this might not be best in all situations that other means of support should be sought.

Some of the social responsibility norms have been accepted, while others

9. One could argue that, if media did present reality, the resulting picture might be even more depressing.

are in formative stages. This normative conception has come from many sources. Important among these sources were the recommendations of the Commission on the Freedom of the Press which, under grants from *Time, Inc.,* and the *Encyclopedia Britannica,* spent two years studying problems of freedom and responsibility in the mass communications industry. While the reports of the Commission were severely criticized by mass media spokesmen as being the work of uninformed outsiders, the Commission said little which had not been anticipated by criticism within the communications industry.

The conception of social responsibility insists that the media be free from governmental control, but that this freedom is too important to be left to chance. It cannot be assumed that men will automatically seek out competing points of view. Nor can every man have "his own" newspaper. Neither will men act, at all times, as rational beings seeking to maintain their liberties and the liberties of others. The perpetuation of freedom and the encouragement of rationality are responsibilities that have to be implemented and promoted by the mass media. If the communications industry cannot actively promote freedom and rationality, then they must be promoted in other ways. The possibility emerges that government, instead of being a threat to freedom, might promote it. On the specific role of government in promoting freedom, however, there is disagreement. Regardless of disagreement over the means, the ends of various groups are often similar — that freedom should be promoted by the mass media since it cannot be assumed to thrive automatically in an industrial society.

The social responsibility of the mass media has two different facets. The mass media must furnish a medium for the expression of differing opinions and provide the raw material for opinion formation through accurate news coverage. This responsibility is the special concern of publishing but it pertains also to broadcasting. Since the movies, radio, and television emphasize their entertainment function, their social responsibilities also include the necessity for providing "good" entertainment.

THE RESPONSIBILITY OF PUBLISHING

The idea of the newspaper responsibility is not new. More than half a century ago, Joseph Pulitzer, one of the most influential of newspaper publishers, wrote: "Nothing less than the highest ideals, the most scrupulous anxiety to do right, the most accurate knowledge of the problems it has to meet, and a sincere sense of moral responsibility will save journalism from a subservience to business interests, seeking selfish ends, antagonistic to public welfare." [10]

10. Joseph Pulitzer, "The College of Journalism," *North American Review,* 178 (May 1904), p. 658.

To implement the social responsibility of the press, the Commission on the Freedom of the Press suggested five measures of press performance.[11]

First, the press should present "a truthful, comprehensive, and intelligent account of the day's events in a context which gives them meaning." It is important for the press to report facts and to separate facts from opinions. One of the real advances in the development of modern newspapers has been the gradual separation of fact from opinion and the attempt to isolate opinion on editorial pages. The Commission suggested, however, that it is no longer enough to report the *facts* truthfully. It is now necessary to report the *"truth about the facts."* Since citizens in an industrial society depend upon the mass media for knowledge about the world, the press must provide the context for interpretation and even try to evaluate for readers the validity of conflicting points of view. This task is difficult, as Elmer Davis indicated.

The good newspaper, the good news broadcaster, must walk the tightrope between two great gulfs — on one side, the false objectivity that takes everything at face value and lets the public be imposed upon by the charlatan with the most brazen front; on the other hand, the "interpretative" reporting which fails to draw the line between objective and subjective, between a reasonably well-established fact and what the reporter or editor wishes were fact. To say that is easy; to do it is hard.[12]

Second, the press should serve "as a forum for the exchange of comment and criticism." This means that the press should present viewpoints *contrary to their own.* In the libertarian view, a newspaper needed only to represent its own view while other papers presented different ones. If papers do not publish different opinions, those opinions do not reach the public; this destroys the very conditions of freedom under which the press operates.

Third, the press should "project a representative picture of the constituent groups in the society." This responsibility is closely related to the previous two. The public makes decisions in terms of their conceptions about reality. If the mass media present stereotypes, the public reacts and forms decisions on the basis of these stereotypes. If Negroes are always presented as servants, if Italians are always presented as gangsters, if scientists are always presented as "mad," if professors are always presented as being impractical theorists, if children are always presented as impertinent brats, and if husbands are always presented as ineffectual nincompoops, the public may believe that these stereotypes represent reality, and they may use them as a basis for judgment, however false that basis may be.

Fourth, the press should present and clarify the goals and values of society.

11. Commission of the Freedom of the Press, A *Free and Responsible Press,* Chicago: University of Chicago Press, 1947, pp. 20–29.
12. Elmer Davis, *But We Were Born Free,* Indianapolis: Bobbs-Merrill, 1954, p. 175.

Most mass media spokesmen probably would agree that this is an important function of the press. However, it would seem that an understanding of some of the historically important values in American society is still not complete. Mack, in a study of college students, asked their opinions concerning the first ten amendments of the Constitution, without identifying them as such. The majority of students disagreed with the intent of several of the amendments — for example, the right to confront one's accuser and the provision preventing double jeopardy. No provision of the Bill of Rights received unanimous acceptance.[13] Public opinion polls have indicated that a large segment of the American public does not accept the right of the press to criticize the government nor that every group within the society should have the right to freedom of speech and press.

Fifth, the press should provide "full access to the day's intelligence." While the Commission acknowledged that many individuals would not utilize the information they receive through the mass media, the press should keep the public informed and this may require the elimination of barriers to the free flow of information. The growth of large complex organizations of both governmental and nongovernmental character in modern industrial society, plus the development of the "art" of public relations with the express purpose of creating favorable press images, places an additional burden on the press to achieve "full access."

Another source of ideas concerning the social responsibility of the press appeared in a statement of the American Book Publishers Council and the American Library Association. In 1953, they published a joint statement which indicated some of the ways in which the publishers and librarians assumed *active* responsibility for the perpetuation of freedom. They "affirmed the following propositions."

1. It is in the public interest for publishers and librarians to make available the widest possible diversity of views and expressions, including those which are unorthodox or unpopular with the majority.

2. Publishers and librarians do not need to endorse every idea or presentation contained in the books they make available. It would conflict with the public interest for them to establish their own political, moral, or aesthetic views as the sole standard for determining what books should be published or circulated.

3. It is contrary to the public interest for publishers or librarians to determine the acceptability of a book solely on the basis of the history or political affiliations of the author.

4. The present laws dealing with obscenity should be vigorously enforced. Beyond that there is no place in our society for extralegal efforts to coerce the tastes of others, to confine adults to the reading matter deemed suitable for adolescents, or to inhibit the efforts of writers to achieve artistic expression.

13. Raymond Mack, "Do We Really Believe in the Bill of Rights?," *Social Problems*, 3 (1956), p. 267.

5. It is not in the public interest to force a reader to accept with any book the prejudgment of a label characterizing the book or the author as subversive or dangerous.

6. It is the responsibility of publishers and librarians, as guardians of people's freedom to read, to contest encroachments upon that freedom by individuals or groups seeking to impose their own standards or tastes upon the community at large.

7. It is the responsibility of publishers and librarians to give full meaning to the freedom to read by providing books that enrich the quality of thought and expression. By the exercise of this affirmative responsibility, bookmen can demonstrate that the answer to a bad book is a good one, and the answer to a bad idea is a good one.

The freedom to read is of little consequence when expended on the trivial: it is frustrated when the reader cannot obtain matter fit for his purposes. What is needed is not only the absence of restraint, but the positive provision of opportunity for the people to read the best that has been thought and said. . . . We realize that the application of these propositions may mean the dissemination of ideas and manners of expression that are repugnant to many persons. We do not state these propositions in the comfortable belief that what people read is unimportant. We believe that what people read is deeply important; that ideas can be dangerous; but that the suppression of ideas is fatal to a democratic society. Freedom is a dangerous way of life, but it is ours.[14]

IMPLICATIONS FOR BROADCASTING

Social responsibility is even more complex for the broadcasting industries than it is for the press, since they provide both information and entertainment. While some of the same responsibilities demanded of newspapers apply to the information function, other standards are necessary to judge entertainment. The scope of this public responsibility, however, has not been clearly defined.

1. *Information and Opinion.* In general, the broadcasting industry has felt that it has been discharging its responsibility in providing information and the discussion of public issues. The industry grants equal time to political candidates. Under the Communications Act of 1934 (Section 315), the licensee is required to give equal opportunity to all candidates for a particular office. This provision raised many questions. Should this time be given free or should it be sold? Should the time given be not only equivalent in length (perhaps 30 minutes) but also equivalent in the time of distribution (9:00 on Friday night, for instance)? [15] If time is given to the two major political

14. American Library Association and American Book Publishers Council, *The Freedom to Read: Statement of Policy*, New York: American Book Publishers Council (May 1953). Reprinted by permission.

15. The Commission in one case, Stephens Broadcasting Company, 11 F.C.C. 61, 3 R.R.I., 1945, said "quantity alone is not the sole determining factor" in determining equal time.

parties, should equal time be given to the Prohibition party, the Vegetarian party, the Socialist Labor party, the Dixiecrats, the Christian Nationalist party, and to other "third" parties?

During the 1960 Presidential election, Section 315 was suspended to allow the networks to present debates between the two major Presidential candidates. Another exception to the equal time doctrine occurred when a candidate for mayor complained that his opponent, the incumbent mayor, had received an advantage because of the coverage of his official duties. The candidate filed a complaint with the FCC demanding equal time. The FCC ruled in his favor, but Congress, encouraged by the broadcasting industry, passed a law which exempted news programs from having to provide equal time. The law exempts newscasts, news interviews, news documentaries, and on the spot news coverage.[16]

The broadcaster who consistently colors news with opinions representing the owner's point of view runs the risk of having his license revoked. Since 1949, however, stations have had the legal right to take sides on an issue if they provide equal time for an opponent. In 1963, 148 stations were exercising that right but the networks have been reluctant to editorialize themselves.

With the right to editorialize seldom exercised, and the rule of offering equal time to opposite sides of controversial issues generally accepted, several observers have insisted that the media have the further responsibility of reporting important events. Broadcasting industry spokesmen have often used this argument when seeking to cover various governmental hearings — that the people have a right to know and that it is the media's responsibility to serve this right. However, during the Army-McCarthy hearings, while some stations carried the full hearings, the larger networks, with heavier commercial commitments, decided the public was not sufficiently interested in the full hearings, and they soon reverted to commercial programming. Observers pointed out that the broadcast industries were sacrificing the public's "right to know" for their own economic advantages to maintain their commercial programming. As Seldes said:

> The right to broadcast can be discussed only in connection with the duty to broadcast. Neither the broadcasters nor the public is ready to define the right and duty, but this is clear: If a network will act on no principle, if it will carry a hearing when convenient and drop it when the cost is excessive, then the networks will have a profound influence on American political life — for the hearing they do transmit will acquire a special value, and those they ignore will be relatively unknown to the public. This has always been true of newspaper reporting, but the press does not use frequencies belonging to the public; nor is the press quite so capable as television of taking events out of the public mind, since out of town newspapers as well as magazines can correct the partiality or partisanship of

16. Associated Press release, *Columbus Dispatch*, September 15, 1959.

the press. But if no network covers a hearing, vast numbers of people will either know nothing of it or consider it negligible — and the power so to manipulate our political responses should not be in the hands of commercial broadcasting.[17]

2. *Entertainment.* The responsibility of the broadcasting industry for maintaining programming standards of "good" entertainment is different from their responsibility for providing information. Assuming that the various media are free to say what they wish, the question shifts to what they will say. Will they say anything worthwhile?

Radio and television have been accused of introducing their audience to crime and violence and to other questionable tastes and values. Since these media are so heavily loaded with violence and sadism, it is often asserted that this encourages and stimulates aggressive tendencies among children. That the media carry a substantial fare of violence is indisputable. One study in Los Angeles covered TV programs for one week up until 9:00 p.m., when smaller children were assumed to go to bed. They found, during that week, 161 murders, 60 "justifiable homicides," 192 attempted murders, 83 robberies, 15 kidnappings, 24 conspiracies to commit murder, 21 jail breaks, seven attempted lynchings, six dynamitings, eleven extortions, two cases of arson, and two instances of torture, not to mention a number of prolonged and brutal fights, threats to kill, maulings, and other unspecified indignities.[18] These portrayals are often justified by the fact that the audience is usually informed that crime does not pay and that evil doing is eventually punished.

Opinions concerning the impact of the mass media upon the lives of children, however, are much more emphatic than is the *research* evidence. The broadcasting media deny a negative impact on their audience, and emphasize their powerful positive impact. Parents, police officials, and others use the mass media as a convenient scapegoat to blame for delinquency, poor school work, and adolescent rebellion. Psychiatrists often vividly describe individual cases in which television seemingly has provided a source for imitating aggression. Assertions about the negative effects of television are plausible in the face of the scarcity of research evidence.[19] But no one knows *how* many people under *what* kind of conditions will accept *what* kind of advice or imitate *what* kinds of behavior from *what* kind of media. The question can be raised whether the continuation of programs of crime and violence can be justified by the fact that it is not known they do any harm — this does not make them "good" programs.

17. Gilbert Seldes, *The Public Arts*, New York: Simon and Schuster, 1956, p. 237. Copyright © 1956 by Simon and Schuster. Reprinted by permission.
18. *Newsweek* (October 13, 1958). Los Angeles has seven channels. It is assumed here that this survey did not cover news shows or the total might have been higher.
19. For one such summary, see Leo Bogart, *The Age of Television*, New York: Ungar, 1958.

A more inclusive criticism of the mass media is that they cater to poor taste. While good taste is difficult to define, such a definition would no doubt include classical and serious modern music, literary drama and forums, discussions and speeches of importance. It is obvious that current programming contains little of good taste but much of what would be considered "bad" taste, including soap operas, a large proportion of popular music, quiz shows, audience participation programs, most mystery and crime shows, and most westerns. Television has been assessed by Newton Minow, then chairman of the FCC, as being a "vast wasteland." John Fischer has stated that "the result is that the best brains in television, its best hours, and its best dollars are dedicated to making the American people fat, dumb and happy." [20]

Most broadcasting media spokesmen reply that critics of programming are intellectual snobs and point out that minority interests are well served by certain types of programs. For example, network officials point out that Richard III was viewed by more people on television than had seen it since Shakespeare wrote it. This defense overlooks the fact that most programs dedicated to "good" taste are placed at hours when the majority audience is assumed to be asleep — either early morning or midnight — or outdoors — on Sunday afternoon. Often the weekly quota of "good" programs are all presented by different channels at the same hour.

The preponderance of programs which exemplify "bad" taste is generally justified by insisting that these programs appeal to the ultimate judge, the public. John Crosby has commented that the dependence upon the judgment of the public as a guide for good programming has its limits.

The public has created a demand for entertainment, education, music, and news on the radio but the quality of that product should be determined by the broadcasters. George Jean Nathan, I think it was, summed it up very neatly about ten years ago in commenting on the unlooked-for success of Lillian Hellman's "The Children's Hour," a distinctly unusual play. The public, he said, doesn't know what it wants until it gets it. Somebody else — I forget who — put it another way. The public, he said, knows what it wants but it doesn't know what it is.

That's why a Hooper rating is very misleading. There may be dozens of unproduced programs with potential Hoopers of twenty points or higher, but they never will be produced if the broadcasters wait for the public to ask for them. Only in the fields of politics and radio is leadership expected to come from the grass roots rather than the other way around. Both fields suffer severely from this upside down notion.[21]

In spite of the fact that they use public acceptance as a justification for their programming, television broadcasters contributed over a half million

20. John Fischer, "TV and Its Critics," Harper's, 219, no. 131 (July 1959), p. 11.
21. John Crosby, Out of the Blue, New York: Simon and Schuster, 1952, p. 270. Copyright 1946 by New York Herald Tribune, Inc. Reprinted by permission of Simon and Schuster and Willis Kingsley Wing.

dollars in 1959 to set up an Information Office with the express purpose of creating a more favorable image of TV — a task which evidently cannot be left to chance.[22]

WHERE SHOULD RESPONSIBILITY LIE?

While the notion that the mass media have a social responsibility is accepted in many segments of America, it is not agreed whether the locus of responsibility lies with government, with the media themselves, or with the public. In the quiz show scandals during 1959, Congressional investigations tried to determine who was responsible for the rigging of quiz shows and discover ways to prevent it from happening again. The Federal Communications Commission claimed that it had no control over actual programming and the Federal Trade Commission claimed that its role was to watch over advertising, not programming. The networks and local stations claimed that they had no control over programming since the shows had been independently produced by advertisers. CBS, however, did announce that it would ban "quiz shows that gave substantial prizes." Certain Congressmen saw the action of CBS as an attempt to stave off further legislation and pointed out that the existence of the scandals was evidence that responsibility has not been sufficiently localized. The incident illustrates the difficulty of determining who has the ultimate responsibility.

1. *Government.* The idea of governmental responsibility is viewed as a threat to freedom of the press by many who subscribe to libertarian norms. Traditionally the press has been viewed as a check on the possible tyranny of government. If the government is allowed to police communications, it is given the power to control those who would limit tyranny.

The government has assumed some responsibility for controlling and setting standards for radio and television. For example, it has used anti-trust laws to maintain competition among the units of the mass media. The Radio Corporation of America was made to sell one of its two radio networks. Anti-trust laws have prevented major motion picture studios from keeping monopolistic control on the distribution of their products to theaters. There are restrictions on the number of stations that a network or any one person or group can own. By these mechanisms, and others, the government has attempted to maintain a free market place of ideas.

The federal government has also entered communications in areas where private media have been unwilling or unable to operate; it operates the United States Information Agency, which speaks for the United States through mass media in foreign countries. State governments enter the field of communication through educational stations. Occasionally there have been suggestions

22. This pattern, however, is no different than in any other industry.

that government units should operate their own newspapers, radio and tele-vision stations, a practice common in many other countries.

In 1946, the Federal Communications Commission issued a statement concerning the "public service responsibilities of broadcast licensees," which declared that government should take some responsibility for the content of programming. In the "Blue Book," as it is commonly called, the Commission recognized that the problem of improving broadcasting service rests primarily with the broadcasting industries and through public pressure from critics, listeners' councils, and the public. But the Commission felt that it had to come to some definition of the "public interest" to assign and renew licenses of broadcast stations. As a guide to this responsibility, the Commission sug-gested four program factors that would influence their judgment.[23] First, each station should devote a reasonable proportion of time to "sustaining" programs. These are programs which are inappropriate for commercial spon-sorship, which cater to minority tastes and interests, and which provide time for religious, agricultural, labor, educational, and other nonprofit organiza-tions. These sustaining programs should be distributed through the broad-cast day. Second, local live programs should be encouraged. Third, programs devoted to the discussion of public issues should be encouraged. Fourth, ex-cesses of advertising should be eliminated, that is, time devoted to advertising should bear a reasonable relation to the amount of time devoted to pro-gramming. This statement by the Commission was met by accusations of "governmental interference." The broadcasters insisted that "freedom" can only be achieved by the extension of the existing programs justified by pop-ularity and economic success.

This negative reaction would seem to be somewhat misplaced. Even if the sole responsibility of government for broadcasting is to issue licenses and not to censor content, some standard must be evolved to choose between various competitors seeking the same channel. Alternative standards could be de-vised. For example, a channel might be given to the applicant who requested it first, or to the one with the most financial backing, or to the one with the best technical equipment, but these criteria have little to do with the obliga-tion to serve the "public interest." The first, richest, or best equipped ap-plicant might broadcast only commercials and thus use the frequency, which is public property, solely for private gain. Since licenses have to be renewed, each station might be required to give some indication of having operated during that time in the "public interest." The standards specified by the "Blue Book" could be used to judge performance.[24] However, in the renewal

23. Federal Communications Commission, *Public Service Responsibility of Broadcast Licensees*, Washington: Superintendent of Documents, 1946, pp. 54–6.
24. Industry spokesmen often complain these standards are too vague. The FCC, in Feb-ruary 1961, adopted new program forms which try to clarify them.

of licenses, the FCC has been content to let these standards operate as *guides* for programming rather than as a basis on which existing licenses can be withdrawn. The Commission has revoked licenses and fined stations which, by their performance, have not given attention to local programming and local issues. While many stations conscientiously attempt to live up to the standards, others only become aware of their responsibilities in the several months previous to reapplication for license and then frantically attempt to give time away to any group that will use it.

The FCC has tried to encourage better program content by setting aside certain channels on TV and FM for noncommercial educational broadcasting purposes. During the rapid growth of radio, from 1921 to 1936, some 202 educational licenses were granted, but during the same period 164 of those licenses were permitted to expire or were transferred to commercial interests.[25] For television, the FCC, in its original allocations, provided 242 channels for noncommercial educational purposes, 12 per cent of the total number allocated. By 1962 there were 64 noncommercial stations on the air. The growth of educational television has been inhibited by high costs, which are viewed with reluctance by state legislators. Many of the frequencies assigned were available only on UHF channels, which could not be received on most sets without conversion. While the addition of UHF frequencies was intended to make more and wider program coverage possible, UHF commercial stations experienced a high mortality rate, which made educators more reluctant to establish stations.[26] However, notable progress has been made by some educational stations. The state of Alabama has built the first educational network providing programs to every part of the state. The significant point is that the FCC has, through the allocation of separate noncommercial channels, attempted to re-emphasize that the "public interest" should be maintained in frequency allocation.

2. *The Media.* The media have generally assumed that the responsibility lies with the mass media themselves, and that the Jeffersonian ideal applies — the less government, the better. Most of the media have developed various codes of their own which attempt to set standards of conduct for the various members of the profession.[27]

In 1923, the American Society of Newspaper Editors adopted the Canons of Journalism, which represented one aspect of the desire of newspapermen for professional status. This document is an eloquent statement concerning not only freedom of the press, but also the responsibilities of newspapers to

25. Llewellyn White, *The American Radio*, Chicago: University of Chicago Press, 1947, p. 101.
26. This will change since manufacturers are now required by law to include UHF channels on new sets.
27. Most of these codes are found in Wilbur Schramm (ed.), *Mass Communications*, Urbana: University of Illinois Press, 1949.

be faithful to public interest and to be accurate, impartial, and decent. This document, however, has never been formally accepted by the publishers, who command the policy of newspapers. The binding nature of the document remains on a moral level, and, as such, it remains a set of rather abstract principles.

While the Canons of Journalism stemmed from a desire for professional status, other codes have been developed as a defense against public criticism. The Motion Picture Producers and Distributors of America adopted a code in 1930, which was administered under the supervision of the "Hays Office." The code was primarily concerned with depictions of violations of morality, for which movies had been severely criticized. The code suggested, among other things, that "adultery must not be presented attractively . . . brutal killings are not to be presented in detail; obscenity in word, gesture, reference, song, joke or by suggestion is forbidden; no film or episode may throw ridicule on any religious faith." The code provided a type of pre-censorship to forestall later censorship. In 1954, the Association of Comic Magazine Publishers developed a similar type of code and administrative system.

In 1929, broadcasters drew up their code of radio practice in the face of the threat of governmental investigation. It has since been revised several times. This code specifies that news reporting should be without bias and that, in the presentation of controversial issues, efforts should be made to present a balance. Other standards are specified for religious programming, for children's programs, and for crime and mystery programs. Other concerns of the code specify certain advertising standards and a maximum time allotted for advertisers during certain time periods and for particular types of programs. In most instances, the emphasis of the code is upon certain things which should *not* be done. For example, "Broadcasting . . . should avoid attacks on religion . . . should make no appeals urging children to purchase a product in order to keep the program on the air, . . . should avoid episodes involving the kidnapping of children, . . . should contain no claims that a product will effect a cure." [28]

While the various codes have been successful in meeting certain types of public criticism, they do little more than keep the mass media out of trouble. They are statements of minimum acceptability — of what the media *should not do* rather than the responsibility of the media for adequate performance. The codes do little to ensure quality. Leaving aside such questions as why ministers should receive complete protection against ridicule, the codes often illustrate the statement quoted earlier — "Sheer inoffensiveness is so small a virtue as to be no virtue at all."

Other mechanisms which might be utilized to increase social responsibility

28. National Association of Radio and Television Broadcasters, *Standards of Practice*, Washington, D.C.: The Association, 1948, pp. 1–8.

might be more professionalization within the occupations connected with the mass communications industry. Occupations which are professionalized generally depend upon long years of training in which attitudes of public service are inculcated. Schramm has suggested that the various media could move toward professionalism by (1) making the various codes of ethics within these occupations a subject of discussion, (2) the encouragement of self-criticism, (3) trying to recruit personnel who are not only "smart" but also informed and (4) in-service training programs to attempt to raise the level of competence within the occupation.[29]

3. *The Public.* The public also may have a part in helping create social responsibility on the part of the various media. The various codes have in most instances been developed by the media. But codes seldom induce good programming. The Commission on the Freedom of the Press recommended a device which might channel public activities. It recommended the establishment of a public agency which would "appraise and report annually upon the performance of the press." The term "press" here included all the mass media. While this recommendation was viewed as being a threat to "freedom of the press" by various newspapers, it is difficult to see how an "appraisal" would constitute such a threat. Such an appraisal might provide more positive direction for the media than do the negative but often petty appraisals by disgruntled individuals and pressure groups.

The public still has some control of printed material by "buying" or "not buying" in the few cases where realistic alternatives actually exist. In the case of radio and television, Siepmann has suggested a "Bill of Rights" for radio listeners which could also be applied to television.[30] This "bill" is based on the idea that the individual citizen has a vested interest in these media. He suggests that individuals can protect their "rights" as part owners of these frequencies by establishing their own images of balanced programming. They can exercise the control they have over their (public) property by listening selectively and by communicating information of good programming both to other listeners and to broadcasters. That individual citizens should become experts in the judgment of good programming might be a desirable goal but it would appear to be a somewhat unrealistic one. In Crosby's words, "the public knows what it wants but it doesn't know what it is."

John Fischer has suggested a "solution" which depends neither on the threat of governmental intervention nor on public apathy. Fischer is concerned with the problem of the responsibility for good programming in TV, which he thinks is impossible under the present commercial system.[31] While

---

29. Schramm, *Responsibility in Mass Communication,* op. cit. pp. 343–52.
30. Charles Siepmann, *The Radio Listeners' Bill of Rights,* New York: Anti-Defamation League of B'nai B'rith, 1948, pp. 45–52.
31. Fischer, op. cit.

admitting some bright spots in programming, Fischer points out that the conflict in radio and television is generally between public service obligations and commercial obligations. If a station uses a "public service" program, it often does so at the expense of a commercial broadcast. (This helps explain why public service programs often are used at 6:00 in the morning or 12:00 at night). The station manager, whose responsibility is to the stockholders, does not often refuse the profit-making alternative. Sponsors, too, are interested in the largest possible audience, so they support westerns rather than the New York Philharmonic. The consequence of this clash is programs of commercial value but often of poor quality.

Commercial interests granted television frequencies often ignore their public service responsibility. The frequency costs them nothing, but it may earn them a fortune. Some licenses, shortly after they have been granted by the FCC, have been sold for as much as ten million dollars. Fischer suggests that "we are letting the broadcasters use valuable public property for free — and they are not delivering in return the public service which they promised."

Fischer suggests that since the FCC is unlikely to enforce its own rules, and because of the political atmosphere in which the commission operates, governmental responsibility is undesirable. Since the commercial interests of existing stations preclude their operation in the public interest, another device must be used. He suggests:

1. The government should rent channels rather than give them away. Each local station might be assessed some percentage (perhaps 10 or 15 per cent) of their annual earnings. That this would not be a heavy economic burden is illustrated by the fact that CBS earned seven million dollars during the first quarter of 1959.

2. The money derived from rental should be turned over to the National Broadcasting Authority — a public body chartered by Congress but isolated from politics. These men would come from responsible positions in education, culture, and information, but not governmental posts.

3. This Board would hire a Program Manager and would provide him with broad policy directives.

4. The main function of the Authority and its manager would be to produce public service programs — news-in-depth, top quality music and theater, documentaries on science, the arts and public affairs. They would be allowed to experiment with new ideas without worrying about their commercial possibilities.

5. Assuming the Authority produced three television programs a week, each program would be carried by one of the major networks and all affiliated stations in the prime evening time — perhaps NBC on Monday, CBS on Wednesday, and ABC on Friday. The time would be donated by the stations

as additional rental. If the viewer did not wish to see the Authority's program on NBC he could turn to the western on CBS, instead of having the choice between the westerns on NBC or CBS.

6. Such a system, Fischer thinks, would be less costly than it might appear. It would relieve the networks and some local stations who try conscientiously to provide public service programs from sacrificing their commercial interests and it would force those stations who evade their public responsibilities to bear a fair share of the cost. Thus broadcasters could deal properly with advertisers and the Authority would be able to explore the implications of public service without having to "water down" programs to appeal to the lowest common denominator.

Whether this plan or a similar one will eventually become operative only time will tell, but norms of social responsibility are increasingly accepted in practice. If social responsibility is not accepted by the various media, however, either voluntarily or in response to public criticism, the government may possibly remain the only source to implement and maintain the freedom of the press. Such are the ironies of social change.

SUMMARY

Early norms regulating the printed word would today be considered authoritarian. Drawing on a number of ideas important in early America, a libertarian conception emerged stressing the importance of newspapers free from governmental control, providing a market place for ideas. Complete freedom was impractical, since limitations were placed on it by libel, obscenity, and the demands of national security. With increasing costs, the concentration of ownership in the media created inherent limitations on the diversity of expression. The growth of new media, radio and television, presented new problems not easily controlled by the old norms.

A newer normative conception has emerged emphasizing the social responsibility of the media. While accepting many prior norms, this conception suggests that freedom is so important it cannot be left to chance. Newspapers are now responsible for publishing a diversity of opinion. While the newer media have an informational function, they also have the responsibility of providing good entertainment, which is not necessarily signified by the popularity of programming. Many of the norms are still being formulated and disagreement exists over who should be responsible for the conduct of the media.

QUESTIONS AND SUGGESTIONS FOR FURTHER STUDY

1. Describe the extent of concentration of the mass media within your community. How many newspapers exist? Does this indicate a historical decline?

Are existing papers independent or part of a chain? What is the pattern of ownership of local radio and television stations?

2. Not all behavior in early America conformed to the libertarian conception. What were the circumstances leading to the development and to the termination of the Alien and Sedition Acts under the Adams administration?

3. Investigate the state laws governing libel and obscenity. Do various cities in the state have provisions for movie censorship? If so, how is this censorship administered?

4. What innovations have been created in American society by the invention and adoption of television? What changes in political, economic, religious, familial, etc., behavior can be attributed to this invention?

5. Describe the pattern of governmental regulation over the various mass media in a country other than the United States.

6. Observe a day's schedule on radio and television; what proportion of the total is devoted to "good" programming? Specify what criterion you use to make the distinction between "good" and "bad" programming.

7. Read a specific newspaper over a period of time. How does its performance compare with the five measures suggested in the discussion of the responsibility of publishing?

8. What types of criticism led to the development of the conception of social responsibility?

9. It has been suggested that as every new medium of communication is introduced into society, its effects are initially overestimated. Why do you think this happens?

10. "If criticism is the healthiest thing in the world, television should be roaring with intellectual, spiritual, and aesthetic health. It has become the national whipping boy." Do you think this statement to be true? Why should it become a whipping boy?

SUGGESTED READINGS

Berelson, Bernard, and Morris Janowitz (eds.), *Reader in Public Opinion and Communication*, Glencoe: Free Press, 1953. A collection of articles containing both theoretical and empirical treatments of issues in communication. Describes some of the methods used in research.

Bogart, Leo, *The Age of Television*, New York: Ungar, 1956. A compilation of studies on the impact of television. It largely depends on data from audience research done by the networks.

Coons, John E. (ed.), *Freedom and Responsibility in Broadcasting*, Evanston: Northwestern University Press, 1961. This collection of essays centers on the legal aspects of the mass media. It contains statements on the role of public interest and on the role of government.

Himmelweit, Hilde T., A. N. Oppenheim, and Pamela Vance, *Television and the Child*, London: Oxford University Press, 1958. Done in England, this is probably the best study on the effect of television on children. The authors were able to observe the behavior of children before and after the impact of television.

Hughes, Helen McGill, *News and the Human Interest Story*, Chicago: University of Chicago, 1940. A sociological analysis of different types of news. In particular, it treats the shift to and the function of the human interest type of "news."

Janowitz, Morris, *The Community Press in an Urban Setting*, Glencoe: Free Press, 1952. Treats the function of the small neighborhood newspapers in integration of urban areas.

Klapper, Joseph, *The Effects of Mass Communication*, Glencoe: Free Press, 1960. A comprehensive summary of the social and psychological effects of the various media. A careful review of the evidence.

McCormick, John, and Mairi MacInnes (eds.), *Versions of Censorship: An Anthology*, New York: Doubleday, 1962.   P   This is an anthology of various documents in the history and practice of censorship. It deals primarily with censorship of literature.

Ohmann, Robert (ed.), *Mass Media and Mass Culture*, New York: Putnam, 1962. A series of articles reprinted from *Daedalus*.

Schramm, Wilbur (ed.), *Mass Communications*, Urbana: University of Illinois Press, 1960. 2nd ed. A collection of essays on various aspects of mass media. Includes sections on the development and the support of communication.

————; *Responsibility in Mass Communication*, New York: Harper, 1957. Prepared for the National Council of Churches, this book elaborates the idea of social responsibility.

Siebert, Fred, Theodore Peterson, and Wilbur Schramm, *Four Theories of the Press*, Urbana: University of Illinois Press, 1957. This sets forth four different conceptions of the press, including the libertarian and social responsibility. It provides interesting contrasts, both historically and cross culturally.

Siepmann, Charles A., *Radio, Television, and Society*, New York: Oxford University Press, 1950. This book describes the growth of radio and TV and their effects on society.

Wright, Charles, *Mass Communications: A Sociological Perspective*, New York: Random House, 1959.   P   A concise sociological analysis of mass communication. A good introduction.

CHAPTER 10 MASS LEISURE:
A NEW SOCIAL PROBLEM

> A California aircraft worker, commenting on an experiment that gave
> employees a three-day weekend once a month: "Look, that long week-
> end was for the birds as far as I'm concerned. That extra day. You know
> how wives are. She planned something for me. I either had to take her
> shopping or I had to change the wallpaper or I had to move the furniture
> or I had to plant some new shrubbery. Always something to do. . . .
> A man shouldn't have all that time with his family. He gets tired of
> them. I tell you, by the time Monday night came I was just dying to
> get back to work." [1]

Large-scale industrialization has revolutionized leisure in the United States.
For the first time in history, free time is available to almost everyone. With
automation and more efficient production methods, the work week has
dropped from sixty hours to forty or less. In some industries the twenty-
hour week is both a dream and a threat.

Not only do more people have more hours away from the job, but they
have more money to spend during these hours. The goods and services that
can be purchased have also increased. These developments have been accompanied by ambivalent attitudes toward the place and use of leisure. Dissensus has occurred between emerging leisure norms and more firmly entrenched ones. Since the United States is work-oriented, leisure is seen in
contrast to work, and is viewed not only as free time but time that has been
earned and paid for. What to do with mass leisure has become a more and
more perplexing problem.

The normative problem: how should leisure be used in an industrial society?

There are several answers to this question. The historical conception challenged any nonwork activity and said, in effect, that leisure is wasteful, if
not sinful, and should be minimized or avoided. Since this normative prescription provides a basis for analyzing present-day leisure conflicts, we shall
start by considering the historical roots of the problem.

1. "Highlights from the Hidden Revolution," *Minutes* (June 1959), p. 6.

Leisure was viewed with suspicion in early America. It was something that should be generally avoided, because work-free hours yielded few, if any, benefits. This negative evaluation has been in evidence longer than any other normative prescription. To understand why this norm became so firmly entrenched, it is necessary to understand the period in which it flourished.

Early Americans saw little value in leisure; this attitude was consistent with the task they faced. In a pioneer era the dominant emphasis was upon work, self-sacrifice, and thrift — not fun, relaxation, or contemplation. It had to be if the early colonies were to survive. Tools were crude, production methods were inefficient, knowledge was limited, and the land was strange.

The extreme emphasis placed on work and the "detestation of idleness" was supported by Puritan theology, which gave moral sanction to economic necessity. Work, especially long hours of physically exhausting work, was regarded as part of God's plan — necessary for divine salvation. Leisure was equated with idleness, and along with the virtues of rising early and keeping busy, everyone was taught also that the devil finds work for idle hands. Time empty of work was regarded as a dangerous thing, and was frequently assumed to be inherently evil and destructive. This conception was buttressed by an economy desperately in need of a long work day, and by a theology admonishing that leisure is sinful. In this setting, a negative evaluation of leisure becomes not only understandable, but can be interpreted as being functional for the era in which it flourished.

Early American life, however, was not totally devoid of play and free time. There were holidays, picnics, turkey shoots, and fairs, but even these events had a utilitarian aspect, and generally were a by-product of work. In short, the life-demands of that era did not permit participation in meaningful leisure pursuits for sheer enjoyment or satisfaction.

When a society survives, it also changes. Changes in the economy were accomplished by corresponding shifts in the normative view of leisure. These norms will be discussed in terms of contemporary and emergent conceptions of the way in which leisure time should be used in an urban-industrial society.

> *Contemporary Normative Conception:* Leisure should be used chiefly as a restorative for work. It should be used as a means to other goals.

During the early twentieth century, mass production began to make its impact on the economy. Cities increased in size, standards of living moved upward, and the work week began to shorten. As shops grew into factories, many people began to work from eight to five, rather than from sunup to sundown. The six-day week became five-and-a-half-day week, and then the five-day week became commonplace. Not only had a large urban population been formed, but for the first time in history, a large proportion of this population was employed in jobs which permitted increasing amounts of free time. The shift from class leisure to mass leisure had begun.

Although industrialization removed the basis for anxiety about man's ability to sustain himself on a new continent, the fears of the earlier era remained. Continuous hard work was still regarded as honorable, and other activities were evaluated in relation to work. After all, an industrial society had been built by work.[2] The idea that less effort was now needed for greater productivity was difficult to comprehend, and not widely accepted. Machine production methods shortened working hours, but these innovations clashed with earlier work norms. When Henry Ford adopted the five-day week in 1926, some opponents of shorter hours, such as John E. Edgerton, president of the National Association of Manufacturers, invoked the Deity to support their views. Speaking that year before the NAM national convention, he pronounced, "I regard the five-day week as an unworthy ideal. . . . More work and better work is a more inspiring and worthier motto than less work and more pay. . . . It is better not to trifle with God's laws." Too many hours away from the job, especially for "the common man," was still viewed with distrust.

However, along with the new products and conveniences produced by an advanced technology, an important change in the *motivation* for work occurred. This, in turn, brought about a change in the normative view of leisure. The pre-industrial emphasis on work as necessary for survival was replaced by a post-industrial emphasis upon vocational success and the acquisition of money and possessions. Obviously, the pioneer, as well as the urbanite, was preoccupied with "making a living" and "getting ahead," but in the urbanite's world, emotional and psychological needs, as well as sustenance needs, became increasingly tied to the world of work. In a work-centered society it is not surprising that one's conception of himself and his life satisfactions became more closely centered in the job. And from this perspective it is not difficult to see why leisure now became defined as desirable *if* it was used as a restorative for more and better work. Thus the contemporary normative conception of leisure is still largely negative. Leisure is regarded as a release from duties or obligations, or more specifically, release from job obligations. Its role, from this viewpoint, is simply "recreational," or consists chiefly of

2. The class composition of immigrant groups also reinforced traditional work norms. As Williams has pointed out, "the population of this country was mainly recruited from the working classes of Britain and Europe; except in a few areas of the South and New England, there was no aristocratic class to give prestige to leisure and to stigmatize manual labor and trade." Robin M. Williams, *American Society*, New York: Knopf, 1960, p. 423.

those activities which give refreshment from toil.[3] In short, the contemporary norm regards leisure as a *means* to other goals.

Industrialization also encouraged a secular view of life. Consequently earlier moralistic admonitions about the inappropriateness of free time failed to make an impression. Leisure, however, was still viewed as a kind of "standing still." As soon as there was more leisure than the amount needed for "healthy recreation," concern mounted. Significantly, during this period the normative criticism of leisure changed. The religious warning that, "he who plays is sinful," was supplanted by the secular admonition that, "he who plays will not succeed," bringing it into line with the emphasis on economic success.

The contemporary view of leisure, as a means to other ends, enabled it to operate *within* the work setting as well as outside of it. With increased emphasis on business success, leisure began to be used in a more direct way to further vocational goals. If success in a bureaucratic-industrial society is achieved largely by impressing other people with one's interests and abilities, then certain types of spare time activities can be utilized more effectively than others as vocational assets. Thus golfing, membership in certain organizations, spending time in certain restaurants and nightclubs, for example, may not be engaged in solely for pleasure, but chiefly as a means of promoting business interests. It is, of course, obvious that all leisure activities cannot be so interpreted, yet it is probable that belonging to a country club, the Chamber of Commerce, a fraternal organization, or similar groups, is frequently used for enhancing occupational status. These techniques, it should be noted, are in keeping with the rise of instrumental, impersonal relationships which accompanied the growth of cities, and a more bureaucratic way of life generally.[4] In fact, business activity itself may become a form of recreation — a kind of competitive sport — for many American males. Writing of Middletown, for example, the Lynds point out that members of the business

3. Speaking of the traditionally oriented person, Riesman has commented that "an attenuated puritanism survives in his exploitation of leisure. He may say, when he takes a vacation or stretches a weekend, 'I owe it to myself' but the self in question is viewed like a car or house whose upkeep must be carefully maintained for resale purposes." David Riesman, Nathan Glazer, and Reuel Denney, *The Lonely Crowd*, New York: Doubleday, 1953, p. 185.
4. Writing on this aspect of urban life, Davis, Bredemeier, and Levy, observe: "Success in our urban-industrial society comes primarily from the manipulation of other persons. They rather than the forces of nature are the obstacles and the means to one's aspirations. Consequently, the individual is forced to develop toward others the same kind of attitude that his agricultural ancestor developed toward tree stumps, rocks, and insects: an instrumental, impersonal attitude. But if he views others in such a way, he must suspect that others view him similarly. He finds it increasingly difficult to enter into the unsuspecting relationships of affectional intimacy that he learned as a child to crave." Kingsley Davis, Harry C. Bredemeier, and Marion J. Levy, Jr., *Modern American Society*, New York: Rinehart, 1949, pp. 711–12.

class significantly refer to their office activities as the "business game" although it is decidedly not customary for members of the working class to refer to their work as the "factory game." [5]

It should also be pointed out that the traditional or utilitarian conception of leisure illustrates the degree to which business and economic norms have "invaded" nonwork or leisure areas of life. Indeed, the often repeated popular version of this norm, that it is desirable to *spend* leisure *profitably*, emphasizes the fact that "the very symbols of group speech swing around economic values." [6]

Before discussing contemporary issues further, some important features of the changing leisure picture should be observed.

CHANGES WHICH HAVE AFFECTED THE CONTEMPORARY CONCEPTION OF LEISURE

1. *Increased Leisure: A Modern Paradox.* Although the impact of industrialization has been widespread, leisure time has not been diffused equally throughout all of the society. A paradoxical situation has developed. Instead of remaining the exclusive characteristic of a privileged class, recent gains in leisure time have been greatest among skilled and semiskilled workers. The occupational groupings in Figure 10-1 show the "middle mass" section of society which now represents the new leisure class. This shift in the distribution of leisure explains why many businessmen and professionals are often unable to understand why there is growing concern about leisure. In today's work-world they are the ones who put in the longest hours. The readers of this book may also find it difficult to understand why increased leisure is a problem. College students often feel that their problem is lack of time and "keeping up" with the demands of each day. There are others who share this feeling. For example, there are many married women, especially mothers with young children, who would be happy for a few extra minutes — by themselves. For persons in these categories — professionals, executives, students, married women, and certainly others who are busily engaged in generally satisfying activities — leisure time may not be a pressing problem. But they have only to wait. Earlier mandatory retirement and early marriage (with offspring now married or away at school) mean that parents — and this includes a lot of people — will be "out of a job" a lot earlier than their parents were, and with many active years ahead of them.

With widespread leisure now a social fact, what impact has it made on the American scene? How has it affected spending patterns, national sports,

5. Robert S. Lynd and Helen M. Lynd, *Middletown in Transition,* New York: Harcourt, Brace, 1937, p. 243.
6. Ibid.

or vacation behavior? Who gets the long vacation with pay? How extensive are these changes? We turn now to these and related concerns.

Fig. 10-1.

	Today's Labor Force	66,316,000
	Professional	8,218,000
	Managers, officials, proprietors (except farm)	7,562,000
	Farmers and farm managers	2,709,000
	Sales	4,277,000
The New Leisure Class	Clerical	10,094,000
The New Leisure Class	Craftsmen, foremen, etc.	8,206,000
The New Leisure Class	Operatives (factory machines and vehicles)	11,627,000
The New Leisure Class	Service workers (except domestic)	6,224,000
The New Leisure Class	Laborers (except farm)	3,156,000
	Farm laborers and foremen	1,788,000
	Private houseworkers	2,453,000

Source: U.S. Bureau of the Census, *Statistical Abstract of the United States*, 1962, adapted from Table 297, p. 226.

2. *Increased Expenditures.* Additional leisure has created additional leisure spending. One indication of the impact which new income and more time to spend it have made on the American economy is reflected in available data. Leisure spending during the past three decades has increased steadily to about $41 billion — approximately the size of the national defense budget. Or stated differently, about one out of every six dollars in personal income is spent for leisure pursuits.[7] The amount spent for domestic recreational travel rose from $5.4 billion in 1947 to $12 billion in 1955, and during these years foreign pleasure travel increased from $600 million to more than $1.5 billion dollars. Georgia's tourist business is now bigger than the cash value of its cotton crop, and Florida's deep-sea fishing, supported mainly by sportsmen, is nearly as big as its citrus fruit and cattle industries combined.

Mass production of mechanical and technical equipment has permitted new opportunities for ever increasing numbers of hobby enthusiasts. For example, there are 60 million cameras being used by nonprofessional photographers, who spend $1.3 billion a year on supplies and equipment, and approximately 100,000 amateur radio operators in the United States whose average investment in equipment is $400. With the increase in home ownership and the availability of home tools, woodworking has gained in popularity,

7. Reuel Denney, "The Leisure Society," *The University of Chicago Magazine* (May 1960), p. 7.

and since 1952 sales have increased from $6 to $60 million. Auto racing, perhaps the best illustration of a sport created by the products of technology, has had a 40 per cent gain in gate receipts since 1952. One of the outstanding nondefense "growth industries" is the pleasure-boating business, which has more than tripled sales since 1951. There are now close to eight million recreational boats in the United States, and on the Fourth of July weekend in 1959 a milestone of some kind was reached when more people were killed in New York State in boating accidents than in highway accidents.[8]

College football has become big business, and the changes that have occurred in the game illustrate the degree to which economic norms have invaded the world of sports. In 1950, it grossed ten times the income of professional football. Using the gate receipts of that year as a basis ($11.2 billion), it has been estimated that a total capital of about $250 million is invested in the college football industry.[9] These figures, obviously, do not include the "invisible" subsidization of football, nor do they hint at the place that football pools occupy in the American betting economy.[10] What started out at the turn of the century as a game with relatively simple rules, stressing sheer physical power, has developed into a complex, highly organized sport characterized by costly operating expenses, specialized personnel, intricate recruitment, and bureaucratic procedure. Accounts of pressures — some subtle and some obvious — exerted on the big-time coach "to win" are commonplace. Commenting on these changes, Denney observes: "It is a game in which anthropologists are hired as scouts, recruits are acquired in a labor market, and Monday-morning TV quarterbacks employ charts that make a Wall Street analyst look amateurish." [11]

The rapid growth of vacations with pay is most evident among production workers. In 1937 only about 40 per cent of this group received paid vacations. During World War II the percentage rose to about 80, and today almost 90 per cent of all production workers receive approximately two weeks' vacation with pay. Vacation leisure represents bulk time, which differs from "bits and pieces" of time gained through the reduction of working hours, into which only a few leisure activities will fit. Bulk time "permits a long trip or paints a large room." Furthermore, it takes on new meaning when applied to persons who are in retirement. A statistical picture of this kind of leisure is revealing:

8. Most of the statistics cited in this paragraph can be found in *Life*, Special Issue, *The Good Life*, 47 (December 28, 1959), pp. 69 ff.
9. David Riesman, "Football in America: A Study in Culture Diffusion," *Individualism Reconsidered*, Glencoe: Free Press, 1954, p. 242.
10. Ibid.
11. Reuel Denney, *The Astonished Muse*, Chicago: University of Chicago Press, 1957, p. 119.

If one retires at 60 and lives five more years, his total of new free time (from 9:00 a.m. to 4:00 p.m. Monday through Friday) comes to over 10,000 hours; if he lives 15 years, he faces over 31,000 free hours of time previously devoted to work. But assume an average Mr. American who retires at 60 and lives to 70. To his bulk of actual retirement hours we must add the 48 hours per week which most of us enjoy on weekends and evenings. This American may anticipate almost 45,000 hours of time to do with as he wishes — a quantity of time, indeed, which is more than all of his previous working hours from the age of 40 to 60. In other words, his free time in retirement equals precisely half of his past working life! [12]

There are almost 16 million persons in the United States who are over sixty, and with medical knowledge increasing the life span, the number of "young" retired persons can be expected to increase annually.

Up to this point we have emphasized the historical setting of the problem, the contemporary normative conception, and some facts documenting the impact of mass leisure. But little has been said about the *meaning* of leisure — other than contrasting it to the world of work. While it is true that economic activities have occupied the greater part of man's time and attention, the fact that abundant leisure is now an integral part of the social scene has meant that this aspect of American society is receiving greater attention. Significantly, much of this interest centers in the meaning of leisure.

3. *Rethinking the Meaning of Leisure.* What is leisure? The plethora of definitions reflect the elusiveness of this concept. At first glance leisure is not a difficult word to define. Most persons would reply that it is "time when I'm not working — free time." This type of response, however, points up the difficulty besetting most definitions of leisure. This definition assumes that all life activities can be neatly divided into work and nonwork. To think in terms of such a dichotomy seriously distorts one's view of contemporary life. In a complex industrial society, work and nonwork overlap and mix. Many occupational roles contain in varying degrees the same qualities that characterize meaningful and satisfying leisure pursuits. Qualities such as friendship, entertainment, and creativeness occur in work-oriented situations as well as in leisure settings. A luncheon with colleagues can be both socially pleasurable and professionally productive.

Leisure is obviously a many-sided concept. The following general picture of an "ideal construct" describes its essential elements.[13]

(a) *Antithesis to Work as Economic Function.* Engaged in leisure I can dig a ditch in my yard to make way for some landscaping project; this may

12. Reprinted with permission from Max Kaplan, *Leisure in America: A Social Inquiry,* New York: Wiley, 1960, p. 12.

13. These dimensions of leisure are adapted from Max Kaplan, *Leisure: A Social Inquiry.* For a further discussion of this conception, see chap. 2, "Leisure as a Social Relationship in Culture."

require more energy than my "job." It is, however, outside of the economic system in the usual way I relate myself to that system. It is, obviously, not altogether unrelated to economics *per se*, for my "labor of love" may deprive a professional "worker" of employment.

(b) *Pleasant Expectation and Recollection.* With this element we eliminate all enforced "leisure" such as unemployment, imprisonment, or sickness. Constructively, we include a psychological attitude moving both forward and backward in time. It is impossible to divorce "vacation," for instance, from the expectation, planning, daydreaming, saving, packing, the "excitement" of going away. Such looking ahead often makes the routine of life more bearable, for then work periods are seen as means toward "life" and "living." Similarly, the recollection of the vacation or leisure activity is often inaccurate, colored by the idealization fostered in the preparatory stage. Research would probably show that many persons on vacation enjoy themselves and look back favorably upon their experience because they cannot emotionally afford to contradict their past hopes and projections. And as a matter of fact, the attitude and expectancy do influence the actual experience itself.

(c) *Minimum of Social Role Obligations.* Social role distinguishes John Smith *as* John Smith from the many "positions" or obligations he has achieved in his society or which he has been given by it: citizen, father, friend, carpenter, Protestant, Mason, and so on. He is only *one* John Smith who plays or possesses *many* roles. In each of the many circles he touches, Smith has rights and obligations. These are obligations, however, which he is more likely to assume voluntarily, and with more pleasant expectations, than such obligations as going to work on January 2nd. He is formally committed to the latter, and for a long period of time. Theoretically, he has greater freedom in deciding whether to be with his family on his "off" time. The observer from the outside can, in specific cases, question such "self-deception"; yet John Smith himself is the one who perceives his relative freedoms, and acts in accordance with his perceptions.

(d) *Psychological Perception of Freedom.* It is the perception of freedom *by the person who participates in leisure* which is the important factor. Thus, there will be considerable variety in the definitions of leisure or of "free time."

(e) *Close Relation to Cultural Values.* If the concept of leisure is equated with re-creation it has no value in itself except as a supplement to work. However, leisure has moved further and further from subordination to work; increasingly leisure is bound up closely with moral, ethical, and thought systems, and with all social institutions.

(f) *Equal Significance for All Areas of Life.* Old associations of work with seriousness and leisure with lightness are now out-dated and theoretically indefensible. Leisure activity can include interests covering the whole gamut of human life; hence the degree of seriousness is irrelevant to the concept of what leisure is or "should be."

In the broadest sense leisure may be defined as an activity or social relationship in which the commitment is relatively voluntary; one in which the participant *perceives* a freedom to become involved or not, to engage in significant activity or not, or to use it as an end in itself or not. It should be noted that this definition purposely does not focus on the *content* of leisure. *Any activity can become the basis for leisure.* Many persons, however, think of leisure as a particular set of recreational activities, and when an activity becomes serious it ceases to be regarded as leisure. This view is rejected here. It should also be noted that this definition treats leisure as something related to but distinct from play or recreation.[14] Leisure is not a peripheral phenomenon, extracurricular to life situations — it is an integral part of society. T. H. Marshall echoed this emphasis when he wrote, "leisure does not mean mere idleness. It means the freedom to choose your activities according to your own preferences and your own standards of what is best." The emphasis here is upon leisure as a type of commitment — a commitment which is more voluntary than a work commitment, one in which there is a maximum freedom to become involved, and one which can (and does) include behavior ranging from the very frivolous to the very serious.

With this conception of leisure serving as a point of reference, let us continue to pursue the leisure problem. Although much leisure behavior reflects the contemporary normative conception, within the last decade a new norm based on different assumptions about the use of leisure has emerged.

> *Emergent Normative Conception:* Leisure should be more than a restorative for work. It is an important part of life and should be regarded as a worthwhile end or goal in itself.

Along with increasing industrial efficiency and productivity there occurred corresponding increases in leisure time. Standards of living continued to rise, the work week shortened, educational levels continued to be raised, urban employment became more specialized, and much physically exhausting work was transferred from men to machines. During World War II, production efficiency reached a new high, and within the last decade automation and

14. It is useful to distinguish between the terms recreation and leisure. Recreation comes from the Latin *recreare*, to restore or refresh, and refers to certain activities (e.g., games, sports, athletics) pursued during leisure, which are designed to revitalize individuals so that they may return to work refreshed. Although the term leisure also refers in part to such activities, the emphasis is on the time element. Leisure time, obviously, can be spent in many ways, and the pursuit of some form of recreational activity is, therefore, only one of the many ways of spending leisure time.

further technological refinements have raised productive efficiency still higher (see Fig. 10-2).

While the effects of pre-industrial Puritanism are still evident, its influence is waning. The image of starving colonists has all but faded from the American scene. With wealth and plenty, a new, less ascetic, philosophy of life has emerged based on industrial triumphs. The successful application of in-

Fig. 10-2. A Measure of Abundance in the United States

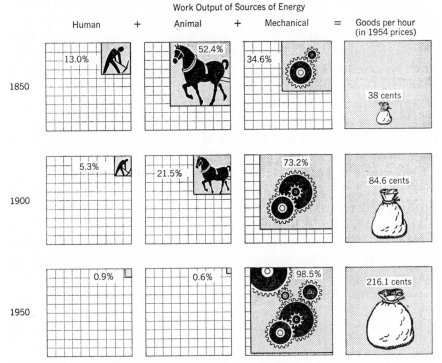

Source: Thomas R. Carskadon and George Soule, *USA in New Dimensions*, Twentieth Century Fund, New York, 1957. Reprinted by permission of the Twentieth Century Fund.

dustrial techniques has meant that the American people of today are living in a fundamentally different social setting. For the first time, a point has been reached where abundance rather than scarcity is the rule. Today most Americans can work fewer hours, produce more goods, and enjoy a higher standard of living than any previous generation. The major problems of production have been solved. In fact, the efficiency with which production problems have been solved is reflected in the fact that no other country in the world has a problem of surpluses, e.g. food and other consumer goods, comparable to the one currently existing in the United States.[15] This does

15. Problems and issues associated with "high production" are obviously complex. Population growth and the cold war alone are sufficient reasons for increasing productivity.

not imply, of course, that all economic problems have been solved. But the fact remains that modern production methods can readily meet basic consumer demands, and in many instances production rates are slowed down so that supply does not surpass demand. This is not to mention the stockpiling of consumer goods which could easily occur if present levels of efficiency were increased. Today, the average American is not "starved" in the same way as was his colonial cousin.

The cumulative effect of these changes has brought about a recent change in the normative conception of leisure. In a society now characterized by economic affluence, Americans are looking upon leisure as something more than a restorative for work. With more time away from the job and more money to spend, leisure has taken on new meanings. It has come to be regarded as an important, legitimate part of modern life. It is regarded as a right; something to be pursued in a meaningful way, apart from utilitarian purposes. The emergent normative conception implies that leisure should be an intrinsically satisfying experience in and of itself — an *end*, not a means to other ends.

Conceptions of leisure are always tied closely to conceptions of work. To understand the new leisure norm it is therefore necessary to understand changing work norms.

The post World War II period has witnessed a re-evaluation of work and a re-definition of leisure. There is evidence that work is becoming less meaningful, and this trend has reinforced the emerging leisure norm. Automation has increased job efficiency but has decreased job enthusiasm. In a highly efficient, industrialized society, many vocational demands are dull and monotonous. Specialization and mechanization mean that working patterns have to be set by machinery,[16] with little room left for spontaneous activity or for

> But it is here that the problem becomes complex. Today the issue is not one of merely producing more goods, or more services. It is largely a matter of producing, in addition to what is now being produced, the particular goods and the particular services that are needed most. This involves serious thinking about what is being produced. For example, hospitals and automobiles can now be built equally well. The further question is: should productivity be increased in terms of more and better equipped automobiles, or more and better equipped hospitals? In his provocative book, *The Affluent Society* (Boston: Houghton Mifflin, 1958), John Galbraith has observed, "To furnish a barren room is one thing. To continue to crowd in furniture until the foundation buckles is quite another. To have failed to solve the problem of producing goods would have been to confine man in his oldest and most grievous misfortune. But to fail to see that we have solved it and to fail to proceed thence to the next task would be fully as tragic."

16. The unskilled laborer and semiskilled machine operator together make the largest category in the labor force. One in four of all those at work are semiskilled or unskilled manual workers. For a further discussion of the social implications of this feature of an industrial society, see Harold L. Wilensky and Charles N. Lebeaux, *Industrial Society and Social Welfare*, New York: Russell Sage Foundation, 1958, pp. 100 ff.

individual creativity. Standardized mass production methods require more self-repression than self-expression, and men "must be serious and steady about something that does not mean anything to them. . . . The work itself . . . offers little change for external prestige and internal self-esteem." [17] Workers, especially in highly automated industries, find it increasingly difficult to relate meaningfully to job activities, and there is evidence that alienation from work is moving upward into executive and professional levels. Consequently, more persons are looking beyond their jobs for satisfying life experiences.

There has occurred a shift from job-centered activities to leisure and home-centered interests. This does not mean that Americans are working less diligently than their predecessors. Work is mandatory if current and envisioned standards of living are to be maintained. Rather, the emphasis has changed. The home and off-the-job activities which traditionally allowed little relaxation have become more meaningful — particularly for the post World War II family — and now, in large measure, justify working hard in the first place. Frequently, husband and wife are both employed and often combine work roles with rearing children and getting an education. Work is important but, again, the emphasis is different. August Heckscher, research director for the Twentieth Century Fund, comments pointedly on this part of the contemporary scene.

Today, I think we're in a sort of middle ground where more and more people are working in order not merely to live but are working in order that they may live well, and the living well becomes the objective of their life, and work therefore becomes a kind of secondary . . . process. Men are not looking for the ultimate satisfactions of life on the job. They are looking for those satisfactions in the free time that comes after the job, or, more and more, in the free years that come after retirement.[18]

The emergent norm, however, has not replaced the contemporary normative view. This reassessment has been — and still is — accompanied by ambivalent attitudes. The point is that *both* normative prescriptions currently compete for adherents. Dissensus exists as to what role leisure should play in the American pattern of living. On the one hand, the press of the past is still strong. Work, especially for the person who can remember the depression years, is still regarded as the most important thing around which to organize his life. He feels guilty if he relaxes and uses his free time in a "nonproductive" way. But on the other hand, he now has to live with more free hours — free hours to do the things he has always wanted to do, free hours to experience satisfactions that increasingly he cannot experience on the job,

17. C. Wright Mills, *White Collar*, New York: Oxford University Press, 1951, pp. 236, 243.
18. August Heckscher, as quoted in *Minutes*, op. cit. p. 20.

and free hours to relax. But again he feels guilty when he begins to enjoy his newly won freedom.[19] He cannot quite accept the emergent leisure norm for fear that others who espouse the contemporary norm, will call him frivolous, pleasure-seeking, or worse, lazy. So he turns to find more work to do to avoid leisure, or he pursues a "leisure" activity strenuously, even though it gives him little enjoyment. This situation, however, is changing. People increasingly question contemporary normative assumptions. The trend toward the emergent normative view will likely continue.

REACTIONS TO INCREASED LEISURE

New leisure has created new problems. These center on two contrasting situations. One involves the issue of excessive enthusiasm and activity, while the other stems from excessive apathy and passivity. In short, one set of issues centers on exhaustive leisure, and the other on boredom.

EXHAUSTIVE LEISURE

Despite the popularity of current advice from physicians who urge Americans to relax, especially during leisure hours, few (including the physicians themselves) seem able to do so. Characteristically, the United States is a nation of energetic, fast-paced people, who "play as hard as they work." Busy urbanites who lead busy lives during the week become even busier during the weekend. Some who arise at 6:30 on weekdays get up at 5:30 on Saturday to play a tension-laden round of golf on an overcrowded course; some doggedly drive long distances to glimpse the ocean or bake in the sun, and return home over the same hazardous highway triumphant if not relaxed. Some play bridge as though the fate of nations depends upon their bid; some compulsively go fishing every Saturday come rain, heat, sleet, or snow; some mow and "manicure" their lawn with clock-like regularity, and some isolate themselves in basements every evening straining to build another cabinet.

These characteristics are perplexing to visitors from other countries, who find it difficult to understand why Americans cannot easily slow down during their leisure time. Miss Santha Rama Rau, a Wellesley-educated writer from India, remarked at a conference on the use of leisure time, "Surely, nowhere else in the world do people fuss about what to do with their leisure. I think it is rather sad that some kind of guilt has been built up in this particular society . . . that people are so tense about the way they spend their spare time. . . . I think it is unfortunate that respect is gone for the man who

19. Commenting on the degree of present-day affluence in the United States, Riesman has observed that "many Americans feel guilty about their luxuries if others are forced to fight and suffer, and so would welcome a kind of edited hardship as an alleviation of their guilt."

simply sits in his rocking chair and thinks, if he happens to feel like it, or does nothing if he happens to feel like it." [20]

Miss Rama Rau's remarks are supported by Russell Lynes, who has observed: "In spite of the statistics which would seem to indicate that none of us does anything but play, most of us when we escape from work do not look for leisure but for other kinds of work." And he adds further,

Already a great many men are playing hooky from leisure by "moonlighting," the practice of taking a second job after one's regular job is done. Economically these second jobs are in most cases not necessary to maintain a decent standard of living, but they keep the hands busy, and they bring in more money with which to buy more labor-saving gadgets to provide still more leisure to the family. It solves not at all the problem of leisure; it only salves the conscience. In removing so much of the tax on the physical and mental efforts which we associate with making a living, we have imposed a tremendous tax in individual ingenuity. *It is obviously much less of a strain for most people to work at prescribed tasks that they believe are productive (if only of a paycheck) than it is for them to think of satisfying ways to occupy themselves.* Consequently into the time vacuum have rushed a miscellaneous lot of leisure activities that are, many of them, more exhausting than work.[21]

Some of the basic normative conflicts of contemporary life are to be found in leisure behavior. The exhausting nature of much spare time activity illustrates again the degree to which competitive economic norms invade noneconomic areas of life.[22] The feeling persists that work is inherently honorable and the enjoyment of leisure for more than a short time is vaguely immoral.

THE PROBLEM OF BOREDOM

To include boredom as a part of the leisure problem may seem strange, especially to those who envision Americans as energetic, highly motivated people constantly on the move and always in a hurry. For many, a problem of this sort appears unreal and remote. Everywhere they turn they see people busily occupied in numerous activities, and seemingly interested in what they are doing; people who are overcommitted, with too many demands upon their time; people without enough hours in the day. Nobody, it seems,

20. Remark by Miss Santha Rama Rau of India made at the Corning Glass Conference, in Eugene Staley (ed.), *Creating an Industrial Civilization*, New York: Harper, 1952, pp. 52–3.
21. Russell Lynes, "The Pressures of Leisure," *What's New*, 208 (Winter 1958), p. 15. Italics added.
22. There is evidence that a similar situation exists in England and other industrialized countries. Malcolm Muggeridge, "The Real Opiate of the Masses," *The New York Times*, November 22, 1959, p. 15: "If we have nothing to do, we must do it vigorously, earnestly and conscientiously."

has "time on his hands." Furthermore, have we not just finished emphasizing the exhaustive, strenuous nature of contemporary leisure? Does this not suggest something other than dullness and monotony, despite the fact that a busy life does not necessarily mean an exciting one? Then who is bored?

An astute observer of the leisure scene has noted that "Human time is a vacuum that has to be filled. If it is not filled with work, it is filled with alternatives to work." [23] How to utilize time in a meaningful way can be a problem. Without great oversimplification, the American people can be divided into two segments: those who do not have enough time, and those who have too much time. While there are probably more who would welcome an extra hour or two added to their day, there are also those — and their number is increasing — who would shudder at such a thought. The first category includes busy professionals, businessmen, and other workers significantly involved in meaningful work and leisure; young married women, especially mothers with preschool children; and those children and adolescents who find life generally an exciting adventure. But these categories are not all-inclusive — there is another side to the coin. There are those who find themselves in dull, monotonous jobs with little hope for advancement, whose occupational boredom spills over into nonwork hours. Indeed those who spend most of their spare time in front of their television sets may not tell us as much about their enthusiasm for passive entertainment as they reveal the degree to which they have seen their dreams and aspirations cut down to the size of the screen that now absorbs them. There are mothers whose children no longer require mothering. Their "children" are now married, or employed, or away at college. These women devoted themselves fully to child-rearing and now they are "out of a job." They are also unprepared for the later stages of family life without children. Consequently, they feel that life is empty — and time passes slowly. There are young people who do not find life very exciting, who have not experienced satisfactory peer-group relationships, and who "can't get interested in anything."

There is also another group for whom time often passes very slowly — and who are also out of a job. They are the aged and the retired. Here again their numbers are increasing daily. The number of people 65 and over approached $17\frac{1}{2}$ million in mid-1962 and continues to increase at the rate of well over 1000 per day.[24] Their despair and apathy stem from a feeling that usefulness is found only in work, and mandatory retirement has deprived them of "their job." This is especially true of males, conditioned by business-world norms, whose lives are organized around their occupations. Play and

23. Lynes, op. cit. p. 14.
24. Report of Special Committee on Aging, Mr. McNamara, Chm. *Congressional Record*, 108, June 14, 1962.

unobligated time are unfamiliar to them. As a result, retirement is often feared, delayed, or disguised, and is seldom approached with wisdom, grace, or pleasant anticipation.[25] They have difficulty in becoming interested in commitments that are not job-oriented, and in most instances have given up the quest to find new interests. Their daily task is reduced to simply "killing time." Apathy and dissatisfaction produce more of the same. They desire new experiences but are unable to realize them.

> Though the bored person hungers for things to happen to him, the disheartening fact is that when they do, he empties them of the very meaning he unconsciously yearns for by using them as distractions. In popular culture, even the Second Coming would be just another barren thrill to be watched till [the next TV show] came on.[26]

There is tragedy as well as irony in the fact that millions yearn for immortality, yet do not know what to do with themselves on a rainy Sunday afternoon.

The impact of industrialization has compounded the problem of the aged, and it is reasonable to assume that this social problem is destined to increase in importance. Institutes of social gerontology will grow in influence and will expand their research programs. Significantly, a recent conference concerned with the pressures of leisure on the older individual observed a fundamental issue.

> All people, but especially older people, are concerned that whatever they do have meaning. Their fear of retirement is largely that the rest of their lives is rendered meaningless. They want more than just to pass the hours. Centers for the aged might do well, therefore, to avoid the term "recreation" in their names and to establish a connotation that the centers cover a whole range of service and opportunity, that in these centers of leisure for creative living, "the human organism is involved in an educative process . . . where our senior citizens may become integrated with their community, alerted to new challenges in the later years." [27]

One study of retired persons related adjustment on the job before retirement to adjustment to retirement roles. Their major finding was unexpected and contains important educational implications. The evidence indicated that those who were satisfied with their occupations made relatively poor adjustments to retirement, while the group who was largely dissatisfied with their

25. In this connection, E. B. White has made the following cogent observation: "To anyone who has always gone some place in the morning, even a place he hasn't particularly liked, retirement seems like the removal of the most steadying thing of all, his destination." Cited in TIDE, 30 (March 24, 1956), p. 24.
26. Ralph Ross and Ernest van den Haag, The Fabric of Society, New York: Harcourt, Brace, 1957, p. 189.
27. Max Kaplan, "Pressures of Leisure on the Older Individual," Journal of Gerontology Supplement, 13 (July 1958), p. 38.

jobs made very satisfactory shifts to retirement roles. Persons who are now in their sixties and seventies may be thought of as pioneers in the new leisure, establishing patterns for successive generations of older people.

FURTHER OBSERVATIONS

We have sought to point out some of the major dimensions of an emerging social problem — mass leisure. To analyze normative dissensus in this area may seem strange to some because, traditionally, leisure patterns have not been subjected to systematic study. A scientific interest in leisure has developed only recently. This is understandable, particularly in a young society such as the United States, which has only recently emerged from an agricultural period where the dominant concern of life had to be with long hours of exhausting work. But it will be recalled that once the frontier was established, the nation's concern centered on the creation of wealth and power. And in a rapidly changing society it is not difficult to see why such fields as engineering, commerce, law, business administration, and similar areas soon came to be regarded as more important than "less practical" areas of knowledge such as the arts and the humanities. As a larger proportion of personal income is invested in leisure pursuits, it is likely that this aspect of American society will receive greater social and scientific consideration. There is also growing recognition of the fact that an understanding of leisure can provide unique insights into human behavior.

What a man *is* can be seen in many ways — his place in the family, his work, his friends, how he votes, what he eats, whether he prays, what he buys, what and how he thinks. But how precious *to* him and how revealing of him are those hours or moments in which he is "himself." He reads, he just sits and smokes, he plays chess with his cronies, he visits a sick friend, he chats with his wife, he writes on his book, he makes furniture, he hunts for a bawdy house, he goes to his club, studies for a better job . . . and each of these, put into perspective of other things he does, and with whom, and how often, and why, can reveal how he sees the world.[28]

The fact remains that historically, greater emphasis has been placed on the role of work — and this emphasis, although changing, still characterizes the United States today. But widespread leisure is already a part of the American scene. "In fact," as Riesman has said, "so great is the sheer quantity of our available leisure and leisure resources, that I do not think we can find very helpful models in other countries." [29]

Yet the accomplishment of this goal involves a curious irony. For centuries

28. Max Kaplan, personal communication.
29. David Riesman, "Some Observations on Changes in Leisure Attitudes," in *Individualism Reconsidered*, Glencoe: Free Press, 1954, p. 204.

man has dreamed of an era where there would be enough time, after daily work tasks were completed, to devote to the things that he really enjoys doing. Through a Puritanical devotion to work for work's sake, Americans have finally succeeded in realizing this cherished dream — leisure time. But now that they have it, there seem to be few who are able to enjoy it. It is difficult for a people to adjust their pattern of living to more leisure than they had anticipated, especially in a society that lacks a tradition for leisure.

It is precisely at this point that the significance of increasing leisure time emerges clearly. The United States is now capable of increasing production levels and increasing available leisure at the same time. Indeed, this has been happening for several decades. But the results can serve to compound problems as well as point the way to new potentialities. When the four-day week arrives, and it appears inevitable, will it contribute to greater happiness or greater anxiety? Will it bring about more enthusiasm or more boredom? Can a meaningful nonwork ethic be developed that will enable Americans to make better use of their industrial achievement? [30]

Unfortunately, the kinds of normative issues which follow full-scale, advanced industrialization have not been anticipated, much less solved. Some searching questions are posed by Kaplan.

What happens, for instance, when the worker is given an option of working four hours per day or six months of full days and six months to fish, loaf or meditate? What happens as jet travel modifies our habits of time and space use? What happens when, and if, as Harrison Brown suggests, 100 billion persons can be supported on earth if we are willing "To be crowded together enough, to eat foods which would bear little resemblance to the goods we eat today . . . if we . . . construct floating islands where people might live and where algae farms could

30. With regard to the impact of work demands upon nonwork activities, Wilensky has described two major hypotheses running through much of the contemporary writing on leisure behavior. The first one he terms the *compensatory leisure hypothesis*: An assembly-line worker, for eight hours gripped bodily to the main line, doing repetitive, low-skilled, machine-paced work which is wholly ungratifying, comes rushing out of the plant gate, helling down the superhighway at 80 miles an hour in a second-hand Cadillac Eldorado, stops off for a beer and starts a barroom brawl, goes home and beats his wife, and in his spare time throws a rock at a Negro moving into the neighborhood. *In short, his routine of leisure is an explosive compensation for the deadening rhythms of factory life.*

An alternative reaction is explained by what is termed the *"spillover" leisure hypothesis*: Another worker goes quietly home, collapses on the couch, eats and drinks alone, belongs to nothing, reads nothing, knows nothing, votes for no one, "hangs around" the house and the street, watches the "late-late" show, lets the TV programs shade into one another, too tired to lift himself off the couch for the act of selection, too bored to switch the dials. *In short, he develops a "spillover" leisure routine in which alienation from work becomes alienation from life; the mental stultification produced by his labor permeates his leisure.* Harold L. Wilensky, "Work, Careers, and Social Integration," in "Leisure and Society," special issue of International Social Science Journal, UNESCO (October 1960), p. 544.

function . . . ?" What happens to the current craving for free time and comfort if the Russians really catch up economically and take over even vaster areas of the world? [31]

In addition to a shorter work week, continuing industrialization will mean that work will become more ordered and secure (if not more meaningful) and income more regular. The home and off-the-job living may well occupy, more than they do now, the central interests of man's life. Significantly, this pattern is now discernible among the younger generation of executives. Although they still put in a longer work day than most other occupational groups, there is evidence that they are beginning to question the assumptions and habits which have led them to work longer hours than their subordinates. And it is not the employees alone who have shaped the pressure for leisure that the executive is beginning to follow. Through advertising and the whole consumer ethic, with its emphasis on leisure for the common man, an image has been created and now employers as well as employees are being affected by it. Although top executives still work long hours — in part perhaps because, being trained in an earlier period, they can hardly help doing so — their younger replacements may be trying to weave together in a more balanced fashion their work and nonwork worlds.

In fact, with a further blending of work and leisure roles, it may be possible some day to retire while working, or enjoy leisure and work together. Otherwise, as one observer notes, "of what human use will automation be . . . or the impending gain of 50 per cent to 100 per cent per capita more leisure?"

Certainly, much of the problem of mass leisure revolves around the attitudes and conceptions of those born into an "economy of abundance" as against those born in a work-centered pre-1920 society. Older persons today have the dubious luck to have outlived the period when their work norm was dominant. This means that they must come to terms somehow with a different kind of economy, an economy in which work as an integrating factor in life has declined, and a search for a new integrating principle, centering in leisure, has begun.

Amid this rapidly changing social scene, perhaps there is need to develop what Peter Drucker has called the "leisure mind." The kind of person "who is not satisfied with the excitement of his immediate work . . . who is not satisfied either with hobbies . . . but who wants to have leisure which is not idle time, which is not play time, which is reflective time." The kind of people "who will be willing to force themselves, despite the appeal of work

31. Max Kaplan, "Creative Values in the New Leisure," paper read at the Contemporary Arts Festival, State University, Potsdam, New York, May 12, 1959 (mimeo), pp. 28–9.

and the hours it gobbles up, to stand back and be human beings and citizens and persons, rather than just specialists and experts and producers." [32]

As industrialization continues, the problem becomes one of finding a more rational balance between work and leisure. Commenting on the problem of how a nation learns to use its leisure without losing its sense of responsibility, Russell Lynes has pointed up the normative issue.

America is a middle-class nation and it is one of our strengths that we have so minimized the differences between the classes in our society that there is almost no lower class, in the nineteenth century sense, and no permanent ruling aristocracy. But we are a middle-class society with a middle-class morality of work and an aristocratic opportunity to make the most of leisure. The question, a hard one indeed, is how does one keep the middle-class backbone of the nation stiff and at the same time give to leisure and its uses the same dignity that we have long given to work? [33]

Leisure time is increasing — and may expand to a point where it will be as important a part of life as work. But in a society dedicated to technology and efficiency, more leisure is still a dream and a threat.

SUMMARY

Today more people in the United States spend more time away from their jobs than any previous generation. Industrial efficiency has steadily shortened the work week for broad segments of the population. The fact that people are living longer and retiring earlier has also increased the proportion of their lives spent in nonwork settings. As a result, large numbers of persons have had to adjust their living to more leisure than they had anticipated. The unexpected occurrence of mass leisure has created perplexing problems.

Historically, the accent has been upon work. It had to be, in a frontier society, and current attitudes still reflect the impact of this earlier orientation. The contemporary normative conception maintains that leisure should be used chiefly as a restorative for more and better work. Leisure, therefore, is viewed as a *means* to other ends or goals.

Along with greater production efficiency, higher standards of living, and more affluence generally, the role of leisure began to be redefined. Since World War II, an emergent conception has appeared which views leisure as more than simply a restorative for work. Leisure is now regarded as an integral part of modern life. The emergent conception says, in effect, that the use of leisure time should be an intrinsically satisfying experience in and of itself.

Attitudes toward leisure are linked closely to the meaning of work, and

32. *Minutes*, op. cit. p. 8.
33. Lynes, op. cit. p. 17.

both are being redefined. Increasing mechanization of work has meant that more persons are now looking beyond their jobs for satisfying life experiences, and as a result there has occurred a shift in emphasis from job-centered activities to leisure and home-centered activities, especially among the younger generation. The emergent norm has not replaced the contemporary norm, and therefore many Americans face a dilemma as to what role leisure should play in their lives. Some feel guilty about additional hours of free time and seek more work to avoid leisure hours, while others strenuously pursue leisure activities that resemble work. Still others, who have been thoroughly conditioned by older norms, find extra hours of free time bring only boredom. They fear additional years of retirement. As the work week is shortened and the weekend is lengthened, the problem ultimately becomes one of finding a more meaningful balance between work and nonwork worlds.

QUESTIONS AND SUGGESTIONS FOR FURTHER STUDY

1. What features of the emergent conception of leisure are most clearly established in contemporary American society?
2. If you were a stranger to this society, and not familiar with American habits and values, what aspects of leisure and recreation would you find it difficult to comprehend?
3. In what ways has the emergence of "bulk" time changed leisure behavior?
4. Explain the statement, "Any activity can become the basis for leisure." What are the reasons some persons might find this statement difficult to understand?
5. In what ways are work roles and leisure activities related?
6. Do you feel that most people would prefer to have a three-day weekend? Who are the individuals or groups who would probably prefer a longer weekend? Who are these who would prefer a two-day or even a shorter weekend? How would you explain these differences?
7. What should be the basic criterion for evaluating activities pursued during leisure hours?
8. Make a study of your family's leisure activities. List the activities (a) in which the entire family participates as a family, and (b) those that are based on individual leisure preferences. In your opinion, which member of your family finds leisure activities (a) most meaningful, (b) least meaningful? How would you explain these differences?
9. Discuss the statement, "Leisure activities are inherently less important than work activities."
10. In what ways is the emergent conception of leisure use consistent with the dominant features of American society? What are some of the inconsistencies between the emergent viewpoint and the major characteristics of our society?
11. Analyze a sample of vacation advertisements appearing in the Sunday edition of the *New York Times*. Do most of them reflect contemporary or emergent conceptions of leisure use?
12. What new goods and services do you feel will be demanded for leisure time activities?

SUGGESTED READINGS

American Journal of Sociology, 62 (May 1957). This issue, entitled, "The Uses of Leisure," contains a wide variety of articles and an annotated bibliography of works on leisure since 1900.

Anderson, Nels, *Work and Leisure*, New York: Free Press of Glencoe, 1961. An insightful examination of the interrelationships between work and leisure in an industrialized society.

Clarke, Alfred C., "The Use of Leisure and Its Relation to Levels of Occupational Prestige," *American Sociological Review*, 21 (June 1956), pp. 301–7. This study, based on five independent samples, explores the frequency of participation in specific leisure time activities.

de Grazia, Sebastian, *Of Time, Work and Leisure*, New York: Twentieth Century Fund, 1962. The author, a political scientist and philosopher, contributes penetrating inquiry into some of the dilemmas leisure poses for a work-centered society.

Galbraith, John K., *The Affluent Society*, Boston: Houghton Mifflin, 1958. Contains some insightful observations on the relation between leisure and work in a wealthy, industrial society. See especially Chap. 24.   P

Kaplan, Max, *Leisure: A Social Inquiry*, New York: Wiley, 1960. A comprehensive sociological analysis of leisure as distinct from recreation.

Larrabee, E., and R. Meyersohn, *Mass Leisure*, Glencoe: Free Press, 1958. A reader containing the contributions of social scientists and literary men regarding the new problem of widespread leisure. Contains one of the most comprehensive bibliographies on leisure yet compiled.

Lundberg, George A., Mirra Komarovsky, and Mary A. McInerny, *Leisure: A Surburban Study*, New York: Columbia University Press, 1934. One of the first comprehensive studies of leisure. Although written before the advent of television, this research is valuable for its methodological approach and as an illustration of the integral part leisure plays in suburban life.

Lynd, Robert S., and Helen M. Lynd, *Middletown in Transition*, Harcourt, Brace, 1937.   P   In Chapter 7 the authors of this classic sociological study present valuable insights into the way in which leisure plays a different role in the lives of "working class" and "business class" people.

Riesman, David, Nathan Glazer, and Reuel Denney, *The Lonely Crowd*, New York: Doubleday, 1953, chaps. 15 and 16.   P   These chapters contain numerous insights into the meaning and significance of leisure in contemporary American society.

Social Problems, 9 (Summer 1961). This issue contains an excellent collection of authoritative, up-to-date articles on different phases of leisure and work.

Veblen, Thorstein, *The Theory of the Leisure Class*, New York: New American Library, 1953.   P   A classic statement of the close relation between social class position and the conspicuous use of leisure.

A generation ago it was widely believed that many minority groups in American society would readily become acculturated to the dominant patterns and, in the course of a few generations, assimilated into the total population. Although racial groups were generally excepted from this thesis, its proponents contended that linguistic and national-origin lines would be obliterated and even religious divisions, unlikely to be eliminated in a society that practiced freedom of religion, would be greatly reduced. In recent years, this thesis has been challenged. Many students of the current scene argue that the process of assimilation is neither inevitable nor desirable. Extensive acculturation can scarcely be denied, but assimilation — the loss of group identity — has become problematic, both as fact and as value.[1]

Minority groups are characterized by similar customs, traditions, language, religion, or physical characteristics. These groups not only define themselves as being different from the majority, but are defined as different (and often, by reason of that difference, inferior) by the majority. Some minorities seek to maintain their uniqueness: others prefer to lose it. Regardless of their preference, these groups usually are the objects of prejudice and discrimination. The term prejudice may be defined as an *attitude* in which an ethnic or racial or religious minority is erroneously prejudged. All members of the minority group, regardless of individual qualities or differences, are disliked or even hated. Discrimination is not an attitude but a form of behavior by which a minority group is treated differently and unfavorably.

Although the term minority technically refers to a limited number or a small percentage of the whole, sociologists use the concept with reference to a group's access to power, status, and prestige within a society. Minority groups, thus, may constitute a numerical majority, as in the case of Buddhists in Viet Nam, Indians in Peru, or Negroes in some southern communities, but still be treated as social inferiors and deprived of political and economic power.

Minority groups can be classified into two types, ethnic and racial. Ethnic groups, often referred to as nationality groups, share a common cultural

1. J. Milton Yinger, "Social Forces Involved in Group Identification or Withdrawal," *Daedalus* (Spring 1961), p. 247.

heritage different from that of the majority. Racial groups, on the other hand, share common physical characteristics which distinguish them from the majority. Often these biological differences are so slight as to be virtually imperceptible. In some states, a person is legally defined a Negro if he has had any Negro ancestry, no matter how remote. Unlike ethnic minorities, racial minorities do not necessarily have a unique cultural heritage. However, some groups in the United States, such as the Indians, Japanese, and Chinese, are both racially and ethnically distinct.

The composition of nationality groups in 1960 is shown in Table 11-1, and Table 11-2 gives a rough approximation of the total immigration to the United States from various nations since 1820. These figures, however, do not reveal the dynamics of the events which affected the immigrants' response to the development of an industrial society. This chapter will concentrate on the problems posed by ethnic diversity. In Chapter 12, racial minorities will be considered.

In recent years the United States has taken great strides toward unifying its diverse minorities into a common American community. Recent movements toward minority group integration have been so forthright that they have brought to the surface many of the basic cleavages that have been glossed over for decades. Populations which have been identified with particular cultural and religious loyalties have been forced to re-evaluate their own identities and their place in the new scheme. In particular, disagreement has arisen over the desirability of retaining such group identifications. Some see the persistence of traditional group identity as a threat to democratic processes because it can create disunity among Americans. Others, who believe that the persistence of group individuality enriches the total society, see the retention of group loyalties as a healthy sign and as proof of the growing maturity of the American community.

The normative problem: should ethnic minorities maintain separate identities in an industrial society?

The earliest answer given to this problem grew out of the social life of the early days of the Republic. The historical reply was "Americanization," which said, in effect, that regardless of differing national origins or cultural backgrounds newcomers to this society should assimilate the patterns appropriate to the American scene. The continuation of alien customs, language, ethical codes, and other symbols of group identity was deemed inimical to the aim of establishing national unity. According to this normative conception, diversity stemming from ethnicity was undesirable.

TABLE 11-1

Nativity and parentage of the foreign white stock
by country of origin, 1960

Country of birth	Number (in thousands)	Per cent
All countries	34,050	100.0
England, Wales, Scotland, Northern Ireland	2,885	8.5
Ireland (Eire)	1,773	5.2
Norway	775	2.3
Sweden	1,047	3.1
Denmark	399	1.2
Netherlands	399	1.2
Switzerland	263	0.8
France	352	1.0
Germany	4,321	12.7
Poland	2,780	8.2
Czechoslovakia	918	2.7
Austria	1,099	3.2
Hungary	702	2.1
Yugoslavia	449	1.3
U.S.S.R.	2,290	6.7
Lithuania	403	1.2
Finland	241	0.7
Romania	234	0.7
Greece	379	1.1
Italy	4,544	13.3
Portugal	277	0.8
Other Europe	492	1.4
Asia	1,142	3.4
Canada	3,181	9.3
Mexico	1,736	5.1
Other America	581	1.7
All others and not reported	391	1.1

Source: U.S. Bureau of the Census, *Statistical Abstract of The United States*, 1962, Table 28.

This historical conception still persists. The courts, the law, the legislative bodies, and the educational system particularly, even today sustain this point of view. English is the universal language of the society, patriotism is encouraged in the schools, and holidays and other ceremonial occasions emphasize the common values that all citizens are enjoined to uphold.

The persistence of this historical "Americanization" norm, however, should not be interpreted to mean that it has been consistently upheld through the intervening decades. Such an interpretation would gloss over the realities of vast changes that challenged it. Since the advent of industrialization, this historical conception has undergone significant modifications. Since the 1880's, America has attracted immigrants and refugees from southern and

TABLE 11-2

Immigrants, by country of origin: 1820–1960

Country	Total, 141 years 1820–1960
All countries	41,840,961
Europe	34,574,632
Austria and Hungary	4,275,847
Belgium	188,969
Czechoslovakia	129,278
Denmark	351,402
Finland	27,021
France	684,928
Germany	6,726,294
Great Britain	3,784,565
Greece	487,189
Ireland	4,676,407
Italy	4,962,375
Netherlands	320,896
Norway	837,890
Poland	432,311
Portugal	283,055
Spain	180,915
Sweden	1,249,810
U.S.S.R.	3,344,479
Yugoslavia	66,588
Asia	1,097,772
China	408,539
Japan	325,396
America	5,753,214
Canada and Newfoundland	3,555,398
Mexico	1,138,655
West Indies	619,787
Africa	47,519
Australia and New Zealand	79,843
Pacific Islands	21,280

Source: U.S. Bureau of the Census, *Statistical Abstract of the United States*, 1961, p. 93.

eastern Europe, from certain parts of Asia, and, more recently, from Latin America, in particular, Mexico and Puerto Rico. Many of these groups have perpetuated significant aspects of their heritage, such as dietary habits, national customs, and particularly religious institutions, and descendants of the immigrants have thereby retained group identity while assimilating American values and patterns of behavior.

Many claim that the resulting cultural mosaic manifests a fundamental strength and unity in the society, despite such symptoms of social disorganization as intergroup discrimination, prejudice, conflict, and tension. The question still remains whether the continuation of this ethnic diversity signifies a strength or a weakness in American society.

Historical Normative Conception: "Americanization" — Ethnic minorities should divest themselves of their cultural traditions and adopt the existing white Anglo-Saxon Protestant heritage.

This historical conception developed mainly out of the experience and cultural background of the English Puritans in the colonies. Thinking of themselves as members of a homogeneous religious community, these settlers wanted to establish in the new country one church, one language, one hierarchy of occupations, one pervasive code of ethics, and one set of ultimate values — an Anglicized version of Calvinist theocracy.

This set of ultimate values served to integrate the religious, economic, political, and social life of the early settlers. The religious values in the Puritan community emphasized the perfectibility of man through salvation, hard work, and individual effort. Consistent with this ideal, great stress was placed on self-discipline, the denial of personal pleasures, and the virtue of deferring immediate gratifications in favor of long-range goals. In the economic realm, emphasis was placed on competition, acquisitiveness, success and a rational approach to economic risk-taking. On the political level, drawing upon their English background, New Englanders attached great importance to the orderly processes of government within an essentially democratic framework. Parliamentary procedures were highly valued. Resolution of conflicts ideally occurred within a framework of due process, discussion, and vote. Although self-reliance was regarded as one of the chief virtues, informal assistance to the losers in the competitive struggle was also part of the way of life.

These values were expressed most visibly in the early New England town, which was built around the green or common, church, and meeting hall. Beyond the town were the fields and woods and beyond these the open countryside. The population was originally composed of a single Puritan congregation, which was made up of autonomous households, each governed by the head of the household. These heads of families, in turn, governed the community in town meetings, hired and fired the clergy, and enforced the previously described set of values. Thus American community life began as an integrated system fusing religious, economic, and political values in the democracy of the town meeting. Public office was rotated among the "pillars of the community." Frequent daily interaction between neighbors and friends was made possible by the spatial arrangement of the town. The way the Sabbath was observed encouraged contacts between even remote neighbors.

This high level of interaction made for a continuous exchange of views and acceptance of a strong and lasting code of ethics.[2]

There were other types of colonial communities, however. Small colonies of Germans and Scotch-Irish settled in Pennsylvania and along the Allegheny frontiers. The Dutch and Swedes came to New Jersey, New York, Pennsylvania, and Delaware. Some French Huguenots were in New England, other Frenchmen settled along the St. Lawrence, and Jews from Spain and Portugal lived in towns along the Atlantic coast. These groups did not assume the religion-based social organization and economic values of the New England Puritans. Before the Revolution their distinct sub-cultures flourished in various sections of the developing colonies.

In the South there developed, among the predominantly British settlers there, still another pattern of settlement and way of life, organized around the plantation economy, including a semi-feudal economic and social organization that emphasized aristocratic traditions of privilege — a society much like that of the landed aristocracy of England at the same period. However, living as "outsiders" on the periphery of this society were Negroes, who were mostly of slave status. Other "outsiders" to colonial life were Indians, who were considered completely inferior culturally, even if they happened to be friendly.

Somewhat similar to the New Englanders in outlook and way of life were the English Quakers, who set the tone of the large and prosperous colony of Pennsylvania. Other English colonies were established on the east coast, and together with southern planters, these colonists were successful in establishing the English language and English institutions in the New World. Though Revolutionary philosophy as it later developed was influenced by French thought, the principal institutions of the new nation early took as their basis English political philosophies and the English common law. The political concepts included the idea of representative government, the concept of limited state power, and the tradition of civil liberties. America looked to Great Britain, rather than to France or Germany, to model its schools, voluntary institutions, businesses, and later, its trade unions. Early national literature, painting, sculpture, and architecture were also influenced by British models.

Victorious in wars with the French and numerically superior to non-British colonists, English settlers thrived. The New England Protestants founded schools, became successful traders and merchants, developed efficient community governments, fostered migrations west from an early date, and became

2. This analysis of New England towns is taken from Conrad Arensberg, "American Communities," *American Anthropologist*, 57 (December 1955), pp. 1148–51.

culturally dominant during the latter colonial period. They extended their influence as the Revolutionary War and subsequent events consolidated the society and established greater national unity.[3]

In retaining their cultural predominance, the English Protestants developed a normative conception which came to be known as "Americanization." Eventually it was expected that any newcomer to the society would soon acquire the English language, the Puritan ethical code, and the political philosophy of the white Anglo-Saxon Protestant, all firmly established by the Colonial and, later, national experiences. Different races and religions were to live under the same government, in freedom and on terms of equality; yet that freedom depended on the stability of the government — and stability depended upon unity. Cultural diversity and ethnic enclaves were to be discouraged in the interests of national unity.

1. *The "Old Immigration."* The first real test of this normative conception came when immigrants from Ireland, Germany, and other parts of northern and western Europe arrived in large numbers. Between 1847 and 1854, more than 100,000 Irish, driven by the potato famines, arrived on these shores each year. The Germans, escaping the disorganization of the abortive German revolutions of 1848, reached a high point of 215,000 immigrants in 1854. Smaller populations, at the rate of two or three thousand per year, came from Scandinavian countries.

At first these immigrants were welcomed for their willingness to provide the labor and industrial skills required by the developing nation. They were needed to man the farms in the prairie settlements, to swell the population necessary to achieve statehood in the western territories, to mine the mineral resources, and to build the railroads and canals of the expanding nation. But while their skills and labor were desired by the older Americans, their cultural traditions were not. These immigrants attempted to maintain their languages, moral codes, religions, diets, and recreational patterns. The Germans, for example, who worked their way through the cities and farms of the Midwest, attempted to establish a separate community life, a different language, and separate schools. The intellectuals of this group had "liberal" ideas on temperance, labor unions, slavery, and other social questions, which were at variance with the dominant codes and institutions. Similarly, in the eastern cities where large numbers of poverty-stricken Irish settled, Catholic churches, and other "alien" institutions were being planted.

2. *Successful Integration of "Old Immigrants."* Despite continuing immigration, the historical normative conception prevailed. A number of conditions made this possible. One was the high birth rate of the native American popu-

3. Thomas Jefferson Wertenbaker, *The Puritan Oligarchy: The Founding of American Civilization*, New York: Scribners, 1947.

lation. Before mass immigration, and during the first half of the nineteenth century, the national population rose sharply from 5.3 million to 23.2 million. This population increase was "home-grown." These increments provided the essential manpower for the westward expansion of American culture as well as for the growing urban centers of the east coast. Thus the seeds of American institutions were planted before the arrival of the great mass of European immigrants. Those who came after 1840 had to adjust to the fact that the "native Americans" had preceded them. The basic outlines of the English-derived, American institutional forms were already set by their predecessors. The immigrants, so long as they were in the minority, had to adjust to or accommodate themselves to the pre-existing normative order.

A second reason for the dominance of the Americanization conception was the conscious attempt to extend tax-supported public schools and compulsory education to all the states. This movement has been described in Chapter 5, so it is sufficient to say here that these common schools played an important role in transmitting to the children of immigrants the common values of American civilization.

A third, and somewhat later, factor was the general growth of the economy and its consequences for social mobility. The Homestead Law of 1862 and later land legislation permitted an immigrant farmer to begin work on land which was almost cost-free. As the vast timber resources and farm crops were being shipped to the population centers by the newly constructed railroads, the city people were also beneficiaries. Success stories and folk heroes spurred thousands of others, both native and immigrant, to strive for wealth and prestige. This was the period when fortunes were being made. As Eric Goldman has written: "Any Irishman could see the future of his family in terms of the life of Charles O'Connor, son of a ragamuffin immigrant from Dublin, apprenticed to a lampblack manufacturer at twelve, a lawyer at twenty, a high-priced counsel in his thirties, and now the recognized leader of the New York bar, the holder of five honorary degrees from universities, and the master of a stately mansion at Nantucket." [4]

There were, of course, some correctives for this idyllic picture. There was the Know-Nothing party of the mid-nineteenth century which played on the anti-Catholic feelings and resulted in "No Irish Need Apply" signs. Nevertheless, the prejudice and discrimination experienced by these immigrants was more tolerable than the persecutions and the limited opportunities in their native countries. For most immigrants, the "good" life was unattainable in the old country. Charles O'Connor, the culture hero just alluded to, summed up the spirit of the times in this manner: "In worn out, king-ridden Europe men must stay where they are born. But in America a man is ac-

4. Eric F. Goldman, *Rendezvous with Destiny*, New York: Knopf, 1952, pp. 8–9.

counted a failure, and certainly ought to be, who has not risen above his father's station in life." [5]

The immigrant learned about the meaning of American life by experiencing at first hand the invigorating period of American industrial growth and opportunity. The expanding frontier and the growth of industrialization were the forces that made possible the social mobility of the immigrants who came from northern and western Europe.

Some scholars have argued that the relative similarity in cultural background favored the rapid assimilation of the "old immigrants." But, as Oscar Handlin points out, this is quite contrary to the facts. Indeed as he has shown, the native American's belief in progress, in man's perfectibility, and in a rational approach to correcting the evils in social institutions were not a part of the heritage of most of these immigrants. They came primarily from peasant backgrounds of Europe where they had accepted their station in life and where "they believed that the world in which they lived was not one that was capable of true reformation, much less perfection. Instead their earthly existence was only the prelude to a more significant life that began after death." [6]

Finally, an important element in the adjustment of the immigrants was the fact that the native Americans had not restricted their voting rights — as the South had done to the Negroes — and more generally did not seriously limit the political rights of the newcomers. The assumption was that any individual, regardless of his background or previous ideological commitments, could become a *bona fide* American by simply being exposed to an American way of life. As Handlin has observed:

The old Americans accepted democracy as a matter of course. Since man was essentially good and reasonable, he was capable of guiding his own actions in affairs of state as in other aspects of his life. As he cast his ballot he made the choices most in accord with his own interest and with the interests of the whole society. For the peasant, by contrast, reason was fallible and man imbued with evil, and democracy was therefore a rank delusion. Each individual occupied that status in life to which he had been called, and it made no more sense that a husbandman should vote on foreign policy than a ruler should plow.[7]

So the immigrant from Europe, in spite of his earlier ideological orientations, learned to exercise his political rights. As later events have shown, the immigrant absorbed a new ideology and justified the faith that had been placed in him.

5. Ibid. p. 9.
6. Oscar Handlin, *Race and Nationality in American Life*, Boston: Little, Brown, 1957, p. 186.
7. From Oscar Handlin, *Race and Nationality in American Life*, Copyright © 1948, 1950, 1953, 1956, 1957 by Oscar Handlin; reprinted by permission of Atlantic-Little, Brown and Company, p. 187.

AMERICANIZATION QUESTIONED

The Americanization conception prevailed until about the 1880's, when a series of significant historical events indicated that the U.S. was now well on its way toward becoming an industrial society. Jacksonian democracy was now a matter of record, and the early immigrants were becoming acculturated. The frontier was closing; there was no more open territory to conquer. Expansion was to take place in the growth of cities, in the rise of the middle class, in the emergence of corporations, and in the exploitation of new energy sources. There were fortunes yet to be made.

But at the same time there were human problems to be solved, problems faced by all rapidly industrializing societies: unsanitary living conditions, crowded urban housing, child labor, long working hours, sweatshop factories, prostitution, high crime rates, alcoholism, and business depressions. In addition to these problems, political machines were rising; graft and corruption were making honest government difficult; and reform movements were suggesting a number of new norms.

Reflecting these unresolved problems, social tensions were evident concerning both ethnic and racial minorities. In the South, the Negroes had been given their freedom, but they were being segregated and were losing their civil rights as the result of new Jim Crow laws. The Ku Klux Klan, in addition to its anti-Negro activities, was engaged in anti-Semitic and anti-Catholic programs. In the Southwest, the whites or Anglos were attempting to enforce segregation on the Mexicans. In California, and elsewhere on the west coast, fear of Chinese and Japanese cheap labor was expressed in unfavorable journalism, discriminatory legislation, mob action, and the lobbying activities of the American Federation of Labor. On Indian reservations in various sections of the country, the government was making half-hearted and patronizing attempts to "acculturate" the "red man," but such measures usually resulted in his further demoralization.

1. *Later Immigration.* News of continuing industrial expansion and a rising standard of living reached even the remotest villages of the most underdeveloped countries of Europe. Attracted by these economic dreams and driven by persecution and dissatisfaction with conditions in the homeland, more than 23 million immigrants came to the United States in the years between 1881 and 1920. This immigration contributed substantially to the population increase in this period — a growth from 50.1 to 105.7 million.

The new immigrants were different from those who had preceded them. They came from eastern and southern Europe, whereas the old came from western and northern Europe. The national backgrounds of these new arrivals were Italy, Greece, Russia, Hungary, Poland, Bulgaria and other countries. Unlike the earlier English and Irish immigrants, they did not speak English and their religious beliefs, moral codes, and customs were substanially different. Their cultural heritage diverged from the American pattern. These differences were perpetuated as most of these immigrants settled in the slums of growing metropolitan areas. Whereas the earlier immigrants were able to disperse in the expanding frontier zones, these immigrants settled in "ghetto-like" clusters, especially along the Atlantic seaboard, where their physical traits, religion, old-country mannerisms, and menial occupations made them conspicuous. "Foreign" restaurants, strange-sounding social clubs, non-Protestant religious groups — Roman Catholic, Greek Orthodox, and Jewish — increased substantially.

Many Americans began feeling uneasy about the wide cultural gap that existed between the old and new immigrants; between the white man and the aboriginal Indians; between themselves and the Orientals; between Protestantism on the one hand and Catholicism and Judaism on the other; and between the wealthy and the poor. In the light of the American creed these obvious differences and the prejudice and discrimination they evoked required explanation and justification.

One justification was the development of a doctrine of cultural inferiority which suggested that certain ethnic groups were incapable of being Americanized. This doctrine, a variation of the doctrine of racism, had important consequences in the subsequent restriction of immigration to the United States. Another response, however, came from minority group members and their supporters. This was the view that America could become a melting pot. As certain minority groups gained a degree of acceptance in America, members often felt secure enough to suggest that they could become contributors to American culture rather than passive recipients of it. It is to these two responses we now turn.

2. *The Doctrine of Cultural Inferiority*. As the proportion of the "native" white, Protestant, Anglo-Saxon stock in the total population declined, members of this dominant group began to feel that the millions from eastern Europe and the Mediterranean basin as well as newer racial minorities were debasing the American heritage. This viewpoint was reflected in the work of writers like Madison Grant, Lothrop Stoddard, and others who affirmed the superiority of the white Anglo-Saxon tradition.[8]

These doctrines of the alleged superiority of Anglo-Saxon biology and heri-

8. The following are some books written by Americans on this racist theme: Madison Grant, *The Passing of the Great Race*, New York: 1916; Clinton Stoddard Burr, *America's Race Heritage*, New York: 1922; Lothrop Stoddard, *The Revolt Against Civilization: The Menace of the Under Man*, New York: 1922; Charles W. Gould, *America: A Family Matter*, New York: 1922; Henry Fairfield Osborn, *Man Rises to Parnassus*, New York: 1927.

tage created bitter controversy in the first two decades of the twentieth century. At least two major "scientific" investigations supported this view. One was the study by Senator Dillingham sponsored by the U.S. Immigration Commission; the other a report by Dr. Harry H. Laughlin, a geneticist of the Carnegie Institute, sponsored by the House Committee on Immigration and Naturalization. The Dillingham study, which took three years of work by a staff of about three hundred, was published in 42 volumes at a cost of one million dollars. Oscar Handlin, who has made a careful analysis of these volumes, writes that the committee, "despite its scientific pretensions," aimed to prove what it had concluded before the investigation began, namely, "that the new immigration was essentially different from the old and less capable of being Americanized." [9]

Dr. Laughlin's report was presented in 1922, less than ten years later. His biases and judgments were clearly indicated by this statement which he made to the House Immigration Committee: [10]

We in this country have been so imbued with the idea of democracy, or the equality of all men, that we have left out of consideration the matter of blood or natural inborn hereditary mental and moral differences. No man who breeds pedigree plants and animals can afford to neglect this thing.

His analysis, was based on crude statistics on feeble-mindedness, crime, epilepsy, tuberculosis, and other evidence of "social inadequacy." His conclusion was "[after] making all logical allowances for environmental conditions, which may be unfavorable to the immigrant, the recent immigrants as a whole, present a higher percentage of inborn socially inadequate qualities than do the older stocks." [11]

The intent of these investigations was to explore restrictive immigration legislation. Until 1880, there had been no serious attempts to stem the tide of immigration. Newcomers were generally welcomed and were able to find their roots in the new society. Restrictions on the inflow of migrants to this country coincided with the rise of the doctrine of "cultural inferiority."

In the 1880's, only undesirables — such as mental defectives, convicts, and those deemed likely to become public charges — were excluded. Then in the 1890's, health standards and literacy standards were imposed as qualifications for immigration. Such measures, however, were not able to stem the flow of newcomers from "non-Nordic" countries, and in 1921 and again in 1924 Congress enacted more stringent laws. These acts established a quota system which allocated the number of future immigrants according to a ratio which

9. Handlin, op. cit. pp. 80–81.
10. Ibid. p. 105.
11. Using Laughlin's own data, Professor Handlin shows that "the data, faulty as they are, simply do not say what Laughlin says they do." Ibid. p. 106.

represented the proportion of nationalities present in the United States before the arrival of the later immigrants. The 1924 act allowed Great Britain
65,000 immigrants and Germany 25,000 but southern European nations like
Italy were allowed only 5645 and Greece 308. Furthermore, the 1924 law
closed the door on racial minorities, e.g. the Japanese, who had been arriving
in small numbers. Chinese immigration had already been stopped by the
Exclusion Act of 1882.

The implications of these restrictions were many and far-reaching. The
restrictions indicated lost faith in the ability of American institutions to
reshape the outlook and to claim the loyalty of immigrants. Restricting immigration on a quota basis was tantamount to saying that some immigrant
stocks were not properly fit to become Americans. Clearly the 1921 and 1924
laws implied that people from Italy, the Balkan states, Poland, and Hungary
were not as desirable as the "Nordic" types from Great Britain, Ireland, Germany, and Scandinavia. Still another implication was that America was striving to achieve some kind of biological homogeneity and racial purity.

In spite of these restrictions, American society already consisted of a tremendous range and variety of people.

In addition to the British, the Scotch-Irish, the French Huguenots, the early
German settlers from the Palatine and the later Germans who left behind the
abortive German revolutions of 1848, many other strains came to America. There
were Irish Catholics, driven by famine and inner restlessness; there were Nor-
wegians, Swedes and Danes, Hungarians, Austrians, Bohemians and Moravians,
Spaniards and Portuguese; there were Swiss, Italians, Serbs, Greeks, and Arme-
nians; there were Russian and Polish peasants, Lithuanians and Finns; there
were Jews, hoping that America would be the last stop in their history of wandering; there were Mexicans and Canadians, crossing not a sea but only a border;
there were Latin Americans; there were Chinese, Japanese, Filipinos.[12]

3. *The Doctrine of the Melting Pot*. The variety of groups and the resistance
of some of these groups to losing their identity created the conditions which
lead to the view of America as a melting pot of nationalities. Fighting back
against the doctrines of cultural inferiority, many ethnic minorities complained that "Americanization" was too one-sided to work. They suggested
that American values were not finalized at the end of the colonial period. The
cultural traditions of all groups, including the new immigrants, could contribute to the continuously emergent American society. Each group, adding
its best cultural traits to the melting pot, would help create a new cultural
synthesis.

The melting pot doctrine can be illustrated by the eighteenth century

12. Max Lerner, *America as a Civilization*, New York: Simon and Schuster, 1957, pp.
    21–2.

agriculturalist Hector St. John de Crèvecœur, who asked, and answered, the question, what is the American?: [13]

He is either an European, or the descendant of an European, hence that strange mixture of blood, which you will find in no other country. I could point out to you a family whose grandfather was an Englishman, whose wife was Dutch, whose son married a French woman, and whose present four sons have now four wives of different nations. *He* is an American, who leaving behind him all his ancient prejudices and manners, receives new ones from the new mode of life he has embraced, the new government he obeys, and the new rank he holds . . . Here individuals of all nations are melted into a new race of men, whose labours and posterity will one day cause great changes in the world."

Similar ideas were expressed by Ralph Waldo Emerson in his Journal of 1845, where he wrote that in this continent the energy of the Irish, Germans, Swedes, Poles, Cossacks and other Europeans, of the Africans, and of the Polynesians "will construct a new race, a new religion, a new state, a new literature, which will be as vigorous as the new Europe which came out of the melting-pot of the Dark Ages . . ." [14]

The historian Frederick Jackson Turner suggested that the various nationalities and ethnic groups in American society had avoided separationist tendencies in favor of blending because the frontier experience had acted to minimize cultural differences: "In the crucible of the frontier the immigrants were Americanized, liberated, and fused into a mixed race, English in neither nationality nor characteristics." [15]

Others have suggested the application of this norm in the urban centers where immigrants concentrated. In New York, in 1908, Israel Zangwill wrote a drama, *The Melting Pot*, which viewed America as a cultural and biological blend of many peoples: "America is God's Crucible, the great Melting Pot where all the races of Europe are melting and reforming!" [16] Each group, the dramatist suggested, would make its contribution, the composite of which would be greater than the sum of its diverse parts.

The reader will recognize that the melting pot conception is a slight revision of "Americanization." Both required that each ethnic group lose its separate identity. While Americanization required that the ethnic group lose its previous values and substitute the common values of the majority group, the melting pot thesis is more "open-minded." It recognizes the potential contributions of the old world cultures to American society. If each immigrant

13. Quoted in Milton M. Gordon, "Assimilation in America," *Daedalus* (Spring 1961), p. 270.
14. Quoted in Frederick Jackson Turner, *The Frontier in American History*, New York: Holt, 1920, pp. 22–3.
15. Ibid.
16. *The Melting Pot*, New York: Macmillan, 1909.

group contributes its own talents and values to the community, a new, more productive cultural synthesis will emerge.

The melting pot doctrine had tremendous appeal in the early decades of the present century; through it the immigrant groups could justify the preservation of part of their heritage without feeling disloyal; while retaining their customs they were making a contribution to the growth of American civilization; and their adjustment to American life would be rather easy, natural, and inevitable.

However, as Berry notes, the outbreak of the First World War shattered this comforting theory.[17]

When the nation began to take stock of itself, the startling fact emerged that there were millions in the country who could neither read, speak, nor write the English language; less than half the foreign-born white males of voting age were citizens; there were thousands of organizations flourishing among the foreign element, and hundreds of newspapers and periodicals published in foreign languages; immigrants were concentrated in "colonies" in the cities, and foreign governments were in the habit of encouraging their nationals to retain their old allegiance, not without some success.

There were also some interesting intellectual movements that helped to discredit the melting pot doctrine. In 1915, Horace M. Kallen, a Jewish immigrant in New York, repudiated the idea in an article entitled "Democracy versus the Melting Pot." [18] Kallen understood democracy to be a "federation or commonwealth" of nationalities, whereas the "melting pot" idea suggested to him a "purification process." Randolph Bourne, a non-Jew, took essentially the same point of view. He called for conscious seeking of a "trans-nationality" in which a "cosmopolitan federation of national colonies" would be established.[19]

Criticism of the melting pot doctrine foreshadowed the emergence of another normative conception — cultural pluralism. But as it was emerging, another attempt at "Americanization" was made. Acceptance of existing American culture had always been suggested as a desirable goal but in wartime it became a necessity. Americanization programs were introduced to incorporate the immigrant into American society; to divest him of his foreign heritage; to substitute English for his foreign language; to have him identify with American institutions and be naturalized. Much of the work to accomplish these aims was done in the public school system. Patriotic societies, women's organizations, public libraries, settlement houses, chambers of commerce, and even industrial plants where immigrants were employed participated in the program.

17. Brewton Berry, *Race and Ethnic Relations*, Boston: Houghton Mifflin, 1958, p. 212.
18. Horace M. Kallen, *Nation* (February 25, 1915), p. 219.
19. Randolph Bourne, "Trans-National America," *Atlantic Monthly* (July 1916).

But in this feverish attempt to change overnight the habits and customs of the immigrants, the basic assumption of the Americanization process was revealed: American culture is superior to the cultures the immigrant brought to this country. It implied that the Anglo-Saxon patterns were a finished product and needed no further improvements. This Americanization program was implemented in a spirit of coercion, patronage, and suppression, and the reaction on the part of the newcomer was resentment and frustration.

> *Contemporary Normative Conception: Cultural Pluralism* —
> Ethnic minorities should strive to maintain their separate identities while sharing common American values and participating in the opportunity structure of the society.

The idea of maintaining cultural diversity was expressed previously by Kallan and Bourne in their criticism of the melting pot. Today the sociological term used for this idea is "cultural pluralism." Charles Marden has defined it:

The "Cultural Pluralism" school advanced the theory that the ethnic groups should be encouraged to retain as much of their traditional heritages as was consistent with their new civic responsibilities and sentiments of loyalty to their adopted country. Spiritually akin to the "melting pot" school, the cultural pluralists nevertheless considered the retaining of ethnic differences a value in the great democratic society.[20]

By referring to a "cultural pluralism school," Marden may leave the reader with an erroneous impression that this was only an academic distinction. Quite the contrary, this normative conception evolved out of real struggles among practical men. Some details of this development are considered here.

1. *The Rise of Ethnic Group Consciousness.* As noted in earlier chapters, the development of industrial societies often produced feelings of individual loneliness, isolation, and powerlessness. To seek security and to exert some measure of control over their environment, men joined together to form voluntary associations along lines of common interests and common goals. Professional organizations, like the American Medical Association, the Bar Association, and trade unions, were the most conspicuous examples, but there were movements to organize almost every special interest.

It was not surprising, then, that ethnic groups followed suit. In the 1920's a number of nationality groups intensified their pride in their respective heritages by organizing or reviving societies of Irish patriots, German patriots,

20. Charles F. Marden, *Minorities in American Society*, New York: American Book, 1952, p. 108.

Italian patriots. The maintenance of ethnic identity emerged as a dominant theme in this period.

Jewish organizations grew profusely in the 1920's. Zionism became respectable and enjoyed widespread support.[21] Although Justice Louis Brandeis was said to have proclaimed in 1905 that habits which tend "to keep alive differences of origin" are "inconsistent with the American ideal . . . and are disloyal," he became, seven years later, the first distinguished non-eastern European Jew to publicly associate himself with Zionism.[22]

Developing concurrently with this growth of ethnic self-consciousness was a general feeling against marriage across ethnic lines. One of the significant consequences of the ethnic chauvinism of the 1920's and 1930's was the negative view of ethnically mixed marriages. The pressures toward ethnic endogamy are still great, as a student of mixed marriages, Milton L. Barron, has observed. He finds that honest research on this matter is quite limited and most of it is influenced by "vested interest, social myopia and wishful thinking." Although today opposition to intermarriage is rarely voiced on the grounds of detrimental biological consequences, he notes that: [23]

. . . There are numerous people who insist on a consequence of overwhelming doom for those who intermarry in social and cultural matters. For example, at the annual conference of the Rabbinical Council of America in January, 1950, Rabbi Israel Tabak of Baltimore, then president of the council, contended that such marriages are 90 per cent unsuccessful and that they "undermine the stability of the home, increase the number of unhappy marriages and bring children into the world with a rift in their souls which can never be healed."

These taboos on intermarriage and the tendency toward ethnic endogamy make sense, if one assumes that it is necessary for each ethnic group to maintain cohesion and exclusiveness and one believes that the transmission of minority experience is worthwhile. Whatever the reasons it appears that in the period since the 1920's, many religious and national origin groupings have closed ranks. Such developments have coincided with the increased significance of voluntary associations found elsewhere in this complex, impersonalized industrial society.

2. *The Rise in Political Power.* The increased group-centeredness of minorities was soon translated into political influence. Here again the actions of minority groups were patterned after those of other special interest groups. Through their organizations they "buttonholed" Congressmen, engaged public relations experts, made "deals" with other organizations on items of mutual

21. Goldman, op. cit. p. 300.
22. Ibid. p. 185.
23. Milton L. Barron, "Research on Intermarriage: A Survey of Accomplishments and Prospects," *American Journal of Sociology*, 47 (November 1951), pp. 249–55.

interest, and watched legislative bodies for bills that were either inimical or beneficial to their cause.

In cities and towns where a particular ethnic group had a sizable population, political candidates and city officials took such facts into account in their campaigns and political activities. The political reality of "bloc votes" on issues that affect minority groups is well-known. A spokesman of the newest American ethnic group, the Puerto Ricans, explained the political realities as follows: [24]

At word that city officials were looking into the conditions of the Puerto Rican slums in New York City, Aberlardo Gonzales, head of one of the airlines that flew the Puerto Ricans in, said: "A long time back everybody was beefing about the Irish when they came over. Then they got themselves a Mayor and a Senator and some Congressmen, and people quit bothering about them. Then came the Jews, and they started kicking about them. They got themselves a Governor and some Congressmen, and they let up on them. Next came the Italians, and they got guys like La Guardia and Marcantonio, and they let up on them. But us? We got nobody, so they pick on us. But just you wait — after a while we'll get some guys, and they'll let up on us, too. That's the way it goes."

The growth in ethnic consciousness and the associated rise in political influence of ethnic groups indicate that there are many who subscribe to a normative conception which demands neither assimilation into a dominant white, Protestant society nor a complete ethnic isolation. Instead such groups favor a normative conception under which peoples of different cultural backgrounds can live harmoniously together on the basis of equality, justice, and mutual respect. This normative conception assumes that each ethnic group will in some degree live apart from other groups. This voluntary segregation is to be maintained without prejudice and discrimination, without feelings of superiority and inferiority, without conflict, and in a spirit of accommodation.

While these ideals are praiseworthy there seems to be some practical limits to their immediate realization. For a pluralistic society to remain harmonious, there must be some fundamental agreement and empathy between the cultures of the different ethnic groups.[25] For example, it is claimed that one reason the American Jew and white Protestant can pursue their pluralistic ideals is that both traditions share democratic values which emphasize the worth

24. *New York Herald Tribune*, November 13, 1947, quoted in Goldman, op. cit. p. 441.
25. The language of pluralism is sometimes used to rationalize the potential conflicts that may exist between ethnic groups. For instance, in the 1890's the "separate but equal doctrine" of the southerners was put forth in the name of pluralism. However, the intent of the dominant white group was quite different, and in actuality the notion of pluralism was subverted to maintain dominance over the Negro minority. Similarly, in the Union of South Africa the theory of *apartheid* is one of pluralism, but its practice is one of enforcing subordination.

of the individual, the right to freedom, and devotion to social justice. But what would be said about an ethnic group which favors totalitarianism?

One of the reasons pluralism could be successful is that to a considerable extent the common values of American civilization have been internalized and accepted by virtually all ethnic, racial, and religious groups in the United States. Fishman, for example, shows that despite the fact that large numbers of Catholic, Jewish, and Negro children attend parochial and segregated schools, they share the dominant values of the larger American community.

> The school in America operates within a complex cultural environment. There exists an "American" society, in no way dependent on Jews or Catholics, Poles or Italians, Negroes or Orientals. The core of that society is white, Protestant, middle class, and it attracts all other particles to it. This is the culture into which the immigrants are assimilated, and it forms the *one accepted set of standards, expectations, and aspirations*, whether they pertain to clothing, household furnishings, personal beauty, entertainment, or child rearing.[26]

Handlin [27] makes similar observations and explains the adherence to the common values of American society by such factors as: (1) the over-riding demands of the organization of American economic, political, and cultural life, which often compel individuals to disregard ethnic lines, (2) the multiple membership of individuals in different social groupings, many of which are not centered in ethnic groups, (3) the fluidity of the social system which makes possible the changing social identities of individuals and groups, and (4) the assimilating role of newspapers, public schools, radio, television, and other mass media elements that address themselves not to ethnic groups but to individuals.

The result is that an inner core of American values has emerged which cuts across religious, ethnic, and racial lines. In brief, acculturation has been achieved to a considerable extent. Most ethnic minorities now participate within the opportunity structure of the society with little prejudice and discrimination compared with previous periods in American history. Jews, both a religious and an ethnic group, do experience some discrimination in housing and employment. Latent anti-Catholicism as well as hostility toward the "Irish Mafia" emerged during the 1960 Presidential elections. But, compared to the prejudice and discrimination against the Negro, these are infrequent enough to make them exceptions, not the rule. Both the majority, and the many organizations which function to protect ethnic integrity, usually repudiate such displays of prejudice. For example, the outbreak of swastika

26. Joshua A. Fishman, "Childhood Indoctrination for Minority-Group Membership," *Daedalus* (Spring 1961), p. 329. (Italics added.)
27. Oscar Handlin, "Historical Perspective on the American Ethnic Group," *Daedalus* (Spring 1961), pp. 220–32.

paintings on synagogues and temples by vandals in the late 1950's and early 1960's was decried by many responsible groups in America.[28]

Pluralism in a complex and heterogeneous industrial society such as the United States requires a delicate balance between the freedom to be different and some overriding common values. Yet in practice it remains a very difficult norm to maintain because it requires agreement on certain ground rules. Berry summarizes the aims and difficulties in institutionalizing this norm: [29]

Pluralism, as a form of adjustment for the differences of racial and ethnic groups, has an especial appeal to those who subscribe to democratic ideals and processes. It is very congenial to those who place high value upon good sportsmanship, fair play, freedom, and the sacredness of human personality. It attracts those who hold that "variety is the spice of life!" and who deplore the modern trend toward uniformity, homogeneity, and standardization. At the same time it must be admitted that pluralism is a delicate form of accommodation, difficult to achieve, applicable only in rare circumstances, and demanding a high degree of mutual tolerance and sympathy.

THE FUTURE — CONTINUATION OF DISSENSUS

American culture expresses both common values and the freedom to be different. From the standpoint of ethnic minorities, the retention of in-group integrity has been important. Yet these groups have not been totally successful in fostering separationism because they have been identified with the promises of the American dream. Despite the emphasis on separate ethnic identity, many individuals cannot be neatly fitted into any single minority box. Individuals have multiple group identifications mixing both ethnic antecedents and achieved roles. No minority group can demand of its membership exclusive attention and commitment to its interests. It must permit considerable latitude for members to define their own fluid patterns of association. No large minority group, despite the desires of some of its leadership, has been successful in total withdrawal or separation from the larger community of American society. Instead there has been a continuous process of adapting and changing traditional doctrines, rites, and social structures of the ethnic group to the ever-shifting conditions of the total society.

Pluralism becomes most difficult to achieve in the "voluntary" relationships within an industrial society. It constantly places the ethnic group member in the position of not knowing when to be similar — accept the "common" values — and when to be different — maintain his own cultural heritage. This dilemma is related to very practical issues. Is the encouragement of

28. Howard J. Ehrlich, "The Swastika Epidemic of 1959–1960: Anti-Semitism and Community Characteristics," *Social Problems*, 9 (1962), pp. 264–72.
29. Berry, op. cit. p. 364.

ethnic endogamy "undemocratic"? Does the existence of Italian, Polish, or Jewish neighborhoods represent clannishness or democratic choice? Are the complaints of non-Protestant ethnic groups concerning religious observance in the public schools petty quibbling or the defense of a crucial principle? Are parochial schools and organizations divisive or desirable? These are the issues that will continue to be debated in the future. With the cessation of large-scale immigration and the effectiveness of the acculturation process, ethnic minorities, for the most part, will in time disappear as an object of dissensus in American life. Their place has already been taken by racial minorities.

SUMMARY

This chapter has been concerned with the problem of maintaining unity in a society which has had to integrate an ethnically diverse population. The problem has been accentuated by the fact that the sheer number of people involved in this experiment has been extraordinarily large and that they came to the United States over a relatively short period of time.

As each wave of immigrants came, there were new problems and new adjustments to be made, for each wave was markedly different from its predecessors. In the process of accommodating almost every new group, a new normative conception was formed or an old one revised.

The historical conception was based on "Americanization," but it was drafted with reference to the "old" northern and western European immigrants. When the "new" immigrants from eastern Europe arrived, this process was more difficult to achieve, since their cultural backgrounds were perceived to be considerably different from that of the "native stock." The "melting pot" doctrine evolved, which asserted that a single unitary culture based on white Protestant values was no longer feasible and suggested that a syncretic culture arising out of the best of "old world" cultures would be the solution.

The melting pot doctrine was first embraced by various ethnic groups but later resisted because its consequence would be to destroy their separate identities. To preserve the ethnic groupings the norm of pluralism emerged; pluralism is the result of the growth of ethnic self-consciousness and the increase in political influence of minorities and today remains in delicate balance with the continuing pressures toward "Americanization."

QUESTIONS AND SUGGESTIONS FOR FURTHER STUDY

1. Interview two or three individuals whose ethnic background is different from yours. Try to establish what normative conception they favor and their reasons for taking the stand they do.

2. Examine over a period of time the editorials in your local newspaper that discuss any aspect of current minority problems. What "solutions" do these editorials suggest for ameliorating ethnic problems?

3. Why do you think there is disagreement on contemporary normative conceptions concerning ethnic groups? What changes in the national conditions would tend to reduce disagreement in this area?

4. Is it necessary to have consensus on the normative conception regarding ethnic groups? Why or why not?

5. Read again the quotation in the "Melting Pot" section which answers the question, what is the American? How would you answer this question? Is your answer different from that given in the quotation? In what respects?

6. In the late 1950's many southern mountain people, the so-called hillbillies, emigrated out of their locale and moved into the northern cities and received much the same treatment as did the alien immigrants a generation or two ago. How do you account for this treatment?

7. Some experts on ethnic relations claim that the reason why there is so little hostility and friction between groups is that most Americans subscribe to the ideals of freedom and equality. If they did not, there would be much more intergroup conflict, some experts claim. What do you think about this?

8. Examine a newspaper or journal article which describes a problem in ethnic or religious conflict such as the Planned Parenthood movement, "released time" for religious instruction, and federal grants to parochial schools. What stand would you take on such issues?

SUGGESTED READINGS

Adamic, Louis, *A Nation of Nations*, New York: Harper, 1944. A general survey of ethnic groups by a long-time student of minorities.

Berry, Brewton, *Race and Ethnic Relations*, Boston: Houghton Mifflin, 1958. Probably the most balanced and comprehensive analysis of the subject. Contains both American and cross-cultural data.

Cole, Stewart G., and Mildred W. Cole, *Minorities and the American Promise*, New York: Harper, 1954. A careful analysis of American minorities.

Gordon, Milton, *Assimilation in American Life*, New York: Oxford University Press, 1964. A more complete treatment of the issues described in this chapter. What we have called Americanization here, Gordon calls Anglo-conformity. See especially Chapters 4, 5, and 6.

Handlin, Oscar, *The Uprooted*, Boston: Little, Brown, 1951. A prize-winning essay on immigration.

———, *Race and Nationality in American Life*, Boston: Little Brown, 1957. An excellent review of the development of racism in America.   P

Herberg, *Protestant-Catholic-Jew*, New York: Doubleday, 1955. Deals with the interplay of ethnic and religious factors.   P

Higham, John, *Strangers in the Land, Patterns of American Nationalism, 1860–*

1925, New Brunswick: Rutgers University Press, 1955. Describes the factors which ultimately lead up to the restrictive legislation on immigration.

Kramer, Judith, and Seymour Leventman, *Children of the Gilded Ghetto*, New Haven: Yale University Press, 1961. An examination of ethnic problems over several generations.

Marden, Charles F., *Minorities in American Society*, New York: American Book, 1952. Case by case description and analysis of minorities in America.

Thomas, W. I., and Florian Znaniecki, *The Polish Peasant in Europe and America*, 5 vols. Boston: R. G. Badger, 1918–20. A classic analysis of various aspects of immigrant problems.

Vander Zanden, James, *American Minority Relations: The Sociology of Race and Ethnic Groups*, New York: Ronald, 1963. Excellent recent treatment of contemporary minority relations.

Wirth, Louis, *The Ghetto*, Chicago: University of Chicago Press, 1928. Another sociological classic, a study of a Jewish community within a community.

CHAPTER 12   MINORITY PEOPLES: RACIAL GROUPS

Today we are committed to a worldwide struggle to promote and protect the rights of all who wish to be free. And when Americans are sent to Vietnam or West Berlin we do not ask for whites only.

It ought to be possible . . . for every American to enjoy the privileges of being American without regard to his race or his color.

Difficulties over segregation and discrimination exist in every city, in every state of the Union, producing in many cities a rising tide of discontent that threatens the public safety.

It is better to settle these matters in the courts than on the streets, and new laws are needed at every level. But law alone cannot make men see right.

We are confronted primarily with a moral issue. It is as old as the Scriptures and is as clear as the American Constitution.

One hundred years of delay have passed since President Lincoln freed the slaves, yet their heirs, their grandsons, are not fully free.

President Kennedy, June 11, 1963

". . . he [the Negro] did not evolve simply because of his inherent limitations. Water does not rise above its source, and the Negro could not by his inherent qualities rise above his environment as had the other races. His inheritance was wanting. The potential did not exist. This is neither right nor wrong; it is simply a stubborn biological fact.

Tom P. Brady, *Black Monday*, 1954

The white man offers us gratuities when we seek dividends, contempt when we seek justice, insults when we seek equality, violence when we seek the right to vote, privileges when we seek rights.

We are sick of evasion, weary of excuses, fed up with promises and want action now, liberty now, equality now.

Dr. James M. Nabrit, Jr., *The New York Times*, July 5, 1962

These quotations point up contemporary dissensus in America over race relations. It is fair to say that it is the most important domestic conflict in the United States. The words of Dr. Nabrit, of Howard University, speaking at an Independence Day rally of the National Association for the Advancement of Colored People, reflect the long-term struggle of the American Negro for civil liberties and his continued search for self-respect. These are words of disappointment, frustration, and impatience.

On the other hand, Judge Brady, a Mississippi circuit judge, justifies the inequalities in the treatment of the Negro, as a racial minority, by addressing himself to what he regards as the innate "biological inferiority" of the American Negro. From this perspective, inequality is equality.

President Kennedy, in a nation-wide address, clearly states the dilemma posed by racial conflict in America. Prodded by the self-conscious Negro demanding first-class citizenship and strenuously resisted by segments of the majority group seeking to maintain the *status quo*, the United States is confronted with its most serious racial crisis since the Civil War.

These statements symbolize the emergence of a new stage in the history of American race relations. The "new" Negro is no longer humbly asking for the privileges of equal status; he now demands this equality. Furthermore, this demand now enjoys the sanction of the United States government and the approbation of the many who are concerned with civil rights in America. The demand is reinforced by many voluntary associations engaged in political and social action to remove all forms of segregation. Moreover, peoples in other nations of the world — most of whom are "colored" — are exerting moral, and political, pressure upon the United States for an early elimination of discrimination.

But not every section of the country, nor every group, favors the present trend. Some, not unalterably opposed to change in race relations, are nevertheless hesitant about its rapidity and militancy: the "Freedom Rides," the "sit-ins," and other mass protests. Some are concerned that civil rights are being handed to Negroes at great expense to their own vested interests. There are still others who do not object to legal changes involving political and civil rights but oppose changes involving greater interpersonal contacts between the races.

These differing conceptions of race relations in the United States reflect various attitudes and points of view that have emerged through the years. As conditions of living change, so do the conceptions of normative order.

Unlike the ethnic minorities, which are confronted with the problem of maintaining their identities in a society which assimilates them more and more readily, the Negro is still striving to gain greater freedom of access in the opportunity system and is still far from achieving educational, political, economic, and legal equality — rights which have long since been achieved by ethnic minorities. As the largest numerical minority, American Negroes have been the subject of greater dissensus than any other ethnic or racial group (see Table 12-1). They therefore furnish the chief focus of this chapter. Other racial groups — the Indian, the Chinese, and the Japanese — will be discussed in less detail. These latter groups have presented somewhat different problems from those of the Negro. The numerical composition of the major racial groups in the United States is shown in Table 12-2.

TABLE 12-1

Races in the United States by per cent, 1860 to 1960

Year	White	Negro	Other races
1960	88.8	10.6	0.6
1950	89.5	10.0	0.5
1940	89.8	9.8	0.4
1930	89.8	9.7	0.5
1920	89.7	9.9	0.4
1910	88.9	10.7	0.4
1900	87.9	11.6	0.5
1890	87.5	11.9	0.6
1880	86.5	13.1	0.3
1870	87.1	12.7	0.2
1860	85.6	14.1	0.3

Source: U.S. Bureau of the Census. *U.S. Census of Population: 1960. General Population Characteristics. United States Summary.* Final Report PC (1) -1B. Washington, D.C., U.S. Government Printing Office, 1961, pp. 1–145, Table 44.

TABLE 12-2

Major racial groups in the United States, 1860 to 1960

Year	Negro	Indian	Japanese	Chinese
1960	18,860,117	508,675	260,059	198,958
1950	15,042,286	343,410	141,768	117,629
1940	12,865,518	333,969	126,947	77,504
1930	11,891,143	332,397	138,834	74,954
1920	10,463,131	244,437	111,010	61,639
1910	9,827,763	265,683	72,157	71,531
1900	8,833,994	237,196	24,326	89,863
1890	7,488,676	248,253	2,039	107,488
1880	6,580,993	66,407	148	105,465
1870	4,880,009	25,731	55	63,199
1860	4,441,830	44,021		34,933

Source: U.S. Bureau of the Census. *U.S. Census of Population: 1960. General Population Characteristics. United States Summary.* Final Report PC (1)–1B., Washington, D.C., U.S. Government Printing Office, 1961, pp. 1–145, Table 44.

The normative problem: should racial minorities be excluded, segregated, or integrated in an industrial society?

The treatment of racial minorities in the United States has varied considerably in the past 300 years. While there have been no well-defined stages, in general the normative conception has shifted from exclusion to segregation to integration. Since each of the racial minorities has had a different history, each is presented here in brief before the discussion of these three normative conceptions.

The Negro. In 1619, when the first twenty Negroes disembarked in Jamestown, they were given the status of indentured servants. Upon the completion of their contracts, it was assumed they would be free. But gradually, as more Negroes arrived in this country, legal decisions and enactments supported by other norms changed their status to one of hereditary, lifelong servitude, or slavery. For over two hundred years, the relations of most Negroes and whites in the United States were those of master and slave. While the Civil War marked the end of slave status for the Negro, a new status was not immediately forthcoming. The post-Civil War years were marked by intense conflict as to what this new status would be. There slowly evolved a newer conception of his place as separate though "equal." Through the development of Jim Crow laws in the South, separateness, but not equality, was achieved, with the patterns of segregation cutting through every segment of community life.

The twentieth century has seen the beginning of a reversal of this pattern of segregation and the gradual development of the conception which has come to be known as integration. This emerging conception, implemented by both legal norms and moral force, is working toward the eventual elimination of restrictions and discrimination in housing, education, public facilities, political activity, and economic opportunity.

The Indian. From the beginning, contact between the Indians and the settlers gave evidence that the Indian was to be excluded from evolving American society. One aspect of this exclusion was the British colonial and later United States government treatment of the various tribes as sovereign powers, recognizing their title to land, paying them for it, and negotiating with them by treaties. This approach led to conflict because the Indians' conception of land and property was quite different from that of the settlers. The conflicts resulted in wars in which large numbers of Indians were exterminated. Even slavery was attempted at times, but Indians were not passive recruits for such status. Gradually, a policy evolved to remove the Indian by mass expulsion, which was sometimes accomplished peacefully by encouraging settlement outside the boundaries of the society; at other times, the Indian was forced to move against his will. A classic example of the latter method occurred in the 1830's when federal troops rounded up more than 10,000 Cherokees and drove them west into what is now Oklahoma.

In the middle of the nineteenth century, there was a change of policy, and Indians were segregated on reservations. Between 1850 and 1880, most of the Indian reservations, of which there are now some 200, were created.

But in time, this pattern also shifted. The newest conception suggested that the Indian be integrated into American life. This could only be accomplished by rapid compulsory assimilation and by the loss of Indian cultural identity. Indian tribal organization, religion, language, and customs were to disappear and the Indian was to be incorporated into the mainstream of American life. Because of persistent cultural differences between Indians and other Americans, the federal government has at different times encouraged both cultural pluralism and integration.[1]

The Chinese. Records show that by 1820 only one Chinese had been admitted to the United States, and by 1850 only 758 were in this country. But during the gold rush period in California, Chinese were welcomed as a source of cheap labor. The American fortune hunter was not inclined to waste his time performing "coolie" labor, and, in 1852, some 20,000 Chinese were admitted. By the time of the 1880 Census subsequent immigration totaled 105,465. As the gold rush subsided, there were railroads to be built using Chinese labor. The joining of the eastern and western railroad links in 1869 meant unemployment for the Chinese at a time of major depression. Their willingness to work for low wages at almost any employment began to change the old American image of the Chinese as industrious and law abiding; now they appeared undependable and shifty. Legislation restricting their economic opportunities, and political campaigns based on anti-Chinese feeling, became characteristic patterns on the west coast. Finally, Chinese immigration became a national issue and Congress passed the Chinese Exclusion Act in 1882, which suspended all immigration for ten years. This ten-year extension was renewed in 1892 and indefinitely renewed in 1902, although some modifications were made in subsequent years.

The Chinese who were already here reacted in a number of ways. Some went back to China; others moved away from the coast. In most instances, they migrated to large cities and "voluntarily" segregated themselves. They withdrew socially, politically, and economically as well as physically. They turned to those occupations which gave them minimal contacts with whites; they opened art and curio shops, restaurants, and hand laundries. They settled their disputes among themselves and tried to preserve their cultural tradition.[2]

Despite this history of exclusion and segregation, there are indications today that the Chinese are being integrated into American society. As a result of the high value the Chinese have placed on education, many second-generation

1. For a detailed treatment of the American Indian see John Collier, *The Indians of the Americas*, New York: New American Library, 1949.
2. For an excellent sociological analysis see Rose Hum Lee, *The Chinese in American Society*, New York: Oxford University Press, 1960.

Chinese children find employment in fields formerly closed to them. The expansion of the economy has also meant new occupational opportunities. The Chinese today, no longer having to bear the hostile feeling of a century ago, are gradually being accepted into the mainstream of American life.

The Japanese. For a long time, Japan opposed its citizens leaving their own country. Thus, there were only 148 Japanese recorded in the 1880 Census. In 1884, the Hawaiian Sugar Planters Association persuaded Japanese authorities to drop their opposition, and Japanese in other countries began to increase. By 1910 there were 72,157 in the United States. Coming in through Seattle and San Francisco, they settled on the west coast. As late as 1940, nearly 90 per cent of all Japanese in the U.S. were in the Pacific coast area — 74 per cent in California and 39 per cent in Los Angeles County. Consistent with previous restrictions on the Chinese, there were early attempts to segregate them. In 1906 the San Francisco school board attempted to place Oriental students in separate schools. The federal government also made informal arrangements with Japan to slow down the rate of immigration by refusing passports except to those immigrants who were coming to join their families. This "Gentleman's Agreement," arranged in 1907, put an end to most immigration, except for the so-called "picture brides" — marriages arranged by men already in this country. In 1924, Congress passed a law effectively barring all Orientals from immigration.

On the west coast, most Japanese lived in urban areas called "little Tokyos." Social, economic, and legal forces effectively restricted them to jobs in hotel and restaurant service, fruit stands, nurseries, and cleaning and dyeing shops. Other Japanese established themselves in small-scale truck and fruit farming. Here again a pattern of segregation, partly voluntary and partly enforced, resulted.

This concentration of Japanese on the west coast had other consequences. The attack by Japan on Pearl Harbor in 1941 gave rise to widespread anti-Japanese prejudice. False rumors concerning Japanese sabotage created a climate which resulted in the compulsory evacuation of Japanese from the Pacific coast and their placement in internment centers.[3] Beginning in 1942, more than 100,000 persons of Japanese lineage were transferred to these centers and placed under guard. Nearly two-thirds of these were American citizens.[4]

The Japanese did not remain in these centers long. Students were allowed to leave to attend high school and college. In 1943, the Army accepted enlist-

3. See Alexander H. Leighton, *The Governing of Men*, Princeton: Princeton University Press, 1945.
4. See Dorothy S. Thomas, *The Salvage: Japanese American Evacuation and Resettlement*, Berkeley: University of California Press, 1946.

ments from this group. In 1944, the ban on returning to the west coast was lifted. Many went back but large numbers chose to settle in other states.

Since World War II, the pressures toward segregation have been reduced. The lessening of Japanese population concentration, diffusion in the country's occupational structure, and the great value placed on education by the Japanese have given them new access to the opportunity structure within the society. Perhaps this process has been speeded by the guilt for what has been called America's "worst wartime mistake" — the relocation of American citizens. In any case, the integration of the Japanese seemingly is being accomplished.

The remainder of the chapter will be concerned primarily with the Negro, about whom normative dissensus has been deepest and most persistent. The Indian, the Chinese, and the Japanese were all numerically smaller minorities than the Negro, and since their differences from Americans were national as well as racial, ideas of cultural pluralism came to influence their treatment for the better during the last few decades. With the Negro there has been no such adjustment.

> *Historical Normative Conception: Exclusion* — White men are endowed by their Creator with certain inalienable rights.

Like many other immigrants, Negroes were first brought to colonial America as indentured servants. Unlike other immigrants, however, Negroes had terms of indenture which were never specified and remained indeterminate. Their relatively low cost and their superior adaptability to certain types of work led to the importation of more Negroes and the development of a slave code. Over time, an elaborate system evolved defining their status, both as persons and as property. This code prescribed that Negroes could not own or possess firearms, could not travel freely or leave their employer's premises without written permission, and could not gather for any purpose without white supervision, or in any way reject white authority.

In addition to these formal legal codes establishing slavery, unwritten rules governing relations between white and black, master and slave, began to emerge in colonial America. This code of racial etiquette, with its delicate shadings and nuances, still persists in sections of the U.S. today as part of the legacy of slavery.

At the outbreak of the Revolutionary War, every colony recognized the institution of slavery. While the Declaration of Independence spoke eloquently of the inalienable rights of all men, slavery with its exclusion of the Negro from the free society was never mentioned. The Constitution subsequently safeguarded slavery without mentioning the word. Congressional seats were apportioned on the basis of population size, and southern states gained seats since they were allowed to count each Negro slave as three-fifths of a person.

Not only was the exclusion of the Negro from active participation in American society indirectly sanctioned in the Constitution, but even the staunchest democrats of the time tended to share this view. Jefferson, for example, writing in his *Autobiography*, said: "Nothing is more certainly written in the book of fate than that these people [Negroes] are to be free; nor is it less certain that the two races, equally free, cannot live in the same government." It was also Jefferson who drafted the Virginia slave bill which coupled the manumission of slaves with their immediate deportation.[5] Negro slaves, in this plan, were to be freed and deported to other parts of the world and their place taken by white settlers.

The ideals of the Declaration of Independence did suggest that slavery was wrong. Based on these ideals, the abolitionist movement gained enough support to force Congress to enact a law preventing the further importation of slaves by 1808, the earliest date allowed by the U.S. Constitution. Almost every northern state either abolished slavery outright or provided for its gradual elimination. Slavery was abolished by the constitutions of Vermont (1777), Ohio (1802), Indiana (1816), and Illinois (1818); by judicial decision in Massachusetts (1793); by interpretation of the state constitution in New Hampshire; and by legal acts stipulating gradual abolition in Pennsylvania (1780), Rhode Island (1784), Connecticut (1784 and 1797), New York (1799 and 1817), and New Jersey (1804). Nevertheless, by 1800, some 30,505 northern Negroes were still slaves, most of them in New York and New Jersey.

In the North, freedom from slavery did not automatically confer citizenship on the free Negro.[6] Most northern whites maintained a careful distinction between granting Negroes legal protection — the right to life, liberty, and property — and political and social equality. The general opinion was that no legislative act could "free" them from their natural inferiority. In most northern states, the Negro's citizenship status was unclear. In some states, they were allowed to pay taxes, but not to vote. The growth of the free Negro population in the North lead to increasing interest in colonization plans for the Negro. In 1816, the American Colonization Society was formed to promote and execute a plan for colonization of Negroes in Africa or in any other place Congress might decide. Its members, which included men such as Francis Scott Key, argued that their plan was the only humane and

5. For a fuller treatment of Jefferson's attitudes see Chapter 4 in Nathaniel Weyl, *The Negro in American Civilization*, Washington, D.C.: Public Affairs Press, 1960.
6. For a discussion of the free Negro in the North see Leon F. Litwack, *North of Slavery*, Chicago: University of Chicago Press, 1961.

just solution. Although colonization appealed to many as the ideal solution to the dilemma posed by the freedom of an "inferior" race, Negro and white abolitionist resistance, governmental apathy, and southern suspicion inhibited the full implementation of such a plan. However, largely through the efforts of the Society, a successful colony for Negroes was eventually established in Liberia.

The South, of course, resisted the movement to free the slaves. Southerners did not see the principles of the war for independence as incompatible with the existence of slavery. This was true partly because the South had a heavier economic investment in the institution, as can be seen from the relative proportion of slaves in 1790 in both regions: [7]

	North	South
White	1,900,616	1,271,390
Free Colored	27,070	32,457
Slaves	40,354	657,327
Total	1,968,040	1,961,174

The reason, of course, for the large slave population in the South was the production of cotton. Cotton was produced fairly efficiently on the plantation with slaves providing the chief source of labor. It was a valuable product because the growing industrial and commercial centers of England and elsewhere sought it as a relatively inexpensive textile material.

The South was becoming more agricultural as the cotton market developed; as a result, the slave population increased. By 1810 it had passed the one million mark. Twenty years later it approached two million, and by 1860 it was close to four million. Conversely, the slave population declined in the North because there was a decreasing need for farm labor — the only work open to slaves — along with an increasing need for industrial workers.

These statistics reflect a crucial cultural gap that had developed during the nineteenth century. The North was progressing along lines signifying the emergence of an industrial society, while the South was not. The South's labor force consisted chiefly of slaves, and a slave was rarely allowed to do any work other than field labor, unless he became a domestic servant. Until the Civil War, southern life remained much as it had been in 1790. The remnants of aristocratic privilege, which elsewhere had been eliminated by Jacksonian democracy, still retained force in the South. The ruling class — that is, the large landowners — maintained absolute control over the slaves and a class influence over the poorer whites. Owning slaves became an important means of social mobility. The politically ambitious southerner would

7. U.S. Bureau of the Census, *Historical Statistics of the United States, 1789–1945,* Washington, D.C.: U.S. Government Printing Office, 1949, p. 27.

buy more slaves to gain prestige. From the large land-owning and slave-owning class were drawn the representatives and senators in Congress, the governors, and other officeholders. By the Constitutional provision for counting slaves, the South had twenty additional Congressmen. This was a particularly important gain in "black" districts where whites were few and the slaveholders could thus easily control the district. This political power was justified on the basis of white supremacy. The slave system, however, continued to pull the South out of harmony with the rest of the society so that by the middle of the nineteenth century, North and South were almost two different countries.

The problems of the slave in the South and the free Negro in the North were reflected in early Congressional legislation. Individual states had to come to terms with Negroes in their own unique settings, but at the same time Congress had to deal with the Negro on the national level. While the issue of the relation between the federal government and the individual states was beginning to be raised, in areas where Congress had clear authority, an exclusionist attitude toward the Negro became evident. In 1790, Congress limited naturalization to white aliens; in 1792, it organized a militia and restricted enrollment to white male citizens; in 1810, it excluded Negroes from carrying the U.S. mails; in 1820, it authorized the citizens of Washington to elect "white" city officials. Moreover, it repeatedly approved the admittance to the union of states whose constitutions severely restricted the legal rights of slaves. On several occasions, exclusionist sentiments prompted Congress to place restrictions on the ownership of land through provisions in homestead bills. In organizing the Oregon and New Mexico territories, Congress agreed to limit public land grants to white settlers.

Since no federal ruling or act specifically defined the Negro's status, each governmental department felt free to determine its own policy. Negroes sometimes benefited from this confusion in that some were allowed to exercise the rights of white citizens. The confusion was ended with the decision by the Supreme Court on Dred Scott. This decision affirmed and justified the exclusion of the Negro.

Dred Scott was a Missouri slave who had been taken into several free states and then back to Missouri. He sued for his freedom and his case was heard in the federal courts because it involved an interstate issue. After extensive litigation, the case was finally appealed to the Supreme Court, by whose decision Scott was ruled to be the property of his master and was returned to him. In the decision (1857), the Court ruled that a slave, or a descendant of a slave, could not be a citizen of the United States. Chief Justice Taney reviewed the previous treatment of the Negro and concluded that Negroes had "been regarded as beings of an inferior order, and altogether unfit to associate with the white race, either in social or political relations; and so far inferior, that they had no rights which the white man was bound to respect." [8] He also observed that state and federal legislation as well as the conduct of the executive department confirmed that Negroes "are not included and were not intended to be included, under the words 'citizens' in the Constitution and can therefore claim none of the rights and privileges which that instrument provides for and secures to citizens of the United States." [9] Taney's decision also suggested that it was the responsibility of Congress to protect, not to prohibit, slavery in the territories since one of its constitutional functions was the protection of property. Other justices disagreed with Taney and the decision was denounced by abolitionist and Negro leaders. Southerners viewed the decision as a validation of their own practices.

The Dred Scott decision was more a summation of how the Negro had been treated in the past than a precedent for the future. With the onset of the Civil War, the whole issue of slavery was raised again. Early in the war, pressure was brought to bear on President Lincoln to declare that the slaves in the seceded states were free. On January 1, 1863, he used the Emancipation Proclamation to free the slaves in areas still fighting against the Union. With the defeat of the South slavery as an institution was effectively ended, and new ways to treat the Negro had to be devised.

THE DECLINE OF EXCLUSION AND THE EMERGENCE OF SEGREGATION

The Civil War had both immediate and long-range effects on the status of the Negro as a participating member of society. The victory of the North compelled the southern states to search for new methods of imposing historic traditions of exclusion on the emancipated Negro. In the period 1865–67, eight states in the South took the lead in passing laws, called Black Codes, which deprived the Negro of his newly acquired civil, political, and economic rights. Negroes could not be licensed for certain occupations — most notably medicine and pharmacy. They could not freely cross state lines. Vagrancy laws were enacted which provided harsh penalties for Negroes found far from home. Negroes could not serve as jurors or testify against whites. And, finally, they could not vote.

These Black Codes were short-lived, for the onset of the Reconstruction period in 1867 compelled the southern states to repeal them and the Reconstruction Congress set out to destroy for all time historic white domination over a powerless Negro minority. Negro civil rights were to be granted and enforced and Negro participation in community life and in the economic and educational institutions encouraged.

8. *Dred Scott v. Sanford*, 19 Howard 403, 407.
9. Ibid. 404–6, 419–22.

In order to achieve these objectives, several important amendments to the Constitution were ratified. These amendments granted the Negro rights as a citizen. The Thirteenth Amendment (December 18, 1865) abolished involuntary servitude and slavery; the Fourteenth (July 18, 1868) conferred citizenship and equal protection of the laws; and the Fifteenth (March 30, 1870) prohibited the states from denying the right to vote for reasons of race, color, or previous condition of servitude. On a level less basic but more practical, Congress adopted in 1867 and 1875 the Civil Rights Acts which, among other things, provided that all persons should be entitled to the full and equal enjoyment of public conveyances, accommodations, and places of public amusement.

In addition to these legal changes, an attempt was made to provide equal status for Negroes in the South. They attended public schools and gained vocational training. They held public offices and, with the aid of northern advisers, participated in local and state affairs. From 1870 to 1901, twenty Negroes as Representatives, and two as Senators, represented their constituents in the United States Congress. At no time, however, were there more than seven Negroes in Congress.

For about fifteen years following the Civil War, the status of the Negro was in flux. The legal patterns excluding the Negro had ended but this did not assure their integration into American life. A number of events in the decades between 1880 and 1920 led to the establishment of a new conception — segregation — and undercut legal and social gains the Negro had made after the Civil War.

First, certain economic conditions affected the Reconstruction gains of the Negro. Among these was a general decline in agricultural prices, especially cotton, in the latter part of the nineteenth century, which grew into a nationwide financial crisis. The resulting depression contributed to the problems of the transitional period in the South, which had already experienced considerable political and social dislocation, not the least of which was the necessity of absorbing millions of Negroes with new citizenship status. The same depression created problems in the North that led to decreasing concern with the reconstruction of the South. The net effect was a seeming indifference on the part of the North to the gradual abrogation of the newly gained rights of the Negro in the South.

In addition, the Negro was poorly prepared for his new legal status. While some effort was made by Congress, through the agency of the Freedman's Bureau, and by northern philanthropic organziations to assist the emancipated Negroes, this did not begin to meet the need. Cultural impoverishment, illiteracy, broken families, and other conditions resulting from slavery left the Negro disorganized and unable to take full advantage of his legal rights.

The Negro quest for civil rights was also met with resistance by an increasingly "solid" South. As E. Franklin Frazier indicates:

A consolidated white South was the final result of the Negro's struggle, with the aid of political allies, to achieve equality. When freed men attempted to assert their right to equal accommodations in public places, they were either violently ejected or the whites offered passive resistance by withdrawing from such places. But violent methods of suppressing the Negro were the rule where he insisted upon asserting his newly acquired rights. Negroes were not only denied civil rights but were also driven from the fertile land, their school houses were burned, and their leaders murdered. Nor is it to be forgotten that the monopoly which the Negro slave labor had enjoyed in the economic organization was broken and competition with "poor whites" often resulted in open conflict. The newly formed trade unions refused Negroes membership and denied them an opportunity for apprenticeship. The solidarity of the whites was only slightly broken during the agrarian movement when "poor whites" were arrayed against the large planters and the financial interests.[10]

The Solid South's resistance to Negro gains was bolstered by the rise of racism. The disorganized Negro of the post-Civil War period lived in squalor and held only the most menial jobs. This way of life contributed to the perpetuation of racial stereotypes and racist beliefs. Many white men and women came to believe that the Negro was the most simple and childlike of all peoples; that he was inherently incapable of intellectual achievement; that he was "irresponsible," "shiftless," and "lazy"; and that he was "unfit" to participate fully in "white man's civilization." These "conclusions" of southerners based on "first-hand observation" were further reinforced by racist literature, which repeated the thesis of white supremacy — an idea generally accepted in the North as well as the South. "Scientific" inquiries also supported the racist ideology.[11] Biologists and other scientists were writing about inherent racial differences among men, the superiority of the whites, and the inferiority of the colored races. With the acceptance of this racist doctrine by many whites, the uneducated Negro came to accept his subordinate position and to react as if he were inherently inferior.

The depressed economic conditions, the poor preparation of the ex-slaves for freedom and the rise of racism combined to produce secondary consequences. One of these was the coalition formed between the two major political parties in the South against the Negro. This coalition between the Populists and southern Democrats became more or less permanent, giving the South a one-party political system. Another consequence was the submission of northern legislatures and courts to southern (white) political pressures on

10. E. Franklin Frazier, "Role of the Negro in Race Relations in the South," *Social Forces*, 19 (December 1940), p. 255.
11. For example, Lothrop Stoddard, *The Rising Tide of Color Against White World-Supremacy*, New York: Scribners, 1920.

questions involving the Negro. Between 1880 and 1910, the United States Supreme Court and the lower courts approved dozens of discriminatory laws enacted by the southern legislatures. One example was the Supreme Court's decision that the Civil Rights Bill of 1875 was unconstitutional. That bill was regarded by many as the culmination of the federal reconstruction acts for it provided that all persons should be entitled to the full and equal enjoyment of public facilities. The Supreme Court nullified it on the ground that it referred to acts of social discrimination committed by individuals. The court claimed that the Fourteenth Amendment gave Congress power to restrain states, but not individuals, from acts of discrimination. The outstanding example of Court backing of the southern attitude, however, is the famous decision of *Plessy* v. *Ferguson* in 1896. The well-known "separate but equal" doctrine was given official approval in this decision. The Court ruled that separate public facilities for Negroes would not be discriminatory if these facilities were equal to those provided whites.

The importance of this "separate but equal" doctrine as a means of keeping the Negro "in his place" can hardly be overestimated. The primary effect of the doctrine was to establish segregation. It was believed that if facilities of equal quality and quantity could be provided for Negroes, the simple fact of separate facilities would not be a violation of the principles of the Fourteenth Amendment. When the Supreme Court of the United States accepted this interpretation in 1896, it eased the misgivings of those who believed in equality yet wanted to keep Negroes separate. The Supreme Court, thus, made *legalized segregation* both respectable and democratic.

With these developments it became clear that in the decades between 1890 and 1920 the normative conception of segregation had been established. However, because of their different histories, the South and the North developed different ways of implementing segregation.

> *Contemporary Normative Conception: Segregation* — Racial minorities, because they are inferior, should be separate.

THE SOUTH

Because segregation is so pervasive and because so much emotion is involved in its preservation, many mistakenly assume that it is an old institution. It is curious, writes Max Lerner, that the South with its "history-obsessed culture" "nourishes an unhistorical delusion." [12] The fact is that segregation did not gain momentum until the beginning of the twentieth century.

In the South, the white supremacy formula was fostered by active and

12. Max Lerner, *America as a Civilization*, New York: Simon and Schuster, 1957, p. 198.

deliberate indoctrination. The press and the speech-maker sensationalized alleged instances of Negro crimes, sexual deviations, arrogance, impertinence, and surliness. The propaganda created a feeling of despair even for civic-minded professional people with a humanitarian bent. According to C. Vann Woodward, they "took a deeply pessimistic or despairing view of the Negro. They laid great stress on the alarming increase in Negro crime as the race flocked to the cities and packed into crowded, filthy slums. They were convinced that the race was rapidly deteriorating in morals and manners, in health and efficiency, and losing out in the struggle for survival. They resolved that the Negro was incapable of self-government, unworthy of the franchise, and impossible to educate beyond the rudiments." [13]

Given this climate of pessimism about the future of the Negro, it is not difficult to understand the proliferation of methods to keep the white and Negro populations apart, in spite of their economic interdependence. Many of these practices were informally established and maintained. City ordinances and local regulations codified other segregation practices into Jim Crow laws. These ordinances went into great detail and sometimes even specified the size of the "whites only" and "colored" signs to be placed before segregated theaters, water fountains, waiting rooms, toilets, and restaurants.[14]

In addition to local ordinances, state legislative bodies passed thousands of regulations. Parks, factories, hospitals, amusement centers, bus and train depots, prisons, and schools came under the scrutiny of different state legislatures in the South for the purpose of regulating the relations between the races.

Residential segregation in the southern cities was established by a variety of techniques, including block-by-block segregation in areas already occupied by both races, zoning certain areas according to race, and restrictive covenants which limited the sale of real estate. The large towns in the South confined Negroes to the slum areas, and smaller towns often completely excluded Negroes by force and intimidation.

The Jim Crow laws and other discriminatory regulations could not have been passed so readily had the Negro been able to vote. Beginning with Mississippi in 1890, all the southern states had passed, by 1915, laws which restricted the voting rights of the Negro. Ingenious methods were devised to

13. C. Vann Woodward, *The Strange Career of Jim Crow* (rev. ed.), New York: Oxford University Press, 1961, p. 79.
14. A number of excellent descriptions of the segregation system and Jim Crow laws are available. See for example, Charles S. Johnson, *Patterns of Negro Segregation*, New York: Harper, 1943; Bertram W. Doyle, *The Etiquette of Race Relations in the South*, Chicago: University of Chicago Press, 1937; E. Franklin Frazier, *The Negro in the United States*, New York: Macmillan, 1949; and Allison Davis, B. Gardner, and M. R. Gardner, *Deep South*, Chicago: University of Chicago Press, 1941.

set up barriers to the Negro vote — property qualifications, literacy require-ments, an "understanding clause," a "grandfather clause," and a "good char-acter clause." But the most effective techniques were the poll tax and the "white primary." The latter prevented any Negro from voting in the primaries, which under the one-party system in the South was the point at which the elections were decided.

Schools, too, were segregated. During the early decades of this century, the budget, the plant facilities, the teachers, and almost all tangible aspects of the Negro school system were not equal to those of the white schools. Even if they had been equal, segregated schools meant that the children were taught only by Negro teachers and associated only with other Negroes. The Negro schools of this period were severely handicapped in that the teachers were poorly paid and poorly trained. At levels higher than the grade schools, a good education became more difficult to obtain because of the low income level of the Negroes and the shortage of Negro schools and colleges. Philan-thropic institutions and religious organizations did make substantial contribu-tions to Negro education, however.

Some Negroes achieved a modicum of success in spite of these difficulties. A few acquired professions by training in the North. These educated Negroes provided the leadership in Negro life, which more or less paralleled the or-ganization of white communities. Thus, the Negroes developed their own clubs, fraternities, sororities, and professional organizations when discrimina-tion excluded them from comparable white organizations. Separate churches, stores, theaters, restaurants, barber shops, newspapers, clinics, and other community services were established. Separate occupational groups emerged, such as Negro carpenters, plumbers, auto mechanics, nurses, and physicians.

From this parallel social structure came some advantages for the Negro de-spite the basic discriminatory feature. The biracial organization permitted considerable occupational diversification and an occupational apprenticeship within the ranks of the Negro. It also developed, as time went on, a social stratification system within the Negro community. Talented Negroes were able to find at least some outlet for their energies and skills within the exist-ing social structure. They could become Negro community leaders even if they could not become community leaders.

Since the dual organization minimized contact, Negroes could avoid some of the ruder forms of discrimination by living almost entirely within the Negro community. From the standpoint of the larger community, however, this type of deliberate avoidance of contact inevitably led to the psycho-logical and cultural isolation of the Negro. The stereotypes each group de-veloped of the other tended to be perpetuated without correction under these conditions.

THE NORTH

Given the conditions in the South, it is not difficult to understand the attraction of the North for southern Negroes. The two world wars were particularly significant in this migration. Labor shortages and related opportunities in the North attracted more than two million Negroes between 1910 and 1940, and the proportion living outside outside of the South rose from 10.3 per cent in 1900 to 23.0 per cent in 1940 (see Table 12-3). Since 1940, the

TABLE 12-3

Per cent distribution of Negro population
United States by regions

	1860	1900	1940	1950	1960
United States	100.0	100.0	100.0	100.0	100.0
Northeast	3.5	4.4	10.6	13.4	16.0
North Central	4.1	5.6	11.0	14.8	18.4
South	92.2	89.7	77.0	68.0	59.9
West	0.1	0.3	1.3	3.8	5.7

Source: Thompson, W. S., *Population Problems*, 4th ed., New York: McGraw-Hill, 1953, p. 127. The data for the 1960 percentages were derived from U.S. Bureau of the Census. *U.S. Census of Population: 1960. General Population Characteristics. United States Summary.* Final Report PC (1)–1B. Washington, D.C., U.S. Government Printing Office, 1961, pp. 1–145.

migration out of the South has continued and the Negroes are now well represented in the urban centers of the North and West. About 40 per cent of all Negroes live outside of the South. As someone observed, the "South is getting whiter all the time."

As the result of this migration, several important changes in the complexion of race relations in the United States took place. One of these was that the North was now faced with the reality of large populations of Negroes in its midst. By 1960, almost 10 per cent of the population of the urban areas of the Northeast and the North Central states were Negroes (see Table 12-4). "To preach a distant reform," observed one South Carolinian, "is very cheap philanthropy — the cheaper in proportion to the distance. The feeling of self-satisfaction exists without the necessity of personal sacrifice." [15]

As the Negro population increased, the North adopted some of the southern attitudes toward the Negro. White southerners who traveled North carried their attitudes with them, and many attempted to impose their customs on northern hotelkeepers, theater owners, and restaurant managers. The

15. Dwight L. Dumond, *Antislavery Origins of the Civil War*, Ann Arbor: University of Michigan Press, 1959, p. 51.

TABLE 12-4

Per cent of Negroes in the total population of regions
and of urban and rural places, 1960

Region	Total	Urban	Rural
Northeast	6.8	8.1	1.5
North Central	6.7	9.3	0.9
South	20.6	20.5	20.6
West	3.9	4.6	1.3

Source: U.S. Bureau of the Census. *U.S. Census of Population: 1960. General Population Characteristics. United States Summary.* Final Report PC (1)–1B. Washington, D.C., U.S. Government Printing Office, 1961, pp. 1–58.

southern Negro also brought with him some of the foot-scraping and hat-tipping behavior he had learned. Some northern whites, while not taking a patronizing attitude toward such behavior, felt uncomfortable and looked upon Negroes as strange and alien. The widespread ignorance, different standards of hygiene, and strange mannerisms of the early migrants helped to perpetuate stereotypes about the Negro in the minds of the Northern whites.

Racial etiquette in the North has never been as sharply defined as in the South, but the stereotypes of Negroes have helped to maintain a marked social distance between the two races. For instance, in high schools and colleges Negroes have often been excluded from dances and social affairs, or if they attended the same functions, they kept separate groupings and members of the two races rarely danced together. Eventually the North developed its own form of school, church, and residential segregation, as well as job discrimination, unequal opportunities for higher education, and less protection than whites from the law enforcement agencies.[16]

Differences should be noted, however, in the attitudes and practices in the North and South. The North has not had segregated buses, trains, and public toilets nor has it enforced a rigid etiquette of subservient behavior. The northerner has accepted the prejudices about intermarriage, but with considerably less emotional involvement than the southerner. He has not generally looked with strong disapproval on the Negro who was ambitious and eager to achieve in the occupational world. Rather there has been a tendency to admire and reward such aspirations.

16. The following studies illustrate segregation patterns in the North: W. Lloyd Warner, B. H. Junker, and W. A. Adams, *Color and Human Nature*, Washington, D.C.: American Council on Education, 1941; E. Franklin Frazier, *Black Bourgeoisie*, Glencoe: Free Press, 1957; St. Clair Drake and Horace Cayton, *Black Metropolis*, New York: Harcourt, Brace, 1945; Frank F. Lee, *Negro and White in a Connecticut Town*, New York: Bookman Associates, 1961.

In the South the stronghold of segregation has been in the rural areas and plantation regions. By contrast most of the problems concerning the integration of Negroes in the North were found in the large urban industrialized areas. The reason is that the vast majority of the in-migrants have settled in the large metropolitan areas: Baltimore, Chicago, Cleveland, Detroit, Los Angeles, New York, Philadelphia, Pittsburgh, St. Louis, San Francisco-Oakland, and Washington, D.C.

As Negroes came into these cities, they had problems finding suitable housing.[17] Even if they could afford it, the polite and sometimes not so polite refusals kept them from apartments and houses they desired. The result was a piling up of the nonwhite population in the cheaper, deteriorating city areas while the whites fled into the suburbs. Chicago's South Side, Detroit's East Side, Philadelphia's "inner city," and New York's Harlem are examples of a nonwhite core surrounded by a "white suburban ring."

Segregation in housing inevitably resulted in school segregation. Most children in the United States attend schools which are located near their homes. Because Negroes are forced to live in certain districts of the cities, the schools in these neighborhoods came to be composed primarily of one race. Housing, then, was the focus of segregation in the North. The lack of freedom to purchase the house he could afford to own contributed to school, church, neighborhood, and social segregation of the Negro.

While segregation existed in both North and South, there was one all-important difference. Negroes in the North had the right to vote. This factor has played an important role in national and local elections and is related to some of the recent progress made toward the integration of the Negro.

Every social pattern has certain consequences. In both the North and the South, segregation has existed long enough to produce definite results. In recent years, those results have undergone an assessment which is making more and more apparent the "cost" of segregation.

CONSEQUENCES OF SEGREGATION

The consequences of segregation to all concerned — the larger society, the white majority and the Negro minority — have invariably been negative. From the point of view of American society, segregation, prejudice, and discrimination have adversely affected the image of this country as a free and democratic society. Apart from our image abroad, the segregation pattern has led to the underutilization of American manpower resources which is costly to the economy. Dual and largely unequal educational facilities, general hos-

17. Robert C. Weaver, "Integration in Public and Private Housing," *The Annals of the American Academy of Political and Social Sciences*, 304 (March 1956), pp. 86–97.

pitals, movie houses, churches, business enterprises, recreational facilities, hotels, and restaurants, often represent a waste of scarce economic resources in the South. Northern segregation patterns, while more subtle, are equally costly.

To the white majority, patterns of segregation, discrimination, and prejudice have also been problematic. Moral ambivalence and feelings of guilt have resulted. The Swedish sociologist Gunnar Myrdal has probably done more to document this moral dilemma than most others.[18] Myrdal contended that the thoughtful white person has difficulty reconciling his religious, social, and moral ideals with his practices toward the Negro minority. It is difficult to preach the brotherhood of man while segregating some men by virtue of skin color. It is equally difficult to reconcile the American dream with the denial of voting rights and economic opportunity. Consequently, psychological stresses and strains are created for the majority group member as well as for the society as a whole.

The consequences of segregation and discrimination are greatest for the Negro minority. It is one thing for a nation to experience a somewhat tarnished international image or a majority group to reconcile a "moral dilemma" but quite another matter for a person to be the object of prejudice and discrimination. The Negro not only suffers in terms of his life-chances but also faces the problem of adjusting to the "inferior" status forced upon him. In terms of life-chances, Negro infant and maternal mortality rates are much higher than those of whites. Negro life expectancy is seven years shorter. The Negro child has only half as much chance of completing high school, a third as much chance of receiving a college degree, a third as much opportunity of becoming a professional man, twice as much chance of being unemployed, and only one seventh the possibility of earning $10,000 a year. Negro life-chances are comparably inferior in most other aspects of life (see Figs. 12-1 to 12-6). On every indicator of employment and earnings, Negroes lag behind (see Fig. 12-7).

Segregation, with its not too subtle use of the doctrine of racial inferiority as justification, has also presented the Negro with psychological adjustment problems. Negro reactions to second-class status and alleged inferiority have varied considerably. Some Negroes have reacted by utilizing stereotyped responses in their contacts with whites. Two such reactions are the abject "Uncle Tom," and the happy-go-lucky fool approach to whites. These approaches are calculated to ease interpersonal relations but the "deferential," or the "buffoon" Negro will act very differently in his relationships with members of his own race. This conscious shifting between the "pretend" and the "real" man

18. Gunnar Myrdal, *An American Dilemma: The Negro Problem and Modern Democracy* (Twentieth Anniversary Edition), New York: Harper and Row, 1962.

Fig. 12-1. White and Nonwhite Life Expectancy in the United States, 1920-61.

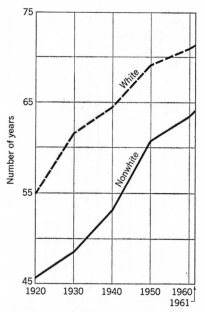

Source: *The New York Times*, June 16, 1963, p. E3.
Copyright by The New York Times. Reprinted by permission.

Fig. 12-2. Percentage of White and Nonwhite High School Graduates, by Age Group.

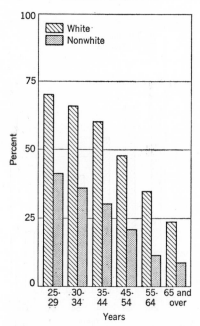

Source: *The New York Times*, June 16, 1963, p. E3.
Copyright by The New York Times. Reprinted by permission.

requires painful adjustments. Still, whites do not object to interaction with Negroes who deliberately confirm their stereotypes.

Other Negro reactions feature withdrawal, overcompensation, and the "oppression psychosis" mentality. Since some Negroes do not wish to expose themselves to interracial contacts which may be psychologically painful, there is the tendency to withdraw into the "black ghetto." This withdrawal approach has led some to extoll the virtues of a separate Negro economy or a "nation within a nation." This response is closely identified with the growth of Negro nationalism, which will be discussed later in this chapter. The difficulty with this withdrawal approach, on the psychological level, is that it makes it relatively easy for the Negro to develop equally uncomplimentary perceptions of whites while denying himself the opportunity of testing these stereotypes against reality. Negroes may also react by "overcompensating" for their alleged shortcomings. Many Negroes spend large sums of money and endless hours attempting to straighten and unkink their hair. Also, a major criterion used by many Negroes in the selection of a marital partner is lightness of skin color. Negro middle-class parents may drill their children by the hour on the middle-class white virtues of cleanliness, orderliness, and respect-

Fig. 12-3. Per cent of White and Nonwhite
College Graduates, by Age Group.

Fig. 12-4. Occupational Distribution of White
and Nonwhite Workers, June 1962.

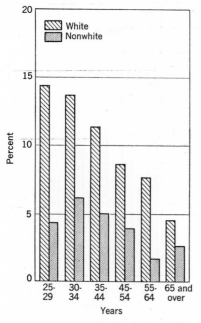

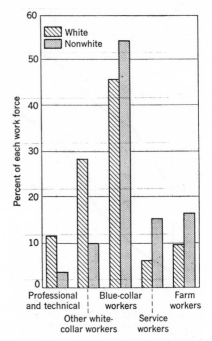

Source: *The New York Times,* June 16, 1963, p. E3.
Copyright by The New York Times. Reprinted by
permission.

Source: *The New York Times,* June 16, 1963.
Copyright by The New York Times. Reprinted by
permission.

ability. This "Black Puritanism" overemphasizes formality, for example, Mr.,
Mrs., Miss, clothing, etiquette. Among lower-class Negroes, overcompensation may take the form of driving a spectacular and expensive automobile or
wearing flashy clothes. Nothing is overlooked in proving that white stereotypes
are indeed without foundation.

Finally, and not without justification, members of racial minorities often
develop the "chip on the shoulder" mentality, in which all problems, even
the most personal ones, are attributed to segregation, prejudice, and discrimination. This attitude set is often referred to as "oppression psychosis." Minority group members may become so preoccupied with looking for evidence
of prejudice directed at them that they become unable to act constructively.
This preoccupation with oppression sometimes takes the form of racial
chauvinism. Thus, Negroes may scan newspapers with the sole aim of finding
news of members of their own race who have done something praiseworthy.[19]

All these reactions to prejudice — the stereotyped, or "Uncle Tom" and

19. For an excellent discussion of reactions to minority status, see Brewton Berry, *Race
    and Ethnic Relations,* Boston: Houghton Mifflin, 1951, chap. 16.

buffoon, responses, withdrawal, overcompensation, and the oppression psychosis — may be psychologically damaging. The target of prejudice may become so preoccupied with his second-class citizenship and the "outrageous" fortune of being nonwhite that he becomes incapable of accepting himself as a man and as a human being. These and other consequences have contributed to the emergence of a new normative conception — integration.

> *Emergent Normative Conception: Integration* — Racial minorities should have equal access to the opportunity structure of an industrial society.

Complete integration refers to a condition in which all individuals are accepted in the opportunity structure on the basis of merit rather than on the basis of their membership in a racial minority. Complete integration obviously does not describe the present status of the Negro in the United States. There are, however, degrees of integration, and a growing movement toward integration has been apparent in recent years. Subsequent sections will describe this process of *desegregation* and the movement toward the condition or state of *integration*.

Fig. 12-5. Per Cent of White and Nonwhite Unemployed Workers, 1954-63.

Fig. 12-6. Salaries and Wages of White and Nonwhite Workers, 1960.

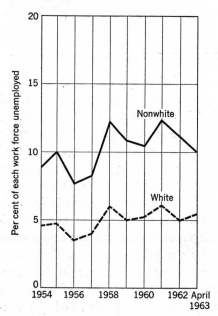

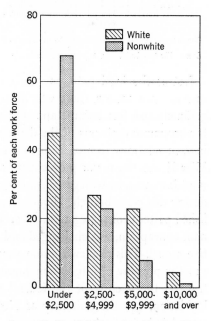

Source: *The New York Times,* June 16, 1963, p. E3. Copyright by The New York Times. Reprinted by permission.

Source: *The New York Times,* June 16, 1963, p. E3. Copyright by The New York Times. Reprinted by permission.

Fig. 12-7. Employment and Earning Patterns of Whites and Nonwhites.

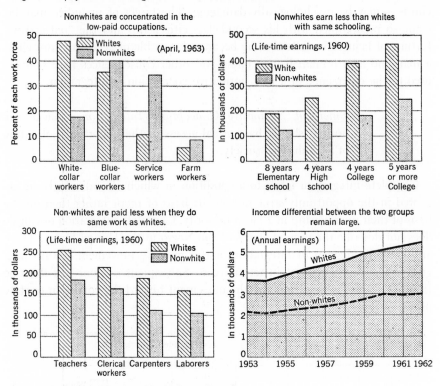

Charts are based on a study released by the Census Bureau.

Source: *The New York Times*, Aug. 4, 1963, section 4, p. 10E. Copyright by The New York Times. Reprinted by permission.

Just as the legal patterns which undergirded segregation emerged slowly in American society, those which implemented desegregation also developed gradually and first became apparent after World War II. During the 1930's, the economic problems of the depression were so overwhelming that changes in race relations seemed comparatively unimportant. In the 1940's, World War II was the major preoccupation. While World War II was fought, in most instances, by segregated American troops, the necessity for national unity during this crisis brought about a temporary relaxation in some of the established patterns of segregation. After World War II, segregation, as the dominant conception, was challenged and integration was offered as a new normative model. This challenge came about for a number of reasons. These were (1) the pressure of international opinion, (2) political changes in this country, (3) the re-entry of the federal government into the area of civil-rights legislation, (4) the militancy of Negro protest organizations, and (5) continued industrialization.

1. *The Pressure of International Opinion.* Since the end of World War II,

the United States has played an increasingly dominant role in world affairs. Because of this role as a world leader, U.S. domestic problems have become intertwined with international problems. With Communist bloc countries citing racial discrimination as an indication of the failure of the American system and with new nations of primarily colored populations having attained independence from former colonial powers, the treatment of racial minorities receives instantaneous publicity in every capital in the world. For example, after one of the "Freedom Rides," Radio Moscow reported:

> Scenes of bloodshed in Montgomery are . . . the worst example of savagery . . . taking place in a country which has the boldness to declare that its way of life is an example for other people. . . . The question of rights of the colored population, the running amuck of racist barbarians . . . who the authorities have no wish to repress and who in many cases are certainly encouraged by authorities, the brutal attack on people [in] anti-segregation demonstrations, have aroused indignation throughout the world. They are particularly enlightening for . . . those countries where people of the Negro races and other colored people live. It would be more than naïve to expect success for the maxim "I hate Negroes at home, but I love them in Africa."

Furthermore, American prestige is damaged when, because of discrimination, diplomats from African nations find it difficult to obtain suitable housing for their families, schooling for their children, and service for themselves in restaurants and in other public accommodations. Desegregation is thus encouraged as a way to increase national prestige abroad and to influence uncommitted and newly emerging nations.

2. *Political Changes.* The practice of segregation has lost support in this country through the decreasing importance of the South in political life and the increasing importance of the Negro vote. Several factors have combined to weaken the influence of the South politically. The "solidarity" of the South as a voting unit has decreased. Many states or sections of states who formerly thought of themselves as "southern" have now changed in identification. Texas has become a western state. The southern parts of Ohio, Indiana, and Illinois, as well as Kentucky and Missouri, are considered midwestern states or at least "border" states. These developments have come about gradually, as the country as a whole has moved away from a regional and toward a national outlook. The "core" South itself has undergone much change in economic and social organization. One of the primary reasons for all these changes has been industrialization, with its tendency to dislocate provincialism and bring an area into contact with other parts of the country. Another reason has been the tremendous advances in transportation and communications. In any case the South is no longer as solid or as significant a political bloc as it used to be. And neither major political party can accede to southern demands with-

out sustaining a considerable voting loss outside the South. The persistance of the one-party system in the South does, however, produce a disproportionate amount of influence in Congress through the control of important Congressional committee chairmanships by southern Democrats who have been unchallenged in elections for years.

In addition, Negro migration to northern cities has created the conditions for electing Negro Congressmen. This is a result of residential concentration, created by housing discrimination in the North. These Negro Congressmen, if they are to represent their districts, must become spokesmen for desegregation. Northern migration of Negroes also has made northern urban politicians sensitive to the voting power of racial minorities. While being a segregationist is a political asset in many sections of the South, it is a political liability in the North. Outside of the "shrinking" South, politicians with state-wide or national political ambitions cannot ignore the Negro vote; even in the South, the gradual demise of voting restrictions will create similar sensitivities in the future.

3. *The Re-entry of the Federal Government into the Area of Civil Rights Legislation.* In recent years, judicial and executive officials and agencies of the federal government have taken an active role in the desegregation process. This re-entry has been called the "Second Reconstruction" since it has involved judicial decisions, Congressional legislation, and administrative action.

Certainly the most widely known of these actions are the Supreme Court decisions of May 17, 1954, and May 31, 1955. In the first of these decisions, the "separate but equal" doctrine sanctioned by the famous *Plessy* v. *Ferguson* case in 1896 was rejected. The 1954 decision argued that segregated public schools could not provide equal educational opportunity even if equalities in buildings, curricula, teacher salaries, and other tangible factors existed. The fact of segregation made schools unequal and thus, the Court ruled that segregated public schools were unconstitutional. The decision of May 31, 1955, ordered the desegregation of public schools to be carried out "with all deliberate speed" and in "good faith." Segregationists had viewed the earlier *Plessy* case as a vindication of their views, and the 1954 decision undercut this legal justification for segregation.

Another effort of the national government in behalf of desegregation was the Civil Rights Act of 1957. This Congressional act authorized the U.S. Attorney General to seek court orders to restrain local officials from denying qualified persons the right to register and vote. It also established a Civil Rights Commission, which seeks the facts about violations of civil rights and recommends appropriate legislation. In 1960, Congress enacted additional legislation to strengthen the 1957 law. Although this legislation precipitated a filibuster, it was a significant departure since civil rights legislation of this magnitude had not been passed by Congress since Reconstruction days.

These legislative acts and court decisions plus hundreds of administrative measures removed any doubt as to the stand of the federal government concerning the Negroes' status in American society. Federal troops have been pressed into service over incidents growing out of school desegregation. The U.S. Attorney General has ordered federal marshals into a southern city to keep peace while "Freedom Riders" protested segregation of facilities at a bus station. Companies with federal contracts have been ordered to eliminate racial discrimination in their employment practices.

This kind of positive action taken by the federal government has changed the context of race relations in the United States. Prior to the Supreme Court decisions, much of the struggle to reduce discrimination and segregation was viewed simply as an inevitable problem of a minority racial group struggling against the dominant racial group. With federal support behind the desegregation movement, the issue has become more than this; it is now a movement in which the prestige and authority of the federal government is involved. No longer a contest between parts of a society, the contest now involves compliance or noncompliance with the law.

The role of the federal government in effecting desegregation has been opposed by segregationists on many grounds. Some objections have, of course, been based on different conceptions of the scope of federal power, the so-called "states' rights" argument. Other persons object on the grounds that legislation will not change the attitudes of those who uphold segregation as "natural." This latter objection overlooks the fact that legislation in various southern states initially created segregation patterns in the South. In addition, experience has shown that the *behavior* of people can be changed without necessarily changing their *attitudes*. While many attempts to change race relations are directed toward reducing *prejudice*, federal action has attempted to eliminate legal *discrimination*. This action by the government is called the administrative approach.[20] It operates on the principle that when rights are well established by law, most people will accept the enforcement of these laws by legitimate authorities. The current strategy is to get legal rights incorporated into public policy by means of ordinances, regulations, and policies. After these policies are enacted, then, responsible officials are compelled to enforce them. When desegregation is enacted and is firmly enforced people tend to concede the legitimacy of the policy although they may not abandon their prejudice. Much of the impetus for utilizing the administrative approach has come from Negro protest organizations. Their role in desegregation will now be examined.

20. Cf. Arnold M. Rose, "Sociological Factors in the Effectiveness of Projected Legislative Remedies," *Journal of Legal Education*, 11 (1959), pp. 470–81. For a series of generalizations describing the effectiveness of the administrative approach affecting school desegregation, see James W. Vander Zanden, "Turmoil in the South," *Journal of Negro Education* (Fall 1960), pp. 445–52.

4. *Negro Protest Organizations.* The use of political pressure by organized groups is a common means of seeking redress of grievances in a complex society. Racial minorities, like other groups, have organized for this purpose. The National Association for the Advancement of Colored People (NAACP) was founded in 1909. Composed of both Negroes and whites, the NAACP claimed over 400,000 members in 1963. This organization accepted as its chief responsibility, the bringing about of the equal application of the law to Negroes and the conformance of all laws to the Constitution. The goal of the NAACP has been to provide a degree of legal security for the Negro through courts of law. The NAACP has had a number of successes in cases tried before the Supreme Court. It was instrumental in outlawing "grandfather" clauses (1915), "white" primaries (1944, 1947), and school desegregation (1954, 1955).

A second organization, founded in 1911, is the National Urban League, first established in northern cities. Chapters of the Urban League attempt to secure economic opportunities, decent jobs, equal pay, and adequate housing for Negroes in their local communities. The organization became increasingly important with larger Negro migrations to the North. The Urban League has not been particularly militant and operates largely by persuasion rather than by demonstration.

In recent years, dissatisfaction with the activities of these organizations in speeding desegregation has produced new leaders, new organizations, and new techniques of protest. These newer organizations have utilized "nonviolent" or passive resistance and have gained public attention because of their dramatic "Freedom Rides," "sit-ins," and other mass protest activities. Negro ministers and professionals have acted as leaders; much of the active support has come from students including some white students. The adult leaders have provided legal and financial assistance and have joined in the demonstrations. The goal of these demonstrations is to draw state and national attention to the persistence of segregation practices in local communities.

A dramatic example of the emergence of new leadership occurred in Montgomery, Alabama, in December 1955, when a Negro woman refused to give her seat on a bus to a white passenger as ordered by the bus driver. The bus driver, acting within Alabama law, had her booked on a charge of violating the segregation laws. This event touched off an effective boycott of city buses by Negroes. Despite harassment by police, Negroes did not retaliate with violence and this passive resistance ultimately proved to be an effective technique in challenging segregation. The leader of the boycott, the Rev. Martin Luther King, Jr., became one of the most important Negro leaders of the century. King and the organization he heads, the Southern Christian Leadership Conference, have continued to concentrate on nonviolent action to eliminate segregation of public facilities in specific communities. For example, in 1963, in Birmingham, under King's leadership, Negroes picketed, boycotted, prayed, demonstrated, and registered to vote, all in a short time, in an effort to win equal access to public facilities and equal job opportunities.

These nonviolent methods have been utilized by other organizations. The Congress of Racial Equality (CORE) — organized in New York in 1942 — gained prominence with Freedom Rides in 1961, and continues to draw national attention to local segregation practices. The Student Non-violent Coordinating Committee (SNCC or "Snick") was born in 1960 as an after-math of the Greensboro, N.C., "sit-in" campaigns. This group sends field workers into various areas to enlist local Negro support to challenge segre-gation. The militancy of these organizations has effected the desegregation of many facilities and forced the older organizations to adopt similar tactics. For example, the NAACP executive secretary was arrested for picketing in Jackson, Mississippi, in 1963. Negro leadership, in general, has been pushed to adopt more aggressive (although nonviolent) tactics.[21] A person active in desegregation activities said, "We must tell our leaders that, if you don't want to do it, get out of the way," or as the executive director of the Urban League said, "Hurry up, there go our followers." The growing feeling among the Negro rank and file seems to be that one hundred years is too long to wait for reconstruction.

5. *Continuing Industrialization.* Still another development contributing to the decline of segregation is the continued growth of industrialization. The U.S. is now a heavily industrialized society. With this has come a series of deep-rooted modifications in race relations. Industrialization has fostered the dispersion and mobility of the American people, shifts in the economic bases of many sections of the country, and the breakdown of regional cul-tures. These facts of social change have tended to fracture the historically established patterns of segregation.

Nowhere has this influence of industrialization on the nature of Negro-white relationships been as evident as it is in the South.[22] Aristocratic planta-tion owners have been replaced by prosperous white conservatives who live in suburban communities, manage their businesses and industrial plants in the cities, and often vote the Republican ticket. Quietly working behind the scenes with local and state government officials, they strive to control the violent

21. For a perceptive discussion of Negro leadership in Southern communities see Daniel C. Thompson, *The Negro Leadership Class,* Englewood Cliffs, N.J.: Prentice-Hall, 1962, and M. Elaine Burgess, *Negro Leadership in a Southern City,* Chapel Hill: Uni-versity of North Carolina Press, 1962.

22. For a discussion of the changing South, see James W. Vander Zanden: "Desegrega-tion and Social Strains in the South," *Journal of Social Issues,* 15, (1959), pp. 53–60; and "Desegregation: the Future?" *The South Atlantic Quarterly,* 60 (Spring 1961), pp. 205–16. See also: E. William Noland, "Industry Comes of Age in the South," *Social Forces,* 32 (October 1953), pp. 28–35; and C. Arnold Anderson and Mary Jean Bowman, "The Vanishing Servant and the Contemporary Status System of the American South," *American Journal of Sociology,* 59 (November 1953), pp. 215–30.

racists and troublemakers. These men, ambitious for their private enterprises to prosper, know that racial violence brings bad publicity which hinders new business and industrial development. Their advice to the militant segregationists is that law and order must be preserved at all costs.

The status system and the power structure are being modified at the same time. Northern capital is moving into the South. Industrial and business interests are challenging the declining large-scale farm owners' influence, while the Negro, with his increased earnings from new industry and greater voting strength through federal government backing, is demanding a stronger voice in government and politics.

The national state of flux that is affecting the South today is nicely stated by the folk saying: "cotton is going West, cattle are coming East, Negroes are going North, Yankees are coming South, money is coming in." [23] Despite nativistic attempts to return to the patterns of the "Old South," traditional beliefs and customs cannot endure without institutional and economic underpinnings. The New South — with its urbanization, industrial developments, and increasing integration of the economy with the rest of the nation — is changing its image of itself by changing the institutions which support it. In defending white supremacy and the old order, segregationists attempt "to defend a memory, not a living institution." [24]

THE PROCESS OF DESEGREGATION

In the preceding section, an attempt was made to sketch briefly the factors underlying changing race relations. Since World War II the desegregation process in the United States has consistently gained momentum. Widespread change in Negro-white relations is now under way in almost every aspect of American life.

1. *Voting Rights.* One of the most significant strides the Negro has made since World War II is the gain in political power. Northern Negro voters — some three million — have become an important factor in both national and municipal elections in the larger northern cities.[25] The large-scale migration of Negroes has meant that, in at least eight industrial states, Negro voters now hold strategic "balance of power" positions. Both political parties have recognized this fact and have sought Negro votes, even at the risk of alienating the segregation-minded white voters of the South. Equally important is the return of the Negro to the polls in the South. While this return has not been total, most estimates place the number at more than a million voters, and

23. Quoted in Max Lerner, op. cit. p. 194.
24. Arnold Rose, *The Negro in America*, Boston: Beacon Press, 1948, p. xxii.
25. James Q. Wilson, "How the Northern Negro Uses His Vote," *Reporter* (March 31, 1960), pp. 20–22.

they are most significant in southern cities and towns. These developments give strong political impetus to the desegregation process.

Despite such gains, the U.S. Commission on Civil Rights in 1961 filed suits in which 17 Southern counties were charged with voting discrimination. The Commission reported that large numbers of Negroes in 100 counties in eight southern states were still not permitted to vote.[26] The chairman of the Commission has stated that in 16 counties in which one-third or more of the population is Negro, not a single Negro has been permitted to register to vote. The remainder of the counties have permitted token voting by non-whites.[27] Nevertheless, there were six times as many registered Negro voters in the South in 1962 as in 1944.[28]

The increase in votes is related to the increase in Negroes who hold public office. At state and local levels Negroes are occasionally elected or appointed to various civic and political offices and even in a dozen or more of the large cities in the South, they have been appointed or elected to school boards and city councils. Reflecting the changing times, southern politicians have become less inclined to appeal to race prejudice in their campaigns. Of course, cases still come before the federal Civil Rights Commission involving Negroes who have lost their jobs, have been refused credit at local banks, and have had insurance policies cancelled as the result of attempting to register to vote.[29]

2. *Education.* No phase of the desegregation process has received more publicity than recent changes that have occurred in the American educational system. In an industrial society, education becomes a matter of great importance since those denied educational opportunities suffer distinct disadvantages even though other influences may be favorable.

The long-term trend has been in the direction of increased educational opportunity for all groups in American society, and desegregation represents the most recent feature of this trend. At the time of the 1954 Supreme Court decision, elementary and secondary schools of 17 states plus the District of Columbia were completely segregated. Early in 1963 more than 30 per cent of the segregated school districts (972 of 3058) had been desegregated. On the university and graduate level, the process of desegregation began before the Supreme Court rulings, and has proceeded further than on the primary and secondary levels. Although the proportion is still small, especially in the Deep South, recent evidence suggests there are now approximately 7000

26. *Encyclopedia Britannica Yearbook*, 1962, p. 164.
27. John A. Hannah, Alson Lectureship, Anti-Defamation League, New York City, December 6, 1959. Mimeographed copy, p. 4.
28. J. Milton Yinger, "Desegregation in American Society: The Record of a Generation of Change," *Sociology and Social Research*, 47 (July 1963), p. 438.
29. *Time* (September 15, 1961), p. 24.

Negro students enrolled in institutions of higher education that a few years ago were completely segregated.[30] And there are also white students enrolled in fifteen of the fifty colleges that were formerly limited to Negro students. The steps taken to implement desegregation of schools to date, however, have been slowed by involved litigations, token compliance with court orders, and in some instances, open violence. If one views the educational picture in terms of the number of persons involved, it is obvious that major desegregation of the schools in the South has not yet occurred. But the more significant fact is that an essentially irreversible process has been set into motion.

The problem of school desegregation in the North has also been extremely difficult to resolve. Outside of the South and the "border" states, school segregation has been primarily a function of residential segregation and the occasional gerrymandering of school districts. Most elementary and junior high schools in the major cities outside the South educate students of only one race. The percent of racially mixed schools in 1963 varied from 13 per cent in Minneapolis, where Negroes constitute 4 per cent of all students, to 65 per cent in New York City, where Negroes comprise 27 per cent of the students in public schools (see Table 12-5).

TABLE 12-5

Integration patterns in public schools, grades 1–9, in selected northern cities, 1963

City	Per cent Negro enrollment in all schools	Number of schools	Per cent integrated schools *
Baltimore	60	144	23
Chicago	45	442	15
Cincinnati	30	90	37
Detroit	53	223	32
Los Angeles	8	483	22
Minneapolis	4	104	13
New York	27	723	65
Philadelphia	54	246	39
Pittsburgh	39	105	46
San Francisco	25	117	51
Washington, D.C.	85	153	22

* Integrated schools are defined as those containing over 5 per cent and less than 90 per cent of enrollment of any racial group.

Recent pressure from Negroes has led school boards in these larger cities to search for new methods of desegregating the schools. Such methods include: open enrollments, so that any student may attend any school in the city; rezoning, to draw students from both white and Negro sections to a

30. J. Milton Yinger, op. cit.

given school; and educational parks, which students from all neighborhoods and all educational levels through high school would attend.

3. *Employment and Economic Gains.* As his political influence and his educational opportunity have increased, the Negro's economic and occupational status has improved. Many Negroes who served in World War II and the Korean War or who worked in defense industries learned new skills and gained occupational experience that served them well. Whereas only 17 per cent of the Negro males were in semi-skilled and skilled occupations in 1940, the number had risen to 33 per cent by 1962.[31] This rise was due, in part, to the President's Fair Employment Practices Commission (FEPC) during World War II, which investigated complaints about discriminatory practices in defense industries. The attempt to make this commission permanent failed to pass Congress in 1947. By 1963, however, twenty states and over forty cities had passed enforceable fair employment practice laws. Approximately one-half of the Negro population resides in cities and states covered by these laws. The labor unions before 1940 had color bars, but by early 1960, all but two of the twenty-one international unions in the AFL-CIO had officially dropped them.[32] The CIO had a National Committee To Abolish Racial Discrimination and a full-time director to run it.

Desegregation has been occurring rapidly for some years in the area of professional sports and athletics. Perhaps the most publicized step in the desegregation of sports occurred in 1946, when Branch Rickey, general manager of the Brooklyn Dodgers, decided to add Jackie Robinson to the team. Negro major league professional baseball and football players, unheard of in the prewar days, now play a prominent role. In the entertainment field the Metropolitan Opera Company has opened its stage door to Negroes. In popular entertainment, the number and prominence of Negro artists have greatly increased in recent years.

Perhaps the rising status of Negroes can best be symbolized by the number named to high government posts. In recent years Negroes have been appointed to the post of administrator of the Housing and Home Finance Agency, and to two federal judgeships. In 1962, the ambassadors to Norway and Finland, the Assistant Secretary of Labor for International Affairs, the Assistant Presidential Press Secretary, the Deputy Assistant Secretary of State for Public Affairs, and a U.S. district attorney were Negroes.[33]

Throughout the armed forces there has been an increase in equal-status con-

31. U.S. Department of Labor, "The Economic Situation of Negroes in the United States," Bulletin S-3, Revised, 1962.
32. Theodore Kheel, "The Gains of Democratic Employment," *New York Times,* Section 10, January 17, 1960, p. 7.
33. For examples of sociological analysis of Negro employment see: Victor Perlo, "Trends in the Economic Status of the Negro People." *Science and Society,* 16 (1952), pp. 115-50.

tact across race lines. With few exceptions, all branches of the military segregated non-white troops before and during World War II. This policy was
discontinued in 1950 when President Truman ordered immediate integration
of all branches of the service after receiving the report of his Committee on
Equality of Treatment and Opportunity. And in 1954 the *New York Times*
wrote that racial integration in the armed forces is "one of the biggest stories
of the twentieth century."

While prejudice has hindered the employment of Negroes in all but menial
jobs in the South, this region has also made changes. In the industries such as
textiles and furniture manufacturing, Negroes remain largely excluded, but
in meat packing and oil refining, for example, they have made substantial
gains. Perhaps a more significant indication of the rise of the Negro's economic
status is suggested by the wholesale movement away from the generally impoverished farms. Farmers and farm workers in the South, in 1940, constituted
50 per cent of employed male Negroes. Ten years later this dropped to 34
per cent and this decline has continued.[34] Considering the total Negro population in the United States, only one out of every eight now is a farmer.
The movement away from farming has resulted in both occupational and geographical mobility, and has carried Negroes to the cities in and out of the
South. L. T. Lawley wrote in 1956: "The cash income of Negroes, over the
last twenty years, has soared about 350 per cent. Their present income of
$15.25 billion represents a sum almost as great as the value of all goods ex-
ported annually by the U.S." [35] By 1963, Negro income exceeded $20 billion
— an increase of $5 billion in the seven years. While the economic gap has
not been closed — Negro median family income is still only three-fifths that
of whites — the Negro is moving upward in the occupational hierarchy, joining the unions, and enjoying a higher income. This change again is in the
direction of equality of opportunity.

4. *Housing*. Desegregation of housing has occurred more slowly than almost any other phase of desegregation. The Commission on Race and Housing has estimated that one-sixth of the American population is restricted to
some degree in their choice of residence. In many ways, residential segregation is a more complicated issue in the North than in the South. Yinger
points out that, "Many Yankees who criticize the South for its segregated
schools defend housing arrangements that have many of the same consequences for race relations and for personality development that school segregation has." [36] Most contractors and developers are interested in building
for white families only, and a very small number are concerned with con-

34. George Simpson and J. M. Yinger, *Racial and Cultural Minorities*, New York: Harper,
      1958, p. 396.
35. L. T. Lawley, "The Negro's New Economic Life," *Fortune* (September 1956), pp.
      128–9.
36. J. Milton Yinger, op. cit. p. 435.

structing integrated projects. Urban redevelopment often increases segregation, since deteriorated housing is likely to be replaced by units too expensive for minority-group families.

Although segregated housing is still the typical pattern, an increasing amount of evidence suggests changes in the direction of desegregation. The Federal Housing Authority and other governmental agencies openly encourage the development of integrated housing projects, and in 1963 President Kennedy, in an administrative order, declared that all new governmentally assisted housing must be rented or sold without regard to race, religion, or national origin. In addition, some state and local laws are now promoting housing integration. Also, some of the labor unions, especially those with interracial membership, have entered the mortgage market, and a large number of churches have circulated open-occupancy covenants. Although the total impact of these developments is difficult to access, it appears likely that in the future housing desegregation will proceed at a more rapid pace.

5. *Public Accommodations.* Since the war years there has also been extensive desegregation in public accommodations. Before the war almost complete segregation in restaurants and hotels was the rule. Even though there were civil rights statutes in most Northern states designed to protect minority group members against discrimination in access to public accommodations, these codes were frequently violated without penalty.

This situation has changed considerably, especially within the past few years. The chief reasons are to be found in the growing economic power and increased political participation of minority group members which has made it more "costly" to reject them. Today all the larger restaurants, hotels, and theaters are desegregated in the major Northern and Western cities. This is less true for the smaller communities in the North and for most areas of the South, where opposition is still strong, but significant changes have nevertheless occurred. The Freedom Riders, the "sit-in" movement, and court decisions upholding civil rights legislation have also opened other public facilities to members of all racial groups.

REACTIONS TO DESEGREGATION

Most Americans — North and South — have acted as spectators to this accelerating desegregation process. Whether welcoming or regretting the trend, they have accepted the mandates of the federal courts and administrative agencies to further desegregation. The great mass of people who passively accept the process are probably more committed to law and order than they are to the principle of integration. Regardless of motivation, this middle range has functioned, by their very passivity, as a brake on racial violence and strife.

The push toward integration is, of course, speeded along by the newer militant Negro protest organizations. This militancy also has its causes. Militancy requires leaders who have been able to survive the degradation and deprivations of segregation. That such leaders have appeared in significant numbers in the 1960's is a tribute to the older generation of white and Negro leaders who, working through the Urban League, the NAACP, Negro and white churches, and other agencies, brought about the reforms that have made this leadership possible. The new agents of change have provided and will continue to provide a rallying point for resolving this "peculiar" American dilemma.

There are still important pockets of resistance to desegregation — those who hope to slow, stop, or reverse the trend. There is great similarity between these forms of resistance. Both the white Ku Klux Klan and the Black Muslims are committed to the same aim — the absolute segregation of the races. Both are secret societies, indulging in mystical, quasi-religious activities. Both have a fondness for parades and rallies in their uniforms and have faith in their ability to intimidate their enemies. Both preach racial hatred and covertly encourage violence.

WHITE RACISM

Racism as an ideology has many historical roots. The basic ideas have appeared at different times in different configurations — to justify slavery and other forms of exclusion as well as segregation. It is not surprising, then, that the desegregation process revived notions of white supremacy and Negro inferiority as a justification for maintaining segregation as a normative conception.

In general, the white racist justifies segregation as being "natural" because it is "instinctive" in human nature for races to live separately. Since it is "natural," racists claim not to be bigoted when defending segregation. Since it is "natural," racial minorities can thrive only under such conditions, and to change them would hinder maximum development.

To the racist, segregation is also justified by the "fact" that Negroes are different kinds of human beings. Some argue that the "facts" point to biological inferiority and try to document this thesis. For example, the Governor of Alabama commissioned a report on the biology of the race problem.[37] This report and other such "scientific" publications usually find some physiological difference between whites and Negroes and then assume that this observable difference is an explanation for difference in levels of culture, in intelligence, in rates of crime, and in evolutionary development. These reports "conclude" that biological differences automatically call for segregation. Other racists, with a greater social science orientation, do not attempt to prove biological inferiority but concentrate on proving cultural inferiority. They are

37. W. C. George, The Biology of the Race Problem (Report prepared by commission of the Governor of Alabama), New York: National Putnam Letters Committee, 1962.

certain that Negroes are culturally different and that this is sufficient to justify segregation. Their thesis is that since Negroes show higher indices of violence, crime, and illegitimacy, they are unable to live in an integrated world without contaminating it.

All these themes culminate in the traditional question, "Would you want your daughter to marry a Negro?" It is assumed by the racist that Negroes, particularly males (hence the form of the question), wish to intermarry with whites and that, if intermarriage occurred on a large scale, the great differences between the racial groups would produce what is called "mongrelization." The taboos against intermarriage are reinforced by an elaborate mythology of Negro sexual behavior. The long-range aim of preventing intermarriage justifies avoiding any type of equal-status contacts between racial groups.

The system of segregation is further defended by the suggestion that, under its undisturbed operation, Negroes are contented and race relations are harmonious. Under such a system, segregationists claim that "some of their best friends" are Negroes. Since this idyllic image of contentment is hard to reconcile with racial demonstrations, it is assumed that any "trouble" is the work of outsiders, Communists, and "uppity niggers." [38]

While elements of this racist ideology are accepted by many, both in the South and the North, two groups have been especially identified with it: The Ku Klux Klan and the White Citizens' Councils. The Ku Klux Klan, organized in the Reconstruction period and revived during the 1910's and 1920's, experienced another revival after the Supreme Court decisions on school desegregation. This revival was followed by an outbreak of bombings, the burning of fiery crosses, torchlight rallies, whippings, beatings, and castrations. The strength of the organization was concentrated in the urban centers of the southeastern Piedmont. Vander Zanden analyzed the occupations of 153 active Klansmen during this revival.[39] The members seemed to be drawn from (1) skilled workers, e.g. mechanics and carpenters, (2) marginal small businessmen, e.g. small contractors, proprietors of small grocery stores and service stations, (3) marginal white-collar and blue-collar workers, e.g. grocery store clerks and service station attendants, and (4) transportation workers (e.g. truck drivers) and unskilled workers in textile, coal, and construction industries. He suggested that most of these occupations were marginal — between the middle and working classes. Klansmen's foothold in the middle class was so insecure and ambiguous that they felt disgruntled, discontented, and frustrated. They could enhance their status in a number of ways. One way was to continue to keep the Negro in his "place." They also created a world with its own elaborate symbols and titles of status — the

38. For an illustration of contemporary racism see Carleton Putnam, *Race and Reason*, Washington, D.C.: Public Affairs Press, 1960.
39. James W. Vander Zanden, "The Klan Revival," *American Journal of Sociology*, 36 (March 1960), pp. 456–63.

Imperial Wizard, Grand Dragon, and Exalted Cyclops. Since they considered themselves to be the perpetuators of 100 per cent Americanism, they blamed their tenuous economic and social status not upon themselves, but upon the Communists, the Jews, the Catholics, foreigners, and, of course, Negroes. While the Klan still persists in specific areas, its membership during the late 1950's was probably not over 10,000 and, while its activities produced fear, its influence was largely dissipated by its irrationality.

The kind of activities that the Klan sponsored did not attract the "better" racists. Originating in Mississippi, a new organization — the White Citizens' Council — emerged which emphasized "racial integrity" and "states' rights." The strength of these local Citizens' Council organizations, estimated to be over 250,000, has been concentrated in the heavily Negro-populated Black Belt counties of the Deep South. The Citizens' Councils claim their leadership is drawn from the "best" and "most prominent, well-educated businessmen" in the community. The Councils forswear violence, although this pledge has been forgotten in several instances. Local chapters engage in a wide variety of activities — supporting segregated Negro colleges, checking voter registration lists to disqualify Negroes, attempting to drop the Urban League from support by local community chests, investigating textbooks for "subversion," and "exposing" the NAACP and other integrationist groups as Communist fronts.

The major activity of the White Citizens' Councils has been to intimidate by economic pressure those who support desegregation. One speaker at an organizing rally in Alabama explained the methods they use in the following way: "The white population of this county controls the money, and this is an advantage that the council will use in a fight to legally maintain complete segregation of the races. We intend to make it difficult, if not impossible, for any Negro who advocates desegregation to find and hold a job, get credit or renew a mortgage." [40]

Such tactics were effectively used when the NAACP, after the Supreme Court decision, encouraged Negroes in 170 southern communities to sign petitions demanding immediate school desegregation. Those who signed the petition were harassed by the White Citizens' Councils and other groups.

BLACK NATIONALISM

Whereas white racism attempts to justify subordinate status for the Negro, black nationalism has arisen out of the conviction that whites will never grant the Negro equality. This fatalism has sporadically spawned movements which seek to disengage from the struggle for equality. In retaliation for years of

40. *Montgomery Advertiser*, December 1, 1954.

subjugation, these movements preach the inferiority of whites and of Western culture, identification with "Asiatic" (non-Western) cultures, and the development of a new image of the Negro — the nonsubservient, self-respecting black man.

Black nationalist movements are not new in this country. As early as 1913 a North Carolina Negro established a "Moorish Science Temple" in Newark, New Jersey, which later expanded to include temples in many cities and at its peak claimed some 20,000 adherents. "Noble Drew Ali, the Prophet," as the originator liked to be called, preached a very simple message. Negro salvation could only occur when black men came to know and take pride in their cultural origins. Negroes should call themselves "Moors" or "Asiatics," hold whites in contempt, and reject Christianity. Some of the "Asiatics" believed in the imminent destruction of all whites via supernatural intervention. The movement was short-lived. The "Asiatics" splintered into small segments after the death of the Prophet and ceased to exist as a mass movement, although isolated groups still function.

Another major movement was led by a Jamaican — Marcus Garvey. The Garvey movement, which began during World War I, was fueled by the resentment of Negroes who had helped "make the world safe for democracy" and returned home to find that nothing much had changed in the way of discrimination and segregation. As one consequence of this resentment, the year 1919 became one of the bloodiest in American race relations. There were some twenty-five race riots in the U.S. including one which lasted for three days in Washington, D.C., and another for thirteen days in Chicago. In the Chicago race riot, 38 people died and over 500 were injured. In that year, too, 75 Negroes were lynched. A few of the victims were publicly burned.

Negroes who despaired of improvement in their status were receptive to the vague doctrines and anti-white militancy of the Garvey movement. Garvey believed that Negroes must establish their own nation and make it strong and vital so as to be a significant world force. The general goal was to make black Africa independent of colonial rule and to settle American Negroes there. This objective brought the Garvey movement into direct conflict with the major colonial powers in Africa, notably England and France, and later helped bring about the collapse of Garveyism. Ironically, the resettlement of Negroes in Africa was strongly supported by white racist groups such as the Klan. Racial problems, like politics, sometimes make strange bedfellows.

To facilitate the ultimate goal of resettlement in Africa, Garvey established the Universal Negro Improvement Association, which at its peak claimed two million members in many world branches. The UNIA published a newspaper, ran a steamship line, and owned and operated scores of business establishments. It set up Negro organizations such as the Black Cross Nurses, Universal African Legion, the Black Eagle Flying Corps, and a "black" church called the African Orthodox Church.

Middle-class and highly educated Negroes were unanimously opposed to the objectives, immediate and long range, of the UNIA as well as to its methods — as were the NAACP and the Urban League. Eight prominent Negroes publicly petitioned the Attorney General to "use his full influence to completely disband and extirpate the vicious movement . . ." The government obliged and prosecuted Marcus Garvey for using the mails to defraud. His conviction, two-year imprisonment (1925–27), and subsequent deportation signaled the end of the movement as an effective force.

In 1930, Wallace D. Fard came to Detroit and established a cult which has since grown into the most powerful of all black nationalist movements — the Black Muslims. Combining some of the pseudo-religious mystique of the Moorish movement with the black nation concept and businesslike approach of the Garveyites, the Black Muslims, under the leadership of Fard's successor, have enlisted over 100,000 members.[41] As in all previous black nationalist groups, the bulk of the membership is drawn from the lowest socio-economic levels in the Negro community and is almost devoid of middle- and upper-class Negro support.

Muhammad, the leader, and his spokesmen preach a very powerful message. The "so-called Negro" can never attain the status of a real man in white society. Black men, which is their preferred term, must unite and develop a racial consciousness. Black men must set up their own nation, primarily by taking over the states that made up the Confederacy. There must be absolute separation of the races in all respects — separate governmental, economic, religious, and educational institutions.

The Muslims contend that since whites are devils, their abuse of black men is not likely to stop now. "White" religion, that is, Christianity, functions to justify the enslavement of black men. Muslims therefore subscribe to Islam and believe that the coming of Allah will put an end to the white race since, whites are innately "murderers and liars" and enemies of righteousness.

In practice, Muslims are urged to pray five times daily, facing east to Mecca; to be ritually clean and abstain from certain foods — pork and cornbread — in order to maintain their purity; to forsake alcohol and tobacco; and adhere to the strictest sexual codes. At least twice weekly temple attendance is required, and male members must "fish for the dead," that is, carry their message to the nonconverted. Temples have mushroomed North and South in areas of Negro concentration. Inside these temples, ceremony is highly valued. Negro recruits are welcomed by dark-suited "brothers," and their names and

41. C. Eric Lincoln, *Black Muslims in America*, Boston: Beacon Press, 1961.

addresses recorded by Muslim "sisters." A paramilitary group serves as honor guard.

While the appeal may be pseudo-religious and mystical, and the unifying theme racial hatred, Black Muslim leadership is also oriented to practical realities. At least two active "parochial" elementary schools (Universities of Islam) are in operation. Various business enterprises are run by and for Muslims and these net substantial profits for the "cause." The Muslim newspaper carries the message to Negroes in all sections of the country. The decision of Muslim leaders to present their views via the mass media — most notably television — has given the "cause" the appearance of a genuine mass movement rather than a mere cult.

Mass movements such as those just described arise and retain their appeal when they speak to and for the perceived basic needs or grievances of people. They lose their meaning when the grievances disappear or when other solutions are more likely to achieve the same goals. As with other such mass movements, the Black Muslims will probably exert less influence in the Negro community as the desegregation process brings improved status to the Negro minority. To the extent that the Negro protest movement succeeds, the violent racist doctrine of the Muslims will probably lose much of its appeal. It may well be that the decline has already begun.

THE FUTURE OF RACIAL DISSENSUS

The treatment of racial minorities in America has illustrated this country's inability to resolve the moral dilemma posed by national commitment to the principle of equality and actual practice of discrimination. While the emergent normative conception is slowly being achieved through the process of desegregation, the end result will probably not take the form that Negro leadership now visualizes. Neither will the forces of resistance stop what is presently visible as a trend toward a new consensus. Rapid industrialization, the gradual integration of the southern economy with that of the nation, new Negro political power, and the increasingly active role of the federal government have set in motion forces that cannot be stopped. Neither the activities of racist groups, the glorification of the Civil War, the glamorization of the values of the "old" South, nor "token" integration will satisfy the Negro and be sufficient to stop desegregation.

While some speak of the move toward integration as a revolution, its goal is opposite to that of revolutions in other parts of the world. Africa, for example, where nonwhites seek to drive out the white man and to shape their destiny on their own terms. America's Negroes, with the exception of the Muslims, do not seek such radical change. They demand only full admission to a white society that has heretofore been closed and that has imposed its standards on them while denying them full access to its benefits. Negroes have accepted the importance of the common values of American life and wish to participate fully in the middle-class society that expresses them.

History and the peculiarities of the political system provide explanations and even excuses for the treatment in the United States of racial minorities. The tragic history of the Negro, his poverty and oppression from slavery through segregation have left a mark which will be difficult to erase. Even with legal rights guaranteed, these past deprivations will have to be recognized and compensated for before many Negroes are able to take advantage of their rights. Second-class citizenship produces second-class citizens. For example, in the past it was assumed that Negroes needed little education (because they were to work in menial jobs), therefore inferior education was provided for them. Now Negroes are criticized because they are under-educated. In many other areas of life, this same "self-fulfilling" prophecy has been fulfilled, creating a segment of the Negro population which is indifferent and apathetic to its new opportunities and rights. Although these conditions were created by segregation, this does not obviate the fact that they exist and will exist after segregation is ended.

Some Negro leaders feel that, in order to overcome these limitations, a reverse type of "discrimination" might be necessary — that Negroes must be "favored" and provided with extra help to overcome the past. In the same fashion that public schools give added attention to the physically handicapped, the society also has a responsibility for those who have been handicapped by historical circumstances.

Controversy over the treatment of racial minorities has occurred at every stage in American history. It has been kept alive by the troubled consciences of some whites and by the agitation of some Negroes challenging the society to fulfill the ideals of the American dream. As one Harlem organizer said,

This long debate may be boring but for 300 years Negroes have been the object of special attention for the purpose of keeping them segregated and excluded. There is nothing wrong with the fact that they now have been the object of special attention for ten years running if the aim is to restore to them the rights of which they have been so long deprived.[42]

SUMMARY

When this nation was founded, the Declaration of Independence declared that all men were created equal and that they have a basic right to equality and justice. These ideals were contradicted by the presence of large groups

42. *Il Mondo*, May 23, 1963, Translated and reprinted in *Atlas*, August 1963, Vol. 6, No. 2, p. 93.

of Negroes who had been brought to this country as involuntary laborers. It soon seemed clear that full participation in the society was meant to be the right of whites only.

The struggle to abolish slavery lasted nearly a century and the emancipation of the slaves was accomplished only after an expensive war. After the power of the slave-holding states was broken in the Civil War, the status of the Negro was changed through Constitutional amendments and Reconstruction legislation.

These measures, however, failed to remove the contradiction between American ideals and American practice, primarily because the freed slaves continued in their customary subservient roles in the southern labor force. A series of Jim Crow laws based upon the separate-but-equal doctrine were passed by the southern states and created patterns of segregation throughout the South. Segregation reached its apex at the turn of the century and still persists.

Segregation spread northward in modified form as Negroes in increasing numbers migrated to seek new employment opportunities. While educational and occupational opportunities were greater in the North, the increasing concentration of the Negroes in larger cities resulted in patterns of discrimination, especially segregated housing.

Many changes in American society suggest that a new conception, integration, is emerging. Consensus seems to be developing, more manifest in the North than in the South, that desegregation should be pursued since equal opportunity and equal treatment are not possible under a segregated pattern of community and social life. This new conception is resisted by racist ideology but it is supported by Negro protest organizations and the federal government, and it is given impetus by increasing social and political change.

QUESTIONS AND SUGGESTIONS FOR FURTHER STUDY

1. Why is the history of the Negro in America so important in understanding his present situation? Would the understanding of other racial groups be greatly aided by the examination of their respective histories?
2. How would you account for the similarities and differences in the treatment of Negroes between the North and the South?
3. From several periodicals select articles concerning the desegregation of Negroes. How do the writers of these articles attempt to explain either (a) why desegregation is resisted or (b) why it should be resisted?
4. From any source, examine a case where the administrative approach to race relations was followed. What specific strategies were used in the case?
5. In the next decade what effects do you think the out-migration of Negroes would have on the southern economy if they continued to leave at the same rate as they have in the 1950–60 decade?
6. In the modern history of the United States, what other comparable kinds of

social problems have been approached by administrative and legislative meth-ods, that is, by changing the laws and by enforcing these laws through the national administration?

7. How large is the Negro population in your community? To what extent has desegregation taken place in this community? What groups of people favor this policy and what groups oppose it?

8. What kinds of national or international events would aid the trend toward desegregation? What would delay it?

9. Why are the desegregation of schools and voting rights considered by many experts two of the most important civil rights issues for the attainment of Negro equality in the United States?

SUGGESTED READINGS

Berry, Brewton. *Race and Ethnic Relations*. Boston: Houghton Mifflin, 1958. A comparative study of race relations in different times and places.

Cox, Oliver C. *Caste, Class and Race in Social Dynamics*. New York: Double-day, 1948. A comprehensive analysis of social stratification patterns.

Davis, Allison, B. Gardner, and M. R. Gardner. *Deep South*. Chicago: University of Chicago Press, 1941. A classic community study of race relations in a Southern town.

Drake, St. Clair, and Horace Cayton. *Black Metropolis*. Harcourt, Brace, 1945. The problems of Negro adjustment in the city and the rising middle class.

Frazier, E. Franklin. *The Negro in the United States*. New York: Macmillan, 1949. An overview of Negro life in America by a Negro.

Handlin, Oscar. *Race and Nationality in American Life*. Boston: Atlantic-Little, Brown, 1957. An excellent study of the rise of racist ideology in America.   P

Lincoln, C. Eric. *Black Muslims in America*. Boston: Beacon Press, 1961. A de-tailed examination of a militant Negro organization that seeks separation from whites.   P

Mendelson, Wallace. *Discrimination*. Englewood Cliffs, N.J.: Prentice-Hall, 1962. Based on the report of the U.S. Commission on Civil Rights, this book dis-cusses racial discrimination — its scope and effect in major aspects of American life.   P

Myrdal, Gunnar. *An American Dilemma: The Negro Problem and Modern Democracy* (Twentieth Anniversary Edition), New York: Harper and Row, 1962. The most comprehensive analysis of Negro life in America yet undertaken. A condensed and revised version is available in paperback: Rose, Arnold, *The Negro in America*. Boston: Beacon Press, 1948.   P

Rabb, Earl (ed.) *American Race Relations Today: Studies of the Problems Be-yond Segregation*. New York: Doubleday, 1962. A recent series of articles probing the future of race relations.   P

Simpson, George, and J. Milton Yinger. *Racial and Cultural Minorities*. New York: Harper, 1958 (rev. ed.). A massive compilation of facts and statistics as well as interpretative comments on several racial and ethnic minorities in America.

Woodward, C. Vann. *The Strange Career of Jim Crow*, rev. ed., New York: Oxford University Press, 1961. A detailed historical review of the rise of segregation patterns in the South.　P

13 THE INTEGRATION OF
INDUSTRIAL SOCIETIES

Modern urban societies are so differentiated that one may wonder
whether it is accurate to impute to them any common values at all. Perhaps all that holds them together is interdependence for sustenance and
the interlinking of groups that results from overlapping memberships.
Certainly in a country like the United States, the members of different
social classes or the people in different regions tend to put their own interpretation on common values. Whether this leaves anything more than
lip service paid to purely verbal symbols is a legitimate question. . . .
But to most students of American society it seems that there is an underlying consensus nevertheless.[1]

The focus so far has been on dissensus in various institutions within American society. Before turning to the second aspect of social problems, deviation,
we wish to raise the question of how industrial societies, characterized by
dissensus, are able to maintain their stability. If American industrial society is
complex, heterogeneous, and changing, can it have any stability? Given the
extent and frequency of dissensus, which make clear normative directions impossible, how can the society continue? Does the image of the isolated,
alienated person mean that individuals have no meaningful associations with
others?

The way society maintains stability is generally covered by the concept of
integration. The last two chapters have been concerned with the integration
of ethnic and racial minorities, but before analyzing the integration in American society generally, certain observations should be made concerning the
earlier chapters. The discussion thus far has probably overemphasized the
lack of integration within the society. The historical perspective we have
been using creates the illusion of greater dissensus than actually exists at any
particular moment. While we have viewed social change, particularly industrialization, as the problem-producing force, institutions are differentially
affected by it. Dissensus may characterize one institution while consensus is
nearly achieved in another. At any one point in time, then, society only experiences a portion of the conflicts catalogued in the previous chapters.

1. Robert Cooley Angell, *Free Society and Moral Crises*, Ann Arbor: University of Michigan Press, 1958, p. 24. Copyright © 1958 by University of Michigan.

The analysis of dissensus has been on the societal level, not on the level of the individual. Since members of the society differ in their active involvement in various institutions, they may experience dissensus in some areas, while they are unaware of it in others. For example, they may experience personal tension as a result of dissensus within the family, but may be unaware of normative problems involving mass media. It is still possible for individuals in industrial societies to internalize one set of norms without being aware that other normative possibilities exist. By carefully selecting their group affiliations, they can shield themselves from dissensus. By leading a folklike existence, they may avoid the personality conflicts which dissensus creates.

For these reasons, the previous discussion of dissensus has probably over-emphasized the lack of integration within American society. It should be observed, however, that by concentrating on dissensus within institutions, we have ignored the degree of strain among the various institutions. As we shall see subsequently, the co-ordination of institutions is one aspect of integration.

The possibility always exists that dissensus will become extreme and result in conflict among groups, threatening the stability of the society — the Civil War is an example of dissensus become group (regional) conflict. Such potentialities have led to the development of mechanisms that minimize or resolve group conflict. Some of these are common to all societies, some are unique, part of the adaptive equipment allowing industrial societies to cope with heterogeneity, complexity, change, and dissensus.

MECHANISMS OF INTEGRATION

Some of the mechanisms that facilitate integration are: (1) cultural integration — the sharing of common values and symbols; (2) institutional integration — the closeness of "fit" among the various institutions within a society; (3) social integration — the network of social relationships which minimize conflict and achieve common purposes among diverse groups; and (4) techniques of conflict resolution — methods of decision-making which establish stability within the society.

1. *Cultural Integration — Shared Values and Symbols.* One mechanism of integration is the sharing of common values among the members of a society. This provides the members with a common orientation — a common world view. Too, since norms are based on values, norms in several institutional areas based on a single shared value provide a degree of consistency throughout the society. Do industrial societies possess common values and symbols? The heterogeneity of modern societies seems to indicate that common values cannot exist. But some observers think that they do.

Some scholars think there is agreement on such values as monogamous marriage, freedom, acquisitiveness, democracy, education, monotheistic religion, and science.[2] Williams has described certain persistent themes within American society pointing to a value system which cuts across many of the subgroups.[3] A few of these themes can be stated here. American culture places great stress on personal achievement, especially in one's occupation. Since occupational success is difficult to measure, wealth is often taken as a tangible evidence of it. There is great emphasis on activity and work. Though the meaning of work and leisure is currently subject to dissensus, leisure activities still tend to "re-create" the energies of the individual for further work. Americans tend to view the world in moral terms — in terms of "oughts." Americans also express a disinterested concern and helpfulness toward others less fortunate. There is national pride in the fact that America has been a haven for the oppressed, and there is civic pride in the welfare activities of the Rotary Club. There is also an emphasis on being scientific, efficient, and practical. A scientific viewpoint toward every aspect of social life, even religion, is encouraged. Practicality is a theme reflected in our earlier discussion of science as technology, and "be practical" is an admonition accepted everywhere. Too, Americans seemingly have faith in progress; "backwardness" only applies to other nations.

There has been a persistent emphasis on equality of opportunity. This theme has been important in both education and race relations. While America has many inequalities of wealth, power, and prestige, equality is embedded in our legal norms and in the manner in which people relate to one another in everyday activities. Freedom, another value, is often coupled with the notion that the individual is capable of deciding things for himself since he is an autonomous, morally responsible agent. Certainly the theme of democracy would have to be added to the common values of American society. Democracy has many dimensions, some of them already implied here — freedom, equality, individualism; it also includes the value of majority rule, government of the people, and a rejection of aristocratic and totalitarian tendencies.

Like every society, America is ethnocentric, but, more than most societies, its citizens see its "morally superior" traits as capable of export to other countries. While this "moral superiority" is emphasized most during wartime, technical assistance to underdeveloped countries and the Peace Corps draw much of their support as practical demonstrations of the exportability of these values. Nationalism and patriotism are reflected in other ways — to some, criticism of American life is close to treason, but to others, loyalty to

2. John F. Cuber, R. A. Harper, and William Kenkel, *Problems of American Society*, 3rd ed., New York: Holt, 1956, pp. 486–7.
3. Robin M. Williams, Jr., *American Society*, 2nd ed., New York: Knopf, 1960, Chap. XI.

the American life rests on its embodiment of the values of democracy, freedom, equality, and the right to dissent.

The degree of actual acceptance of these values among the various subgroups within American society is unknown, but it can be inferred that they are widely shared and that American society does possess a degree of value consensus. Some of these values also function as common symbols.

Symbols have something of an advantage over values in that they act like sponges — they can absorb almost any meaning. Certain terms, such as democracy and freedom, may only be shared symbols and not shared values. It is obvious that when Americans and Russians talk about "freedom," quite different meanings are involved. One should also recall that, while there was emphasis on freedom in early America, it was also possible to institutionalize slavery and to disenfranchise whole groups. Symbols, however, can become rallying points for the members of a society. Some symbols may be consciously developed to create a degree of cohesion, like a flag or a national anthem; others may emerge from the cultural tradition, like folk heroes and holidays. Symbols often take on a quality of sacredness. Few people openly complain of the difficult melodic line of the national anthem and Southern Democrats refrain from criticizing Lincoln. Stuart Chase suggests some of the common word symbols in American society:

> Let us glance at some of the queer creatures created by personifying abstractions in America. Here in the center is a vast figure called the Nation — majestic and wrapped in the Flag. When it sternly raises its arm we are ready to die for it. Close behind rears a sinister shape, the Government. Following it is one even more sinister, Bureaucracy. Both are festooned with the writhing serpents of Red Tape. High in the heavens is the Constitution, a kind of chalice like the Holy Grail, suffused with ethereal light. It must never be joggled. Below floats the Supreme Court, a black robed priesthood tending the eternal fires. The Supreme Court must be addressed with respect or it will neglect the fire and the Constitution will go out. This is synonymous with the end of the world. Somewhere above the Rocky Mountains are lodged the vast stone tablets of the Law. We are governed not by men but by these tablets. Near them, in satin breeches and silver buckles, pose the stern figures of our Forefathers, contemplating glumly the Nation they brought to birth. . . . Higher than Court, Flag, or the Law, close to the sun itself and almost as bright, is Progress, the ultimate God of America.[4]

Many observers have commented on the increasing mechanization and standardization of modern life. While much of this is a by-product of bureaucratization and industrialization, some standardization undoubtedly emerges from the sharing of common values and symbols. As economic activity moves from the local market to the national level and as political

4. Stuart Chase, *Tyranny of Words*, New York: Harcourt, Brace, 1938, p. 23. Reprinted by permission.

democracy shifts from local to national and international concerns, a common value system becomes possible if not necessary. With urbanization and mass education, different segments of the population come into more frequent contact with each other and with common values and symbols. Too, the emergence of new class and status interests minimizes the span of stratification; in many societies, there is a large gap between those at the top and those below. While class conflict is reflected in political conflict, it is domesticated and restricted by this reduction in span and by common values.

Common values and symbols can be more effectively communicated since the development of the mass media. Isolation inhibits the sharing of values and symbols but the mass media can diffuse them throughout the society. In the past, these media have played an important role in the socialization of immigrants. American society has received over 35 million immigrants throughout its history; the newspaper, and later the movies, radio, and television have all played an important role in providing them with a "window to the new world." The mass circulation newspaper, the comic strip, and the movies developed most rapidly during the peak years of immigration. In a sense, every child born is an "immigrant" and the mass media help to teach him the right kind of breakfast food to eat and the right kind of values and symbols to accept. With their parents, children see certain common themes through the mass media. For example, holidays, both religious and patriotic, become national celebrations as well as commercial rituals. One's obligations to the nation are suggested by spot announcements on the Fourth of July, and business establishments broadcast best wishes to the public at Christmas. One's responsibility to the less fortunate is stressed during a minute of humility after an hour of hilarity by a Jerry Lewis or a Danny Thomas. While the values and symbols communicated tend to be vague, this may be the only level at which all Americans can agree. Being against sin and for motherhood may be superficial, but these attitudes still represent a degree of consensus.

The mass media frequently ignore ideas contradicting shared values. Movies seldom present controversial subjects, and those that do are termed "classic," attesting more to their infrequency than to their quality. While radio and television do, at times, present disagreement as a part of their "public service," one point of view is neatly balanced with the equal time of another, giving the illusion that one opinion is as valuable as another. More frequently, radio and television avoid controversy by emphasizing entertainment. Newspapers, too, withdraw controversy from public examination. When Warren Breed analyzed various American community studies made by sociologists and anthropologists for behavior he felt would be ignored and not reported by the press, his judgment of the kinds of stories that would be excluded was later confirmed by experienced newsmen.[5] The various mass media, then, tend to emphasize common values and symbols and to "protect" the society from dissensus and deviation.

2. *Institutional Integration.* Societies do not contain random collections of institutions. Studies of cultural diffusion show that innovations are accepted or rejected by a society in terms of its prevailing values. When a particular innovation is "compatible" with existing values, it is likely to be accepted, and a degree of consistency is maintained. Similarly, there is consistency among the various institutions in a society. This consistency, an essential part of integration, is created by (a) institutional compatibilities, (b) institutional dominance, and (c) the co-ordination of institutional elites.

(a) *Institutional compatibilities.* Certain structural and normative arrangements are compatible while others are not. For example, the extended family system is the predominant form in pre-industrial societies. With industrialization, occupational roles are removed from the family, and the necessity for a large, extended kinship structure is decreased. Since children are no longer economically helpful, there are developments toward the small, nuclear family. Since industrial occupations require specialization and technical skill, families can no longer train children for economic roles. This necessitates the development of separate organizations to transmit these skills. And, since status, in large part, is not given, but must be achieved, this educational system is often public and open to all. With industrialization, the economic system becomes more complex. The larger the units of production become, the more interdependent they are and the state is drawn into establishing normative regulations for economic activity. Too, the direction of economic production depends in large part on political considerations — war or the threat of war. Therefore, a big economy creates a big government, and, in turn, the ends of the state dictate much of economic activity. Just as pre-industrial societies developed a degree of consistency among various institutions, so industrial societies have developed a differentiated but still compatible institutional system.

(b) *Institutional dominance.* Integration is also facilitated by the dominance of certain institutions. Not all institutions carry equal weight; some influence, while others are influenced. Dominant institutions create the conditions to which other institutions must adapt and thus create a degree of integration. The dominant institution may differ from one society to another and from one period of history to another. The importance of institutional dominance for integration can be seen in the following questions, which direct attention to the location of dominance.

5. Warren Breed, "Mass Communication and Socio-Cultural Integration," *Social Forces,* 37 (December 1958), pp. 109–16.

1. What institutions in a society change first? Do changes in economic institutions precede changes in family structure?

2. How do individuals within a society resolve conflicts between institutional obligations? Confronted with conflicts between the demands of the family and the demands of the economic institutions, what choice do individuals make?

3. What variable explains the greatest amount of behavior within a society? Can political behavior be explained independently or does it have to be explained in terms of religious, family, educational, or economic factors?

4. What institutions make the most demands on the time and energy of individuals within a society? Are individuals preoccupied by political, religious, educational, economic, or family activity?

5. Which institutions control the scarce rewards in a society? On what basis are power and prestige awarded within a society?

6. What institutional leaders are consulted when a planned change is contemplated within a society? What interests are considered more relevant and due more consideration when change is anticipated?

The intent here is not to make a complete assessment of dominance. The Industrial Revolution signalizes the emergence of economic institutions to a position of dominance in the Western world. C. Wright Mills, in describing what he called the "power elite" in America, locates dominance in both the economic and governmental (political and military) realms:

Within American society, major national power now resides in the economic, the political, and the military domains. Other institutions seem off to the side of modern history, and, on occasion, duly subordinated to these. No family is as directly powerful in national affairs as any major corporation; no church is as directly powerful in the external biographies of young men in America today as the military establishment; no college is as powerful in the shaping of momentous events as the National Security Council. Religious, educational, and family institutions are not autonomous centers of national power; on the contrary, these decentralized areas are increasingly shaped by the big three, in which developments of decisive and immediate consequence now occur.

Families and churches and schools adapt to modern life; governments and armies and corporations shape it; and, as they do so, they turn these lesser institutions into means for their ends. Religious institutions provide chaplains to the armed forces where they are used as a means of increasing the effectiveness of its morale to kill. Schools select and train men for their jobs in corporations and their specialized tasks in the armed forces. The extended family has, of course, long been broken up by the industrial revolution, and now the son and the father are removed from the family, by compulsion if need be, whenever the army of the state sends out the call. And the symbols of all these lesser institutions are used to legitimate the power and the decisions of the big three.[6]

6. C. Wright Mills, *The Power Elite*, New York: Oxford University Press, 1956, p. 6.

(c) *Co-ordination of institutional elites.* Institutional integration is also facilitated by a degree of co-ordination among the leaders in each institutional area. Each institution develops a degree of autonomy. Institutional interests are represented in specific organizations which protect them and resist encroachment from other groups. From these organizations and groups emerge an elite who exercise leadership for the institution. The institutional elites can be seen most clearly on a local level. The superintendent of schools is part of the educational elite, and the mayor, part of the political elite. To understand the nature of the local community one must have a knowledge of the connections among the various institutional elites. Community activity is a consequence of co-ordination among the institutional elites. A contemplated change in one institutional area requires the "approval" of the other elites. Thus, the various institutions are integrated through the co-ordination of the elites. This co-ordination is somewhat simplified in industrial societies since institutions are nationally, rather than locally, integrated. Speaking of American society, Mills says, "During the past century, local society has become part of the national economy; its status and power hierarchies have come to be subordinate parts of larger hierarchies of the nation." [7]

3. *Social Integration.* Complexity has a positive function in the integration of industrial societies. The types of social relationships alleged to "dehumanize" man actually contribute to cohesion within the society. While individuals and groups may lack common values and may have conflicting interests, they are still bound together by the very complexity of the division of labor. Any individual who works for a large-scale organization — and this constitutes an increasingly large part of the population — is connected to others in a complex set of relationships. Regardless of whether other ties exist among the employees, they are bound together by common participation in the organization; their "lives" depend upon it. Too, a division of labor always implies a degree of mutuality. A store owner needs a salesman as much as the salesman needs employment. Similarly, the steel manufacturer is necessary to the automobile manufacturer. And automobiles cannot be produced without workers, and workers cannot work without "tools" supplied by the organization. This interdependence allows individuals and groups with separate and even antagonistic interests to achieve their goals. It should not be overlooked, however, that even these economic relationships are normatively defined. There is consensus on the norms guiding these activities in which other differences are excluded. The fact that the salesman is a Democrat and the store owner a Republican is irrelevant. Most relationships within the division of labor are specific, restricted to narrowly defined limits. This

7. Ibid., p. 39.

creates the impersonality characteristic of modern societies, but it allows a heterogeneous population to enter into stable social relationships, facilitating the integration of the society.

Complex societies minimize potential conflict in other ways. Groups with unique, divergent normative patterns are often able to maintain them by isolation. Religious groups, like the Amish and Hutterian Brethren, have been able to maintain their distinctive customs. Among other groups, association mainly with those who share similar evaluations avoids conflict with those who differ. Integrationists talk to other integrationists; Catholics talk to other Catholics; Republicans talk to other Republicans. This type of isolation also can accentuate normative differences among groups, but even this effect can be minimized. In industrial societies, a number of formal and informal roles emerge which mediate and minimize potential conflict. Racial, ethnic, and religious leaders often serve as a bridge from their groups to the larger society. Mediators have become an integral part of governmental structure to deal with labor-management conflict. These mediating roles allow dissensus to exist and demands to be accommodated so the interdependence in the society is not broken.

Even where normative differences exist, other devices allow interaction to continue. In the armed forces, what is called military courtesy allows one to salute the uniform, not the man. Etiquette, courtesy, and tact are techniques which overcome differences. When we tell a hostess we had a wonderful time at a party, we wish not to alienate her, regardless of our private feelings. A complex society inevitably brings divergent people together and often leaves them with no clear norms governing behavior. In such situations, people must depend on their skill and knowledge in anticipating the reactions of others. These skills are informally learned and are even taught in courses on "how to win friends and influence people," or as the cynic might describe them, "how to exploit and manipulate people." There is a premium placed upon the ability to size people up quickly. These skills are part of the personality which Riesman has described as "other-directed." [8] One of the techniques one learns in "influencing people" is to avoid controversial topics of conversation. It is standard advice to avoid politics and religion, two perennial areas of dissensus. This avoidance makes much public conversation superficial, confining it to the state of the weather, the fortunes of baseball, and the mysteries of sex.

All of the types of social relationships, criticized by some for their superficiality and impersonality, allow the diverse individuals necessary in an industrial society to carry on the functions essential for its continuation. The division of labor and the interdependence it reflects integrate society in such

8. See David Riesman, *The Lonely Crowd*, New Haven: Yale University Press, 1950.

a fashion that some have concluded that common values and symbols are no longer essential to the survival of an industrial society.

4. *Mechanisms of Conflict Resolution — the Emergence of Democracy.* The integration of industrial societies is also facilitated by democratic government. While dictatorships provide another kind of integration, democracy seemingly provides a flexibility that knits diverse groups together. As Lipset states, "Democracy in a complex society may be defined as a political system which supplies regular constitutional opportunities for changing the governing officials, and a social mechanism which permits the largest part of the population to influence major decisions by choosing among contenders for political office." [9] Stable democracies seemingly are possible only at certain levels of economic development. At a certain degree of industrialization, per capita wealth, urbanization, literacy, and education, democratic forms of government become possible and provide some of the mechanisms whereby industrial societies are integrated.

As the analysis of institutional areas has shown, normative dissensus often becomes political conflict. Support of specific norms, however, is seldom embodied in any one political party. Stable democracies seemingly depend on a situation in which all of the major political parties include supporters from many segments of the population. Each party must appeal to diverse groups and interests, so party loyalty cuts across groups within the society. Certain parties do attract greater support from some groups. In American society, laborers, Catholics, and Jews tend to vote Democratic while those with higher income, education, and occupational status tend to vote Republican. There are, however, contradictions which prevent the total allegiance of any one group to a specific party. A Democrat might find that his fellow union member votes Republican, but their animosity is mitigated by their common union membership. Too, individuals may belong to groups and categories with differing political allegiances. A person may be a Catholic with high occupational status. This in itself will reduce the intensity of his feeling on the issues upon which these groups differ. He responds to the cross pressures of multiple group memberships, as does everyone in an industrial society.

In American society, the voter is limited to two realistic alternatives: the Democratic and the Republican parties. On occasions, voters have had a third alternative, but the history of third parties shows a singular lack of success. Change in power between the two parties is accomplished with a minimum of difficulty. The losers in an election vacate their offices; contenders for political power do not attain it by force, nor do winners attempt to sup-

9. Seymour M. Lipset, *Political Man, The Social Bases of Politics*, New York: Doubleday, 1960, p. 45.

press their opposition, except at the polls. The existence of political parties was not anticipated by the Founding Fathers, nor are their relationships embedded in the legal structure of the society. However, regardless of the legal status of parties, normative rules exist which govern the relationships between the parties. That these norms are effective in maintaining a degree of stability within the society is seen by comparing behavior after an election in the United States with the revolutionary seizures of power in many other societies. One might suggest that the most important agreement among the members of American society is that the loser of an election vacates his office.

Democratic forms of government provide a flexibility that helps achieve consensus. Louis Wirth, speaking particularly about American society, has said:

. . . We have developed patience to endure heresies and sufferance to endure transitory annoyance in the hope that minorities can, under freedom, develop themselves into majorities, and we have come to believe that for most purposes of life it is more economical, though perhaps less interesting, to count noses than to break heads.

But modern societies, whether they are autocratic or democratic, have learned that in the face of their size and complexity and their internal heterogeneity, the engineering of public consent is one of the great arts to be cultivated. Democracies, as distinguished from autocracies, seem to have taken the longer view by recognizing, as did Machiavelli, that the pseudoconsensus that is achieved by force cannot long endure and weather crisis, when he said: "It cannot be called talent to slay fellow citizens, to deceive friends, to be without faith, without mercy, without religion; such methods may gain empire but not glory." Democracies proceed on the assumption that even if the contending parties fight it out violently there is no assurance that the problem over which they fought won't remain after the stronger has suppressed the weaker. Even military conquest uses the technique of undermining the will to fight of the enemy, and nowadays, even after the enemy has surrendered, we send public opinion pollers among them to learn how best to govern them. The believers in the democratic principle have learned not to be impatient in the process of reaching agreement and that society can go on as long as we agree not to settle our disagreements by resort to force. They have had to learn that society can remain democratic only as long as we recognize and respect that essential residue, the freedom and dignity of every personality, which is no less important then it was before merely because it seems to have become a cliché. They have come to know also, as a contemporary philosopher has put it, that "lacking the consensus a legal crime may be a social virtue and religious heresy a moral duty."

Consensus in mass democracies, therefore, is not so much agreement on all issues, or even on the most essential substantive issues, among all the members of society, as it is the established habit of intercommunication, of discussion, debate, negotiation and compromise, and the toleration of heresies, or even of indifference, up to the point of "clear and present danger" which threatens the life of the society itself. Rather than resting upon unanimity, it rests upon a sense of group identification and participation in the life of a society, upon the willingness to allow our representatives to speak for us even though they do not always faithfully represent our views, if indeed we have any views at all on many of the issues under discussion, and upon our disposition to fit ourselves into a program that our group has adopted and to acquiesce in group decisions unless the matter is fundamentally incompatible with our interests and integrity.[10]

INTEGRATION AND RELIGIOUS DIVERSITY

The integration of American society has many dimensions. We can illustrate one aspect which has led to the disintegration of other societies. Religious diversity in American society has been the subject of much comment. In an earlier chapter, dissensus within Protestantism and Judaism was discussed, as was dissensus over the role of Catholicism. This represents only a part of the potentialities within American society for dissensus and group conflict on religion. There are over 250 religious bodies, and, to the extent these groups represent different religious values, they constitute a significant problem for the integration of American society. A religious commitment seldom allows compromise; the religious wars and the Inquisition attest to this fact. Given this explosiveness and its dangers for the integration of a society, what factors tend to minimize the potentials for conflict in religion and what factors knit the diverse groups together?

Cultural integration. Religious groups in the United States share a number of common religious values and symbols as well as religious beliefs. The Judeo-Christian tradition is considered one of the formative influences in Western culture. The pairing of Jews and Christians implies that the two traditions share many ideas and practices. Christianity borrowed a number of items from Judaism — the name of the deity, the view of creation, the Ten Commandments, original sin, the Kingdom of God, and the fatherhood of God are a few examples. The Old Testament, of course, is a Jewish book and almost all of the New Testament was written by Jewish Christians. Many of the patterns of worship are shared also. Even before Christianity, Judaism had public worship with preaching, singing, Scripture reading, teaching, baptizing, and sharing a sacred meal. Both religions have retained a strong ethical concern.

Protestantism and Catholicism, of course, share a common history until the sixteenth century and thus share many of the early creeds of the Church and the doctrines contained in them. Both believe in the power of sin, the need for grace, and the need for faith. They both have congregational meeting for worship led by pastors, and they share two sacraments, baptism and the Lord's Supper.

These common aspects of the various heritage are often evoked when dif-

10. Louis Wirth, "Consensus and Mass Communication," *American Sociological Review,* 13 (February 1948), pp. 1–15. Reprinted by permission.

ferences arise. Points of similarity would be much more difficult to find if a society had to integrate Catholicism and Islam, or Protestantism and Hinduism, or Judaism and Buddhism.

Religious groups also share common secular attitudes and symbols, among them tolerance. This attitude seems to be necessary in all industrial societies and is both a cause and a result of diversity in the United States. Members of religious groups, like those outside a religious tradition, accept the validity of democracy, the importance of occupational success, and other secular values. In fact, a number of observers have suggested that these secular values — the "American way of life" — are so widely shared that they override religious commitments.[11] Religion, as it is incorporated in individual behavior rather than as it is stated ideally in creeds, is frequently used as a means to achieve secular goals and aspirations. Since American society sees occupational success as important, God is often visualized as a friend and helper — One who encourages you when you are discouraged with your progress toward success. Since national security is a current preoccupation, many Americans insist that, along with intercontinental ballistic missiles, religion is a potent weapon in the fight against Communism. If mental health is valued, the church tries to give psychiatric aid to its members. This use of religion as an instrument to help achieve secular goals may be due either to the strength of secular values or to the weakness of the religious ones, but the end is similar: common values are emphasized while dissensus and conflict are minimized.

Institutional integration. Two aspects of institutional compatibility can be indicated here. Protestantism has been the dominant religious pattern in the United States. Max Weber has suggested that the ethics which characterized certain Protestant sects played an important part in the development of capitalism, that is, of an industrial society.[12] These religious groups developed what Weber called an "inner worldly asceticism." Calvinism, in particular, rejected easy assurance of man's salvation. Man could no longer be certain he would be saved since his salvation was predestined by God. Given this uncertainty, a devotion to work and one's success in work were taken as an index of salvation. Individual self-discipline was stressed. Money was to be saved and not to be spent on vain display. This created a type of asceticism enacted, not in a monastic setting, but in "the world." It was present in everyday behavior and particularly in one's work. As we indicated earlier, these attitudes toward work are an integral part of American culture. Weber suggested that this asceticism subordinated the individual's personal needs to the demands of work and provided the "spirit of capitalism." By exercis-

11. See, for example, Will Herberg, *Protestant–Catholic–Jew*, New York: Doubleday, 1955.
12. Max Weber, *The Protestant Ethic and the Spirit of Capitalism* (trans. by Talcott Parsons), New York: Scribners, 1930.

ing industry, thrift, sobriety, and restraint and avoiding the "excesses" of the flesh, individuals often accumulated money. This accumulation was sometimes viewed as an indication of one's predestined salvation. The wealth could not be wasted since thrift was valued, so it was reinvested rationally, providing the basis for industrial enterprise. Weber suggested this relationship since Protestantism appeared on the historical scene at the same time as capitalism and Protestants were prominent among business and industrial leaders in capitalist countries. The importance here is that in American society the predominant religious heritage was Protestant, and here as elsewhere individualism and the emphasis on work were compatible with the demands made by economic institutions.

The compatibility of Protestantism extended to other institutions. The development of capitalism created a middle class. This class acted as a catalyst to the development of democratic forms of government. Protestant emphasis on individual responsibility also facilitated the acceptance of many democratic values. Lipset, in studying the many factors which give rise to a stable democracy, makes the following statement: "Men may question whether any aspect of this interrelated cluster of economic development, Protestantism, monarchy, gradual political change, legitimacy, and democracy is primary, but the fact remains that the cluster does hang together." [13]

The predominant religious pattern in American society, Protestantism, "fits" with other institutions. This is not to imply that Judaism and Catholicism are "un-American," but their adaptation to American society was conditioned by the priority and numerical superiority of Protestantism. Nor does this imply that religion was the dominant institution. Mills indicates in the quotation earlier in this chapter that now religious institutions adapt to life rather than shape it. Economic factors often can explain differences in religious behavior.[14] Thus, religion's compatibility with other institutions and its adaptation to dominant institutions facilitate integration and minimize conflict.

Social integration. Members of all religious groups are bound together in the division of labor. In spite of periodic instances of religious discrimination, occupational positions and tasks require knowledge and skill, not particular religious beliefs. Relations among people usually are specific to the task in which they are mutually involved. A Protestant driver does not care whether the owner of a gas station is a Protestant, Catholic, Jew, or non-believer. His choice of station is based on brand, on location, and on the fact that he needs gas. In all those situations where individuals from different backgrounds come

13. Lipset, op. cit. p. 71.
14. See, for example, Russell R. Dynes, "Church-Sect Typology and Socio-Economic Status," *American Sociological Review,* 20 (October 1955), pp. 555–60.

into contact, Americans try not to talk about "religion and politics." Such controversial subjects are avoided since they separate people "needlessly." Everyone can agree that "religion," or "having a belief," is important, but no one ventures to specify what one should believe.

The many religious groups in the United States could pose a threat to social integration in this country. In part, religious conflict has been minimized by the relative isolation of religious groups. Protestantism has been traditionally rural, while Catholicism and Judaism are urban religions. This means that members of particular religious groups live primarily among others who believe as they do. For example, over 50 per cent of all American Jews live in New York City. Even in religiously heterogeneous areas, residential and associational "segregation" makes the friendship group coincide with religious affiliation. For example, one study showed that among sectarian Protestants, three out of their five best friends belonged to the same church.[15] Many secular groups are formed along religious lines; there are Jewish War Veterans, Catholic War Veterans, and other, predominantly Protestant organizations.

There are also overt indications of co-operation among religious groups. Both theological and social factors have played a part in what is called the ecumenical movement within Christianity. Some religious leaders believe that the diversity of religious groups distorts the unity of Christianity and that all religious groups must bear blame for it. In addition, many of the factors that created diversity have lost their importance. Certain nationality loyalties are no longer important, and regional differences, often reflecting different attitudes toward race relations, are losing their ability to divide. The ecumenical movement got its start in interdenominational meetings concerned with the duplication of effort in missionary activities. It was furthered when the National Council of Churches of Christ was formed. This provided a precedent for the formation of the World Council of Churches in 1948. Both of these organizations are federations of churches, including Protestants, Anglicans, Orthodox, and Old Catholics. The Roman Catholic Church has remained aloof from these attempts, but the ecumenical council called by Pope John in 1962, opened up some possibilities of co-operation. A more direct expression of the ecumenical movement has been the merger of some Protestant bodies. In 1939, three branches of Methodism came back together. In 1961, three denominations formed the American Lutheran Church and four more made tentative plans to form a Lutheran Church in America. Also, in 1961, the Congregational Christian Churches formally met with the Evangelical and Reform Church as the United Church of Christ. And a leader in the United Presbyterian Church in the U.S.A. has suggested a merger of that body

15. Russell R. Dynes, "The Consequences of Sectarianism for Social Participation," *Social Forces*, 35 (May 1957), pp. 331–4.

with the Protestant Episcopal Church, the Methodist Church, and the United Church of Christ. These events indicate that, in spite of different organizational structures and beliefs, many religious groups feel a unity with other Christian groups. Jews, of course, have not been included in Christian ecumenical attempts. There are, however, interfaith organizations, of which the best known is probably the National Conference of Christians and Jews. Organized in 1928, primarily to combat anti-Semitism, it provides some opportunity for co-operative action.

Mergers of religious groups may have unanticipated consequences. The presence of many groups may actually minimize the intensity of religious conflict. Conflict among many small religious groups has the effect of reducing the potential for other, more massive, conflict. Although the ecumenical movement may reduce conflict within Protestantism, it might intensify Catholic-Protestant tension. Evidence supporting this was presented in Chapter 6.

Methods of conflict resolution. The potential explosiveness of religion is minimized in American society since it is somewhat independent of political life. The separation of church and state was written into many state constitutions and into the First Amendment of the U.S. Constitution. Belief in this separation may be traced to several sources. Some of the Founding Fathers, like Jefferson, were influenced by Deism, which taught that God was detached from the universe and that men should rely on reason, not on religious authority. Too, there were already many religious groups in colonial America, and this made the establishment of a state church impractical. Strong groups often opposed giving religion political authority, both on theological grounds and on the basis of their experience in Europe. The combination of these factors resulted in the constitutional separation of religious and political action.

The initial settlement pattern reflected religious diversity, and the subsequent distribution of people along the expanding frontier continued it. No religious group was able to maintain a regional monopoly. Non-Protestant groups did settle down in the cities of the East, but Jews were not numerous and Catholics dominated few cities.

The constitutional structure and the settlement pattern meant that religious groups could not utilize political authority effectively. In folk societies, religion permeates every aspect of social life and is not embodied in a separate organization. In American society, religious interests were embedded in the churches. This localization of interest "removes" religion from other institutional involvements and is one manifestation of secularization. It means that political, economic, and other types of behavior within the society may "ignore" religion, and conflicts within other institutional areas do not also become religious conflict. This means, in addition, that the roles of individuals in various types of institutional behavior do not form a consistent "package." When roles coincide, individuals feel intensely toward others with differing roles; but when roles do not coincide, they become somewhat apathetic toward others. In other words, party affiliation, region, occupation, and nationality have never been consistently related to religious affiliation. Since these group affiliations have run at cross purposes, they have reduced conflict among religious groups and among other groups as well.

INTEGRATION AND DEVIATION

There are situations where consensus exists within a society on clearly and consistently defined norms. Some individuals are unwilling or unable to follow these agreed-upon norms. Earlier we termed this phenomena behavioral deviation.

Deviation and deviants are another hindrance to the integration of industrial societies. Dissensus may be considered a "normal" condition; members of a society can disagree concerning the applicability of certain norms without creating extreme cleavages. Deviant behavior, however, presents a threat to integration by threatening the whole normative order. In addition, deviation frequently harms the deviant, others, or both. There is a need, then, to reduce and eliminate deviation or to minimize the consequences of deviation for the integration of society.

In all industrial societies, separate governmental organizations are assigned the responsibility to enforce certain norms. The police are expected to enforce the legal normative regulations and to apply the sanctions stipulated by the law. The existence of these roles reminds the other members of a society of their obligations to the normative order.

As science developed, there were efforts to understand the etiology of deviant behavior. It was assumed that, as causes are understood, deviation can be eliminated. Partial knowledge often becomes the basis for programs intended to reduce deviation. For example, many community activities in American society — the establishment of a park, the addition of a police car, or the installation of street lights — are expected by their sponsors to lead to a reduction in the rate of criminal deviation.

Since deviation is not easily prevented, deviants have traditionally been removed from the society so that their lack of conformity does not provide an example for others to follow. Deviants are commonly removed by imprisonment, banishment, or execution. For example, in early eighteenth-century England, over 200 crimes carried the death penalty. One should also recall that some of the people who were burned as witches in Salem were probably mentally ill. In addition, deviants have been stigmatized, for example, by being forced to wear a "scarlet letter" or by cutting off a hand to give others fair warning to shun the deviants. In more recent times, deviants have been put into institutions. Both prisons and mental hospitals isolate deviants from the larger society.

With increased understanding, another, somewhat contradictory, approach has been taken toward deviation. Removal does little to change deviant behavior. In fact, isolating deviants from the norms of the larger society and placing them with other deviants may inhibit rather than facilitate conformity. Men who have served prison sentences are likely to return to prison because, during institutionalization, they have had an opportunity to reinforce their deviancy and to learn new types of deviant behavior. These factors have encouraged attempts to treat deviants not in the isolation of an institution, but in "controlled" situations. Probation and parole for criminals and outpatient treatment for the mentally ill are manifestations of these attempts. Integration of deviants with the society is to be achieved by bringing the deviants into contact with, not isolating them from, the dominant norms of the society and by attempting to "supervise" their conformity.

Deviation can be minimized by redefining the norm so that it applies to a much narrower range of behavior. Widespread deviation has the potentiality of threatening the maintenance of the normative patterns. If substantial segments of the population can be classed as deviant, condoning the deviation would make it impossible to retain the norm but condemning it would involve punitive action against a large and perhaps powerful segment of the population. The usual response to this dilemma is to redefine the norm so most of those previously considered deviant are then excluded. For example, the Biblical injunction "Thou shalt not kill" has been redefined so that a person who does not wilfully kill others — who kills in war, in the performance of police duties, by negligence, in self-defense, under duress, when he cannot distinguish between "right" and "wrong," or when he is too young to understand and behave otherwise — is not considered a murderer. The deviant act of killing is thus redefined and circumscribed. In this fashion, the norm is "upheld" but its applicability is restricted.

Another way in which deviation is handled so that it does not threaten the integration of society is to develop patterned ways to evade it. This is likely to occur in situations where large and powerful groups act in deviant ways. Particularly in complex societies, various segments of the population want different, contradictory things. Given this situation, a "compromise" is worked out which allows each segment to get what it wants. One of the best examples of this phenomenon was Prohibition. The "drys" got Prohibition, but the "wets" still got alcoholic beverages. Those supposed to enforce the legal norms faced a real dilemma. The police had to make an attempt to enforce the laws. If they enforced the laws too rigorously, however, they would alienate an important segment of the population, the "wets." What actually occurred was sporadic enforcement which ritualistically affirmed the norm but never eliminated the "needed" alcoholic beverages. A similar situation now exists with reference to prostitution and gambling. These activities violate legal norms, but they exist in every major community. Completely enforcing the laws would make some "respected" members of the community deviant. The periodic closing of houses of prostitution and of gambling establishments creates the impression that the legal norms are being enforced. Those who engage in these activities look upon their arrests as one of the "costs" of doing business. Our concern here is not with the morality of the situation but with its functions: it enables groups wanting different norms to co-exist. One group is assured that the "official" norms are enforced, and the other is allowed to continue, with periodic interruptions, to behave in what it considers "acceptable" ways.

One final aspect of the relation of deviation to integration has been suggested by a number of observers. The very fact of deviation evokes a situation in which the norms must be remembered and reaffirmed. Deviants remind the other members of the society of their normative obligations. They are reminded that there are certain prohibited behaviors. Even when punishment is directed toward the deviants, the existing normative order is affirmed for deviants and for the "punishers" as well.

Deviation constitutes the second major aspect of social problems. In subsequent chapters, we will treat two different categories of deviation, mental illness and criminal deviation. Mental illness is a type of deviant behavior in which the individual does not conform to the expectations of occupational and familial roles and behaves in ways harmful to himself and others. While diagnosis has become a psychiatric undertaking, persons who are mentally ill are characterized by an inability to perform adequately. Criminal deviation presents a clearer illustration. While consensus on some norms may be lacking, for the most part crimes are violations of legal norms. Since there are many different types of legal norms, there are many types of criminal deviation. The subsequent discussion will describe the extent and social location of deviant behavior. Various etiological theories will then be defined and evaluated. In addition, attempts at prevention of deviation, and rehabilitation and therapy of deviants will be discussed. Since etiological theories differ, deviation also involves dissensus concerning treatment. So, throughout the discussion of deviation, examples of dissensus also appear.

SUMMARY

Normative dissensus in various institutional areas disturbs the integration of a society. Every society, however, contains certain mechanisms facilitating integration. Members of a society share common values and symbols which function as a cohesive factor. The transmission of these is facilitated by the development of the mass media. A degree of stability is also achieved by institutional integration. The various institutions are, to a degree, compatible. This, in part, is created by the dominance of some institutions and by the co-ordination of institutional elites. The division of labor in a society creates interdependence among people in spite of their normative differences. Too, certain types of social relationships allow interaction to continue among individuals with differing normative conceptions. The emergence of democratic forms of government allows an increasing proportion of the population to participate in political decision-making and provides a political mechanism which minimizes the destructive potential of conflict while emphasizing the development of integration and consensus. The various mechanisms facilitating integration were illustrated by the way religion, a traditionally disintegrative force, is handled in American society.

Deviation also provides a threat to the stability of a society. Various mechanisms that reduce its consequences were discussed. The following chapters will focus on two categories of deviation — mental illness and criminal deviation.

QUESTIONS AND SUGGESTIONS FOR FURTHER STUDY

1. Many foreign observers of American culture comment on its standardization and mechanization; others are amazed by its diversity. Which of these observations do you think can best be supported?
2. Analyze a television program or series to find whether the content communicates common values or symbols?
3. Choose a product and trace the various steps necessary to put it on the market. Describe the web of social relationships this process requires.
4. What examples of patterned evasions, other than Prohibition, gambling, and prostitution, can be given? Are there other situations which reflect a gap between the normative requirements and actual behavior? Why do these situations exist? What role do they place in the integration of the society?
5. Some observers have described religion in the United States as being at a "low temperature." Does this description reflect the ways in which religion is handled within the society? What would be the consequences of a "high temperature?"
6. Read Robert S. and Helen M. Lynd's *Middletown in Transition*, with the purpose of determining whether the values expressed in Middletown at that time (1937) still persist in American society?
7. Read a history of the ways in which the criminal or the mentally ill has been handled to ascertain whether these ways have been concerned with protecting the deviant or the society?

SUGGESTED READINGS

Angell, Robert Cooley, *Free Society and Moral Crises*, Ann Arbor: University of Michigan Press, 1958. One of the few books devoted to a discussion of the maintenance of the normative order, it deals with the punishment and reorientation of the deviant, as well as with institutional factors.

Coser, Lewis A., *The Functions of Social Conflict*, Glencoe: Free Press, 1956. Conflict is often viewed as disintegrative, but Coser suggests its contributions to the stability of social relationships.

Durkheim, Emile, *The Division of Labor in Society* (trans. by George Simpson), Glencoe: Free Press, 1947. A classic treatment of the integrative effects of the division of labor.

Graham, Saxon, *American Culture*, New York: Harper, 1957. An analysis of the various facets of American culture.

Lipset, Seymour Martin, *Political Man, The Social Bases of Politics*, New York: Doubleday, 1960. This book explores the conditions which facilitate democracy, using many comparative studies. It shows how both consensus and cleavage play a part in maintaining order.

Lerner, Max, *America as a Civilization*, New York: Simon and Schuster, 1957. An encyclopedic work which attempts to give an over-all interpretation of America's emergence as a civilization. Combines insights from many disciplines.

Martindale, Don, *American Social Structure*, New York: Appleton-Century-Crofts, 1960. An analysis of American society, both past and contemporary, in terms of regional, rural, urban, ethnic, and status groups.

Williams, Robin M., Jr., *American Society*, 2nd ed., New York: Knopf, 1960. An excellent sociological interpretation of American society. It is particularly good in its treatment of the integrative factors.

III BEHAVIORAL DEVIATION

14 MENTAL ILLNESS:
TYPES AND EXTENT

> Madness severs the strongest bonds that hold human beings together. It separates husband from wife, mother from child. It is death without death's finality and without death's dignity.[1]

Mental illness represents a social problem in the following respects. First, the behavior of the mentally disturbed deviates from the normative prescriptions of society. The mentally ill are unable to perform their usual roles to conform with the expectations of others, though a great deal of normative dissensus exists over the types and severity of aberrations which are to be defined as mental disease. Second, dissensus exists as to the treatment to be accorded those who are mentally ill.

DEFINITION OF THE PROBLEM

Despite the fact that persons are diagnosed daily as mentally ill, mental illness and mental health are difficult to define.[2] There are several reasons for this. First, some mental illnesses are organic or physical in nature while most are not. Second, the term mental illness covers an extremely broad range of behaviors and symptoms — sometimes very mild and sometimes totally incapacitating. Third, any definition tends to violate the theories of one or another school of thought. Thus, some psychiatrists have suggested that most persons are to some extent deviant. Others define deviation only in terms of inability to perform minimal everyday functions. Fourth, anthropologists add to the confusion by pointing out the enormous cultural variations in the content of mental illness in different cultures. By American standards, almost all persons in some societies would be defined as mentally ill, since their cultures expect or demand some behaviors — chronic suspicion of other persons, much hostility and aggression, trance-like conduct, and delusions — which American psychiatrists would classify as psychiatric impairment.[3] For these and

1. R. S. deRopp, *Drugs and the Mind*, New York: St. Martin's, 1957, pp. 167–8.
2. Marie Jahoda, *Current Concepts of Positive Mental Health*, Report to the Joint Commission on Mental Illness and Health, no. 1, New York: Basic Books, 1958.
3. Abram Kardiner and Associates, *The Psychological Frontiers of Society*, New York: Columbia University Press, 1945. Ernest M. Gruenberg, "Socially Shared Psychopathology," in *Explorations in Social Psychiatry* (Alexander Leighton, John Clausen, and Robert Wilson, eds.), New York: Basic Books, 1957, Chap. 7.

other reasons no one has yet come up with a definition universally applicable or satisfactory. Mental illness and mental health are generally defined in terms of (1) whether there are glaring psychological and social symptoms; (2) whether the behavior departs from some statistical concept of normality; (3) whether the behavior is injurious to self or others; and (4) whether it violates conventional norms.

A Joint Commission on Mental Illness and Health, after extensive investigation, issued a report in 1958 on the definition of mental disorder. This report made the following points:

1. Mental health is an individual and personal matter. It involves a living human organism or, more precisely, the condition of an individual human mind. A social environment or culture may be conducive either to sickness or health, but the quality produced is characteristic only of a person, therefore it is improper to speak of a "sick society" or a "sick community."

2. In speaking of a person's mental health, it is advisable to distinguish between attributes and actions. The individual may be classified as more or less healthy in a long-term view of his behavior or, in other words, according to his enduring attributes. Or, his actions may be regarded as more or less healthy — that is, appropriate — from the viewpoint of a single, immediate, short-term situation.

3. Standards of mentally healthy, or normal, behavior vary with the time, place, culture, and expectations of the social group. In short, different peoples have different norms of appropriate behavior.

4. Mental health is one of many human values; it should not be regarded as the ultimate good in itself.

5. No completely acceptable all-inclusive concept exists for physical health or physical illness and, likewise, none exists for mental health or mental illness. A national program against mental illness and for mental health does not depend on acceptance of a single definition and need not await it.[4]

CLASSIFICATION OF MENTAL DISORDERS

Not only is it difficult to define mental health and mental disorder, but it is almost equally difficult to determine the precise type of illness of a patient. Studies indicate there are fads and fashions in diagnosis and, except in very clear cases, diagnoses tend to vary widely. This imprecision is attributable to the same basic causes as the lack of precision in definition. For example, the American Psychiatric Association has a Diagnostic and Statistical Manual, 128 pages in length, which lists literally hundreds of classifications and subclassifications of mental disease.[5] One Appendix in this volume presents a partial list of no less than 300 terms associated with or descriptive of one or more types of disorder.

4. Jahoda, op. cit. pp. x–xi.
5. *Mental Disorders: Diagnostic and Statistical Manual*, The Committee on Nomenclature and Statistics of the American Psychiatric Association, Washington, D.C.: American Psychiatric Association Mental Hospital Service, 1952.

In view of the diversity and range of possible classifications, little is gained from an analysis of all the intricacies and problems of classification and diagnosis. It is sufficient to suggest that all disorders may be described as either psychotic or nonpsychotic, and within the designation of psychotic as either organic or functional. Psychotic disorders are generally characterized by varying degrees of loss of contact with reality, and sometimes by disorientation and confusion as to time, place, and person; in extreme cases by regressive behavior such as incontinence and loss of control over bodily functions; by personality disintegration; by difficulty in interpersonal relationships and in communicating with others; and, in some, by such other behaviors as hallucinations, delusions, withdrawal and isolation, depressions and other mood disturbances, stupors, increased or inhibited motor responses, and perceptual difficulties. Depending upon the type of psychosis and the specific case, different combinations of these and other symptoms may be manifest.[6]

The term organic psychosis is largely self-explanatory. Etiologically, disorders of this type are brought about by a physical or organic impairment to brain tissue and/or the central nervous system. There is, in short, little dispute about their origin. The origins of the more numerous functional psychoses are largely unknown. Scientific attempts to specify physical causes and structural changes in the brain for these disorders have thus far failed. There is some reason for believing that with additional research, disorders currently classified as functional may prove to be organic.

Nonpsychotic disorders, on the other hand, may be as disturbing to the patient and others as psychotic disorders but are seldom incapacitating enough to warrant institutionalization. These ailments, if treated at all, are usually handled by private psychiatrists, clinical psychologists, and psychiatric social workers on an outpatient or private basis. They feature a variety of symptoms ranging from anxiety, somatic or physical complaints, compulsions and obsessions, depression and chronic fatigue, to the inability to respond adequately to a work situation or to assume even minimal responsibility for one's behavior. Given the variety and the vagueness of these symptoms, it is not surprising that there is dispute as to the extent of these disorders in the population.

Most mental diseases, despite the variations, may be grouped into six major categories.[7] The first three are psychoses — the first is organic, and the other two are functional. The last three are nonpsychotic disorders. The six types

6. For a more detailed description of these disorders, see Robert A. White, *The Abnormal Personality*, New York: Ronald, 1948. Also, Roy M. Dorcus and G. Wilson Shaffer, *Textbook of Abnormal Psychology*, 3rd ed., Baltimore: Williams and Wilkins, 1945.
7. See *Mental Disorders: Diagnostic and Statistical Manual*, op. cit. pp. 14–50. See White, op. cit. pp. 276–561. See, also, Norman Cameron, *The Psychology of Behavior Disorders*, Boston: Houghton Mifflin, 1947.

are as follows: (1) Acute and chronic brain syndromes; (2) Affective disorders; (3) Schizophrenia; (4) Psychoneuroses; (5) Psychophysiologic-visceral-autonomic disorders; (6) Characterologic or personality trait disturbances.

PSYCHOSES

1. *Acute and Chronic Brain Syndromes.* The acute and chronic brain syndromes are organic in nature. These diagnoses are made when damage to brain tissue has been substantiated. This damage may be temporary or permanent and may range from gross to very mild. Whatever the source or origin of the damage — senility, infections, drugs, poisons, trauma, cerebral arteriosclerosis, or syphilis — it is sometimes irreversible. This damage to the brain and central nervous system is reflected in impairments in various areas of functioning. These impairments are most likely to occur in the areas of orientation, memory, intellectual functioning, judgment, and affect.

Diagnoses of this type are being made with increasing frequency. In 1959, one-third of all patients in state mental hospitals were 65 years of age or older.[8] There are several important reasons for this. First, as the life span is lengthened and the per cent of aged in the population increases, chronic disorders of all types become more likely. Since the aged are often without money or family, the mental hospital has tended to become a nursing home. Second, in an industrial society, the risk of injury to the brain or nervous system, as in auto accidents is an important one. Third, the widespread use of alcohol and drugs is a major contributing factor. Fourth, improvements in medical techniques which aid in diagnosis, such as electroencephalography, make diagnoses easier and more reliable. Fifth, and extremely important in explaining the increase in this classification, is the increasing ability to keep people alive for longer periods in hospitals through care and medication.

2. *Affective Disorders.* The affective disorders are at present considered to be functional in nature. These psychoses are usually characterized by severe distortions in mood (affect) which are reflected in thought and behavior. Specific diagnostic symptoms may include delusions, hallucinations, periods of depression or elation, speech and motor excitation or inhibition, anxiety, insomnia, agitation, guilt, and paranoid ideas.

Affective disorders tend to be diagnosed during the age period of 30–55 and the rates for females exceed those for males. Unlike some other psychoses, the prognosis is usually favorable for the affective disorders. Institutionalization is often short and with the newer drugs — tranquilizers and psychic energizers — and electro-shock, the per cent of patients who return home is reasonably high. Unfortunately, recurrence in these disorders is frequent.

The affective disorders provide an example of fad and fashion in diagnosis.

8. *Fact Sheet,* Joint Information Service of the American Psychiatric Association and the National Association for Mental Health, no. 14 (January 1961), p. 2.

In the past, they constituted a sizable proportion of the diagnoses. In 1950–55, they represented a minor diagnostic group. The reasons for this decrease are not clear. Patients formerly classified as affectives now are probably spotted earlier in life and are more likely, therefore, to be designated as schizophrenics. Too, some are probably classified as psychoneurotics.[9]

3. *Schizophrenia.* The functional psychosis affecting the largest group of institutionalized patients is schizophrenia. Some psychiatrists prefer to use the plural term schizophrenias to indicate that there may be several disease entities which are difficult to separate from each other. This classification was formerly called *dementia praecox* (psychosis of adolescence). Laymen often speak of *split personality* when referring to schizophrenia, but there is no justification for this description.

Schizophrenia is usually diagnosed by the presence of such symptoms as difficulty in perceiving reality, a tendency to distortion of and withdrawal from reality, isolation from interaction with others, distortions in the stream of thought and its expression, generally inappropriate behavior, regression to lower levels of psychological integration, and deterioration in intellect. The schizophrenic may be unaware of his surroundings and of others and live in a private and personal world. He may have great difficulty in understanding and responding to very simple questions. His speech may be idiosyncratic and almost impossible to understand. Muteness occasionally is encountered. Body control and co-ordination vary from no observable impairment to total rigidity. In extreme cases, control over eating, elimination, speech, and perception may be lacking, and only with great difficulty can presently available therapies restore them.

The Diagnostic Manual of the American Psychiatric Association lists nine types of schizophrenic reactions. Five of these are most likely to be encountered: the *simple, hebephrenic, catatonic, paranoid,* and *chronic undifferentiated subtypes.*

Simple schizophrenia as a sub-classification unually implies moderate detachment from reality, apathy, indifference, isolation and poor interpersonal relationships. This private world is unshareable. In time, and in the absence of treatment, deterioration in mental functioning tends to occur.

The *hebephrenic* subtype is quite different. Here, isolation from reality is accompanied by a silliness in response, girlish and wholly inappropriate

9. For a discussion of fads in diagnosis see, Richard J. Plunkett and John E. Gordon, *Epidemiology and Mental Illness*, Report to the Joint Commission on Mental Illness and Health, No. 6, New York: Basic Books, 1960, pp. 25–7. Also, Benjamin Pasamanick, Simon Dinitz, and Mark Lefton, "Psychiatric Orientation and Its Relation to Diagnosis and Treatment in a Mental Hospital," *American Journal of Psychiatry*, 116 (1959), pp. 127–32. Also, Morton Kramer, Earl S. Pollack, and Richard W. Redick, "Mental Disorders in the United States: Current Status and Future Goals," in *Comparative Epidemiology of the Mental Disorders* (Paul S. Hoch and Joseph Zubin, eds.), New York: Grune and Stratton, 1961, pp. 68–79.

giggling and laughter, inappropriate gestures and mannerisms, and hallucinations. Serious and somber statements, as well as innocuous ones, are sufficient to bring a response of laughter. Attempts by outsiders to "enter" this private world are extremely frustrating.

A highly publicized subtype is *catatonia*. Patients of this type may swing from complete withdrawal characterized by speechlessness, stupor, lack of control over arms and legs and general rigidity, to excitation and violence. Sometimes catatonics are reduced to a state of vegetation.

The *paranoid* type of schizophrenia is typified by transitory as opposed to the relatively fixed states of persecution or grandeur that belong to another disease called paranoia. Paranoid schizophrenics may express feelings of being hunted, poisoned, deceived, and killed on the one extreme or being God-like, brilliant, creative, and masters of strategy on the other.

In contrast to these subtypes of schizophrenia is one designated as *chronic undifferentiated*. This term is used when symptoms are not clear cut. It is a sort of taxonomic repository for cases which cannot otherwise be meaningfully classified. Psychiatric categories contain many such subtypes, indicative of the present state of confusion with regard to both the nature of mental disease and its classification.

Schizophrenia is more frequent among young, unmarried persons. The peak years seem to be before 35 and many are found prior to age 21. Males probably predominate. This may be due to the fact that women are not as frequently involved in the world of work and can more easily escape detection. Schizophrenics marry less frequently than other people and many avoid early detection by being shielded by parents.

Until the advent of shock therapy, the newer medications, and other special programs, most institutionalized schizophrenics were likely to remain hospitalized for the balance of their lives. As late as the 1920's, fewer than one in five were ever released and, after a year or two in a mental hospital, a schizophrenic had only one chance in a hundred to leave the hospital with a discharge. By 1960, some 60 per cent of hospitalized schizophrenics could be expected to return home.[10] Part of this success is due to earlier detection and to decreasing social stigma, so that less severely impaired schizophrenics are being hospitalized, helped, and released. With research, prognoses may be expected to continue to improve. Even the severely regressed "backward" cases are no longer hopeless.

NONPSYCHOTIC MENTAL DISORDERS

4. *Psychoneuroses.* More disagreement exists over the psychoneuroses, or, more simply, the neuroses, than over most other mental diseases. Here, a

10. *Facts about Mental Illness*, National Association for Mental Health, 1960.

diagnostician's training, orientation, and theories of mental disorder determine whom and how many he classifies as neurotic.

Technically, psychoneurotics retain a firm grasp on reality. There are no delusions, hallucinations, or other distortions of this type. The isolation of the schizophrenic and the distortions in mood of the affective or manic-depressive are absent. Instead, the psychoneurotic is characterized by overwhelming anxiety, which is sometimes focused but often diffuse. This anxiety is usually accompanied by feelings of guilt, shame, and hostility. Sometimes this anxiety is "acted out," resulting in aggressive behavior, but more often it takes other and more subtle forms. In short, the terms neurosis and anxiety are inseparable in the lexicon of psychiatry.

Depending upon the symptoms and the manner in which the anxiety is expressed, a diagnosis may involve one of several subtypes of psychoneuroses. Five of these will be described. When the anxiety is diffuse and without specific focus, the classification is usually that of anxiety state. The patient is irrationally anxious and tense. Occasionally this diffuse anxiety takes a somatic form and the patient suffers from general malaise including fatigue, poor eating practices, and insomnia.

A second type of neurotic classification is the dissociative reaction. Relatively rare, the anxiety may take the form of stupor, amnesia, a dreamlike state, or sleepwalking. The patient seems to dissociate himself from his problems. A third type is known as conversion reaction or hysteria. Anxiety is focused on bodily organs over which the patient formerly exercised control. Examples of conversion hysteria include blindness, paralysis, deafness, tics, and tremors. Cases of conversion hysteria are likely to be encountered under conditions of extreme anxiety such as those in wartime. In World War II, battlefield personnel suffering from conversion reactions were at times accused of malingering. Such accusations point up some of the prejudices and lack of knowledge about mental illness.

In obsessive-compulsive reactions, individuals express their anxiety by fixing on a repetitive idea or performing a repetitive act. Although the neurotic may be aware of such irrationalities as constant handwashing and wiping all door handles with a handkerchief before touching them, he cannot control them. These compulsions may also take the form of criminal acts like arson and kleptomania. In extreme instances, the rituals come to dominate the life of the patient to the extent that he cannot organize himself sufficiently to carry out his usual duties.

Phobic patients, on the other hand, translate their anxiety into specific fears of people, places, or things. Common phobias include fears of open and closed spaces, height, water, thunder and lightning, elevators, and the like. Not only are these fears unsound but, in phobic types of neurotics, they may come to dominate life and disorganize other activities. Irrational fears may also play a role in the lives of mentally healthy persons. They are manageable and restricted in the healthy person, while they are disruptive and predominant in the neurotic.

Neuroses may be encountered at any age level. Most diagnoses, however, are made in the middle years of life — primarily because persons in this age range can afford to seek and receive treatment. Similarly, persons of relative wealth are more likely to receive such a diagnosis. Females are more frequently diagnosed as neurotics than are males.[11]

Neurotics constitute a relatively small per cent of patients institutionalized in public mental hospitals. Those receiving treatment are overwhelmingly patients of psychiatrists and other private therapists.[12] Since such cases are not officially recorded, there is no method of determining the extent of neurosis in the general population. However, various estimates, based on research studies, will be presented later.

Standard treatment with neurotics involves establishing a patient-therapist relationship through which the patient gains understanding or "insight" into his neurosis. This process is costly and lengthy and, since no general records are maintained, it is difficult to evaluate its success.

5. *Psychophysiological-Visceral-Autonomic Disorders.* This impressive classification covers a variety of illnesses better known as the "psychosomatic" disorders. In these disorders — in theory at least — the patient's emotions find expression in vulnerable physical organs or general physiologic processes. In time these organs or processes may undergo structural change and may be temporarily or permanently impaired. This implies that certain organic impairments are of psychological origin. Repair of these organs or processes must be preceded by removal of the psychological problems.

Certain diseases or patterns of malfunctioning are often attributed to psychological stress, anxiety, or guilt and would fall into this classification. These include diabetes mellitus, asthma, stomach ulcer, colitis, bladder trouble, essential hypertension, hay fever, heart conditions, neuralgia, arthritis, and skin rashes and hives.[13] Clearly, there are other bases for some or possibly all of these conditions. Nevertheless, psychological factors are believed by many

11. Benjamin Pasamanick, Dean W. Roberts, Paul W. Lemkau, and Dean B. Krueger, "A Survey of Mental Disease in an Urban Population," in *Epidemiology of Mental Disorder* (Benjamin Pasamanick, ed.), Washington, D.C.: American Association for the Advancement of Science, 1959, pp. 183–201.

12. August B. Hollingshead and F. C. Redlich, *Social Class and Mental Illness*, New York: Wiley, 1958.

13. These 11 conditions are subsumed under the designation psychophysiological-visceral-autonomic disorders which are sometimes also called the "organ neuroses." See, *Mental Disorders: Diagnostic and Statistical Manual*, op. cit. pp. 29–31, for additional descriptions and differentiations of these disorders.

psychiatrists to be either the primary precipitants of these disorders or to play a causative role.

Even less is known about "psychosomatic" disorders than about most other types of mental disorder. Few such patients are ever institutionalized. Many are completely undetected. When treatment is sought, it is usually from a family physician or a medical specialist rather than from a psychiatrist. In addition, many persons with such impairments would fear being stigmatized if their impairment were attributed to psychological factors.

6. *Characterological or Personality Trait Disturbance Disorders.* The characterological or personality trait disturbances include a diversity of people and behaviors which are placed together because (a) no other classification seems suitable and (b) the persons so described cannot tolerate stress without losing their emotional equilibrium or stability. These persons have, in psychiatric terminology, failed to achieve emotional maturity. Many feel inadequate and insecure and have difficulty managing their emotions. Many are irresponsible in fulfilling job and family obligations. Some seek escape from the pressures of life by drifting from place to place or by means of alcohol or drugs. Some appear to be almost amoral in their conduct and particularly in their sexual behavior. Almost all have trouble making decisions. Some seem devoid of goals and their conduct is therefore controlled by impulses. A few may be aggressive, but most are not. There is rarely any indication of intellectual or other deterioration or loss of contact with reality — only an inability to operate within prevailing social and legal norms.

In the past, and to a lesser extent now, the terms psychopath and sociopath were used to describe many of these patients. Psychopaths, among them the "bad seeds," include persons who deviate in terms of personal qualities such as those enumerated above. Sociopaths deviate normatively.

Little is known about these disturbed persons. Few are hospitalized. Most remain in the community or are caught in the revolving door of our jails and workhouses. Under these circumstances, data on the prevalence of these disorders are lacking.

THE EXTENT OF MENTAL DISORDER

Estimating the prevalence (the per cent of cases in the total population at a given time) of these and other specific mental diseases in the United States is not an easy task.[14] Mental patients may be institutionalized in public mental hospitals, VA hospitals, private hospitals, or, on occasion, in psychiatric wards of general hospitals. Some are not institutionalized but receive therapy in out-patient facilities, from psychiatrists in private practice, and from other physicians. With the exception of the 270 public (state and county) hospitals

14. Plunkett and Gordon, op. cit. pp. 12–13.

which account for some 88 per cent of the known resident patients and the
41 VA hospitals which house another 9 per cent, records on the patients in
310 private psychiatric hospitals and the 789 psychiatric sections of general
hospitals as well as on other hospitalized and nonhospitalized patients are
scarce, scanty, and generally unreliable.[15] Since even the public and VA
hospitals often do not strictly adhere to standard recording and reporting
procedures, this leads to a paucity of reliable data and results in different estimates of the extent of mental illness.

In a report of the Joint Commission on Mental Illness and Health it is estimated that 1,070,000 Americans are admitted and institutionalized in public and private mental hospitals and in the psychiatric wards of general hospitals during the course of a year. When a daily census figure is used, some
650,000 persons are in hospitals with mental disorders. This means that on
any given day as many or more hospital beds are occupied by the mentally ill
as by persons suffering from all other types of diseases combined. The Joint
Commission also reports that at least 379,000 other nonhospitalized patients
are annually treated in mental hygiene and health clinics; and from 365,000
to 451,000 are annually seen by private psychiatrists. Many others are seen
by physicians other than psychiatrists, and by social agencies, clergymen,
and psychologists.[16]

Public hospital data do provide clues to the extent of mental disease. On
the basis of these partial data, five trends are apparent. First, mental hospital
admissions are increasing at a rate of 2 per cent per year while the general
population increases at a lower rate of 1.6 to 1.8 per cent per year. In a short
time already overcrowded facilities will be more crowded. The resident population will be 35 per cent higher in 1975 than in 1955.[17] Second, acting as a
counterforce is the trend toward increased and earlier release of hospitalized
patients because of drug therapies. This trend first became prominent in 1955
with the widespread adoption of tranquilizers and will no doubt continue. The
effect of these drugs can best be illustrated by the fact that there are now
52,000 fewer resident patients than was predicted earlier.[18] Third, the composition of the hospitalized mentally ill is changing. Older persons, 65 and
over, suffering from senility and related afflictions, constitute an increasing
proportion of the mental hospital population. Projections indicate that first
admissions of the aged to public mental hospitals will rise from 32,615 in 1955
to 47,878 in 1975.[19] Fourth, psychiatric facilities in general hospitals will play

15. *Action for Mental Health*, Final Report of the Joint Commission on Mental Illness
    and Health, New York: Basic Books, Science Edition, 1961, p. 173. Also Kramer,
    Pollack, and Redick, op. cit. pp. 87–8.
16. Plunkett and Gordon, op. cit. p. 41.
17. Kramer, Pollack and Redick, op. cit. p. 86.
18. Ibid. p. 73.
19. Ibid. p. 80.

Fig. 14-1. Number of Resident Patients, Total Admissions, Net Releases, and Deaths. Public Mental Hospitals. United States, 1939-'59.

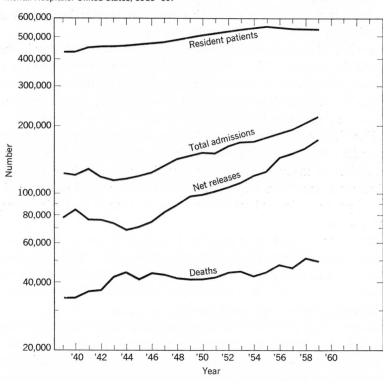

Source: *Mental Health Statistics, Current Reports,* U.S. Department of Health, Education and Welfare, Public Health Service, National Institute of Mental Health, (January, 1960).

an increased role in the care of the mentally disturbed. In 1955, 35 per cent of the total admissions in carefully selected reporting areas went to general hospitals and this per cent will probably increase.[20] Fifth, the diagnoses of hospital admission cases are changing. From 1940 to 1950, the number of diagnoses of schizophrenia increased 32 per cent, of psychoses attributable to syphilis decreased 59 per cent, of psychoses involving alcoholism increased 20 per cent, and of patients without psychosis increased 45.2 per cent. In 1950 schizophrenics accounted for 21 per cent of the first admissions and manic-depressives for 4.7 per cent. Comparable figures in 1940 were 15.9 and 7.6 per cent respectively.[21]

THE EPIDEMIOLOGY OF MENTAL DISORDERS

Hospital data fail, of course, to present a complete picture of the problem. For this reason various epidemiological studies have been undertaken to arrive at a more reliable estimate of the incidence and prevalence of these dis-

20. Ibid. p. 88.
21. Ibid. Table 1, pp. 66–7.

orders. Epidemiologic studies are also concerned with the distribution of disorders by population characteristics (age, sex, race, and social class) and by
geographic area. Accurate data of this type can provide hypotheses about
the etiology or causation of the mental illnesses.

A number of epidemiologic investigations have been conducted. Five of
these will be discussed. These were selected because they indicate the range
of interest of specialists in mental health and the different methods of study
possible. The five studies were conducted in Chicago, several areas in the
northern great plains, in New York, in Baltimore, and in New Haven.

1. *The Faris and Dunham Study.*[22] This study of the urban distribution
of first admission cases to all public and private hospitals in the Chicago area
was the first of many such investigations. Later studies have corroborated
the findings in most if not all details.[23] This study plotted the areas of residence of patients admitted for the first time to mental hospitals during the
years 1922–34.

Examination of these areas revealed an almost perfect gradient tendency.
Beginning with the central business district (downtown Chicago), concentric
zones of one mile each were plotted from the city center and the ratio of hospitalized cases to population in these zones was calculated. The results showed
that beginning at the center and moving through the zone of transition toward the periphery of the city, the rates for all mental illness per 100,000 population decreased. From the center of Chicago southward the rates were: 362,
337, 175, 115, 88, 74, and 71. All other segments or directions from the center
followed the same trend.

Admissions for schizophrenia showed the most persistent gradient tendency. The alcoholic psychoses were most heavily concentrated in the zone of
transition. Only the manic-depressive (affective) psychosis failed to adhere to
this pattern, appearing to be randomly distributed throughout the city.

These results led to three hypotheses concerning the nature of mental illness. First it was suggested that precipitants of mental illness, such as poverty,
slums, homelessness, and area disorganization, were concentrated in the center of the city and decreased toward its periphery. Persons residing closer
to the center were consequently more subject to these stresses and their rates
reflected the personal consequences of this social disorganization. The more
disorganized the area, the higher the rates.

Second, precisely the reverse interpretation was suggested by those with
a biological explanation. They posed the "drift" hypothesis which suggests

22. For a more detailed analysis of this pioneering work see, Robert E. L. Faris and H.
    Warren Dunham, *Mental Disorders in Urban Areas,* Chicago: University of Chicago
    Press, 1939.
23. H. Warren Dunham, "Current Status of Ecological Research in Mental Disorder," in
    Mental Health and Mental Disorder (Arnold Rose, ed.), New York: Norton, 1955.

that impaired persons from all areas in and outside the community, tend to drift into the center of the city and concentrate there.[24] The deteriorated areas characterized by impersonality and anonymity act as a magnet, pulling in persons unable to adjust in other areas. There is one other aspect of this hypothesis which deservs mention. It is suggested that, in these deteriorated areas, the more "healthy" succeed in moving out while the less "healthy" remain. These latter persons, plus those who have "drifted in," account for the disproportionately high rates for mental disorders in urban slum areas.

Third, it has been suggested that the gradient tendency in mental hospital rates is an artificial creation of economic and class factors. At the periphery of a community, residents are more highly educated and economically affluent and are better able to afford private psychiatric care. As a result they are less likely to be hospitalized in public institutions. Mental hospitals therefore become repositories for those who are unable to pay for other types of care. If opportunities for early, private, out-patient care were equally available to all segments of the population, the gradient tendency would largely disappear.[25] Whatever the merit of these interpretations — and probably all three account for a part of the variation in rates — the Faris and Dunham study opened new vistas for exploration.

2. *The Hutterites*.[26] While Faris and Dunham studied urban areas, Eaton and Weil studied a sharply contrasting area. The Hutterites are a German Anabaptist sect who live in small communities in the northern great plains area of the United States and Canada. They are primarily involved in agricultural pursuits and in community life closely approximate a folk society; large families, the communal care of children, strong community and religious ties, and isolation from urban areas characterize this folk group. Under these conditions, one might predict that they would be relatively free of mental disorder if mental disease is related to the complexities of urban life.

A team of researchers investigated the mental health of over 8000 Hutterites scattered in more than 90 local communities in the United States and Canada. Over 2000 Hutterites were interviewed and, of these, the staff psychiatrist saw 298 persons. The results were equivocal. While the Hutterites did have a lower rate for the psychoses and neuroses than urbanites, the rates were high enough to cast doubt on the role of stress and tension in modern

24. A large number of studies have considered this problem of the "drift" hypothesis and its corollary, the "social selection" hypothesis. For a review of some of this work, see H. Warren Dunham, "Social Structures and Mental Disorders," in *Causes of Mental Disorders: A Review of Epidemiological Knowledge*, New York: Milbank Memorial Fund, 1961, pp. 244 ff.
25. This suggestion is implicit in many of the ecological and community studies.
26. For a more detailed analysis, see Joseph Eaton and Robert J. Weil, *Culture and Mental Disorders*, Glencoe: Free Press, 1955.

life in causing mental disorder. While the "simple" life may reduce the extent of neuropsychiatric disorders, it does not eliminate them.

3. *The "Midtown" Study in New York*.[27] "Midtown," in New York City, is a complete contrast to Hutterite society. It is a densely populated, congested area in Manhattan composed of a variety of social classes, a variety of ethnic groups, a variety of occupational and educational attainments, and a variety of about every other sociocultural dimension. The ties of kinship and community are, at best, tenuous. The area is impersonal and anonymous and the pressures of life are great. What, then, are the consequences of such an area for the residents? How much mental disorder is to be found in this type of community?

From census data, the investigators carefully selected a sample of 1660 persons for study. This 1.7 per cent sample was representative of the entire population of the area in terms of age, sex, marital status, social class, religion, rural-urban background, and national origin. All except 13 per cent of the sample were successfully interviewed. The interview schedule contained 120 specific items dealing with psychologic symptoms as well as other items pertaining to childhood and demographic factors. In addition, it was determined whether the respondents had received previous psychiatric care or treatment and whether they were listed in the New York Social Service Index.

By classifying symptoms by number, quality, and severity, the sample was divided into six groupings. These were: well (free of important symptoms), mildly disturbed (some symptoms but fairly good behavior), moderately disturbed (a greater number and qualitatively more important symptoms but everyday functioning was still good), marked disturbance (important symptoms having some effect on performance), severe disturbance (symptoms made a real difference in performance), and incapacitation. Persons falling into the first three of these groups, by virtue of the lack of overt disability, were further classified as unimpaired. The latter three groups constituted the impaired. *The results indicated that nearly a fourth (23.4 per cent) of the sample was impaired*.[28] Since the sample represented the general population of the area under study, the inevitable conclusion is that nearly one out of every four persons in "Midtown" was experiencing symptoms that interfered with functioning.

Caution should be exercised in using this prevalence percentage because every form of mental disorder was included. No distinction was made between the psychoses and other disorders which are less clearly defined. It is

27. For a more detailed analysis, see Leo Srole, Thomas S. Langner, Stanley T. Michael, Marvin K. Opler, and Thomas A. C. Rennie, *Mental Health in the Metropolis: The Manhattan Midtown Study*, Vol. I, New York: McGraw-Hill, 1962.
28. Ibid. p. 138.

probable that psychotics did not exceed 10 per cent of the sample. If the less severe disorders are excluded, or analyzed separately, the prevalence diminishes greatly. Such is the case in the next, and perhaps the best, study to be reported.

4. *The Baltimore Study.*[29] From 1952–55, the Commission on Chronic Illness, an agency jointly sponsored by the Ameircan Hospital Association, the American Medical Association, the American Public Health Association, and the American Public Welfare Association, conducted a study of the prevalence of chronic illness in Baltimore, Maryland.[30] The first phase of this investigation consisted of a survey of some 4000 carefully selected Baltimore households containing 12,000 people. This phase attempted, through interviews, to arrive at some estimate of the prevalence of such chronic diseases as heart disease, diabetes, and arthritis as well as of mental disorders. The second and unique phase consisted of examining, at Johns Hopkins Hospital, some 809 respondents. In 86 cases, a finding of mental disorder was made and substantiated by a psychiatrist who reviewed the data obtained in the clinical evaluation. Rates by diagnosis were then calculated for the population. This revealed that the prevalence rate of noninstitutionalized psychotics was 0.4 per cent; for neurotics, 5.3 per cent; and for the "psychosomatic" disorders, 3.7 per cent. The total rate for these disorders alone, then, was 9.4 per cent.

This rate fails, of course, to include the state hospital, private hospital, and Veterans' Hospital patients. Pasamanick was able to obtain data from all three of these sources for these years. Adding the institutional rates to the noninstitutional rates provides the closest approximation to a true rate for mental disorders. This rate for Baltimore was 9.8 per cent. In other words, one person in ten was mentally ill at the time in Baltimore. This rate was distributed as follows:

(a) One per cent of the population was psychotic; half were institutionalized and the other half were not. Of those in hospitals, almost all were in state, rather than private, facilities.

29. The results of the Baltimore study were published in a series of articles. See, Benjamin Pasamanick, Dean W. Roberts, Paul W. Lemkau, and Dean B. Kreuger, "A Survey of Mental Disease in an Urban Population: I. Prevalence by Age, Sex, and Severity of Impairment," *American Journal of Public Health*, 47 (1957), pp. 923–9; "A Survey of Mental Disease in an Urban Population: II. Prevalence by Race and Income," in *The Epidemiology of Mental Disorder* (Benjamin Pasamanick, ed.), Washington, D.C.: American Association for the Advancement of Science, 1959, pp. 183–201; "A Survey of Mental Disease in an Urban Population: III. Prevalence and Demographic Distribution of Some 'Psychosomatic' Disorders," Washington, D.C.: American Psychiatric Association, 1960, pp. 245–53; Benjamin Pasamanick, "A Survey of Mental Disease in an Urban Population: IV. An Approach to Total Prevalence Rates," *Archives of General Psychiatry*, 5 (1961) pp. 151–5.
30. *Chronic Illness in the United States: Chronic Illness in a Large City*, Vol. 4, Commission on Chronic Illness, Cambridge: Harvard University Press, 1957.

(b) Over 5 per cent were neurotic. The number institutionalized was only 0.07 per cent of the general population.

(c) The psychophysiologic-autonomic-visceral disorders ("psychosomatic") had a rate of nearly 3.8 per cent. Not one person was institutionalized for these disorders.

(d) One person in every 40 in Baltimore, or 2.5 per cent of the total population, was severely or totally disabled by these psychiatric difficulties.

(e) No other group of diseases approached the psychiatric disorders in the number of severely and chronically disabled persons.

There were other findings. For example, the prevalence of mental disorders increased systematically with age — from 0.35 per cent for those under 35, to 1.3 per cent among those aged 35 to 64, to 4 per cent of those over 65 years of age. Males had a much higher rate for the psychoses, but not as high a rate for the other major disorders. Somewhat surprising was the finding concerning race. Whites had far higher rates than nonwhites for the psychoses, psychoneuroses, and psychosomatic disorders. These findings attest to the importance of studying noninstitutionalized subjects in order to estimate prevalence rates for mental disorder.

5. *The New Haven Study.*[31] One of the most provocative of all the epidemiological investigations is the work of Hollingshead and Redlich and their associates in the New Haven, Connecticut, metropolitan area. This sociologist and psychiatrist team tested several hypotheses dealing with the relation of social class to treated mental illness. Hollingshead and Redlich hypothesized that social class should make a difference in the percentage of persons treated for mental illness and that it would be a factor in diagnosis and therapy.

In order to test these hypotheses, it was necessary to determine the characteristics of treated patients in the New Haven area. Six state hospitals, five veterans' hospitals, eleven general hospitals with psychiatric wards, and seven clinics in the area made their records available on the medical and social characteristics of their patients. Forty-six out of 66 private practitioners also co-operated. Totally unrecorded, however, were the cases known to non-psychiatric agencies.

Since the census data failed to provide the necessary data, an extensive survey had to be conducted to establish the characteristics of the population in the total community. This was done by selecting every twentieth address from the City Directory and interviewing the occupants. Of the 3608 household units thus selected, interviews were conducted with occupants in 3559 homes.

31. For a detailed analysis of the New Haven study, see August B. Hollingshead and F. C. Redlich, *Social Class and Mental Illness,* New York: Wiley, 1958.

The two populations — treated patients and the 5 per cent sample of the households in New Haven — were then stratified into five class categories. The categories were determined by area of residence within New Haven and by occupation and education. One per cent of the patients and 3 per cent of the nonpatients fell into Class I, the New Haven upper class. Seven per cent of the patients and 8.4 per cent of the nonpatients belonged to Class II, or the upper middle class. The middle-middle class (III) contained 13.7 per cent of the patients and 20.4 per cent of the nonpatients. The lower-middle and upper-lower class (IV) contained 40.1 per cent of the patients and 49.8 per cent of the nonpatients. The lower class (V) had 38.2 per cent of the patients and 18.4 per cent of the nonpatients.

Class V persons thus appear twice as frequently as expected among treated patients. All other classes are under-represented in the patient population. This same class pattern persists, with minor variations, in spite of differences in sex, race, marital status, and religious affiliation. After weighting the sample differences by age and sex, there were 553 treated patients in every 100,000 Class I-II persons, 528 in Class III, 665 in Class IV, and 1668 in Class V. The rate for all classes was 808 treated patients per 100,000 persons.

Class was found to be related not only to prevalence but to other important dimensions. The rate of diagnosed neurotics decreased almost consistently from Class I–II to Class V, and the rate for psychotics increased sevenfold from Class I–II to Class V. Within the psychoses, treated organic cases were over 26 times more common in the lower than in the upper and upper-middle classes; senile schizophrenics and psychotics were over eight times as frequent; and affective psychotics two and a half times as common in Class V as in Class I-II. Psychotics in the upper classes were only infrequently hospitalized in public facilities. In Class I-II, a half or more of all psychotics in treatment were utilizing private facilities. At the other extreme, Class V, over 98 per cent of the schizophrenics, all senile psychotics, 98 per cent of the organics, and 94 per cent of the affectives were in state or veterans' hospitals.

Class I-II patients received psychotherapy, which is considered to be the preferred therapy more frequently for every type of disorder than did patients in Class V. The opposite, custodial care, was given most often to lower class patients and least frequently to the upper and upper-middle class cases. The use of organic therapy, of which electro-shock is most common, varied among the classes but was more frequently applied at the lower socio-economic levels.

Considering length of treatment and cost, lower class patients were institutionalized far longer than Class I-II cases for all psychoses except the affective. On the other hand, Class I-II nonpsychotic patients were in treatment for longer periods than Class V cases. The expenditures, by class, varied even more. The mean cost per psychotic patient varied in 1950 from $3961 in Class I-II to $1704 in Class III, $1347 in Class IV and $1289 in Class V. For nonpsychotics, the expenditures ranged from $2765 per patient at the upper socio-economic levels to $956 per Class V patient. These costs are, however, largely deceptive. Class V patients are sent almost exclusively to state mental hospitals where treatment generally consists of "custody" for long periods at low per diem cost. Class I-II patients avail themselves of private psychiatrists and hospitals and public clinics. They receive preferred treatment — psychotherapy — at relatively high costs for short periods. In the long run the higher costs to Class I-II patients, because they reflect treatment and not mere custody, may be less expensive than the costs to the state for the custody of long-term Class V patients.

In conclusion, Hollingshead and Redlich demonstrated that social class is related to the prevalence, types, treatment, and costs of mental disorders. In so doing, they also called attention to the very distinct possibility that socio-cultural variables play a major role in the etiology of mental disease.

SUMMARY

In this chapter, the problem of the definition of mental disease and classification of the various disorders was discussed. Mental disease defies adequate definition. A diagnosis of mental illness is usually made when there are glaring psychological symptoms, when the individual is thought to be dangerous to himself and others, and when his aberrations prevent him from performing his usual duties.

Mental illness takes many forms. There are the psychoses and the nonpsychotic disorders. Within the psychoses, some disorders are organic in origin and others are functional. Six types of disorders were discussed: the organic psychoses, the affective disorders, schizophrenia, the psychoneuroses, the psychosomatic diseases, and the personality trait disturbances.

The extent of these mental diseases and their distribution in the population was discussed. Mental disorders were shown to be the most prevalent and debilitating of all chronic diseases. They require as many or more hospital beds as all other diseases combined. Over one million persons are admitted to mental hospitals each year. The combined data of reported and unreported mental illness indicated that one in ten persons suffers from some mental or emotional disturbance.

The chapter concluded with an analysis of five community studies. These studies dealt with the distribution of mental disease by age, sex, race, class, and geographic area. From the evidence of these studies we deduced the amount of unreported mental illness and the differentials in diagnosis and treatment by class position.

QUESTIONS AND SUGGESTIONS FOR FURTHER STUDY

1. Why is it that mental disease is considered a form of deviation whereas other chronic illnesses are not?
2. Trace the changes in public attitudes toward mental illness and the care and treatment given mental patients. Read *The Mind That Found Itself* and *The Snake Pit* for further information.
3. Why is it so hard to develop an adequate definition of mental illness?
4. Distinguish the psychoses from the nonpsychotic disorders.
5. What is meant by a functional mental disorder?
6. Take a field trip to a state mental hospital.
7. Invite a speaker from the local Mental Health Association to speak to your class on the treatment facilities available in your community.
8. Read Hollingshead and Redlich's volume on mental illness in New Haven and evaluate this work and its implications.
9. Read *Action for Mental Health* and discuss its recommendations for the prevention and treatment of mental disorder.
10. What do you think ought to be done about mental illness? How can we arrive at some consensus about its definition? How would you go about modifying public attitudes toward the mentally ill?

SUGGESTED READINGS

Eaton, Joseph, and Robert J. Weil, *Culture and Mental Disorders*, Glencoe: Free Press, 1955. A provocative description and analysis of the problems of mental illness among the Hutterites. The Hutterites are an interesting religious sect tenaciously adhering to sacred values in the face of social change.

Faris, Robert E. L., and H. Warren Dunham, *Mental Disorders in Urban Areas*, Chicago: University of Chicago Press, 1939. This is the pioneering study of the ecological distribution of mental disorders in an urban population. It is still the finest work on this subject.

Hollingshead, August B., and F. C. Redlich, *Social Class and Mental Illness*, New York: Wiley, 1958. This volume describes the relation of social class to the incidence, prevalence, diagnosis, and therapy of treated mental illness in New Haven, Conn. This is the standard work on social class as a variable in mental disorder.

Jahoda, Marie, *Current Concepts of Positive Mental Health*, Report to the Joint Commission on Mental Illness and Health, No. 1, New York: Basic Books, 1958. In this slim volume, Jahoda attempts to arrive at a satisfactory definition of mental illness based on the most current information in the field.

Plunkett, Richard J., and John E. Gordon, *Epidemiology and Mental Illness*, Report to the Joint Commission on Mental Illness and Health, No. 6, New York:

Basic Books, 1960. This work contains an abbreviated and systematic review and analysis of the major community studies of mental illness. Both readable and informative.

Srole, Leo, Thomas S. Langner, Stanley T. Michael, Marvin K. Opler, and Thomas A. C. Rennie, *Mental Health in the Metropolis: The Manhattan Midtown Study*, Vol. 1, New York: McGraw-Hill, 1962. The most recent attempt to assess the extent of the mental disorders among a heterogeneous population of urban dwellers. The findings are interesting and controversial.

15 MENTAL ILLNESS: ETIOLOGY,
TREATMENT, AND FUTURE TRENDS

The nonconformist — whether he be foreigner or "odd ball," intellectual or idiot, genius or jester, individualist or hobo, physically or mentally abnormal — pays a penalty for "being different," unless his peculiarity is considered acceptable for his particular group, or unless he lives in a place or period of particularly high tolerance or enlightenment. The socially visible characteristic of the psychotic person is that he becomes a stranger among his own people.[1]

Epidemiologic investigations such as those described in the preceding chapter have provided considerable information about mental illness as a form of deviation. They have also led to many hypotheses about the etiology or causation of mental disorders. Despite these studies and experimental and laboratory research, the causation of mental and emotional deviancy and nonconformity remains a major mystery.[2] Without knowledge of the specific etiologic agents in mental disorder, treatment and therapy remain arbitrary and often ineffective. Intelligent discussion of the problem of deviant behavior, as represented by the mental disorders, requires, therefore, an understanding and evaluation of the competing theories of causation.

THE ETIOLOGY OF MENTAL DISORDERS

Theories of the etiology of mental disorders have focused on organic, psychogenic, and sociocultural factors. In organic theories, emphasis has been placed on defective heredity, physical constitution, biochemical and physiological malfunctioning, endocrine difficulties, and on brain pathology resulting from injury and infections. Psychogenic theories have considered psychological and interactional factors leading to faulty socialization of mentally ill persons. Sociocultural conceptions have dealt with the impact of differential pressures, tensions, norms, and elements of social disorganization on individual functioning. Organic theories have more frequently been used as explana-

1. *Action For Mental Health,* Final Report of the Joint Commission on Mental Illness and Health, New York: Basic Books, Science Edition, 1961, p. 59.
2. The amount of current research on the etiology of mental disorders is staggering. The 1961 *Research Grants Index* contains a 681-page listing of 13,500 projects in progress costing $280,900,000. In 1951, there were only 1695 research projects, involving $17,-129,554. See *Research Grants Index,* U.S. Department of Health, Education and Welfare, 1961.

tions in the psychoses; psychogenic and sociocultural theories, in the non-pyschotic disorders.

ORGANIC THEORIES

1. *Genetic Theories.* The importance of heredity as a causative factor in the functional psychoses has been a matter of persistent controversy. The possible hereditary nature of schizophrenia and the affective psychoses has been extensively investigated; these psychoses have been found to occur far more frequently in persons from families in which there is a history of mental illness than in persons without such a history.[3] Some researchers have cited probabilities for the occurrence of schizophrenia and the affective psychoses based on detailed analyses of family histories. The usual rates for schizophrenia are approximately 1 to 3 per cent of the population.[4] Yet the rate for children born to families in which at least one parent is schizophrenic is 7 to 16 per cent. Among siblings of schizophrenics, the rate is 7 to 15 per cent, and for the parents of schizophrenics, 5 to 10 per cent.[5] For fraternal twins, the rate of concordance is 10 to 17 per cent, and for monozygotic (identical) twins, 76 to 91 per cent.[6] In identical twins, then, schizophrenia in one is accompanied by the same disease in the other in at least three cases out of four. For the affective psychoses, the concordance rate for parents, children, and siblings is approximately 10 to 15 per cent.[7] This is very much higher than general population rates.

Two possible interpretations exist for these findings: first, that there is some genetic mechanism that is causative; second, that some form of infection, physiologic malfunction, virus, or as-yet-unknown organism is more common to some families than to others.

2. *Biochemical, Physiological, and Endocrine Theories.*[8] Many of these

3. A review and analysis of many of the recent European and American studies on this subject is to be found in Jan A. Böök, "Genetical Etiology in Mental Illness," in *Causes of Mental Disorders: A Review of Epidemiological Knowledge*, New York: Milbank Memorial Fund, 1961, pp. 14–50.

4. Ibid. p. 26.

5. Ibid. p. 26.

6. Very careful research in the U.S. on the concordance rates of schizophrenia in twins has been reported by Franz J. Kallmann, "The Genetic Theory of Schizophrenia: An Analysis of 691 Schizophrenic Twin Index Families," *American Journal of Psychiatry* 103 (1946), pp. 309–22. See, also, Franz J. Kallmann, *Heredity in Health and Mental Disorder: Principles of Psychiatric Genetics in the Light of Comparative Twin Studies*, New York: Norton, 1953.

7. Böök, op. cit. p. 30.

8. For a discussion of some of these theories, see Arnold R. Kaplan, "Biochemical Studies in Schizophrenia: A Review," *Eugenics Quarterly* 5 (1958), pp. 86–94, and Ronald R. Kroegler, Edward Colbert, and Samuel Eiduson, "Wanted: A Biochemical Test for Schizophrenia," *California Medicine* 94 (1961), pp. 26–9.

theories, which have recently come to some prominence, are almost wholly incomprehensible to laymen. This provides them with a scientific aura, as does the fact that these theories derived from laboratory research. The success of drugs in the treatment of non-neuropsychiatric diseases has also given these theories, and the organic viewpoint in general, special credence.

One of the most persistent biochemical hypothesis is that, during a psychosis, the organism produces a toxic substance that is thought to be directly responsible for the disorder. The evidence for this thesis is logical but tenuous.[9] In 1943 it was accidentally discovered that when a drug — lysergic acid diethylamide (LSD) — is consumed in very small doses by human beings, it will produce a reaction similar to a psychotic episode. The subject experiences vivid hallucinations and distortions of time, place, and person. Other drugs, such as mescaline, have similar effects.[10] If minute quantities of LSD can have these consequences, is it not logical to assume that a toxic substance exists in the brain in "natural" mental disorders? The difficulty with this thesis is that, despite extensive research, no such substance has yet been found. There have been reports from various laboratories about the successful isolation of a substance in the blood or urine of psychotics, but each time careful investigation indicated these reports to have been premature and based on questionable scientific procedures. In addition, drug injections are not the only method of inducing pseudo-psychotic episodes. Experiments have shown that sensory deprivation also brings pseudo-psychotic reactions. Floating a person in water without outside stimulation or isolating him in a soundproof room devoid of objects will often produce a "model" psychosis. These sensory-deprivation experiments imply that environmental stresses as well as toxic substances may be involved in the psychoses.[11]

A second theory in the biochemical and physiologic area suggests that the psychoses are precipitated by or related to metabolic changes in the organism. The most persuasive evidence for this thesis is that a large proportion of early and chronic cases of all psychoses show some difficulties with carbohydrate tolerance. Schizophrenics also show resistance to insulin and thyroid preparations.[12] No one seems to know why this is so or what its etiologic significance.

The endocrine glands play a part in a third theory. The hypothalamo-

9. See Some Biological Aspects of Schizophrenic Behavior (D. V. Siva Sankar, ed.), New York: Annals of the New York Academy of Sciences, 96 (1962), Part I, pp. 5–160.
10. Leo E. Hollister, "Drug Induced Psychoses and Schizophrenic Reactions," ibid. pp. 80–92.
11. Sensory Deprivation (Philip Soloman et al., eds.) Cambridge: Harvard University Press. 1961.
12. The Etiology of Schizophrenia (Don D. Jackson, ed.), New York: Basic Books, 1960, pp. 124–38.

pituitary-adrenal axis, in particular, is thought to be related to mental disorder. The human brain is likened to a computer that receives, stores, interprets, and transmits messages to other parts of the organism.[13] It does this electro-chemically. As with every other machine, some kind of control must be exercised over its operation. This control presumably is exercised by the endocrine glands, whose secretions flow directly into the blood stream. The endocrine system is fallible. When mistakes or malfunctions in the endocrines occur, pathological conditions, including mental disorders, may then follow.[14]

The difficulty with this theory is that it emphasizes mechanisms within the organism and neglects environmental forces creating stress on the endocrine and nervous systems. Its virtue, however, lies in focusing on organic change as the principal mechanism in mental and emotional pathologies. If proved, this theory will provide a basis for developing chemical and surgical therapies to rectify the faults or errors in the system.

3. *The Brain Pathology Theories.* The most likely place to search for the etiology of mental disorders is in the brain. Damage to brain tissue and brain lesions have, of course, been found to be causative for the organic psychoses. The major dispute, therefore, concerns brain and nervous system pathology as a causative factor in the functional mental disorders.[15] While no one has as yet been able to demonstrate such a cause in functional disorders, at least one theory of this type deserves some consideration.

This theory asserts that from the moment of conception, and particularly during the first trimester of pregnancy when the development of the central nervous system is most critical, the organism is subject to stress and injury which may result in impairment. These external stresses may be brought about by poor nutrition in the mother, toxemias during the pregnancy, viruses and other infections, and many other conditions. Injuries to the brain and central nervous system at birth may range from extremely minor ones to those so gross that they result in deformity and death. Minimally and moderately damaged persons are likely to develop a variety of difficulties in childhood; these conditions might include hearing, reading, and speech disorders, inability to concentrate or to sit still for a reasonable length of time, and tics, tremors, and motor problems. In later life, this early damage might

13. See Norbert Wiener, *Cybernetics*, New York: Wiley, 1948, and *The Human Use of Human Beings*, New York: Doubleday, 1954.
14. Harold Goldman, Rudolf Kaelbling, and Lewis Lindner, "Stress: Some Physical, Physiological and Psychological Correlates," unpublished paper, Columbus Psychiatric Institute and Hospital, August 29, 1961.
15. Brian MacMahon and James M. Sowa, "Physical Damage to the Fetus," pp. 51–120, and George James, "The Epidemiology of Mental Disorder Associated with Damage to the Brain after Birth," pp. 121–52, both in *Causes of Mental Disorders: A Review of Epidemiologic Knowledge*, New York: Milbank Memorial Fund, 1961.

lower resistance to environmental pressures and thereby help produce psychiatric disorders.[16]

Since women in the lower socio-economic strata are more likely to experience difficulties such as toxemias during pregnancy and are more likely to have inferior nutrition and less adequate medical care, it is reasonable to assume that children born to lower class parents stand a greater chance of acquiring these subtle injuries. From this it would follow that these factors and other might lead to higher rates for psychoses in the lower socio-economic groups.

PSYCHOLOGICAL THEORIES

Psychological theories of mental disorder are considerably more abstract. They are also considerably less specific in identifying the mechanisms through which normal behavior becomes deviant. In general, these theories attempt to explain personality and its formation and adaptability rather than to explain pathological manifestations *per se*. They assume that, once the general principles underlying personality are understood, pathological conditions such as the psychoses and neuroses will also be understood. In attempting to arrive at these generalizations about human personality, psychological theories have been developed which range from the bio-psychological on the one extreme to the socio-psychological on the other. Rather than explore the entire spectrum, we will discuss only the psychoanalytic and the neo-Freudian.

1. *Psychoanalytic Theories*.[17] These stem from the creative efforts of Sigmund Freud and his disciples. A practicing physician in Vienna, Freud was confronted by patients with problems in which no known organic involvement could be found. These ailments often featured hysterical symptoms such as paralysis of one or more limbs and compulsive and obsessive reactions. Because standard medical procedures were inadequate, Freud became

16. See Benjamin Pasamanick and Hilda Knobloch, "Epidemiologic Studies on the Complications of Pregnancy and the Birth Process," in *Prevention of Mental Disorders in Childhood* (G. Caplan, ed.), New York: Basic Books, 1961, pp. 74–94; Hilda Knobloch and Benjamin Pasamanick, "The Syndrome of Minimal Cerebral Damage," *Journal of the American Medical Association*, 170 (July 1959), pp. 1384–7; Benjamin Pasamanick and Hilda Knobloch, "Complications of Pregnancy and Neuropsychiatric Disorder," *Journal of Obstetrics and Gynecology of the British Empire*, 66 (1959), pp. 753–5; and Benjamin Pasamanick and Hilda Knobloch, "Brain Damage and Reproductive Casualty," *American Journal of Orthopsychiatry*, 30 (1960), pp. 298–305.
17. For an analysis of the psychoanalytic theories of mental disorders, see Ruth Munroe, *Schools of Psychoanalytic Thought*, New York: Dryden, 1955. Also, Calvin S. Hall and Gardner Lindzey, *Theories of Personality*, New York: Wiley, 1957, Chaps. 2 and 3. For a first-hand account, see Freud's *The Psychopathology of Everyday Life*, New York: Random House, 1938, and *An Outline of Psychoanalysis*, New York: Norton, 1949.

interested in newer approaches. For a time he experimented with hypnosis as a technique, and later he developed the method of free association. This method — despite many alterations and elaborations since his early experimentation — is still a basic technique utilized by most psychoanalysts in treatment.

Not only was Freud a well trained and creative physiologist but he was also a classical scholar — as much at home in the classics, Greek mythology, philosophy, and comparative religion as in biology and medicine. With these orientations he was peculiarly well prepared to synthesize these various conceptions of man into an integrated theory. For half a century, until his death in 1939, he worked to improve and alter his theory in accord with scholarly and clinical findings. Unfortunately, some modern disciples have reified his conceptions instead of using them as constructs to be tested and verified.

Freudian theory is complicated and subtle. Its major postulates are these:

(a) All behavior, no matter how bizarre, is motivated toward the satisfaction of basic instinctual needs. All humans have the same needs because all humans are alike in their instinctual endowment.

(b) The individual is not conscious of these instinctual needs. Even if he were aware of them, he could not successfully modify them.

(c) These instinctual biological needs, whose psychic counterpart Freud called the *id*, are of two major types — the so-called erotic instincts and death instincts. The former are primarily but not exclusively sexual, that is, concerned with the pleasure derived from various zones of the body and the latter are primarily but not exclusively aggressive and destructive. These two sets of wishes are in conflict with each other on the unconscious level, and both must somehow be satisfied. Such is the very complex biological endowment of man.

(d) In order to contain these primitive instinctual wishes, the human being in the process of being socialized begins to develop an *ego*, or self. This ego is extremely vague in Freudian theory, but it is, at least, the set of socialized impulses which each person individually elaborates in the confrontation between the primitive instinctual impulses and the realities of everyday existence. One of the functions of the ego is to keep the wishes of the *id* in check. To the extent that the ego remains strong and dominant, the cruel, gratification-seeking, unconscious biological urges of the *id* are subject to control.

(e) A third mechanism or aspect of human personality is the *superego*, or conscience, which represents the normative aspect of personality. It consists of the unconscious internalization of the norms of society. Its function, like that of the ego, is the channeling of biological energies into socially acceptable behaviors and thoughts. Violations of these internalized norms, as well as of the more individual impulses of the ego, result in anxiety. This anxiety may be experienced as guilt, as shame, or in many other ways.

(f) While all persons are subject to these inherent conflicts — both bio-logical and socio-biological — some are better able to resolve them than others. The critical difference is to be found in personality development. The nature of this development and the dynamic experiences of the process of socialization provide the bases for mental health or mental illness.

(g) The personality (or psychosexual) development of humans begins at birth and progresses through several stages derived from different erogenous zones of the body. The biological animal is moulded, frustrated, satisfied, and socialized in these stages so that, at or near puberty, it becomes a human being with fixed and relatively permanent adaptive mechanisms, characteristics, and problems.

The earliest is called the oral stage and is essentially narcissistic. The term narcissism derives from the name of the mythological hero who fell in love with his image while gazing into a glass-smooth pond. The infant, like Narcissus, is totally self-centered, and its sole concern is the immediate gratification of biological urges. It learns to love and hate (unconsciously) as these needs are satisfied or frustrated. It learns to identify with the source of gratification — the mother or surrogate. The ego and superego begin their development and are elaborated as urges are tested against reality; norms become superimposed on biology.

The second stage is the anal, with pleasures derived from the process of elimination. The third stage is the phallic, with pleasure derived from the genital area without regard for other persons or objects. The fourth or last stage is the genital, characterized by normal heterosexual relations with regard for a partner.

(h) Different problems arise at each of the psychosexual stages resulting in the development of defense mechanisms by the personality. At the earliest stage the problem involves differentiation of self from others and from the external world. Among the central problems in the anal stage is the control of bodily functions in a socially acceptable manner. In the third stage the major difficulty is the Oedipal problem.

The term Oedipal derives from the Greek myth about Oedipus, a king of Thebes. Reared in another kingdom without knowing his parents, Oedipus as an adult encountered and unwittingly slew his father, the monarch of Thebes, and married his mother. From this tale, Freud drew the inspiration for his description of the Oedipal state. The thesis is that the young child, 3 to 5 years of age or so, becomes enamored of the parent of the opposite sex and comes to hate the parent of the same sex. To solve this dilemma, the child represses these feelings, thrusting them into his unconscious. Just as

repression serves as the solution for the Oedipal problem, so other defenses
— denial, obsessions, and displacement — develop to handle other psychosexual problems.

The etiology of the neuroses, therefore, is to be found in the unsuccessful
resolution of the Oedipal and/or earlier psychosexual difficulties and the anxiety thereby generated. In the neurotic, this anxiety brings about the maladap-
tive manifestations characteristic of obsessive, compulsive, hysterical, and
other neurotic behaviors and problems. In channeling this anxiety through
these symptoms, the patient limits the disorder to only a part of his life activities.

The etiology of the psychoses is another matter. Freud believed that in
many cases the psychoses were of organic origin. In those in which the
psychosis was not organic, the etiology derived from conflicts in the very
earliest period of life — even before the Oedipal period. To escape from
intolerable conflicts generated in the oral stage, the psychotic withdraws
into himself in disregard of the external world. This regressive behavior makes
the patient akin to the infant in handling and evaluating events and stimuli
from the outside world.

The psychoses are viewed as quantitatively different from the neuroses.
The etiology, however, is essentially the same. Both types of disorders stem
from faulty psychosexual development and the inner conflicts between man's
biological and instinctual needs and the realities of the external environment.

2. *The Neo-Freudians.* The neo-Freudians accept some of Freud's theories
and reject others. They de-emphasize the instinctual and biological motivations in man and shift the focus to the social conditions of modern life. Society, by shaping persons to fit the "standardized" model it has created, is
responsible for inducing the anxieties and tensions, the guilt and hostilities,
of modern man.

Fromm has probably stated this position as clearly as any neo-Freudian.[18]
In contrast to those psychoanalysts who argue that man's motivation is instinctual, Fromm suggests that his motivations are social and include needs
for identity, relatedness, rootedness, and the like. These needs unfortunately
may be warped and frustrated by the society in which he lives. This leads to
alienation, isolation, and despair. Industrial societies, by forcing man into roles
which violate his needs — such as turning him into a mere cog in a bureaucratic or industrial machine — tend to drive him into deviant behavior.
Neuroses and anti-social behaviors result when man is no longer capable of
coping with alienation or isolation and no longer capable of achieving the
productive expression of his needs. There is only one solution to this "human

18. Erich Fromm, *Escape From Freedom*, New York: Rinehart, 1941; and Erich Fromm,
The Sane Society, New York: Rinehart, 1955.

condition." Instead of attempting to mould man to fit into a "sick" society, society should be altered to fit better the needs of man.

Horney is another psychiatrist who accepts Freud's concepts of psychological determinism, the irrationality of motivation and the unconscious, but rejects almost everything else in psychoanalytic thought.[19] Her major thesis is that the neuroses are a by-product of the deficiencies of parent-child relationships in early life. The psychological mistreatment of the young child may take such forms as too little or too much parental love, rejection, indifference, and domination, and this mistreatment causes basic anxiety in the child. The insecure child develops one of three irrational strategies in escaping his feelings of rejection and helplessness: an exaggerated need for love, independence, or power. Neurotic persons have developed these mechanisms. Healthy parent-child relationships produce normal adults, whereas unfortunate relationships with parents produce neurotic personalities. In addition, Horney argues that conflicting norms which confront adults may also result in neurotic manifestations. Her focus on the inconsistencies in society as causative in neuroses is an important departure from Freudian thinking, which emphasizes almost exclusively the earliest years of life as the basis for both inner conflicts and neuropsychiatric disorders.

The third of the major neo-Freudians is Sullivan. His theory of the etiology of the neuroses and psychoses is not as complete as those of either the psychoanalysts or the neo-Freudians.[20] Nevertheless his influence on neo-Freudian thinking and concepts warrants his inclusion. From Sullivan's point of view the single most important fact of life is one's interpersonal relationships. It is in these relationships with other persons — beginning with the mother in infancy — that one develops a self or self-system. This self-system consists of the patterned mechanisms which defend the person against insecurity and anxiety. Different neuropsychiatric disorders feature different mechanisms. Hysteria, for example, involves the mechanism of amnesia. In compulsive and obsessive neuroses, the self defends against deep-rooted anxiety stemming from unsatisfactory interpersonal relationships by invoking the mechanism of personal magic. In schizophrenia, too, the origin of the malady is to be found in the lack of security and in profound anxiety. Instead of substituting less satisfactory patterns for more satisfactory mechanisms as in the neuroses, the schizophrenic regresses to more primitive and less satisfactory patterns.

19. Karen Horney, *The Neurotic Personality of Our Times*, New York: Norton, 1937; Karen Horney, *Our Inner Conflicts*, New York: Norton, 1945; and Karen Horney, *Neurosis and Human Growth*, New York: Norton, 1950.
20. Harry S. Sullivan, *The Interpersonal Theory of Psychiatry*, New York: Norton, 1953, and *Conceptions of Modern Psychiatry*, Washington, D.C.: W. A. White Psychiatric Foundation, 1947.

SOCIOCULTURAL THEORIES

Sociocultural theories are considerably more general than the psychological theories. They focus on environmental conditions which presumably are conducive to mental health and illness. No attempt is made to specify why some and not other persons become disturbed or the precise mechanisms through which this selective process operates. In general, sociocultural theories have suggested that mental illness may be a function of or related to the stresses society places on its members, the types of social sanctions employed to achieve conformity, the clarity or ambiguity of roles, the smoothness of transition from one role to another, the nature of child-rearing patterns and the influence of various elements of social organization. At least three specific sociocultural theories have been developed to explain mental illness. These are the discontinuity, social isolation, and social cohesion or integration theories.

1. *The Discontinuity Theory.*[21] The discontinuity theory was developed by anthropologists on the basis of observations of and participation in folk societies. In these societies, the roles which individual members play are generally found to be well defined and unambiguous. There is adequate preparation given to individuals so that, in moving through life from one status to another, a person is able to play each new role satisfactorily. Life is a relatively smooth process without abrupt breaks occasioned by the transitions from childhood to adulthood, single estate to marriage, childlessness to parenthood, and adulthood to old age. Various transitional stages may be marked by ceremonials or *rites de passage*, and every status offers its rewards and gratifications. Human life becomes an unfolding and each transition an achievement. The new roles, like the old, are sufficiently structured so that their obligations and responsibilities and their rewards and limitations are clear to the individual. Under these circumstances, the stresses normally associated with role transitions and role behaviors are minimized.

In industrial societies, role discontinuity is marked. The transitions from infancy to childhood, childhood to adolescence, adolescence to young adulthood, adulthood, and old age are sharp, unstructured, and often exceedingly painful. Adolescence and old age, in particular, are difficult stages, and retirement and the "empty nest" periods are often traumatic. Life becomes a series of abrupt and discomfiting changes causing stress.

In addition, the various roles played by persons are often in conflict with each other. The roles of housewife, glamour girl, career woman, and community leader, when simultaneously held by one woman, are inconsistent and call for subtle role distinctions. The husband-father-breadwinner-handyman

21. See Ruth Benedict, *Patterns of Culture*, Boston: Houghton Mifflin, 1934 and Margaret Mead, *Growing Up in New Guinea*, New York: Morrow, 1930. Also Margaret Mead, *Sex and Temperament in Three Primitive Societies*, New York: Morrow, 1935.

roles, though not quite as discontinuous, are often equally problematic for the male. These discontinuities and conflicts in roles and in the values and goals attached to the roles are seen as precipitants of the functional mental disorders and particularly of the neuroses.

2. *The Social Isolation Theory.*[22] Some anthropologists have stated that schizophrenia, like many other forms of deviant behavior, is generally absent in certain types of folk societies.[23] They have attributed this relative absence of schizophrenia not only to the lack of cultural and role discontinuities but also to the social organization that prevents persons from withdrawing from social interaction. The meaningful interpersonal and group involvement of all members of all ages and sexes is believed to prevent persons from withdrawing from reality and creating specialized and unshareable worlds of their own.

Sociologists have also invoked this theory. Faris and Dunham attempted to explain the high rates of mental disorder, in and near the hub of Chicago in precisely these terms.[24] Disorganized areas, and those containing polyglot populations and large numbers of single persons, are areas with a high degree of impersonality and anonymity. The residents of such areas are often excluded from meaningful participation with others and, hence, tend to become isolated socially. Since schizophrenia, in particular, is a disease characterized by social isolation, the privatization of one's world, and the difficulties in communication with others, the social isolation theory seems to have some merit.[25]

3. *The Social Integration Theory.*[26] The social integration theory is in many ways similar to the social isolation theory. Durkheim, in attempting to account for differentials in suicide by age, sex, and religion, concluded that suicide could not be explained by understanding suicidal individuals alone. The amount of suicide seemed to be related to the social cohesiveness or integration of the group. Thus, some forms of suicide were a function of too much group identity and social cohesion. These ritualistic suicides (hari-kari, suttee) occurred because the individual was so well integrated that he preferred to die for the sake of the group and its goals. On the contrary, egoistic suicides occurred when the individual placed his own problems above the norms and values of the group.

In extension of this theory, then, the psychoses and characterologic dis-

22. Robert E. L. Faris, "Cultural Isolation and the Schizophrenic Personality," *American Journal of Sociology*, 40 (1934), pp. 155–64.
23. S. Kirson Weinberg, *Society and Personality Disorders*, New York: Prentice-Hall 1952, pp. 228–32 and 255–8. See also N. J. Demareth, "Schizophrenia Among Primitives," in *Mental Health and Mental Disorder* (edited by Arnold Rose), New York: Norton, 1955, pp. 215–22.
24. Robert E. L. Faris and H. Warren Dunham, *Mental Disorders in Urban Areas*, Chicago: University of Chicago Press, 1939.
25. For criticism of this thesis, see M. L. Kohn and John A. Clausen, "Social Isolation and Schizophrenia," *American Sociological Review*, 20 (1955), pp. 265–73.
26. Emile Durkheim, *Suicide: A Study in Sociology*, Glencoe: Free Press, 1951.

orders may be said to correspond in etiology to the egoistic or personal suicides. Insufficiently integrated groups fail to develop cohesiveness among their members to prevent the privatization of problems and the creation of unique personal worlds. Neuroses, on the other hand, might be likened to the altruistic suicides. Great social cohesiveness may result in feelings of guilt, shame, and anxiety when norms are violated — and in typically neurotic manifestations.

THE TREATMENT OF MENTAL ILLNESS

Since the etiology of neuropsychiatric disorders, with the exception of the organic psychoses, remains largely speculative, treatment must of necessity depend upon clinical judgment and trial and error. Specific and reliable treatment procedures are largely absent. As would be expected in these circumstances, most treatment procedures derive in whole or in part from the etiological theories. Biologic theories have resulted in the widespread acceptance of the shock and chemical therapies; the psychoanalytic theories are associated almost exclusively with the use of psychotherapy; and the neo-Freudian and sociocultural theories have resulted primarily in the utilization of milieu therapy.

ORGANIC THERAPIES

Organic therapies take two major forms — shock and drugs.

1. *Shock Treatment.*[27] It was not until the 1930's that methods of traumatizing a patient through physical shock *for therapeutic purposes* were instituted. One retrospective theory behind the use of shock is that a patient confronted with a biological emergency or trauma will often tend to undergo a personality reorganization. A newer theory of the effect of shock is based on one of the biochemical theories of the etiology of functional disorders. From this point of view, the brain is an elaborate electro-chemical computer. In mental illness the computer becomes jammed so that there is no meaningful relationship between the information that is fed in and the output. The function of shock therapy, then, is to unjam the mechanism. Shock acts as a circuit breaker. Another theory is that shock therapy works selectively or unevenly for memory. By deadening memory for recent events, shock may induce the patient to experience amnesia for the events and conflicts that precipitated the psychotic episode.

The earliest method of creating shock was through the administration of insulin to schizophrenics. When fully developed, the method consisted of intramuscular injections of insulin on a daily basis for as long as three months. The effect of the insulin on the patient is to induce something resembling a

27. Robert W. White, *The Abnormal Personality*, New York: Ronald, 1948, pp. 554–60.

seizure followed by a deep coma. After perhaps an hour of coma, the patient is awakened by an administration of glucose which restores the blood sugar content to its normal level. After prolonged treatment, the mental state of the patient tends to show minor to marked improvement. The remarkable re- mission rates originally attributed to insulin shock have now been considerably tempered. This fact, plus inherent difficulties in the method, led to its par- tial replacement by a second drug, metrazol.

Metrazol therapy had certain advantages. It does not require very much time; the convulsion is extremely short in duration; the nursing care require- ment is minimal; and it need be given only about twice a week as against once a day for insulin. It has two shortcomings; it is not very effective with schizo- phrenics, and patients fear it. For these reasons it has been almost wholly replaced by the electro-shock method.

Electric shock treatment (EST), or electro-convulsive therapy (ECT), was introduced in 1938.[28] Like all other shock techniques, ECT is probably most effective in the affective (manic-depressive) disorders and is particu- larly useful in treating psychotic depressions. It is only modestly successful in schizophrenia. The technique consists of strapping an electrode to each temple of the patient and passing a current through the brain. A very small current is used and the time period is less than one second. Patients are often sedated before treatment. There is no pain connected with this therapy since the electric current travels so rapidly that the patient is unconscious before he can experience pain. The shock results in a *grand mal* convulsion fol- lowed by sleep. The immediate effects of the shock may last half a day before the patient can resume his normal activity. Other effects such as difficulties with memory may last considerably longer.

Electro-shock treatments are given twice or three times weekly, often for protracted periods. Although regressed schizophrenics may receive as many as 200 treatments, shock treatments are generally used sparingly because of possible brain damage.

Of the three methods, electro-shock has come to dominate the field. Al- though it is detested by psychoanalysts because of its "punitive" nature, its use often reduces patient hospital time. It is also valuable in sufficiently im- proving patient mental status so that other techniques may be more effectively utilized.[29]

28. Dugal Campbell, "The Psychological Effects of Cerebral Electroshock," in *Handbook of Abnormal Psychology* (H. J. Eysenck, ed.), New York: Basic Books, 1961, Chap. 16.
29. *Surgical Treatment.* At one time, every large mental hospital had patients who pre- sented management problems to the staff. Some of these were agitated cases, many of whom had suffered irreversible brain damage, and the prognosis for their recovery was negligible. More as a management than a therapeutic technique, a surgical method called prefrontal lobotomy was widely adopted in the 1940's to treat these patients. The surgical technique utilized in lobotomies is relatively safe and easy. It involves

2. *Tranquilizing Drugs.*[30] These drugs were first used in the treatment of mental patients in 1952. By 1955, they had been widely adopted in state and veterans' hospitals and, since that time, have revolutionized patient care and treatment both in and out of mental hospitals. The first tranquilizer was reserpine and it is ironic that the effects of this natural substance, derived from a plant, *Rauwolfia serpentina*, have been known for centuries in India. The second type of tranquilizer is chlorpromazine, which was synthesized for use as an antihistamine. Almost all succeeding tranquilizers followed from the chlorpromazine model rather than the alkaloid model exemplified by reserpine. New tranquilizers are being developed and produced at such a rate that few psychiatrists can keep track of them. The original drugs now have been replaced by newer variants which eliminate some of the undesirable side effects found in early tranquilizers.

As with the shock therapies, no one is certain why tranquilizers work. It is generally agreed, however, that they act on the central nervous system to calm the patient without producing or inhibiting sleep. They also ameliorate such symptoms as hallucinations, delusions, aggression, overactivity, and tension and anxiety. Except in very heavy dosages they have little effect on motor behavior, perception, and intellectual functioning. While tranquilizers do not "cure" the psychosis or neurosis they make the symptoms more tolerable both for patients and those responsible for the patients. Tranquilized patients rarely present management problems. Because of this, supplementary therapies can now be introduced where once these were almost impossible.

With tranquilizers, fewer patients need be hospitalized, the hospitalized patients are easier to work with, the mental hospital begins to resemble a general hospital and loses its bars, personnel can be more readily attracted, treatment more easily implemented, and patients more rapidly discharged. Discharged patients using tranquilizers after release may keep from being rehospitalized or may be able to remain in the community for longer periods than previously. Patient posthospital functioning is also likely to be better with tranquilizers than without them. It is still too early to predict their ultimate

---

severing the connections between the frontal lobes or between other sections of the brain, notably the thalamus and hypothalamus. The results are not nearly as drastic as they might seem. The principal changes which occur seem to come in the mood or affect of the patient. Remarkably little damage seems to be done to intellectual functioning. Nonetheless, certain secondary consequences make this method undesirable.

30. For a review of the chemical revolution in the treatment of mental disorders, see Frank J. Ayd, Jr., "Phenothiazine Tranquilizers: Eight Years of Development," *The Medical Clinics of North America* 45 (1961), pp. 1027–40. A more general statement of the effects of drugs can be found in D. Tronton and H. J. Eysenck, "The Effects of Drugs on Behaviour," in *Handbook of Abnormal Psychology,* op. cit. Chap. 17.

effect on treatment and on public attitudes toward mental illness. Nonetheless, and if only their immediate consequences for hospital care are evaluated, the tranquilizers have been an important breakthrough in the treatment of mental illness.

3. *The Psychic Energizers (Antidepressive Drugs)*.[31] Another aspect of the pharmacological revolution in the treatment of mental illness was the development and diffusion of the psychic energizers in 1957. These drugs are well suited for the treatment of depressions and of those disorders which feature impairments in affect. Antidepressive drugs may be used alone or in combination with tranquilizers. They seem to alleviate some of the more profound symptoms of depression and withdrawal. There is some improvement in motor activity and responsivity, a reduced need for sleep, and often an improvement in appetite. These effects are accomplished by such drugs as iproniazid and others in the monamine oxidase inhibitor group which stimulate central nervous system activity. The side effects of these drugs may be countered by the tranquilizers and vice versa. The real hope for these drugs is that they may replace electro-shock in the treatment of depressions.

Despite early enthusiastic reports of the effectiveness of the energizers in depressions and in some forms of schizophrenia, more study will be required before these drugs can be conclusively evaluated. With so much research effort currently expended for the development of new chemical agents, the current tranquilizers and energizers may be replaced by still other groups. There is every reason to believe that more effective drugs will be forthcoming.

In concluding this section on drug therapy, it should be stressed that the tranquilizers and energizers do not cure mental illness nor prevent its onset. At best, they ameliorate some of the symptoms and are helpful in reducing the length of hospital stay. In making patients more tractable and less aberrant in behavior, drugs may help overcome the stigma which has been attached to mental disorders for centuries.[32]

---

31. John C. Saunders, "Antidepressives: The Pith of Affective Therapy," *Diseases of the Nervous System* 22 (1961), pp. 1–4; and B. B. Brodie, F. Sulser, and E. Costa, "Psychotherapeutic Drugs," *Annual Review of Medicine* 12 (1961), pp. 349–68.

32. *Other organic methods.* Various other organic techniques have been tried or are currently being tried. One of the earlier ones which has regained some popularity in the late 1950's and early 1960's is narcosis or sleep therapy. Reports indicate that experiments with sleep therapy are also being conducted in several European countries. In sleep therapy, the patient is given a chemical agent, previously ether and later sodium amytal and similar drugs, which produces a state of deep sleep lasting for 20 or more hours per day. This therapy is applied over a period of time. The theory is that the precipitating trauma may thus be relieved or that the circuits may unjam during this induced sleep. The results of this method have not been impressive.

Another method which is still largely in the early experimental stage of development takes as its point of departure the Pavlovian concepts of cortical excitation and inhibition in behavior. This technique will theoretically involve some form of conditioning of patients.

PSYCHOTHERAPY

Psychotherapy as a method emerges from Freudian theories about the etiology of mental disorder. Almost all psychoanalysts and clinicians use some variant of psychotherapy in their treatment of patients. It is a costly and time-consuming method and, hence, is most often used in private practice and but rarely used with state hospital patients. Since the method depends on verbal communication between patient and therapist, schizophrenics and psychotics generally, with their privatization of worlds and of language, are the least eligible for this therapy.

All methods of psychotherapy make one assumption in common; that the only cure for nonorganic disorders is for the patient to obtain insight into the nature and basis of his condition. This insight is not mere intellectual knowledge. Insight requires that the patient feel as well as intellectually understand the hostilities, drives, and other unconscious factors he has repressed. This insight into his problems, it is held, can be obtained only through an abstract reliving of his previous experiences. It is the function of the therapist to help the patient relive his critical earlier life experiences and thereby achieve insight. Fromm-Reichmann has stated these goals of psychotherapy as practiced by psychoanalysts as follows:

> The aim of psychoanalytic therapy is to bring these rejected drives and wishes, together with the patient's individual and environmental moral standards, which are the instruments for his rejections, into consciousness and in this way place them at his free disposal. In doing this the conscious self becomes strengthened, since it is no longer involved in the continuous job of repressing mental content from his own awareness. The patient can then decide independently which desires he wants to accept and which he wishes to reject, his personality no longer being warped or dominated by uncontrollable desires and moral standards.[33]

The methods of psychotherapy are many. These may include such techniques as catharsis (allowing the patient to talk freely about his difficulties and anxieties, resulting in his feeling "better"), encouragement, reassurance, hypnosis, free association, and dream analysis. Depending upon the "depth" of the problem and the orientation of the therapist, psychotherapy may represent something akin to a confessional or it may involve something as complicated as the reconstruction of the traumatic life history of the patient. The more psychoanalytically oriented the therapist, the "deeper" he delves. This very deep probing of the unconscious and its reconstruction may require sessions of an hour a day once, twice, or even as many as five times a week. Psychotherapeutic precedures may be continued for three years or more.

Psychotherapeutic methods are almost impossible to evaluate in terms of

33. Frieda Fromm-Reichmann in Ruth Munroe, *Schools of Psychoanalytic Thought*, op. cit. p. 520.

their effectiveness. There is little doubt that mere interest in a troubled personality may make a difference in some cases. Similarily, providing a setting devoid of judgments of good and evil where the patient may "ventilate" his conflicts may be therapeutic for some. In the most successful situation, that in which the patient is able to achieve "insight," modifications in behavior and in habit patterns are likely to follow. Since these techniques, however, are always employed in a patient-therapist relationship, there are few measures of effectiveness which can be used. For one thing, there can be no control group of comparable and untreated patients against whom the change in patient functioning as a result of therapy may be measured. For another, it is impossible to determine the effects of other changes on the outcome of therapy. Such changes might be biological or they might be environmental. Further, so sacrosanct is the therapeutic relationship between patient and clinician that the attempt to study it is said to change, modify, and even to destroy its value. For these and other reasons, no one can state with any reasonable degree of assurance how valuable psychotherapy is in treatment.[34]

MILIEU THERAPY [35]

Milieu therapy is environmental or situational therapy. Its origin is to be found in the "humane" treatment idea — that patients are people to be treated with dignity, respect, and warmth. Its theoretical justification stems from the interpersonal theory of Sullivan. Its increasingly widespread use, however, may be attributed to necessity rather than theory. Two practical reasons led to its implementation. First, there are not enough psychiatrists to deal with patients individually. Second, most hospital wards, even since the introduction of the drug and shock therapies, are custodial units. The concept of therapy on these wards was often a dream, not a reality. The simplest and most feasible way to transform custodial into treatment wards was, therefore, to introduce milieu therapy.

In theory, milieu therapy, or the therapeutic community as it is often called, presupposes that the ward relationships among patients, between patients and staff, and among staff members can be structured for the maximum benefit of all concerned. The goal is to create a conflict-free, warm, encouraging, reassuring environment which produces a minimum of stress for the patients. In this environment, patients can participate more freely in activities, can help and guide one another, can gain "insight" into the nature of their disabilities through meaningful interaction with others, and can test their

34. H. J. Eysenck, "The Effects of Psychotherapy," in *Handbook of Abnormal Psychology*, op. cit. Chap. 18.
35. See, for example, Maxwell Jones, *The Therapeutic Community*, New York: Basic Books, 1953; Alfred H. Stanton and Morris S. Schwartz, *The Mental Hospital*, New York: Basic Books, 1954.

behavior against the "reality" of involvement in group living.[36] Proponents of milieu therapy argue that individual psychotherapy lasts but one hour a day at most, yet the patient is confronted with other experiences at all other times. Unless the remaining hours of the day are also therapeutic, much of the benefits derived from psychotherapy are likely to be lost. Finally, proponents of milieu therapy believe that mental disorders result from previous and unfortunate interpersonal experiences. The effects of these poor relationships can best be overcome by establishing or re-establishing meaningful and satisfying ones.

"Therapeutic communities" may feature a number of attributes. They are usually "open" so that patients are, within limits, free to move through the hospital. Bars, closed doors, isolation rooms, and other devices which stigmatize the patient are removed. Male and female patients are free to interact with one another as they would on the outside. Patients and staff wear civilian clothes and often cannot be differentiated from one another. Within limits, patients are permitted to make the rules that govern their hospital lives, are encouraged to conduct "gripe" sessions with staff, to see visitors at almost all times of the day and evening, to avail themselves of facilities such as occupational and recreational therapy, and to develop their interests and potential. Group therapy sessions and various other techniques, such as psychodrama and sociodrama, may also be used. The ward or hospital "climate" is warm and democratic and every effort is made to eliminate indignities and reduce rules to a minimum.

There can be little argument with these methods. In an industrial society in which patients and non-patients alike are confronted with the loss of identity and individuality, providing patients with this type of pressure-free environment has much to recommend it. Despite this, however, there is little valid evidence to indicate the effectiveness of these methods.[37] Difficulties in evaluating the effectiveness of "therapeutic communities" are of the same type as those encountered in evaluating psychotherapy. The selectivity of patients, the non-specificity of the methods, and the lack of adequate control groups make it necessary to reserve final judgment on the efficacy of the "therapeutic community."

MENTAL ILLNESS: PRESENT STATUS OF THE PROBLEM

Despite tangible progress in the treatment of neuropsychiatric disorders with the development of the tranquilizers and energizers and with the therapeutic community, much remains to be changed in this area of deviant behavior. Decades and even centuries of neglect and abuse cannot be remedied over-

36. Morris Schwartz, "What is a Therapeutic Milieu?" in *The Patient and the Mental Hospital* (M. Greenblatt et al., eds.), Glencoe: Free Press, 1957, pp. 130–44.
37. Simon Dinitz, Mark Lefton, et al., "The Ward Behavior of Psychiatric Patients," *Social Problems*, 6 (1958), pp. 107–15.

night. The critical problem, therefore, involves reducing the accumulated lag which presently characterizes the approach to and treatment of mental disorders.[38] This lag between scientific knowledge and its practical application is particularly pronounced in the area of public attitudes toward mental illness and in public treatment facilities for the care of the mentally disturbed.

PUBLIC ATTITUDES TOWARD MENTAL ILLNESS

Religious, economic, and other cultural factors have combined over the centuries to create a negative public image of the mentally disturbed, which is difficult to modify. The earlier image of the mentally ill as witches, as beset by devils and demons, as dangerous and repugnant tends to persist. Mental illness stigmatizes the hapless patient and his family and creates a heavy economic burden. Former patients are still discriminated against socially and economically. Sympathy normally granted to the physically sick is usually denied the mentally ill. Few people are willing or able to tolerate the aberrations of the mentally ill, while many continue to think of his symptoms as involving sinful behavior.

The public response to mental illness remains one of rejection.[39] In 1950, Roper conducted a survey of the attitudes of persons in Louisville, Kentucky, on mental health.[40] Six questions were asked of a sample group of 3971 respondents. The responses to these questions indicated that 59.4 per cent believed that "the trouble with most people who are mentally ill is that they just don't want to face their problems;" 50 per cent believed that "the experts themselves often can't agree on whether a man is mentally ill enough to be put in an insane asylum or not;" and over 80 per cent agreed that it is advisable to seek "a psychiatrist's help when someone begins to act queerly or get strange ideas." In addition, most respondents believed that mental illness is not inherited (71.8 per cent), that there are an insufficient number of physicians and hospitals to care for the mentally ill (63.8 per cent), and that the hospitalized mentally ill are not treated very badly (46.6 per cent). Nearly a third of the respondents did not answer this last question, probably because they had no knowledge about the nature of hospital treatment.

The answers to other questions are also interesting. For example, three-fifths of the respondents thought that sex criminals should be sent to a hospital rather than to jail. If a family member were to become mentally ill, 43.8 per cent of the respondents would tell their friends and acquaintances, while 46.8 per cent would keep it quiet. Of four occupational groups whose responses were analyzed — lawyers, doctors, clergymen, and teachers — 67.5

38. For a discussion of this lag see *Action for Mental Health,* op. cit. pp. 3–23.
39. Ibid. pp. 59–85.
40. Elmo Roper, *People's Attitudes Concerning Mental Health: A Study Made in the City of Louisville* (September 1950), pp. 152–206.

per cent of the lawyers, 47.2 per cent of the doctors, 45.7 per cent of the clergymen, and 50.4 per cent of the teachers, would keep it quiet. Even these more "enlightened" groups in the community continued to confer a degree of "shame" on the families of the mentally disturbed.

In other studies, respondents were asked to evaluate various thumbnail sketches of different types of mental disturbance. An example of such a sketch is the following.[41]

Now I'd like to describe a certain kind of person and ask you a few questions about her. She is a young woman in her twenties — let's call her Betty Smith. She has never had a job and she doesn't seem to want to go look for one. She is a very quiet girl, she doesn't talk much to anyone — even her own family — and she acts like she is afraid of people, especially young men her own age. She won't go out with anyone and whenever someone comes to visit her family, she stays in her room until they leave. She just stays by herself and daydreams all the time and shows no interest in anything or anybody.

In 1950, only 34 per cent of 3500 respondents recognized this sketch of a simple schizophrenic as involving mental illness.[42] In a later study in 1955, only 36 per cent of the 540 respondents recognized it.[43] These results imply that most are unaware of the nature of mental illness. Perhaps this unawareness suggests that persons would like to deny the existence of such a problem by refusing to recognize even the most obvious symptoms.

Other studies demonstrated that those who treat patients are granted status only reluctantly. Of all medical specialties, psychiatrists are accorded lowest status by the general public. Psychiatrists who are in private practice and thus deal with neurotics are rated somewhat higher than those who work in public mental hospitals.[44] Thus, even those who work with mental patients suffer from the public's negative image of psychiatric disorders.

Positive changes in public attitudes, however, may be coming rapidly. In 1960, a study in Baltimore reported a number of surprising findings.[45] For example, a majority of the 1736 respondents considered all three case sketches used — the paranoid, the simple schizophrenic, and the alcoholic — to be indicative of mental illness. In particular, 78 per cent thought the schizophrenic girl described above was mentally ill. Even more surprising were the findings that (a) half the respondents said they could conceive of themselves

41. Shirley A. Star, "The Public's Ideas about Mental Illness," mimeographed paper, National Opinion Research Center, University of Chicago, 1955.
42. Action for Mental Health, op. cit. pp. 75–6.
43. Elaine Cumming and John Cumming, Closed Ranks, Cambridge: Harvard University Press, 1957.
44. Benjamin Pasamanick and Solomon Rettig, "Status and Work Satisfaction of Psychiatrists: A Comparative Study of Psychiatrists in State Employ and Private Practices," Archives of Neurology and Psychiatry 81 (1959), pp. 399–402.
45. Paul V. Lemkau and Guido M. Crocetti, "An Urban Population's Opinion and Knowledge About Mental Illness," American Journal of Psychiatry 118 (1962), pp. 692–700.

as "falling in love" with someone who had a history of mental disorder; (b) half the respondents would be willing to share a room with a former mental patient; (c) eight out of ten respondents would not object (hesitate) to work on a job with a former patient; and (d) 62 per cent disagreed with the statement that "almost all persons who have a mental illness are dangerous." Since the respondents in this study were comparable in socio-economic status and education to the respondents in studies reported earlier, it appears that public attitudes may have undergone modification from 1950 to 1960. If so, we may stand at the threshold of a new era in the handling of the mentally ill.

THE MENTAL HOSPITAL

The mental hospital developed in the nineteenth century as the most plausible method of removing mentally ill persons from a society then in the process of rapid industrialization and urbanization. At the time of their development, the mental hospital and the prison were considered far more humane than treatment previously in vogue — allowing the ill to wander around the countryside, banishment, and death. Massive institutions were built and located at a distance from urban centers. At worst, these institutions were literal "Bedlams" in which patients lived in unspeakable filth and degradation.[46] At best, they were humane custodial institutions from which only a very few could ever hope to emerge. Therapy for patients was not demanded and even the best hospitals did not provide it. So little was known about the etiology and treatment of mental disorders that only custody could be provided.

With budget and salaries extremely low, less competent personnel were attracted to positions in these hospitals. Even these persons soon left and the staffs came to consist of a cadre of untrained, unskilled, and often uninterested persons. Periodic political changes in state governments resulted in placing political appointees in important positions of hospital administration. Occasionally corruption complicated this already dismal picture. Buildings and grounds aged and deteriorated and were not replaced or renewed. In the last few decades the fortress architecture of the institutions became dysfunctional, but the bars, doors, and burly attendants remained until the advent of the drug therapies. In a few institutions, there was remarkably little change even after the newer therapies came into use. An overwhelming per cent of public institutions are still understaffed at all levels, operate on inadequate budgets, too often serve as political playthings, are too large and unwieldy for the purpose of effective therapy, and lag behind available knowledge and techniques.

46. A great deal has been written on the mental hospital. See, for example, Albert Deutsch, *The Mentally Ill in America*, New York: Columbia University Press, 1949; Clifford W. Beers, *A Mind That Found Itself*, New York: Doubleday, 1921.

Only recently have major modifications been made. Physicians, nurses, social workers, psychologists, occupational, vocational, and recreational personnel, and better trained attendants have been added to hospital staffs. Research programs have been brought into hospital settings. Smaller, more modern, short-term, intensive therapy hospitals have been built. A discussion of some of these changes follows.

1. *Personnel and Patients.* Since World War II public mental hospitals have increased their ratios of staff personnel to resident patients. In 1959, there were less than half as many patients per hospital physician as in 1945; a tenth as many patients per psychologist, and less than half as many patients per graduate nurse, social worker, and attendant. Table 15-1 portrays this enormous improvement in the personnel situation. In 1959, a hospital physician was responsible for an average of 132 patients, a psychologist for 601, a graduate nurse for 63, a social worker for 146, and a non-graduate nurse or attendant for 6 patients.

TABLE 15-1

Patient to staff ratios in public mental hospitals
in 1945, 1950, 1955 and 1959

	No. patients to each staff member			
	1945	1950	1955	1959
Physician	299	214	201	132
Psychologist	6312	1447	1106	601
Graduate nurse	169	106	82	63
Social worker	366	247	163	146
Non-graduate nurse and attendant	13	8	7	6

Source: *Fact Sheet*, Joint Information Service, American Psychiatric Association and National Association for Mental Health, no. 1, March 1957, and no. 16, September 1961. Reprinted by permission.

Assuming, however, that these personnel worked a 40-hour week and that therapy of any type required one hour per patient per week, a hospital physician could treat each patient less than once per month and a psychologist might see a case once in every 15 weeks. According to the intensive treatment standards of the American Psychiatric Association a maximum of 30 patients per physician, 100 patients per psychologist, 5 patients per registered nurse, 70 patients per psychiatric social worker, and 4 patients per attendant is recommended.[47] The 1959 patient-personnel ratios were still more or less custodial. Extending the trend line from 1945 to 1959, it will be 1974 before hospitals are staffed for therapy rather than custody.

47. *Fact Sheet*, Joint Information Service, American Psychiatric Association and National Association for Mental Health, No. 1 (March 1957), p. 4.

The situation has improved, but staffs are still inadequate to handle the numbers of patients. Only three states had enough hospital physicians in 1959 to meet minimum APA standards. No state had sufficient graduate nurses and only one state had enough hospital social workers to meet minimum standards. Some states were extremely low in all staff categories and other states approached staff adequacy in all categories. Regional differences were pronounced. The Midwestern states of Kansas and Nebraska and the northeastern and Middle Atlantic states rated fairly well. States in the deep South, supporting segregated institutions, rated poorly. A state-by-state analysis of the ratio of personnel to minimum personnel standards is presented in Table 15-2.

2. *Expenditures and Costs.* Data on the costs of mental illness are scarce. The closest approximation to reliable data is found in a report of the Joint Commission on Mental Illness. In this report, Fein estimates the direct costs of mental illness to be $1.7 billion per year.[48] Annual direct and indirect costs, such as lost wages, amount to $2.4 billion as a minimum estimate. State expenditures for public mental hospital patients alone exceeded $900 million in 1961. A state-by-state analysis reveals wide differences in the willingness and ability to expend funds for the mentally disturbed. Thus, in 1961 all states spent an average of $5.02 per resident hospital patient per day. At the extremes, Alaska spent $8.97 and Kansas $8.75 while Mississippi expended $2.67 and Alabama spent $2.85. Table 15-3 contains the average daily and yearly expenditures per patient by state in 1961.

Although taxes are used to maintain mental hospitals, almost all states require payment from patients and their families when this is possible. In addition, for patients in private psychiatric hospitals, in general hospitals, in out-patient centers, and under private psychiatric but non-hospital care, the costs can easily become burdensome. A month's care in a private psychiatric facility may cost a thousand dollars or more. Since mental disorders are usually long-term problems, the total costs of psychiatric care can be staggering. Few insurance plans defray the expenses incurred. Insurance coverages for nervous and mental disorders are not only costly but extremely restricted in applicability. Of the 83 Blue Cross plans in the United States and Canada in 1961, 25 contained no significant nervous and mental disease coverage while 58 provided for varying amounts of such coverage. In many of the latter, coverage is added as a rider or endorsement and involves additional cost. Only 13 of the 83 Blue Cross plans offered nervous and mental care coverage which was as inclusive as that offered for most other diseases.[49]

48. Rashi Fein, *Economics of Mental Illness*, Report to the Joint Commission on Mental Illness and Health, No. 2, New York: Basic Books, 1958, p. x.
49. *Fact Sheet*, Joint Information Service, American Psychiatric Association and National Association for Mental Health, no. 15 (May 1961).

FUTURE PROSPECTS: AN EMERGENT NORMATIVE CONCEPTION

While mental illness has been treated here as a type of behavioral deviation, social norms also exist which specify how deviants should be treated. Elements of previous norms have already been cited: the mentally ill should be banished, shunned, or isolated. No attempt is made here to state earlier normative conceptions. These norms have shifted with new theories of etiology and perhaps are more dependent upon knowledge than are other norms. If scientific knowledge plays such an important part in normative change, one can forecast certain changes based on existing knowledge not yet accepted by the public and on future knowledge to emerge from continued research.

The medical-technological revolution was late in arriving on the scene. Not until most of the infectious diseases had been conquered or neutralized did researchers turn their attention to the "dirtier" and less specific chronic diseases. Aided by research grants from the National Institute of Mental Health, a federal granting agency associated with the Department of Health, Education and Welfare, expenditures for scientific equipment and research have increased every year since 1955. These projects have probed almost every aspect of the problem from etiology to treatment. In addition, NIMH has supported the training of specialists through fellowship grants. While no single project is likely to "pay off," the accumulation of new and basic knowledge will probably alter present ideas about mental illness and perhaps provide the methods whereby some or all of the neuropsychiatric disorders will be effectively treated and perhaps be prevented.

Anticipating this increase in knowledge, it is possible to suggest certain

TABLE 15-2

Adequacy of staff in public mental hospitals, by state, 1959

| | Per cent of adequacy | | | | |
State	Physicians	Psychologists	Registered nurses	Social workers	Other nurses & attendants
U.S.	63.0	83.3	24.2	39.8	88.0
Ala.	15.8	40.8	6.5	25.0	67.9
Ariz.	41.2	62.5	19.4	27.8	102.7
Ark.	43.8	70.7	12.1	15.7	87.2
Calif.	76.4	114.3	31.7	43.1	94.7
Col.	91.7	66.7	20.2	11.0	90.2
Conn.	90.8	87.2	24.5	34.7	110.6
Del.	103.4	206.9	41.1	55.2	118.1
Dist. of Col.	94.4	43.8	60.7	51.7	93.9
Fla.	33.4	33.5	18.2	20.3	93.4
Ga.	33.6	16.9	10.0	5.7	53.9
Hawaii	83.3	125.0	44.7	0.8	81.8
Idaho	49.2	250.0	19.0	63.0	107.9

			Per cent of adequacy		
State	Physicians	Psychologists	Registered nurses	Social workers	Other nurses & attendants
Ill.	48.4	87.3	15.1	38.5	63.5
Ind.	53.7	159.1	23.7	86.6	96.2
Iowa	155.6	244.4	23.3	46.6	120.9
Kansas	205.9	333.3	37.7	92.7	129.0
Ky.	75.6	79.1	28.7	55.7	93.4
Louisiana	24.8	53.6	8.5	29.7	76.7
Maine	42.7	172.4	15.8	51.4	96.1
Md.	80.8	160.2	12.4	50.8	100.8
Mass.	89.0	83.9	49.8	58.1	93.2
Mich.	81.8	92.4	17.6	57.5	86.2
Minn.	27.5	96.3	22.5	24.1	79.0
Miss.	55.3	39.2	7.9	8.6	89.5
Missouri	47.2	83.0	6.4	44.9	107.4
Montana	34.4	176.5	10.6	44.6	100.5
Neb.	94.2	162.8	37.7	101.6	127.7
Nevada	31.7	—	19.9	—	86.0
N.H.	55.0	78.4	5.8	46.8	110.0
N.J.	83.6	67.0	28.8	55.0	98.8
N.M.	44.6	16.0	12.8	25.4	141.0
N.Y.	67.1	45.0	30.8	40.5	95.5
N.C.	35.3	46.6	18.6	11.4	54.8
N.D.	58.0	100.0	14.7	23.6	90.1
Ohio	67.7	146.6	22.7	56.9	85.0
Okla.	No Report	No Report	No Report	No Report	No Report
Oreg.	71.2	100.0	23.5	22.0	103.7
Pa.	52.0	71.2	35.3	33.0	80.2
R.I.	78.6	14.9	25.2	22.9	93.4
S.C.	37.7	85.9	13.5	25.3	58.8
S.D.	45.0	30.3	24.3	25.0	87.4
Tenn.	49.5	90.9	12.5	37.9	61.4
Tex.	68.9	75.9	14.0	34.6	86.1
Utah	35.7	260.9	14.1	65.0	130.3
Vt.	65.7	181.8	26.3	47.1	109.2
Va.	37.7	81.4	11.3	28.9	82.3
Wash.	72.2	73.5	10.8	14.2	117.6
W. Va.	34.0	64.8	8.9	19.1	55.5
Wis.	33.4	53.5	19.6	40.0	80.4
Wyo.	66.7	166.7	14.3	78.9	91.1

Source: *Fact Sheet*, Joint Information Service, American Psychiatric Association and National Association for Mental Health, no. 16, Sept. 1961. Reprinted by permission.

directions treatment will take in the future. They reflect emerging normative conceptions of what treatment should be.[50]

1. Mental illness will be detected earlier than it is now. This will keep many patients from being institutionalized. Patients, whenever possible, will remain in the community under drug and other therapies. These early cases,

50. See, for example, President John F. Kennedy, Special Message to the Congress on "Mental Illness and Mental Retardation" (February 1963).

and perhaps even chronic cases, will remain under medical and nursing supervision while at home.

2. Out-patient clinics will expand to supplement the home care of patients. These clinics will also provide additional help to patients after hospital discharge.

3. General hospitals will assume greater responsibility for the treatment of acute mental patients. This care will be intensive and short term. Patients will be released within a few days or weeks after admission and will convalesce at home. Mental illness will be treated in substantially the same way as other ailments that require hospitalization.

4. For specialized cases and for purposes of research, public-supported, short-term treatment centers will be expanded. Newer therapies will be tested

TABLE 15-3

Daily and yearly per capita maintenance expenditures
at public mental hospitals, by state, 1961

| | Maintenance expenditures | |
State	Daily	Yearly
U.S.	5.02	1,833.44
Alabama	2.85	1,042.05
Alaska	8.97	3,275.21
Arizona	5.11	1,863.59
Arkansas	3.37	1,229.09
California	6.41	2,337.98
Colorado	5.69	2,075.03
Connecticut	7.56	2,760.47
Delaware	5.29	1,929.51
Dist. of Columbia	7.88	2,874.80
Florida	3.98	1,451.39
Georgia	2.93	1,070.35
Hawaii	6.00	2,188.57
Idaho	6.21	2,266.81
Illinois	4.75	1,734.61
Indiana	5.21	1,901.21
Iowa	7.11	2,594.44
Kansas	8.75	3,193.75
Kentucky	4.46	1,629.42
Louisiana	3.59	1,310.59
Maine	4.63	1,698.69
Maryland	5.54	2,022.17
Massachusetts	6.11	2,229.49
Michigan	5.73	2,089.90
Minnesota	4.85	1,768.59
Mississippi	2.67	973.15
Missouri	5.19	1,894.96
Montana	4.35	1,588.17
Nebraska	6.37	2,326.18
Nevada	5.15	1,878.16
New Hampshire	4.90	1,787.77

| State | Maintenance expenditures | |
	Daily	Yearly
New Jersey	5.55	2,026.45
New Mexico	5.62	2,051.87
New York	5.14	1,875.43
North Carolina	4.40	1,604.87
North Dakota	4.46	1,627.19
Ohio	5.36	1,957.95
Oklahoma	3.87	1,413.95
Oregon	4.56	1,664.03
Pennsylvania	4.50	1,643.36
Rhode Island	5.74	2,093.28
South Carolina	2.98	1,088.63
South Dakota	4.12	1,503.54
Tennessee	2.89	1,053.87
Texas	3.71	1,353.09
Utah	6.83	2,493.63
Vermont	5.15	1,878.04
Virginia	3.47	1,265.36
Washington	6.66	2,432.12
West Virginia	2.96	1,079.50
Wisconsin	5.08	1,852.71
Wyoming	5.78	2,110.77

Source: *Mental Health Statistics, Current Reports,* U.S. Department of Health, Education and Welfare, Public Health Service, National Institute of Mental Health (January, 1962), Table 2.

in these institutions in what will essentially amount to clinical research wards.

5. There is also likely to develop a whole new series of institutions — day hospitals, night hospitals, sheltered workshops, and halfway houses. These institutions will serve as intermediate settings between the mental hospital and the community. They will provide quiet environments and therapy for patients who do not as yet function sufficiently well to resume all of their normal daily activities but who function too well to require 24-hour hospitalization.

6. Finally, the traditional mental hospital will eventually give way to smaller, better staffed institutions with perhaps a few hundred rather than a few thousand patients. The older hospitals will house and treat the more chronic and difficult patients. It is likely that they will eventually serve primarily as a nursing home for the aged and senile persons for whom treatment will not be feasible. In fact, they are already in the process of becoming repositories for the rejects of an industrial society — the aged.

SUMMARY

This chapter dealt with three aspects of the problem of mental illness. First, major approaches to the etiology of mental illness were discussed. These explanations included biologic, psychiatric, and sociocultural positions. From the biological point of view, genetic, physiological, and endocrinological factors as well as brain and central nervous system pathologies may be causative elements in mental disorder. Two psychiatric theories — the psychoanalytic and the neo-Freudian — were explored. Although quite different in many respects, both approaches attribute mental illness to faulty development in early life and the dynamisms involved therein. The sociocultural theory of mental illness was described as emphasizing elements in the social structure which resulted in social isolation and in a breakdown in social integration.

Second, the chief treatment methods — organic therapy, psychotherapy, and milieu therapy — were examined. Organic methods are espoused by persons adhering to biological explanations. These methods include electro-shock and chemotherapy. The latter consists most frequently of the tranquilizing drugs and the energizers or anti-depressants. The psychoanalytic point of view gave rise to the method of psychotherapy. The essence of psychotherapy is the attempt to get the patient to achieve "insight" into the early, unconscious, and painful origins of his illness. Psychotherapy is utilized most consistently in the treatment of the neuroses. The neo-Freudian and sociocultural approaches provide the theoretical rationale for milieu therapy. The latter consists of structuring mental hospital wards in such a way as to create a warm, accepting climate. In this climate, and through group-therapy procedures, the patient can "work through" his conflicts and problems.

Third, public attitudes toward the etiology and treatment of mental disorders were described. The consequences of historic rejection of the mentally ill were reviewed in some detail. Some of these consequences were and are inadequate facilities, personnel, research, and expenditures for patient care. Recent changes and modifications in these negative attitudes and in patient care practices were discussed. The chapter concluded on the emerging normative conception of mental illness.

QUESTIONS AND SUGGESTIONS FOR FURTHER STUDY

1. What is meant by a "model psychosis"?
2. How would you evaluate the work in the genetics of mental illness? Are there any alternative explanations for the "family aggregation" of schizophrenia and the affective psychoses?
3. Discuss the point of view which posits "a continuum of reproductive casualty" in explaining the neuropsychiatric disorders.
4. Describe the major assumptions of the Freudian position on mental illness.
5. Contrast neo-Freudian and psychoanalytic viewpoints.
6. Discuss the origin of the "social isolation" theory.
7. Why and how well does electro-shock work?

8. What is chemotherapy and how successful has it been in the treatment of mental disorders?

9. Describe milieu therapy.

10. Read Beers's book, A Mind That Found Itself, and discuss it in class.

11. Visit a large state mental hospital and a small intensive therapy center and contrast the treatment of patients in these institutions.

12. Use the description of the simple schizophrenic and see how many of your fellow students consider her mentally ill.

13. Check to see how many and how adequate are the facilities for treating mental disease in your community.

14. Invite a hospital psychiatrist, a psychologist, a psychiatric nurse, a psychiatric social worker, an occupational therapist, and a mental hospital attendant to speak to your class on the role of each of these specialties in the treatment of mental disorders.

SUGGESTED READINGS

Action for Mental Health, Final Report of the Joint Commission on Mental Illness and Health, New York: Basic Books, Science Edition, 1961. A readable, complete, official report on the status of the problem of mental illness in the United States. This volume summarizes the entire range of activities dealing with mental disorders and contains a blueprint for the organization of services in the field of mental health.

Causes of Mental Disorders: A Review of Epidemiologic Knowledge, New York: Milbank Memorial Fund, 1961. A number of experts describe the status of knowledge in their specialities. The volume covers genetics, brain injury, family, social stress, social change, and cultural variables in the causation of the mental disorders.

Deutsch, Albert, The Mentally Ill in America, rev. ed., New York: Columbia University Press, 1949. A thorough and scholarly work on the history of the mental hospital in the United States. The pioneering efforts of "reformers" of the mental hospital are treated at length.

Goffman, Erving, Asylums, New York: Doubleday, 1961. A penetrating social-psychological analysis of the meaning of institutionalization to the institutionalized and to those who care for them. The major themes are developed by the author in a series of essays on the "total institution." Equally pertinent to the mental hospital and the prison.   P

Jones, Maxwell, The Therapeutic Community, New York: Basic Books, 1953. The original treatise on the meaning and significance of "milieu therapy" in the treatment of mental patients.

Munroe, Ruth, Schools of Psychoanalytic Thought, New York: Dryden, 1955. This is the most complete and systematic exposition and critique of the major psychoanalytic theories and their development currently available.

> Men are not bad, men are not degraded, because they desire to be so;
> they are degraded largely through circumstances.
>
> Justice Brandeis

Every society, from the simplest folk type to the most highly industrialized, complex, and populous type, develops and elaborates norms to guide the behavior of individual members. These norms protect society against disruptions, facilitate interpersonal relationships, prevent or minimize strife among members, and preserve the basic structure and values of the society. These norms reflect the consensus as to what should or ought to be. They embody both prescriptions and proscriptions. These norms impose various social sanctions — from ridicule to death — to penalize deviation.

All norms are not equally important to society. The most important norms are those that deal with crucial social values and on which, therefore, the highest degree of consensus exists. It is the violation of these — whether they are formalized as mores or as criminal codes — that we call behavioral deviation. Thus crime provides an excellent example of deviant behavior.

There are various technical definitions of crime, none of which is wholly satisfactory. At least three major conceptions of crime exist: the legal, the behavioral, and the conduct norm definition. Each focuses attention on a somewhat different aspect of crime. Together, they present a comprehensive view of criminal deviation.

THE LEGAL DEFINITION [1]

Legally, a crime is a violation of one or more criminal statutes. It is an act which is injurious to the public as distinguished from a private wrong or "tort" or civil injury. A crime is an offense against the entire community

---

1. Edwin H. Sutherland and Donald R. Cressey, *Principles of Criminology*, 6th ed., New York: Lippincott, 1960, pp. 3–23; Herbert A. Bloch and Gilbert Geis, *Man, Crime and Society*, New York: Random House, 1962, pp. 1–137; Jerome Hall, *General Principles of Criminal Law*, 2nd. ed., Indianapolis: Bobbs-Merrill, 1960; Jerome Michael and Mortimer J. Adler, *Crime, Law, and Social Science*, New York: Harcourt, Brace, 1933; and William L. Marshall and William L. Clark, "The Legal Definition of Crime and Criminals," in *The Sociology of Crime and Delinquency* (M. Wolfgang, L. Savitz, and N. Johnston, eds.) New York: Wiley, 1962, pp. 14–19.

446

rather than against specific persons within the community. As a consequence, it is the state or nation which seeks redress in the form of punishment. In civil law, on the other hand, an injury or infringement to the rights of a person or his property is considered a private matter and the injured party may sue for damages.

1. *Characteristics of Criminal Statutes.* Crime, then, is a public wrong which violates a criminal statute and is redressed in the name of the public. Since crime is the commission of wrong as defined in criminal statutes, it is necessary to examine these statutes in some detail. Criminal statutes have four major characteristics: (a) penal sanction or punishment provisions, (b) political origin, (c) specificity, and (d) uniformity.[2]

The chief distinction between a criminal statute and any other social norm is that criminal codes *specify* that any violation of the code shall be punished. The sanctions specified may include a fine, jail or prison sentence, or death. It is necessary to emphasize this punishment aspect of the definition of crime since many persons contend that offenders should be reformed and rehabilitated rather than punished. Many argue that reformation of the offender and punishment are diametrically opposed goals which logically and empirically preclude one another. Rehabilitation cannot, they hold, take place within a punitive legal framework.[3] The law, however, is unequivocal on this point. All other goals such as the deterrence of crime, the protection of society, and the reform of the offender are subsidiary to the goal of punishment as stipulated in the criminal statutes.

A second characteristic of criminal codes is their political origin. Criminal statutes are enacted by duly constituted legislative bodies. Since a legislative body can both enact and repeal criminal statutes, crime resolves itself to a matter of what types of norms are legislated, by what kinds of people, with what kinds of values, under what kinds of pressure, and when. It is true, of course, that the most persistent norms in Western civilization have been derived from the Judeo-Christian tradition. The statutes dealing with homicide, rape and theft are therefore representative of "core" values, and while there have been changes in the penalties for these deviations, they have not ceased to be normative violations.

Criminal codes do, however, change in time and vary with place. In this sense, crime is man-made and subject to man-made revision and change. Hundreds of thousands of new statutes dealing with new crimes have been enacted since the turn of the century.[4] Examples include the possession of nar-

2. For a discussion of these characteristics, see Sutherland and Cressey, op. cit. pp. 5–9.
3. Donald R. Cressey (ed.), *The Prison: Studies in Institutional Organization and Change*, New York: Holt, 1961.
4. It is estimated that three-fourths of the inmates in our prisons in 1931 would not have been criminals had they committed the same act in the period before World

cotics, income tax evasion, violation of Prohibition, gambling (and its rather indefinite status), and crimes involving the automobile. The most important changes have occurred in the sphere of public welfare, where criminal statutes have been enacted and are still being enacted regulating public safety, public morality, business, labor, professional practices, and the use of natural resources.[5] In the future, some behavior acceptable by present standards may be prohibited by legal enactments, and other behavior presently considered criminal may be redefined as nondeviant.[6]

A third aspect of criminal statutes is the requirement of specificity. A criminal statute is specific in two respects. First, it defines the behavior that is proscribed as illegal. Second, it includes the specific penalty to be meted out to offenders. For example, statutes dealing with theft normally detail the kind of theft proscribed and the conditions under which behavior is to be so construed. Burglary, for example, involves illegal breaking and entering. No money need be stolen in the process. The attempt to break and enter is equally a crime. Certain differentiations, however, are made: Was the entry attempted during the day or the night? Was the property a dwelling or business establishment? Inhabited or not? In at least one state, attempting to illegally enter into an inhabited dwelling during the "night season" carries a life sentence on conviction. Burglarizing an unoccupied business establishment by day is a much less serious offense and carries a milder sentence upon conviction. A number of problems also exist with regard to the specificity of a criminal act. For example, how are we to define a suspicious person? By dress, by activity, by location? What constitutes bribery and differentiates it from innocent gift-giving? These illustrations indicate that criminal statutes require specific statements as to the nature of the illegality before behavior can be defined as criminal.

The fourth characteristic of criminal statutes is uniformity. The statute must apply equally to all persons in the political jurisdiction. In practice, of course, statutes frequently apply unequally. To provide the simplest illustration, the same act — burglary — is a crime when committed by an adult and not a crime in the legal sense when perpetrated by a juvenile offender.[7] Many breaches of this precept of uniformity are necessary and valuable.

War I. See Harry Elmer Barnes and Negley K. Teeters, *New Horizons in Criminology*, 3rd ed., New York: Prentice-Hall, 1959, p. 74.

5. Edwin H. Sutherland and C. E. Gehlke, "Crime and Punishment," in *Recent Social Trends in the United States* (William F. Ogburn, ed.), New York: McGraw-Hill, 1933, pp. 1116–20.

6. Hermann Mannheim, *Criminal Justice and Social Reconstruction*, New York: Oxford University Press, 1946.

7. For a review of the legal problems and court decisions in juvenile delinquency, see, Sheldon Glueck (ed.), *The Problem of Delinquency*, Boston: Houghton Mifflin, 1959, pp. 255–510.

Others represent deliberate attempts to maintain the *status quo* by creating statutes which apply solely to minority groups.

2. *The Overt Act and Criminal Intent.*[8] To repeat, crime may be defined as a violation of one or more criminal statutes. These codes feature four main characteristics: penal sanction, political origin, specificity, and uniformity. Legally, a criminal offense also involves two other qualities. These are (1) an *overt act*, and (2) *intent*, or technically what is called *mens rea*.

In Western culture, the doctrine that a crime is an overt act of commission or omission in violation of a criminal statute appears self-evident. Less obvious, though no less important, is the requirement that a criminal act must be intended or willful. There can be no crime without criminal intent, or *mens rea*. The *mens rea* doctrine means that a person must have a "guilty mind" before a judgment of criminality can be made against him. Violators must be capable of willful wrongdoing and consciousness of the act which they commit in order for the act to qualify as a crime.

The concept of *mens rea* assumes that an individual chooses to act as he does. If he violates the law, he has intended it and is, therefore, criminally responsible for his conduct. It is for this reason that some persons and some violations do not qualify as criminal even though overt violation of the law has occurred. These exclusions include violations which are purely chance occurrences or so-called acts of God; violations committed by persons of "tender age"; by persons who are mentally retarded; by persons who commit compulsive acts; by persons acting under duress; by persons acting in ignorance of the true facts in the situation; by persons who are negligent; and by those who are legally insane.

The latter two exceptions to criminal responsibility — negligence and insanity — are particularly interesting. A ruling of negligence is principally found in crimes involving automobile and other vehicular fatalities and injuries. The legal logic is that although a death may have occurred, the driver did not intend this result. His crime was the result of violations of other statutes — speeding, reckless operation, or driving while intoxicated — which were intended. Consequently, the offense is manslaughter by negligence and not homicide.

Insanity as an exception to *mens rea* is a complex problem and has led to difficulties between the legal and medical professions. Insanity is not a medical term. It was coined in the process of attempting to arrive at legal decisions involving major crimes such as homicide. Its origin was in a decision enunciated in England in 1843. In this decision, which has come to be known as the M'Naghten rule, the doctrine was established that a person could not be held criminally responsible for his acts if, at the time he com-

8. Marshall and Clark, op. cit. pp. 16–19.

mitted them, he could not distinguish between right and wrong.[9] This so-
called right and wrong test almost immediately introduced problems. How
is one to determine whether the perpetrator of a major offense could distinguish between right and wrong at the time he violated the law? Or, is it
not possible for a person to verbally make this distinction without being able
to translate such knowledge into action? Too, what of the emotional components or motives that are unconscious? These and other questions raised
issues which could not readily be resolved.[10] In time, therefore, still another
principle came to supplement the right and wrong test. The second principle
held that if the behavior in question was motivated by an irresistible impulse,
then there was no criminal responsibility.[11] Again, what is an irresistible impulse and how does one substantiate its existence in any given crime? As a
result, two newer ideas have been proposed. A recent court decision held
that no criminal responsibility could be established if the act was a product
of mental illness or mental incapacity.[12] Psychiatrists could certainly testify
to this question even though they may disagree in specific cases. It has also
been suggested that criminal responsibility occurs only when a violator is
able to appreciate the consequences of his actions and has the capability of
conforming to the requirements of the law. Despite these newer approaches,
the issue of *mens rea* and its relation to mental illness remains unresolved.

Legally, then, a crime is a violation of one or more criminal statutes which
is subject to legal action resulting in punishment. A violation includes both
an overt act and intent, or *mens rea*.

THE BEHAVIORAL DEFINITION [13]

The behavioral definition of crime accepts and builds on the legal definition.
From the behavioral point of view, the actual violation of a criminal statute
is an incomplete definition of crime. Behaviorally, a violation or offense must
be *reported* to legitimate authorities before a judgment of criminality can
be rendered. The focus is on the reporting of the offense. Unless reporting of
a violation takes place and legal action is initiated, the violator may just as

9. The decision resulted from an attempt on the life of the British Prime Minister by
   Daniel M'Naghten. The Prime Minister's secretary was fatally wounded in the attempt. M'Naghten was acquitted by reason of insanity. See Sheldon Glueck, "Mental
   Illness and Criminal Responsibility," *Journal of Social Therapy*, 2 (Third Quarter,
   1956), pp. 134–57.
10. Manfred S. Guttmacher and Henry Weihofen, *Psychiatry and the Law*, New York:
    Norton, 1952, p. 409.
11. Fifteen states include this provision, which was first initiated in Ohio in 1834 and
    consequently antedates the M'Naghten rule.
12. This definition was a consequence of the Durham decision which was given in 1954.
    See William O. Douglas, "The Durham Rule: A Meeting Ground for Lawyers and
    Psychiatrists," *Iowa Law Review*, 41 (Summer 1956), pp. 485–95.
13. For a more complete discussion of this approach, see Walter C. Reckless, *The Crime
    Problem*, 3rd ed., New York: Appleton-Century-Crofts, 1961, Chap. 2.

well not have committed the offense at all. This emphasis on reporting directs attention to the idea that it is not the violation per se but rather the social definition of it that is crucial. Almost all persons violate criminal statutes at some time. The typical urban dweller may violate a large enough number of statutes each and every day to warrant, if he were convicted, fines in the amount of $5000 and jail sentences of as much as five years. If each of these violations were reported and officially acted upon, the crime problem would become overwhelming. Consequently, a legitimate concern centers on differentials in reporting. Are there crimes which are normally reported and those which are not? Are there any principles which apply in differential reporting?

1. *Nonreporting of Crime.* Two reasons have been offered for the nonreporting of criminal offenses. These reasons are the *invisibility* of some offenses and the *unwillingness* of victims and spectators to report others.[14] Many conventional crimes — particularly larceny offenses — go undetected. It is very difficult, for example, for a large retail outlet, a supermarket, or a department store to detect all shoplifting and shoplifters and it would be almost impossible for these same establishments to detect employees who pilfer merchandise. Other offenses are equally difficult to detect: embezzlement, fraud, some burglaries, drug peddling, and some auto thefts. Even personal offenses are not always visible. Homicide may be confused with either suicide or death from natural causes. Nonassaultive sexual offenses entered into voluntarily — homosexuality, for example — also generally escape detection. The least visible and detectable violations are those which, for shorthand reference and to distinguish them from conventional crimes, are referred to as white collar crimes. Examples include income tax evasion, the mislabeling of products, the overweighing and misgrading of goods, the adulteration of products, fee-splitting, antitrust violations, and many others. Many criminal offenses, then, particularly those of an unconventional nature, simply go undetected.

The invisibility of various offenses is frequently complemented by the unwillingness to report others.[15] There are, of course, many legitimate reasons for the unwillingness to report offenses. Some offenses are sociologically inoperative — dissensus may exist as to whether an act constitutes deviation in the first place. Almost all gambling offenses — from bingo to numbers — go unreported. Persons who gamble are not very likely to report something they consider acceptable behavior. The police, too, may consider the behavior acceptable. So most gambling, except in some election years when investiga-

14. Ibid. p. 24.
15. Thorsten Sellin, *Research Memorandum on Crime in the Depression*, New York: Social Science Research Council, 1937, pp. 69–70.

tions are made, remains unreported. The same applies to liquor violations, minor violations of municipal statutes, and most visible white collar crimes. In American society, there is probably greatest normative consensus on personal crimes, less consensus on conventional crimes, and least consensus on crimes against the public welfare. Personal crimes like homicide, when identified as such, are invariably reported. Conventional property offenses are less likely to result in reports and legal action. The nonconventional crimes and more minor offenses are least likely to be reported and officially acted on. This situation has not always prevailed. Prior to widespread industrialization and urbanization, property offenses were considered as important as personal crimes and were probably as likely to be reported and to result in severe punishment including the death penalty.[16]

2. *Victim Proneness and Victim Instigation.*[17] The behavioral definition also stresses the interactional aspects of crime and the necessity for understanding the contexts in which violations occur. Unlike the legal approach, the behavioral viewpoint is as interested in the victim and the spectators to a crime as it is in the perpetrator. This interest is classified under the general heading of victimology. There are two aspects to victimology — victim proneness and victim instigation. The former concerns the observed fact that some types of persons and establishments are victimized far more frequently than chance alone would dictate. While precise evidence is lacking, it appears that victim-prone persons and establishments have at least one attribute in common — relative defenselessness. The defenseless are found in various social categories: Females, as opposed to males; old persons more than young adults; minority group members in contrast to those in the majority group; lower class persons more than middle and upper class persons.[18] The most likely category to include the victim prone consists of persons who are themselves deviant. Sex offenders, drug addicts, and criminals make excellent victims since they perceive themselves to have little recourse to enforcement agencies. Thus, crime is not a random phenomenon and such attributes as age, sex, minority status, and personal deviancy may to some degree determine who becomes a victim.

Similarly, some types of establishments are more prone than others to be burglarized or robbed. Those which have late closing hours and which are one-man operations are peculiarly subject to robbery. The same gas station or bar may be robbed several times in a very short period. Suburban banks, un-

16. Eric R. Calvert, *Capital Punishment in the Twentieth Century*, 2nd ed., London: G. P. Putnam's Sons, 1927.
17. Hans Von Hentig, *The Criminal and His Victim*, New Haven: Yale University Press, 1948.
18. Ibid. pp. 404-38.

like the massive and well-protected downtown banks, face the same problem and account for a significant increase in the bank robberies since 1955.[19]

In victim instigation, as opposed to victim proneness, the victim plays a role in triggering the offense.[20] This instigating role is nearly always unknown to the victim. Murders, for example, are commonly committed against friends or relatives — rarely against someone unknown to the assailant. The nagging wife, the lecherous husband, the love triangle, a simple argument at a bar, and many other common interactional relationships may trigger a personal offense. In every case, the law is primarily concerned with the perpetrator; the criminologist with the interactional setting.

Instigations exist for property offenses, too. Stolen cars are often those in which the keys have been left. Families going on vacation may stimulate burglaries by leaving "signs" around noting when they are leaving and how long they will be gone. It was once stylish for women to carry handbags which dangled from their shoulders by straps so purse snatchers, using a sharp cutting tool, easily separated many women from their purses. Confidence men operate on the axiom that a totally honest man cannot be taken. In all these illustrations, the essential point is that, wittingly or unwittingly, a victim may provoke an offense.

Thus, the behavioral definition forces attention on three aspects of crime generally overlooked in purely legal conceptions. The behavioral conception looks at the problem of the reporting and nonreporting of offenses, considers the reasons underlying this differential reporting, and sees crime as the product of an interactional relationship.

DEFINITION OF CONDUCT NORMS [21]

A third approach is to view criminal behavior not as a violation of law, whether or not reported, but rather as a violation of the conduct norms of the groups in which one holds membership. In large industrial societies legal statutes incorporate the norms of certain groups, but these norms may not be accepted by other groups and, indeed, may be repugnant to them. Conduct defined as deviant and criminal by the larger society may be wholly acceptable to persons in specific subcultures. Can an act, therefore, be classed as deviant when it is considered perfectly reasonable behavior by a subgroup? From this

---

19. See *Uniform Crime Reports*, U.S. Department of Justice, Annual Reports, 1955–61.
20. Marvin Wolfgang, "Victim Precipitated Criminal Homicide," in *The Sociology of Crime and Delinquency*, op. cit. pp. 388–96. Also, Hans Von Hentig, op. cit. pp. 383–5.
21. See Thorsten Sellin, *Culture Conflict and Crime*, New York: Social Service Research Council, 1938; and George B. Vold, *Theoretical Criminology*, New York: Oxford University Press, 1958, Chap. 11.

point of view, crime can only be defined in terms of violations of specific subcultural norms.

This position is best illustrated by Southern Appalachian migrants to the
midwestern cities of Ohio, Illinois, and Michigan, by the migrations of nonwhites to northern urban communities, and by the unusually rapid migration
of Puerto Ricans to New York. In each instance, the values and norms of the
migrant group are substantially different from those of the host communities.
In time, these normative differences will largely disappear, but is it equitable
to judge the behavior of members of these groups in terms of existing legal
standards? Legal norms regarding the expression of aggression, drinking,
sexual behavior, and various kinds of theft simply do not make sense to
persons reared in a different normative order, particularly when, as in the case
of Puerto Ricans, language presents a major barrier.

This does not imply that antisocial behavior should be accepted by society
if engaged in by subcultural groups. The problem is one of understanding
and not one of accepting or rejecting. It is fair to say, however, that deviant
behavior and crime, as concepts, are most meaningful when normative consensus exists. When subcultural norms differ from those of the larger or more
general culture, it is difficult to consider behavior acceptable to the subculture as being criminal or deviant.

This conception of crime is also exemplified by the problems of religious
sects such as the Amish in Ohio, Pennsylvania, and elsewhere. These groups
refuse to recognize the validity of the state, refuse to pay taxes, refuse to send
their children to school beyond the eighth grade, refuse to serve in the armed
forces, and specify different, and by other standards illegal, norms for
conduct. Is this behavior criminal? — legally yes, but subculturally no. In practice, judges and prosecutors will often be aware of these subcultural variations and treat violations committed by members of these groups accordingly. The law, however, makes no provision for such normative differences.

All three approaches — the legal, the behavioral, and the conduct norm
conceptions — define crime as antisocial conduct. They differ, however, in
specific aspects of this definition. For the remainder of this chapter crime
will be viewed behaviorally and will be defined as any behavior that violates
one or more criminal statutes and is reported and acted upon by appropriate
agencies.

REPORTED CRIME

There is no way of determining the actual extent of lawlessness in the
United States since a substantial, although unknown, proportion of all violations remain unreported. Further, vagaries in reporting make it difficult to
determine whether crime has been increasing or decreasing over time. With

only minor changes in reporting and administrative procedures, it is possible to create crime waves and, by the same token, to eradicate them. This unreliability of reporting is a problem in any type of deviant behavior.[22]

Crime data are regularly reported by police authorities and compiled and published by the FBI in the *Uniform Crime Reports*. The FBI, following the legal definition, divides reported crimes into two classes. Part I crimes are felony offenses and Part II offenses include both felonies and misdemeanors. A felony offense is a major crime which presently carries a minimum sentence of one year or more in a state prison. At one time felony offenses were punishable by death. A misdemeanor is a minor offense which is punishable by a fine or sentence of imprisonment not exceeding one year. The FBI publishes reports on the seven Part I offenses which are most consistently recorded by the police. These are: murder and non-negligent manslaughter, forcible rape, aggravated assault, robbery, burglary, larceny, and auto theft. Part II offenses are reported only when they result in an arrest. So numerous are Part II offenses and so inadequate is the reporting that police jurisdictions keep few meaningful records on them. Part II offenses include assaults, forgery and counterfeiting, embezzlement and fraud, handling stolen property, offenses dealing with the illegal possession of weapons, prostitution and vice, sex offenses except rape, offenses against family and children, vagrancy, gambling, narcotics violations, drunkenness, disorderly conduct, suspicion, and auto violations.

Measurement of the extent of crime in the United States is thus restricted to the aforementioned seven major offenses. In 1961, it was estimated that 1,926,119 Part I violations occurred. There were 8599 murders, 16,012 forcible rapes, 91,659 robberies, 133,020 aggravated assaults, 852,506 burglaries, 498,117 larcenies of $50 and over, and 326,206 auto thefts.[23] These figures only partially reveal the extent of major conventional crime. For example, there were many more rapes than the listed number of 16,012. The unlisted rapes are nonassaultive — that is, statutory in nature. A statutory rape is one in which the female is under the legal age of consent. Listed larcenies accounted for only about 38 per cent of all reported larcenies. The unlisted larcenies involved thefts of under $50 each.

In 1961 the "cost" of robberies, burglaries, larcenies, auto thefts, and other offenses exceeded $591 million.[24] Auto thefts alone accounted for a quarter of this valuation. The police recovered about 52 cents on each dollar stolen; recoveries were primarily automobiles. To put this monetary picture

---

22. For a discussion of the difficulties in obtaining adequate reports, see Ronald H. Beattie, "Problems of Criminal Statistics in the United States," *Journal of Criminal Law, Criminology and Police Science* 46 (July–August 1955), pp. 178–86.
23. *Uniform Crime Reports*, 1961, p. 33.
24. Ibid. p. 1.

into further perspective, the average "take" per robbery in 1961 was $266; per burglary, $187; larceny, $74; and auto theft, $828.[25] Compared with the average "take" from embezzlement, gambling operations, or white collar crimes, conventional property offenses are hardly worth the effort and risk.

NONREPORTED CRIME

In order to estimate the actual extent of committed crime, as opposed to reported crime, a number of small studies have been undertaken. The findings in these studies suggest that criminality is more extensive than the FBI reports indicate. If the data in these studies are valid, crime is far from being a unique and statistically deviant form of behavior.

1. *The Law Abiding and the Law Violators.*[26] In 1947, Wallerstein and Wyle reported the admitted criminal violations of a sample of respondents in the New York City area. These authors compiled a list of 49 punishable offenses in questionnaire form and asked randomly selected respondents to indicate whether or not they had committed any of these violations after reaching the age of 16. Responses were received from 1020 men and 678 women. Analysis of the responses indicated that (a) almost all respondents had committed at least one of the 49 punishable offenses, (b) male respondents averaged 18 offenses, (c) female respondents averaged 11 offenses, and (d) 64 per cent of the men and 29 per cent of the women admitted the commission of at least one felony. Eighty-nine per cent of the men and 83 per cent of the women admitted committing larceny. For grand larceny ($50 and over) the percentages for male and female were 13 and 11 respectively. For burglary, the percentages were 17 and 4. Auto thefts were admitted to by 26 per cent of the males and 8 percent of the women. Even robbery was admitted to by 11 per cent of the males and 1 per cent of the females. Such offenses (Part II) as assault, malicious mischief, income tax evasion, and sexual offenses were reported by as few as 40 per cent of the male respondents and as many as 85 per cent, depending upon the offense category. In each case, fewer females reported violations.

Despite the obvious limitations — who responds to such a questionnaire, who is unwilling to do so, problems of recall, and problems of exaggeration — Wallerstein and Wyle concluded that, "the number of acts legally constituting crime is far in excess of those officially reported." How far in excess remains unknown.

2. *The Cambridge-Somerville Study.*[27] A second study is even more re-

25. Ibid. p. 89.
26. See James S. Wallerstein and Clement J. Wyle, "Our Law-Abiding Law-Breakers," *Probation,* 25 (April 1947), pp. 107–12.
27. Fred J. Murphy, Mary M. Shirley, and Helen M. Witmer, "The Incidence of Hidden Delinquency," *American Journal of Orthopsychiatry,* 16 (October 1946), pp. 686–96.

vealing. Instead of dealing with adult offenders, the problem of hidden delinquency was investigated. In the Cambridge-Somerville study, which dealt with the feasibility of preventing delinquency, there was an analysis of the criminal violations of 61 officially nondelinquent and 40 officially delinquent boys. Although young, 11–16 years old, these boys, from slum neighborhoods, admitted 6416 offenses, or an average of over 64 violations per boy, over a five-year period. Of these 6416 violations, 1400 were found to be relatively minor and consisted of the breaking of municipal ordinances. In addition, 4400 misdemeanors were committed by the 101 boys. Of these, so few were reported that only six-tenths of 1 per cent ended in prosecution. Finally, the 101 boys admitted to committing 616 serious offenses. Of these, only 11 per cent were prosecuted.

It was largely a matter of chance whether these lower-class slum boys were classed as delinquent or nondelinquent. The delinquents and nondelinquents averaged about the same number and same degree of seriousness of violations, and the difference in classification as delinquent or nondelinquent rested on whether the violations resulted in official action. Only 95 of the 6416 offenses ended in such action.

3. *Other Studies*. The evidence obtained in the Cambridge-Somerville study has been corroborated for other groups as well. Bloch found that 91 per cent of 340 college upperclassmen from middle-class homes admitted a considerable number of felony and misdemeanor offenses.[28] Porterfield developed a check list of 55 violations comparable to that in the Wallerstein and Wyle study. This check list of violations was administered to 337 college students in Texas and every student admitted to the commission of at least one of the violational categories.[29] This evidence indicates that official statistics are quite unreliable and that it may be necessary to utilize admitted, rather than reported, violations for studying deviant and criminal behavior.

THE DISPOSITION OF REPORTED CRIMES

Criminal behavior — even serious criminal behavior — has been shown to be far more extensive than crime statistics indicate. Using Part I reported offenses only, it is also possible to demonstrate that relatively few violations result in conviction and imprisonment. The purpose of the discussion which follows is to indicate that persons convicted and sentenced to an institution probably represent a selected and biased sample of those who violate the law.

Table 16-1 indicates the situation in 1961. Column 1 presents the estimated number of Part I offenses reported or known to the police. These figures were

28. Herbert Bloch and Frank T. Flynn, *Delinquency: The Juvenile Offender in America Today*, New York: Random House, 1956, pp. 11–14.
29. Austin L. Porterfield, *Youth in Trouble*, Austin: Leo Potishman Foundation, 1946, pp. 38 ff.

presented previously. Column 2 indicates the percentage of known offenses which resulted in an arrest. Column 3 contains data on the number of persons charged or held for prosecution relative to the number of known offenses. Column 4 contains data on convictions for the reported offenses. Column 5 contains data on acquittals and Column 6 indicates the percentage of offenses referred to juvenile courts.

TABLE 16-1

The disposition of part 1 crimes, 1961

Offense category	Estimated no.	Per cent cleared by arrest [a]	Number charged per 100 crimes [a]	Per cent convicted of those charged [b]	Per cent acquitted of offense charged [b]	Per cent referred to juvenile court [b]
Murder and non-negligent manslaughter	8,599	93.1	95.9	50.7	18.7	3.5
Forcible rape	16,012	72.6	78.4	43.9	23.4	14.2
Aggravated assault	133,020	78.7	62.1	43.4	33.3	8.1
Robbery	91,659	41.6	45.8	45.3	16.2	20.9
Burglary	852,506	30.0	21.6	36.7	8.1	44.0
Larceny $50 & over	498,117	20.8	15.7	45.3	11.0	37.3
Auto theft	326,206	27.8	24.0	27.4	7.8	54.2
Total	1,926,119					

[a] Based on data from 2313 cities; total population 75,642,090, Table 9, p. 85.
[b] Based on data from 1279 cities; total population 31,538,019, Table 10, p. 86.
Source: *Uniform Crime Reports*, 1961.

From the data in Table 16-1, and from other sources, it is possible to conclude that: (a) most known offenses do not result in an arrest, (b) arrests for known offenses are most frequent in personal crimes and least frequent in property offenses, and (c) prosecution of property offenses more often results in conviction or in referral to another court than does prosecution of personal offenses. In summary, convictions occur in less than half of the known murders and non-negligent manslaughter cases, a third of the forcible rapes and aggravated assaults, a fourth of the robberies, a seventh of the burglaries and auto thefts, and a tenth of the grand larcenies.

Even these statistics fail to reveal the actual disposition of crimes. The reason lies in the incompleteness of FBI data. As a consequence, Van Vechten tried to improve the accuracy of these statistics by coupling Uniform Crime Report data with census data. In combining these statistics he arrived at the conclusion that of every 100 known Part I offenses, only 25 are cleared by arrest; in only 20 is anyone ever charged with the offense (held for prosecution); in only 7 does actual prosecution take place; in only 5.5 is there a conviction; and in only 3.5 does imprisonment occur.[30] To reverse these data, 75 out of every 100 known serious crimes remain unsolved, 80 never proceed as far as the stage of charging, 93 never get to the stage of prosecution, 94.5 never end in conviction, and 96.5 never result in a prison sentence.

Under these circumstances several conclusions are possible. First, police and court procedures are simply unable to cope with major criminality to the point where most crimes are solved and penal sanctions imposed. Second, crime waves can be readily "manufactured" by improving the efficiency of the police and courts. Conversely, criminality can be "reduced" by inefficient police and court procedures. Third, if only 3.5 out of every 100 Part I offenses result in conviction and imprisonment, then prisoners probably represent a biased and highly selected sample of law violators. Fourth, it is an axiom of penologists that for punishment to be efficacious it must be certain, swift, and equitable.[31] These and other data indicate that for major crimes in this country, punishment is far from certain.

POLICE AND LEGAL PROCEDURES [32]

In order to understand this overwhelming loss of cases between the report of violations to the police and the sentencing of offenders, it is necessary to examine the procedures involved in handling cases of major crime. For simplicity these procedures in major offenses may be outlined as follows:

1. Complaint or report is made to the police by victim or spectators.

2. Police investigate complaint and attempt to ascertain when and how offense occurred and other information as to type and amount of property stolen.

3. Police launch search for suspects using whatever techniques are required. In a fourth of the major crimes investigation results in the arrest of one or more suspects.

4. Suspect is booked by police. This includes fingerprinting and photographing. Questioning of suspect may follow.

5. Suspect may be held in jail for later prosecution, or released on bail bond. Suspect may also be released outright for lack of evidence or for other reasons.

30. Courtland C. Van Vechten, "Differential Criminal Case Mortality in Selected Jurisdictions," *American Sociological Review*, 7 (December 1942), pp. 833–9.
31. Max Grünhut, *Penal Reform: A Comparative Study*, Oxford: The Clarendon Press, 1948.
32. Any standard volume in criminology contains a section on police administration and criminal and legal procedures. See, for example, Barnes and Teeters, *New Horizons in Criminology*, op. cit.

6. Suspect, if not released, is brought to preliminary court hearing (arraignment or charge). Case may be dismissed at this point if evidence is scant, or evidence may warrant continuation of case.

7. If case is continued, suspect is bound over to grand jury. Bail may be granted while awaiting grand jury action. If suspect cannot meet bail requirements, he is confined in jail.

8. Grand jury has two alternatives. It may indict (return a "true bill") or fail to indict the suspect. Case proceeds if true bill is returned.

9. Case comes to trial in local court. Judge alone or jury may hear case. Suspect may be convicted or found not guilty.

10. If a conviction is obtained, sentence may be suspended, bench parole granted, a jail sentence or fine imposed, or a prison sentence may be ordered.

Although this procedure may vary among jurisdictions, it does in general outline the various steps between the complaint and the outcome. This procedure is a product of a long historical development and is surrounded by guarantees designed to prevent "railroading" of suspects to prison. Its very cumbersomeness and relative inefficiency operates in favor of the offender. This procedure also accounts for much of the loss of cases between arrest and conviction.

THE INSTITUTIONALIZED CRIMINALS

Despite this case loss, prisons and jails do not lack for inmates. In 1959, for example, 207,513 persons were confined in prisons in the U.S.[33] Of this total, over 89 per cent were imprisoned in state institutions and the remainder were in federal institutions. Male prisoners constituted over 96 per cent of the inmates.

In 1959, 167,826 inmates were admitted or readmitted to our prisons and only a slightly lesser number were discharged.[34] Of prisoners discharged as first releases (released for the first time on their current sentences), over 60 per cent were paroled. As in sentencing and other procedures, variations in parole rates for first releases were enormous. The State of Washington paroled 99.6 per cent of first releases while the State of Vermont paroled only 7.7 per cent of first releases.[35] Discrepancies of this magnitude are by no means unusual. A state-by-state breakdown of paroles is presented in Figure 16-1.

In the last two sections, we have considered the extent of crime — both known and unreported — and the legal procedures involved in dealing with known criminal offenses. Unfortunately, the criminologist knows little about

33. "Prisoners in State and Federal Institutions," 1959, *National Prisoner Statistics*, Federal *Bureau of Prisons*, No. 24 (July 1960), Table 1.
34. Ibid. Table 2.
35. Ibid. Chart 2.

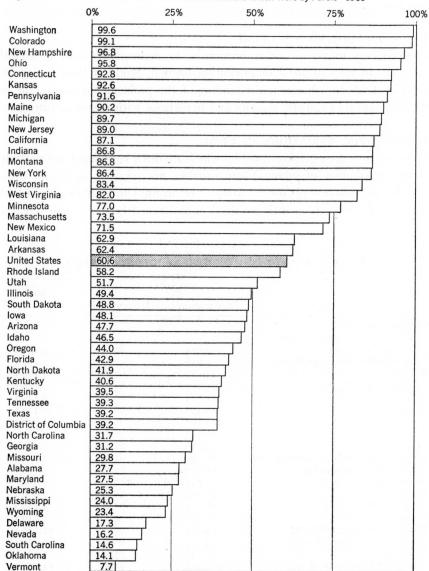

Fig. 16-1. Per Cent of First Releases From State Institutions Which Were by Parole—1959

Washington	99.6
Colorado	99.1
New Hampshire	96.8
Ohio	95.8
Connecticut	92.8
Kansas	92.6
Pennsylvania	91.6
Maine	90.2
Michigan	89.7
New Jersey	89.0
California	87.1
Indiana	86.8
Montana	86.8
New York	86.4
Wisconsin	83.4
West Virginia	82.0
Minnesota	77.0
Massachusetts	73.5
New Mexico	71.5
Louisiana	62.9
Arkansas	62.4
United States	60.6
Rhode Island	58.2
Utah	51.7
Illinois	49.4
South Dakota	48.8
Iowa	48.1
Arizona	47.7
Idaho	46.5
Oregon	44.0
Florida	42.9
North Dakota	41.9
Kentucky	40.6
Virginia	39.5
Tennessee	39.3
Texas	39.2
District of Columbia	39.2
North Carolina	31.7
Georgia	31.2
Missouri	29.8
Alabama	27.7
Maryland	27.5
Nebraska	25.3
Mississippi	24.0
Wyoming	23.4
Delaware	17.3
Nevada	16.2
South Carolina	14.6
Oklahoma	14.1
Vermont	7.7

Source: National Prisoner Statistics, 1959, Federal Bureau of Prisons, No. 24, July, 1960.

the people who commit the offenses. Information must be gathered at a level once removed from the crime itself — that is, at the level of arrest. This proves to be a disadvantage, in that only about 25 out of every 100 Part I offenses result in an arrest. In dealing with the epidemiology of crime, through rates of arrest, biases of all kinds may be operating. Nevertheless, arrest rates are the only ones available. They provide the basis for much of the discussion that follows.

THE EPIDEMIOLOGY OF CRIME

Epidemiology refers, as noted previously, to demographic and ecological variations in rates of arrest or institutionalization. Study of these variations not only leads to a better understanding of the problem but may result in the elaboration of testable theories and hypotheses with regard to causation.

DEMOGRAPHIC VARIATIONS IN CRIME

There are four demographic variables which are often considered in the study of the distribution of crime. These variables are sex, age, race, and class.

1. *Sex Distribution of Arrests.* Arrests rates in the United States reveal that males are far more frequently involved in violational behavior than females.

TABLE 16-2

Ratio of male to female arrests by city police, 1961

Offense category	Total number [1]	Per cent male	Ratio male to female
Criminal homicide:			
A) Murder and non-negligent manslaughter	4,625	82.0	4.6 to 1
B) Manslaughter by negligence	1,618	90.1	9.1 to 1
Robbery	33,175	95.1	19.4 to 1
Aggravated assault	55,355	84.8	5.6 to 1
Other assaults	141,784	89.4	8.4 to 1
Burglary	126,477	96.7	29.3 to 1
Larceny	228,067	82.0	4.6 to 1
Auto theft	58,547	96.4	26.8 to 1
Embezzlement	34,286	83.3	5.0 to 1
Stolen property; buying, receiving, etc.	10,745	91.3	10.5 to 1
Forgery and counterfeiting	21,613	82.5	4.7 to 1
Forcible rape	7,143	100.0	—
Prostitution	26,843	28.1	0.4 to 1
Other sex offenses	46,204	81.5	4.4 to 1
Narcotic drug laws	25,080	84.6	5.5 to 1
Weapons; carrying, possessing, etc.	34,985	93.8	15.1 to 1
Offenses against family & children	35,017	88.8	7.9 to 1
Liquor laws	99,048	85.6	5.9 to 1
Driving while intoxicated	164,222	93.4	14.2 to 1
Disorderly conduct	434,886	85.9	6.1 to 1
Drunkenness	1,399,293	92.0	11.5 to 1
Vagrancy	147,526	91.2	10.4 to 1
Gambling	108,571	91.7	11.0 to 1
All other offenses	480,099	84.1	5.3 to 1
Suspicion	125,616	88.1	7.8 to 1
Total	3,851,825	88.7	7.9 to 1

Source: These data compiled from *Uniform Crime Reports*, 1961, Table 22. Ratios are based on arrests by city police in 2776 cities with a total population of 85,158,360 people.

Of the twenty-four Part I and II offense classifications on which city police forces maintain sex distributions, there is only one category in which the male rate does not appreciably exceed the female. In Table 16-2, the sex ratios by offense category are reported. For all offenses in 1961, males were arrested eight times more often than females; in the conventional property offenses, male rates were over 19 times as great for robbery, 29 times as great for burglary, and 27 times as great for auto theft. The only offense in which female arrest rates exceeded those of males was, of course, prostitution.

Explanations of these differences are numerous.[36] Females are not likely, in terms of their biological and social roles, to become involved in the more aggressive types of offenses, except perhaps as accessories. The image of a dainty female staging a robbery or burglarizing an establishment violates more than a legal norm. Such an image does violence to normative conceptions of the female role. Apart from the role discrepancy, females are more infrequently arrested because, even in slum areas, the female is more carefully watched and more thoroughly socialized. Her range of permissible behavior is more elaborately circumscribed and supervised. When she deviates, it is usually in terms of sexual misconduct. There are also no norms which can justify her deviance as male deviation is justified by subcultural norms. In accounting for these lower female rates, consideration must also be given to the greater leniency accorded women by the police and courts. Police are reluctant to arrest women and juries are loath to convict them.

Still, differential rearing patterns, socialization, self-conceptions, and roles may not present the whole picture. At least one criminologist believes that female crime is significantly more extensive than arrest ratios would indicate. Pollak's contention is that female criminality tends to be "masked" or hidden by the roles females play in society.[37] Probably the most extensive female crime — involvement in abortion — is almost never reported. Women, in their normal role as shoppers, are frequently able to escape detection for shoplifting whereas a male carrying a shopping bag is sometimes suspect. Women can abuse children in their normal roles as mothers with relative impunity. Domestics can often loot a house without an official complaint being lodged. Finally, women sexual offenders are rarely reported.

2. *Age Distribution of Arrests.* Conventional crime in this country, and since World War II in other countries as well, appears to be a preoccupation of relatively young persons. Over the last few decades, and certainly since the turn of the century, adolescents and young adults have constituted an increasing proportion of total arrests. Table 16-3 shows the situation in the

36. See Reckless, op. cit. pp. 37–9.
37. Otto Pollak, *The Criminality of Women*, Philadelphia: University of Pennsylvania, 1950.

TABLE 16-3

City police arrests of persons under 18, under 21, and under 25 years of age, 1961

Offense charged	Number of persons arrested				Percentage		
	TOTAL	Under 18	Under 21	Under 25	Under 18	Under 21	Under 25
TOTAL	3,851,825	566,682	892,245	1,270,088	14.7	23.2	33.0
Criminal Homicide:							
(a) Murder and non-negligent man-slaughter	4,625	384	871	1,511	8.3	18.8	32.7
(b) Manslaughter by negligence	1,618	115	305	557	7.1	18.9	34.4
Forcible rape	7,143	1,363	2,949	4,381	19.1	41.3	61.3
Robbery	33,175	7,775	14,439	21,138	23.4	43.5	63.7
Aggravated assault ..	55,355	7,189	12,658	20,029	13.0	22.9	36.2
Burglary — breaking or entering	126,477	61,508	81,479	96,783	48.6	64.4	76.5
Larceny — theft	228,067	113,619	141,149	160,819	49.8	61.9	70.5
Auto theft	58,547	35,714	45,735	51,016	61.0	78.1	87.1
Other assaults	141,784	15,089	27,699	47,504	10.6	19.5	33.5
Embezzlement and fraud	34,286	834	2,594	6,989	2.4	7.6	20.4
Stolen property; buying, receiving, etc. .	10,745	2,940	4,603	5,997	27.4	42.8	55.8
Forgery and counter-feiting	21,613	1,422	3,814	7,488	6.6	17.6	34.6
Prostitution and com-mercialized vice ...	26,843	544	2,948	9,574	2.0	11.0	35.7
Other sex offenses (includes statutory rape)	46,204	10,012	14,847	21,003	21.7	32.1	45.5
Narcotic drug laws ..	25,080	1,701	4,898	10,456	6.8	19.5	41.7
Weapons; carrying, possessing, etc ...	35,985	6,860	11,970	17,379	19.1	33.3	48.3
Offenses against family and children	35,017	1,070	3,567	8,775	3.1	10.2	25.1
Liquor laws	99,048	18,700	47,615	55,137	18.9	48.1	55.7
Driving while intoxicated ...	164,222	1,207	7,719	23,824	.7	4.7	14.5
Disorderly conduct ..	434,886	55,627	107,383	163,750	12.8	24.7	37.7
Drunkenness	1,399,293	14,207	56,222	144,532	1.0	4.0	10.3
Vagrancy	147,526	10,143	25,469	40,307	6.9	17.3	27.3
Gambling	108,571	1,352	4,715	14,944	1.2	4.3	13.8
All other offenses ...	480,099	176,203	222,199	270,561	36.7	46.3	56.4
Suspicion	125,616	21,104	44,398	65,634	16.8	35.3	52.2

Source: *Uniform Crime Reports,* 1961, Table 21, p. 95. Data based on reports of 2776 cities with a total population of 85,158,360.

major cities of the United States in 1961. Persons under 18 contributed 48.6 per cent of the arrests for burglary, 49.8 per cent for larceny, and 61.0 per cent for auto theft. They also contributed 14.7 per cent of arrests for all crimes. Since 1940, arrests of persons under 18 have doubled, whereas the population in the 10–17 group has increased 32 per cent.

In 1961, individuals under 21 contributed over two-fifths of all robbery arrests, slightly less than two-thirds of the burglary arrests, over three-fifths of the larceny arrests, and over three-fourths of the arrests for auto thefts. Those under 25 contributed over half of all the arrests for robbery, burglary, larceny, auto theft, stolen property offenses, forcible rapes, liquor law violations, suspicion of a crime, and "all other offenses." From these and other data, it would appear that the age variable is as highly related to arrests for conventional crimes as any other single factor.

In interpreting these results it is necessary to examine the changing American social structure that has resulted in important age discontinuities.[38] In economic, political, social, legal, as well as in biological terms, late adolescence and early adulthood represent periods of cultural discontinuity. Traditional roles, duties, obligations, and responsibilities break down. The labor of young persons is not desired, expected, or highly rewarded. Such employment as they are able to gain is usually unskilled and poorly paid and at the very bottom of the status pyramid. Unless they are oriented toward higher education — and many still are not — the major route to status and monetary advancement is closed. Family ties are often insufficient to control the adolescent. Community controls are also relatively weak in the urban setting. The physical mobility conferred on young persons by the automobile and other means of rapid transit further attenuate, family, neighborhood, and community controls.

Frustrated in attaining the material aspirations and status which he had hoped to achieve, the adolescent or young adult turns to his peers for status and security. From this interaction a peer group culture develops, which, in lower class areas, is often expressed through delinquent, criminal, and other deviant behavior.

The problem of the adolescent or young adult is further complicated by differential handling by the public, police, and legal authorities. Young persons tend to be more frequently reported for almost all offenses. A young adult in a slum area seen wearing a cape or a motorcycle jacket and cap is a prime suspect for nearly any offense. Far from being coddled, as is often charged by the press, adolescents and young adults are often treated by law enforcement officers with undue and unusual severity.

The involvement of young persons in criminal activities is, if anything,

38. Reckless, op. cit. pp. 363 ff.

likely to increase in the future. By present projections, 20 per cent of all
males and 8 per cent of all females will experience some contact with the
police and courts prior to reaching 18 years of age.[39] With increasing "drop-
outs" from schools at 16, increasing teen-age marriages and divorces, increasing material aspirations, increasing difficulty in finding employment
without education or skill, continuing growth of slums despite efforts at slum
clearance, and many other disturbing trends, the arrest picture as it pertains
to young persons may become far worse in the years ahead. Piecemeal efforts
at amelioration so far have proven ineffective. Whether more effective approaches can be instituted remains to be seen.

3. *Racial Distribution of Arrests.* In 1961, Negroes constituted approximately 10 per cent of the population of this country. Negro arrests, however,
accounted for 28.0 per cent of all arrests, or nearly three times as many as
would be expected by chance.[40] In some offenses, Negro arrests accounted
for half or more of all arrests. In 1961, violations in which an actual majority of
all those arrested were Negroes were murder and non-negligent manslaughter,
aggravated assault, robbery, forcible rape, weapons offenses, and gambling.

Of the twenty-four offense groupings, there was not a single category in
which the per cent of Negro arrests did not exceed the per cent of Negroes
in the population in 1961. Negroes were most over-represented in offenses in
which violence was or could be involved. On the other hand, they were least
over-represented in offenses which require some legitimate access to funds.
The latter point is readily seen in an examination of Negro rates for embezzlement and fraud and for forgery. These figures are presented in Table 16-4.

In assessing these findings, criminologists have stressed several major
points. First, the role of prejudice and discrimination enhances the risk for
arrest, prosecution, conviction, and imprisonment, especially since policemen, prosecuting attorneys, judges, and others concerned with criminal and
legal matters are overwhelmingly white.[41] Negroes also often cannot afford
legal representation. But prejudice cuts both ways. Minor violations and
even more serious offenses are, at times, less likely to be processed when they
involve nonwhites as both perpetrators and victims.[42]

Second, crimes of a conventional type are classically associated with lower
socio-economic status. Negroes, despite improvement in economic status,
remain essentially lower class. The median income of Negro families is still

39. *Juvenile Delinquency,* Report of the Committee on the Judiciary, U.S. Senate, 85th
    Congress, U.S. Government Printing Office, 1957, p. 24.
40. *Uniform Crime Reports,* 1961, Tables 23 (p. 97) and 29 (p. 103).
41. See, for example, William H. Kephart, *Racial Factors and Urban Law-Enforcement,*
    Philadelphia: University of Pennsylvania Press, 1957.
42. Guy B. Johnson, "The Negro and Crime," *Annals of the American Academy of Politi-
    cal and Social Science,* 217, (September 1941), pp. 93–104.

TABLE 16-4
Negro arrests as per cent of total arrests Part ı and Part ıı offenses, 1961

Offense type	Per cent Negro arrests of total
Murder and non-negligent manslaughter	53.8
Manslaughter by negligence	18.4
Robbery	50.1
Aggravated assault	55.7
Other assaults	39.0
Burglary	28.1
Larceny	28.8
Auto theft	19.3
Embezzlement and fraud	14.7
Stolen property; buying, receiving	29.5
Forgery and counterfeiting	15.4
Forcible rape	50.1
Prostitution and commercialized vice	46.2
Other sex offenses	24.7
Narcotic drug laws	33.0
Weapons; carrying, possessing	50.9
Offenses against family and children	27.6
Liquor laws	27.4
Driving while intoxicated	14.2
Disorderly conduct	36.9
Drunkenness	22.8
Vagrancy	26.3
Gambling	69.5
All other offenses	26.0
Suspicion	35.3
Average	28.0

Source: *Uniform Crime Reports*, 1961, Tables 23 (p. 97) and 29 (p. 103).

only three-fifths that of white families in the United States. Low socio-economic status is associated, of course, with slum living, poor education, large families, divorce, desertion, and disease. The underprivileged have little stake in society and its norms. Their children are likely to be inducted into the criminal and delinquent subculture of the slum neighborhood. It is probable that Negro arrest rates will decline as nonwhites move into middle class occupations and more desirable neighborhoods.[43] Middle class Negroes tend to overinternalize white norms in their style of life.[44]

Third, family disorganization tends to be pronounced among lower class Negro families. High illegitimacy rates, a considerable amount of desertion, and common law marriages are part of this family instability. Much of this

43. E. Franklin Frazier, *The Negro Family in the United States,* Chicago: University of Chicago Press, 1939, pp. 371 ff.
44. E. Franklin Frazier, *Black Bourgeoisie*, Glencoe: Free Press, 1957.

disorganization, historically, is attributable to the slavery period. Male responsibility for and to the family was minimal and this became part of the cultural heritage of the Negro. In addition, in the post-slavery period, and even now, Negro females can more readily find employment than can Negro males. Negro females meet little competition for employment from whites. Out of these experiences, the Negro lower class family has evolved as a matricentric family — the only such family type in any known subculture in the United States. In this family type, children are normally without a male role model since the father role is clearly not a strong, responsible one. With both parents out of the home, children are left with neighbors, grandmothers, or often to their own devices. The neighborhood and the school are incapable of supplying the controls and restraints that the family fails to provide. Nor can these agencies provide the satisfactions and security lacking in the family.[45]

These factors — discrimination, low socio-economic status, and family disorganization — are only three areas in which to seek explanations of the high rates of Negro involvement in crime. Others — the tradition of violence characteristic of the early southern plantation social structure, the rapid transition of the Negro from a landless peasant to an urbanite, the effects of Negro ghetto culture — have also been described as criminogenic.

4. *Class Distribution of Arrests.* The class variable is so pervasive that it is difficult to separate its effect from the age, sex, and race variables. In addition, the police do not keep any records on socio-economic status as such. As a result, information about class as a risk for arrest is usually obtained in two ways. These are (1) the characteristics of the census tract in which the offender lives and (2) research studies using occupational and educational data which are collected by the police and the courts. These are frequently supplemented by community studies such as those described in Chapter 14.

By using data from these sources it is possible to conclude that the class variable is intimately related to arrests for conventional criminal behavior. Warner, in his study of a New England town, found that persons of lower class standing contributed 90 per cent or more of all arrests — and very nearly all of the arrests for the more serious property offenses.[46] A review of the 1960 juvenile court cases in Franklin County (Columbus), Ohio, indicated that over 85 per cent of those brought to court were of the lowest socio-economic strata. Data on multiple offenders (two or more separate offenses in a two-year period) from this same court showed that all were lower class.

While the evidence on the role of class in conventional crime is beyond

45. See Ernest W. Burgess and Harvey J. Locke, *The Family: From Institution to Companionship,* New York: American Book, 1945, Chap. 5.
46. W. Lloyd Warner and Paul S. Lunt, *The Social Life of a Modern Community,* New Haven: Yale University Press, 1941, p. 376.

dispute, the explanations of this phenomenon are debatable. Any number of interpretations have been posited. These include differential child-rearing patterns which presumably lead to greater aggressiveness and less adequate internal controls on the part of lower class persons; lower aspirations at the lower class levels; fewer legitimate opportunities for achievement; the pressures of an adverse cultural and physical environment; slum social codes; the possibility that lower class persons are more likely to be intellectually, emotionally, and physiologically impaired; and, of course, differential reporting and treatment.

Middle and upper class persons, on the other hand, are not likely to commit conventional crimes but rather the "white collar" offenses. These are "masked," and because of the nature of our legal statutes sometimes do not come to the attention of the police or result in arrests. It may be that crime would be distributed more normally across class lines were these offenses to be included.

ECOLOGICAL VARIATIONS IN CRIME

Arrests are not only unevenly distributed by population characteristics but by geographic variables as well. Three such variables will be examined. These are rural-urban differences, variations by size of city, and variations within cities.

1. *Rural-Urban Differences.* With several exceptions — negligent manslaughter, embezzlement and fraud, forgery and counterfeiting, and offenses against family and children — urban arrest rates exceeded rural arrest rates in all Part I and Part II offense categories in 1961. For all offenses, urban rates were over twice as high as rural rates. The degree of disparity varied with the offense. The greatest differentials occurred in such offenses as prostitution and vice, drunkenness, vagrancy, and gambling — all of which are more typically urban violations. The data for Part I offenses are presented in Table 16-5.

Rural-urban differences may be attributed to several factors: differential police activity; greater disorganization, impersonality, and anonymity of the urban community; greater mobility within the urban setting; and increased opportunities for property offenses in urban areas. Clinard and others have shown that rural offenders tend to be mobile and isolated from local community participation.[47] In this sense, they were approaching the situation of the urban offender. In fact, the differences between rural and urban life are lessening as a result of increased mobility, exposure to the mass media, more nearly comparable educational facilities, and the decline of the farm as a

47. Marshall B. Clinard, *Sociology of Deviant Behavior*, New York: Rinehart, 1957, pp. 63–4.

TABLE 16-5

Size of community and arrest rates per 100,000 population,
Part I offenses, 1961

Size of city	Total rate	Murder and non-negligent man-slaughter	Man-slaughter by neg-ligence	For-cible rape	Rob-bery	Ag-gravated assault	Bur-glary	Lar-ceny	Auto theft
Rural	318.5	4.2	3.1	6.7	9.5	28.1	109.0	124.1	33.8
Urban	570.1	5.4	1.9	8.4	39.0	65.0	148.5	267.8	68.8
Over 250,000	681.3	8.4	2.1	13.3	70.7	98.9	183.0	283.1	87.2
100,000–250,000	609.0	5.5	2.5	7.8	28.1	67.9	158.3	309.4	71.8
50,000–100,000	490.0	3.8	2.0	4.9	20.0	44.6	121.7	251.3	60.6
25,000–50,000	497.4	3.2	1.8	4.6	15.1	34.3	123.1	272.8	53.0
10,000–25,000	412.6	2.7	1.3	4.1	10.8	30.6	109.0	236.1	46.5
Under 10,000	411.4	1.4	1.4	3.1	8.5	29.1	110.8	213.0	47.4

Source: *Uniform Crime Reports*, 1961, Table 19, pp. 92–3.

family operation and its alteration into a major industrial enterprise. As a consequence, rate differentials may be expected to decline. Changes in the last few decades make this almost inevitable.

2. *Size of City and Arrest Rates.* Table 16-5 contains arrest data by city sizes for Part I offenses in 1961. It appears from this table that arrest rates for Part I offenses decrease with decreasing community size. Rates in cities of 250,000 persons or more are at least three times higher for personal offenses, eight times greater for robbery, and about one and a half times more for the property offenses than in cities of less than 10,000 population.

The explanations for these variations are essentially the same as for rural-urban differences. Less community disorganization, stronger family, neighborhood, and religious ties, an older population, less impersonality, and a more traditional way of life remain more characteristic of the smaller urban centers than of the larger ones.

3. *Intra-City Arrest Rates — The Gradient Tendency Effect.* In Chapter 15 the gradient tendency effect in mental disease rates was discussed. In crime rates, too, there is a decline in arrests as one moves from the center of an urban community to its periphery. This decline can be documented in terms of (1) the location of the reported offense and (2) the residence addresses of the offenders. Using Cook County (Chicago) juvenile court statistics, Shaw and McKay calculated the rates for each two-mile concentric zone from the center of the city outward in all directions. For the period 1927–33, the rates from the center of the city going north were: 7.9 in Zone

I, 5.1 in Zone II, 2.6 in Zone III, and 1.7 in Zones IV and V. Moving due west from the center, the two-mile zonal rates were 9.8, 6.7, 4.5, 2.5, and 1.8. Moving south from the center, the zonal rates were 11.9, 8.8, 5.7, 3.3, and 1.9. These 1927–33 rates were also found to be highly correlated with rates for the same zones in 1917–23 and in 1900–1906.[48] These results have been duplicated and validated in many other major cities in the United States. In cities in South America, Asia, Africa, and elsewhere, however, this gradient tendency does not appear, primarily because slum areas ring the outskirts of a city rather than permeating the core.

Three explanations of the gradient tendency effect were discussed in the section on mental illness. These included the social disorganization thesis, the "drift" hypothesis, and the interpretation that the gradient tendency may be an artifact of economic and social considerations. The disorganization theory suggested that high rates for deviancy are a function of the breakdown of group norms in deteriorated areas. Community social controls are insufficient to keep legal and behavioral deviation in check. The "drift" hypothesis explained intra-urban rate variations in biological terms. Personally disorganized, sick, and deviant persons from other areas tend to gravitate to the slums and thereby create a condition of disorganization. The third explanation — namely, that an examination of other variables would modify or eliminate entirely the gradient effect — is particularly appropriate for the crime and delinquency problem. If white collar and nonconventional crimes were included, the zones might well show less disparate rates.

THE ETIOLOGY OF CRIMINAL BEHAVIOR

Epidemiological variables are helpful in understanding deviant behavior; they do not, however, constitute causation. When the etiology is known as, for example, in many infectious diseases, the distribution becomes unimportant. The causes of crime and delinquency, as well as those of mental illness, are not known. For this reason, epidemiologic variables are carefully investigated. For the same reason, a multitude of general and specific theories have been developed. These theories range from the biological and constitutional, on the one hand, to the sociological, on the other. These theories will be discussed in some detail in the remainder of this chapter.

For hundreds of years crime was thought to be the product of sin and the machinations of the Devil.[49] If behavior is a matter of evil or supernatural forces, it cannot be attributed to man's will. In time, these demonologic theories were replaced by naturalistic ones. Man had certain innate capabili-

48. Clifford R. Shaw and Henry D. McKay, *Juvenile Delinquency and Urban Areas*, Chicago: University of Chicago Press, 1942.
49. For an excellent summary of these early theories, see Vold, *Theoretical Criminology*, op. cit. pp. 3–26.

ties, including the ability to act rationally. Deviant behavior could, therefore, be attributed to the rational choices which man made — particularly the choice as to whether to behave according to normative prescriptions. Crime became a personal rather than a supernatural matter. Once the idea was accepted that behavior could be understood in a rational and "this-world" context, it then became possible to begin the search for causes. Late in the nineteenth century, this search became empirical. Speculative assertions now had to be justified by observable evidence. The obvious place to begin this search was with man himself. Thus, the earliest of the modern theories came to focus on the importance of biological factors in criminality.

BIOLOGICAL THEORIES OF CRIME

1. *"Constitutional Inferiority."* Cesare Lombroso is credited with being the founder of "modern criminology." [50] As a physician, Lombroso concentrated on the human organism and employed anthropometric measurements — head length, head breadth, cephalic index — in comparing convicted Italian criminals and Italian soldiers. These research methods constituted a significant departure from the speculation of the past and also served to test his theory of the etiology of crime. This theory, in essence, held that: [51]

1. The criminal represents a born physical type. The propensity for criminality is consequently an inherited (inborn) quality.

2. This born criminal type can be recognized by certain physical anomalies or "stigmata." These "stigmata" include an asymetrical cranium, (flat head), a large jaw featuring a receding chin or one which is unusually long, a distorted nose, big and protruding ears, large lips, unbalanced face, unusual teeth formation, long arms, squat trunk, and many, many others.

3. These "stigmata" indicated that the criminal type was *atavistic* — a reversion to an earlier evolutionary stage in human development. The criminal type was subhuman.

4. With these inherited characteristics, the born criminal type, even under the most advantageous social circumstances, has difficulty refraining from deviant behavior.

This theory, archaic by present standards of etiological thinking, was first published in 1876 — less than a century ago. It is amazing, however, how tenaciously it has persisted in lay thinking. Movie villains are still type cast to conform to the Lombrosian model, and students visiting a prison are sometimes surprised that inmates look like real people. Even Lombroso rejected many aspects of his theory and modified others. In his later modifica-

50. Ibid. pp. 28–32.
51. Cesare Lombroso, *Crime, Its Causes and Remedies* (trans. by H. P. Horton), Boston: Little, Brown, 1912.

tions, he contended that only about one-third of all criminals represented this atavistic type. Another third were composed of insane persons (epileptics, psychotic, mentally retarded), and a final third of "criminaloids," or more or less normal persons who, under adverse conditions, became criminals.

The Lombrosian theory underwent significant modifications in the work of other members of the so-called "Italian" or "Positivist" school, but it was not refuted until Charles Goring conducted a careful study of 3000 British convicts and compared them with noncriminal Englishmen.[52] This study, published in 1913, could find no evidence in support of Lombroso's assertions, with the one exception that the criminal population was shorter in height and lower in weight (This latter finding could be explained in terms of the lower socio-economic status origins of inmates). Goring summarized his eight-year study in these words: [53]

Our results nowhere confirm the evidence [of a physical criminal type], nor justify the allegation of criminal anthropologists. They challenge their evidence at almost every point. In fact, both with regard to measurements and the presence of physical anomalies in criminals, our statistics present a startling conformity with similar statistics of the law-abiding class. Our inevitable conclusion must be that *there is no such thing as a physical criminal type*.

As a result of the work of Goring, the Lombrosian theory was relegated to the status of a scientific oddity. It did not, however, retain this status very long. In the United States a number of studies have attempted to verify the Lombrosian contentions.[54] The most famous of these studies was conducted by the late Ernest Hooton, a renowned physical anthropologist whose findings were published in 1939.[55] This research involved 33 anthropometric measurements of 13,873 criminals, white and nonwhite, native and foreign-born, and inmates of prisons, reformatories, and jails. The same measurements were taken of 1976 noncriminal controls consisting of college students, firemen, policemen, and hospital patients as well as of 1227 mental hospital patients. This massive effort resulted in the following findings:

1. Criminals, or at least inmates in penal institutions, were significantly different from the control population in 19 of the 33 measurements taken.

2. The inmates were clearly inferior in nearly all measurements.

3. The inferior criminal constitution is characterized by such things as a compressed face and narrow jaw, high pinched nasal roots, nasal bridge either

52. Charles Goring, *The English Convict: A Statistical Study*, London: His Majesty's Stationery Office, 1913.
53. Ibid. p. 173.
54. Vold, op. cit. pp. 55–9.
55. Ernest A. Hooton, *The American Criminal: An Anthropological Study*, Cambridge: Harvard University Press, 1939, vols. I, II and III. See, also, Ernest A. Hooton, *Crime and the Man*, Cambridge: Harvard University Press, 1939.

too wide or too narrow, blue-gray eyes, thin eyebrows, thin lips, small, protruding ears, long thin neck, and sloping shoulders.

4. These physical inferiorities are important because they connote mental inferiority.

5. Most important of all, these inferiorities are results of defective heredity and not social circumstances. There can be no doubt either of the organic inferiority of the criminal constitution or of its transmission through the germ plasm.

Based on such findings, some have drawn conclusions with regard to the treatment of the inferior criminal type. Garofalo, for example, suggested that society should eliminate the biologically unfit criminal type. His recommendations included the death sentence, and life and long-term imprisonment for some of the "born" criminals, and the transportation to undeveloped areas of some others. For the "criminaloid" group, enforced reparation was suggested.[56] Hooton was even more positive in his approach. He urged either elimination of the criminally unfit or their permanent isolation from society.[57] These suggestions make it clear that the school of criminal biology cannot accept the proposition that reformation and rehabilitation are likely for those who are constitutionally inferior.

These theories have been criticized severely by persons adhering to other etiologic positions. The essence of these criticisms is as follows: [58]

1. Imprisoned criminals do not necessarily represent the criminal population. It is conceivable that inmates do, indeed, represent the failures — physical, mental and emotional — in crime.

2. The control groups which have been used are not even approximately typical of the noninstitutional population. Firemen and policemen, for example, are required to pass stringent physical examinations. College students, on the other hand, are drawn from the higher socio-economic status groups in society. The hospitalized insane are surely atypical of the population.

3. In what sense do a narrow face, a compressed jaw, high pinched nasal roots and the frequent presence of blue-gray eyes testify to biological inferiority?

4. Even if inferiority in terms of these physical criteria are granted, why are not all persons with these characteristics criminal? Many control subjects in all these studies have some of these questionable "anomalies." How is it possible for them to avoid criminality?

2. *Body Type Theories.* A slightly different biological approach to the

---

56. B. Raffaele Garofalo, *Criminology* (trans. by Robert W. Miller), Boston: Little, Brown, 1914.
57. Hooton, *The American Criminal*, Vol. i, op. cit. p. 309.
58. Vold, op. cit. pp. 63–5.

etiology of crime is represented by the body type or morphological theory.[59] Body type theory maintains that differing physical structures react differently to external tensions and pressures. Psychological and emotional traits as well as interests, abilities, and other aspects of personality, are believed to be fundamentally related to physical structure. Some types of physical build are predisposing to deviant behavior. This approach differs from the constitutional inferiority theory in that general structure rather than specific physical characteristics indicates criminal potential. It also plays down the idea of criminal inferiority.

According to William Sheldon, each body structure contains three major components — endomorphy, mesomorphy, and ectomorphy — in different proportions.[60] The extent to which each of these components characterizes a person influences the psychological and emotional behavior of that person and his propensity for criminal conduct.

The terms endomorphy, mesomorphy, and ectomorphy are derived from the embryonic states of life in which three tissue layers become the basis for later physical development. The inner layer — endoderm — eventuates in the development of the viscera; the middle layer — mesoderm — in bone and muscle and tendons; and the outer layer — ectoderm — in the nervous tissue system and skin. By definition, therefore, an endomorphic type of build is one characterized by fat. The endomorph tends to be small-boned, well-rounded, short-limbed. The mesomorph shows a predominance of muscle and bone in his physique. He has a large trunk, and large hands, wrists, biceps. Motor organs are well developed, resulting in good coordination and athletic potential. The ectomorph, on the other hand, is a lean, fragile, delicate-looking type. Facial and body features are likely to be small. He is a skin-and-bones type.

These physiques have associated temperament or personality characteristics. The endomorph theoretically tends to be visceratonic in temperament. His body build gives rise to a personality which features love of comfort and luxury, and an extroverted and nonaggressive approach to others. Physical activity rarely appeals to such persons. The mesomorph build features associated temperament traits and qualities classified under the designation somatotonic. The mesomorph-somatotonic type is active, dynamic, assertive, and aggressive. He is outgoing and delights in physical activity. His type might be ex-

---

59. See Ernest Kretschmer, *Physique and Character* (trans. by W. J. H. Sprott), London: Kegan Paul, Trench and Treubner, 1925.
60. For a more detailed discussion of the body type approach see William H. Sheldon, et al., *The Varieties of Human Physique*, New York: Harper, 1940; William H. Sheldon and S. S. Stevens, *The Varieties of Temperament*, New York: Harper, 1942; and William H. Sheldon, *Varieties of Delinquent Youth*, New York: Harper, 1949.

emplified by the hand-shaker who leaves only a semblance of a hand after a greeting, or the effusive back-slapper, or the bar-bell pusher. He is a restless, active type. The ectomorph build, on the other hand, is associated with a cerebrotonic temperament. The ectomorph-cerebrotonic tends to be an introverted, nonaggressive, sensitive soul given to bodily complaints. His pleasures are in pursuits of the "brain" rather than the "body" or the digestive viscera. In popular terminology he can be described as an "egghead" type. These qualities of temperament are shown in Table 16-6.

In applying this system William Sheldon studied 200 problem boys, aged 15–21, who were residents at the Hayden Goodwill Institute in Boston during 1939-1949. Many of these boys had a history of delinquency and were known to various social agencies, to the police, and to the juvenile court. Others were dependent and neglected boys rather than delinquents. Each of the 200 boys was typed as to physique, using various anthropometric measurements and special types of photographs. Each was given a complete medical examination. I.Q. tests were given, temperament and psychiatric evaluations made, and family histories taken. From all this data a standard evaluation was made.

The results of all this effort indicated that the 200 boys were primarily mesomorphic in physique. Using a score of 1–7 for each component of build (the higher score signifying a greater degree of the component), the 200 boys were listed as being 3.5 to 4.6 to 2.7 in physique on the endo-, meso-, and ectomorphic components. They were unbalanced in build with the mesomorphic component (4.6) predominating. There were sixteen serious delinquents in the group. Their measurements were 3.4 to 5.4 to 1.8, even more unbalanced in favor of mesomorphy.[61] The conclusion seemed obvious. The more dynamic, active, aggressive mesomorph is more likely, by virtue of his physique and its corresponding personality characteristics, to violate legal norms.

Reference should also be made to the research of Sheldon and Eleanor Glueck, who compared matched groups of delinquent and nondelinquent boys. There were 500 boys in each group. Using the techniques developed by Sheldon, the Gluecks found that 60 per cent of the delinquents were mesomorphic in physical structure, but only 31 per cent of the nondelinquents were. The masculine component was also stronger in the delinquents. The delinquents also had narrower faces, wider chests, larger and broader waists, and greater forearms anld upper arms.[62] Other studies have also tended

61. Sheldon, *Varieties of Delinquent Youth*, op. cit. p. 727.
62. See Carl C. Seltzer, "A Comparative Study of the Morphological Characteristics of Delinquents and Non-Delinquents," in Sheldon and Eleanor Glueck, *Unraveling Juvenile Delinquency*, Cambridge: Harvard University Press, 1950, pp. 307–50; also, Sheldon and Eleanor Glueck, *Physique and Delinquency*, New York: Harper, 1956.

TABLE 16-6

The scale for temperament

I Viscerotonia	II Somatotonia	III Cerebrotonia
1. Relaxation in posture and movement	1. Assertiveness in posture and movement	1. Restraint in posture and movement, tightness
2. Love of physical comfort	2. Love of physical adventure	2. Physiological overresponse
3. Slow reaction	3. Energetic characteristic	3. Overly fast reactions
4. Love of eating	4. Need and enjoyment of exercise	4. Love of privacy
5. Socialization of eating	5. Love of dominating, lust for power	5. Mental overintensity, hyperintentionality, apprehensiveness
6. Pleasure in digestion	6. Love of risk and chance	6. Secretiveness of feeling, emotional restraints
7. Love of polite ceremony	7. Bold directness	7. Selfconscious motility of the eyes and face
8. Sociophilia	8. Physical courage for combat	8. Sociophobia
9. Indiscriminate sociability	9. Competitive aggressiveness	9. Inhibited social address
10. Greed for affection and approval	10. Psychological callousness	10. Resistance to habit, and poor routinizing
11. Orientation to people	11. Claustrophobia	11. Agoraphobia
12. Evenness of emotional flow	12. Ruthlessness, freedom from squeamishness	12. Unpredictability of attitude
13. Tolerance	13. Unrestrained voice	13. Vocal restraint, and general restraint of noise
14. Complacency	14. Spartan indifference to pain	14. Hypersensitivity to pain
15. Deep sleep	15. General noisiness	15. Poor sleep habits, chronic fatigue
16. The untempered characteristic	16. Overmaturity of appearance	16. Youthful intentness of manner and appearance
17. Smooth, easy communication of feeling, extraversion of viscerotonia	17. Horizontal mental cleavage, extraversion of somatotonia	17. Vertical mental cleavage, introversion
18. Relaxation and sociophilia under alcohol	18. Assertiveness and aggression under alcohol	18. Resistance to alcohol, and to other depressant drugs
19. Need of people when troubled	19. Need of action when troubled	19. Need of solitude when troubled
20. Orientation toward childhood and family relationships	20. Orientation toward goals and activities of youth	20. Orientation toward the later periods of life

Source: William H. Sheldon, *Varieties of Delinquent Youth* (New York: Harper, 1949), pp. 26–7.

to confirm the predominance of the mesomorphic component in delinquent populations.[63]

The question, of course, is how to interpret these results. In this respect a number of problems arise. For example, is it the physique itself or the social interpretation given to physique which makes a difference? Are persons more likely to lodge complaints, police more willing to arrest, and judges more willing to sentence a boy who is athletic and muscular as opposed to a boy who is small-boned and scrawny? In what way does physique operate to determine personality? Why are not all mesomorphs, particularly middle class mesomorphs, involved in deviant behavior? While the morphological thesis conforms to the folklore about physique and behavior, the nexus between build and behavior remains dubious and awaits further testing and evidence.

PSYCHOLOGICAL THEORIES

Psychological theories of the etiology of crime have taken many forms. In essence, all of them have sought to arrive at certain psychological characteristics associated with a criminal type. Of the many theories that fall into the psychological category, two will be examined briefly. The first deals with the relation of intelligence to crime and the second with personality traits and characteristics.

1. *I.Q. and Crime.* An incarcerated population presents an excellent group for study. Like college students, prisoners have been tested in a variety of ways and for a variety of purposes. Soon after the advent of the I.Q. tests, prison inmates began to be tested extensively. Such tests now are routinely administered for classification and research purposes. The results of early I.Q. tests seemed to indicate that a substantial proportion of the inmate population was either defective or "dull normal." [64] For a time, mainly during the 1920's, criminality came to be viewed as a product or by-product of intellectual inadequacy. The term criminal moron became a catchy newspaper phrase and considerable discussion concerned the treatment possibilities for criminal defectives. Some psychologists contended that low I.Q. was the single most important etiologic factor in crime.

Later evidence refuted this contention, however, and by 1940 the low I.Q. theory had largely disappeared. The criminal population has only a slightly larger percentage of low I.Q. persons than does the general population. Feeble-

---

63. Based on as yet unpublished results obtained in the Ohio State University Delinquency Project in a study at the Boys Industrial School, Lancaster, Ohio.
64. Henry H. Goddard, *Feeblemindedness: Its Causes and Consequences,* New York: Macmillan, 1914.

minded criminals constitute an insignificant proportion of the inmate population.[65]

This theory, like the Lombrosian approach, indicates the propensity and desire of professional and layman alike to single out a variable and assign it a major causative role in deviant behavior. It often takes years of systematic effort to undo the damage created by seemingly logical, but scientifically erroneous, approaches.

2. *The Personality Trait Approach.* Since crime is an act committed by an individual, it has always seemed reasonable to probe into the personality and character of criminals in order to explain their behavior. Such probing is justified on the grounds that personality traits and needs, being relatively fixed and stable, constitute the motivation for behavior. Literally hundreds of such traits and needs have been specified and studied over time. Criminals, or at least inmates in institutions, have been subjected to a variety of tests — pencil and paper, projective, performance — in order to arrive at some kind of criminal personality configuration. Traits, qualities, sentiments, needs, and drives such as aggression, nonaggression, introversion-extroversion, achievement, autonomy, abasement, egocentricity, sociocentricity, masculinity, deference, succorance, honesty, tolerance, anxiety, and many others have been studied and restudied. Some of the testing procedures have been ingenious; others routine. Some have focused on one or more traits, others on total configurations.

These efforts have failed thus far to present any conclusive evidence to the effect that (a) there is a criminal personality type or (b) that any traits or qualities are the special property of deviants and criminals. This does not imply that psychological tests are of little or no use for the prediction and classification of individual offenders. It does mean that, from an etiologic standpoint, it remains to be demonstrated that criminals are unique or different from nonoffenders in personality makeup. To evaluate the present status of the personality trait theory, Schuessler and Cressey analyzed 113 studies which had used some 30 different tests to assess the personalities of criminals.[66] These tests have measured some of the aforementioned traits and such others as emotional maturity and emotional stability. The results, however, have been equivocal. In a majority of the studies, 58 per cent, the criminal populations did not differ from the general population norms. In the remaining studies, 42 per cent, some differences were evident but the results were often contradictory. Criminal populations, for example, have been found

65. Simon H. Tulchin, *Intelligence and Crime*, Chicago: University of Chicago Press, 1939.
66. Karl F. Schuessler and Donald R. Cressey, "Personality Characteristics of Criminals," *American Journal of Sociology*, 55 (March 1950), pp. 476–84.

to be both overly aggressive and overly passive. Under these circumstances, positive conclusions about the personality aspects in crime causation seem unwarranted.

PSYCHOANALYTIC THEORIES

Psychiatric and psychoanalytic theories of deviant behavior have received extensive treatment in the section on mental illness. This discussion will therefore be limited to a general summary of the major tenets of this approach in regard to crime causation. Some of these major points are: [67]

1. Delinquent behavior and criminal behavior are caused by emotional problems which disorganize the individual personality. These emotional difficulties and problems make it necessary for the person to resort to behavior patterns which are not only illegal or immoral but also fail to satisfy the basic urges, drives, and needs of the criminal and the delinquent.

2. These emotional problems consist of deep and often unconscious feelings of insecurity, inadequacy, inferiority, and of being unwanted and unloved or rejected.

3. In turn, these emotional problems are caused or created by inner conflicts or turmoil. The basis of this inner turmoil is to be found in the conflict between the expression of basic biological needs and urges such as sex and aggression and the frustration of these urges by social norms. In psychoanalytic terms this conflict is the pleasure versus the reality principle.

4. Inner conflicts that lead to personality disorganization (a) originate early in life and (b) rest below the level of individual consciousness. Hence the person is generally incapable of understanding why he deviates from the legal norms or how to rectify his behavior.

5. The most important relationships in life are those that occur in the family situation during the formative years of life. These relationships — with the mother, father, and sibs — become the prototypes of all future relationships. Consequently, unsatisfactory and frustrating early childhood experiences leave an almost indelible imprint on personality — which often eventuates in deviant behavior.

6. Deviant behavior, including crime and delinquency, represents patterns of conduct which are merely symptoms or symbols of underlying emotional problems. Crime and delinquency are symptomatic in the same sense that a fever is symptomatic of physical illness. To treat crime and delinquency as a reality and not as a symptom is to deal with the surface problem rather than the causes. Effective treatment requires a restructuring of the personality and a lessening of inner conflict and turmoil.

67. For a discussion on elaboration of this material, see Marshall B. Clinard, *Sociology of Deviant Behavior*, op. cit. pp. 125–36.

From this point of view the criminal act represents the triumph of the id over the ego and superego, of the pleasure principle over the reality principle; of the aggressive, instinctual nature of man over social and community controls. It represents a faulty personality development and unfortunate childhood experiences in the family. Finally, it represents a symptom of a "sick" or pathological state of mind. Delinquent or criminal behavior is an unsatisfactory "solution" to inner turmoil.

Although extremely popular as a theory, this approach is difficult to evaluate.[68] The theory, as noted in the previous chapter, makes certain assumptions about the nature of man and society and the development of human personality which defy empirical verification. The critical assumption concerns man's instinctual impulses which provide the motivating element for all behavior. This presupposition, though central to the theory, cannot be tested by any known method. Equally critical, and equally untestable, assumptions include the "depth" of human conflict, the stages of human development, the fixed nature of human personality which develops in childhood, and the insignificance attributed to other motivations — economic, status — underlying human conduct. Despite these inherent limitations, psychodynamic theories have served to remove some of the stigma surrounding crime and delinquency, have emphasized the "hidden" motivation of conduct, have offered a coherent, if unverifiable, analysis of human behavior, and have emphasized the possibilities of treatment and rehabilitation.

ECONOMIC THEORIES

Economic theories of the etiology of crime focus attention on factors external to the individual. The emphasis is on economic and social forces as being "deterministic" in human conduct. Although the individual may have some choice in directing and controlling his behavior, these choices are severely limited by the external, environmental context in which he operates. People are neither good nor bad as such. They merely respond to the requirements of these impersonal forces. These approaches, of course, are diametrically opposed to the biological, psychological, and psychiatric viewpoints. The last considers forces external to the person as a backdrop against which the uniquely endowed individual can be clinically evaluated. The economic and sociological positions reverse the procedure and emphasize the commonalities of men responding to forces external to themselves.

1. *The Poverty Theory.* In the aftermath of the industrial revolution, impoverished peasants flocked to the cities in increasing numbers. The condi-

---

68. For an extremely critical evaluation of this viewpoint, see Michael Hakeem, "A Critique of the Psychiatric Approach to Crime and Correction," *Law and Contemporary Problems*, 33 (Autumn 1958), pp. 650–82.

tions under which they lived and worked were indescribably brutal. The simplest amenities were lacking, malnutrition was rampant, housing consisted of hovels, and economic exploitation, long hours of labor, and bare subsistence were the fate of many. Humanitarian and enlightened citizens were appalled by this degradation of men, women, and children, much as modern man is repelled by the conditions of existence in the *favelas* of Latin America and the cities and villages of Asia and Africa.[69] Seeing the slums filled with unskilled illiterate laborers living in the most sordid of circumstances, with little chance for escape into a better life, one could conclude that impoverishment was the cause of the demoralization, deviancy, and criminality of the slum dweller. This demoralization could not be attributed to the biological impairments or psychic traumas of the organism. Men were the victims of economic and social changes and their behavior could only be understood in this context.

Those of all shades of economic and political opinion have suggested that economic factors, and especially impoverishment, caused deviant behavior. Marx, Bonger, and other communist and socialist political economists believed that poverty, and therefore personal disorganization, was inherent in capitalism. The solution to crime and its associated evils — prostitution, vagrancy, alcoholism — could only be achieved through the reorganization of the means of economic production and distribution and the development of a classless society.[70] Other political economists were equally convinced of the effects of poverty as the causative agent in crime. They viewed poverty as an inevitable consequence of the operation of "natural" economic laws and believed that any interference with these "laws" would disrupt social "progress." The unemployed, impoverished slum dwellers were failures in the natural struggle of men to survive in a competitive world.

There, of course, is ample evidence to indicate that illegal deviant conduct is most concentrated among those in the lowest socio-economic strata of society. But a number of problems arise in shifting the association to the etiologic level. If economic deprivation and its correlates of poor housing and low education are causative in crime, why is it that only some persons become violators in these circumstances while many others do not? Why is it that white collar crimes (embezzlement, conspiracies in violation of the law) occur specifically among the more well-to-do groups in society? This explanation, like every other, singles out only one of many variables and disregards all others. What is obviously required is a systematic explanation which includes many variables and the assignment of specific weights to each of these factors. Such a system remains to be found.

69. For a recent appraisal of the anthropology of poverty, see Oscar Lewis, *Five Families: Mexican Case Studies in the Culture of Poverty*, New York: Basic Books, 1959.
70. See, for example, William A. Bonger, *Criminality and Economic Conditions* (trans. by Henry P. Horton), Boston: Little, Brown, 1916.

2. *The Business Cycle Approach.* Another way of determining the role of economic factors in crime and deviancy is to relate fluctuations in economic activity to fluctuations in crime rates. If high unemployment rates, for example, are related to high crime rates and periods of relative prosperity to low crime rates, then economic factors may be said to exert an influence on deviancy. Many studies here and abroad have attempted to do this. These studies were especially popular during the great depression. However, with the advent of post-World War II affluence, interest in this relationship has waned. Rather than review these studies, this discussion will focus on their major findings instead. These findings are as follows: [71]

1. There seems to be little, if any, relationship between over-all economic fluctuations and crime rates.

2. Offenses against property (burglary, larceny) appear to increase during periods of recession and depression but the increase is not consistent. In some studies almost no increase was shown to have occurred while in others a marked upward trend was found.

3. Crimes against persons (murder, aggravated assault, rape) show no fluctuations of any consequence. Personal crime rates seem to be largely unrelated to economic conditions.

4. Crimes against public morality (such as drunkenness and disorderly conduct) show no consistent trend when related to the economic cycle. In a few studies, these offenses were found to increase slightly during prosperous times. In others, they were found to increase slightly in periods of depression. In still others, no variations were found.

5. The only form of deviant behavior which exhibits a consistent trend line is suicide. Self-destruction occurs with increased frequency in periods of economic depression.[72]

These results do not, of course, rule out the role of economic fluctuations in influencing the crime rate. Part of the difficulty lies in patterns of reporting and police activity and changes occasioned in these by economic fluctuations. In prosperous times, police forces are likely to be at less than full strength because the salaries paid to civil servants lag behind those in private industry. In depressions or less severe recessions, civil servants are more secure economically and police forces are able to attract and to keep personnel. Other confounding variables also make it difficult to assess the exact impact of economic fluctuations on criminality.

SOCIOLOGICAL THEORIES

The most systematic efforts to formulate etiologic statements about crime and delinquency have occurred in the field of sociology. Largely by accident,

---

71. Sellin, *Research Memorandum on Crime in the Depression,* op. cit.
72. Andrew F. Henry and James F. Short, *Homicide and Suicide,* Glencoe: Free Press, 1954, pp. 23–45.

the study and teaching of criminology became an integral part of sociology departments in American universities. In Europe, by contrast, criminology is taught in law schools. This accidental development, coupled with the early interest of sociologists in social reform and in the amelioration of social problems, has given American criminology a distinctive sociological coloration. As a consequence, the major theories of crime causation have tended to focus on social norms, social roles, social organization, social structure, social conflict, social processes, and social change, as the contexts within which deviant behavior becomes meaningful. All sociologic theories focus on the structuring of society, and on its values, norms, and institutions as the causative context for crime. In principle, sociological explanations reject the ideas of constitutional inferiority or morphology, reject dynamic and personality trait theories, and reject all other individualistic interpretations of causation. From the sociological point of view, the deviant is a product of his social milieu and his adjustments to this milieu are different only in substance from other and noncriminal forms of adjustment. Deviancy is "normal" and comprehensible in specific social contexts.

Two general and competing paradigms have been utilized by sociologists in studying the context of deviant and criminal behavior. The first of these posits an equilibrium theory of society. In a static state, society tends toward order, integration, and organization. All the parts mesh. Goals are appropriate to the available means of achieving them. Values and norms are consistent and unidirectional. Personality and social structure are two sides of the same coin. Social institutions reinforce one another. Life, therefore, represents a meaningful unfolding and a member of such a stable society is conscious of the appropriate roles and status conferred upon him. In this kind of a stable, organized, or integrated society, deviant behavior has little or no basis for existence. It is, or would be, dysfunctional for both the person and the larger social order.

The conditions presupposed by this analytic scheme are ideal-typical and static. But society is dynamic. Change, innovation, technology, culture contact, and other internal and external forces serve to produce conflict, role discrepancies, and a lack of integration. Norms and values clash; subcultural groups based on occupation, material acquisitions, racial, religious, age, and sex differences emerge; and roles become ambiguous and inconsistent. The older normative order decays and in the transition to a new consensus, individual conduct comes to reflect this disorder and disorganization of the society. Men become alienated and disaffected with the breakdown of the social structure. They search for new meaning and identity and for new and rewarding roles. Personal disorganization and deviancy become legitimate responses to social confusion and despair. The form of this response may vary.

It may be aggressive and directed outward as in property offenses and in the behavior of criminal gangs. It may be passive and escapist as in alcoholism and drug addiction.

Out of this equilibrium concept have emerged several general theories which argue implicitly or explicitly that crime reflects and is caused by a breakdown in the normative order. Thomas and Znaniecki, for example, studied Polish peasants who had come as immigrants to Chicago. The disruption to their lives occasioned by the transition from a stable, folk society to an urban setting, featuring anonymity, impersonality, and an emphasis on material values, was often translated into crime and vice. The new arrivals had not yet learned and internalized the new normative patterns and their previous norms and values were unsuitable or dysfunctional as guidelines for behavior.[73] Others have described the adjustment problems of delta Negroes who migrated to the Chicago Black Belt in similar terms.[74] The adjustment problems experienced by migrants from the southern Appalachian regions to northern cities and by Puerto Ricans and Negroes in New York are other illustrations of the applicability of the disorganization approach.[75]

The second analytic scheme starts from a different set of assumptions. Crime and other forms of deviancy are not the result of a breakdown in norms but rather an integral part of the normative structure itself. For example, in a society in which material goals are accepted by almost everyone but the means of achieving these goals are limited, deviant behavior is to be anticipated as an outcome.[76] Illegitimate means will be devised or innovated in order to achieve these goals. Similarly, race conflict is inevitable in a society which specifies equality but sanctions discrimination.

From the sociological frame of reference, therefore, "society is the patient." The difficulty with this theme lies in its failure to specify the mechanisms through which social pathologies are translated into individual deviancy. As a result, several specific theories have emerged to bridge the gap between general social conditions and individual criminal behavior. These are the differential association theory, the subculture theories, and the limited access theory.

1. *The Differential Association Theory*. The late Edwin H. Sutherland, one of the foremost students of the crime problem, developed the differential association theory.[77] Drawing heavily upon the earlier work of Gabriel Tarde,

73. William I. Thomas and Florian Znaniecki, *The Polish Peasant in Europe and America*, New York: Knopf, 1927.
74. St. Clair Drake and Horace R. Cayton, *Black Metropolis*, New York: Harcourt, Brace, 1945.
75. Oscar Handlin, *The Newcomers: Negroes and Puerto Ricans in a Changing Metropolis*, Cambridge: Harvard University Press, 1959.
76. Robert K. Merton, *Social Theory and Social Structure*, Glencoe: Free Press, 1949.
77. Sutherland and Cressey, op. cit. pp. 74–80.

the French jurist and criminologist, and on emerging theories of learning in psychology, Sutherland stated his position in the form of a series of nine hypotheses. The essence of these statements is that criminal patterns are learned and transmitted from one person to another through interaction or contact. Criminal patterns, like fashions in clothes, music, art, and literature, and in food preferences and other social customs, are socially transmitted through exposure and contact. Prolonged and extensive exposure to deviant norms in primary group relationships — the family, school, neighborhood — will result in the internalization of these norms and in deviant and criminal behavior. Isolation from carriers of these deviant norms will result in "insulation" from criminality. In Sutherland's terms: [78]

1. Criminal behavior is learned.

2. Criminal behavior is learned in interaction or association with other persons in a process of communication.

3. Learning of criminal patterns takes place principally in primary or intimate groups.

4. The learning of criminal patterns includes criminal techniques and the specific and necessary attitudes, motives, drives, and rationalizations.

5. The learning of criminal patterns also includes definitions of the legal codes as favorable (those to be observed) and unfavorable (those which can be violated).

6. A person tends to become a criminal or a delinquent when he has internalized an excess of definitions favorable to violation over definitions which are unfavorable to violation.

7. Differential associations vary in priority (how early in life exposure to criminal patterns occurs), frequency (of exposure), duration (length of exposure), and intensity (meaningfulness of exposure, prestige or status of sources of criminal patterns).

8. The learning of criminal patterns involves precisely the same process and mechanisms as the learning of noncriminal patterns. The contents of the learning and not the method differ.

9. The learning of both criminal and noncriminal patterns are an expression of the same needs and values. The motivation for both is the same but the expression of these needs and values is the basis of the difference between criminal and noncriminal.

The differential association theory has been both widely acclaimed and criticized. It accounts for certain known facts — the concentration of deviant and criminal behavior in subcultural groups, the peer relationships in crime, the early onset of criminal and deviant behavior, the relatively unimportant role of secondary contacts in criminality (movies, comic books), and the con-

78. Ibid. pp. 77-9.

centration of deviancy in some families and neighborhoods. All of us, to a greater or lesser extent, internalize and act on the values and norms to which we have been exposed. Nevertheless, the differential association theory is incomplete and inadequate in many respects.[79] First, it is difficult to test empirically many of the hypotheses. Second, the theory fails to account for the selective factor in associational patterns. May not those who are potentially deviant be attracted to criminal associations and delinquent and criminal gangs? Third, the theory seems inapplicable to certain categories of criminals including personal offenders (homicide), sex offenders, compulsive violators (arson, kleptomania), and even to some types of property offenders (embezzlers and naïve check forgers). There are many other criticisms of a technical nature which need not concern us here. Despite these criticisms, however, the differential association theory remains the most systematic sociological conceptualization of crime causation.

At least one attempt has been made to modify differential association theory so as to eliminate some of its alleged shortcomings while retaining its central thesis. Glaser calls his revision differential identification which suggests that criminality occurs as a consequence of one's identification with criminal persons and patterns who serve as role models.[80] The problem remains of determining why, with all of the potential role models available, some persons select a deviant role model (a robber rather than a cop) to emulate.

2. *Subcultural Explanations.* After years of relative inactivity occasioned by World War II and the cold war which followed, concern with the development of theories of the etiology of crime and delinquency began with renewed vigor in the latter half of the decade between 1950 and 1960. The accelerated rate of technological innovation and diffusion, the "population explosion," increased urbanization, urban blight, the continued migrations to cities, the expansion in the mass media of communication and particularly of television, the continuing disorganization in family life, and the plight of our educational establishments, have served to renew interest in the problem of deviation. Despite economic affluence reported rates of crime and delinquency continue to increase more rapidly than population. In this context a renewed interest in deviancy has been generated. This interest has found expression in subcultural and structural theories of deviancy. The work of Cohen, of Miller and Kvaraceus, and of Ohlin and Cloward exemplifies this trend.

(a) *The "inversion" of middle class norms.* The essence of this subcultural

79. Donald R. Cressey, "The Development of a Theory: Differential Association," in *The Sociology of Crime and Delinquency,* op. cit. pp. 85–90.
80. Daniel Glaser, "Criminological Theories and Behavioral Images," *American Journal of Sociology* 61 (March 1956), pp. 433–4.

thesis, as posited by Cohen, lies in its assumptions about the spread of the middle class ethos in American life and the polarization of the American class structure into middle class and working (lower) class strata.[81] Working class boys in a lower class neighborhood have a series of difficult choices. Through higher education, they may attempt to shed their lower class way of life and, in its place, substitute a conventional middle class orientation and style of life. A few are able to make the transition despite the handicaps involved. The more common response of lower class boys to environmental adversities, however, is to accept, consciously or otherwise, their status. These boys "insulate" themselves as much as possible from middle class cultural patterns and perpetuate their accustomed way of life. These boys remain relatively free of delinquency and crime. In later life, they are likely to become skilled, semiskilled, and unskilled workers. To a large extent, these boys constitute the "good" or "insulated" group in the high delinquency areas.[82] Some boys, however, cannot make either of these adjustments. Their response consists of lashing out at middle class standards which are unattainable and, consequently, undesirable. This group becomes the backbone of the delinquent gang subculture. The origin of this delinquency subculture is therefore to be found in the rejection of middle class norms and values. This rejection is exemplified by five characteristics of the delinquent subculture. These characteristics include: [83]

Nonutilitarian behavior. The behavior of delinquent gang members has no purpose beyond the delinquency itself. Economic motivation is absent. Stolen goods are often deliberately thrown away. One popular game involves stealing from a series of establishments and leaving the stolen property obtained from one establishment in a different one. The fun or game is in taking rather than using stolen articles. This type of behavior would be incomprehensible to delinquents in economically impoverished societies where theft is for use, not fun. Nonutilitarian behavior is a tribute to the affluence of our society and, in a way, makes "sense" in a society in which the planned obsolescence and destruction of goods are extolled as economic virtues.

81. Albert K. Cohen, *Delinquent Boys: The Subculture of the Gang,* Glencoe: Free Press, 1955.
82. On this issue, see the studies of Walter C. Reckless and Simon Dinitz dealing with the "insulation" against deviant patterns among slum youth. Walter C. Reckless, Simon Dinitz, and Ellen Murray, "Self-Concept as an Insulator Against Delinquency," *American Sociological Review,* 21 (December 1956), pp. 744-6; Frank R. Scarpitti, Ellen Murray, Simon Dinitz, and Walter C. Reckless, "The 'Good' Boy in a High Delinquency Area: Four Years Later," *American Sociological Review,* 25 (August 1960), pp. 555-8; and Simon Dinitz, Frank R. Scarpitti, and Walter C. Reckless, "Delinquency Vulnerability: A Cross Group and Longitudinal Analysis," *American Sociological Review,* 27 (August 1962), pp. 515-17.
83. Albert K. Cohen, *Delinquent Boys: The Subculture of the Gang,* op. cit. pp. 25 ff.

Malicious behavior. Delinquent gang members delight in discomfiting others. They enjoy slashing tires or using a spike to remove paint on a new car. This malicious destruction of property, as in the case of vandalism, is a hallmark of the delinquent gang subculture.

Negativistic behavior. Negativistic behavior is that in which delinquent gang members invert middle class norms. If a certain kind of behavior is appropriate or acceptable to middle class society, it is rejected by gang members and its opposite becomes the appropriate standard.

Short-run hedonism. Delinquent gang members have no long-range desires or aspirations for achievement, even in crime. Behavior is based on spur-of-the-moment whims, and pleasure conferring activities. Planning for the future, saving, the postponement of immediate gratifications, and other orientations of middle class life are totally rejected.

Group autonomy. Delinquent subculture members reject conventional authority figures such as parents, teachers, and policemen. Authority resides in the gang itself and its leadership. Consequently, gang members are difficult to reach through conventional techniques such as recreation centers, religious and character building organizations, the school, and social agencies.

(b) *Lower class focal concerns.* The Miller-Kvaraceus *focal concerns theory* is derived from their work for the National Education Association on the problem of delinquency.[84] Unlike Cohen, who specifies that delinquency is a product of the inversion of middle class norms, Miller and Kvaraceus view deviancy as an inherent aspect of the lower class system of norms. From their point of view, two normative systems co-exist in our society. One—the middle class normative system—specifies values, which when internalized, practically guarantee "insulation" against delinquency and many other forms of deviancy. These values include an emphasis on achievement, work, responsibility, ambition, education, long-range goals, material goods, planning for the future, and the acquisition and maintenance of property, among others.

Lower class members, constituting from two to three-fifths of the population, have focal concerns or values different from those of the middle class. These focal concerns include a preoccupation with trouble, toughness, smartness, excitement, fate, and autonomy. The life chances of lower class existence make these values just as reasonable or functional to persons in this stratum as middle class values are to the middle class way of life. The difference is that these lower class values or focal concerns are tailor-made to operate as etiologic agents in crime and delinquency.

(c) *Differential opportunity structures.* Many sociologist have called attention to the role of the social structure in providing and preventing legiti-

---

84. William C. Kvaraceus and Walter B. Miller, *Delinquent Behavior: Culture and the Individual,* Washington: National Education Association, 1959.

mate avenues of access to the goals of individuals in society and to the significance of this blockage for deviant behavior. To the extent that society limits the opportunities to certain subcultural groups, expedient but illegitimate means develop to achieve socially approved goals. For lower class youth, the problem of adjustment lies in channeling the frustrations inherent in the disparity between their social and economic aspirations and the inadequate legitimate means available to them for achieving these goals. Out of this frustration arises the delinquency subculture. Actually, according to Ohlin and Cloward, lower class youth become alienated from legitimate social norms and invest "illegitimate" norms with moral rectitude.[85] Using the alternatives available to them, they develop a criminal subculture (organized crime), a conflict subculture (the lower class gang), or a retreatist subculture (drug users). The etiology of deviancy, therefore, lies in the frustrations imposed on slum dwellers by their limited access to culturally approved goals. There are two possible solutions — either a change in culturally approved goals and a lowering of aspirations or an opening up of new avenues through which the underprivileged have a reasonable opportunity to satisfy their culturally induced aspirations.

The three subcultural theories discussed above focus on the etiologic role of the social structure in creating deviancy. The chief criticism of all of these theories lies in their inability to specify why some slum dwellers accept their subordinate status while others reject this status and violate the law. Neither can they help us predict who will accept this status and who will not, nor why persons of economic wealth and high social status involve themselves in illegal activities. On the positive side of the ledger, however, they do explain the emergence of the delinquency and criminal subculture, and the persistence of this subculture. They also underscore the idea that the deviant response is simply one of a variety of alternatives to external and environmental pressures. Under comparable circumstances many law-abiding middle class persons would resort to these same alternatives. Far from being abnormal or inferior or emotionally disturbed, criminality and delinquency may simply be mechanisms for rationalized adjustment to adversity.

SUMMARY

This chapter has discussed four aspects of the problem of criminal deviation. These included a consideration of (a) the definition and nature of crime, (b) its scope and volume in the United States, (c) demographic and ecological correlates of crime, and (d) theories of the etiology of criminal devia-

---

85. For a more detailed analysis, see Richard A. Cloward and Lloyd E. Ohlin, *Delinquency and Opportunity*, Glencoe: Free Press, 1961.

tion. This chapter also traced the procedures and discussed the difficulties in the handling of criminal violations — from the initial report to the police to the final disposition of the offense.

Three approaches to the definition of crime were examined and evaluated. Each of the approaches — the legal, the behavioral, and the cultural — emphasizes a different aspect of the problem. The legal definition views crime as a violation of a criminal statute; the behavioral definition is concerned with the reporting of the violation, and the cultural definition deals with crime from the standpoint of normative dissensus.

The volume and scope of crime in the United States was discussed largely in terms of the known major (felony) offenses. Included were statistics dealing with the number of offenses reported and the number resulting in arrest, prosecution, and conviction. Several conclusions were reached about the volume and processing of criminal violations. First, both major and, more particularly, lesser offenses are grossly under-reported. Second, the percentage of major offenses that results in a conviction is extremely small. An overwhelming percentage of the property offenses do not even result in an arrest. Third, criminals who are institutionalized for their offenses may represent a biased sample of those who commit crimes.

An analysis of the major demographic and ecological variables related to criminal deviation included age, sex, race, social class, rural-urban residence, size of community, and residence location within a city. The chapter concluded with a discussion and evaluation of competing etiologic explanations of criminal behavior. These included the various biological, psychological, psychiatric, economic, and sociological theories.

QUESTIONS AND SUGGESTIONS FOR FURTHER STUDY

1. Define criminal deviation.
2. Discuss the major characteristics of criminal statutes.
3. What is the chief distinction between criminal laws and other social norms?
4. Discuss the concept, *mens rea*. What are some of the exceptions to this concept?
5. What was the major provision of the M'Naghten rule? What problems have resulted from this provision?
6. What are some of the major problems in the reporting of crime?
7. Discuss the three chief approaches to the definition of criminal deviation.
8. Cite the findings of at least one study that deals with the reporting and non-reporting of criminal violations.
9. Clarence Darrow is reputed to have said that even if we released all present prison, reformatory, and jail inmates, the crime problem would not change appreciably. Discuss the reasons for and significance of this assertion.

10. What are the major epidemiologic variables in crime?
11. Discuss the chief conclusions or major theoretical postulates of Lombroso, Hooton, Sheldon, Sutherland, Cohen, and Ohlin and Cloward.

SUGGESTED READINGS

Cloward, Richard A., and Lloyd E. Ohlin, *Delinquency and Opportunity*, Glencoe: Free Press, 1961. This volume presents a sociological theory of the etiology of delinquency as a consequence of limited legitimate opportunities available to slum youths. The thesis is well worth pondering.

Cohen, Albert K., *Delinquent Boys: The Subculture of the Gang*, Glencoe: Free Press, 1955. A very readable volume on delinquency as a subcultural phenomenon among lower class boys. A genuine contribution to the understanding of a special order of delinquency.

Shaw, Clifford R., and Henry D. McKay, *Juvenile Delinquency and Urban Areas*, Chicago: University of Chicago Press, 1942. The original ecological analysis of juvenile delinquency in metropolitan communities. This is a companion volume to the Faris and Dunham work on mental disorder.

National Prisoner Statistics, Federal Bureau of Prisons, Washington, D.C. The source of all official statistics on prisoners, and prisoner movement, in all federal and state institutions.

Reckless, Walter C., *The Crime Problem*, 3rd ed., New York: Appleton-Century-Crofts, 1961. A standard and complete text in Criminology. Chapters 1–4 and 12–18 are especially pertinent to the material on the definition, reporting, epidemiology, and etiology of criminal behavior.

Uniform Crime Reports, U.S. Department of Justice, Washington, D.C. The source of all official statistics on reported crime in the United States.

Vold, George B., *Theoretical Criminology*, New York: Oxford University Press, 1958. A precise and scholarly exposition of the theories of the pioneers in the development of criminological theories. Excellent as an introduction to criminologic thought from classical to modern times.

Wolfgang, Marvin E., Leonard Savitz, and Norman Johnston (eds.), *The Sociology of Crime and Delinquency*, New York: Wiley, 1962. A group of articles from professional journals on various aspects of the crime problem. The readings cover a wide range of subjects, both theoretical and empirical.

17

We welcome almost any break in the monotony of things and a man has only to murder a series of wives in a new way to become known to millions of people who have never heard of Homer.

Robert Lynd

a suicide is a person who has considered his own case and decided that he is worthless and who acts as his own judge jury and executioner and he probably knows better than anyone else whether there is justice in the verdict

Don Marquis

These are vices of mankind, not of the times.

Seneca (A.D. 5–65)

All criminals are similar in one major respect — their violation of a legal norm. Behaviorally, however, criminals may have little or nothing in common. Some offenders commit violations that require skill, talent, experience, and sophistication. Others commit offenses that require little skill or sophistication. Some offenders commit crimes while under the influence of narcotics or alcohol, or as an expression of uncontrollable impulses. Others are calculating, looking upon criminal violations as a career. This enormous diversity partly accounts for the limited applicability of etiologic theories. To understand criminal deviation, it is also necessary to classify different kinds of offenses and offenders. While an adequate typology is still to be devised, one attempt to deal with specific orders of criminality merits consideration.

Lindesmith and Dunham attempted to reconcile psychiatric and sociological theories of etiology by arraying types of criminal behavior along a continuum.[1] One end of this continuum includes offenses and deviations in which compulsion or psychiatric impairment is of greatest etiologic significance. The other extreme includes offenses which are part of a career in crime. These latter offenses could be analyzed best in a sociological framework. Deviants and offenders can be placed on this continuum in terms of four criteria: (a) the amount of skill and criminal learning necessary for the commission of the

1. Alfred R. Lindesmith and H. Warren Dunham, "Some Principles of Criminal Typology," *Social Forces*, 19 (March 1941), pp. 307–14.

offense, (b) the direction of the offense — whether against persons or property, (c) the role of companionship in the offense — whether it is a "lone wolf" operation or one characteristically involving confederates and, consequently, an organized operation, and (d) the extent to which psychiatric elements or cultural and learning factors are predominant in the motivation of the offender.[2]

Using these criteria, "individual" crimes include homicide and suicide, sexual offenses and aberrations, and offenses attributable to narcotics and alcohol. The "social" deviations include ordinary offenses such as burglary, robbery, and auto theft; professional crimes such as counterfeiting, pickpocketing, safe-cracking, and confidence games; and highly organized violations such as gambling, prostitution, and racketeering.

In this chapter some of the "individual" crimes will be discussed. The next chapter will deal with the "career" and social types.

MURDER

With the possible exception of kidnapping, no offense commands as much interest as homicide. Newspapers devote considerable space to reporting it — from the original report, to the search for suspects, to the arrest, indictment, trial, and conviction. There is nothing quite like a homicide as a feature story. A cursory appraisal of television offerings in prime viewing hours will convince even the most skeptical person that murder is a salable commodity. Similarly, homicide has been a recurring theme in literature — from classics to pulp. Measured in terms of human interest, murder far outdistances any combination of other offenses. There are many reasons for this. First, homicide violates the most important of our legal norms. Second, homicide represents finality — the victim never reappears alive, and death is a sacred matter in all societies. Third, homicide occurs infrequently and interest can therefore be sustained. Fourth, most persons are incapable of consciously identifying with the perpetrator and, hence, ascribe a certain mystique to the event. Fifth, some psychoanalysts maintain that we vicariously satisfy our own thinly veiled aggressive impulses in the act of murder. Whatever the reasons, killing is of tremendous concern to the public. Much less public concern is shown for persons who die "impersonally" in wars, in traffic accidents, and as suicides.

Definition of homicide. According to our criminal statutes, there are four types of homicide.[3] These are murder, manslaughter, justifiable homicide, and excusable homicide. Murder involves the wilful and premeditated killing

2. Marshall B. Clinard, *The Sociology of Deviant Behavior*, New York: Rinehart, 1958, pp. 200–201.
3. *Uniform Crime Reports, U.S. Department of Justice*, 1961, p. 29. See also Roy Moreland, *The Law of Homicide*, Indianapolis: Bobbs-Merrill, 1952.

of a person. Murder normally is charged in degrees, depending upon the amount and type of intent, premeditation, or malice aforethought. Except in a few states, first degree murder is subject to the death penalty, although a sentence of life imprisonment is more likely to be imposed. Second degree murder is normally punished by a life sentence or less, and usually less. Murder in the second degree is often classified as non-negligent manslaughter. *Non-negligent manslaughter* differs from murder in that no malice aforethought is involved. This offense may be charged when a death is the outcome of an altercation between the perpetrator and victim, such as in a barroom brawl or a gang rumble. *Manslaughter by negligence* is charged in deaths in which the perpetrator was grossly negligent. The degree of manslaughter depends on the circumstances surrounding the death. *Justifiable homicide* is usually defined in terms of death resulting from legitimate law enforcement procedures. This includes a policeman killing a felon, a prison guard killing an escaping inmate, and a private citizen killing an assailant. *Excusable homicide* most often is defined in terms of self-defense and involves the reasonable use of force to protect oneself. Neither justifiable nor excusable homicide is a crime.

Aggravated assault, which is similar to murder, is defined as assault with intent to kill or to inflict severe bodily injury.[4] The difference between murder and aggravated assault often lies in a chance factor — whether the victim lives or dies. Parenthetically, the declining murder rate in the United States has been attributed not to a lessening of violence but rather to improved medical services, communication, and transportation. Victims who earlier might have died are now rushed to hospitals and often survive.

The extent and methods of murder. About 8500–9000 murders are committed annually in the United States.[5] The murder rate is approximately 4.7 per 100,000 persons. From 1933 through 1944, the rate dropped steadily. It was 9.7 per 100,000 in 1933 and about half that great, 4.9, in 1944. After World War II the rate rose to 6.3, in 1946, but by 1950 it was down again to 4.6 per 100,000 population. This rate has remained fairly stable since 1950.[6] Most English-speaking countries, with the exception of South Africa, have rates much lower than those in the United States. England, for example, has maintained a murder rate which is only about a tenth as great.[7] Different traditions and population groups probably account for some of this discrepancy.

Within the United States there are major regional variations in murder

4. *Uniform Crime Reports*, 1961, p. 29.
5. Ibid. p. 2.
6. Herbert A. Bloch and Gilbert Geis, *Man, Crime and Society*, New York: Random House, 1962, pp. 258–9.
7. Ibid. pp. 259–60.

rates. In 1961, the New England states reported a rate of 1.3 per 100,00 persons; the Middle Atlantic states, 3.0; the East North Central states, 3.7; the West North Central states, 2.5; the South Atlantic states, 8.2; the East South Central states, 9.4; the West South Central states, 7.4; the Mountain states, 4.4; and the Pacific states, 3.4 per 100,000 population. Even within these regions, marked variations occur. All the Pacific states have low rates except Alaska, while all the South Atlantic states have high rates except West Virginia. The lowest rates belong to New Hampshire and South Dakota. Alabama, South Carolina, and Alaska are among the states with the highest rates.[8]

In 1961, the FBI added a Supplementary Homicide Report in collecting crime data from law enforcement agencies. This report, based on a sample of 3008 murders, indicated that the chief weapon used was a gun (52.5 per cent); knives or other cutting instruments were used in 24.1 per cent; blunt objects in 6.6 per cent; and "personal" weapons (beating and strangulation) in 11.2 per cent. Poison accounted for only nine of the 3008 murders (0.3 per cent) while explosives and miscellaneous techniques accounted for the rest. Of 7348 aggravated assaults, shooting occurred in 12.7 per cent; stabbing in 44.0 per cent; blunt objects were used in 24.0 per cent; "personal" weapons in 12.3 per cent; acids or poison in 1.2 per cent, and miscellaneous devices in 5.8 per cent. These results are shown in Table 1.

A *profile of murderers.* Arrested murderers are generally older than other offenders. In 1961, the median age was 30–34 years. Only 7.8 per cent were juveniles under 18; over 18 per cent were under 21 and about 22 per cent were under 25 years of age.[9] The age distribution of murderers was similar in urban and rural areas. In 1961, males constituted the overwhelming majority of murderers, as is usually the case — 82.5 per cent.[10] Negroes contributed 53.8 per cent of the murders.[11] In a five-year study of 588 criminal homicides in Philadelphia, Wolfgang found that 82 per cent were male and 75 per cent of the offenders were Negroes (compared to a population base of 18 per cent).[12] In addition, Negro females had higher rates than white males, leading Wolfgang to conclude that race is a more important correlate of homicide than is sex. The data also dispel the prevalent myth that homicide is committed across racial lines. Over 94 per cent of all homicides were committed against members of the same race.[13]

8. *Uniform Crime Reports*, 1961, Table 2, pp. 34–7.
9. Ibid. Tables 20 (p. 94) and 27 (p. 101).
10. Ibid. Tables 22 (p. 96) and 31 (p. 105).
11. Ibid. Tables 23 (p. 97) and 29 (p. 103).
12. See Marvin E. Wolfgang, *Patterns in Criminal Homicide*, Philadelphia: University of Pennsylvania Press, 1958, Chap. 2, pp. 31 ff.
13. In addition to the Philadelphia study on homicide, see also Guy B. Johnson, "The Negro and Crime," *Annals of the American Academy of Political and Social Science,*

TABLE 17-1

Weapons used in 3008 murders and 7348 aggravated assaults, 1961

		Murder					
	Gun	Knife or other cutting instrument	Blunt object (club, hammer, etc.)	"Personal" weapon (strangulations and beatings)	Poison	Explosives	Other
Per cent .. 100.0	52.5	24.1	6.6	11.2	0.3	0.1	5.3
Total 3,008	1,578	725	198	336	9	2	160

		Aggravated assault					
	Gun	Knife or other cutting instrument	Blunt object (club, hammer, etc.)	"Personal" weapon (hands, fists, feet, etc.)	Poison or acid	Explosives	Other
Per cent ... 100.0	12.7	44.0	24.0	12.3	1.2	[1]	5.8
Total 7,348	931	3,230	1,760	906	90	2	429

[1] Less than 1/10 of 1 per cent.

Source: *Uniform Crime Reports*, 1961, p. 13.

The Philadelphia study also revealed some interesting sidelights on the problem of homicide. These are: [14]

1. Murders are most likely to be committed on weekends. Saturday night is the least safe night of the week. Tuesday is the safest of all.

2. Half of all murders occur between 8 p.m. and 2 a.m.

3. Over half the murderers had been drinking (some quite heavily) prior to the offense. Data from other countries corroborate this finding. Drinking is, of course, related to the high rate of homicide on weekends.

4. The least expected finding was that 64 per cent of the offenders had previous arrest records. Of those with arrest records, almost half had been involved in at least one aggravated assault. This finding is in direct opposition to the results of previous research, which has indicated that all but a very few murderers are first offenders.

A profile of victims. In almost every demographic respect, victim and as-

217 (September 1941), pp. 93–104. Johnson found that in Richmond, Va., only six of 220 homicides committed in the years 1930–39 were interracial; only 22 homicides of 330 in five North Carolina counties during the same period were interracial; and only three of 95 in Fulton County, Georgia, in a 20-month period, 1938–39, were interracial. Only 25 of the 645 homicides involved a Negro as offender and a white as a victim.

14. Marvin E. Wolfgang, *Patterns of Criminal Homicide*, pp. 99, 106, 108–9, 136, and 175.

sailant are much alike. In 1961, as reported by the FBI on a limited sample of 3008 murders, most of the victims were males (72.3 per cent). The majority were also nonwhites (54.8 per cent). The age of the victims ranged from under one year (2.0 per cent) to 75 years and over (1.8 per cent). The typical victim was 35–39 years old.[15] The Wolfgang data on Philadelphia victims adds other dimensions.[16] Nearly half of the victims had been drinking prior to the offense. A fourth of the victims had previous arrest records for personal offenses, and 21.6 per cent more had arrest records for other than personal crimes. Most importantly, Wolfgang contends that 34 per cent of the victims precipitated the offense. By "victim-precipitated offenses" is meant that the victim was the first to show or use a weapon or the first to resort to physical violence. A few examples, all of which resulted in charges of homicide, follow: [17]

A husband accused his wife of giving money to another man, and while she was making breakfast, he attacked her with a milk bottle, then a brick, and finally a piece of concrete block. Having had a butcher knife in hand, she stabbed him during the fight.

During a lover's quarrel, the male (victim) hit his mistress and threw a can of kerosene at her. She retaliated by throwing the liquid on him, and then tossed a lighted match in his direction. He died from the burns.

A drunken victim with knife in hand approached his slayer during a quarrel. The slayer showed a gun, and the victim dared him to shoot. He did.

Contrary to popular opinion, the overwhelming majority of victims are relatives and friends, and homicides most often occur in the home or its vicinity. According to the Uniform Crime Reports for 1961, 27 per cent of the 3008 killings occurred within the family — the wife or husband most often being the victim. Quarrels with friends, lovers, enemies, and rivals accounted for more than half of the total. About 10 per cent involved the killing of police officers or private citizens (probably during the course of a robbery or burglary). One per cent were juvenile gang slayings.[18]

A number of detailed studies support these FBI data. Wolfgang found that close friends accounted for over 28 per cent of the victims; family members for about a fourth of the victims; acquaintances for over 13 per cent; lovers, prostitutes, and homosexual partners for a tenth of the victims; and

15. *Uniform Crime Reports*, 1961, p. 90.
16. See Marvin E. Wolfgang, "Victim-precipitated Criminal Homicide," in *The Sociology of Crime and Delinquency* (ed. by Marvin Wolfgang, Leonard Savitz, and Norman Johnson), New York: Wiley, 1962, pp. 388–96.
17. Ibid. Reprinted by permission of the publishers.
18. *Uniform Crime Reports*, 1961, pp. 12–13. According to this same source, 65 per cent of the aggravated assaults were committed by members of the victim's family or by friends and neighbors.

enemies and rivals for about 7 per cent. Strangers, police officers, and by-standers represented 14 per cent of the victims. Wolfgang also found that 51.2 per cent of the victims were at home at the time of the offense.[19]

Another study found that of 489 homicides in Houston, Texas, four areas, populated chiefly by nonwhites and Mexicans and geographically close to each other and the center of the city, accounted for over 27 per cent of the crimes. In over 32 per cent of the crimes the victim and perpetrator lived in the same block or house. Nearly nine out of ten had known each other prior to the offense.[20]

Explanations of murder: Another case of normative dissensus. Two points of view vie for public acceptance as explanations of murder. The first is the so-called "soft line" taken by many psychiatrists and related professional groups. This approach contends that the murderer is often, if not always, a sick person. The murder represents a symptom of his mental illness. Frederic Wertham, a pyschoanalyst, who has testified as an expert witness at many murder trials, maintains that deep, unconscious, and uncontrollable urges impel the murderer to commit his offense.[21] Even murders which start out as something quite different like armed robbery are, at the deepest levels, motivated by the urge to kill. Murder, therefore, represents one facet of mental disorder and should be treated as such. One implication of this theme is that each of us, because of biologic endowment, is perfectly capable of committing murder. Further, none of us knows under what kinds of stress situations these inherent urges might find expression. When homicide occurs, it must be attributed to failures in the social nature of man — the ego and superego structures. From this frame of reference all murders — whether committed by a hired killer, by a person suffering from paranoid delusions, by a young child, by a sexual deviant, or by almost anyone — represent one facet of the larger picture of mental disorder.

The opposing viewpoint — the "hard line" — is held by many law enforcement personnel and by a significant section of the public. The "hard line" maintains that murderers are not usually sick or mentally disturbed persons. Their behavior is usually wilful, and premeditated, and should be dealt with punitively.

A third point of view is offered by Wolfgang on the basis of his studies of homicides in Philadelphia. This sociological position maintains that, in

19. Marvin E. Wolfgang, "Victim-Precipitated Criminal Homicide," op. cit. Table I, pp. 390–91.
20. Henry A. Bullock, "Urban Homicide in Theory and Fact," *Journal of Criminal Law, Criminology and Police Science* 45 (January–February 1955), pp. 565–75.
21. See Frederic Wertham, *The Show of Violence*, New York: Doubleday, 1949; and David Abrahamsen, *Crime and the Human Mind*, New York: Columbia University Press, 1944.

lower socio-conomic strata, among nonwhites and other groups, a "subcul-ture of violence" exists. This subculture does not conceive of physical violence as being morally or legally repugnant when it is expressed in response to certain stimuli. This subculture not only tolerates but often encourages violence. Violence is accepted as a part of the normative order.[22] In this sub-culture, parents often use violence to discipline children; wife-beating is common; brawls of one kind or another are a fact of life; teen-age rumbles occur; and the possession of weapons is common. Street corners and tenement dwellings are the slum equivalents of "boot hills" or burial places of the Old West.

The outcome of murder. A deviation as serious as murder usually results in an equally severe penalty — death, life imprisonment, or a sentence to in-carceration for 99 years or longer. The reason for a sentence exceeding a life term is that a life sentence makes an offender eligible for parole in 15 or 20 years, but a certain percentage of time, a third or more, must be served under a sentence of a fixed number of years before eligibility to parole.

Murder, as well as other capital offenses such as rape, rarely results in the death penalty. The 8600 murders and non-negligent manslaughter cases re-ported to the FBI in 1961 culminated in the imposition of 112 death sen-tences. A total of 33 persons were executed for murder.[23] Of these, 15 were nonwhite. Table 17-2 lists the actual number of executions in the United States for murder and for all other offenses for every year since 1930. The total number of executions was 47 in 1962 — murder (41), rape (4), and all others (2). The median age of those executed was 28 years and all were males.

As indicated in Table 17-2, each decade since 1930 has witnessed a sub-stantial decline in executions for homicide. There are several possible reasons for this. First, although only eight states — Maine, Rhode Island, Michigan, Wisconsin, Minnesota, North Dakota, Alaska, and Hawaii — do not have a death penalty, many other states have, in fact, given up the use of the death penalty. Seven states with a death penalty have not had an execution since 1955 and nine others have executed one or two persons each since 1955.[24] Life imprisonment has usually been imposed as a substitute. Second, prose-cuting attorneys often are willing to accept a plea of guilty to a lesser offense, like second degree murder, rather than to try to obtain a first degree convic-tion. Third, juries over the years have become increasingly wary of a death

22. Marvin E. Wolfgang, *Patterns of Criminal Homicide*, op. cit. p. 329. See, also, Andrew F. Henry and James F. Short, *Suicide and Homicide*, Glencoe: Free Press, 1954.
23. "Executions, 1961," *National Prisoner Statistics*, No. 28, U.S. Department of Justice (April 1962).
24. "Executions, 1962," *National Prisoner Statistics*, No. 32, U.S. Department of Justice (April 1963), Table 3.

TABLE 17-2

Prisoners executed under civil authority in the United States,
1930 to 1962

Year	All offenses	Murder
	Total	Total
All years	3812	3298
1962	47	41
1961	42	33
1960	57	45
1959	49	41
1958	49	41
1957	65	54
1956	65	52
1955	76	65
1954	81	71
1953	62	51
1952	83	71
1951	105	87
1950	82	68
1949	119	107
1948	119	95
1947	153	129
1946	131	107
1945	117	90
1944	120	96
1943	131	118
1942	147	116
1941	123	102
1940	124	105
1939	159	144
1938	190	155
1937	147	133
1936	195	181
1935	199	184
1934	168	154
1933	160	151
1932	140	128
1931	153	137
1930	155	147

Source: "Executions, 1962," *National Prisoner Statistics* (April 1963), Table 1.

penalty verdict and have increasingly suggested mercy. Fourth, governors are resorting to commutations of sentences to reduce death penalty sentences to long-term imprisonment. Fifth, psychiatric evaluations of homicide perpetrators have led to an increasing number being placed in institutions for the mentally ill and criminally insane.

The murderer in prison and on parole. Murderers serving life terms are considered by most correctional authorities to be "model" inmates after an initial period of adjustment. Many become prison trusties and are employed in activities outside the prison compound. The reasons for their generally exemplary behavior include the fact that many were never imbued with the criminal culture and were relatively law-abiding persons prior to committing a crime of passion. A more important reason, perhaps, is that aside from a pardon the only way lifers can achieve freedom is via parole, and few will engage in behavior that will jeopardize that hope.

Not only are murderers model prisoners but they also constitute the best risks for parole. In Ohio, for example, 142 first-degree and 464 second-degree life-termers were paroled in the decade 1949–59. Of every 17 life termers sentenced for first-degree murder, 14 were eventually paroled. Prior to being granted parole, the first degree murderer had spent an average of 23 years in prison; the second-degree murderer, an average of 13 years and five months. Of 169 first-degree murderers released on parole since 1945, only two committed new offenses. Eight others were returned for technical violations of parole. This success rate — 94.1 per cent — is the highest for any known offense group.[25]

These results in Ohio are not unique. In New York, of 36 lifers paroled, many of whom had originally been sentenced to death, only two were returned to prison. In Michigan, of 164 lifers paroled since 1938, only four were reinstitutionalized and only one for a new offense.[26] The reasons for these low recidivism rates are three in number. First, murderers are very carefully selected for parole. Second, the age of lifers who get paroled (50–55 years) is high. Third, murder is usually a one-time proposition and, after years of imprisonment, most men are more than ready to "settle down" and to start anew.

SUICIDE

Any consideration of homicide as a type of deviant behavior almost inevitably leads to a comparison with suicide. Suicide is the opposite of murder in most respects. Some of these differences are: [27]

1. Suicide involves the channeling of aggression against the self; homicide consists of aggression against others.

2. Suicide is only rarely defined as a crime. In many European countries and many states in the United States, attempted suicide is not a crime. Homicide is everywhere a serious offense. On the other hand, both homicide

25. *Capital Punishment*, Staff Research Report No. 46, Ohio Legislative Service Commission (January 1961), pp. 81–2.
26. *Capital Punishment*, op. cit. p. 82.
27. See Walter C. Reckless, *The Crime Problem*, 3rd ed., New York: Appleton-Century-Crofts, 1961, pp. 129–51.

and suicide — successful or unsuccessful — violate religious and moral norms.

3. Suicide and homicide are also opposites in that the rates for one are inversely related to the rates of the other. When suicide rates are high, homicide rates are low and vice versa. High suicide rates, for example, are characteristic of white, older persons, of both high and low socio-economic status. High murder rates are more characteristic of Negroes, young adults, and persons of low socio-economic status. Cities, states, and countries with low suicide rates are most likely to have high homicide rates.

These differences, coupled with the fact that suicide and homicide both result in death, have intrigued sociologists, psychiatrists, and psychologists for many years. Unfortunately, the reporting of homicides is probably more reliable than of suicides. This reporting difficulty has frustrated efforts to test theories of the etiology of suicide.

The extent and methods of suicide. Twice as many persons each year commit suicide as commit murder. An additional 100,000 persons each year are unsuccessful in suicide attempts. In the United States, 18,633 persons committed suicide in 1959 and 19,450 did so in 1960. The 1959 rate was 10.6 per 100,000 population and in 1960, 10.8 per 100,000.[28] This contrasts with a murder rate of 4.7 per 100,000 persons. Unlike the murder rate, which has declined since 1930, the suicide rate, except for the depression years of 1930 to 1939, when it increased sharply, has remained fairly constant. The suicide rate in 1920 was almost identical with the 1960 rate.[29]

In many countries, including the United States, suicide ranks high among the leading causes of death. At the end of the decade of the 1950's, suicide was the eleventh leading cause of death in the United States.[30] It stood comparably high in Japan and in some of the Scandinavian and Central European countries. In most South American and Middle Eastern countries, suicide is a minor cause of death.

The chief method used in suicide is the same as that in homicide. About half of all suicides occur through the use of firearms. Hanging, a method almost never employed in murder, accounts for over a fifth of the self-inflicted deaths. Poisoning, gas, and similar techniques, also rare in homicide, occur in less than a fifth of the suicides. The remainder of the suicides employ still other techniques — drowning, jumping from buildings and bridges, and stabbing.[31]

28. *Statistical Abstract of the United States*, U.S. Department of Commerce, 1961, Table 62, p. 61.
29. *Statistical Abstract of the United States*, 1961, p. 61.
30. *Leading Causes of Death: U.S. and Each State, and Hawaii, Puerto Rico, and the Virgin Islands*, 1959, National Office of Vital Statistics, Vol. 54, No. 2 (May 1961), Table 1, p. 50.
31. *Mortality from Each Cause: United States*, 1957–1959, National Office of Vital Statistics, Vol. 54, No. 1 (April 12, 1961), p. 38.

THE EPIDEMIOLOGY OF SUICIDE

Sex. Suicide in the U.S. varies enormously with demographic and ecological variables. Males, for example, have higher rates at all age levels than females. In 1959, the male rate was approximately three and a half times as great as the female rate (16.6 versus 4.7 per 100,000 population). In addition, and as shown in Table 17-3, the rate discrepancy between males and females increases with age. Male rates keep rising with age up to age 80. Female rates, however, reach their peak in the 55–69-year-old range and then decline. As a result, at age 80 and over, the rates for men are over ten times as great as those for women.

However, suicide statistics in Detroit indicate that women attempt self-destruction twice as often as men.[32] The clinical impression of physicians and others who work in emergency rooms in hospitals is that women are brought in for self-inflicted injuries up to ten times as often as men. There are several possible explanations for this relative lack of success of women in committing suicide. First, women resort more often to methods which are not as lethal or as adequate for the purpose at hand, such as sleeping pills, poisons, and gas, compared to guns and knives used by men. Second, women are more likely to attempt suicide for its effect on others. The genuine intention to destroy herself may be lacking.

Race. One of the real puzzles about suicide is the white-nonwhite differential in rates. In 1959, the rate for whites was 11.3, or over twice that of the nonwhites (see Table 3). In addition, the rate for whites systematically increased with age, while the nonwhite rate, except for a few minor variations, tended to remain fairly constant after age 25–29.

Age. In a youth-oriented society like ours, it is reasonable to expect that age will be one of the more critical demographic correlates of suicide. The 1959 data indicated that (a) there are almost no suicides under age 10, and (b) from 10 years of age on up, suicide rates increase systematically with each five years of age span (see Table 3). In some countries, most notably Japan, the suicide rate peaks in young adulthood (20–24), falls until about age 50, and accelerates upwards thereafter.

Marital status. Marital status also appears to be an important correlate of suicide. National statistics indicated that for the period 1949–51, the suicide rate per 100,000 population of single persons (unadjusted by age or sex) was 4.7; of married, 13.4; of widowed, 24.9; and of divorced, 45.8. When these

32. See F. C. Lendrum, "A Thousand Cases of Attempted Suicide," *American Journal of Psychiatry*, 13 (November 1933), pp. 479–500. See, also, a recent study of successful and attempted suicides in Seattle by Calvin F. Schmid and Maurice D. Van Arsdol, "Completed and Attempted Suicides: A Comparative Analysis," *American Sociological Review*, 20 (June 1955), pp. 273–83.

statistics are controlled for age, however, the married and widowed had the lowest rates, single persons were intermediate, and the divorced were highest at all age periods after 25. Single persons had rates two to four times as great as married persons, depending on the age category examined.[33]

Occupation. While the evidence on occupation is scanty and largely unofficial, there is reason to believe that the distribution of suicide by occupation is bimodal. Persons in the lower occupational, income, and status echelons and those at the upper levels exhibit high rates. In a comprehensive study in Tulsa, Oklahoma, during the years 1937–56, Powell determined the following average annual rates (per 100,000) for suicide, by occupation, of the male white population: professionals and managers, 35.4; clerical and sales, 11.6; skilled workers, 14.3; semi skilled workers, 20.5; and unskilled workers, 38.7. Suicide rates, by occupation, indicated that among professionals, pharmacists had a rate of 120; physicians, 83; nurses, 38; lawyers, 36; engineers, 15; and accountants, 7. Blue collar occupations were arranged from cab drivers (87) through welders (25), machinists (17), truck drivers (12), and mechanics (10) to carpenters (5).[34]

Religion. There is substantial evidence, gathered mostly in pre-World War I European countries, that the suicide rate of Protestants is generally higher than that of Catholics and Jews. Some of the lowest rates of all are those for Moslems. United Nations demographic data indicated that in 1959 England and Wales had a suicide rate of 11.5, while in Catholic Ireland it was 4.1 per 100,000 population. The rate in Poland in 1958 was reported as 6.1; in Portugal in 1959, as 9.2; and in Italy in 1958 as 6.3. On the other hand, some Catholic countries in Europe had extremely high rates. For example, Austria in 1959 reported a rate of 24.8, which was the second highest reported rate of any country in the world.[35] So while the analysis of suicide in relation to religion is contaminated with many other variables and at points is contradictory, it is nevertheless possible to suggest that religious identification may be related to suicide.

Ecological correlates. Without presenting all or even many of the detailed studies on the subject, certain conclusions will be drawn about the ecological correlates of suicide. First, highly industrialized nations have higher rates than underdeveloped countries. In part, this may be attributed to the longer life span of persons in industrial societies and, consequently, their greater risk for suicide. Where life expectancy is 35 or even 40 years of age, suicide is not as probable as in countries where the life expectancy exceeds 70 years of age. In

33. *Suicide Rates by Marital Status in the U.S.*, 1949–51, National Office of Vital Statistics, Vol. 39, No. 7 (May 8, 1956), pp. 370, 426.
34. Elwin H. Powell, "Occupation, Status and Suicide; Toward a Redefinition of Anomic," *American Sociological Review*, 23 (April 1958), pp. 131–9.
35. United Nations Demographic Yearbook, 1960. Table 19.

part, also, underdeveloped folk or peasant societies are more integrated than modern industrial societies. Strong social controls are undoubtedly a preventive for suicide.

Second, in the United States at least, urban rates are slightly higher than rural rates. The differential is of the order of 1 suicide per 100,000 population. Third, larger cities have slightly higher rates than smaller communities. In 1950, the difference between the largest and smallest cities was 5 suicides per 1,000,000 population. Fourth, within large cities, there is a gradient tendency effect. In general, suicide rates decline as the distance from the center of the city increases.[36]

EXPLANATIONS OF SUICIDE

Two major approaches — the psychoanalytic and the sociological — dominate etiologic thinking about suicide. Freud suggested the original psychoanalytic theory of suicide and Emile Durkheim first enunciated the sociological theory of suicide.

The psychoanalytic approach to suicide. Psychoanalytic theory postulates a built-in death wish as part of the original biological endowment of man. In Freud's original thesis, about the origin of depression, a person becomes a suicide when he has identified with another person toward whom he is extremely ambivalent (simultaneous feelings of love and hate). Since this unconscious hatred (sadistic, destructive) cannot be directed against the source of the hatred (and love), these impulses are redirected against the self and result in self-destruction.[37] Some analysts have also suggested that suicidal persons are characterized by extreme unconscious hostility and also, by the incapacity to love. Still others see the threat of suicide as a means by which emotionally deprived persons attempt to punish others. The greatest elaboration of this psychoanalytic approach is to be found in the work of Karl Menninger. Suicide, to Menninger, is composed of three sets of impulses — the wish to kill, the wish to be killed, and the wish to die.[38] All three components, in different proportions, are held to be characteristic of suicide. The wish to kill is derived from feelings of hatred. The wish to be killed is derived from guilt, masochism, and feelings of worthlessness. The wish to die is derived from hopelessness and despair.

36. For an analysis of intercity and interstate variations see, Austin L. Porterfield, "Indices of Suicide and Homicide by States and Cities," *American Sociological Review* 14 (August 1949), pp. 481–90. For an analysis of gradient tendency, see Calvin F. Schmid and Maurice D. Van Arsdol, "Completed and Attempted Suicides," op. cit. pp. 274–5.

37. Don D. Jackson, "Theories of Suicide," *Clues to Suicide* (Edwin S. Shneidman and Norman L. Farberow). New York: McGraw-Hill (Blakiston Division), 1957, pp. 11–19.

38. Karl L. Menninger, *Man Against Himself*, New York: Harcourt, Brace, 1838.

Farberow and Shneidman collected over 700 suicide notes and attempted to classify them in terms of Menninger's tripart formulation. About 20 per cent of the notes emphasized the wish to kill, about 15 per cent the wish to be killed, and some 40 per cent the wish to die. Nearly a fifth of the notes could not be classified in these terms at all.[39] An example of suicide notes in each of these categories follows: [40]

The Wish To Kill

Jane:
    You 25¢ chippy, I hope this makes you happy. All the time that you could spent here you had to be shacked up with someone else ....
You have brought this on yourself ....

The Wish To Be Killed (Female, married, age 24)

I've proved to be a miserable wife, mother and homemaker — not even a decent companion. Johnny and Jane deserve much more than I can ever offer. I can't take it any longer. This is a terrible thing for me to do, but perhaps in the end it will be all for the best. I hope so.

Mary

The Wish To Die (Male, divorced, age 50)

To the Police—
    This is a very simple case of suicide. I owe nothing to anyone, including the World, and I ask nothing from anyone. I'm fifty years old, have lived violently but never committed a crime.
    I've just had enough. Since no one depends upon me, I don't see why I shouldn't do as I please ....

Unclassifiable (Female, widowed, age 70)

In case of my death notify Charles Smith, Smith Funeral Home, 100 Main Street.
    This letter to be opened by him.

Mary Jones

It is my wish that my funeral be strictly private. Just a minister to say a prayer for me.

The sociological approach to suicide. The classical sociological position on the etiology of suicide derives from the work of Emile Durkheim. After analyzing variations in European rates, Durkheim concluded that *"suicide rates vary inversely with the degree of integration of the social groups of which the individual forms a part."* [41] In general, the more socially cohesive the group,

39. Norman L. Farberow and Edwin S. Shneidman, "Suicide and Age," *Clues to Suicide,* op. cit. p. 45
40. Norman L. Farberow and Edwin S. Shneidman, "Suicide and Age" in *Clues to Suicide,* New York: McGraw-Hill (Blakiston Division), Copyright © 1957, pp. 43–4. Used by permission.
41. Emile Durkheim, *Suicide: A Study in Sociology* (trans. by John A. Spaulding and George Simpson), Glencoe: Free Press, 1951, p. 209.

the fewer the suicides. The less tightly knit the group, the higher the suicide rate. From this law, Durkheim proceeded to develop a typology of suicide. This typology includes *altruistic, egoistic,* and *anomic* suicide.[42] Altruistic suicide is a predominately non-Western, folk, cultural pattern in which suicide occurs ritualistically and is prompted by the individual's overidentification with the welfare of the group. The motive for suicide is social, not personal. Examples of altruistic suicide include the tradition of *hara-kiri* in Japan, the *suttee* in India, and the suicide of old and infirm persons in Eskimo and other folk cultures. In Japan, *hara-kiri* occurs when the victim has suffered disgrace. The honorable way to avoid inflicting this "shame" on the family is through ritually ending one's life. In many folk societies, a wife had to ritualistically destroy herself following the death of her husband. In India, the accepted cultural norm was for the wife to throw herself upon a funeral pyre. The British, and the Westernization and industrialization of India, finally succeeded in eliminating this tradition of *suttee.* In Eskimo society, persons who for reasons of age or infirmity became a liability to the survival of the group were expected to kill themselves. In these illustrations of altruistic suicide, the motive for self-destruction was neither a wish to kill, to be killed, nor to die. Nor was the suicide a by-product of mental illness. Instead, altruistic suicide implied conformity with the norms of the society and was a tribute to the individual's integration in this society.

Egoistic suicide is at the opposite end of the continuum in Durkheim's typology. It is individually motivated and violates social and cultural norms. In modern society egoistic suicide occurs because persons are insufficiently integrated into the group so that their own welfare takes precedence over the welfare of the group. Egoistic suicide is often triggered by failures in love, in health, and in fortune. In modern Japan, students who are rejected by the university for training or young persons who are prevented by parental pressures from marrying the partner of choice may resort to suicide. Menninger's concept of the wish to be killed comes close to describing the concept of egoistic suicide.

Anomic suicide is the third type. It, too, is motivated by individual rather than group needs. Anomic suicide generally occurs as an aftermath of depression or of defeat in war. The individual becomes "alienated" from his society and feels that life is meaningless. The social norms to which he owed allegiance, and which he had internalized, break down, and he feels lost and helpless. The *anomie* or normlessness of society is translated into personal loss of identity and meaning. Anomic suicide, in the final analysis, is a function of the lack of consensus.

42. Ibid. pp. 152 ff.

TABLE 17-3

Suicide rates by age category, sex, and race

1959

Category age	All rates	White	Nonwhite	Male	Female
Total	10.6	11.3	4.6	16.6	4.7
1–10	0.0	0.0	0.0	0.0	0.0
10–14	0.5	0.5	0.3	0.9	0.1
15–19	3.4	3.5	2.5	5.1	1.6
20–24	6.6	6.7	6.1	10.6	2.8
25–29	9.1	9.0	9.4	13.0	5.2
30–34	10.6	10.9	8.1	13.8	5.7
35–39	12.3	12.9	6.9	18.5	6.4
40–44	15.1	16.0	6.8	23.0	7.6
45–49	17.8	18.9	8.0	28.1	8.0
50–54	21.4	22.8	8.1	33.9	9.4
55–59	24.1	25.5	9.9	39.0	10.0
60–64	24.6	25.8	9.5	40.5	10.0
65–69	26.2	27.2	13.0	43.8	10.6
70–74	27.4	28.7	7.9	48.8	9.2
75–79	27.1	28.1	12.8	52.4	7.5
80–84	29.7	31.3	10.1	61.2	6.5
85 and over	26.9	29.5	4.3	58.6	4.0

Source: *Mortality from Selected Causes by Age, Sex and Race*, 1959, National Office of Vital Statistics, No. 54, September 22, 1961.

DRUG ADDICTION

So much confusion in the definition of drug addiction has existed that various national and international bodies have attempted to arrive at some kind of agreement. The chief reason for this confusion lies in the fact that drug addiction is one thing legally, medically quite another, and socially and morally yet another.

Legal Definition: Origin and Present Status. Narcotic drugs such as opium, cocaine, and marihuana (hashish) have been known and used for a very long time. Their use was sometimes condemned and outlawed and sometimes condoned. They were valued for their effects and feared for their consequences. Many an early physician developed a reputation as a healer by systematically prescribing them. Nevertheless, narcotic addiction remained a minor problem in Western society until the American Civil War. In the 1850's, the hypodermic needle had been widely adopted. In order to ease the pain suffered by war casualties, the practice of administering morphine hypodermically became widespread. Many men became victims of the "Army disease" — narcotic addiction. With the cessation of hostilities, medically created addicts could obtain drugs at moderate prices from almost any supplier. No definition of criminality was involved in either the sale, possession, or use of narcotic drugs. In 1898, heroin was synthesized in Germany and initial reports extolled it as a drug which had all the virtues of opium and morphine but was not addicting.[43] The initial reports were erroneous.

Various nations soon thereafter became concerned about the international traffic in drugs and its consequences for national welfare.[44] A series of international conventions, beginning in 1909, was called to discuss the problem. It was recommended that participating nations pass restrictive laws governing the manufacture, sale, and use of narcotic drugs. Congress passed the Harrison Narcotics Act in December, 1914. There were approximately 264,000 addicts in the United States at the time. The stated purpose of the act was to raise revenue. Nevertheless, Section 2 of the act made it a crime to sell, trade, or barter narcotic drugs. A physician, according to a later Supreme Court decision involving the Harrison Act, could prescribe narcotics only when medically required and "in good faith and in the course of his professional practice." He could not prescribe maintenance dosages for addicts. A series of later Supreme Court decisions affirmed the fact that prescribing drugs for addicts except for medical purposes could not be justified legally. The net effect of these decisions and of the enforcement practices of the Federal Bureau of Narcotics, which had been created to enforce the Harrison Act, was to make drug addiction a crime. The drug addict-patient had been transformed into the drug addict-criminal.

Legally the *possession* of any quantity of narcotics became a federal offense unless the person was legally authorized to possess such drugs. Since addicts cannot be given drugs legally and since they must possess the drug in order to use it, drug addiction is in fact a crime.

Medical Definition. The medical definition of drug addiction focuses on the effect of narcotics on the organism. According to the World Health Organization: [45]

Drug addiction is a state of periodic or chronic intoxication, detrimental to the individual and to society, produced by the repeated consumption of a drug (natural or synthetic). Its characteristics include:

43. For a historical review of the problem of drug addiction, see David W. Maurer and Victor H. Vogel, *Narcotics and Narcotic Addiction*, Springfield, Ill.: Charles C. Thomas, 1954, pp. 3–9. See, also, Charles E. Terry and Mildred Pellens, *The Opium Problem*, New York: Committee on Drug Addiction, 1928, Chap. 2.
44. For a review of the laws and court decisions concerning narcotics addiction, see Alfred L. Tennyson, "Medical and Legal Problems Involved in Narcotic Addiction," *Proceedings: Medicolegal Symposiums on Narcotic Addiction*, Chicago: Law Division, American Medical Association, 1959, pp. 48–70.
45. United Nations Expert Committee on Drugs Liable To Produce Addiction, Reports 6–7, World Health Organization Technical Report Series No. 21, 1950. For other viewpoints, see, *Drug Addiction: Crime or Disease?* Interim and Final Reports of the Joint Committee of the American Bar Association and the American Medical Association on Narcotic Drugs; Bloomington: Indiana University Press, Appendix A (by Morris Ploscowe), pp. 33–45.

1. an overpowering desire or need (compulsion) to continue taking the drug and to obtain it by any means;

2. a tendency to increase the dose;

3. a psychic (psychological and sometimes physical) dependence on the effects of the drug.

These three characteristics have also been referred to by others as *habituation, tolerance* and *dependence. Habituation* is defined as the emotional or psychologic need for the drug as a substitute for other kinds of adaptive behavior. *Tolerance* refers to the decreasing effect of the same drug dosage. This means that higher and higher dosages are required to achieve a previous effect. *Dependence* implies an altered physiologic state and the necessity for continuing the use of the drug in order to prevent the onset of the abstinence syndrome.

The central medical aspect of drug addiction is the withdrawal or abstinence syndrome. After injection of a narcotic, the addict is likely to experience a feeling of well-being (euphoria), and a reduction in anxiety, pains, and aches. Under the influence of the narcotic, he feels "normal." This euphoria, as well as the other effects of the narcotic, lasts for a few hours. Unless the addict takes another "fix," the abstinence syndrome will follow. Addicts fear the pain and consequences of withdrawal and will seldom hesitate to commit criminal violations to obtain narcotics in order to prevent withdrawal.[46]

Abstinence symptoms vary in intensity with the type of drug, the length of addiction, the frequency of administration of the drug, and the drug dosage. Initial withdrawal symptoms of restlessness, tension, and depression begin about 8–14 hours after the last administration of the drug. In "mild" cases these introductory symptoms will be followed by yawning, watering eyes, sneezing, sweating, and a running nose. Additional symptoms of loss of appetite, dilated pupils, tremors, and goose flesh will characterize more intense withdrawal cases. In marked withdrawal, there is also fever, insomnia, increased blood pressure, deep breathing, extreme restlessness, and twitching. Finally, in very severe cases, weight loss (5–15 pounds or more, in 24 hours) diarrhea, and vomiting also occur. These acute symptoms increase in intensity until 36–48 hours after the last administration of the drug. Three days — 72 hours — after the last shot, the symptoms begin to abate and the addict is left with feelings of restlessness, weakness, and insomnia which may last as long as six months.[47]

46. It is Lindesmith's contention that addiction to opiates is largely determined by fear of withdrawal distress rather than the positive euphoric effects of narcotics. See Alfred R. Lindesmith, *Opiate Addiction*, Evanston: Principia Press, 1947.

47. See Maurer and Vogel, op. cit. pp. 164–71. See, also, Extract from Treasury — Post Office Department Appropriation Hearings for 1963, Subcommittee of the Committee on Appropriations, House of Representatives, 87th Congress, Second Session, Jan. 30, 1962, pp. 293–4.

In rapid (abrupt) withdrawal, the process of "drying out" the addict may take 3–14 days. Prolonged withdrawal, a process in which the dosage is gradually reduced, may take several weeks or months. The former is used when the addict has not been taking substantial amounts of "pure" drug. The latter is used when the dosage level preceding withdrawal has been substantial.

Addicting Drugs. The problem of drug addiction is largely restricted to the natural and synthetic narcotics. While other drugs may exhibit addicting properties, they are, with only minor exceptions, less important than the narcotics.

Natural narcotics. All narcotic drugs, natural and synthetic, have two properties in common. They have an *analgesic* effect — they kill pain — and an *anesthetic* effect — they produce sleep. They produce these results by depressing the entire central nervous system. They also slow the heart function and respiration, and produce a number of side effects, such as dilation of the pupils.

Four major natural narcotics are generally used, of the 90 or so which are known. These are opium, morphine, heroin, and codeine.[48] All derive from the gummy substance extracted from the opium poppy. Opium is prepared by boiling the gum opium and successively filtering out the impurities. Depending upon the process, opium can be produced as a paste, powder, in granules, or in solution. It is known by many different names in the addict world — tar, mud, button, black stuff — and can be smoked, sniffed, tasted, and drunk (when in solutions such as paregoric).

Morphine, a second derivative, is a valuable medical drug. Known in addict culture as M, junk, bindle, paper, and by many other names, it is processed into white, odorless, extremely bitter crystals, powder, or lumps. It can be injected subcutaneously, mainlined (injected intravenously), or taken by mouth.

Heroin is the third and most important of the derivatives for opiate addiction. It has no medical use. Referred to by any word beginning with the letter H (horse, Harry), it is twice as potent as morphine. This makes it exceptionally important in the illicit trade. Heroin is usually adulterated in processing. The "cutting" agent is milk sugar. By the time it is peddled to users, the heroin content may be as little as 2 to 5 per cent. This accounts for the enormous profits made by processors and organized criminals handling illegal narcotics. Heroin is used in much the way morphine is — by mouth, injection, or sniffing. It is produced in capsules, powder, or tablet form.

Codeine is the fourth and least important derivative of opium. It is the least addicting of the major derivatives and is only about one-sixth as potent

48. This discussion of opiates and their synthetic equivalents is largely derived from Maurer and Vogel, op. cit. pp. 47–77.

as morphine. Codeine is widely used in cough preparations. Addicts rely upon it only in the absence of stronger preparations and when combined with terpin hydrate.

Synthetic narcotics. Synthetic (laboratory developed) narcotics have essentially the same properties as the natural narcotics, including the properties leading to addiction. The two best known synthetics are *demerol*, also known by various other names, including meperidine, and *methadone* (dolophine). Synthetics come in powder, capsule, and other forms and are administered hypodermically or orally, as in a syrup.

Vogel, Isbell, and Chapman rated the various narcotics in terms of effectiveness as pain relievers and sleep-producers. On both counts, heroin was most effective and codeine least effective. In terms of three criteria of addiction — physical dependence, emotional dependence, and tolerance — the natural narcotics, with the exception of codeine, were found to be more addicting than the synthetics.[49]

Non-opiate addicting drugs. Non-opiate addicting drugs include some stimulants, barbiturates, and bromides. Two of the better known drugs are cocaine (a stimulant) and marihuana.[50] Cocaine, and other stimulant drugs such as peyote and benzedrine, have the opposite effect of the narcotics. Stimulants produce sleeplessness and alertness and relieve fatigue and hunger. They also increase nervous irritability. Their analgesic effect is limited.

Cocaine, the most important of the stimulants in addiction, is processed from coca leaves and generally comes in a powder known as "coke." Like the narcotics, it is either sniffed or injected intramuscularly or intravenously. Addiction to cocaine as such is not a very important problem. However, cocaine is often used by addicts in conjunction with heroin. The term for this is "speedball," and the reason for combining the two is that heroin acts to control the anxiety, irritability, and other unpleasant side effects inherent in the use of cocaine. In undiluted form, cocaine can have serious effects, such as delusions and excitement, with the possibility that violence will be a consequence.

Marihuana is a drug whose characteristics and use are much disputed. Not until 1937, with the Marihuana Tax Act, was it included under the heading of a proscribed drug. There is a great deal of argument concerning its addiction potential. Generally speaking, it is not considered to be addicting because it cannot produce tolerance in the user. It is outlawed largely because its use may easily be a stepping-stone to narcotic addiction. The drug itself comes from a hemp plant (cannabis) which can and does grow without cul-

49. Ibid. pp. 63–4.
50. For a discussion of the stimulants and of marihuana see Maurer and Vogel, op. cit. pp. 91–7, 104–7.

tivation in almost every part of the world. Marihuana (hashish, reefer, loco weed, tea) consists of any part of the plant, but most particularly the seeds or the resin. It is usually smoked but can also be ingested in liquid concoctions. Marihuana is not used medically since its depressant effect is unstable. It is, however, the most widely used drug among novices (joy-poppers).

The extent of addiction. Because of the unusual amount of misleading publicity devoted to narcotic addiction, several facts warrant mention. First, drug addiction is not a numerically important problem. Second, the number of drug addicts has probably declined substantially since the turn of the century. Third, while adult addiction has systematically decreased, experimentation with drugs (marihuana, morphine, and heroin) by youth seems to have increased significantly.

In 1961, police agencies reported 29,122 arrests for narcotic law violations — a rate of 25.2 per 100,000 persons.[51] Obviously not all of those arrested were addicts. Some were pushers and peddlers and a very few were probably professional persons illegally dispensing drugs. Arrests for narcotic violations constituted 0.69 per cent of all arrests. Over the years, arrests for nacotics violations have rarely exceeded 1 per cent of all arrests. Of the 24 offenses listed by the FBI, narcotics arrests are usually third to fifth from the bottom numerically.

The Federal Bureau of Narcotics maintains a register of "active" addicts. Active addicts are presumably those who are kept under some type of surveillance. In December 1961 this register contained 46,798 names. Allowing for the vagaries of reporting, there are probably some 50,000 addicts in the United States and this number is considerably smaller than previously. At or near the turn of the century there were estimated to be some 264,000 addicts. By 1924, surveys of physicians and official statistics led to an estimate of 150,000.[52] One draftee in every 1500 examined was rejected as an addict in World War I whereas only one in 10,000 was rejected in World War II. Although these figures indicate a marked decrease in addiction, the United States rate is still substantially greater than that of any European country. In England there were only 333 known addicts in 1956, approximately 100 of whom were medical personnel. A survey in Sweden in 1954 reported 500–600 addicts, 20 per cent of whom were medical personnel. In that year 130 persons received treatment as addicts. Norway estimated some 700 addicts out of 4,000,000 persons in 1955. Switzerland reported 109 known addicts in 1954; France, 129 in 1953 and 93 in 1954; and West Germany, 4374 in 1957, of whom 14 per cent were medical personnel.[53]

51. *Uniform Crime Reports,* 1961, pp. 92–3.
52. *Drug Addiction: Crime or Disease?,* op. cit. p. 28.
53. Ibid. pp. 126–53.

Fig. 17-1. Active Narcotic Addicts Reported in the United States as of December 31, 1961

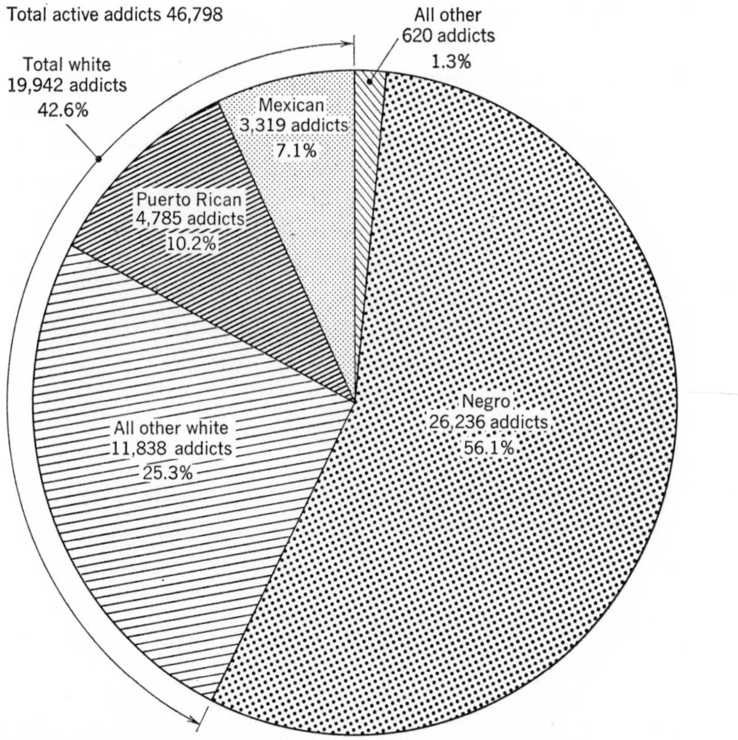

Federal Bureau of Narcotics

Source: Subcommittee of the Committee on Appropriations, House of Representatives, Jan. 1962, p. 258.

THE EPIDEMIOLOGY OF DRUG ADDICTION

The demographic and ecological characteristics of American addicts have undergone considerable change since World War II. Addiction now is overwhelmingly concentrated among impoverished groups, as are the arrests for narcotics law violations.

Sex and race. Narcotics arrests in 1961 were five times as great for men as for women. Men also constitute from 75 to 85 per cent of the treated addicts. This proportion seems to have existed since the 1920's. Prior to the Harrison Act, females were thought to have outnumbered male addicts because of their presumably greater utilization of elixirs containing narcotics.

The race composition of those arrested for narcotic violations in 1961 was approximately 62 per cent white and 37 per cent Negro. The Narcotics Bureau register, on the other hand, lists over 56 per cent of the addicts as Negro, 10 per cent as Puerto Rican, 7 per cent as of Mexican descent, and only 25 per cent as native white (see Fig. 17-1). A Chicago study in 1952 found that

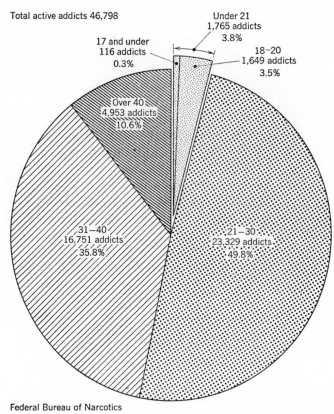

Fig. 17-2. Age of Active Narcotic Addicts as of December 31, 1961 in the United States

Total active addicts 46,798

Under 21
1,765 addicts
3.8%

17 and under
116 addicts
0.3%

18–20
1,649 addicts
3.5%

Over 40
4,953 addicts
10.6%

31–40
16,751 addicts
35.8%

21–30
23,329 addicts
49.8%

Federal Bureau of Narcotics

Source: Subcommittee of the Committee on Appropriations, House of Representatives,
Jan. 1962, p. 259.

84.1 per cent of the addicts were nonwhite.[54] The Public Health Hospital at Lexington currently lists about 40 per cent of its patients as Negro — a substantial increase over the 10 per cent who were patients in the late 'thirties. This change may be due to factors other than race itself, such as knowledge of the existence of the hospital and willingness to use the facilities.

Age. A major change in addiction patterns has been in age. In 1961, 6.8 per cent of those arrested for narcotics offenses were under 18; 19.5 per cent were under 21; 41.7 per cent were under 25.[55] The age distribution of active addicts is shown in Figure 17-2. Addicts are considerably younger now, according to the admissions records at the Public Health Hospital at Lexington. In the late 1930's, under 10 per cent of the admissions were under 25, while

54. Ibid. p. 30.
55. *Uniform Crime Reports*, 1961, Table 20, p. 94.

in the 1950's a third or more were under 25.[56] In Chicago in 1952, one-third of some 5000 drug users were found to be under 21. Of 1844 new drug user cases found in New York in 1949–1952, a majority were found to have become addicted in their late teens.[57] Drug addiction appears to have become a teen-age problem. This means that many new users are being inducted into the drug culture early in life. Whereas previously many became addicts as a result of poor medical practices, now it is more a matter of street-corner culture.

Ecological correlates. Narcotic addiction is largely restricted to a dozen or so of our largest metropolitan areas. Of the 46,798 "active" narcotic addicts in 1961, some 21,813 were listed as living in New York State (and nearly all of these in New York City itself), 7592 were located in California (Los Angeles and San Francisco), 6924 in Illinois (Chicago). Almost all of the other addicts were in major cities (see Fig. 17-3). In 1956, some 9000 arrests for narcotics violations occurred in Chicago; New York and Los Angeles contributed over 5000 each, Detroit police arrested over 2600 offenders, and the remaining major cities had less than 500 each.[58] No other type of deviation is as highly localized.

Even within the major cities, drug addiction is heavily concentrated in a very few census tracts. These tracts invariably are slum areas heavily populated by Negroes and persons of Mexican and Puerto Rican descent. One interesting aspect of this distribution is that tracts with high rates are the poorest of even the slum sections of the community. This intra-city distribution does not appear to have changed significantly over the years. In Dai's study of 2439 addicts who were arrested in 1928–34, nine tracts or neighborhoods (of the 120 in Chicago) contributed half of the drug users.[59] In a New York City study in the 1950's, three-fourths of the adolescent narcotic users were concentrated in 15 per cent of the city's census tracts.[60]

Explanations of drug addiction. As with any other form of deviant behavior, considerable disagreement exists among professional students of the problem as to the etiology of narcotics addiction. Careful research on the subject since the 1930's has identified several types of addicts. The difficulty with these classifications is that they describe men and women who are already addicts. This means that the basis of their problem must be recon-

56. John A. Clausen, "Drug Addiction," in *Contemporary Social Problems* (Robert K. Merton and Robert A. Nisbet, eds.), New York: Harcourt, Brace, and World, 1961, p. 190.
57. Robert A. Felix, "Medical and Legal Problems Involved in Narcotic Addiction," in *Proceedings: Medicolegal Symposiums on Narcotic Addiction,* op. cit. p. 131–2.
58. *Drug Addiction: Crime or Disease?,* op. cit. pp. 32–3.
59. Bingham Dai, *Opium Addiction in Chicago,* Shanghai: Commercial Press, 1937.
60. Isidor Chein, "Studies in Narcotics Use Among Juveniles," *Social Work,* 1 (April 1956), pp. 50–60.

Fig. 17-3. Active Narcotic Addicts Reported in Several Selected States as of December 31, 1961

Total active addicts 46,798

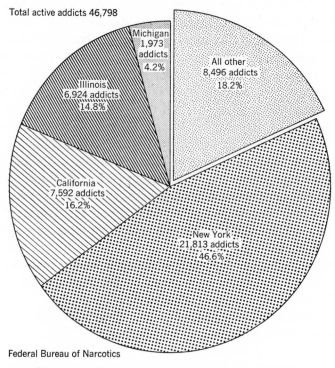

Federal Bureau of Narcotics

Source: Subcommittee of the Committee on Appropriations, House of Representatives, Jan. 1962, p. 257.

structed. Retrospective etiological statements are subject to distortion. Despite these limitations, three classications of addicts have been proposed on the basis of presumed etiology. These are: the accidental or medical, the emotionally disturbed, and the socially processed types.[61]

Accidental addicts are those who were treated with narcotic drugs for physical illness, became addicts, and continued using narcotics to satisfy the addiction. Some experts contend that medically addicted addicts are a very small proportion (no more than 5 per cent) of treated addicts. Others contend that even this type has underlying emotional problems.

The neurotic, psychotic, and characterologically disturbed constitute a much larger segment of the addict population. The neurotic uses narcotics to relieve anxiety and guilt. Like alcohol, narcotics provide an escape from inner problems. The psychotic uses drugs to make adjustment a little easier. Interestingly, in some addicts of this type the mental disorder becomes ap-

61. See *Drug Addiction: Crime or Disease?*, op. cit. pp. 50–59.

parent only after the addict has been "dried out" or forced to abstain. Pescor contends that perhaps only 6 or 7 per cent of addicts are neurotic and only a handful are psychotic.[62] Most addicts are characterologically disturbed. They are simply inadequate personalities. Their inadequacies consist of what Felix calls a "touch-and-fly" approach to life's problems and an inability to tolerate discomfort.[63] Others have considered the addict to be a hostile and aggressive personality who resorts to drugs to relieve his frustrations.

The socially processed addicts include those who come from a cultural climate that favors experimentation with drugs — in other words, from the subculture of the addict. This subculture involves the search for "kicks" and the willingness to experiment with marihuana and heroin. In this subculture the user of marihuana has to be taught (a) how to smoke reefers for the desired effect; (b) to recognize the effect; and (c) to enjoy the sensations he is supposed to get.[64] Most of the sensations are hardly pleasurable as such — dizziness, tingling — hence the need to define them as desirable. The same type of definition is involved in the use of heroin, alcohol, or cigars, pipes, or cigarettes. Neither alcoholic intoxication nor the dizziness accompanying the initial use of tobacco is inherently pleasurable.

Not all street-corner gangs in very deprived neighborhoods experiment with drugs. In gangs in which experimentation does take place, most gang members eventually become concerned about the future and leave these youthful preoccupations.

But for those gang members who are too disturbed emotionally to face the future as adults, the passing of adolescent hell-raising leaves emptiness, boredom, apathy and restless anxiety. In a gang where there are many such members, experimentation with drugs for "kicks" will soon lead to frequent and, later, habitual use, cliques of users will grow quickly. Enmeshed in the patterns of activities revolving around the purchase, sale, and use of drugs and the delinquent efforts to get money to meet the exorbitant cost of heroin, the young users can comfortably forget about girls, careers, status and recognition in the society at large. Their sexual drive is diminished, they maintain a sense of belonging in the limited world of the addict, they remain children forever. They may give up all sense of personal responsibility for their lives and conveniently project the blame for their shiftless existence on the "habit." [65]

62. Michael J. Pescor, "The Kolb Classification of Drug Addicts," *Public Health Reports*, Supplement No. 155, 1939.
63. Felix, op. cit. p. 135.
64. Howard S. Becker, "Becoming a Marihuana User," *American Journal of Sociology*, 59 (November 1953), pp. 235–43. See also Alfred R. Lindesmith, *Opiate Addiction*, op. cit.
65. Daniel M. Wilner, Eva Rosenfeld, Robert S. Lee, Donald L. Gerard, and Isidor Chien, "Heroin Use and Street Gangs," reprinted by special permission of the *Journal of Criminal Law, Criminology, and Police Science*, Vol. 48, No. 4. Copyright © 1957 by Northwestern University School of Law.

Drug Addiction and Crime. Since the Harrison Narcotics Act, the possession of proscribed drugs is itself a crime. So addicts are criminals. In addition, since drugs are illegal, the costs involved to addicts are prohibitive, and the profits to those who control the drug traffic are sensational. Clinard has calculated the hypothetical profits on 35 ounces (one kilogram) of heroin. One kilogram of 86 per cent pure heroin would cost about $1000 in Italy and as much as $5000 more to smuggle into the United States. After adulteration with 90 per cent milk sugar, the original 35 ounces will be made into about 20,000 capsules which will contain one and a half grains of mostly milk sugar. Each capsule will sell for from $2 to $3, for a total of $40,000 to $60,000.[66]

Addicts will, of course, bear the entire burden of this mark-up. To "get by" and keep constantly supplied, they will spend from $40 to $150 per week, depending upon the length and extent of their addiction. A ten-grain-a-day addict, taking four shots, will spend $14 to $21 per day. Although many addicts suffer from symptoms related to malnutrition, and live in impoverished circumstances, they have to engage in predatory criminal activities to support their addiction. Their criminality is likely to consist of property offenses (males) and prostitution (females). For addicts there is simply no alternative to property crimes as a means of maintaining their expensive addiction. The public misconception that narcotics addicts commit violent personal crimes has no basis in fact. In 1951 the Narcotics Bureau of the Chicago Police Department gathered records on the offenses for which addicts had been arrested. A contrast of these records with those for the remainder of the arrests in Chicago revealed that 84.9 per cent of the offenses of addicts involved larceny, robbery, or burglary. The same three offenses accounted for only 47.7 per cent of the arrests of nonaddicts. Sex offenses contributed only 1.6 per cent of the arrests of addicts and 11.0 per cent of the arrests of nonaddicts. The figures for aggravated and other assaults were 1.3 for the addicts and 19.7 for non-addicts.[67]

Treatment of Addicts. The treatment of addicts — juvenile and adult — is probably less effective, and results in higher readmission rates, than treatment of any other known type of deviancy except possibly that of abnormal sexual offenders.

In 1935, the Public Health Service established the first hospital for narcotic addicts in the United States at Lexington, Kentucky. A second hospital was later opened in Fort Worth, Texas. The latter facility, however, receives other types of patients as well. The hospital at Lexington, with a present capacity of 1050 patients, has handled some 70,000 patients since opening, and of

66. Clinard, op. cit. p. 276.
67. Harold Finestone, "Narcotics and Criminality," *Law and Contemporary Problems* 22 (Winter 1957), pp. 69–85.

these about 60 per cent have been first admissions. Of the 3500 addicts admitted each year, 10 per cent are federal prisoners (sent from other institutions) and the remaining 90 per cent are voluntary patients from states east of the Mississippi.[68] Those from states west of the Mississippi go to the Fort Worth Hospital. Many voluntary patients come to Lexington because their tolerance level is so great that they can no longer support their addiction, even through theft. The average length of stay of voluntary patients is approximately five months, although it may exceed a year. Treatment is divided into three phases: (a) withdrawal of the narcotic, which averages one week; (b) orientation and evaluation, during which time the patient is seen by staff personnel (psychiatrist, psychologist, social worker, vocational and/or educational counselor, and psychiatric aide) — this evaluation may take two weeks to a month and results in a treatment plan; and, (c) transfer to a continued treatment unit ward for individual or group psychotherapy and psychiatric supervision, and for educational and vocational training and work assignments.[69]

The results of this treatment have never been evaluated rigorously. One early follow-up study of 4776 addicts six months after discharge revealed that 13.5 per cent had remained abstinent. Nearly 40 per cent could not be evaluated as to addiction status.[70] In a California study of 584 cases treated in a state narcotics hospital, only 15 per cent of the addicts were later found to be abstinent.[71] Most had reverted within 18 months after discharge. Lindesmith cites a German study, prior to 1930, of 800 treated addicts, in which 81.6 per cent relapsed in one year, 93.9 per cent within three years, and 96.7 per cent within five years.[72] Finally, a follow-up study of 247 adolescent narcotics users treated at Riverside Hospital in New York concluded that 86 per cent had returned to drugs, crime, or both. Of 147 of these patients who allowed themselves to be interviewed, *eight*, who had been joy-poppers, were free of addiction, and all the rest were addicted.[73]

EMERGENT CONCEPTIONS IN THE TREATMENT OF ADDICTION: NORMATIVE DISSENSUS

The treatment of addicts is grossly ineffective because (a) many addicts are unwilling and unable to face an abstinent future and (b) the environments to which addicts return are the same ones in which they developed ad-

68. John A. O'Donnell, "The Lexington Program for Narcotic Addicts," *Federal Probation*, 26 (March 1962), pp. 55–60.
69. Ibid.
70. Michael J. Pescor, "Follow-up Study of Treated Narcotic Addicts," *Public Health Reports*, Supplement 170, 1943, pp. 1–18.
71. *Drug Addiction: Crime or Disease?*, op. cit. pp. 90–91.
72. Lindesmith, *Opiate Addiction*, op. cit. p. 49.
73. See Clausen, op. cit. p. 211.

diction. Many proposals have been presented for handling the addiction problem.

In the period immediately subsequent to the passage of the Harrison Act (1919–23) over 40 clinics were established by cities and states to meet the problem. The clinics were to provide ambulatory treatment for addicts since physicians were barred from treating addicts except for other medical problems.[74] These clinics aroused the antipathy of the Federal Bureau of Narcotics and of the American Medical Association and were abandoned. No evaluation of their effectiveness is available since most of them were so short-lived.

In 1954 a resolution was submitted to the AMA by Dr. Andrew E. Eggston of the New York delegation, which revived the clinic idea. It called for: [75]

(1) The establishment of narcotics clinics under the sponsorship of the Federal Bureau of Narcotics.

(2) Registration and fingerprinting of addicts; provision for the keeping of accurate records.

(3) Administration of optimal doses to addicts at regular intervals at cost or free of charge.

(4) Prevention of self-administration of drugs by addicts.

(5) Rehabilitation through voluntary hospitalization.

(6) The avoidance of forcible confinement.

Along the same lines, the New York Academy of Medicine espouses two major points in a six-point program. These are: [76]

1. Define the addict as a sick person and not as a criminal.

2. Remove the profit from the illegal traffic in drugs by furnishing drugs to addicts at low cost and under federal control.

The implementation of this second proposal would involve establishing clinics attached to general hospitals which would operate on a 24-hour day, seven days a week. Addicts would be hospitalized in order to evaluate their drug needs, after which the clinic would provide the necessary dosage at cost. The clinic would dispense no more than a two-day supply of the narcotic. Abuses by addicts would result in commitment to a hospital. Enforcement against the illicit trade would be continued.

Another proposal, which is equally or even more strongly opposed by law enforcement agencies, is called the "British Plan." The essence of this plan, as it has operated in Great Britain for many years, is that treatment of addiction is the prerogative of the individual physician. Doctors may administer and prescribe morphine and heroin when (a) patients are gradually being

74. Ibid. pp. 209–10.
75. *Drug Addiction: Crime or Disease?*, op. cit. pp. 94–5.
76. Ibid.

withdrawn from their dependence on narcotics, (b) the severity of the abstinence syndrome precludes withdrawing the drug in safety, and (c) it has been demonstrated that the patient who can lead a normal and useful life on minimum dosages of narcotic becomes incapable of this when the drug is discontinued. Before an addict is placed on a narcotic regimen, a second physician may be, and often is, consulted. Also, addicts under such treatment are usually reported to the responsible government agency so that there is nothing *sub rosa* about the arrangement and both physician and addict are more or less protected from prosecution.[77]

Similar plans have been recommended by various professional and advisory groups. They appear foredoomed to failure, however, unless the definition of the addict as criminal is replaced by a new definition of the addict as victim and patient.

ALCOHOL AND ALCOHOLISM

Certain important similarities characterize drug addiction and alcoholism. Both have a history as problems reaching back into antiquity. Both are compulsive afflictions. Both are defined medically as abnormal. Both are morally repugnant. Both violate legal codes — directly or indirectly. Both are related to and often causative of other social problems — mental and physical disorders, personal and property crimes, suicide, divorce, desertion, unemployment, and poverty. Both have resulted in attempts to legislate them out of existence and have created problems of dissensus. Finally, both have defied effective treatment, prevention, and control.

But alcoholism differs from opiate addiction in several important respects. First, in terms of sheer magnitude of the problem, the excessive use of alcohol dwarfs narcotic addiction. Second, in terms of its consequences — poverty, unemployment, homelessness, divorce, automobile accidents, and physical disorders — the excessive use of alcohol is one of the major concerns and problems in Western society. Third, whereas the use of opiates is illegal, the use and even abuse of alcohol is perfectly legal. Fourth, whereas consensus exists in the definition of the use of narcotics as immoral and illegal, no such consensus exists as to the use of alcohol. In fact, part of the problem of alcohol is that it is extolled as a socially useful substance and at the same time feared for its consequences. On the one hand, drinking has become a deeply imbedded social pattern. Social gatherings, parties, and business deals are incomplete without the ever-present cocktail or other alcoholic beverage. On the other hand, lingering Calvinistic traditions define its use as immoral.

77. Ibid. pp. 126–39. For a negative appraisal of the British system, see Malachi L. Harvey, "Medical and Legal Problems Involved in Narcotic Addiction," in *Proceedings: Medicolegal Symposiums on Narcotic Addiction*, op. cit. pp. 91–127.

Thus, alcohol presents two problems: a normative problem, which has flared from time to time in the United States, and at one point resulted in Prohibition, and a problem of behavioral deviation.

HISTORICAL ANTECEDENTS OF ALCOHOL AS A NORMATIVE PROBLEM

In Western history, the problems connected with the use and misuse of alcohol have been difficult.[78] Alcohol, particularly wine and beer, was used in the earliest Western civilizations. The ancient Egyptian, Babylonian, Greek, Roman, and Hebrew civilizations contain references to intoxication and demoralization. Despite these problems, alcohol remained a socially important and acceptable adjunct to conviviality throughout the ages and well into the early Industrial Revolution. The Industrial Revolution, and the urban squalor that followed, plus the discovery of a cheap alcoholic beverage — gin — led to stern protests against the use of alcoholic beverages and to the first repressive laws against its sale and use. Calvinistic moral and religious conceptions provided the normative framework for opposition to the use of alcohol. The problem was no longer behavioral deviation as represented by excessive drinking and alcholism; the focus had shifted so that drinking itself had become a moral and normative issue.[79]

The early American colonists reflected this moral concern. To the Puritans, particularly, all alcoholic beverages were anathema. Stringent rules and regulations governed the use of alcohol and emerging cities, particularly Boston, were viewed as threatening the moral fiber of decent, God-fearing citizens. Nevertheless, the consumption of alcohol — particularly distilled spirits — showed no appreciable signs of decreasing. The turning point in American history came shortly after the Civil War. The influx of various ethnic groups — the Germans, Scandinavians, and Irish — who were morally, behaviorally, and traditionally "wet" — aroused considerable antipathy. The emergence of the saloon as a drinking and social establishment, and the excesses to which it gave rise, caused even more concern. The widespread introduction of beer led to hostility toward drinking in general, and toward the saloons, bars, and taverns in which it occurred. The morality of the use of alcohol became a major source of contention and a focal point in the conflict between the native white, rural Protestants and the politically emerging, urban Catholic, im-

78. For an analysis of the patterns of use and problems of alcohol in preliterate societies, see Donald Horton, "The Functions of Alcohol in Primitive Societies," *Quarterly Journal of Studies on Alcohol*, 4 (1943), pp. 199–320; and Donald Horton, "Alcohol in Primitive Societies: A Cross-Cultural Study," in *Alcohol, Science and Society*, New Haven: *Quarterly Journal of Studies on Alcohol*, 1945, Lecture 13, pp. 153–77.

79. For a historical review of the problem, see Simon Dinitz, *The Relation of the Tavern to the Drinking Phases of Alcoholics*, unpublished doctoral dissertation, University of Wisconsin, 1951, Chap. 3.

migrant groups. The conflict was heightened even more when immigrants from southern and eastern European countries began their mass migrations to the United States. The newer groups, although differing from the earlier ones in their drinking patterns, were unmistakably and outspokenly "wet." [80]

The issue was finally joined politically with the formation of organized "dry" groups, such as the WCTU and the Anti-Saloon League, which applied pressure on state legislatures to enact state-wide Prohibition laws. These maneuvers were countered by the "wets" and the result was a maze of conflicting laws and statutes.[81] The net effect was that the rural states went "dry"; the urban states remained "wet." Many states vacillated between the two, being "wet" and "dry" by turn. Finally, a sufficient degree of consensus was achieved to enact Prohibition as the Eighteenth Amendment to the Constitution. Prohibition became law in January 1920.[82] It was repealed, by the Twenty-first Amendment to the Constitution in December 1933.

In the intervening thirteen years, the issue of total abstinence was debated vigorously.[83] Despite Prohibition, drinking remained a major pastime. In certain urban areas and for certain classes of people, drinking acquired a romantic aura far beyond that which it had ever possessed. Legal proscription proved to be no match for this traditional, and in some cases, newly acquired, need to drink. Those who had used alcoholic beverages, and those whose cultural heritage included the traditional and social use of alcohol, experienced only minor difficulties in quenching their thirst. The quality and price of the alcohol, however, left much to be desired. Persons who had been abstinent by conviction were hardly affected by the "noble experiment," as Prohibition was called. These persons, no doubt, would have remained abstinent regardless of the legality or illegality of drinking. Prohibition did present a grave moral problem for the fence-sitter — one who by conviction and practice, was neither "wet" nor "dry." It was persons in this latter group who eventually sealed the fate of Prohibition.

An important element in the repeal of Prohibition was the growth of organized syndicates of criminals, who circumvented the law with relative impunity. These men evolved from petty neighborhood hoodlums into wealthy

---

80. Dinitz, op. cit. pp. 64 ff.
81. Peter H. Odegard, *Pressure Politics: The Story of the Anti-Saloon League,* New York: Columbia University Press, 1928.
82. A number of other countries tried Prohibition, also. The Swedish "noble experiment" lasted five weeks in 1909. Iceland was "dry" from 1915 to 1935; Newfoundland from 1915 to 1924; Norway from 1916 to 1927; Russia from 1916 to 1925; Turkey from 1920 to 1924. Eight Canadian provinces attempted Prohibition during the period 1916–27.
83. Herbert Asbury, *The Great Illusion,* New York: Doubleday, 1950. For an opposing viewpoint see Irving Fischer, *Prohibition at Its Worst,* New York: Alcohol Information Committee, 1928.

and powerful gangsters through profits from illicit liquor traffic operations. From this base of operation, they extended their networks to include gambling, and racketeering.

The problem of drinking has never been the locus of the intense social conflict it was during the first third of the twentieth century. Since 1940, interest in the problems of alcohol has gradually shifted from the social conflict level to the scientific level. States and universities have supported research organizations to study every aspect of the drinking problem. Originally feared by both "wets" and "drys," these organizations for the scientific study of alcohol and its problems are now accepted as serving a necessary and useful purpose.[84]

NATURE AND EFFECTS OF ALCOHOL: THE SOURCE OF THE NORMATIVE PROBLEM

Alcohol is a rapidly acting *depressant*. In suppressing the higher brain controls, alcohol reduces inhibitions and may permit the individual to behave in a manner that would be unacceptable to him when sober. The loss of internalized social controls (superego) led Karen Horney to remark that, "The superego is that part of the personality which is soluble in alcohol." [85] For this reason — the loss of inhibition — alcohol is often mistakenly assumed to be a stimulant.

Alcohol, like water, does not require digestion. When it reaches the stomach, some of it is absorbed directly into the blood stream. The remainder is absorbed through the small intestine. The rapid response of the organism to alcohol is a direct consequence of its quick absorption into the blood stream. The blood stream carries the alcohol to the liver, at which point some of it is detoxified. In opposition to the rapid effects of alcohol on the organism is its relatively slow rate of elimination from the body. This lingering of alcohol in the blood stream has made it possible to devise "drunkometers" to test for intoxication of drivers involved in auto mishaps and violations.[86] Another consequence is that a small amount of alcohol taken after an interval of nondrinking will reinduce the effects of the previous drinking.

Several variables are related to the level of alcohol in the blood and its effects. These are the rates of absorption and elimination — this varies to some extent for different people — the amount and nature of the food in

84. Morris E. Chafetz and Harold W. Demone, *Alcoholism and Society*, New York: Oxford University Press, 1962, pp. 109–45.
85. Quoted in Chafetz and Demone, op. cit. p. 9.
86. H. R. Hulpieu and R. N. Harger, "The Alcohols," *Pharmacology in Medicine*, 2nd ed. (Victor A. Drill, ed.), New York: McGraw-Hill, 1958, pp. 195–212.

the stomach at the time of drinking, the rate of drinking, the quantity consumed, and the percentage of alcohol in the beverage.[87]

When ingested in moderate quantities, alcohol is a cheap and relatively nontoxic tranquilizer. It functions to reduce anxiety, tensions, worry, and depression. It eases fatigue and facilitates social relationships. These effects have been valued for ages. When consumed in greater quantities, alcohol impairs judgment, discrimination, reaction time, and muscular co-ordination. When consumed to excess, the results may be stupor and asphixiation. Generally speaking, and using a 150-pound person as the norm, the first behavioral symptoms attributable to alcohol will occur when the alcohol level in the blood reaches 0.05 per cent. Intoxication occurs at a 0.15 per cent alcohol concentration. Ot 0.50 per cent the person is "dead drunk" or unconscious, and a concentration exceeding 0.60 per cent is usually lethal. Reduced to drinking terms, two ounces of whiskey or two bottles of beer will result in a 0.05 per cent concentration of alcohol in the blood and six ounces of whiskey or six bottles of beer will result in legal intoxication — 0.15 per cent blood alcohol. Other countries, notably Norway, Sweden, and Denmark, set the legal intoxication limit at from 0.05 to 0.10 per cent blood alcohol. It is likely that many United States communities will eventually follow suit.[88]

THE EXTENT AND EPIDEMIOLOGY OF DRINKING

Official statistics on drinking and alcoholism in the United States are lacking. As a result, most of the available information is based on community and sample population surveys. These surveys find that approximately two-thirds of all adults (21 years of age and older) drink some type of alcoholic beverage. Nearly three-fourths of all men and a half or more of all women indulge.[89] A study in the State of Washington revealed that 3.6 per cent of the population drank each day; 15.4 per cent drank intoxicating beverages at least once a week; 26.1 per cent once a month, and 18.2 per cent at least once a year. The remainder, 36.7 per cent, were abstemious. The frequency of drinking was significantly greater for men than women.[90]

Drinking patterns have been found to vary not only with sex but with social class, religion, ethnic group, age, and occupation. In addition, drinking patterns also vary with rural-urban status, community size, and region within the United States.

87. Clinard, op. cit. p. 287.
88. Hulpieu and Harger, op. cit. p. 204–5.
89. John W. Riley and Charles F. Marden, "The Social Pattern of Alcoholic Drinking," *Quarterly Journal of Studies on Alcohol*, 8 (September 1947), pp. 265–73.
90. Milton A. Maxwell, "Drinking Behavior in the State of Washington," *Quarterly Journal of Studies on Alcohol*, 13 (June 1952), pp. 220–21.

Class patterns. In the United States, drinking appears to be distributed bi-modally by class. It is probably more common at the upper and lower levels than in the middle class. In addition, Dollard found that attitudes toward and behavior during drinking are correlated with class standing.[91] At the upper class level drinking is not a moral issue. Both sexes participate in it. Even drunkenness is tolerated if it does not lead to antisocial conduct (brawls, aggression). Members of the "lower-upper" class, presumably because of status anxiety, may tend to become excessive and "destructive" drinkers.

The upper-middle class is neutral in attitude toward drinking. Women indulge sparingly, if at all. In the lower-middle class, drinking is to some extent taboo inasmuch as those at this class level desire to differentiate themselves from lower-class persons. In the lower class, on the other hand, drinking is acceptable and pervasive and few taboos surround it. Drunkenness and chronic inebriety are common, and aggressive behavior under the influence of alcohol is expected.

Social class drinking patterns also differ in terms of (a) the type of alcoholic beverages commonly consumed, (b) the place, time, and circumstances surrounding drinking, (c) the quantity consumed, (d) the speed of consumption, and (e) in the goals or reasons for drinking.[92]

Religious and ethnic patterns. In a national survey, Riley and Marden found that 41 per cent of the Protestants, 21 per cent of the Catholics, and only 13 per cent of the Jews abstained from the use of intoxicating beverages.[93] Ethnically, the Irish lead all groups in their propensity to consume alcohol. In both World War I and World War II, draftees of Irish descent were rejected more frequently for alcoholism than were members of any other ethnic group. In World War I, the Irish rate was twenty times higher than the Jewish or Italian rates.[94] Not only is alcohol an integral part of the customs and traditions of Irish life but even excessive drinking has been considered almost inevitable. These patterns, however, have been modified to some extent in the last decade. As persons of Irish descent ascend the socio-economic ladder, their drinking practices tend to assume the same character as those of other middle-class persons. There is reason to believe that drinking will eventually play a less important role in this group.

While almost all first-generation Italian adults in the United States drink, the character and circumstances surrounding the drinking are different from the Irish patterns.[95] In the Italian community, wine is an integral part of

91. John Dollard, "Drinking Mores and the Social Classes," *Alcohol, Science and Society*, op. cit. pp. 99–100.
92. Mass Observation, *The Pub and the People*, London: Gollancz, 1943.
93. Riley and Marden, op. cit. pp. 265–73.
94. Chafetz and Demone, op. cit. p. 77.
95. Giorgio Lolli, Emido Serianni, Grace M. Golder, and P. Luzzatto-Fegiz, *Alcohol in*

eating and is consumed in significant quantities at meals, often including breakfast. Initiation into drinking occurs early in life — between six and ten. The reasons for drinking are subsumed under traditions, health, and pleasure. Intoxication is rare and alcoholism rates are negligible.

In the second and third generations, the American influence has shifted the patterns considerably. Wine is less commonly used, being replaced by the stronger intoxicants (distilled spirits) and by beer. Alcohol is no longer restricted to meal time. The reasons for drinking also change. Sociability and taste are more frequently cited than traditional reasons. Intoxication is more common and alcoholism becomes a possibility.

In Jewish communities in the United States and elsewhere drinking is common.[96] Alcohol in all forms is used. Orthodox Jews, because of their generally lower-class standing and for traditional and ceremonial reasons, are more likely to use wine and certain types of distilled spirits. Conservative and Reform groups are likely to conform to the social class patterns at their level in the use of alcoholic beverages. Drinking in moderate amounts is traditional for all groups and historically was closely connected with religious activities. One drinks on certain occasions because it is necessary and appropriate to do so. There is no connotation of sociability or pleasure involved and alcohol is not employed as a means of reducing anxiety or as an "escape." Although studies of Jewish college students indicate that these patterns are changing, there is as yet no indication of increasing alcoholism. So strong are the internalized cultural controls that Jewish alcoholics are rare specimens.

Age patterns. One of the interesting aspects of drinking practices is the negative relationship between age and drinking. Survey results indicate that the percentage of persons who consume alcohol decreases with age. About 75 per cent of those between 21 and 29, two-thirds of those between 30 and 49, and only half of those 50 years of age and older drink.[97] Drinking at the college level is more frequent, with 80 per cent of the males and 61 per cent of the females occasionally using alcoholic beverages.[98] On the basis of these figures, alcoholism will probably become an even more serious problem in the future.

Other correlates. Drinking and alcoholism are known to be more common in some occupational categories — seamen, salesmen, manual workers — and to be less frequent in others — ministers and certain types of white collar workers.

Italian Culture: Food and Wine in Relation to Sobriety among Italians and Italian-Americans. New Haven: Yale Center of Alcohol Studies, and Glencoe: Free Press, 1958.

96. Charles R. Snyder, *Alcohol and the Jews: A Cultural Study of Drinking and Sobriety,* New Haven: Yale Center of Alcohol Studies, and Glencoe: Free Press, 1958.
97. Clinard, op. cit. p. 297.
98. Robert Straus and Selden D. Bacon, *Drinking in College,* New Haven: Yale University Press, 1953.

Drinking is also more pronounced in urban than in rural areas, and in larger as opposed to smaller urban communities. Finally, regional differences indicate that the percentage of abstainers is greatest in the Protestant rural Midwest and least in the urban, Catholic, and heavily ethnic New England and Middle Atlantic states.[99]

ALCOHOLISM AND RELATED PROBLEMS

About 70 million Americans use intoxicating beverages with varying frequency. They spend 5 per cent of their budgets for alcohol — a sum approximately equivalent to the total annual cost of education in the United States.[100] The overwhelming number of these 70 million — some 65 million — are social drinkers. For them, alcohol presents no major problem, inasmuch as they "can take it or leave it." They may on occasion become inebriated and "hung over," but this is the exception rather than the rule. They may occasionally drive their cars under the influence of alcohol, but this is not the usual situation. They use alcohol for its pleasurable effects and for sociability.

The remaining five million — one in fourteen — are problem or excessive drinkers. For them, alcohol has become a necessity. They drink not for pleasure or sociability or conviviality but because they have lost most or all of their ability to control their intake of alcohol. Of these excessive drinkers, one million are chronic alcoholics — men and women who have passed the point at which they can manage their problem. Alcohol is the most significant element in their lives. It dominates their thinking, interferes with their jobs, disrupts their family life, creates physical and mental problems, and sometimes involves them in crime.

Excessive drinkers and alcoholics, and occasionally social drinkers as well, account for the single largest number of arrests in the United States. Of the total of 4,214,826 arrests in 1961, 35.7 per cent were for drunkenness; 11.1 more for disorderly conduct; 4.9 for driving while intoxicated; and 2.9 for liquor law violations. Thus, intoxication or related offenses accounted for 54.6 per cent of all arrests in 1961.[101] Intoxication was also a factor in other offenses — both personal and property. As already noted, Wolfgang found that drinking had been involved in 64 per cent of the homicides in Philadelphia. In a study in Columbus, Ohio, of 882 persons arrested during or immediately after the commission of a felony offense, it was found that 64 per cent had a significant percentage of alcohol (0.10 per cent) in the blood stream.[102] Jails and workhouses are "revolving doors" through which problem

99. Clinard, op. cit. pp. 296–7.
100. Chafetz and Demone, op. cit. p. 12.
101. *Uniform Crime Reports*, 1961, pp. 92–3.
102. Paul Tappan, *Crime, Justice and Correction*, New York: McGraw-Hill, 1960, p. 157.

drinkers pass with regularity. Other institutions — TB sanitaria and mental hospitals — make secondary diagnoses of excessive drinking or alcoholism in many admission cases. In Massachusetts, the figure was 30 per cent.[103]

The process of becoming an alcoholic. Unlike narcotics addiction, in which the onset may occur in a few weeks or months, the process of becoming alcoholic is a lengthy one. Most alcoholics begin as social drinkers and pass through a series of stages. At about age 40, after two or more decades of increasingly heavy and more frequent drinking, they lose most or all of their control over alcohol.[104] Retrospective studies of alcoholics indicate that many were introduced to alcohol prior to age 15. Most had become "regular" or frequent social drinkers by age 19. After approximately seven years of social drinking, the alcoholics entered the excessive drinking phase. As excessive drinkers they experienced frequent "blackouts," or amnesia; "sneaked drinks"; were concerned with maintaining and protecting the supply of alcohol; went on "weekend drunks"; had frequent "Blue Mondays"; experienced midweek intoxication; drank on the job; had tremors; attempted to change their drinking patterns; from time to time went on the "wagon"; felt remorse, shame, and guilt; and became alienated from friends and family members.[105]

In the alcoholic phase, many engaged in (a) solitary drinking; (b) morning drinking, usually justified to themselves as the best method of "sobering up" and facing the day's problems; (c) "benders" and "prolonged" drinking "sprees" which were often curtailed only through lack of money, the onset of acute illness, or arrest by the police; and (d) experienced feelings of resentment and hostility to others for their failure to "understand." Above all, the alcoholics felt an intense need to drink and marked discomfort in the absence of alcohol.[106]

In the early stages of alcoholism, few alcoholics will admit to themselves or others that they cannot control their "problem." Most delude themselves about their ability to stop drinking or at least to drink moderately. Few seek professional help unless they are pressured into it by their families or employers or by the threat of commitment to a mental hospital. Some of the more affluent may voluntarily go to a private sanitarium for a week or two each year to "dry out." In general, however, the uncontrolled drinking continues until "bottom" is reached, and this may involve different things to different alcoholics. For some, "bottom" in a flop-house on the local "skid row";

103. Chafetz and Demone, op. cit. pp. 12–13.
104. Simon Dinitz, *The Relation of the Tavern to the Drinking Phases of Alcoholics*, op. cit. pp. 200–204.
105. E. M. Jellinek, "Phases in the Drinking History of Alcoholics," *Memoirs of the Section of Studies on Alcohol*, No. 5, New Haven: *Quarterly Journal of Studies on Alcohol*, 1946.
106. Ibid. pp. 37 ff.

for others, divorce, rejection by family and friends, unemployability, physical impairments, or a proprietary interest in a jair cell. It is only after reaching "bottom" that some become amenable to treatment.

THE ETIOLOGY OF ALCOHOLISM

With the advent of scientific interest in "alcoholism as a disease," the problem has been studied in terms of its physiological, endocrinological, psychological, psychiatric, and sociological concomitants.[107] Etiologically, alcoholism has been held to be intimately associated with adrenal deficiency in the cortex; and with nutritional and metabolic disturbances. On the psychological and emotional level, alcoholism has been viewed as being associated with sociopathic and neurotic traits and "deep personality problems." Psychoanalysts have generally attributed alcoholism to one or more of the following "causes": fixation at or regression to the "oral" stage; sexual problems, and particularly latent homosexuality, in which the guilt is assuaged in alcohol; as a substitute for suicide, as self-destruction, as a means of self-punishment; as a means of escaping "inner conflicts," as a technique for managing anxiety; and as a method of handling feelings of insecurity and inadequacy. On the sociological level, alcoholics have been found to be socially isolated persons.[108] It has also been suggested that the extent of alcoholism is a function of several aspects of social existence: the extent to which a society creates tensions, pressures, and anxieties in its members; the extent to which it defines alcohol as a satisfactory method of releasing these pressures; the customs and prescriptions and practices that evolve around drinking behavior; and the extent to which society provides and prescribes substitutes for drinking.[109]

THE TREATMENT OF ALCOHOLISM

Present treatment methods of alcoholism, as in drug addiction, are largely nonspecific. These techniques may be classified under three headings: general, aversive, and psychotherapeutic (individual or group). The general treatment methods are designed to separate the alcoholic from alcohol as rapidly and painlessly as possible. Some alcoholics must be treated at the same time for nutritional deficiencies and for organic problems occasioned by their lack of desire and inability to eat normally while on a "bender." The cumulative effects of this abuse to the organism over twenty or more years can be massive and may require prolonged care. Once the alcoholic has been sobered up, and his physical condition improved, other methods can be used.

107. E. M. Jellinek, *The Disease Concept of Alcoholism*, New Haven: Hillhouse Press, 1960.
108. For a review of these etiologic theories, see Chafetz and Demone, op. cit. pp. 33–61.
109. Robert F. Bales, "Cultural Differences in the Rate of Alcoholism," *Quarterly Journal of Studies on Alcohol* (December 1945–46), pp. 482–98.

1. *Aversive Techniques.* Aversive methods are based on the well-known principle of stimulus-response conditioning. The initial application of this principle in alcoholism probably occurred in ancient Rome. Legend has it that a Roman physician treated his alcoholic patients by forcing them to drink wine into which he had put live worms. The result was a rather crude form of conditioning. The "recidivism" rate based on this technique was never divulged.

Conditioned reflex therapy. The same idea was introduced in the United States in 1940 and is called conditioned reflex therapy. Its purpose is to create aversion to the sight, smell, taste, and thought of alcohol. Drugs which produce nausea and vomiting — apomorphine and emetine — are administered to the alcoholic. Before the onset of these and other unpleasant symptoms, the patient is given his favorite alcoholic beverage. The expected occurs and the patient becomes quite ill. This treatment is repeated daily or every other day for five to ten days or more. "Booster" treatments are given at various intervals, and at the end of six months, a year, or whenever the patient experiences a recurrence of the urge to drink. The results of this therapy vary considerably from study to study. In a follow-up study of 4096 private patients treated with conditioned reflex therapy, three-fifths remained abstinent for a year, 51 per cent for at least two years, 38 per cent for five years, and 23 per cent for a decade or more. Of 878 relapsed patients who were treated a second time, 39 per cent remained "dry." [110] Despite these excellent results with private, economically well-off patients, there is some evidence to indicate that for the more nearly "typical" alcoholic, who is farther along in his drinking pattern, conditioned reflex therapy may not be as efficacious.

Antabuse. In the late 1940's, two Danish scientists accidentally discovered a drug — disulfiram, commonly known by its trade name, Antabuse — which showed extraordinary promise in the treatment of alcoholism. The action of Antabuse on the organism is well understood — up to a point. It blocks the ability of the organism to oxidize alcohol. Thus, a very small amount of alcohol will have the same consequences as considerably larger amounts. Within a short time, five to ten minutes, after ingesting a small amount of alcohol, a patient taking Antabuse will feel extremely hot and intensely flushed. The redness or flush will appear on the face, chest, and upper limbs. There will be a feeling of throat irritation, some constriction in the throat, and considerable coughing. Taken in larger amounts, alcohol will produce nausea and vomiting, a drop in blood pressure, and feeling of uneasiness. Other symptoms may include dizziness, blurred vision, headache, heart palpi-

110. Frederick Lemere and Walter L. Voegthn, "An Evaluation of the Aversion Treatment of Alcoholism," *Management of Addictions* (Edward Podolsky, ed.), New York: Philosophical Library, 1955, pp. 173–80.

tations, chest pain, and numbness in the hands and feet. These effects usually wear off after several hours of sleep.[111]

The purpose of Antabuse is to keep problem drinkers from using alcohol. It works very well as long as the alcoholic continues to take Antabuse regularly. After a few months of sobriety, however, some alcoholics stop using the drug. Relapse to inebriety is the usual consequence. Another difficulty with Antabuse is that not all alcoholics are eligible to use it. Certain physical and emotional problems make its use inadvisable.

Neither Antabuse, conditioned reflex therapy, nor the other organic treatment methods, such as elevation of the blood sugar count and vitamin therapy, will "cure" alcoholism. Their function is to prevent or reduce the craving for alcohol. They fail, of course, to deal with the root causes of the problem, which, for the present, remain speculative. Nevertheless, these methods are valuable in that they curb the craving to drink or preclude the satisfaction of this urge. When coupled with individual or group therapy methods, such as Alcoholics Anonymous, organic methods are reasonably effective in treating alcoholics.

2. *Alcoholics Anonymous: Social Therapy.* Alcoholics Anonymous is an organization of alcoholics which attempts to do more than curb the alcoholic's compulsive appetite for intoxicating beverages. A.A. serves its members in many ways: by helping them to reintegrate themselves into the conventional social order; by giving them insight into their problems; by standing by them (supportive therapy) when the going gets difficult and the desire to drink becomes overwhelming; by "picking them up" and starting them over after a failure experience, known as a "slip"; by providing fellowship with others who share the same problem; by demonstrating that social activities can be meaningful without alcohol; and by helping the families of alcoholics understand them better. A.A. is important to the alcoholic member in other ways, too. It provides examples of men and women who have achieved sobriety after overcoming drinking problems as great or greater than that of the new member. It makes it possible for a member to change his concept of himself from that of a "drunk" or "lush" to that of a person with a disease who, with help, can overcome his difficulties.[112]

Alcoholics Anonymous began in Akron, Ohio, in June, 1935. There are several versions of its origin. Two men, a New York stockbroker and an Akron physician met, by accident or design (depending upon which version one accepts), and decided that alcoholics could, by helping each other, help themselves to achieve sobriety. The early growth of the group was painfully slow.

111. Chafetz and Demone, op. cit. pp. 209–12.
112. For a more detailed exposition of Alcoholics Anonymous, see, Simon Dinitz, *The Role of Alcoholics Anonymous as a Therapeutic Agent*, unpublished master's thesis, University of Wisconsin, 1949; and Chafetz and Demone, op. cit. pp. 146–65.

In two years there were 40 members. By 1939, there were 100 members. A book written by these 100 members and containing the purposes, procedures, and methods of A.A., and testimonials from their own experiences, was published in that year. A national publication did a feature story on the group in 1939. As a result of favorable publicity, membership grew rapidly. In 1940 there were about 800 members. A year later membership had increased tenfold. It rose to 150,000 in 1950, and to more than a quarter of a million in over 4000 local chapters in all parts of the world by 1960.

The A.A. program is based on principles outlined in the Twelve Steps. These are: [113]

1. We admitted we were powerless over alcohol — that our lives had become unmanageable.
2. Came to believe that a Power greater than ourselves could restore us to sanity.
3. Made a decision to turn our will and our lives over to the care of God "as we understood Him."
4. Made a searching and fearless moral inventory of ourselves.
5. Admitted to God, to ourselves, and to another human being, the exact nature of our wrongs.
6. Were entirely ready to have God remove all these defects of character.
7. Humbly asked Him to remove our shortcomings.
8. Made a list of all persons we had harmed, and became willing to make amends to them all.
9. Made direct amends to such people wherever possible, except when to do so would injure them or others.
10. Continued to take personal inventory and when we were wrong promptly admitted it.
11. Sought through prayer and meditation to improve our conscious contact with God "as we understood Him," praying only for knowledge of His will for us and the power to carry that out.
12. Having had a spiritual awakening as the result of these steps, we tried to carry this message to alcoholics, and to practice these principles in all our affairs.

These Twelve Steps involve the admission on the part of the alcoholic that he is incapable of handling alcohol, that he has defects, that he has harmed other people and that he must make amends for previous shortcomings. Many of these ideas were adapted from those of the Oxford Movement, to which both the original founders had belonged.

A.A. emphasizes the group approach to therapy. It espouses Twelve Traditions as organizational guides. These Traditions are: [114]

1. Our common welfare should come first; personal recovery depends on A.A. unity.

113. *Alcoholics Anonymous*, New York: Works Publishing Co., 1939, pp. 71–2.
114. Bill, "Twelve Suggested Points for A.A. Tradition," A.A. *Grapevine*, 2 (1946), pp. 2–3.

2. For our group purpose there is but one ultimate authority — a loving God as He may express Himself in our group conscience. Our leaders are but trusted servants; they do not govern.

3. The only requirement for A.A. membership is a desire to stop drinking.

4. Each group should be autonomous except in matters affecting other groups or A.A. as a whole.

5. Each group has but one primary purpose — to carry its message to the alcoholic who still suffers.

6. An A.A. group ought never endorse, finance, or lend the A.A. name to any related facility or private enterprise lest problems of money, property, and prestige divert us from our primary purpose.

7. Every A.A. group ought to be fully self-supporting, declining outside contribution.

8. A.A. should remain forever nonprofessional, but our service centers may employ special workers.

9. A.A., as such, ought never to be organized, but we may create service boards or committees directly responsible to those they serve.

10. A.A. has no opinion on outside issues; hence the A.A. name ought never be drawn into public controversy.

11. Our public relations policy is based on attraction rather than promotion; we need always maintain anonymity at the level of press, radio, and films.

12. Anonymity is the spiritual foundation of our traditions, ever reminding us to place principles before personalities.

Alcoholics Anonymous, as an organization, is the single most effective method yet devised to deal with the problem drinker. It helps resocialize him to a conventional way of life and it provides meaning in his life. In carrying his message to other alcoholics, it constantly confronts him with an image of himself — as he was — and makes new members ("babies") dependent upon him. The important principle that the "sick can lead the sick" has been widely copied and adapted for different purposes. Recovery Incorporated was founded in 1937 to provide discharged mental patients with group support. Narcotics Anonymous was organized in 1950 and various groups oriented toward other problems — obesity, stuttering — have also been formed. One other organization — Al-Anon — should be mentioned. This group, founded unofficially in 1949, is unique in that it includes family members of alcoholics and is designed to help them understand better their common problem — an alcoholic family member. Al-Anon has achieved remarkable growth in its first decade and in 1960 consisted of over 1300 local chapters.[115]

The success of these organizations has not and cannot be evaluated precisely. The reason for this is the anonymity of members and the consequent lack of records for follow-up purposes. A number of small investigations over limited time periods have been attempted. The results of these studies in-

115. Chafetz and Demone, op. cit. pp. 166–71.

dicate that A.A. may be successful in "arresting" the drinking of about half the alcoholics who join the organization. The longer the membership in A.A., the fewer the "slips" and the greater the period of time between relapses. The primary consequence of the A.A. movement, wholly apart from its success in treating alcoholics, has been its role in redefining the status of chronic inebriety — from "deviation" to "illness." In the process of altering public attitudes, A.A. has played a major role in the development of federal and state programs for the study and treatment of "alcoholism as a disease."

SUMMARY

This chapter considered four specific kinds of personal deviations: homicide, suicide, drug addiction, and alcoholism. In each instance, special attention was devoted to definition of the problem, its extent, distribution in the population, etiology, treatment, and prevention.

Homicide and suicide were described as polar opposites. In one, the aggression is directed outward, and in the other, toward the self. It was also noted that whenever the homicide rates are high, suicide rates are low. Two major explanations of homicide and suicide — the psychoanalytic and the sociologic — were discussed. The former emphasizes the individual origins of aggressive impulses and the latter attempts to understand the sociocultural factors which control and channel them. The discussion of homicide also dealt with the role of the victim in precipitating the violence, the methods used in perpetrating the offense, and the disposition of convicted murderers.

The use of narcotics was legal prior to the passage of the Harrison Narcotics Act in 1914. As a consequence of the Harrison Act, the addict, by legal definition, became a criminal deviant. Narcotics addiction was discussed in terms of the numbers and location of addicts; the types, sources, and costs of their drugs; and the medical aspects of addiction. A special section was devoted to an analysis of various methods of treatment and the general lack of success of these procedures. In conclusion, two recommendations to ameliorate the addiction problem were described: to establish clinics to dispense narcotic drugs to addicts; and to make it possible for physicians to prescribe narcotics to patients in his care who are addicts.

Alcoholism was discussed from two points of view — first, the normative problem concerning the use of alcohol itself, and second, the problem of deviation involved in excessive drinking. In discussing the normative problem, a brief historical review of drinking as a moral issue in Western society up to and including the Prohibition movement was presented. The point was made that, with two-thirds of the population favoring the use of alcohol, the problem of dissensus has been largely resolved. Instead, the problem today is one of excessive drinking and its ramifications for crime and other forms of disorganization. Treatment programs of alcoholism such as aversive conditioning, drug therapy, and group therapy were described and evaluated.

QUESTIONS AND SUGGESTIONS FOR FURTHER STUDY

1. Describe the Lindesmith-Dunham typology of criminal deviation.
2. Discuss the differences among the various kinds of homicide.
3. Discuss the extent of murder in the United States and the variations in these rates by age, sex, and race.
4. How similar or different are the victims and perpetrators in homicide?
5. What are the major explanations of homicide?
6. Why is the death penalty invoked less often now than in previous years?
7. Compare and contrast homicide and suicide.
8. What are the major correlates of suicide?
9. Compare the psychoanalytic and sociological approaches to the etiology of suicide.
10. Differentiate the legal and medical definitions of drug addiction.
11. What is the abstinence syndrome?
12. What does the term, narcotic drug, imply in terms of the action of that drug?
13. Why is society concerned about the use of marihuana and not concerned about the use of cigarettes?
14. How many people are known to be drug addicts and what are their characteristics?
15. What proposals have been offered for the amelioration of the drug addiction problem, and how would you evaluate these suggestions?
16. There are actually two aspects to the problem of alcoholism. What are they?
17. Discuss the extent and distribution of drinking behavior in the United States.
18. What is the process of becoming an alcoholic and how long does it usually take?
19. What are the chief methods used in treating alcoholics?

SUGGESTED READINGS

Chafetz, Morris E., and Harold W. Demone, *Alcoholism and Society*, New York: Oxford University Press, 1962. A readable up-to-date analysis of the problems of alcoholism. Contains a fine section on treatment and prevention. Some interesting case histories are presented at the end of the volume.

Drug Addiction: Crime or Disease? Interim and Final Reports of the Joint Committee of the American Bar Association and the American Medical Association on Narcotic Drugs, Bloomington: Indiana University Press, 1961. An excellent and very readable volume on every phase of the narcotics problem. Contains a section on drug laws, regulations, and policies in other countries.

Durkheim, Emile, *Suicide* (trans. by John A. Spaulding and George Simpson), Glencoe: Free Press, 1951. The classic sociological statement about the relationship of social cohesion and suicide.

Henry, Andrew F., and James F. Short, *Suicide and Homicide*, Glencoe: Free Press, 1954. This volume develops a theory about the expression of aggression as homicide or suicide. An attempt to reconcile the psychiatric and sociological viewpoints, buttressed by recent statistical data.

Schneidman, Edwin S., and Norman L. Farberow, *Clues to Suicide*, New York: McGraw-Hill, 1957. A slim volume of articles by experts on every aspect of suicide. Many of the articles are based on clinical considerations in the management, prevention, and treatment of potentially suicidal persons.

Wertham, Frederic, *The Show of Violence*, New York: Doubleday, 1949. A series of case histories of murderers. The dynamics of homicide as seen through the eyes of a psychoanalytically oriented expert.

Wolfgang, Marvin R., *Patterns in Criminal Homicide*, Philadelphia: University of Pennsylvania Press, 1958. This volume contains an analysis of 588 criminal homicides in Philadelphia and develops a theory to explain murder.

Successful and fortunate crime is called virtue
Seneca

At the opposite end of the individual-social continuum of criminal deviation are the career violators. Unlike murderers, suicides, narcotics addicts, alcoholics, and sexual deviants, criminal careerists are interested in making a living out of crime. Their violations are not usually expressions of inner drives, compulsions, and uncontrollable passions, and they are often not malicious, "escapist," or pathological. Rather careerists engage in violational behavior much as law-abiding persons engage in legitimate occupations. To careerists, crime is a vocation that provides them with a living and involves certain risks including arrest and incarceration. As in all occupations, some careerists bring intelligence, resourcefulness, and finesse to their work, while others — by far the majority — are largely inept and unsuccessful.

Career criminals have many characteristics in common.[1] First, they normally are property offenders. Theirs are crimes of gain. They are in the business of crime for a livelihood. As a consequence, the use of force and violence is resorted to only when absolutely necessary. It is one thing to serve a "rap" for a property offense and quite another to add a personal crime sentence to the property violation.

Second, career criminals tend to specialize or pattern their violations. Racketeers do not commit burglary and pickpockets do not "heist" safes. This is no different from specialization in legitimate activities. Criminal *argot* attests to this specialization. In the language of the underworld, "yeggs" are safecrackers, "paperhangers" are forgers, "cannons," "dips," "hooks," and "wires" are pickpockets, and "second story" men are topnotch burglars. Criminal lingo also identifies "boosters," "shills," "heavies," and "con" men. This patterning of criminal activities serves to confer a degree of immunity from arrest, but it also facilitates police activity by providing leads which they might otherwise not have.

Third, criminal specialization requires skill and experience which, as in any other occupation, take years to develop. This is particularly the case with

1. See Walter C. Reckless, *The Crime Problem*, 3rd ed., New York: Appleton-Century-Crofts, 1961, Chaps. 9 and 10, pp. 153–206.

professional criminals — pickpockets, sneak thieves, counterfeiters — and less so with organized and ordinary criminals. This level of skill has to be learned and few can acquire these skills without tutoring by other careerists. Jails, reformatories, and prisons often provide the necessary contacts for learning these skills.

Fourth, career offenders accept a *way of life* which is different from that of most other occupations. Career offenders cannot escape the fact that their liberty and livelihood are constantly in jeopardy. As a result, they are often highly mobile and move from place to place to escape detection and arrest. Career criminals are usually unmarried or divorced and without familial responsibilities. They are suspicious of and isolated from legitimate persons in society. Because of these characteristics, it is difficult to reintegrate career criminals into conventional social and occupational channels.

Fifth, career criminals are characterized by unique backgrounds. The majority come from slum neighborhoods and a large number are from unstable and broken homes. Few complete high school. Most have little or no interest in education or in vocational training. Experiences with the police and courts for truancy, theft, running away from home, and incorrigibility, occur early in their lives. After several such contacts many are placed in industrial schools and become recidivists after release. This progressive involvement in crime and deviant behavior results in occasional arrests and incarceration. By early adulthood, with several "stretches" in institutions, career crime becomes plausible. Given this background, most career criminals continue crime until such time as advancing age, fortuitous circumstances, or perhaps marriage, a family, and a job, result in their rehabilitation. In the Glueck studies, about 88 per cent of ordinary career criminals reverted to illegal activities after imprisonment.

Sixth, as noted above, career criminals are not "sick" people. They do not exhibit glaring emotional disturbances. Their behavior can be explained, if at all, in cultural and social terms. There are some 25,000 or more occupations in the United States, ranging from those which command status and prestige and in which the qualifications are difficult to achieve to those which require little training and offer few rewards. Just as some prepare for the high prestige occupations, so others prepare for criminal involvement.

Three career types of criminal deviation will be discussed in this chapter: ordinary, professional, and organized crime. In addition, a quasi-career type, white collar crime, will be analyzed. Before describing these in detail it should be noted that at least two criteria distinguish ordinary, professional, organized, and white collar crimes and criminals from each other. These are (1) the nature of the criminal deviation itself and (2) the methods used in commiting the offense.

1. *The nature of the crime.* Ordinary offenders, whether members of a group or "lone wolves," specialize in the conventional offenses. These consist principally of robbery (armed or unarmed), burglary, larceny, safecracking, hijacking, forgery, illegal check passing, and also of such rare offenses as kidnapping. Professional criminals specialize in confidence games, pickpocketing, shoplifting, sneak thievery (a professional type of burglary), and counterfeiting. Organized criminals specialize in any activity which can be run as a large-scale business operation. Gambling (numbers games, pools, bookmaking, slot machines), narcotics, vice, bootlegging (in the 'twenties) and business and labor racketeering represent special areas of organized crime. White collar criminals are the least restricted in terms of the nature of their violations. Such offenses as income tax evasion, expense account padding, false advertising and selling, fee-splitting, commercial bribery, the misapplication of funds, violations of antitrust laws, conspiracies to rig the prices of stocks and bonds, and patent and copyright infringements illustrate the wide range of white collar crimes.

2. *The methods used.* The methods of ordinary criminals are crude. Their crimes are highly visible and frequently reported. Professional criminals, on the other hand, avoid force and violence at all costs. They rely instead on manual dexterity, intelligence, and skill. Their approach is "soft" and indirect. As one consequence, professional crimes are less visible and rarely reported to the authorities. Organized or syndicate criminals employ precisely the opposite tactics. Force, violence, and intimidation buttressed by bribery and corruption are used to develop or take over illicit or legitimate activities. The gangster and "torpedo" are the "enforcers" in the system. White collar criminals are the most difficult to categorize. They manipulate, operate, promote, and defraud. Their techniques are mostly illegal extensions and variations of legitimate business practices.

There are other distinctions as well. Ordinary offenders come from the lowest socio-economic stratum of society and are uneducated and unskilled. Professional criminals, while frequently lower class in origin, are also recruited from the middle class. They are better educated, more urbane, and sophisticated. Organized criminals are recruited from the lower class members of various ethnic groups — Italians, Irish, Jews. Organized criminals sometimes simply move into the family "business" when they become part of a syndicate. White collar criminals are different. Almost all are of respectable backgrounds, and if not always of well-to-do families then certainly of families in comfortable economic circumstances. Most attended or graduated from college and almost all are in high status and responsible positions or professions.

ORDINARY CAREER CRIME

Ordinary criminals represent the lowest rung of career crime. They are the least successful, skilled, and sophisticated of career offenders. They do not plan or execute their offenses with the precision of the professional nor are they sufficiently well organized to avoid arrest, conviction, and imprisonment as is often the case with organized criminals. Ordinary criminals populate our prisons and generally are highly recidivous after release. Perhaps as many as half of all prison inmates are of this type. The crimes commited by ordinary property offenders involve repeated thefts which generally net small sums of money.

The following case history illustrates the method by which an ordinary criminal careerist made a living at forgery and theft.[2]

PREVIOUS COURT RECORD

Date	Offense	Court	Disposition
12– 5–35	Stealing	Juvenile, Y., Ohio	Complaint Withdrawn
10–27–39	Viol. Alcohol Bev. Control Act (Misdemeanor)	X. X., Calif.	$50.00 or 25 days
12–29–39	Petty Theft	X. X., Calif.	60 days
5–13–40	Petty Theft	X. X., Calif.	6 months
1–11–41	Petty Theft	X. X., Calif.	Released
11–11–43	Illegally wearing uniform of Captain, U.S. Army	Federal, Y., Ohio	6 mos. & 300.00 fine. Fed. Correctional Inst. Released 4–18–44 on expir. of sentence.
10–11–44	Hold for Navy	Y., Ohio	Paupers' Oath filed
6– 9–47	Failure to Provide	Police	Released to Naval authorities Costs remitted and referred to Prob. Dept. $15.00 a week support

(Defendant has used five aliases.)

A holder is on file by the authorities at B., Ohio on the charge of obtaining money by false pretense. A holder is on file by the U.S. Marshal, Y., Ohio, on the charge of interstate transportation of a stolen motor vehicle.

Offense. Indictment No. xxx (Y., Ohio), concerns a $50 bad check issued by the defendant and cashed by R.J., night club operator, on 1–11–48. Indictment No. xxx concerns a $52.00 bad check issued by the defendant and cashed by the N.Y. Hotel on 1–14–48. Indictment No. xxx concerns a $72.50 bad check issued by the defendant and cashed by the N.Y. Hotel on 1–17–48. Indictment No. xxx

---

2. Condensed from Walter C. Reckless, *The Crime Problem,* 3rd ed., New York: Appleton-Century-Crofts, 1961, pp. 154–9. Reprinted with permission of the publisher.

concerns clothing belonging to C.C., acquired by the defendant and placed in pawn by him. Sometime between 11–10–47 and 11–15–47 Mr. C. gave the defendant some clothes to take to the dry cleaners. Later the defendant returned to C's home during the latter's absence and took out additional clothes. The defendant did not take them to the cleaners as requested, but pawned them instead. The total value of the clothing as indicated in the indictment is $125.00. The defendant admits fully his participation in all of the above offenses. On 3–30–48 the defendant entered a plea of guilty to the charge of forgery and grand larceny and the case was referred to the Probation Department for a preliminary investigation and report.

Mitigating and Aggravating Circumstances. In addition to the above offenses the defendant is involved in other charges not covered by the indictment. On or about 11–29–47 T.S. cashed a $100.00 check issued by the defendant which was dishonored by the bank. This charge was ignored by the grand jury as the complainant was out of town at the time the case was heard and could not testify. On or about 12–20–47 the defendant stole T.S.'s Oldsmobile car and wrecked it. Riding with him at the time of the accident was a show girl by the name of P.D., who was seriously injured, requiring medical care at the S. Hospital. She incurred a bill there of $120.05 which has not been paid. The owner of the other car involved in the accident was J.F., of X., Ohio. It has been reported that the damages to his car amounted to between $611.00 and $724.00. No reply has been received to a letter addressed to this man concerning the bill and it is possible that some insurance company made good his loss. Following the accident, the defendant sold the wrecked car to B.A., in B., Ohio. Mr. A is connected with the O. Garage in that city. A holder by the authorities at B. concerns this fraudulent transaction. The holder filed by the U.S. Marshal concerns the theft of a 1946 Plymouth Sedan from W., N.Y. on 10–18–47. The car was recovered in Y., Ohio and claimed by the X. Fire Insurance Company. The defendant admits that he had this car in his possession for about four weeks, having been loaned to him by a friend who was taking a vacation in Florida. With the exception of the last named alleged offense the defendant admits the facts as outlined concerning all of the others. In connection with the theft of the Oldsmobile, the Y. Guarantee and Fidelity Company paid a claim of $3000.00 to the owner. Through the sale of the wrecked car, of which they took possession, the insurance company realized $800.00 which leaves the sum of $2200.00 as the net amount of their loss. The following represents the various amounts of restitution to be considered:

Name	Amount
R.J.	$ 50.00
N.Y. Hotel	124.50
T.S.	100.00
Y. Guarantee and Fidelity Company	2200.00
B.A.	1000.00
S. Hospital	120.05
C.C.	125.00

The U.S. Secret Service has on file two one-hundred dollar checks which the defendant acquired by intercepting his former wife's mail. The defendant got hold of these checks, forged and cashed them and used the proceeds for his own benefit. The U.S. Secret Service Agent advises that the government will not initiate prosecution on these checks as the defendant and his wife were not divorced at that time, although they were separated.

ANALYSIS OF ENVIRONMENT

Personal History. The defendant was born 8–5–19 in S., Indiana and has been a resident of Y., Ohio for 17 years. The defendant was married but is divorced and is the father of two minor children.

Education and Early Life. The defendant attended schools in Y. He graduated from the B.R. school. The defendant also claims that he attended the University of X.X., Cal. for a period of one year in 1939 but his former wife advises that she doubts very much if this is true. The defendant is the son of Italian-born parents who are now divorced. During the defendant's early years there was considerable domestic trouble in the home and the parents separated frequently. The father is said to have exercised rigid discipline, whereas the mother was said to be more lenient. There is nothing to indicate that the family has not always been in satisfactory financial circumstances and they have had very little contact with social agencies in this city.

Family and Neighborhood. The defendant's father, age 62, is a native of Italy and came to the United States in 1916. He operates a tailor and dry cleaning shop. The father was interviewed and implied that there was nothing that he could do to assist the defendant. He indicated that a penal sentence might be the best thing for the defendant. The mother, age 48, is also a native of Italy and came to the United States in 1906. She has had an 8th grade education. She has been employed for years as a tailoress and works at the present time at the C. Clothing Company. The parents were divorced in 1943 and the mother has married T.W., age 60. They were married in 1945 and he has been employed for many years as a clerk at the Postal Annex. The mother and stepfather occupy a very comfortable home at X. Avenue. The mother was interviewed and, although she asked that the defendant be given favorable consideration, she had no constructive suggestions to make in regard to the future. The defendant has one sister, B.L., age 30, who is said to be connected with a night club in D., Florida. The defendant married R.J., age 23, in 1941. She is a native and life resident of Y., Ohio. They have been separated since he returned from the service and were divorced in October, 1947. Since the marriage the wife has lived mostly with her people at X. Street and has been considerably dependent upon them. There are two children, a son, born 9–22–41, and a daughter, born 1–6–44, who are in the care of the defendant's former wife. The wife seemed to be a very nice person and was able to discuss the defendant in a dispassionate manner. With the exception of the period when the defendant was in the service and she was receiving regular allotment checks, he has never done very much in regard to supporting the family. Although the defendant gives his home address as that of his mother, he has not actually lived there for more than a total of one month since his discharge from the Navy. He has been traveling about the country a great deal, living well from the proceeds of fraudulent transactions.

Industrial History. The defendant's record of legitimate employment is practically non-existent. For a period of two weeks in the early part of 1947 he was employed by the K. I. Collection Agency. Although the defendant had the opportunity to work into a very good job, Mr. *I* advised that the defendant started pilfering small sums of money almost immediately. Moreover, Mr. *I* had cashed one of the $100.00 checks mentioned in connection with the Secret Service and was out this amount of money. The only other employment the defendant has had was with various book-making establishments and for a period he claims as a professional boxer on the West Coast. His former wife states that she does not know of any legitimate employment that the defendant has had since she has married him. It does not seem likely that the defendant could be induced to settle down to the regularity of a legitimate and steady job.

ANALYSIS OF PERSONALITY

Physical and Mental. The defendant is a 28 year-old white man who measures 5′ 7½″ in height and weighs 165 lbs. The jail physician reports that an examination discloses that the defendant is in satisfactory physical condition. The defendant advises that he is in good health and that the only defect he has is poor vision in one eye. No psychiatric examination has been made and there is no indication that the defendant has ever been given a psychometric test. He appears to be an individual of normal intelligence.

Character and Conduct. The defendant advises that he drinks only moderately and none of the persons interviewed have disclosed otherwise. The defendant admits gambling to excess and there is reason to believe that this tendency is a contributing cause. He denies any sex irregularities and states he has never had a venereal infection. The defendant is of Catholic faith but attends church only occasionally. The defendant is a dynamic individual who has the earmarks of becoming an accomplished confidence man if his fast-moving career is not brought to a halt. He has a record of arrests for rather serious offenses dating back to 1939. He has run up a formidable series of escapades recently in a relatively short period of time. The defendant has a tendency to frequent night spots and represent himself as being widely acquainted with people and places and this probably indicates a desire on his part to be lionized. His philosophy seems to be come-easy and go-easy and if he were as diligent in legitimate employment as he is in unlawful activities he could probably be eminently successful. The defendant appears to be crafty, erratic, contemptuous of the rights of others, and scornful of lawful authority. At the present time he seems to find it expedient to be resigned to the inevitability of a penal sentence. He is deferential when interviewed and has apparently not falsified information unduly. Some of his exploits have been characterized by considerable ingenuity and effrontery. For instance in W., N.Y., he is reported to have stolen the luggage of a man from Bermuda by the name of R. Having R's papers in his possession he learned that this man's father was a prominent banker in Bermuda. Representing himself as the owner of the baggage, the defendant wired the banker for several hundred dollars, with instructions that it be sent in care of an attorney. It was the defendant's intention then to represent himself as the attorney. When arrested in S., Ohio the defendant had this baggage in his possession and at first tried to identify himself to the police as R. Another incident which would illustrate the defendant's audacity is reported to have occurred in X., Ohio. In this instance he represented himself to the manager of a theatre as Lieutenant Jones of the Vice Squad of the X., Ohio

Police. By means of this subterfuge the defendant is said to have obtained $30.00 from the manager for the purpose of betting on the horses, the defendant claiming that he had certain connections. When the defendant brought to the manager a check for $300.00 representing winnings and he suggested that he split with the defendant, the manager failed to cooperate previous to clearance of the check. On his second visit to the manager, the defendant had race results with him showing horses which would have won $300.00 on the amount bet. In addition to the instances in which he has victimized others, it is obvious that he had failed to meet his obligation in regard to his children and has actually defrauded his family of money of which they were in need.

The persistence of ordinary offenders in crime is demonstrated in the case history of a burglary which follows. This offender developed an interesting *modus operandi* in the course of his very long history of criminal activity.[3]

Edward Henry Wheeler, convicted burglar who two weeks ago began a new Ohio Penitentiary sentence, admitted stealing an estimated $100,000 worth of loot from about 2000 apartments in an 18-month cross-country spree.

Sentenced this time on charges of jailbreak, larceny and breaking and entering in the night season, Wheeler, 37, has detainers awaiting his release in Columbus; Baton Rouge, La.; Memphis, Tenn.; Mobile, Ala., and Cleveland.

Detectives here said they have received an estimated 100 inquiries about Wheeler from cities throughout the country.

Wheeler, who has a long police record, told Columbus detectives he began traveling about the country burglarizing apartments after his latest release from confinement in February, 1961.

According to detectives who questioned Wheeler:

His "working" hours were from about 10 a.m. until 4 p.m. He would seek out "nice" apartments where he found mail in mailboxes indicating no one was at home.

At each apartment he would ring the doorbell or knock loudly at the door. If someone answered, Wheeler would pretend to be looking for a friend's apartment.

If no one answered, he would go to work with a plastic ruler which he could usually slip between the door and the door frame to trip the lock.

Once inside, Wheeler said he would take anything he thought he could pawn or take to an auction to sell.

Wheeler told detectives he always burglarized apartments because he felt there were good chances no one would be home, since many men and wives living in apartments both work.

Wheeler's police record dates back to 1940 when he was sentenced to Boys Industrial School on 23 charges of burglary and petty larceny and one of auto theft. He has served previous prison sentences in Ohio, Arizona and Tennessee, records show.

Although this burglar showed some ingenuity, his criminal pattern cannot compare with the professional criminal's approach to the same type of crime. The latter will be described in the section which follows.

3. *Columbus Evening Dispatch*, August 21, 1962, p. 1.

PROFESSIONAL CRIME

Professional criminals are aristocrats among criminal entrepreneurs. Professionals are accorded great prestige by other offenders pincipally because of their ability to steal considerable sums of money while avoiding arrest and imprisonment. This does not mean that professionals are never apprehended or imprisoned. It does mean that they have developed techniques which, for the most part, keep them out of prison. These techniques and methods include putting in a "fix" before a crime is committed; reimbursing their victims, if necessary, to prevent them from complaining to the police; and using ingenious procedures in committing offenses.

Professional criminals differ from other careerists and especially from ordinary criminals in several ways. First, they are more skilled. Second, they shun violence and strong-arm methods. Third, they are better educated, more urbane, and from better family and economic backgrounds. Many held skilled and white collar employment before gravitating to, or being recruited into, professional criminality. The case of a master jewel thief which follows illustrates these points. It also indicates the specialized nature of professional crime and some of the characteristics of this exceptionally successful and currently rehabilitated offender: [4]

Arthur Barry was an incomparable second-story man. . . . Second-story men are not often in the news today, but there was a time when they were aristocrats among thieves and when Barry himself was a king. There are elderly detectives still active today who regard him as the greatest jewel thief who ever lived. In the 1920's Barry "collections" were valued somewhere between $5 and $10 million. He rarely robbed anyone who was not in the Social Register, his manners were impeccable and his working uniform was often a tuxedo. He seldom carried a gun or a knife, never indulged in violence and almost invariably left a favorable impression upon his victims, whom he called clients.

Barry attributed his downfall in the main to simple physiological mischance; he matured too early and was full-grown at 13. The companions he sought out were of his own size but considerably older, and in his efforts to ingratiate himself with his elders he presently found himself running errands for some "sinful" people. One of these was a "peteman," in the language of the trade, a master safecracker named Lowell Jack, who was then in semiretirement and made his living by manufacturing special tools and nitroglycerin. Lowell Jack had no difficulty making the nitroglycerin: he simply heated dynamite and water in a bucket on the kitchen stove and bottled the essence. But he needed a good delivery boy who would not drop the stuff in a public place and damage a number of bystanders. He employed young Barry, at $4 or $5 per delivery, and sent him on trains to other New England cities. Barry did just as he was told and soon be-

4. Robert Wallace, "Confessions of a Master Jewel Thief," *Life* (March 12, 1956), pp. 121–36. Copyright © 1956 Time, Inc. Condensed and reprinted with permission of the publisher.

came a trusted member of the small-time Worcester underworld. As he rode from city to city, a quiet, manly youngster of 14 in knickers, with his bottle of nitroglycerin in a cotton-filled suitcase between his knees, he was the perfect picture of the noble lad of whom people say, "If we only had more fine boys like this one."

Barry committed his first burglary at 15, a small job that netted him less than $100 but a thoughtful and deft one all the same. His victims were a middle-aged couple who ran a dry goods store and brought the day's receipts home with them each evening, there being no night depositories at the Worcester banks in those days. For several days before the robbery, while the couple was at work, Barry entered their house through an unlocked window and prowled about, looking for a place where, if he were a middle-aged man who ran a dry goods store, he would hide the money. Eventually he found it, an empty desk drawer that seemed to have the smell of cash lingering in it. On the night of the burglary he entered the house through the same unlocked window, tiptoed directly to the drawer, removed the money and tiptoed out.

"No, I was not frightened," he says. "If they had awakened, the advantage would have been all mine. I was wide awake, they were groggy. I knew what was behind every door as well as they did. I could have been halfway down the block before they got organized." Careful preparation and a fine grasp of the probabilities were Barry's greatest business assets. They made violence unnecessary.

Barry committed a number of other minor burglaries during his formative years, then interrupted his career to serve in the Army in World War I. He was wounded in action and recommended for a Silver Star, but went AWOL before he could get it. After the war he settled in New York. It had never seriously occurred to him to follow any honest profession; his problem was merely to decide what kind of thief he would be. Safecracking and bank robbery did not appeal to him, and ordinary burglary and holdups struck him as unprofitable and somehow disreputable. Although he had only a high school education, Barry was a polished individual, a good conversationalist and something of a dandy. There was only one specialty that seemed appropriate for him: jewel theft.

Jewel theft was attractive because of the ease with which, in the 1920's in New York, a thief could dispose of his loot. "Why," Barry says, "there were fences in those days who could have got rid of the Statue of Liberty. Sometimes they had to send the big, recognizable jewels to Amsterdam to have them recut, but not often. I do remember that they once sent over a big emerald of mine, the size of a walnut, and some thief in Amsterdam stole it. But usually they were very reliable." At that time it was also possible for fences, many of whom operated as "private detective agencies," to deal directly with insurance companies. "They'd go to the company, say they had accidentally found the jewels in a hollow tree, and sell them to the company for 10% or 20% of the insured value. This was better than a total loss for the company."

Having decided what to steal, Barry had only to decide whom to steal it from. "I noticed that a lot of wealthy women who came into New York shopping used to wind up their afternoons at the casino up in Central Park. So I'd go up there myself to look them over. When I spotted a woman who had plenty of diamonds on her, I'd follow her out to her limousine and take the license number. Then all I had to do was go to the nearest phone, call up the police traffic bureau and say, "This is Patrolman Schultz, badge number 465786. I've got an accident up here, and I need the name and address of a Cadillac sedan, New York plate number XYZ-123! The traffic bureau never took the time to check on Patrolman Schultz. They'd simply give me the name and address."

Barry also selected his victims from the society columns, paying particular attention to announcements of wedding and engagement parties in the estate section on the North Shore of Long Island, his favorite hunting ground. On the afternoon of a party he would drive out to the Island, park his car near the estate in question and change into formal clothes. Then he would crash the party. Lawn parties were particularly easy for him since he had only to climb unnoticed over a wall or through a hedge, pick up a drink and canapé from a passing waiter and mingle with the guests. Thereafter it was easy for him to get into the house, wander upstairs and make a mental sketch of the floor plan. Often he was able to enter the master bedroom and locate likely hiding places for jewelry, although on such preliminary forays he never stole anything. Sometimes he unlocked a half-dozen windows in strategic spots, hoping that they would remain unlocked for a day or two, and occasionally he cut off the burglar alarm system. If he was discovered wandering about the house, he pretended to be a drunk looking for a place to lie down. No one ever challenged him. His stage presence was faultless, his taste in clothes excellent and his grammar good enough to fool the King of England — which, as a matter of fact, it did, at a time when Edward VIII was Prince of Wales.

Barry encountered the prince on an evening at a speakeasy on 59th Street and made a very favorable impression on him. They had several drinks in the course of two or three hours, during which the prince chatted gaily and perhaps a little too informatively. A few days later, early on the morning of Sept. 9, 1924, a thief entered the home of Mrs. Joshua Cosden at Sands Point, Long Island and made off with $150,000 worth of jewels, including some which belonged to guests of the Cosdens, the prince's cousin, Lord Louis Mountbatten, and his wife. It was almost as though someone in the vulgar phrase, had fingered the job.

The proceeds of a $150,000 robbery could not support Barry in the style to which he was accustomed for long. He could sell only the most valuable jewels and for only a fraction of their worth. His usual procedure was to break up the compound pieces, such as necklaces, pins and brooches, at once and throw away the gold and platinum settings and the smaller stones. The safest depository for these, he decided, was New York Bay. He was a frequent passenger on ferryboats, a fine-looking gentleman standing by the rail flicking what appeared to be cigaret ashes into the water.

Because his cash realizations were low in relation to the value of what he stole, Barry was obliged to make numerous business trips to the suburbs. After the Cosden affair he paid a call at the home of a Social Registerite named John C. Greenleaf of Hewlett Bay Park, Long Island, and took $10,000 worth of jewels. He had also stopped at the residence of Mr. Harold E. Talbott, who would some day become President Eisenhower's Secretary of the Air Force, and took $23,000 worth. Because he knew that Major Tommy Hitchcock, the polo player, was a man of substance, Barry visited him as well but got away with jewelry worth only $900. As he examined it during his getaway, Barry was so miffed that he threw much of it into a brook.

Despite occasional disappointments of this sort, Barry did well during the mid-'20's, averaging about a half a million dollars in thefts per year. He extended his territory up into Dutchess County in New York and in that area in 1926 he performed a feat that aroused real awe in police circles. Having discovered that the master and mistress of a large estate kept their jewelry in a 150-pound safe in their bedroom closet, Barry climbed into the bedroom on a ladder, tiptoed to the closet and silently hoisted the safe on his shoulder, (although he stands only 5 feet 8 inches, Barry was and still is a man of astonishing physical strength). Without a sound he withdrew the way he had come.

Silence and deftness also characterized the great Hotel Plaza robbery on Sept. 30, 1925, in which jewelry valued at $750,000 disappeared in broad daylight from the six-room suite of Mrs. James P. Donahue, daughter of F. W. Woolworth. Among the objects stolen were a 10-carat diamond ring worth more than $50,000 and a rope of pearls valued at $450,000. These were taken from a dressing table in Mrs. Donahue's bedroom while she sat in a tub in a bathroom only a few feet away. A maid was in a nearby room and a masseuse in another. No one heard a sound. No arrest was ever made for the theft and the jewels were recovered by an insurance detective not long afterward and returned to the police. "Whoever took those pearls," a police captain remarked at the time, "really knew what he was doing. There were five ropes in the drawer, four imitations and the real one. The imitations were good enough to fool an oyster."

"The easy way to tell a real pearl from an imitation," Barry says with a reflective smile, "is to rub it gently across your teeth. A real pearl produces a somewhat grating, sandpapery sensation, but a fake is smooth and slippery."

The only one of his 150 major thefts for which Barry was prosecuted, convicted and jailed was the stealing of some $100,000 in jewelry from the late Jesse Livermore, the Wall Street operator, whose summer home was in Kings Point, Long Island. It took place early in the morning of May 29, 1927, and was a double-headed operation: the Livermores had some house guests at the time and Barry robbed them too.

During the Livermore burglary, as in many others in which he could not handle all the details by himself, Barry had an accomplice, a strongarm named "Boston Bill" Monaghan. Barry did the thinking and talking while Monaghan stood ready to take care of anyone who interrupted the proceedings.

It was not a professional blunder that brought about his arrest but, as he supposes today, a woman. Although he was married, Barry was a formidable ladies' man. "That's where all the money went," he explains.

Barry suspects that one of his girls, in a fit of monogamous jealousy, went to the police and told them that he had committed the Livermore burglary. At any rate someone did, and he was arrested by a platoon of cops at the railroad station at Ronkonkoma, Long Island, at 7:30 o'clock on a summer Sunday evening. He was sentenced to 25 years in Auburn Prison.

As he began his sentence Barry was 31 years old and might have been released on parole, if he had behaved well, at the age of 47 or 48. But he did not behave well. On July 28, 1929 he shot his way out of Auburn in one of the boldest, wildest jailbreaks in U.S. prison history.

For more than three years Barry was a successful fugitive. He made his way south to New York, then to New Jersey, where he settled in a small town not far from Flemington. His wife joined him there. He took the name of a man he had once known, James Toner, and became a salesman of windshield wipers. He committed no more burglaries, kept the peace admirably and attracted no attention. But on the night of Oct. 22, 1932, there came the inevitable pounding on his door.

"Do you know what it was?" he says indignantly. "The Lindbergh kidnapping. The cops and the FBI had been going through every town near Flemington checking the background of every new resident. They weren't even looking for me."

For a time Barry was the prime suspect in the Lindbergh case and in a half-dozen other major crimes that had taken place during his vacation from Auburn. But after examining Barry closely, Dr. J. F. ("Jafsie") Condon, the celebrated middleman in the kidnapping, announced firmly that Barry was not the man to whom he had given the ransom money.

"Police chiefs from all over the place came to question me," Barry says, "including a nice guy from Greenwich, Conn. He figured I must have robbed the Percy Rockefeller house in his town in 1926 and he wanted to know how I did it. Of course I told him I didn't know a thing about it, and he said, 'Now look, Arthur. We're alone in the room. I'm not saying you did it or didn't do it. But let me tell you about it. That house is surrounded by a big stone wall, and between the wall and the house there are two of the toughest watchdogs you ever saw. I went out there with a couple of detectives and we tried to go over the wall, just to see if it was possible, and the dogs damned near killed us. Now if you were going to get into a place like that, what would you do?' "

"I told the chief it was all confidential and hypothetical, and then I said I'd try horsemeat. Throw it over the wall and see what happened.

"And then I said that if the dogs didn't like horsemeat, if they were sophisticated dogs, I'd try steaks. And if this didn't work either, I'd try something else. By this time the chief was hopping up and down in his chair. 'What?' he says. 'WHAT would you try? I've been busting my brains over this for six years.'

"Well, I said, if I were going to commit a dastardly crime like that, I'd go to a kennel and I'd buy a female dog in heat. Then I'd tie a rope around her collar, tie the other end to a tree outside the wall, and I'd lower her over the wall. After about five minutes I'd climb over the wall myself, walk into the house and steal $20,000 worth of jewelry. On the way out, so there wouldn't be any evidence, I'd pull my dog up over the wall after me, and drive back to New York.

"I thought the chief was going to die, but after a while he stopped laughing and said he would send me a box of cigars after I got back to jail. I got them an hour later."

Barry spent the next 17 years in jail, most of them in Attica Prison in New York and five of them in solitary confinement as punishment for his escape. Upon his release in 1959 he went home to Worcester and got a job with a boyhood friend who operates a chain of four restaurants. During the period of his parole, one of his chores involved collecting the receipts from all four restaurants and carrying them unguarded to the bank. "I never thought I would live to see the day," a Worcester policeman recently remarked, "but I have seen it, and there's no doubt of it. He's an honest man." Barry is not only honorably employed but has some active extracurricular interests as well. Recently, with the members having full knowledge of his past, he was elected commander of a local veterans' organization.

Criteria of the profession of theft. As the preceding case illustrates and as Sutherland initially suggested, professional criminals — regardless of specialty — have five characteristics in common. These are: skill, status, consensus, differential association, and organization.[5] The criterion of *skill* is obvious and includes not only proficiency in the theft itself but also in planning the offense, leaving the scene of the crime, disposing of the stolen property, and having the necessary contacts and acumen to "fix" the whole affair. The concept of *status* involves the idea that one becomes a professional thief only when one is recognized as such by other professionals. This is not unique since baseball players, for example, speak of "pros" and of "bushers," or journeymen ball players who have not yet made the "big leagues." In other professions, as well, the granting of status is by common agreement as indicated by such terms as a lawyer's lawyer or a teacher's teacher. By *consensus*, Sutherland meant that professional thieves share common values, beliefs, attitudes, hostilities, symbols, and loyalties. Their attitudes toward life, criminality, the police and legal machinery, and their victims are derived from commonly shared values and rationalizations. In short, professional thieves have developed and perpetuate a subculture which is different from that of legitimate society and from that of other types of offenders. This consensus is partly responsible for their continuation in criminal behavior.

As in the case of any value system, the professional criminal's values are learned through *differential association.* The concept of differential association implies systematic interaction with other deviants and a relative lack of interpersonal relationships with law-abiding persons. Professionals isolate themselves from conventional society except to use the services of legitimate persons as necessary adjuncts to their criminal careers. They may have a few personal friends and acquaintances who are law-abiding but in the main restrict their interrelationships to those who share their way of life.

Few professional criminals can survive as "lone wolves." Most, therefore, develop the rudiments of *organization*, embracing confederacy and partnership. The organization of professional criminals, however, is much less structured, demanding, and permanent than that of organized crime. The basis for the survival of professionals is their skill, while that of organized criminals lies in the nature of the organization. The professional thief is like a successful small business entrepreneur; the organized criminal similar to an executive in an industrial enterprise.

Types of professional criminals. The many varieties of professional theft include the confidence game; pickpocketing; shoplifting; sneak thievery (from

5. Edwin H. Sutherland, *The Professional Thief,* Chicago: University of Chicago Press, 1937.

stores and offices); "pennyweighting" (stealing by substitution of cheap articles for expensive ones); professional gambling; passing of illegal checks, money orders, and other negotiable securities (paperhanging); counterfeiting; and professional extortion ("badger" games and others).[6] All of these types, with the possible exception of counterfeiting, can also be engaged in by non-professional criminals, amateurs, and even delinquents. The difference, of course, is in the *modus operandi* — the method of operation — of the professional criminal.

The "con" game. The confidence game stands at the zenith of criminal behavior and the confidence man is the most highly respected of all professional criminals. The "take" is large and perhaps as many as 90 per cent of the victims or "marks" are too embarrassed by their own cupidity or too deeply implicated in the crime itself to complain to the police. Even when complaints do occur, the charge is usually grand larceny and the sentence fairly light. Maurer estimates that a confidence mob operating in the Denver area during the years 1919–21 fleeced 190 victims of nearly $4.25 million. The largest individual loss was $45,000 and the smallest was $5000. Known victims came from as far away as England.[7]

"Yellow Kid" Weil who, by his own account, swindled victims out of some $8 million and served only one five-year sentence in prison, has stated the rationale underlying all confidence games: [8]

The men I fleeced were basically no more honest than I was. One of the motivating factors in my action was, of course, the desire to acquire money. The other motive was a lust for adventure. The men I swindled were also motivated by a desire to acquire money, and they didn't care at whose expense they got it. I was particular. I took money only from those who could afford it and were willing to go in with me in schemes they fancied would fleece others.

Classic "big con" games proceed through a series of steps or stages culminating in the swindling of the victim. In such historically famous games as the "rag" (stocks and bonds), the "wire" (racing) and the "payoff" (also a racing swindle) which developed around the turn of the century, the unfolding of the swindle followed these steps: [9]

1. Locate and investigate a well-to-do victim (Putting the mark up).
2. Gain the victim's confidence (Playing the con for him).
3. Show the victim how he can make a large sum of money illegally (Telling him the tale).

6. Ibid. p. 43.
7. David W. Maurer, *The Big Con: The Story of the Confidence Man*, New York: Pocket Books, 1940, pp. 133–5.
8. Joseph R. Weil and William T. Brannon, *"Yellow Kid" Weil*, Chicago: Ziff-Davis, 1948, p. 293.
9. Maurer, op. cit. pp. 3–4.

4. Let the victim win some money (Giving him the convincer).
5. Determine how much money the victim will "invest" (Giving him the break-down).
6. Play him against a big store (fake gambling establishment or stock brokerage house) and fleece him (Taking off the touch).
7. Get rid of victim (Blowing him off).
8. Prevent or forestall action by the law (Putting in the fix).

Traditional "con" games involving a fake establishment set up for the purpose of swindling victims are no longer important. In fact, although the principles still apply, con games presently operate without much parapher-nalia. An effective yet relatively simple "con" game, which bilked "get rich quick investors" of an estimated $15 million, is the famous Charles Ponzi swindle described below: [10]

One of the oldest swindles known to man is that of paying high dividends or interest to early investors with the money of late comers, and skipping other busi-ness operations completely. The effectiveness of this sham was demonstrated in the early 1920's by Charles "Get Rich Quick" Ponzi. Mr. Ponzi, a dapper little man who sported a cane and cocky smile, took in some $15 million in less than a year on the simple promise to make Boston folks rich. He wooed money-happy secretaries and workers with a slogan of "50% return in 40 days, double your money in 90."

While a $15-a-week stock boy at an export concern, the Italian-born Mr. Ponzi noted that a postal reply coupon bought in Spain at one cent was redeemable in the U.S. for a nickel. Mr. Ponzi maintained that he could convert these coupons, designed to provide return postage when a letter-writer desired a reply, into cash. He solicited $250 from friends, returned them $375 in a few days and the swindle was on. The natural flow of such breathless investment possibilities was helped along by hired agents who spread the word.

By the spring of 1920, he was taking in $250,000 a day from eager investors. In less than a year, he collected an estimated $15 million and became the best known financial figure in the nation. The exact amount of his take was not known, since he kept no books.

Mr. Ponzi's dealing in postal coupons was only for a short time and the amount was not great. It was simpler to pay off early investors with the funds of later ones. In the span of a few months, he discarded the gear of a $15-a-week clerk for an estate, which he furnished at a cost of $500,000, a custom blue limousine and a cellar of fine wines. He also bought the brokerage firm that had employed him as a stock boy three years before.

The Boston Post lit a fuse under Mr. Ponzi when it confronted him and the public with the fact that the entire issue of postal reply coupons over the prior six years totaled only about $1 million; Mr. Ponzi supposedly had accumulated close to $15 million worth in a few months. In August, Montreal police identified

10. Kenneth Slocum, "Master Swindlers: Estes Case Recalls Great Swindles of Past," *The Wall Street Journal*, May 23, 1962, p. 12. Copyright © 1962 by Dow Jones & Company, Inc., and reprinted with their permission.

him as an ex-convict sentenced on a forgery charge, and Federal agents seized him a short time later.

Indicted on 86 counts of larceny and mail fraud, he was convicted and served about 10 years. From his jail cell, he sent Christmas cards to his victims with the wish that the "recent miscarriage of your investment should not mar the spirit of the Christmas season." Among letters he received in return was money which people asked him to invest on their behalf. He was deported to Italy after his jail term. In 1949, partially blind and paralyzed, he died in a hospital charity ward.

"Con" games and professional thefts of all types change with the times. Technological change put an end to many of the standard confidence games and, at the same time, introduced modern variations such as that exemplified by the "golf larceny" swindle which follows: [11]

The gentle arts of the confidence game, which thrives on prosperity and the element of larceny deep in most human souls, are enjoying a renaissance today against a most unlikely backdrop — the clubhouses and greens of the nation's golf course. In the years since World War II its polite and well-dressed practitioners have proved, beyond any reasonable doubt, that there is no safer and more effective method of separating a sucker from his money than inveigling him into a friendly game of golf.

Although his motives are as shady as those of a three-card monte dealer, the golf hustler operates in surroundings which reek with respectability. Unlike the oldtime con man, he needs no police protection. He incurs none of the expense that goes with setting up the "big store," the con man's once-essential front which used to take such forms as a complete but entirely phony brokerage office, a sham Western Union shop or a bogus bookie joint populated by stooges going through the motions of betting huge sums. Today's "big store" is the golf course itself.

Golf hustling all stems from the flaw in human nature which made old con game victims jump at a dishonest stock or horse-betting deal. The human urge to get in on something good, especially if it is slightly illegal, is the basis for all confidence work. The "mark," as a victim is known, is made to think he is getting away with something while actually he is being deftly mulcted of his money. In golf the mark is allowed to think that he is getting away with lying about his handicap when he makes a bet on a game.

Successful golf hustlers all have one distinguishing characteristic. They wear a deep, uniform tan. Among themselves they joke about being "too tan" for one another and refer to their victims, especially at winter resorts in the South, as "palefaces." Even the lowest-grade hustler, roping his prey on the public links, would blush through his sunburn if he failed to average at least $50 a day. The elite of the profession, who mix with millionaires and belong to the very best clubs, sometimes take in more in a single day than their lowly colleagues do in an entire year.

They work deftly and in a variety of ways, carefully setting up their victims for the kill. By the time the hustler and his victim go off the first tee, the gullible mark is sure that he has made a shrewd bet, and the hustler works diligently to preserve this illusion. By regulating his game to that of the victim, he creates the

11. Marshall Smith, "Larceny on the Links," *Life* (March 26, 1956), pp. 141–52. Condensed and reprinted courtesy *Life* Magazine. Copyright © 1956 Time, Inc.

impression of a close match that persists to the very last putt. "If you win by more than one stroke, you lose them," explains one hustler.

When the match is over, the mark feels he has lost only because of a missed putt or what the sympathetic hustler describes as "the rub of the green." The bit is administered so artfully that thousands of marks are running loose on U.S. golf courses without even knowing they have been bitten.

The first great hustlers to take advantage of the palefaces appeared in 1930. A man of pleasing personality, LaVerne Moore, alias John Montague, on the lam from Syracuse, set up headquarters in a Los Angeles rooming house and began working the public courses. Almost simultaneously Alvin Clarence Thomas, alias Titanic Thompson, also turned his creative genius against unsuspecting golfers.

Titanic Thompson was the more diversified and ingenious. Tall, handsome and quick with a story, he considered well-to-do Texans his special prey. Sometimes he would spend weeks fattening them up for the kill. He gave them the "convincer," allowing his marks to win a few matches for modest stakes, but even during such periods Ti worked skillfully at winning back his bait. He would bet that he could bounce a golf ball into a water glass (a trick he practiced by the hour) or guess the weight of a hat-check girl (which he had carefully ascertained the day before). He regaled his victims with funny stories, bemoaned his own golf game and kept saying, "I've got to get even."

At just the right moment he began getting even. Each day the stakes would get higher and the more he won the more merciless he became. When the groggy victim had been taken for just about all he was worth, Titanic had a final trick for squeezing still more out of him. "I'm a fair man," he would say condescendingly. "I'll play you left-handed — double or nothing."

When he had won this too, being a natural southpaw, he moved on to another course. He drove Cadillacs and wore pearl-handled pistols which could be seen protruding from his hip pockets on the putting green.

The great upsurge of the golf con on a nationwide scale began immediately after the war. It rode the coattails of the business boom and the openhanded prosperity that came with it. Some fine "touches" were taken off in this buoyant era. The owner of a Florida newspaper was conned so successfully that he sold his paper to get more money to bet—and lost that too. Several gullible members of the Westchester Country Club were taken for a sum totaling almost $400,000.

There is ham in every good hustler, and it pays dividends. In Miami a paleface from Philadelphia dropped $1600 but was so hoodwinked by the hustler's fine performance that he was back the next day looking for more "action." Another has been getting cut up two or three times a week for several years. He is the pet mark of a strawberry-blond lady hustler. This willingness to be taken again and again simply bears out the old confidence game maxim, "You can't knock a good mark."

Many con routines require a special kind of acting. The Whisky Drinker keeps swigging from a bottle in his golf bag, growing more congenial and unsteady on his feet with every swig. At the end of nine holes he tipsily demands that all bets be doubled and seldom encounters much resistance, for who is to guess that the amber "Scotch" in the bottle is actually tea? The Invalid who excites larceny in a victim with a limp and talk of a bad back always manages to survive the painful ordeal and win by one stroke. Charlie the Blade's specialty is playing with only one club, a four iron. An operator out of Kansas City stimulates curiosity and cupidity by offering to play sitting in a chair or, better yet, on one foot. In Jacksonville one day this expert fired a brilliant 71 with one foot off the ground to win a $1000 bet.

Golf's con men, like all craftsmen, are highly stratified. The brothers who pull gang jobs and cheap tricksters like the Whiskey Drinker constitute the lowest order. They are viewed by members of the next level with the same fine contempt bankers show for pawnshop brokers. That level, in turn, is tolerated but not accepted by the highest order of hustlers who, of course, are members in good standing of the very swankiest country clubs.

The highest order of hustlers operates in exclusive elegance in such places as Palm Beach, Fla. and Palm Springs, Calif. Its members cannot be distinguished from those they prey on except that they have no visible source of income but golf winnings. They blend into the surroundings by impersonating casual and relaxed golfers and are basically just good gamblers, inside the clubhouse and out. They stoop to no cheap tricks such as improving bad lies and have no cheap lines of chatter. They do not even have to be championship golfers, but they seldom lose.

The biggest and most dramatic exchange of currency at golf's upper level took place at White Sulphur Springs, W. Va. four years ago. A rich oilman played one hole for $100,000 and lost by three-putting. But that was only a portion of the bundle he dropped in one disastrous week. When he settled up he sat behind a card table in a hotel room with close to half a million dollars in cash stacked before him in neat piles. He dispensed it with complete calm, saying, "Here's yours" as he handed $130,000 to one hustler, $80,000 to another, and so on. "I don't know how I was cut up," he said, "but if you can't protect yourself, you don't belong out there."

ORGANIZED CRIME

In sharp contrast to the nonviolent methods and the entrepreneurship of professional criminals, stand the violent, unskilled, politically protected, syndicate criminals. While TV describes the efforts of G-men, T-men, grand juries, racket squads, customs agents, sheriffs, marshalls, city police, real Senate investigating committees and the Justice Department, organized crime continues to bilk the American public of millions and possibly billions of dollars annually. In all probability, organized or syndicate crime will increase in influence and significance in future years. In order to grasp the magnitude of the organized crime problem, it is necessary to understand its origins and development.

HISTORICAL DEVELOPMENT OF SYNDICATE CRIME [12]

Prior to the turn of the century, organized crime in its present form did not exist. Instead, metropolitan communities — New York, Chicago, New Or-

12. See Virgil W. Peterson, *Barbarians in Our Midst*, Boston: Little, Brown, 1952; Martin Mooney, *Crime Incorporated*, New York: McGraw-Hill, 1935; Courtney R. Cooper, *Here's to Crime*, Boston: Little, Brown, 1936; Robert F. Kennedy, *The Enemy Within*, New York: Harper, 1960.

leans, St. Louis, and others — spawned local criminal gangs.[13] These gangs existed in the slum areas and were composed of persons of the same ethnic background. There were Irish, Italian, Jewish, and other ethnic groups. The main activity of these gangs — in addition to warring with one another — consisted of supplying and controlling the illegal activites in their neighborhoods. Their major revenue came from gambling activities, organized houses of prostitution and vice, control over the distribution of beer and liquor, and from the protection rackets which they established. These enterprises were lucrative and the strong-arm competition among hoodlum gangs was vicious. In addition to economic competition, part of the animosity among gangs stemmed from old-world ethnic and religious conflicts which had been transplanted into American life. The gangs thrived despite these rivalries because they supplied services which were illegal but which at least part of the public desired. They thrived, too, because they were able to establish firm political connections in their communities and were protected by those in power.[14]

Shortly after the turn of the century, and at about the same time that small business enterprises and small labor unions began to merge into larger and larger units with greater economic resources and power, gangs also began to consolidate. Using the crudest of methods — outright violence — gang wars dominated the scene. The weaker were eliminated and the stronger grew more powerful. This continued for many years. Eventually men like Capone and the Chicago syndicate came to dominate the rackets in the Midwest, and another syndicate dominated on the east and west coasts.[15]

The major growth of these syndicates occurred after Prohibition became law. The unbelievable profits (several hundred per cent) involved in producing, distributing and selling liquor, coupled with allied interests in gambling and racketeering, made the syndicates into major empires wielding enormous economic and political power. Since these empires were interstate and international, local law enforcement was incapable of controlling them. Federal laws and enforcement procedures proved ineffective. As a consequence, organized crime expanded into some legitimate business activities and into some segments of the labor movement.

A new era in the history of syndicate crime was ushered in by the repeal of Prohibition and the loss of the illegal liquor revenues, plus national resentment at the widespread corruption and brutality associated with organized crime and the so-called "gangster" and "hoodlum" penetrations into legitimate activities. There is reason to believe that the two major syndicates merged and were streamlined into one national organization under the con-

13. Herbert Asbury, *The Gangs of New York*, New York: Knopf, 1927.
14. Lincoln Steffens, *Autobiography*, New York: Harcourt, Brace, 1931.
15. See Fred D. Pasley, *Al Capone: The Biography of a Self-Made Man*, New York: Ives, Washburn, 1930.

trol and direction of the heirs of the Chicago and east coast syndicates. The new organization reputedly developed its own enforcement arm of "torpedoes" — Murder, Inc., and later the Mafia — to keep peace within the organization and to bring recalcitrant victims into line.[16]

At the present time, and despite genuine attempts by the federal government to halt organized criminal activities, the successful prosecution of organized crime remains a hope rather than a reality. Judging from the affluence of the fifty-eight organized crime leaders who gathered for a "convention" at an estate in Appalachin, New York, in 1957 and were accidentally discovered by a state trooper who became suspicious of the unusual number of Cadillacs in the area, plus the revelations of the Kefauver and McClellan Senate investigating committees, organized crime seems more firmly entrenched than ever.[17] Its chief source of revenue is gambling — a diversion on which Americans spend an estimated $26 billion annually. The three major contributions to gambling revenue are illegal bookmaking ($8 billion), the numbers game ($6 billion), and slot machines ($3 billion).[18] By comparison, the amount of money from racketeering, narcotics, and from "hoodlum" infiltration into, and ownership of, seventy types of legitimate enterprises such as hotels, resorts, race tracks, breweries, and juke boxes, is small.[19]

THE ORGANIZATION OF SYNDICATE CRIME

The unparalleled growth and success of organized crime is largely attributable to the nature of the syndicate itself. Syndicate crime exhibits these organizational characteristics: [20]

1. A hierarchical structure in the form of a pyramid.
2. A feudal pattern of relationships.
3. The use of legitimate activities as fronts for criminal activities.
4. Tie-ins with local and state political machines.
5. Employment of expert legal and tax counsel.

HIERARCHICAL STRUCTURE AND FEUDAL RELATIONSHIPS

Like other large-scale enterprises, the organized criminal syndicate and its various branches are hierarchically structured. Unlike legitimate enterprises, however, the incumbents of the various positions in the table of organization are unknown. At the bottom of the pyramid are the "flunkies" — numbers

16. Burton B. Turkus and Sid Feder, Murder, Inc., New York: Farrar, 1951; and Ed Reid, Mafia, New York: Random House, 1952.
17. Frederick Sondern, Brotherhood of Evil: The Mafia, New York: Farrar, 1959, pp. 3–17; and Estes Kefauver, Crime in America, New York: Random House, 1951.
18. Harry E. Barnes and Negley K. Teeters, New Horizons in Criminology, 3rd. ed., New York: Prentice-Hall, 1959, pp. 30–31. See, also, Kefauver, op. cit. p. 35 ff.
19. Kefauver, op. cit. p. 16.
20. Reckless, op. cit. pp. 192–201.

runners, narcotics peddlers, prostitutes, and others who deal directly with the public. At the very top are a few individuals who make the decisions and run the organization. These men are usually unknown to persons at the lower levels and, in terms of their daily activities, do not seem to be officially involved in the organization at all. Since no records are kept, and since all transactions are in cash and no one in the organization is likely to turn state's evidence, the leadership remains free from arrest and conviction.[21]

More important, perhaps, than this chain of command and anonymity is the pattern of relationships that characterizes the syndicate. Burgess has called this system a feudal pattern. The term feudal implies a system of master-serf relationships "held together by powerful leaders, by intense personal loyalties, by the gangsters' code of morals, by alliances and agreements with rival gangster chiefs, and by their common warfare against the forces of organized society." [22] This feudal pattern is founded on strong kinship ties. Control of the rackets has become a family proposition. Part of the intense intra-group loyalty is based on the fact that one is being loyal to his relatives in the syndicate.[23] The McClellan committee prepared a listing of the family ties of major racketeers in the Detroit-Cleveland, Pennsylvania-upstate New York, and New York-New Jersey areas. With few exceptions, the top hoodlums in these areas are related to each other and to underworld overlords in other parts of the country. Nepotism of this kind makes for a strong conspiracy, and in the face of tough and honest law enforcement, for a silent one.

FRONT ACTIVITIES AND INVASION OF LEGITIMATE BUSINESS

The interlocking activities of organized crime, the invasion of legitimate businesses and the pervading cloak of secrecy make it difficult to pinpoint the precise responsibilities of the overlords of syndicate crime. They remain more or less anonymous behind legitimate business or labor union façades. Ownership of or partnerships in real estate firms, insurance agencies, construction companies, and distributing companies for various products serve as covers — and also provide income — for these overlords. *Life*, reconstructing the testimony before a Senate investigating committee, illustrates the problem in terms of a hypothetical cocktail lounge or restaurant in Chicago: [24]

To run a restaurant every owner needs services and supplies. He needs someone to deliver food and drink, bartenders and waiters to serve it, maintenance men for vending machines and someone to haul off garbage. When the syndicate moves

21. Kefauver, op. cit. pp. 308–33.
22. Illinois Association for Criminal Justice, *The Illinois Crime Survey*, Chicago, 1929, p. 1094.
23. Gus Tyler, *Organized Crime in America: A Book of Readings*, Ann Arbor: University of Michigan Press, 1962, pp. 19–37.
24. *Life* (February 23, 1959), p. 25. Reprinted courtesy *Life* Magazine. Copyright © 1959 Time, Inc.

in, the owner finds he is forced to pay heavily for these services and even to take on additional ones he does not want.

If he balks, the syndicate can harass him by ordering pickets to scare off customers. If this fails, the mob, which controls waiters and bartenders union locals, can call members out. Since the mobsters also control Teamster locals who deliver, they can put the owner out of business by cutting off his supply of beer or by stopping his garbage pick-up.

Equally pertinent, the companies supplying these services are "fronts" for the overlords. Thus, in this same restaurant or cocktail lounge the following products and services are supplied by racketeer-owned or dominated companies: linen supplies and laundry, the steam-cleaning of beer tap coils, juke box operations, bottled beer, liquor, cigarette, and other vending machines, meat supplies, glassware, and glass-washers. In addition, through local labor union control, some bartenders and delivery drivers handling everything used in the restaurant are controlled by racketeers. The racketeers who provide these services, and thereby obscure their real criminal involvement, constitute a Who's Who of organized crime. These "companies" give them legitimate status and legitimate earnings for income tax purposes.[25]

POLITICS AND INADEQUATE LAW ENFORCEMENT

Syndicate crime is one of the major economic enterprises in the nation, but it could never have achieved its present state of affluence without political connections and lax law enforcement. In the heyday of the political machine, organized crime provided the personnel to get out the votes, to stuff the ballot boxes, to intimidate "reform" minded candidates and voters, and to provide the funds necessary for running election campaigns. Politcians, judges, prosecutors, and others, including policemen, were not infrequently on the syndicate's payroll. Once compromised, office holders were obliged to reciprocate by overlooking the operations of the syndicate.

The political machine is, of course, no longer the important institution it once was. Nevertheless, organized crime continues to contribute heavily in election campaigns, and through bribery and other devious devices, maintains its immunity.[26] A former lieutenant governor in New York not too long ago was forced to resign because he visited a friend — a notorious mobster — while the friend was serving time in prison. A former governor of Florida refused to testify before a Senate committee investigating syndicate crime in that state. Every so often the public becomes aroused about what the press euphemistically calls a "scandal" involving politicians and the syndicate. This interest and concern sometimes results in a "reform" candidate being elected. The scandal is soon forgotten, however, and after an appropriate interval of

25. Ibid.; see also Kefauver, op. cit. pp. 170 ff.
26. Kefauver, op. cit. pp. 14–15.

time during which the "heat" is applied, the community returns to normal.

Similarly, some law enforcement officials at all levels have been corrupted by syndicate "gifts." In some cities police corruption may become so blatant that periodic housecleanings occur. The most highly publicized case in recent years concerned a police captain who estimated his net worth to be $360,000 and the dividends on his stocks and bond holdings to be over $40,000 annually. At the time of the hearings before the Kefauver committee, this captain was chief investigator of the State's Attorney's office in Cook County (Chicago), Illinois.[27] A CBS documentary on a "bookie" joint in the Boston area revealed that the police not only knew of its existence but that many patronized the establishment on a regular basis. One can only surmise about the amount of "pay-off" involved. There is no question about the "gifts" for police protection in New York. The Gross bookmaking empire paid over a million dollars a year to corrupt police according to sworn testimony.[28] In Philadelphia over $150,000 each month went to personnel in 38 police districts in the city.[29]

Aside from the public officials who succumb to the blandishments of organized criminals, perfectly legitimate legal and other professional talent is employed to protect and defend the organization. Perhaps the best illustration is to be found in the testimony of a tax accountant who, while working for the Bureau of Internal Revenue, was responsible for the conviction of a racketeer and his sentence to a four-year prison term and a $15,000 fine. After release from prison, the racketeer approached the accountant, who was by that time in business for himself, and offered him the job of making out his (the racketeer's) income tax returns. The accountant accepted and became involved in the illegal machinations of his client. When pressed by committee counsel to explain the reason for this tie-in, the accountant's explanation was curt and to the point: "For the almighty dollar! The same as you are doing, the job you are doing right now — ." [30]

THE SUCCESS OF ORGANIZED CRIME: OTHER FACTORS

There are other factors which make syndicate crime so difficult to counteract. First, organized crime thrives because it continues to supply goods and services which many people desire but which cannot be obtained legally. Various forms of gambling — slot machines, off-track betting, and numbers — are cases in point. So are narcotics, alcohol in "dry" areas, joints and dives of all types and descriptions, and prostitution. The discrepancy between what people are willing to pay for and what they may legally have, presents a

27. Ibid. pp. 58–60.
28. *The New York Times*, May 19, 1951.
29. Kefauver, op. cit. p. 225.
30. Ibid. p. 204.

vacuum which syndicate crime has filled to its great profit. Thus, normative dissensus plays an important role in the survival of organized crime.

Second, organized crime survives because it is able to use fear, intimidation, force, and violence to further its own ends. Operating on a divide and conquer principle, the syndicate is able to infiltrate and establish itself as a silent partner in one enterprise after another without encountering substantial resistance.

Third, not only is law enforcement sometimes corrupt but it is also often poor since local authorities cannot cope with an organization national and international in scope. Even when one community is successful in eliminating syndicate activities, operations continue elsewhere. Even at the national level, enforcement is hampered by inadequate laws and the possibility of infringing on the rights of local communities and states. Consequently, organized criminals are often prosecuted for (a) income tax evasion, (b) deportation as undesirable aliens, and (c) contempt of various committees of Congress. It is ironic that organized criminals must be dealt with in these terms rather than prosecuted for their major crimes.

While society views organized crime and syndicate criminals as undesirable and is constantly investigating the "hoodlum" empire, it shows less concern about an even more serious type of criminal deviation — white collar crime.

WHITE COLLAR CRIME

White collar crime is the most serious and extensive form of crime in the United States. No other violational behavior involves as great a financial loss to the public nor undermines faith and morale to a comparable degree.[31] Yet while there is consensus that ordinary, professional, and organized crime is reprehensible and should be dealt with sternly, white collar is subject to normative dissensus. To some, white collar crime represents shrewd, sharp, clever, and admirable behavior. To others, white collar crime is the most cynical and deleterious type of criminal deviation. As a result of this dissensus, white collar criminals enjoy greater immunity from arrest, prosecution, and imprisonment than other types of criminals including racketeers and syndicate hoodlums.

While white collar crime is a relatively new concept, it describes violations which came into prominence long before the Industrial Revolution. The term itself was first used by Edwin Sutherland in 1939 as a means of differentiating upper class crime from conventional criminality. It was Sutherland's contention that studies of white collar criminals would document the absurdity of attributing criminal deviation to biological, psychological, and emotional

31. Edwin H. Sutherland, "White Collar Criminality," *American Sociological Review,* 5 (1940), pp. 2–5.

factors. Such factors as poverty, indigency, and family instability are not characteristic of white collar criminals and certainly cannot be invoked as explanations of this form of deviation.[32]

DEFINITION AND TYPES OF WHITE COLLAR CRIME

White collar crime may be defined as a violation of one or more criminal statutes by persons of middle and upper socio-economic status in the course of their business, professional, or occupational roles.[33] This definition emphasizes that (1) white collar crime is real crime and violates criminal statutes in the same sense that conventional crimes do; (2) the so-called criminals are men of relative wealth and high status in their communities and beyond reproach in their private lives; and (3) white collar criminals commit their violations within the normal course of their occupational roles. Unlike conventional and organized criminals, white collar violators commit offenses as part of their legitimate business or professional activities. This tends to make white collar violations invisible as crimes.

All white collar crimes have one element in common. All represent *violations of trust*. White collar offenders not only commit criminal acts but also betray their positions of trust as business or professional men. This violation of trust undermines public confidence in existing institutions. Businessmen who conspire to fix prices, to establish monopolistic practices, to violate anti-trust laws, to divert funds from their companies into their own pockets, to short-weight and misgrade products, to obtain business through bribery, and to evade income tax assessments do more than violate the law. They bring the entire economic structure into disrepute. Physicians who engage in fee-splitting (a criminal violation in many states and an unethical professional practice), involve themselves in "ghost-surgery," enter into collusion with patients so that they can collect workmen's compensation although perfectly capable of working, perform illegal abortions, prescribe narcotics illegally, testify falsely in accident cases, and cheat on their income taxes, corrode public trust in the medical profession. "Ambulance chasers" and "shyster" lawyers do the same for the legal profession. Labor union leaders who dip into union welfare funds for their own enrichment, and who accept "gifts" from employers to keep the workers "in line," undermine confidence in the labor union movement. Every profession and occupation offers criminal possibilities such as those described. These violations of trust moved Al Capone, an offender of some distinction, to speak of the "legitimate rackets" in referring to white collar criminality.

32. Edwin H. Sutherland, *White Collar Crime*, New York: Holt, Rinehart and Winston, paperback edition, 1961, pp. 6–10.
33. Ibid. p. 9.

Thus, to a greater or lesser extent, all white collar crimes inherently violate trust. These violations take two forms: *misrepresentation* and *duplicity*.[34] By misrepresentation is meant that an individual lies, cheats, or steals in violation of law. Income tax evasion, false and misleading advertising, and overcharging for, underweighing, and mislabeling goods, would be examples of misrepresentation. Duplicity is more involved. It may be defined as a double-cross, double-dealing, or working against one's position of trust. It involves betraying the organization for which one works. Examples include embezzlement, misapplying funds, faking expenses, and defrauding the organization.

MISREPRESENTATION

The more common practice, misrepresentation, drains incalculable millions from the pockets of innocent victims who neither know nor can defend themselves against these depredations. A few illustrations might emphasize this point better. A classic case concerns a manufacturer who deliberately and systematically reduced the weight of the product he was selling by the weight of its wrapper. The difference in the net weight of the product was undetectable and resulted, over time, in very substantial profits to the manufacturer. Again, the *Reader's Digest* in 1941 conducted an investigation of automobile garages, radio repair shops, and watch repair establishments. Investigators took their automobiles into 347 garages in 48 states after deliberately disconnecting a coil wire in the car. In 63 per cent of the garages, the investigators were overcharged, unnecessary work was done on the car, charges were made for work which was not done, unnecessary parts were installed, and other fraudulent practices were perpetrated. In studying the "honesty" of radio repair stores, investigators loosened a tube in an otherwise perfect radio. About two-thirds of the 304 shops into which these radios were taken for "repair" deliberately cheated the investigators. Over half the watch repair shops which were similarly investigated, misrepresented their services.[35] This picture of the "integrity" of these entrepreneurs helps destroy public trust in business establishments generally.

There are other, and perhaps even more important, illustrations of misrepresentation. The examples which follow are taken from several different areas and are largely self-explanatory. The first concerns misrepresentation in the field of charity.[36]

34. Reckless, op. cit. p. 209.
35. Roger W. Riis, "The Repair Man Will Gyp You If You Don't Watch Out," *Reader's Digest*, 39 (July 1941), pp. 1–6; and Roger W. Riis, "The Radio Repair Man Will Gyp You If You Don't Watch Out," *Reader's Digest*, 39 (August 1941), pp. 6–10.
36. *Time* (December 28, 1953), pp. 12–13. Reprinted courtesy *Time*. Copyright © Time, Inc. 1953.

In Manhattan's County Courthouse in Foley Square, a committee headed by New York State Senator Bernard Tompkins and Assemblyman Samuel Rabin listened in stunned silence as a parade of witnesses, many of them very reluctant, unfolded a sordid talk of profit in the name of charity. Items:

The National Kids Day Foundation, Inc., a West Coast organization headed by Hollywood Gossipist Jimmy Fidler, collected $3,978,000 in five years, disbursed a total of $302,000 for charitable purposes. The rest — 82% of the take — went into the pockets of professional fund-raisers (Fidler receives no salary). Whimpered Fidler: "It seems like they're picking on us for publicity."

Slick Chicago promoters started a "snowball" campaign by mailing 2000 crisp dollar bills to "sucker lists" (with an appeal to match the dollar, or better), eventually got back a clear $630,000 for a nonexistent "National Cancer Hospital." The cost of fund-raising: $435,000. Another Chicago outfit raised $2,531,000 for the relief of war widows and orphans aided by Gold Star Wives of America, Inc. After fund-raising expenses were deducted, the widows' mite was $309,000.

The Kings County (Brooklyn) Council of the Marine Corps League collected $67,244 for veterans' welfare. The net take: $4000. The rest went into the bank accounts, one hidden, of the promoters.

The Disabled American Veterans collected $21,480,000 over a period of three years with a series of splashy contests and a campaign to flood the mails with unsolicited trinkets. Out of this sum, the expenses of the fund-raisers amounted to $14,529,000, "administrative costs" ate up another $2,400,000, and $3,837,000 more went for D.A.V. lobbying. Not a cent went for the direct aid of a needy veteran. The D.A.V. does maintain 1,800 local chapters, which help veterans, for example, with their claims against the Government.

An unestimated mountain of "clothing for Korea" was sold on the secondhand market and the profits pocketed by the pitchmen.

The names of dozens of celebrities, it turned out, had been freely taken in vain. The D.A.V. campaigns used the names of President Eisenhower, former President Truman, and Generals Omar Bradley and Douglas MacArthur in unauthorized "endorsements," until they were stopped by the threat of a mail-fraud trial. The National Kids Day appeal featured a "testimonial" from Bing Crosby, although Crosby made affidavit that he had never given permission to use his name.

But the U.S. public, which freely contributes to such hoaxes as the relief fund for "The Unknown Soldier's Widow," showed no signs of tightening its purse strings. U.S. charities of all kinds will receive more than $4 billion this year.

A different aspect of misrepresentation plus a variety of other violations is illustrated in the case of a millionaire commodity speculator who attempted to corner the soybean market in the Chicago area by buying up 94 per cent of the deliverable soybeans, shipping them out of the Midwest, and circulating false rumors of a shortage in this commodity. According to the Commodity Exchange Authority, this deception worked extremely well. Soybean prices rose almost a dollar a bushel. When the new crop started coming in, however, the price broke from $4.08 to $2.50 per bushel. In order to get cash, to cover large losses in declining coffee futures, he called two long-time customers and sold them $4,400,000 worth of soybeans. After paying for the beans, a routine check showed that they had never been delivered. The two companies sued for the "nonexistent" soybeans; he was also suspended from trading on the major commodity exchanges.[37]

Apart from filing fraudulent income tax returns there is probably no other aspect of "creativity" (misrepresentation) equal to that in filing an expense account form. The following excerpts from an article by Havemann makes this point well.[38]

This is the Age of the Expense Account, an institution which taxation has inflated into almost appalling importance. The Bureau of Internal Revenue recognizes that travel and a "reasonable" amount of entertaining are necessary in the ordinary course of business; all these expenses can be deducted from a company's taxable profits. To a company which pays the current 52% corporate income tax plus an additional 30% under the excess profits tax, as a lot of them have been doing, a dollar spent on entertainment thus saves 82¢ in taxes and costs only 18¢ in real money. (The publicity women's $40 lunch, for example, cost her company only $7.20 net.) Giving an employe the privilege of entertaining business associates on an expense account is practically painless to the corporation and at the same time is a sort of windfall to the employe. If a salesman gets a $1000 raise, for example, he can spend only what is left of it after the extra personal income tax that it costs him. But if he draws $1000 on an expense account, he pays no extra taxes and can spend every cent having fun with his business friends.

There is every likelihood that the first American to operate on an expense account was also the first man to pad one, for there is something about an expense account that brings out the latent rascality, rapacity and mendacity in even the otherwise most honorable man. Expense account forms have long been known affectionately by their fond possessors as "swindle sheets." Filling out an expense account itemization has been regarded as a kind of contest of wits with the company auditor, in which it is perfectly justifiable to use the most outrageous half-truths, little white lies and outright fantasies, anything at all which the auditor, regardless of how outraged he might be, cannot absolutely prove to be false. You say you spent it. The auditor can only take your word for it or get you fired, and the amount is rarely enough for any punishment quite that drastic.

Jokes about expense account cheating are legion. Possibly the most famous of all concerns Author Gene Fowler, in the days when he was a New York newspaperman. According to legend, he was sent to Northern Canada to find some lost aviators, and in the process he spent some $3000. Back in his office, hard put to account for it all, he invented the purchase of a mythical dog team, then the mythical illness of a dog requiring expensive medical care, and finally the death and funeral of the dog. Finding himself still short at this point, Fowler finally made up the difference by entering the item: "Flowers for bereft bitch, $60."

There is also the story of the World War II correspondent who, flushed by his

37. *Time* (April 4, 1955), p. 90.
38. Ernest Havemann, "Tax Deductions 'For Business Purposes' Make It Cheap To Live Off the 'Swindle Sheet' — But It Proves a Dubious Blessing," *Life* (March 9, 1953), pp. 140–52. Reprinted with the permission of the author.

success and the scarcity of good men at that time, sent in a monthly statement reporting $150 for taxicab fares. This was extremely annoying to his boss, especially since the boss happened to know that he had spent the entire month as guest of the Navy aboard an aircraft carrier. The boss therefore cabled angrily, "How can you spend cab money on a carrier?" The correspondence cabled back with significant insolence: "Big carrier."

Such legends contain a good core of truth. Any bigtime salesman, advertising man or press agent operating on an expense account soon develops a kind of sixth sense for what the traffic will bear. He knows how much seniority he has in the company, how much work he has been turning out and how he stands with his boss at the moment. On this basis, and depending on how cocky and inventive he is by nature, he makes out his monthly account. Records of this sort are hard to keep anyway; if a man starts out to cocktails with a couple of customers and winds up buying them scrambled eggs at 4 o'clock the next morning, he has a hard time remembering every single drink, tip, taxi fare, cigaret pack and quarter for the keeper of the men's room. So he makes some approximation of what he has spent on company business, adds whatever else he thinks he can get away with and proceeds to list some ways in which he might logically have got rid of the money.

There is one New York radio man who puts down dinners every month for four prominent people who have recently died; so long as this obvious prevarication is not challenged, he feels he is in solid with his network. There is another New York executive who has worked up a highly entertaining and almost poetic five-minute speech about how he makes out his account. He can do it, he claims, only by locking his office door, shutting off all phone calls and turning on some soft music, because, as he says, the preparation of an expense account is a highly creative art, far too delicate for the usual hurly-burly of the business office. As one cynical executive has said, "Our men give their talent to the company and their genius to their expense accounts."

DUPLICITY

Whereas misrepresentation consists of defrauding other persons, duplicity involves double-crossing one's own business organization, labor union, or professional group. Instances of duplicity usually result in the resignation of the trust violator. Rarely does prosecution take place. Crimes of duplicity involve millions and sometimes billions of dollars and are referred to as "scandals," a term deemed more appropriate than crime by the press. These "scandals" include such diverse crimes as embezzlement, the misapplication of funds, and fraudulent practices within an organization. The most notorious scandal in government was the Teapot Dome government oil reserve fiasco in which several cabinet members and other high government officials were involved.[39]

For high level government scandals, Teapot Dome up to the present time has had no peer. It produced front page headlines for most of the 1920's and remains to this day as the synonym for graft and malfeasance in public office.

The scandal, which unfolded slowly in the summer of 1923, when Calvin

39. Slocum, op. cit. p. 12.

Coolidge became President following the death of President Harding, resulted in the resignation of three cabinet members appointed by President Harding.

The central figures were Albert B. Fall, Interior Secretary, and two oilmen, Harry F. Sinclair and Edward L. Doheny. All three went to trial on criminal conspiracy charges in Government leasing of U.S.-owned oil reserves to companies controlled by the two oilmen. All were acquitted of charges of conspiracy. Mr. Sinclair served a brief jail term on charges of tampering with the jury — an act that resulted in a mistrial. In 1929, Mr. Fall got a year's prison sentence on a separate charge of accepting a bribe. It has been alleged that he accepted $100,000 from Mr. Doheny. It also had been alleged out of court that he got $300,000 plus other favors from Mr. Sinclair. Mr. Fall insisted these were loans. One key fact was that Mr. Fall previously had been deeply in debt. In return for the oil leases, estimated by the oil men to be worth $200 million, the U.S. Navy was to get some oil tanks at Pearl Harbor.

The first whiff of scandal came in the spring of 1922 when Senators and Congressmen began getting rumors that leases had been executed on two Navy oil reserves, the so-called Teapot Dome area of Wyoming and the Elk Hills reserve in California. An investigation resulted. The facts were that Interior Secretary Fall had, a short time earlier, secretly granted the leases — Elk Hills to the Doheny interests and Teapot Dome to Sinclair interests. A year earlier, less than two months after Mr. Harding took office, the President had ordered transfer of the reserves from the Navy to the Interior Department at the insistence of Mr. Fall. In 1929, the U.S. Supreme Court upheld a lower court decision revoking the leases.

Direct misapplication of funds is illustrated in the case of Musica-Coster who duped his own company out of an estimated $8 million in over a decade of manipulation.[40]

F. Donald Coster was a quiet, home-loving family man, who spent as many as 16 hours a day at his job and whose only hobby was raising show dogs. But before he was through, he perpetrated a classic Wall Street swindle.

Mr. Coster, whose real name was Philip Musica, dribbled some $3 million into his personal kitty by conjuring a fake drug division to a real company, McKesson & Robbins, Inc., of which he was president. Other illicit escapades brought his total illegal take to an estimated $8 million.

Prior to his big time thievery, Mr. Coster broadened his experience by such skullduggery as gyping Uncle Sam out of import duties on cheese and borrowing bank money on trumped up securities. In prohibition days, under the guise of a dandruff-remover business, he acquired denatured alcohol through bogus orders and peddled it to bootleggers.

Armed with $1 million, he bought control of McKesson & Robbins in 1926. The company, small with a good name, grew speedily, becoming the world's third largest drug producer in a few years. Most of the company's operations were delegated to lower executives, supposedly to give Mr. Coster full time to devote to the crude drug division, which he handled alone. McKesson & Robbins' speculative investments in crude drugs soared, on the books at least, to $21 million in little

40. Ibid.

more than a decade. The profit the ghost division invariably showed on paper was "plowed back into more drugs."

But the Italian-born Mr. Coster, who was listed in Who's Who and was on the board of two banks, actually neither bought nor sold crude drugs. Through a bewildering array of figures on the ledgers, he merely gave the impression of dealing in crude drugs, while he siphoned into his own pockets funds slated for sales commissions and other expenses of the bogus division.

His plot involved fictitious names of wholesale concerns, to which he supposedly sold drugs, and an accomplice, a brother who utilized one secretary with seven typewriters to send letters to his non-existent division. For instance, when McKesson & Robbins' auditors, the highly esteemed firm of Price Waterhouse & Co., wrote a fictitious Canadian warehouse concern asking for verification of inventories, the letter was forwarded to the hole-in-the-wall New York office of Mr. Coster's brother. There, it was promptly answered and sent to a Canadian contact, who mailed it to the auditors so it would have an appropriate postmark. The masquerade worked for ten years.

"I live for this company," Mr. Coster was fond of telling his McKesson & Robbins executives. "I'm not interested in money." His salary as president of the company was a modest $40,000 a year.

Mr. Coster met his downfall not because of auditors, suspicious employes or clever police work but because of hard times. In 1937, the hard-pressed board of McKesson & Robbins, which had grown to $150 million in annual sales, began casting about for more cash and ordered Mr. Coster to liquidate part of his non-existent inventory of crude drugs. When he failed to act, directors stumbled onto the truth. In December, 1938, Mr. Coster killed himself.

The Coster experience brought massive changes in accounting practices. McKesson & Robbins, while hard hit by the thefts, survived.

A more recent case and one which is illustrative of both misrepresentation and duplicity concerns the activities of Lowell M. Birrell who in 1954–59 extracted $14 million from his own companies and the public and now lives on a grand scale in Brazil.[41]

Not all free-wheeling corporate looters have been forced to pay the penalty for their activities. A case in point is Lowell M. Birrell, very much alive and enjoying life in Brazil.

Mr. Birrell, a razor-witted attorney with a penchant for booze and pretty girls, allegedly made off with some $14 million of funds in various companies in the mid-1950's. A New York grand jury indicted him in 1959 on 69 counts of grand larceny. He has not faced his accusers, since the U.S. has no extradition agreement with Brazil.

The 200-pound, 55-year-old Mr. Birrell, whose high living currently makes him somewhat of a tourist attraction in Brazil, was unusually successful in one technique. In a typical operation, he acquired control of Swan-Finch Oil Corp., New York, in 1954, then began a widely ballyhooed program of expansion and diversification. He negotiated mergers that gave Swan-Finch, established to distribute sperm oil products, ownership in gas and uranium fields in addition to

41. Ibid. pp. 12 and 19.

grain storage facilities. He ran huge ads in New York papers announcing that "we're expanding from fish oil to fission." While he increased shares to 60 times the number outstanding when he took over, market price of the stock declined only to about half the original market price.

With the stock moving briskly, he then flicked a million shares into his own pocket, according to New York authorities. He had Swan-Finch issue 300,000 shares of stock, then worth $2 million at open market prices, to acquire a small loan company which he had picked up personally for $250,000. Similarly, in 1957, some 700,000 shares of Swan-Finch were issued to acquire a drilling company that Mr. Birrell had acquired at a sheriff's auction for a few hundred dollars. Most of his Swan-Finch shares were posted as collateral for $1.5 million in loans and were sold by lenders when he defaulted on payment.

Mr. Birrell, whose dislike for shareholders took such turns as turning off the air conditioning at annual meetings, also is accused of making off with several million dollars of stock of Doeskin Products, Inc., New York, a producer of facial tissues that he controlled.

Mr. Birrell ran into trouble in 1957, when, with his loans overdue, lenders began unloading on the market the Swan-Finch shares deposited as collateral. The sudden flow attracted Securities and Exchange Commission officials who halted sale of the stock. Mr. Birrell, handed a subpoena as he alighted from a plane from Canada, climbed aboard an outboard aircraft the same day and skipped the country. Swan-Finch later filed bankruptcy proceedings.

Mr. Birrell, on arrival in Brazil, was jailed by the authorities there for entering the country on a false passport. However, he immediately launched through his attorneys a publicity campaign, spiced with numerous cocktail parties, to spread the word that he had come to Brazil to invest his $14 million. Brazilians also were told that his troubles back home involved mainly a matter of income tax, an item for which Brazilians traditionally have had little regard. New York authorities, who originally were confident of returning Mr. Birrell to this country, found relations with Brazilian authorities becoming cooler and cooler. There's no indication that Mr. Birrell ever will be ordered back to this country.

The biggest looter of all time (both misrepresentation and duplicity) was a highly respected millionaire who manipulated the public out of $500,000,000 in the normal course of his business activities. Known as the "Puritan of Finance" and as a banker to government, Ivar Kreuger exemplifies the problem of white collar crime.[42]

For sheer size, geographical scope and complexity of operation, probably no swindle in history compares with the illicit financial maneuvers of Swedish-born Ivar Kreuger. And because of tough new laws, probably none ever will. From 1917 until he killed himself in 1932, the international financier, who at one point controlled three quarters of the world's match production, took in some $650 million, mostly from sales of securities. Although he left assets of $200 million, claims against his enterprises totaled $1,168,000,000. After 13 years of investigation, officials estimated that he probably bilked shareholders and money lenders out of some $500 million.

42. Ibid. p. 12.

A silent, self-reliant man, he founded a Swedish building concern, Kreuger & Toll, in 1908, and in three years expanded it into Sweden's biggest building company. In 1913, he combined 10 tiny match companies in Sweden and four years later, through expansion and merger, he controlled production in the nation.

While these operations seemed honest enough, there were certain departures from recognized bookkeeping procedures. Annual reports, for instance, often identified the source of two-thirds of the net income as "various transactions." As the world was to find out later, he also was switching assets and liabilities between companies to fit the occasion and was creating fictional assets when existing ones ran short.

Over the years, as he pyramided company upon company, funds flowed into his own pockets through the simple procedure of transferring them abroad. For instance in 1923, International Match Corp., a Delaware concern he founded, had an initial stock offering of $15 million. Mr. Kreuger, then the president, pocketed $13 million by charging it off to "A.B. Russia," a dummy company abroad that was little more than a personal savings account. Between 1923 and 1932, International Match sold $148 million in securities and Mr. Kreuger transferred $143 million of it to Europe.

In the late 1920's, the "Puritan of Finance," as newspapers called him, exuded prosperity from his empire of 250 match factories in 37 countries. Mr. Kreuger loaned money freely to poor European countries, receiving match monopolies in return. He was on friendly terms with international leaders, including President Hoover, and was generally conceded to be the world's top financier. While he worked 18 hours a day manipulating his empire, shareholders were kept happy with big dividends, paid mostly out of capital.

But while his stock held up relatively well in the early days of the great depression, the squeeze was on for more funds to cover up his thefts. With this in mind, he agreed in 1931 to a merger of one of his companies, L. M. Ericsson Telephone Co. of Sweden, with International Telephone & Telegraph Corp., New York, which paid a preliminary sum of $11 million.

A few months later ITT discovered that much of the information given on Ericsson was fabricated, tried to call off the merger and demanded its $11 million back. Mr. Kreuger already had spent the funds shoring up his other operations. In the final months before the crash of his empire, he lost an estimated $50 million in the stock market in an attempt to recover. He also personally forged $142 million in Italian government bonds and notes, which he planned to use for collateral to raise funds.

It was never determined what happened to many Kreuger millions, although much of it obviously went to pay huge shareholder dividends to attract more investment. Friends said also that he apparently paid many millions in blackmail, not only to cover up his thefts but to hide his decidedly unpuritanical private life. Mr. Kreuger, a bachelor, maintained a list of 30 women "friends" together with prices and graded rating scale, and he lived in constant fear of tarnishing his facade of respectability.

THE EVIDENCE FOR WHITE COLLAR CRIME

Corporation violations. Apart from these dramatic cases, there is systematic evidence about white collar crime. Edwin Sutherland pioneered in the effort to collect such data. To secure information on the crimes of persons of high socio-economic status, Sutherland examined court and administrative commission decisions against 70 of the 200 largest American corporations. These 70 corporations were involved in manufacturing, mining, and mercantile operations. They had been in existence for an average of 45 years.[43] These 70 corporations had a total of 980 adverse decisions levied against them, an average of 14 each. Each of the 70 corporations had at least one adverse decision rendered against it. Of the 980 adverse decisions, 16 per cent were made by criminal courts, 30 per cent by civil courts, and the rest by equity courts and various administrative commissions.[44] The "crimes" consisted of restraint of trade; misrepresentation in advertising; patent, trademark, and copyright infringements; rebates; unfair labor practices; financial manipulations and misrepresentations; and tax evasion. Sutherland's conclusion was that these violations are normal operating procedure, that they are wilful, and that they are comparable to professional criminality.

The seriousness of white collar crime was recently demonstrated in what has come to be known as the "electrical conspiracy." In 1961, twenty-nine manufacturers of heavy electrical equipment were charged with price fixing and with determining, in advance, the share of the market each would control. Countless millions of dollars were involved, and in 1962, General Electric made its first out-of-court settlement for $7.41 million. One interesting feature of this conspiracy was that the executives who participated met in secret and developed a secret code for pricing their products and controlling the market. Some of these meetings and activities came perilously close to the meeting of the organized syndicate members who convened at Apalachin, N.Y., ostensibly to visit their sick friend and host. Another interesting aspect was that all of the participants knew that they were violating the law and many had been doing so for twenty-five years or more. A third feature of the conspiracy was that all of the executives rationalized their violations in precisely the same terms that conventional criminals rationalize burglary, robbery, confidence games, and other criminal pursuits. This major conspiracy was reported by *Time* as follows: [45]

In a tense and packed Philadelphia courtroom last week, a drama took place that U.S. business will long remember — to its shame. The cases before him, said Federal District Judge J. Cullen Ganey, were "a shocking indictment of a vast section of our economy." They were more than that. They showed clearly that the executives of a mighty industry, publicly devoted to the concept of competition, had privately conspired to rig prices to the detriment of their

43. *White Collar Crime*, op. cit. p. 17.
44. Ibid. pp. 20–28.
45. *Time* (Feb. 17, 1961), pp. 84–5 (Italics added). Courtesy *Time*; copyright *Time*, Inc. 1961.

customers on a scale so vast that it embraced everything from the Tennessee Valley Authority to the private utilities that supply the nation's light and power.

Up for sentencing were 29 electrical-equipment companies, headed by the industry's two "competitive" giants, General Electric and Westinghouse, and 44 of their executives. Long ago, faced with incontrovertible evidence gathered by the Eisenhower Administration's relentless trustbusters, the companies and individuals had pleaded guilty or *nolo contendere* (no contest) to charges that they conspired over the past seven years to fix prices and rig bids in the sale of some $7 billion worth of heavy electrical equipment. Now the moment of reckoning had come. First before the court came the lawyer for John H. Chiles Jr., 57, a vice president of Westinghouse, to plead for mercy. His client, said the lawyer, while Chiles bowed his head, was a vestryman of St. John's Episcopal Church in Sharon, Pa. and a benefactor of charities for crippled children and cancer victims. "These men," the lawyer pleaded, "are not grasping, greedy, cutthroat competitors."

In antitrust cases, executives may be fined but are rarely jailed. Judge Ganey sentenced Chiles to 30 days in jail. Chiles began automatically to return to his seat, but was startled to be seized by two armed deputy U.S. marshals and hustled off to the marshal's office to be fingerprinted.

Behind the Door. One by one, as the sentencing went on, lawyers rose to describe their clients as pillars of the community. William S. Ginn, 45, vice president of General Electric, was the director of a boys' club in Schenectady, N.Y. and the chairman of a campaign to build a new Jesuit seminary in Lenox, Mass. His lawyer pleaded that Ginn not be put "behind bars with common criminals who have been convicted of embezzlement and other serious crimes." Judge Ganey thought the company appropriate, gave Ginn 30 days in jail. The lawyer for Charles I. Mauntel, Westinghouse division sales manager and a man prominent in charitable and community affairs in Drexel Hill, Pa., asked: "What difference does it make if the Government recommends 30 days or 60 days or more? What matters is crossing the prison door at all." Judge Ganey recommended 30 days behind the door.

Despite other pleas attesting to the public usefulness and position of the defendants, the federal judge handed out the greatest number of jail terms ever in an antitrust proceeding. He gave 30-day sentences to George E. Burens, 55, G.E. vice president and division manager, Lewis J. Burger, 49, G.E. division manager — both demoted from those positions since the indictment — Edwin R. Jung, 58, vice president of Clark Controller Co., and John M. Cook, 56, vice president of Cutler-Hammer, Inc. He fined the 29 electrical companies a total of $1,787,000, levied fines ranging from $1000 to $12,500 on the individuals, and gave 21 other executives suspended 30-day jail sentences — advising some that they would also have gone to jail except for reasons of age and health.

Balmed Conscience. Judge Ganey confined jail sentences to those he felt had "ultimate responsibility for corporate conduct" — but he made it clear that he did not think that all the guilty parties were in court. Though the Government could not get enough evidence against them, he said, the "highest echelons" of each company "bear a grave responsibility." Most of the defendants, said the judge, "were torn between conscience and an approved corporate policy, with the rewarding objectives of promotion, comfortable security and large salaries — in short, the organization or company man, the conformist." Even to those whom he did not send to jail, the judge gave no verbal mercy. When the lawyer for M. A. deFerranti, a former G.E. manager, tried to defend his client, Judge Ganey snapped: "But here again is the classical company man. He balmed his conscience for a salary of $60,000 a year."

What aroused Judge Ganey's indignation was not only the conspiracy but also the efforts of almost everyone involved to justify his misdeeds as part of a prevailing business morality. "What is really at stake here," said the judge, "is the survival of the kind of economy under which American has grown to greatness, the free-enterprise system." Many of the executives pleaded through their lawyers that they were victims of corporate policy and morality. G.E., declaring that sympathy for the arrested was misplaced, denied that it had any "business policy or alleged conformity" that would lead its executives into violations of the law; it then called the defendants "nonconformists" who deliberately broke G.E.'s "Directive Policy 20.5" insisting on strict obedience to the antitrust laws. Judge Ganey said that it would be "naive" not to believe that top company officials knew what was going on in such vast and prolonged shenanigans, noted that G.E.'s rule "was honored in its breach rather than in its observance."

Identical Bids. The Government said that the conspiracy had been going on for nearly 25 years. The companies involved might have got away with it even longer had not TVA — which bought from the companies such equipment as the $16.1 million, 500,000-kw. turbogenerator for its Widows Creek steam plant in Alabama — become aroused over a succession of almost identical bids. It tipped off the Justice Department, which began digging into the conspiracy in 1959 under the direction of Republican Trustbuster Robert Bicks (who recently entered private law practice). Often the Government has a hard time gathering evidence in antitrust cases, but this time it got a break. In October 1959, four Ohio businessmen were sentenced to jail for antitrust violations, the first in history to go to jail after pleading *nolo contendere* in an antitrust case. (One of them committed suicide on the way to jail.) This news sent a chill through the electrical-equipment executives under investigation, and some agreed to testify about their colleagues under the security of immunity. With the evidence gathered from them (most are still with their companies), the Government sewed up its case.

The threads wove a fantastic pattern. Top electrical-equipment executives, gathering together at conventions or in hotels, homes and resorts, worked out common prices, split up markets as if they were personal property, and devised ingenious systems for rigging bids on contracts, such as the "phase of the moon" system in which each firm knew when to bid low or high, taking its turn in rotation at the low bid. With most of the industry represented, the conspiracy directly or indirectly affected almost every dam built, every power generator installed and every electrical distribution system set up in the U.S., even reached into the new and vital field of atomic energy.

Many of the executives complained that they had to go along with the conspiracy if they hoped to keep their jobs or have a chance for promotion. Some, even after indictment, openly defended what they had done. F. F. Loock, president and general sales manager of Milwaukee's Allen-Bradley Co., who was slapped with a $7,500 fine and whose company was fined $40,000, maintained that "*no one attending the gatherings was so stupid he didn't know they were in violation* of the law." Then he added, in a surprising *non sequitur:* "But it is the only way a business can be run. It is free enterprise."

Handcuffs & Guards. G.E. has already demoted, shifted or cut the pay of 48 employees involved in the antitrust violations, including 16 who were indicted. Several of the G.E. men indicted who drew fat salaries ranging from $60,000 to $125,000 have had their salaries cut as much as $50,000. But G.E. made no move at all to discipline its most important figure in the trial: Vice President Ginn, head of G.E.'s important turbine-generator department at a salary of $125,000 a year. G.E.'s lame reason: Ginn's illegal activities in the transformer field were outside the company's own three-year statute of limitations for antitrust violations. Westinghouse demoted none of its executives, noted that its employees' punishment "already is harsh," and announced that "no further penalties would serve any useful purpose."

At week's end Westinghouse's Chiles and Mauntel were led off in handcuffs to begin their sentences in a county jail in Norristown, Pa. The others, except for one who got permission to remain free another week to attend his daughter's engagement party, were to begin their sentences this week.

More Trouble. The companies' troubles will not end with the paying of fines, the completion of jail sentences, or the issuance of public relations disclaimers. The antitrust law gives defrauded customers the right to sue for as much as treble damages — and many customers are spoiling to get at the conspirators. More than a dozen cities, including New York and Chicago, are considering suits, and the National Institute of Municipal Law Officers may seek treble damages for many of the 171 cities who bought price-fixed and bid-rigged equipment. The Justice Department announced that it will bring suit within two months for damages on behalf of some 20 federal agencies that could amount to more than $250 million in claims.

All told, the suits against the companies involved in the conspiracies could total as much as $1.7 billion. To collect, their customers must first prove that they were charged more than they would have been without the conspiracy. But the Government charges that the manufacturers raised prices by mutual agreement, and the records show that the companies started cutting their bids as soon as the Government began investigating. TVA had paid $34 per kilowatt for its Widows Creek turbogenerator; because of foreign competition and other factors, the price for similar generators has since dropped to about $14 per kilowatt. So worried are the companies about their chances that some have already agreed to negotiate claims out of court: G.E. has offered to negotiate privately with anyone who feels that he was cheated.

The Black Market. The most dramatic evidence of white collar crime was found in the widespread violations of law which occurred during the shortages and rationing of the Second World War.[46] Shortages existed in a number of consumer products — gasoline, meat, coffee, cigarettes, tires, building material, apparel, grains, poultry, fuel oil, and rental housing.[47] To insure that all Americans had access to the limited quantities of these goods, it was nec-

46. Marshall B. Clinard, *The Black Market,* New York: Rinehart, 1952.
47. Ibid. p. 39.

essary to institute rationing and to restrict prices and wages by government and legislative fiat. Almost immediately a black market developed. The black market consisted of illegal business transactions. These illegal transactions involved over-ceiling price violations, evasive price violations, rationing coupon violations and rent ceiling violations. The violations included overcharging on products, "cash-on-the-side" or under the table payments, charges for goods not delivered, tie-in sales, misgrading of products, theft of ration stamps, charging more stamps than required, and the general misuse of ration currency.[48]

These practices naturally penalized those at the lowest socio-economic levels most and resulted in huge profits to the black market operators. So extensive were these violations that from 5 to more than 40 per cent of the items checked in retail food stores by the Bureau of Labor Statistics were being priced or sold in violation of the law. About one-fifth of the meat supply was estimated as going into the black market. The American Meat Institute estimated that five out of six meat stores in major metropolitan areas were in violation of the law. In 1944, official statistics revealed that 57 per cent of the business firms investigated were in violation of OPA regulations.[49] At least 5 per cent of the available gasoline was diverted into black market channels. Major black market operations also flourished in sugar, coffee, and retail apparel. So far-reaching were these black market operations that in June 1946, *Fortune* wrote: [50]

In the U.S. in 1946, the historians will write, it was possible to get anything you can imagine — for a price. The black-market quotations were fairly level across the land, too; for $7.50 you could get a pair of nylon stockings in any city; for $1 to $1.50 you could buy a pound of butter. It was said and not denied that if OPA really enforced the law, all the building-materials business men in Boston would be in jail. In the South, 1,250,000 pounds of black-market sugar went to the highest bidders — the moonshiners. Throughout the U.S. trucks were sold by "tie-ins"; for as much as $1000 over the ceiling price the customer got some extra piston rings or two front fenders. Carpenters' nails were scarce, with the ceiling at $5 a keg in twenty-five keg lots, they were selling at two or three times the ceiling price. . . . The black market in farm machinery was one of the wildest: used tractors, OPA priced at $2000, sold at $3400. Lumber got around the OPA everywhere by a variety of new grading methods; one lumber buyer grumbled: "If you can pick a board up by both ends without breaking it in the middle, it's No. 1 Select."

The criminal division of OPA conducted over one million investigations of alleged black market activities. These resulted in just over a quarter of a mil-

48. Ibid. pp. 16–27.
49. Ibid. pp. 28–48. See, also, Frank E. Hartung, "White Collar Offenses in the Wholesale Meat Industry in Detroit," *American Journal of Sociology*, 56 (July 1950), pp. 25–32.
50. "The Boom," *Fortune* (June 1946), pp. 258–60. Courtesy of Fortune Magazine.

lion "actions" against nonconsumers — mostly manufacturers, wholesalers, and retailers. Of these 259,966 "actions," only 19,126 were turned over to the courts for prosecution. Some 11,600 cases ended in conviction and of these, 2970 in imprisonment. The others — 8630 — received suspended sentences or probation or were fined.[51]

THE PRESENT STATUS OF WHITE COLLAR CRIME

Despite the pervasive and socially and economically costly depredations of white collar criminals, consensus on white collar crime as constituting real crime does not yet exist. Criminal statutes and enforcement procedures are more lenient with white collar offenders than with other violators, including juvenile delinquents. Even professional criminologists cannot agree amongst themselves that white collar crime is real crime and not simply unethical or shrewd and calculating behavior.[52] Three objections have been raised by some criminologists to the concept of white collar crime. First, white collar criminals for the most part are not tried in criminal court. Instances of white collar crime are disposed of by government agencies such as the Federal Trade Commission, the Interstate Commerce Commission, the Securities Exchange Commission, and other administrative agencies. If there is no conviction in criminal court, but rather administratve decisions in these cases, can the behavior be labeled as criminal? The real problem is that white collar crime *can* be tried in criminal court but, like juvenile delinquency, is treated as a special type of violation. The issue, then, involves conviction versus convictability. Sutherland maintains that a violation of a criminal statute which *can* end in a conviction is a real crime. Others insist that conviction must take place before the behavior can be defined as criminal.

Second, some crminologists argue that neither the public nor the white collar offenders define white collar violations as criminal. This is comparable to public attitudes toward other technically illegal activities such as gambling. The issue is whether or not an act can be described as criminal when the public and those who engage in it do not conceive of it as criminal?

Third, a number of criminologists believe that white collar crime is so rampant that most or all persons in positions of trust engage in it. White collar crime is so deeply embedded in the social structure that a substantial segment of the population must engage in these violations in order to remain competitive. Under these circumstances is it possible to speak of crime at all? From this point of view, the deviant actually conforms to existing business practices while violating legal statutes.

Given these objections, it is little wonder that white collar criminals fare so well under the law. Nevertheless, the increasing complexity of an urban,

51. Clinard, op. cit. pp. 32 ff.
52. For a detailed analysis of this controversy, see Reckless, op. cit. pp. 225–8.

industrial society is beginning to compel reassessment of the problem of white collar crime. Because all persons, to some extent, cannot protect themselves against white collar criminality it is likely that more stringent laws and better enforcement of these laws will occur in the future. White collar crime is likely to be viewed as an increasingly serious form of criminal violation. Dissensus is already giving way to consensus on this issue. This trend is likely to result in the treatment of white collar crime as real crime.

SUMMARY

Four types of criminal activity were discussed in this chapter. These forms — ordinary, professional, organized, and white collar crime — are the most costly and serious of all criminal behavior. In common, the four types include persons who view crime as a means of earning a livelihood or supplementing income from other sources. These persons are not "sick" and crime is not a means of expressing their resentments, hostilities, or psychopathologies. Instead crime is a career or a quasi-career, and is rationalized as a perfectly normal and reasonable way to make a living.

Ordinary criminals are generally slum born and bred, with little education, and no known legitimate occupations. They begin their criminal careers early in life and become progressively involved in more serious property violations as they grow older. As career criminals, they exhibit little sophistication and skill. Many serve repeated sentences for such offenses as burglary, larceny, robbery, and forgery. Their life patterns in crime, contacts with other criminals, resentment at institutional treatment and isolation from legitimate members of society predispose them to a high recidivism rate.

Professional criminals come from better backgrounds than ordinary violators. They often have had legitimate occupational backgrounds before being recruited into professional crime. As professionals, they enjoy the highest prestige of any criminal type. Rarely arrested and imprisoned, professionals shun violence in their offenses. Their chief tools are manual dexterity, intelligence, resourcefulness, and specialized training. Their chief offenses are confidence games, pickpocketing, sneak thievery, shoplifting, counterfeiting, and various types of fraud. Professionals are difficult to rehabilitate since they are fairly successful in their criminal activities and see little reason for reforming.

Organized criminals come from the same impoverished and unstable backgrounds as the ordinary career offenders. They are usually members of an ethnic minority and gradually gravitate into criminal activities which are operated and run as a business. Organized crime is characterized by a tightly knit hierarchical structure with feudal relationships between members; by anonymity of the overlords who hide behind legitimate fronts, by interlocking activities; and by political connections and protection. Syndicate or organized crime derives its revenue primarily from gambling, prostitution and vice, and narcotics and racketeering. Syndicate crime is increasingly getting more money from its incursions and investments in legitimate business enterprises. Inadequate laws, poor enforcement, public apathy, and many other factors make it difficult to control syndicate crime. Organized criminals are largely immune to arrest and imprisonment.

White collar criminals, unlike the ordinary, professional and organized types are men of high incomes and status, and enjoy great repute in their communities. They commit offenses within their occupational or professional roles. These crimes always violate trust and involve either misrepresentation, or duplicity or both. White collar criminals do not conceive of themselves as offenders and usually are not thought of as such by the public. Their violations rarely end in arrest and imprisonment since civil and administrative rather than criminal procedures are invoked against them. White collar offenders drain more money from the public than any other offender group. These offenders attest to the inadequacy of biological, psychological, and social theories as explanations of deviant behavior.

The last five chapters have been devoted to a discussion of two major forms of deviation. In Chapters 14 and 15 deviation was defined as occurring when persons are unable to function in accordance with the minimal social and psychological expectations of others. These persons — the mentally ill — deviate from the norms concerning appropriate behavior. In Chapters 16, 17, and 18, the deviation discussed was the violation of one or more criminal statutes. Criminal deviation was shown to vary widely and to include homicide, suicide, drug addiction, various aspects of alcoholism, conventional property offenses, and the ordinary, professional, organized and white collar offenses. Deviation, however, cannot be understood unless it is placed within the framework of social values and norms. Dissensus concerning the definition, treatment, control, and prevention of deviant behavior make it exceedingly difficult to deal intelligently and vigorously with problems of deviation in our changing society.

QUESTIONS AND SUGGESTIONS FOR FURTHER STUDY
1. What are the characteristics of career crime?
2. Why are ordinary, professional, organized and white collar crimes described as social types of deviation?
3. Distinguish between an ordinary and a professional criminal?
4. What are the characteristics of professional theft as described by Sutherland?
5. Describe the principles operating in confidence games.

6. How do you account for the propensity of Americans to be swindled in confidence games?
7. What is organized crime and how does it differ from ordinary and professional crime?
8. Describe the chief organizational characteristics of syndicate crime.
9. To what factors do you attribute the success of organized crime?
10. What methods have been used in prosecuting organized criminals?
11. Define white collar crime.
12. Distinguish between misrepresentation and duplicity.
13. Discuss the objections raised by some criminologists to the concept of white collar crime.

SUGGESTED READINGS

Clinard, Marshall B., *The Black Market*, New York: Rinehart, 1952. This is the definitive work on the black market which flourished in the U.S. during the latter years of World War II. The author, a criminologist, served as Chief of the Analysis and Reports Branch of the Enforcement Department of OPA. An attempt is made to interpret the meaning of the black market in the context of white collar crime.

Kefauver, Estes, *Crime in America*, New York: Doubleday, Inc., 1951. As chairman of a Senate Investigating Committee on organized crime, Senator Kefauver had access to the sworn testimony of organized criminals as well as law enforcement personnel. The highlights of this testimony provide the basis for this book. The final chapter is devoted to an enumeration of the types of laws needed in combating syndicate crime.

Kennedy, Robert F., *The Enemy Within*, New York: Harper, 1960. This volume, detailing the activities of the Senate Select Committee on Improper Activities in the Labor and Management Field, updates the Kefauver Report. An authoritative book on racketeering in the U.S.   P

Maurer, David W., *The Big Con*, New York: Pocket Books, 1949. *The Big Con* was originally published in 1940. It deals with the nature, participants, and victims in confidence games. An excellent and exciting volume about the élite in crime.   P

Sutherland, Edwin H., *The Professional Thief*, Chicago: The University of Chicago Press, 1937. This volume contains an account of professional crime written by Chic Cornwell — a professional himself. The material was organized and interpreted by Sutherland.   P

———— *White Collar Crime*, New York: Holt, Rinehart and Winston, Paperback Edition, 1961. Edwin Sutherland states his case for the recognition of white collar crime as a major form of criminal deviation. Originally published in 1949, this volume has aroused considerable controversy among criminologists and laymen regarding the nature of criminal deviation.   P

SOCIAL SCIENCE AND THE SOLUTION OF SOCIAL PROBLEMS

The primary role of social science is to analyze the "results" of certain normative patterns and to concentrate on what *is*, not what *should* be, but the social scientist, as scientist, cannot make judgments that one normative pattern is better than another and should be more widely accepted. Neither can social science "solve" deviation. The social scientist may tell us *how* criminals might be rehabilitated but he cannot tell us whether they *should* be rehabilitated. Increasing knowledge about the etiology of deviant behavior does allow increased prevention and control. But *should* questions are matters to be decided within a society and are not within the province of science.

But, as sociologists insist, people play many roles. Certain roles involve analysis and objectivity and others involve choice and commitment. Though social scientists attempt to rule out certain commitments in their scientific activities, as citizens they do have notions about what society should be or become. And they have, by their scientific activity, already accepted a normative position — that one should inquire and learn. By their occupational choice, they are committed to attaining and maintaining the conditions that facilitate such scientific endeavor. They believe science and the knowledge gained from it represent an important advance in man's adjustment to the world. And they feel that scientific evidence has relevance for an individual's decisions about what society should be. Simply because science has no authority to make the choices necessary to achieve consensus and conformity, it does not follow that the social scientist (as a teacher or as a private citizen) or the student should abjure making choices in these matters. A method of analysis cannot be substituted for a personal philosophy, which always necessitates normative choice.

Social problems are solved by achieving consensus and conformity, and this does not mean that all members of a society must behave identically or agree on everything. Most industrial societies provide their members with some areas of free action, but this, too, is the result of a consensus within the society that freedom is important. Consensus and conformity are unlikely to be achieved in complex societies, though particular problems may be solved. There is no longer dissensus on whether to keep men as slaves, and one could say the problem of slavery has been solved. But it has been replaced, because of the change inherent in industrial societies, by problems in other areas, where norms once "settled" become the subject of dissensus. Social problems, in the collective sense, cannot be solved; only particular problems can.

Since industrial societies, by their very nature, are productive of problems, this does not mean that they are "worse" than other societies at other periods of history. Technological innovations, the rapid communication of ideas, and the complexity of living provide the raw materials for continuing dissensus and deviation. So the *benefits* of society produce social problems. To the traditional inevitabilities of life, death and taxes, can be added a third—social problems. More readily than death and even taxes, social problems change their form.

AUTHOR INDEX

SUBJECT INDEX

Aged, 111–12
Alcoholics Anonymous, 534–7
Alcoholism
  epidemiology and extent of, 527–30
  effects of, 526
  history of, 524–6
  related problems, 530–31
  stages of, 531–2
  theories of, 532
  treatment of, 532–7
American Association for the Advancement
  of Science, 197–8
American Council of Christian Churches,
  159
American Federation of Teachers, 146
American Medical Association, 228
Americanization, 310–21

Behavioral conformity, defined, 7
Behavioral deviation, defined, 7
Behavioral revolution, 25–9
Black Muslims, 367–9
Black nationalism, 366–9
Bureaucratization, 26

City planning, 63–4
Communications revolution, 29–31
Community, Chapter 3
  consequences of suburbanization, 80–84
  contemporary normative conception, 70–
  80
    contemporary small town, 70–74
    suburbia, 74–84
    urbanism, 57–70
  future of, 84–5
  growth of, 53–7, 62–8, 72–4, 78–80
  historical normative conception: the small
    town, 52–3
  normative problem, 52
  personal relationships in, 58–9, 70–71,
    76–7
  problems of, 59–62, 71–2, 77–8
Congress of Racial Equality, 357
Consensus, *see* Normative consensus
Crime
  behavioral definition, 450–53

conduct norms, 453–4
criminal statutes, 447–9
demographic variations, 462–9
differential association, 485–7
disposition of, 457–9
ecological variations, 469–71
epidemiology of, 462
institutional population, 460–62
legal definition, 446–50
legal procedures, 459–60
nonreported, 456–7
ordinary, 543–7
organized, 558–64
professional, 548–58
rates of, 462–71
reported, 454–6
subculture, 487–90
theories of:
  biological, 472–8
  economic, 481–3
  psychoanalytic, 480–81
  psychological, 478–80
  sociological, 483–90
victimology, 452–3
white collar crime, 564–80
Cultural pluralism, 321–5

Desegregation, 358–63
Deviation, behavioral and criminal, *see*
  Chapters 16, 17, and 18
Dissensus, *see* Normative dissensus
Divorce, 112–16
  comparative rates, 114
  and nuclear family, 115–16
  trends in United States, 113–14
Drug addiction
  and crime, 520
  and dissensus, 521–3
  epidemiology of, 515–17
  extent of, 514
  legal definition, 509–10
  medical definition, 510–11
  theories of, 517–19
  treatment of, 520–21
  types of drugs, 512–14